UNIX
Internals
A Practical Approach

UNIX
Internals
A Practical Approach

Steve D Pate

ADDISON-WESLEY

Harlow, England · Reading, Massachusetts · Menlo Park, California · New York
Don Mills, Ontario · Amsterdam · Bonn · Sydney · Singapore
Tokyo · Madrid · San Juan · Milan · Mexico City · Seoul · Taipei

Cover designed by Chris Eley, Reading, England.
Illustrations and typesetting by the author.
Printed and bound in The United States of America.

First printed 1996

ISBN 0–201–87721–X

British Library Cataloguing-in-Publication Data
A catalogue record for this book is available from the British Library

Library of Congress Cataloging-in-Publication Data is available

To Eleanor, Ashley and Sam

Foreword

The UNIX operating system (hereafter "UNIX") started its life as a research project in Bell Labs in 1969, designed to provide a flexible and easy-to-use development environment for Bell Labs' in-house developers. Despite many protestations to the contrary, in the 27 years since then UNIX has matured into a highly successful, industrial-strength operating system. Today authorised versions and derivatives of UNIX can be found in all walks of life, from powering point-of-service environments found in local stores to forming the backbone of large multi-mainframe systems which multinational businesses depend upon to run their operations.

Over the years a number of different variants of UNIX have been developed by its then-current owners and by such owners' licensees, reflecting both its portability to new hardware platforms and the desire of users to extend its basic functionality. It has not only been adopted by computer manufacturers such as HP, DEC, ICL and IBM, but has also enabled the growth and acceptance of 'Open Systems' as a pragmatic and reliable way for users to procure systems. SCO has been a leading contributor to both the success of UNIX and the acceptance and adoption of UNIX by the IT industry, initially as the first to deliver a 'shrink-wrap' UNIX system, and subsequently as the leading supplier of systems for the Intel platform.

Along with the incredible growth of the UNIX industry, the size and complexity of UNIX has expanded as the IT industry expects more and more functionality to be provided by the base operating system. This has included expansion in the breadth of hardware platforms and peripherals supported, plus development to support the needs of the commercial business user.

At the heart of the UNIX system is its kernel, and although it has developed as the system has evolved, the workings of the UNIX kernel remain to many an unsolved mystery. This is due to both its complexity and the lack of published documentation. In the past, if you ever wanted to find out how it worked, reading the source code was the only option – often made more complex by the profusion of IFDEF'd code segments! Now, with this book, you can find out not only what goes on under the hood of the world's most popular version of UNIX, but also how the kernel interacts with the Intel family of processors.

By providing the means for users to gain practical insight into the UNIX kernel without access to source code, this book presents a new and innovative approach which I am sure will appeal to all UNIX enthusiasts.

Gary Daniels,
Vice President, Platform Products Division,
The Santa Cruz Operation, Inc.

Preface

Introduction

This book describes the internals of SCO OpenServer Release 5, the version of the UNIX operating system supplied by The Santa Cruz Operation. Unlike other books on UNIX internals which concentrate on kernel algorithms and data structures, this book demonstrates the flow of control through the kernel using `crash`, `adb` and other features provided by the operating system to demonstrate the subject matter being described. This allows readers to see what happens inside the kernel when they run programs, invoke system calls, send signals and so on.

The book also shows how the features of the UNIX kernel utilise the capabilities of the Intel 80x86 and Pentium family of processors to demonstrate how the kernel makes use of features such as memory management, context switching, time and interrupt management. Where applicable a description of the underlying hardware components is provided.

Since many people will not have access to a system on which to use `crash` or the other system tools and interfaces described here, all examples provide sessions showing the commands typed and the output displayed.

While the book is based on SCO UNIX, which in turn is a derivative of System V Release 3.2, I have attempted to capture many of the topics in a manner which can be applied to other versions of UNIX. The approach that many of the examples take, while written for SCO UNIX, should be applicable for other versions of UNIX.

Organisation

Chapter 1 briefly describes the history of UNIX, showing how the different versions have evolved since the inception of UNIX in 1969. This is followed by an overview of the UNIX programming environment in chapter 2, which provides an introduction to the system call and library functions supported by the operating system.

Chapter 3 describes the techniques that can be used to extract information from the kernel as it runs, including use of `crash`, `nlist()` and `/dev/kmem`.

Chapter 4 describes bootstrap and initialisation of the UNIX kernel, covering the stages followed from power-on of the machine, through kernel initialisation to the login prompt being displayed in multi-user mode.

Chapter 5 describes the format of the disk-based kernel image which is constructed as a COFF object file. After, describing how COFF files are constructed, the chapter concludes with how the `nlist()` library function works.

Chapter 6 describes the memory requirements of executable ELF object files, where the different ELF components are placed in memory and the kernel routines used to construct the memory image. This chapter also describes the memory management capabilities of the Intel 80x86 and Pentium family of processors.

Chapter 7 describes the process management subsystem, describing how processes are created and managed by the kernel. This chapter describes system call handling, time management, context switching, scheduling, signals, use of copy-on-write when creating processes, process groups and sessions and the various methods of process termination including the generation of core files.

Chapter 8 describes the file management subsystem showing the separation between filesystem dependent and filesystem independent layers of the kernel including handling of file descriptors, the system file table, inode table and the filesystem switch. The chapter then describes the main paths followed between the user and filesystem, showing how files are accessed through read and write system call interfaces as well as memory mapped files. The chapter also provides an introduction to `fsdb`, the filesystem debugger.

Chapter 9 describes the I/O subsystem, covering the buffer cache, character and block device drivers, the TTY subsystem, pseudo TTYs and interrupt management. A number of device drivers are presented with instructions on how to link them into the kernel.

Chapter 10 describes the STREAMS subsystem, showing the main structures and algorithms together with an example STREAMS driver and module.

Chapter 11 describes the main methods of inter-process communication, concentrating on System V IPC, covering shared memory, message queues and semaphores. The chapter also describes the different pipe implementations provided in the kernel.

Chapter 12 describes different memory management policies implemented by the kernel for paging and swapping, together with details of how the kernel manages memory and handles memory management related faults generated by the processor.

Chapter 13 briefly describes the facilities offered by the `adb` debugger which is used throughout the book for setting breakpoints and single stepping processes to see the effect on the kernel.

Chapter 14 describes the `crash` utility, the commands available, the type of output displayed and cross-references to where the commands are used throughout the book.

Wherever possible, the text throughout the book is accompanied by examples to demonstrate the topic being discussed.

Toolkit examples

Most chapters provide a set of toolkits, self-contained examples which provide a practical insight into the subject matter described.

Many of the examples presented in the book require superuser privileges to run. This includes all examples that use crash(ADM), device drivers and programs that access kernel virtual memory through /dev/kmem.

Unfortunately, for the many who do not have superuser privileges, the examples cannot be tried. For this reason all examples carefully show the user interaction at the terminal with the commands entered and output displayed. In nearly all cases both the sources and output in the examples have been taken from the system on which they were tried, without modification.

Since the goal of the examples is to demonstrate the subject matter being described there is little or often no error checking performed, which helps to reduce the size of some examples. Where errors are detected from system calls, instead of the often used perror(S) function which is usually followed by exit(S), a call is made to pexit() as in the following example:

```
fd = open("/dev/kmem", O_RDONLY) ;
if (fd < 0)
    pexit("kmem") ;
```

This maps onto the following code:

```
void
pexit(const char *ermsg)
{
    perror(errmsg) ;
    exit(-1) ;
}
```

All examples were run on the SCO OpenServer Release 5 operating system. The output shown in the text is the output displayed by the programs, crash sessions and the like. Where applicable, output has been annotated to ease reading.

Typographical conventions

Program listings, UNIX commands, function names, system calls and variables are all displayed in fixed width font.

UNIX commands, system calls and library functions are followed by their manual page section in parentheses. For example, crash(ADM) indicates that the manual page for the crash command can be found in section ADM of the *System Administrator's Reference Manual*.

Where UNIX commands are entered, the prompt which precedes the command indicates whether the command needs to be run as root (#) or any UNIX user ($). All user input is displayed in a **bold fixed width font** with output displayed in fixed width font as shown:

```
# crash
dumpfile = /dev/mem, namelist = /unix, outfile = stdout
> proc ! grep crash
  70 p  3666  3659  3666 13583  35  18          crash       load ntrc
```

The terms SCO UNIX and SCO OpenServer are used interchangeably throughout the book. When features or algorithms that are specific to OpenServer Release 5 are described they are explicitly marked, otherwise SCO UNIX or just UNIX is used.

When referring to the Intel 80x86 and Pentium families of processors the term i386 is used to cover all processors. If features described are specific to one or other of the processors they are clearly stated.

Audience

This book will appeal to people with a number of different disciplines. Apart from the usual group of kernel engineers and device driver writers, the book should also appeal to system administrators, hardware designers, students and people with a general interest in operating systems.

It is assumed that the reader will have knowledge of both the UNIX operating system and the C language. Any knowledge of the Intel 80x86 or Pentium family of processors and assembly language will be useful although not essential.

Acknowledgements

The person I would like to thank most is Eleanor, whose patience, understanding, support and encouragement over the last year and a half have been instrumental in transforming those early thoughts into print.

Both Peter Kettle and Jonathon Webb have spent many hours reviewing the book for both technical accuracy and readability. I hope I have done justice to their comments.

At SCO I would particularly like to thank Nadeem Wahid who has answered many questions. Many others at SCO have also answered my questions including Ashley Baumann, Hugh Dickens, David Edmonson, Donald Page, John Farley and David Simons. I would also like to thank Doug Michels, Mike Davidson and Richard Hughes-Rowlands for providing me with an insight into SCO's history.

Finally I would like to thank Steve Prior who taught me a great deal. He has always put others first, is happy to share his experiences and knowledge and is quite simply one of the best people I have ever worked with.

While reading the book, if you have any comments, questions or bug fixes, please send email to spate@sco.com.

Steve D. Pate
July 1996

Contents

1

The history of UNIX

This chapter provides an insight into the history of UNIX since its inception in 1969 by Ken Thompson and Dennis Ritchie at Bell Laboratories in New Jersey.

It starts by describing the main events that occurred, the formation of different UNIX-based organisations and main variants of UNIX that have been released over the past 25 years.

The major standards that have emerged out of the UNIX community are then described, including the POSIX and X/Open bodies on which the interfaces provided by many operating systems are now based.

The chapter then briefly describes the history of The Santa Cruz Operation (SCO), the versions of UNIX produced by SCO including OpenServer Release 5 on which this book is based, the acquisition of the UnixWare business by SCO and the merging of the two main releases of UNIX into a single common operating system.

1.1 Introduction

With almost 30 years now behind it, UNIX has seen many changes from the initial implementation for a PDP-7 with 4096 words of memory to the now wide range of implementations from single board PCs to massively parallel processors with fault tolerant and mainframe capabilities.

Many of the original concepts, commands, utilities and languages are still very much intact today showing the strength of the original design and simplicity of the UNIX operating system.

Many thousands of people across the world have contributed to the development of UNIX. With the advent of cheap, PC-based computers and the Internet, this distributed form of development continues at an even more alarming pace.

1.2 A UNIX chronology

This section provides a chronology of UNIX from the initial release within Bell Labs in 1969 to the release of UnixWare 2.0 in 1995. Section 1.4 describes the transition of the UnixWare business to SCO and the merging of both the SCO OpenServer and UnixWare versions of UNIX.

1.2.1 The dawn of UNIX

Ken Thompson and Dennis Ritchie, two members of Bell Telephone Laboratories (BTL or Bell Labs) technical staff, both worked on the MULTiplexed Information and Computing Service (MULTICS) project, a joint development with General Electric to create a time-shared system capable of supporting thousands of users simultaneously. Bell Labs withdrew from the MULTICS project in 1969.

Thompson started work in mid-1969 on what was eventually to become UNIX. Constructed using many features from MULTICS and other operating systems, the first version was written in assembler for a GE-645 machine which had previously been used for MULTICS development. Shortly after, Thompson was joined by others including Dennis Ritchie.

Releases of UNIX within Bell Labs started in 1971 with *First Edition UNIX* which was also the year in which the first *UNIX Programmer's Manual* became available. Written by Thompson and Ritchie, the manual was divided into a number of different sections such as system calls, commands and file formats, a structuring which remains largely intact today.

1.2.2 The birth of the C language

Soon after the first assembler versions of UNIX, Thompson started work on a Fortran compiler which was quickly transformed into a compiler for the language B, a cut-down version of the BCPL language developed by Martin Richards.

A B compiler was available with First Edition UNIX and although a few of the programs available with First Edition UNIX were written in B, the operating system itself remained written in assembler.

Ritchie then started to extend the features of the B language over the next two years resulting in a C compiler that became available in Third Edition UNIX for the PDP-11 in 1973. It was five years later when the C programming language (1978) was first published. By the release of Fourth Edition UNIX in 1973, the kernel had been rewritten in C, and by Sixth Edition UNIX in 1975 nearly all of the operating system had been rewritten in C.

The standardisation of C was complete in 1989 resulting in the ANSI Standard X3.159-1989 (1989) and was subsequently adopted by the International Standards Organisation as ISO/IEC 9899:1990.

1.2.3 The 10 research editions of UNIX

There were a total of 10 editions of UNIX released by Bell Labs between 1971 and 1989, each distinguishable by a separate *Programmer's Reference Manual*. The following main features and milestones are associated with each edition:

First Edition	1971	There were a large number of features available in First Edition UNIX including a B compiler, and many of the well-known commands including `cat`, `chdir`, `chmod`, `chown`, `cp`, `ed`, `find`, `mail`, `mkdir`, `mkfs`, `mount`, `mv`, `rm`, `rmdir`, `wc` and `who`.
Second Edition	1972	This included a comment in the *Programmer's Reference Manual* that the number of UNIX installations had grown to 10!
Third Edition	1973	A C language compiler accessible via the `cc` command first appeared in Third Edition UNIX by which time the number of UNIX installations had grown to 16. This edition of UNIX first introduced the UNIX pipe mechanism.
Fourth Edition	1973	This was the first release of UNIX where the kernel was written in C.
Fifth Edition	1974	Following Ritchie and Thompson's ACM paper, The UNIX Timesharing System (1974), Fifth Edition UNIX, including source code, was made freely available to universities for educational purposes.
Sixth Edition	1975	Also known as the UNIX Timesharing System and V6, this edition was the first release which was widely available outside Bell Labs. At this stage, most of the operating system had been written in C.

This version was installed by Thompson at the University of California in Berkeley and based upon the Sixth Edition; distributions of BSD UNIX (Berkeley Software Distribution) started soon after.

Seventh Edition	1979	This included the Bourne shell and a K&R compliant C compiler as defined in Kernighan and Ritchie (1978). The kernel was also largely rewritten to make it more portable to other machine architectures.

Seventh Edition UNIX was licensed by Microsoft who used it to develop their XENIX operating system which was subsequently jointly developed by SCO.

Soon after the Seventh Edition, UNIX was handed over to the UNIX Support Group (USG).

Eighth Edition	1985	Enhancements were added from 4.1BSD to produce Eighth Edition UNIX which was also used in the development of System V Release 3 (SVR3) used by a large number of vendors including SCO.

The most significant enhancement added to Eighth Edition UNIX was the STREAM I/O mechanism described in Presotto and Ritchie (1985).

Ninth Edition	1986	This contained enhancements made available with 4.3BSD UNIX.
Tenth Edition	1989	This was the last release of UNIX from Bell Labs.

1.2.4 System V UNIX

The UNIX Support Group (USG) took over responsibility for UNIX soon after the release of Seventh Edition UNIX. After a number of internal only releases, System III UNIX became the first version of UNIX to be released externally by USG. It had a number of enhancements including features added from the Programmer's Work Bench (PWB) and the 32V (Seventh Edition) version of UNIX.

In 1984, USG became the UNIX System Development Laboratory (USDL) and subsequently released System V Release 2 (SVR2) which included paging, copy on write semantics, shared memory and file locking.

The USDL group then became AT&T Information Systems (ATTIS) and released System V Release 3 (SVR3) in 1987. A wide range of features was added to SVR3 including:

- The STREAM I/O subsystem introduced in Eighth Edition UNIX.
- The File System Switch (FSS) allowing multiple, different filesystem types to be supported simultaneously.
- Remote File Sharing (RFS) allowing distributed, coherent file access.

- Shared libraries.
- The Transport Layer Interface (TLI).

System V Release 3.2 was used by SCO as their base technology for their Open Desktop products and for SCO OpenServer Release 5. Section 1.4 describes some of the enhancements added by SCO to produce OpenServer Release 5.

1.2.5 System V Release 4.0

The next major release of UNIX, System V Release 4.0, took place in 1989. This time there was a large rewrite of the kernel to incorporate many of the features provided by SunOS, namely the Virtual File System (VFS) interface (commonly referred to as *vnodes*), a radically different memory management architecture and the Sun Network File System (NFS).

SVR4 was produced by AT&T's UNIX Software Operation (USO) under the direction of UNIX International (UI). In addition to adding features from SunOS, it also incorporated features from BSD UNIX, System V Release 3 and XENIX in addition to new features specified by UI.

The main features provided with SVR4 in addition to the list of SVR3 features described earlier were:

- The C and Korn shells.
- Symbolic links.
- STREAMS-based console I/O and TTY management.
- The BSD UFS fast file system.
- Job control.
- Sockets.
- Memory mapped files.
- NFS and support for RPC and XDR.
- Real-time scheduling and partial kernel pre-emption.

1.2.6 Novell and UnixWare

UnixWare was first released in 1992 as a result of a joint venture between Novell and USL called Univel. Novell completed its acquisition of USL in 1993 and both Univel and USL were folded into the Novell UNIX Systems Group.

The UnixWare 1.0 and 1.1 releases were based on System V Release 4.2. In 1995 UnixWare 2.0 was released based on a much changed 4.2 MP (Multi-Processing) kernel which was multi-threaded, fully pre-emptable and supported Symmetric Multi-Processing.

1.2.7 The Berkeley Software Distribution

Fourth Edition UNIX was first installed at the University of California at Berkeley in 1974 on a newly purchased PDP-11/45.

Based on Sixth Edition UNIX, the first version of BSD UNIX, called BSD, became available in 1978 which included a Pascal compiler and the ex text editor developed by Bill Joy. This was soon followed by the creation of vi and termcap by Joy which were included in releases of 2BSD which followed soon after.

Based on Seventh Edition UNIX, or 32V as it was also known, 3BSD was released in 1979. This was the first version of BSD UNIX to run on the VAX. It included virtual memory support and demand paging.

The release of 4BSD, which included job control and reliable signals, took place in 1980. Owing to its support of a wide number of third-party peripherals, 4BSD became very popular, particularly within universities.

There were a number of releases of 4BSD. In 1981, 4.1BSD was released, including TCP/IP and the fast file system, now called UFS. 4.2BSD, released in 1983, became the standard research operating system for the VAX and included many additional features.

Owing to the large number of features added to 4.2BSD there were a number of bugs and performance problems. This resulted in 4.3BSD in 1986 which was much more reliable and offered better performance. A number of releases of 4.3BSD between 1986 and 1990 saw more features added including NFS, VFS/vnodes, a kernel debugger and enhanced networking support.

The 4.4BSD and the following BSD Lite version were the last releases of UNIX from Berkeley before the closure of the Computer Systems Research Group (CSRG) in 1993.

1.2.8 Microkernel-based implementations of UNIX

The goal of microkernels is to reduce the services provided and actions taken by the core kernel to an absolute minimum, allowing the main operating system components to be built on top of microkernel constructs.

There have been two main players in the microkernel world over the past 10 years, both supporting various flavours of UNIX in addition to the real-time embedded environments where a small memory footprint, real-time, pre-emptive kernel is highly suited:

- The Mach microkernel, originally developed at Carnegie Mellon University (CMU), is now used in DEC's OSF/1 operating system for its Alpha-based products. Mach is also used as the basis for IBM's Workplace OS.

- The Chorus microkernel has been used successfully in a number of different environments, from the real-time embedded, telecommunications industry to high end, massively parallel database servers.

Chorus/MiX V.3 and Mix V.4 provide a *severization* of SVR3 and SVR4 UNIX on top of the microkernel where the UNIX kernel has been split into a number of different *servers* which can either reside on the same machine or be distributed across multiple nodes.

At the time of writing Chorus Systems and SCO are working together to produce a microkernel-based implementation of UnixWare code-named MK2.

For further details on the activities followed by OSF, see `http:/www.osf.org/` and for details on the Chorus microkernel and microkernel-based products and research see `http://www.chorus.com/`.

1.2.9 Free UNIX

There have been free versions of UNIX available for a number of years. With the introduction of cheap, PC-based hardware, UNIX is now available in one form or another to just about everyone.

One of the most successful versions of PC UNIX called Minix was written by Andy Tanenbaum (1987) which accompanied his book on operating system design. This book also included a complete source listing and an optional set of diskettes to run Minix on an 8086-based PC. Minix was also successfully ported to other machine architectures.

Comer (1984) provided a version of UNIX called XINU (Xinu Is Not Unix) which ran on the LSI-11/2, 16-bit microcomputer. XINU was very popular in universities for which the host machine used to drive Xinu, a PDP-11, was often available.

In recent years, the most commonly used and available version of free UNIX is Linux, written by Linus Torvalds, a research assistant at the University of Helsinki. Linux, originally written for the Intel i386 family of processors, has now been ported to a number of other architectures including DEC's Alpha. Each month sees an ever-increasing number of books on Linux covering all aspects of the system.

1.3 UNIX and the standards bodies

UNIX was one of the first truly portable operating systems, resulting in its success. Both the early editions of research UNIX from Bell Labs were available free of charge, as were BSD UNIX from the University of California, Berkeley and an emerging number of PC or single board versions of UNIX such as Minix and Xinu, and a number of commercial versions of UNIX started to appear covering a wide range of hardware platforms.

This widespread usage of UNIX in research and commercial environments resulted in not only an ever-increasing number of enhancements but also deviations from the released Bell Labs or BSD versions of UNIX. With a large number of commercial versions of UNIX appearing, it soon became apparent that there needed to be co-ordination and standardisation of the interfaces provided across the different UNIX implementations in order to ease application portability. The result has been an explosion in standards bodies, some of which are described in the following sections.

1.3.1 IEEE and POSIX

A group of individuals formed /usr/group in 1980 with the intention of standardising the interfaces provided by UNIX in order to ease porting of applications between the many different versions of UNIX.

The /usr/group standard was agreed in 1984 and was used by the ANSI X3J11 committee, who were standardising the C language, as a basis for the library section. However, as the number of versions of UNIX increased and diverged the /usr/group standard became less effective. Only a year later, in 1985, the Portable Operating System Interface for Computing Environments, or POSIX for short, was created from a technical committee of /usr/group and the /usr/group standard was used as the base working document.

The outcome of the group, POSIX 1003.1-1988, was the first adopted POSIX standard which offered an Application Programming Interface (API) that has been used by many operating systems both within and outside the UNIX community. The text of the standard was revised over the next three years resulting in IEEE Std 1003.1-1990.

There have been a number of additional adopted POSIX standards including:

POSIX 1003.2-1992   This adopted standard includes a specification of the UNIX shell and utilities.

POSIX 1003.1b-1993   Formerly POSIX.4, POSIX.1b includes additional features above POSIX.1-1990 mainly in the area of real-time support.

POSIX 1003.1c-1995   This standard covers thread extensions commonly known as POSIX threads or pthreads.

At the time of writing there are a number of other POSIX working groups still in existence. For further details see http://stdsbbs.iee.org/.

In 1989, the /usr/group organisation changed its name to Uniforum.

1.3.2 X/Open

Many European computer companies formed the non-profit-making X/Open organisation in 1984 with the same goals as /usr/group, to provide a common set of interfaces that vendors could adopt on multiple operating system variants, thus reducing the porting costs of various applications both across one version of the operating to the next and across different vendors' operating systems.

The main goal of X/Open was to adopt a set of de facto or established standards as part of a single, common API and environment for applications. The result was the X/Open Portability Guide (XPG), of which the most commonly known version is XPG3, released in 1992.

XPG3 included both POSIX 1003.1-1988 and the X Window system developed at the Massachusetts Institute of Technology (MIT).

In the same year, XPG3 was extended to produce XPG4 in order to bring XPG more in line with other standards including POSIX.1, POSIX.2 and ISO C.

The interfaces of XPG4 have been extended based on industry feedback, the core APIs of 4.3BSD UNIX and SVID version 3, and STREAMS interfaces. The resulting standard incorporates what was previously known as Spec 11/70 and is now called XPG4.2 (1994).

1.3.3 The System V Interface Definition

Following the release of SVR2 in 1984, USG released the System V Interface Definition (SVID) version 1 in 1985 and version 2 in 1986 which documented, in two volumes, the external interfaces that were provided with System V UNIX. This de facto standard allowed USG and other providers of System V UNIX to provide a common application interface.

To accompany the SVID, USG also released the System V Verification Suite (SVVS), a collection of test programs and utilities, which allowed vendors to ensure that their System V interfaces conformed to the SVID. For vendors to use the name System V UNIX, they were required to conform to the SVID and therefore ensure that they could pass SVVS.

With the introduction of SVR4, the third edition of the SVID, this time a four-volume set, was released in 1992 together with a new version of SVVS.

Both versions of the SVID have played a major role in the definition of the X/Open Portability Guides (XPG).

1.4 The history of SCO

The Santa Cruz Operation (SCO) was formed in 1979 by Larry and Doug Michels as a technical management consulting business. Through the consulting work in which SCO was involved it became obvious that UNIX would play an ever-increasing and important role in the business world. SCO then changed its focus from consulting to the custom porting of UNIX system software and applications.

1.4.1 Pre-XENIX

The first version of UNIX which SCO developed and sold was called Dynix, a name subsequently used by Sequent. The operating system was based on Seventh Edition UNIX and ran on the PDP-11.

At the same time a port was also made to the LSI-11 single board computer based on the PDP-11. The LSI-11 is described by Comer (1984) who used it as the base for his Xinu operating system which was popular as a teaching aid in many universities.

1.4.2 Microsoft, XENIX and the emergence of the PC

Microsoft licensed Seventh Edition UNIX from AT&T in 1978 to produce the XENIX operating system initially for the PDP-11.

In 1982, a joint development and technology exchange agreement was reached between SCO and Microsoft bringing together engineers from SCO and Microsoft to further enhance the XENIX operating system which was increasing in popularity. Microsoft and SCO worked together with Logica in the UK and HCR in Canada, producing enhancements to XENIX and porting XENIX to other platforms.

In 1984 a port of XENIX was made to the Apple Lisa by SCO and Microsoft, and was subsequently sold successfully by SCO as their first binary product, showing the success of the shrink-wrapped market. A port was also made to the Tandy model 16B.

In 1983 the PC emerged. SCO started porting to the 8088 but concentrated on the 8086, producing a release of SCO XENIX in 1984 which ran in 640 Kbytes with a 10 Mbyte hard disk. The release could support three or more users simultaneously, had multiscreen (virtual console) facilities, Micnet local area networking and enhancements added from 4.2BSD.

In 1985 Microsoft and AT&T jointly announced plans for implementing changes to bring XENIX into conformity with the SVID released in the same year. SCO became the pilot participant in AT&T's verification suite for conformance to the SVID. Later that year, SCO announced the release of SCO XENIX System V for both 8088/8086 and 80286-based PCs.

In 1986 SCO bought the Software Products Group of Logica to form a new company, The Santa Cruz Operation Limited, a fully owned subsidiary of SCO Inc. The company, now based in Watford, England, formed the kernel group responsible for the kernel components of SCO Open Desktop 3.0 and SCO OpenServer Release 5.

SCO XENIX for the Intel 80386 was released in 1987 following the introduction of the SCO XENIX 386 Toolkit, allowing developers to start developing 386 applications on both 286 and 386 platforms. This included the Cmerge C compiler, a 386 version of adb and a link kit to allow integration of 386 device drivers.

Motivated by unprecedented customer demand, SCO released XENIX/386 version 2.3.4 in 1991, the last release of XENIX made by SCO.

1.4.3 UNIX System V Release 3.2

In 1987, AT&T and Microsoft announced their intention to merge XENIX and System V versions of UNIX, providing a new version of UNIX incorporating support for applications developed for both UNIX and XENIX.

In 1988 SCO, Microsoft and Interactive Systems developed System V/386 Release 3.2, allowing support for both XENIX System V and UNIX System V binaries without recompilation. In the same year SCO and AT&T jointly announced that SCO would license the UNIX trademark in calling future releases of the operating system SCO UNIX System V/386.

Later that year, SCO announced SCO UNIX System V/386 Release 3.2, providing support for both UNIX and XENIX binaries.

1.4.4 SCO Open Desktop

In 1989 SCO released Open Desktop (ODT) based on the System V/386 Release 3.2 operating system with the X11 Window system and OSF/Motif graphical user interface. Included in this release were TCP/IP, NFS and Locus's Merge 386 technology allowing support for DOS-based applications.

In the same year, SCO MPX was also released allowing SCO UNIX System V/386 Release 3.2 to run on shared memory multi-processing machines. This was the first version of UNIX to take advantage of Symmetric Multi-Processing (SMP) machines offered by Compaq and Corollary.

1.4.5 SCO OpenServer Release 5

SCO OpenServer Release 5.0 emerged in 1995, providing a vast range of new features above the previous ODT 3.0 release. SCO OpenServer Release 5, code-named Everest, represents three years of development in Santa Cruz, Toronto and Watford and runs on 900 different machines, including 60 SMP machines, and supports over 2000 peripheral devices.

During the development of SCO OpenServer, the kernel was largely rewritten to support a number of features including:

- Memory mapped files.
- Dynamic kernel tuneables.
- The transaction-based HTFS filesystem and DTFS data compression filesystem.
- Conformance to the base and kernel extensions components of SVID 3.
- Real-time scheduling and POSIX.1b semaphores.
- Advanced power management.

1.4.6 Acquisition of the UnixWare business

In December of 1995, SCO completed the purchase of the UNIX business from Novell. In addition, SCO recruited many of the technical staff at Novell who worked on the development of UnixWare and previous releases of UNIX from USL.

In 1996 SCO released version 2.1 of UnixWare which, with SCO OpenServer Release 5, will provide the basis for the next generation of UNIX operating systems from SCO, code-named Gemini. This operating system will provide the best technologies from both UnixWare and OpenServer providing support for binary applications from both operating systems.

For further information, see SCO's World Wide Web site: `http://www.sco.com/`.

1.5 Summary and suggested reading

This chapter provides a brief description of UNIX from an historical perspective since its inception almost 30 years ago. The main UNIX variants, organisations and players have been presented together with the various forums and standards bodies.

There are a number of different books, Web sites and magazines devoted to UNIX. For those interested in the historical aspects, Salus (1994) describes the first 25 years of UNIX, providing a detailed account of the events that have taken place, interviews with the key players and even photographs of some of the early UNIX pioneers.

Although there are many books on most aspects of UNIX there still remain only a handful of books describing UNIX internals. Bach (1986) was the first book available which described the internals, structures and algorithms of UNIX. Although based on System V Release 2 the book provides some coverage of the features added to System V Release 3. While this version of UNIX predates the base technology from which SCO OpenServer Release 5 was developed, many of the basic algorithms and structures remain very similar.

Leffler *et al.* (1989), some of the key designers of BSD UNIX, describe the design and implementation of 4.3BSD UNIX.

Goodheart and Cox (1994) describe the implementation of UNIX System V Release 4.0 on which the UnixWare products were derived and from which many of the features of forthcoming versions of UNIX from SCO will be based.

One of the most useful sources of information is, of course, the Internet. Using World Wide Web search facilities such as Webcrawler (`http://www.webcrawler.com/`) and typing specific keywords can reveal many interesting facts about UNIX.

2

The UNIX programming environment

This chapter describes the main features provided by the UNIX system call interface, the mechanism by which user processes request services from the UNIX kernel. Although this chapter is not a complete reference of all the system calls available, many of the common calls are described with working examples where appropriate.

It is important when describing UNIX internals to understand the expectations of user processes, the initialisation and termination of a process, parameter handling, and the interpretation of errors returned by the kernel. This chapter provides the necessary background required.

The chapter provides an introduction for readers who may wish to learn about UNIX internals but have had little experience of the UNIX programming environment.

2.1 Introduction

This chapter provides an introduction to the main aspects of the UNIX programming environment. Emphasis is placed on the system call interface, the method by which user processes request services from the kernel, and low level library routines. The chapter presents numerous programs showing how to use the calls available.

It is important to obtain a good understanding of the user programming environment in order to understand kernel internals fully. The flow of commands and data across the system call interface largely dictates the structure and functionality provided by the UNIX operating system.

All of the programs use the dialect of C defined by the ANSI committee, details of which can be found in the ANSI C language definition (1989). Where applicable, cross-references are given to the appropriate sections in this book where the kernel internal functions underpinning the appropriate calls are described.

2.1.1   Which manuals?

There are a large number of reference manuals for SCO UNIX, each divided into a number of sections which group related functions, commands or other entities together. For example, commands and utilities can be found in section (C), file formats in section (F) and hardware specific details in section (HW).

To locate the manual page for a particular command, for example the vi(C) editor, the man(C) command should be invoked as follows:

```
$ man C vi
```

If the C argument is omitted then man will search the entire set of on-line manual pages section by section and display the first entry it finds. This default search is usually sufficient for most commands, utilities and functions. Where there may be multiple manual pages with the same name, the -k option to man(C) allows a keyword search to be performed.

This chapter concentrates on section (S) which contains the system calls and library functions. System calls are direct calls into the UNIX kernel. Library routines are often built on top of system calls but may perform their required functionality without direct support from the kernel. For example, the fopen(S) library function invokes the open(S) system call whereas the getenv(S) library function does not require any kernel services.

The Intro(S) manual page introduces the system calls, library functions and error codes of all system calls and library functions provided in section (S). It also describes the libraries in which all the system calls or library functions can be located.

The Routines(S) manual page lists the complete contents of the (S) section: the function name; whether it is a system call or library function; the appropriate manual page entry; a brief description of the function and the specification of any libraries that are needed at link time.

Other sections of the manual set of particular interest to programmers are:

(CP)   Programming commands including compilers, assemblers and debuggers.

(F)   The format of various system files and archive formats.

(FP)   Programming file formats such as directory entries, application core files, kernel virtual memory and filesystem formats.

(HW)   Device drivers and hardware specific information.

2.1.2 Header files

Calling one of the functions in section (S) usually requires inclusion in the user program of one or more of the system header files which declare the function to be called including its type, the arguments required and the type of each argument. Most header files can be found in either /usr/include or /usr/include/sys.

The appropriate manual pages in section (S) indicate which header files need to be included. For example, the declaration for the read(S) system call is as follows:

```
#include <unistd.h>

ssize_t read(int fildes, void *buf, size_t nbyte);
```

This specifies that the caller must include the unistd.h header file. A header file such as user.h is located in the /usr/include/sys directory and would be included in the program by use of #include <sys/user.h>.

2.1.3 The compilation phase

The compilation path for most applications is shown in Figure 2.1. The user has a number of program source files including header files for predefined types and system calls or library function prototypes. The user's source files pass through the phases of compilation controlled either by *makefiles* or by command-line options to the compiler.

The C compiler cc produces a set of intermediate object files. These object files are linked with default libraries, for example libc, the standard C library, or user-specified libraries. The output of the linking phase is the executable object file which by default is the file named a.out.

For many programmers, the procedures covered here are usually sufficient to produce a full working application. Some examples of how the compilation paths are used are shown on the next page for completeness. Note that cc(CP) is the front end to the C compiler and ld(CP) is the link editor. Also, typing the following command:

```
$ make myprog
```

produces an executable file named myprog from the source file myprog.c and is usually sufficient when creating small test programs.

```
# to produce an executable file called a.out from file.c
$ cc file.c
```

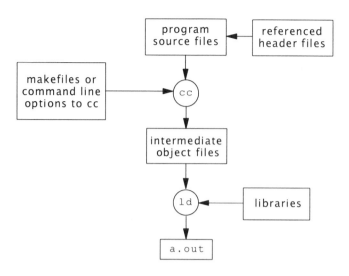

Figure 2.1   The basic compilation path

```
# to produce an executable file called myout from file.c
$ cc -o myout file.c
# to produce an intermediate object file called file.o
$ cc -c file.c
# to link file.o and libc.a to create an executable file called myout
$ ld -o myout file.o /usr/lib/libc.a
```

When using cc, the C compiler informs ld to link the standard C library libc.a and therefore users do not usually have to concern themselves with the C library. Without specifying it as an argument to ld, the link edit will fail due to unresolved symbols since it does not automatically link libc.a.

2.2 Running C programs in the UNIX environment

This section introduces the startup and initialisation of C programs under SCO UNIX, the arguments passed to the program, the shell environment variables to which the program has access and the methods by which the program can exit.

2.2.1 Programs and processes

A program refers to one or more physical files, whether it is a collection of source files, intermediate object files or the executable file itself. To run the program the kernel first creates an *environment* in which the program can run, for example memory resources, access to a terminal for I/O and access to the kernel to request services.

The term used for this environment is a *process*. A process can be thought of as a set of kernel-maintained structures which describe the memory image of the program prior to invocation of the `main()` function, part-way through execution or after the program has terminated but has not yet been removed from memory.

The memory image of the process contains, at a minimum, the instructions and data produced by the compiler and a stack used to create automatic variables as program execution flows from one function to another.

2.2.2 C program startup

The function `main()` is guaranteed by the operating system to be the first, user defined function to be called in a C program unless the programmer explicitly specifies another entry point to the program. The traditional prototype for `main()` in most UNIX environments is:

```
main(int argc, char *argv[], char *envp[]) ;
```

The first argument, `argc`, is the number of arguments passed to the program including the program name. Pointers to each of the arguments are passed in the `argv[]` array such that `argv[0]` points to the name of the program, `argv[1]` points to the first argument and so on up to `argv[argc-1]`.

The `envp[]` array contains pointers to the shell environment variables passed to the program. Each variable is a string of the form `name=value`.

The ANSI C standard (1989) defines only the `argc` and `argv[]` arguments. Although the POSIX.1 standard (1990) recognises the `environ[]` array, it states that the declaration of `environ` should be declared global as follows:

```
extern char **environ ;
```

Declaring `environ` either as an argument to `main()` or as an external pointer will work. It is better however to follow the POSIX.1 method for declaring `environ` in order to maximise portability between different UNIX platforms. The following program uses this format to print the first 10 environment variables it finds in addition to the value of `argc` and the arguments passed to the program through `argv[]`:

```
#include <stddef.h>

extern char **environ ;

main(int argc, char *argv[])
{
    int x ;
    printf("argc = %d\n", argc) ;
    for (x=0 ; x<argc ; x++)
        printf("argv[%d] = %s\n", x, argv[x]) ;
    for (x=0 ; x<10 ; x++)
        if (environ[x] != NULL)
            printf("environ[%x] = %s\n", x, environ[x]) ;
}
```

The `printf(S)` library function from `libc` formats and prints its arguments to the *standard output stream*. When a program is invoked it is passed three streams corresponding to standard input, standard output and standard error. Section 2.5.2 describes I/O streams in more detail.

The output of the program for one particular run is shown below. Note that the content and order of the environment variables will change depending on the user, the shell type and which variables have been set.

```
$ a.out one two three
argc = 4
argv[0] = a.out
argv[1] = one
argv[2] = two
argv[3] = three
environ[0] = _=args
environ[1] = LANG=C_C.C
environ[2] = XFONTS=/usr/lib/X11/fonts/misc;/usr/lib/X11/fonts/75dpi
environ[3] = HZ=100
environ[4] = PATH=/bin:/usr/bin:/usr/bin/X11:/home/spate/bin:.
environ[5] = COLUMNS=80
environ[6] = LEVEL=wait
environ[7] = WINDOWID=8388621
environ[8] = LOGNAME=spate
environ[9] = MAIL=/usr/spool/mail/spate
```

The total space allowed by both the `argv[]` array and the `environ[]` array is limited to `ARG_MAX` as defined in the `<limits.h>` header file. A user program may call the `sysconf(S)` function to find the value of this and other system limits.

There are two library functions available for extracting and setting environment variables, namely `getenv(S)` and `putenv(S)`. As an example, the following program uses `getenv(S)` to extract the current value for the variable `PS1`, prints its value and then sets it to the argument passed to the program using `putenv(S)`. Initially, it prints the value of `ARG_MAX` as returned by `sysconf(S)`.

```c
#include <unistd.h>

main(int argc, char *argv[])
{
    char buf[32] ;

    if (argc != 2)
        exit(-1) ;

  printf("The value of ARG_MAX = %d\n", sysconf(_SC_ARG_MAX)) ;
    printf("current value for PS1 = %s\n", getenv("PS1")) ;
    sprintf(buf, "PS1=%s", argv[1]) ;
    putenv(buf) ;
    printf("new value for PS1 = \"%s\"\n", getenv("PS1")) ;
}
```

The value returned by `sysconf(S)` differs from the value `ARG_MAX` defined in `<limits.h>`. The POSIX.1 standard (1990) defines the value returned to be at least the size of its equivalent value in `<limits.h>`.

Running the program gives the following output:

```
$ a.out "trivia > "
The value of ARG_MAX = 102400
current value for PS1 = $
new value for PS1 = "trivia > "
```

One problem that most UNIX programmers encounter at some stage is a need to set one of the shell's environment variables while executing a program invoked from the shell prompt and for the value of the variable to remain set when the program exits.

It should be noted that each time a process is created, a copy of its parent's environment variables is made and these copies are visible only to the process being run. For the newly created process, the environment variables reside in the data segment of the process so altering the contents of the environment variables is visible only to the process which altered them and to any subsequent child processes.

When a program is linked, the link editor `ld` specifies that the routine called `_start` should be the first function called. The `_start` function initialises the process by establishing the process stack frame, setting the environment variables and arguments to `main()` and then finally calling `main()`.

When the shell is created after logging into UNIX, a number of environment variables are passed to it so that the shell can at least understand the basic context in which it is running. If the program above were used as the user's login shell and specified in the `/etc/passwd` file in place of a common UNIX shell, the output would look similar to:

```
argc = 1
argv[0] = -msh
environ[0] = LOGNAME=jonwe
environ[1] = TZ=ESTE5EDT
environ[2] = HZ=100
environ[3] = PATH=/bin:/usr/bin
environ[4] = HOME=/usr/jonwe
environ[5] = TERM=ansi
environ[6] = SHELL=/tmp/msh
environ[7] = MAIL=/usr/spool/mail/jonwe
environ[8] = HUSHLOGIN=false
```

A login for the user called `jonwe` was created and the shell as specified in the `/etc/passwd` file was run. UNIX shells will typically add new environment variables which are subsequently passed to programs that the user invokes on the command line.

Section 4.3.4 describes in more detail the steps taken when a user logs into a UNIX system. Later in this chapter there is an example shell which has access to the environment list as shown above.

2.2.3 C program exit

There are a number of ways by which a process can voluntarily exit. The process can exit by simply returning from `main()` or by calling the `exit(S)` or `abort(S)` library functions from anywhere within the program.

The argument passed to `exit(S)` is returned to the caller of the process. In the following example, the program is invoked from the shell and the return value displayed using the shell's `$?` variable.

```
$ cat exit.c
main()
{
    exit(7) ;
}
$ cc exit.c
$ a.out
$ echo $?
7
```

By convention, programs return 0 to indicate success and any other value to indicate failure although there are no conventions for programs which return non-zero values. Testing for zero allows constructs available in the shell to be used as follows:

```
$ cat x.c
main()
{
    exit(0) ;
}
$ cc x.c
$ a.out && echo success
success
$ a.out || echo fail
$
```

In addition to returning the value passed, `exit(S)` will invoke a number of cleanup procedures before the process finally exits, such as flushing buffered file data and closing file streams. As an alternative to `exit(S)`, the `_exit(S)` system call may be called which circumvents the cleanup procedures.

The `_exit(S)` system call was defined by POSIX.1 (1990) since the semantics of the `exit(S)` call as defined by the ANSI-C standard included functionality beyond the scope of the POSIX.1 specification.

A `return()` may be called from `main()` which has the same effect as calling `exit(S)`. If the `exit(S)` or `_exit(S)` calls are not made, reaching the end of `main()` has the same effect as calling `exit(S)` with an unspecified value.

A process may register up to 32 *exit handlers*, functions which are called after `exit(S)` has been invoked but before the process terminates. The `atexit(S)` library function registers the functions which are placed on a LIFO (Last In First Out) queue.

Exit handlers are invoked only if the process exits normally, for example by implicit return from `main()` or by explicit return from `main()` through the `return()` or `exit(S)` functions. If `_exit(S)` or `abort(S)` is called or a signal is received which will terminate the process, no exit handlers will be invoked. See section 2.6 for details on UNIX signals.

Exit handlers are created through use of the `atexit(S)` function. The following program registers two exit handlers, `ex1()` and `ex2()`, and then calls the `exit(S)` library function.

```
int
ex1()
{
    printf("ex1 called\n") ;
}

int
ex2()
{
    printf("ex2 called\n") ;
}

main()
{
    atexit(ex1) ;
    atexit(ex2) ;
    printf("About to call exit()\n") ;
    exit(0) ;
}
```

As the output below shows, the exit handlers are executed in LIFO order:

```
$ a.out
About to call exit()
ex2 called
ex1 called
```

There are two other methods by which a process can exit. The first method is use of the abort(S) library function which sends a SIGABRT signal to the calling process. The second method is the result of receiving a signal for which the default action is to kill the process, in which case the kernel will make a call to an internal kernel exit function on behalf of the process. The use and control of signals is described in detail in section 2.6.

2.3 The process environment

This section describes in more detail the environment of the process: its layout in memory; methods of identification; relation to other processes; and the constraints within which the process runs.

2.3.1 Process types

There are two types of UNIX processes, those which are associated with a user's login session and *daemon* processes. A daemon is a process which runs in the background and is not directly controllable by the user. Daemons are usually started early during system initialisation but can be created by directly back-grounding themselves. The steps needed to transform a normal user process into a daemon are shown in section 2.9.1.

2.3.2 Memory layout

A process consists of a number of *memory segments*. The size, content and position in memory of each segment is dependent on both the program contents, for example libraries used, the size of the program's instructions and data, and the type of the

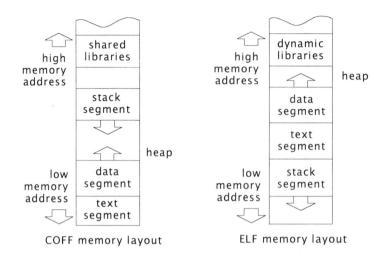

Figure 2.2   Memory layout of COFF and ELF processes

executable file including COFF (*Common Object File Format*) and ELF (*Executable and Linking Format*).

Figure 2.2 shows the basic layout in memory of both COFF and ELF object files when a process has been created. The COFF format is described in chapter 5, the ELF format in chapter 6.

Although the ordering of segments in memory differs between the two formats, the main building blocks of each are very similar. Both formats have text, data and stack segments, library segments including static shared libraries for COFF and ELF and dynamic libraries for ELF. The term *text* is used to refer to a program's instructions.

The data segment comprises *initialised data* which is loaded from the executable file on disk and *un-initialised data* which is guaranteed to be zero filled prior to the program starting. The un-initialised data area is commonly referred to as the BSS.

BSS is an acronym for *Block Started by Symbol*, a pseudo assembly operator in a Fortran-based assembly language for the IBM 704, 709, 7090 and 7094 machines. The bss instruction defines a label and sets aside space for a given number of words.

The space that the data segment grows into is called the *heap*. Expansion of the data segment occurs as a result of memory allocation requests. Functions available for allocation of memory are described in section 2.3.4.

2.3.3 Process identification

Each process has a number of associated *identifiers*. If a process is invoked from the shell then it will be assigned the user ID and group ID of the user who invoked the command. The user ID and group ID are defined for each user in the /etc/passwd file.

For example, the password entry for user spate on one machine is:

```
spate:x:13583:50:Steve Pate:/home/spate:/bin/ksh
```

In this entry, the user ID is `13583` and the group ID is `50`. The format of each line in `/etc/passwd` is defined by the `passwd` structure, declared in the `<pwd.h>` header file. Those fields of the structure which are POSIX.1 compliant are shown in Table 2.1.

Table 2.1   Fields of the `passwd` structure

passwd structure field	Description
`char    *pw_name`	The user's name.
`char    *pw_passwd`	The encrypted password.
`uid_t   pw_uid`	The user ID.
`gid_t   pw_gid`	The user's group ID.
`char    *pw_comment`	Contents of the comment field.
`char    *pw_dir`	The user's home directory.
`char    *pw_shell`	The shell to be invoked after login.

There are a number of library functions available for retrieving information from `/etc/passwd`. Table 2.2 summarises the functions available. The `getpwent(S)`, `getpwuid(S)` and `getpwnam(S)` functions all return a pointer to a `passwd` structure as defined in the `<pwd.h>` header file. The first time `getpwent(S)` is called it returns a pointer to the first entry in the file. The next time it is called it returns the second entry and so on.

Table 2.2   Password retrieval functions

Function name	Description
`getpwent(S)`	Return a pointer to the next `passwd` structure.
`getpwuid(S)`	Search `/etc/passwd` for matching user ID.
`getpwnam(S)`	Search `/etc/passwd` for matching user name.
`setpwent(S)`	Rewind to allow repeated searches.
`endpwent(S)`	Close the password file once processing has been completed.
`fgetpwent(S)`	Return a pointer to the next `passwd` structure.

The `setpwent(S)` function resets the file pointer used back to the start of the file to allow repeated searches while the `fgetpwent(S)` function returns a `passwd` structure from a user specified file stream. Section 2.5.2 describes file streams in more detail.

The following program demonstrates the use of the `getpwnam(S)` library function. It calls `getpwnam(S)` with the user name passed to the program and prints the contents of the `passwd` structure returned.

```
#include <pwd.h>

main(int argc, char *argv[])
{
    struct passwd *pw ;

    if (argc != 2)
        exit(-1) ;
```

```
    pw = getpwnam(argv[1]) ;
    if (pw != 0) {
        printf("Details for user %s\n", argv[1]) ;
        printf("   pw_passwd  = %s\n", pw->pw_passwd) ;
        printf("   pw_uid     = %d\n", pw->pw_uid) ;
        printf("   pw_gid     = %d\n", pw->pw_gid) ;
        printf("   pw_comment = %s\n", pw->pw_comment) ;
        printf("   pw_dir     = %s\n", pw->pw_dir) ;
        printf("   pw_shell   = %s\n", pw->pw_shell) ;
    }
    else
        printf("No match found for %s\n", argv[1]) ;
}
```

The output of the program for one particular run is as follows:

```
$ a.out spate
Details for user spate
  pw_passwd  = jA16qVCZJVPg6
  pw_uid     = 13583
  pw_gid     = 50
  pw_comment = Steve Pate
  pw_dir     = /home/spate
  pw_shell   = /bin/ksh
```

The library function crypt(S) can be used to encrypt a text string passed as an argument. When the login(M) program runs, it disables echoing to the terminal, requests that the user enters the password and calls crypt(S) to encrypt the entered password. This can then be compared with the encrypted password stored in the /etc/shadow file to test whether the password is correct and thus whether the user can login or not.

The entry for the group ID (50) in the pw_gid field shown above is called the *numeric* group ID. For each numeric group ID there is a corresponding *symbolic name* which is stored in the file /etc/group. There are a number of functions shown in Table 2.3 which allow access to the /etc/group file.

Table 2.3   Functions available for reading /etc/group

Function name	Description
getgrent(S)	Return a pointer to the first and successive group structures.
getgrgid(S)	Search /etc/group for matching group ID.
getgrnam(S)	Search /etc/group for matching group name.
setgrent(S)	Rewind the file pointer to allow repeated searches.
endgrent(S)	Close the group file once processing has been completed.
fgetgrent(S)	Return a pointer to the next group structure.

The getgrent(S), getgrgid(S) and getgrnam(S) functions all return a pointer to a group structure as defined in the <grp.h> header file. The first time getgrent(S) is called it reads the first group entry in the file and returns a pointer to the data read. The next time it is called it returns the second entry and so on.

The setgrent(S) function resets the file pointer used back to the start of the file to allow repeated searches while fgetgrent(S) returns a group structure from a user specified file stream. Both file pointers and the standard I/O library are described in more detail in section 2.5.2.

The contents of the group structure are shown in Table 2.4.

Table 2.4   Fields in the group structure

group structure field	Description
char *gr_name	The group name.
char *gr_passwd	The encrypted password (not used).
gid_t gr_gid	The numeric group ID.
char *gr_mem	List of all users allowed in this group.

The following program demonstrates use of the getgrgid() library function. Passed a numeric group ID as an argument, it retrieves the symbolic name of the group.

```
#include <grp.h>

main(int argc, char *argv[])
{
    struct group *grp ;

    if (argc != 2)
        exit(-1) ;

    grp = getgrgid(atoi(argv[1])) ;
    printf("group name = %s\n", grp->gr_name) ;
}
```

Since the group ID is passed to the program as a string, the atoi(S) function is called to convert the string argv[1] into an integer.

Running the program gives the following output:

```
$ a.out 50
group name = group
```

2.3.4 Memory allocation

The memory used by a process's data and stack segments is allocated in a number of different ways both during process creation and dynamically during process execution. There are five methods by which memory is allocated:

1. A program variable is declared as global and assigned an initial value within the program source, for example:

    ```
    char *error_message = "Access rights not granted" ;
    ```

The string for `error_message` is stored in the initialised data section of the binary file on disk and is allocated memory during process creation.

2. The value of a global variable is unknown during compilation, for example:

```
char error_message[26] ;
```

In this example, the space required for `error_message` is not stored in the binary file but is allocated as part of the process's BSS within the data segment during process creation and is guaranteed to be zero filled.

3. Automatic variables used within the program's functions use the process's stack. Space is allocated on the stack for automatics when the function is entered and is then de-allocated prior to return from the function. For example:

```
myfunc()
{
        int         a ;
        char*       pw ;
        static int x = 4 ;
        .
        .
        .
```

The variables `a` and `pw` are allocated space on the stack. The variable `x` is allocated space within the initialised data segment and loaded from the disk copy either during process creation or as part of demand paging. For further information on demand paging refer to section 6.4.7 and chapter 12.

4. Memory is explicitly requested from the system via one or more system calls or library functions. For example, the `malloc(S)` library function requests additional memory and is called to allocate space for data structures, file buffers and so on. The `getpwnam(S)` function described earlier allocates memory within the library function in order to read the `passwd` structure from disk and return a pointer.

5. A *stack overflow* occurs where the stack grows down over the amount of memory allocated. This results in the kernel allocating additional stack space.

Recall from section 2.3.2 that the memory is allocated from the heap, the area of memory above the data segment which grows to accommodate memory allocation requests. The address of the first location beyond the end of the data segment is called the *break address* or *break value*. There are two system calls, `brk(S)` and `sbrk(S)`, which allow a process to manipulate its break address.

The prototypes of both system calls are:

```
int brk(char *endds) ;
char *sbrk(int incr) ;
```

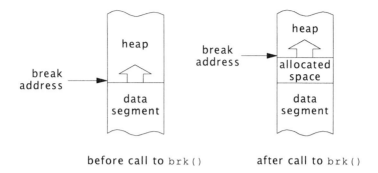

before call to brk()   after call to brk()

Figure 2.3   Allocating memory dynamically from the heap

The brk(S) system call sets the break address to endds and either allocates or de-allocates the memory accordingly. sbrk(S) adds the increment incr to the break address. If incr is negative then memory can be de-allocated. The library functions malloc(S), free(S) and realloc(S) are constructed using the brk(S) and sbrk(S) system calls.

In the program below, sbrk(S) is first called with an argument of 0. This returns the current break address. The sbrk(S) function is then called again with an argument of 32 bytes. The new break address is returned and the difference between the new and old values is printed.

```
main()
{
    char *obrk ;
    char *nbrk ;

    obrk = sbrk(0) ;
    printf("current break address = 0x%x\n", obrk) ;
    nbrk = sbrk(32) ;
    printf("new break address      = 0x%x\n", nbrk) ;
    printf("   difference          = %d bytes\n", nbrk - obrk) ;
}
```

The output of the program for one particular run is as follows:

```
$ a.out
current break address = 0x401ca4
new break address      = 0x402ca4
   difference          = 4096 bytes
```

Note that although only 32 bytes were requested, the system allocated 4096 bytes. This is the size of a physical page of memory on the Intel i386 family of processors and therefore the smallest unit of memory that can be allocated by the kernel. For details on i386 memory management see chapter 6.

The allocation of space through use of brk(S) is shown in Figure 2.3.

As shown in Figure 2.2, the amount of memory that is available for dynamic allocation is bounded by the starting address of library text and data for the memory image of ELF object files or the bottom of the stack in the memory image of COFF object files. There are also system limits on the amount of memory that individual processes can allocate. Section 2.8.2 describes the limits, including memory constraints, within which a process executes.

2.4 Error handling

In section 2.1.1, the difference between system calls and library functions was described. One additional difference between the two types of call is the method by which errors are returned. System calls usually return -1 if the call failed and set the global variable errno to the error returned by the kernel. Library functions do not generally set errno on failure. The individual manual pages should be read carefully to determine the return value and whether errno is set or not.

The possible values that errno can take, including a brief description of each error, can be found in the <sys/errno.h> header file. The Intro(S) manual page provides a more detailed description of each error code.

In order to access errno it must be declared as an extern int prior to being accessed. Alternatively, the <sys/errno.h> header file should be included within the program which declares errno internally.

The program below attempts to open a file which does not exist in order to show the error value returned from the open(S) system call. To see which other errors can be returned refer to the open(S) manual page.

The perror(S) library function can be used to display a message describing the error associated with the value in errno. The string passed to perror(S) is always displayed first.

```
#include <fcntl.h>
#include <stdio.h>

extern int errno ;

main()
{
    int fd ;
    fd = open("This_file_does_not_exist", O_RDONLY) ;
    if (fd == -1) {
        printf("fd = %d, errno = %d\n", fd, errno) ;
        perror("errno meaning") ;
    }
}
```

The file requested is to be opened read only (O_RDONLY). If open(S) fails then it returns -1 and sets errno to the appropriate error value passed back by the kernel. The open(S) system call is described in detail in section 2.5.1. Note however that printf(S) may also fail, resulting in a different value being placed in errno. The value of errno should therefore be checked immediately following the call to open(S).

The output of the program, assuming the file does not exist, is shown as follows:

```
$ a.out
fd = -1, errno = 2
errno meaning: No such file or directory
```

The following are some of the more common error return codes that can be returned by the kernel following an error:

E2BIG	An argument list longer than ARG_MAX bytes was passed to a member of the exec(S) family of routines. The argument list limit is the sum of the size of the user specified arguments to exec(S) plus the size of the environment's exported shell variables.
EACCES	An attempt was made to access a file in a way forbidden as a result of a comparison of attributes of the process (process ID and effective user IDs) and the access attributes of the file.
EALREADY	An operation was attempted on a non-blocking object that already had an operation in progress.
EBADF	A file descriptor does not refer to an open file, a read request is made to a file that is open only for writing or a write request is made to a file that is open only for reading.
EBADFD	A file descriptor does not refer to an open file or a read request was made to a file that is open only for writing.
EBUSY	The device or resource is currently unavailable.
ECHILD	A wait(S) system call was executed by a process that has no existing children or children for which a wait has not already been issued.
EDEADLK	A deadlock situation with respect to file and record locking was detected and avoided.
EEXIST	An existing filename was passed as an argument, for example to the link(S) system call.
EFAULT	The system encountered a hardware fault in attempting to use an argument of a routine, for example a pointer argument is passed an invalid address.
EFBIG	The size of a file exceeded the maximum file size, FCHR_MAX.
EINPROGRESS	An operation that takes a long time to complete was attempted on a non-blocking object.
EINTR	An asynchronous signal, for example interrupt or quit, which the user has chosen to catch, occurred during a system service routine. If execution is resumed after processing the signal, it will appear as if the interrupted routine call returned this error condition.

EINVAL	An invalid argument was specified.
EIO	A physical I/O error has occurred.
EISDIR	An attempt was made to perform an operation not appropriate for a directory, such as `write(S)`.
ELOOP	Too many symbolic links were encountered in a pathname traversal.
EMFILE	The number of open file descriptors exceeds OPEN_MAX.
ENAMETOOLONG	The length of a pathname argument exceeds PATH_MAX, or the length of a pathname exceeds NAME_MAX while _POSIX_NO_TRUNC is in effect.
ENFILE	The system file table is full (SYS_OPEN files are open, and temporarily no more files can be opened).
ENODEV	An attempt was made to apply an inappropriate operation to a device (for example, read a write-only device, open a device not yet allocated).
ENOENT	A file name is specified which should exist but doesn't, or one of the directories in a pathname does not exist.
ENOEXEC	A request is made to execute a file which has an invalid format.
ENOMEM	During execution of an `exec(S)`, `brk(S)`, or `sbrk(S)` system call, a program asks for more space than the system is able to supply.
ENOSPC	While writing to an ordinary file or creating a directory entry, there is no free space left on the device.
ENOSR	During a STREAMS `open(S)`, no STREAMS head data structures or queues were available.
ENOTDIR	A non-directory name was specified where a directory is required.
ENOTTY	A call was made to the `ioctl(S)` system call specifying a file that is not a special character device.
ENXIO	I/O on a special file refers to a sub-device which does not exist, or exists beyond the limit of the device.
ERESTART	An interrupted system call should be restarted.
ESRCH	No process can be found corresponding to the process identifier specified.

For full details of the values that `errno` can take see `Intro(S)`.

2.5 File management

There are two main interfaces for file I/O: low level routines which access the kernel directly and the standard buffered input/output library functions defined by the standard input/output library, `stdio`.

Since the buffered I/O routines are constructed using the lower level, system call interfaces, this section concentrates on the system call interface. Section 2.5.2 describes how the standard I/O library works.

2.5.1 File access functions

In this section, the basic system calls available for file I/O are presented. It is this set of calls, shown in Table 2.5, which provides the basis for the standard I/O library.

Table 2.5   Basic file operations

System call	Description
open(S)	Open the specified file for reading and/or writing.
creat(S)	Create a new file or overwrite an existing file.
close(S)	Close the file using the handle returned from open() etc.
dup(S)	Duplicate an open file descriptor.
dup2(S)	Duplicate an open file descriptor specifying the target.
lseek(S)	Set the file pointer to a specific byte offset within the file.
read(S)	Read a specified number of bytes from the file.
readv(S)	Read the file contents into multiple buffers.
write(S)	Write a specified number of bytes to the file.
writev(S)	Write to the file using a specified number of buffers.
pipe(S)	Open a bi-directional communication channel.
fcntl(S)	Provide file control over an open file.

Each of the system calls is described with examples below.

The open(S) system call

The prototype for open(S) is:

```
#include <fcntl.h>
int open(const char *path, int oflag, mode_t mode);
```

The `path` argument is a pointer to the pathname of the file. The pathname can be either *relative* (starts from the current working directory) or *absolute* (starts from the root directory). The `oflag` argument is used to specify how the file should be opened and is formed as a bit-wise OR of the flags shown in Table 2.6. The `mode` argument is used only when creating a new file and is therefore optional.

Table 2.6   Flags passed to open(S)

oflag	Description
O_RDONLY	Open the file for reading only.
O_WRONLY	Open the file for writing only.
O_RDWR	Open the file for both reading and writing.
O_APPEND	Set the file pointer to the end of the file prior to each write.
O_CREAT	If the file exists, this flag has no effect otherwise the file is created with the owner equal to effective user ID and group equal to effective group ID. The file permissions are specified by mode.
O_EXCL	The open will fail if the file exists.
O_NOCTTY	Prevent the file from becoming the controlling TTY if the pathname refers to a terminal device.
O_SYNC	All subsequent writes will force the data and file meta-data to be written to disk before the write returns.
O_TRUNC	If the file exists and is a regular file then the size of the file is truncated to zero.
O_NONBLOCK	This effects subsequent reads and writes by specifying that read and write operations will not block if data is not available to be read or the process needs to sleep on resources to write the data.

If the call to open(S) is successful, a non-negative file descriptor is returned. The process can then use the file descriptor for any subsequent references to the file.

If the O_CREAT flag is set, the file will be created if it does not already exist. Here, the mode argument passed to open(S) is used to create the file mode creation mask. Details of file access permissions are described in section 2.5.5.

Only one of the flags O_WRONLY, O_RDONLY or O_RDWR can be passed to open(S). The O_SYNC flag ensures that any data to be written will be written to the physical file on disk before the write(S) call returns.

The kernel maintains a cache of data that has been read from disk or is about to be written to disk called the *buffer cache*. Usually a write will only write the data into the buffer cache before returning. The buffer cache is described in detail in chapter 9.

The O_TRUNC flag is used to ensure that any data that existed in the file before the open(S) system call will be removed before the call returns. This flag is set when opening files where the previous contents are not required.

The O_NONBLOCK flag is used so that subsequent reads and writes will return immediately with errno set to EAGAIN if the kernel cannot return any data to be read or requires that the process goes to sleep when writing data.

The creat(S) system call

The creat(S) system call is used to create a new regular file or to modify an existing file to take on properties specified by the arguments to creat(S). The prototype is:

```
#include <fcntl.h>
int creat(const char *path, mode_t mode) ;
```

The `path` argument specifies the file to be created and the `mode` argument is used to create the file mode creation mask. For further details of file permissions see section 2.5.5. If the call is successful, a non-negative integer, namely the file descriptor, will be returned.

If the file already exists then the size of the file is truncated to zero and the existing mode and owner are unchanged. The `creat(S)` system call is identical to the `open(S)` system called invoked with the following arguments:

```
open(path, O_WRONLY|O_CREAT|O_TRUNC, mode) ;
```

The `close(S)` system call

The `close(S)` system call breaks the association between a file descriptor and its associated open file. The file descriptor can then be allocated by the kernel on subsequent calls to `open(S)`, `pipe(S)`, `fcntl(S)` or `dup(S)`. The prototype for `close(S)` is:

```
#include <unistd.h>

int close(int fildes) ;
```

If the call to `close(S)` is successful, 0 is returned. Otherwise −1 is returned and `errno` set to indicate the reason for failure.

Many programs including most of the examples throughout the book do not close files explicitly before returning from the program. Although not explicitly described by the `exit(S)` manual page, all forms of exit from a process will involve an implicit close of open files either by user level libraries or by the kernel before it terminates the process.

The `dup(S)` and `dup2(S)` system calls

The `dup(S)` system call is used to duplicate an already existing file descriptor. The prototype is:

```
int dup(int fildes) ;
```

The file descriptor must have been previously created by a call to either the `open(S)`, `creat(S)`, `pipe(S)`, `dup(S)` or `dup2(S)` system calls. If the call to `dup(S)` is successful, the new file descriptor allocated by the kernel is returned. The newly allocated file descriptor and the file descriptor passed to `dup(S)` both refer to the same file, they both share the same file pointer and the same access mode.

The `dup2(S)` system call provides similar functionality to `dup(S)` but gives the caller more flexibility with the choice of the new file descriptor returned. The prototype for `dup2(S)` is:

```
int dup2(int fildes, int fildes2) ;
```

The file descriptor to be duplicated is passed in `fildes` and the new file descriptor is set to be `fildes2`. If the file descriptor referred to by `fildes2` is already used then it is closed first. If successful, the new file descriptor is returned by `dup2(S)`.

The `getty` program invoked soon after kernel initialisation opens the specified terminal line receiving a file descriptor of 0 (`stdin`). The file descriptor is then duplicated twice resulting in file descriptors 1 (`stdout`) and 2 (`stderr`) before the `login` program is called.

The `lseek(S)` system call

A file descriptor is used to reference a file pointer which is an offset into the file where the next read or write will start. When a file is first opened the file pointer is either set to 0 or to the size of the file if `O_APPEND` is specified to `open(S)`. However, direct access to any part of the file can be achieved through use of the `lseek(S)` system call which alters the file pointer to a specified offset. The prototype for `lseek(S)` is:

```
#include <unistd.h>

off_t lseek(int fildes, off_t offset, int whence) ;
```

The `offset` is interpreted according to the `whence` argument which can take one of the following values:

SEEK_CUR	(0)	The file pointer is set to its current value plus `offset`.
SEEK_END	(1)	Set the file pointer to the end of the file plus `offset`.
SEEK_SET	(2)	Set the file pointer equal to `offset` bytes.

If the call to `lseek(S)` is successful, a non-negative integer indicating the file pointer is returned. For example, the following call:

```
sz = lseek(fd, 0, SEEK_END) ;
```

will set the value of `sz` to the size of the file specified by the file descriptor `fd`.

The `read(S)` and `readv(S)` system calls

The `read(S)` and `readv(S)` system calls are used to read from a file using a file descriptor returned by the `open(S)`, `creat(S)`, `dup(S)`, `dup2(S)` or `fcntl(S)` system calls. The prototypes for `read(S)` and `readv(S)` are:

```
#include <unistd.h>

ssize_t read(int fildes, void *buf, size_t nbyte) ;

#include <sys/types.h>
#include <sys/uio.h>

ssize_t readv(int fildes, struct iovec *iov, int iovcnt) ;
```

The arguments to the read(S) system call specify that nbyte bytes of data should be read from the file identified by fildes using the current file pointer. The data read should be copied by the kernel to the buffer pointed to by buf. The file pointer will be incremented by the number of bytes read.

The readv(S) system call allows iovcnt reads to be performed with the same system call. The iov argument points to an array of iovec structures whose elements are:

```
void        *iov_base;
size_t       iov_len;
```

The number of bytes read is returned from both read(S) and readv(S) which should be verified by the caller.

The following program demonstrates the use of both the lseek(S) and read(S) system calls to read alternate lines of a text file. To simplify the program, the number of lines (nlines) and the size of each line (LINESZ) is already known to the program.

Using the same framework provided in this program, it is possible to construct a similar program which invokes a single readv(S) system call to obtain all the data requested. Another alternative is the use of memory mapped files described in section 2.5.4.

```
#include <unistd.h>
#include <fcntl.h>

#define LINESZ 11
char    buf[LINESZ+1] ;
int     nlines = 10 ;

main()
{
    int fd, ln=nlines ;

    buf[LINESZ] = '\0' ;

    fd = open("testfile", O_RDONLY) ;
    if (fd < 0)
        pexit("open") ;

    for (ln = 1 ; ln <= nlines ; ln += 2) {
        if (lseek(fd, ln*LINESZ, SEEK_SET) < 0)
            pexit("lseek") ;
        if (read(fd, buf, LINESZ) < 0)
            pexit("read") ;
        printf("line %d = %s", ln, buf) ;
    }
}
```

The contents of the testfile are shown below. Note that the line size is 11 characters since it includes the newline character in addition to those characters visible here. After opening the file, the program loops for the number of lines in the file divided by two. For each iteration, an lseek(S) call is made using SEEK_SET to set the file pointer to the byte from which the next read should take place. The `read(S)` system call is made after seeking to read the line and the data read is then printed.

The `testfile` and the output of the program are as follows:

```
$ cat testfile
**line 1**
**line 2**
**line 3**
**line 4**
**line 5**
**line 6**
**line 7**
**line 8**
**line 9**
**line 10*
$ a.out
line 1 = **line 2**
line 3 = **line 4**
line 5 = **line 6**
line 7 = **line 8**
line 9 = **line 10*
```

The `write(S)` and `writev(S)` system calls

The `write(S)` and `writev(S)` system calls mirror the `read(S)` and `readv(S)` system calls. They are used to write data to a file using a file descriptor returned by the `open(S)`, `creat(S)`, `dup(S)`, `dup2(S)` or `fcntl(S)` system calls. The prototypes for `write(S)` and `writev(S)` are:

```
#include <unistd.h>

ssize_t write(int fildes, const void *buf, size_t nbyte) ;

#include <sys/types.h>
#include <sys/uio.h>

ssize_t writev(int fildes, const struct iovec *iov, int iovcnt) ;
```

The arguments to the `write(S)` system call specify that nbyte bytes of data should be written to the file identified by `fildes` starting at the current file pointer. The data to be written, and therefore accessed by the kernel, is located in the buffer pointed to by `buf`. When the write has completed, the file pointer will be incremented by the number of bytes written. The number of bytes written is returned by `write(S)`.

Similar to `readv(S)`, the `writev(S)` system call allows multiple writes to be performed with the same system call using the array of `iovec` structures as defined above. The number of bytes read in total is returned from `writev(S)`.

As with the `read(S)` and `readv(S)` system calls, the number of bytes written should always be checked on return from `write(S)` and `writev(S)`.

The `pipe (S)` system call

The `pipe (S)` system call creates a single duplex I/O channel called a pipe which allows two related processes to communicate. The prototype for `pipe (S)` is:

```
#include <unistd.h>

int pipe(int fildes[2]) ;
```

Two file descriptors are returned in `fildes[]` such that `fildes[0]` is used to read data from the pipe while `fildes[1]` is used to write data into the pipe. The following simple program demonstrates the basic principles of using pipes:

```
#include <unistd.h>
#include <string.h>

#define BUFSIZ 256

char *message = "data to be sent through the pipe" ;
char buf[BUFSIZ] ;

main()
{
    int fd[2], nread ;

    if (pipe(fd) == -1)
        pexit("pipe creation:") ;

    if (write(fd[1], message, strlen(message)) < 0)
        pexit("pipe write:") ;

    nread = read(fd[0], buf, BUFSIZ) ;
    printf("nread=%d, data read = [%s]\n", nread, buf) ;
}
```

The output of the program is shown below. Note that if a process reads from the pipe while no data is present, the process will sleep indefinitely or until interrupted by a signal, for example the `SIGINT` signal generated by hitting the `Delete` key. The `fcntl(S)` system call described in the next section can be used to prevent the process from blocking if no data is available. Signals are described in section 2.6.

```
$ a.out
nread=32, data read = [data to be sent through the pipe]
```

Note that the traditional method for buffering data within the pipe is to allocate space on disk within the filesystem. While this mechanism can still be used, a high performance pipe filesystem `HPPS` provided with the OpenServer Release 5 version of SCO UNIX can be used in its place to gain better performance. With `HPPS`, all data is buffered in memory avoiding the overhead of reading and writing the data to or from disk.

The implementation of both pipe mechanisms is described in chapter 11.

The `fcntl(S)` system call

Once a file has been opened, it can be controlled in a number of ways. The `fcntl(S)` system call defined below allows a number of different commands to be performed on the file descriptor `fildes` passed as the first argument.

```
#include <fcntl.h>
int fcntl(int fildes, int cmd, ...)
```

`fcntl(S)` usually has a third argument whose type and value is dependent on the `cmd`. The values that `cmd` can take are as follows:

F_DUPFD   Return a new file descriptor whose value is greater than or equal to `arg`, the third argument. The file descriptor returned will point to the same open file or pipe referenced by `fildes`.

F_GETFD   Return the close-on-exec flag associated with `fildes`. If the low order bit is 0 then the file is remains open across an `execve(S)` system call, otherwise the file is closed across `execve(S)`. See section 2.7 for details of the various `exec(S)` system calls.

F_GETFL   Retrieve the file status, the flags set by `open(S)`.

F_SETFD   Set the file's close-on-exec flag.

F_SETFL   Set the file status flags to `arg`, the third argument.

F_GETLK   Return file lock information.

F_SETLK   Set or clear a file segment lock.

F_SETLKW   As for F_SETLK but may result in the process sleeping.

For further details on each of these commands see chapter 8.

The `ioctl(S)` system call

Although a little out of place in this chapter since it deals with devices and STREAMS, the `ioctl(S)` system call operates on an open file descriptor in a similar manner to the `fcntl(S)` system call.

```
#include <unistd.h>
int ioctl(int fildes, int request, int arg) ;
```

The file descriptor refers to a device and the `request` argument refers to a device specific control function. As with `fcntl(S)`, the additional argument may be used depending on the device's interpretation of the `request` argument.

2.5.2 The standard I/O library

Although I/O mechanisms are not part of the C language, nearly all programs need to read from and write to physical devices such as terminals and printers. The I/O functions presented above are not part of the C language but represent the I/O interface between applications and the UNIX kernel where the physical I/O is actually performed.

Many UNIX programmers rarely use the low level mechanisms described in the previous sections and use the facilities offered by the standard I/O library instead. The functions supported by this library perform what is usually called *buffered I/O*. To use these functions, the header file <stdio.h> should be included in the caller's program.

A complete description of the standard I/O library can be found in the manual page stdio(S). This section highlights its implementation.

The terms *standard input, output* and *error* are commonly used within C and UNIX environments and are represented by the symbolic names stdin, stdout and stderr. The terms *file streams* and *file pointers* are used interchangeably to represent file handles used for buffered I/O. For example, issuing the command:

```
$ cat file | mycat
```

can be defined as follows: send the standard output from cat file to the standard input of mycat. By default, when a program starts running, the first three file pointers are already assigned to the standard I/O streams shown in Table 2.7.

Table 2.7   Assignment of standard I/O streams

File descriptor	File stream	Description
0	stdin	Standard input.
1	stdout	Standard output.
2	stderr	Standard error.

The choice between using buffered I/O or the I/O system calls described earlier is dependent on a number of factors including portability, flexibility and how much direct control is needed over I/O. For example, consider the following two calls:

```
write(1, "hello world\n",  12) ;
printf("hello world\n") ;
```

For the write(S) system call, the file descriptor used for standard output must be explicitly stated, which loses portability since it makes an assumption about the assignment of stdout to the file descriptor 1. Also, the size of the data to be written must be explicitly stated since there is no assumption made about the type of data being written, for example a null-terminated string.

The `printf(S)` function is identical to the `fprintf(S)` library function called with the additional `stdout` argument as follows:

```
fprintf(stdout, "hello world\n") ;
```

This uses the `write(S)` system call internally but removes the complication of knowing which file pointer corresponds to `stdout` and what the size of the data should be.

Each file pointer references a `FILE` structure which contains the associated file descriptor, the buffer associated with the stream and supporting information. An example `FILE` structure will contain fields similar to the following:

```
struct FILE {
    int     _fd ;
    int     _cnt ;
    char    *_buf ;
    char    *_ptr ;
    int     _flag ;
} ;

extern FILE _iob[NFILE] ;

#define stdin   (&_iob[0]) ;
#define stdout  (&_iob[1]) ;
#define stderr  (&_iob[2]) ;
```

When a user declares a `FILE` structure and invokes `fopen(S)` as follows:

```
FILE *fp ;

fp = fopen("myfile", "r") ;
```

one of the `_iob[]` array entries will be allocated, the file opened via `open(S)` and a buffer allocated to hold data to be read. Subsequent calls to `getc(S)`, `fread(S)` and so on will pre-read data to the size of the buffer such that following calls may not need to access the kernel to satisfy the call.

A more complete description of the standard I/O library and examples of how the buffered I/O library functions use the I/O system calls is described in Kernighan and Ritchie (1978).

2.5.3 File links

Each file within a filesystem has an associated *link count*, a count of the number of physical links to the file. For example, the files `/home/log` and `/usr/log` have different pathnames but may access the same physical file and therefore file contents. In this case the file has a link count of 2.

Whenever a file is removed the link count is decremented. If the link count reaches zero, the file is removed. This type of link is called a *hard link* as opposed to a *symbolic link*. For example, if the file `/usr/bin` is a symbolic link, the contents of the `/usr/bin` file is a pathname which is used to locate the real file.

Although two separate directory entries will be created for hard linked files, only one physical file exists, thus removing the file via rm(C) will decrement the link count but not remove the file.

The link(S) system call is used to create hard links. The prototype for link(S) is:

```
int link (char *path, char *newpath) ;
```

Creating a link performs two operations. Firstly, a directory entry is created for the name which contains the *inode* number of the file to be linked, a number used by the filesystem to identify the file uniquely. Secondly, the link count of the inode is increased. For further details on file management including inode management see chapter 8.

The effect of the link(S) system call can be seen with the following commands:

```
        $ touch file1
        $ ls -li file1
1       98 -rw-r--r--   1 spate      group      0 Jun 10 11:43 file1
2       $ ln file1 file2
        $ ls -li file1 file2
3       98 -rw-r--r--   2 spate      group      0 Jun 10 11:43 file1
4       98 -rw-r--r--   2 spate      group      0 Jun 10 11:43 file2
        $ rm file1
        $ ls -li file2
5       98 -rw-r--r--   1 spate      group      0 Jun 10 11:43 file2
```

The touch(C) command creates the empty file1. The directory entry for file1 is then displayed with the ls -li command on line 1. There are two fields of interest here; the first field (98) is the file's inode number. The field following the file's permissions, 1, is the link count of the file.

A hard link is made from file2 to file1 by using the ln(C) command on line 2 which calls the link(S) system call internally. file2 is created and shares the same file data and meta-data contents as displayed on lines 3 and 4 where the inode of each file is identical and the link count has been increased from 1 to 2. Finally, file1 is removed and the directory entry for file2 is displayed again on line 5. The file still remains although the link count has been decremented.

The rm(C) command invokes the unlink(S) system call. The prototype for unlink(S) is shown below. The path argument specifies the file to be unlinked.

```
int unlink(char *path) ;
```

A system call to remove a file explicitly is not feasible since there may be many hard links to the file and some of the directory entries associated with each link may not be accessible by the process invoking the call.

If there is more than one hard link to a file, utilities such as fsck(ADM) must be able to determine all directory entries which point to the file in order to maintain filesystem integrity. This means that a hard link cannot span multiple filesystems.

The symbolic link briefly mentioned above allows one file to point either to another file within the same filesystem or to a separate file within another filesystem. A symbolic link is created by issuing the `ln -s` command which invokes the `symlink(S)` system call.

```
int symlink(char *path, char *newpath) ;
```

The `path` argument specifies the location of the file to which the symbolic link specified by the argument `newpath` should point. Consider the following two arguments:

```
path = /home/spate/bin/myshell
newpath = /home/peterk/shlink
```

Following a call to `symlink(S)` the file `shlink` can be displayed as follows:

```
$ ls -l /home/peterk/shlink
lrwxrwxrwx 1 peterk group 23 Jun 10 19:37 /home/peterk/shlink ->
/home/spate/bin/myshell
```

When a system call is invoked which needs to access the file through `open(S)`, `read(S)` and so on, `shlink` is used only to reference the target file. Thus, the file that the symbolic link refers to can be a regular file, directory, pipe, device file or even another symbolic link. The contents of the symbolic link can be read using the `readlink(S)` system call:

```
int readlink(char *path, char *buf, int bufsiz) ;
```

The `path` argument specifies the symbolic link to read. The kernel returns up to `bufsiz` characters of the link name in the buffer pointed to by the `buf` argument. The following program reads the contents of the `shlink` symbolic link created above:

```
#define BUFSIZ 256

main()
{
    char buf[BUFSIZ] ;
    int  nread ;

    nread = readlink("/home/peterk/shlink", buf, BUFSIZ) ;
    if (nread < 0)
        pexit("readlink") ;

    buf[nread] = '\0' ;
    printf("nread  = %d\n",nread);
    printf("symlink = [%s]\n", buf) ;
}
```

Note that `readlink(S)` does not null terminate the contents of the link read. The output of the program below shows the correct link being returned:

```
$ a.out
nread  = 23
symlink = [/home/spate/bin/myshell]
```

2.5.4 Memory mapped files

The mmap(S) system call provides an alternative method of file access to the read(S) and write(S) system calls. Instead of explicitly invoking read(S) or write(S) to read or write specific amounts of data at specified offsets from or to a user supplied buffer, the user can *map* parts of the file's contents into its address space. The file can then be accessed by reading and writing from or to memory.

Thus, the effect of issuing a single store instruction has the same effect as calling the write(S) system call with a single byte. The prototype for mmap(S) is as follows:

```
#include <sys/types.h>
#include <sys/mman.h>

caddr_t mmap(caddr_t addr, size_t len, int prot, int flags, /
             int fd, off_t off) ;
```

This requests that the kernel establish a mapping starting at the address addr for len bytes from the file specified by fd at offset off bytes from the start of the file. The file must be opened prior to invoking mmap(S) with the appropriate permissions which correspond to the prot argument.

Although it is usual for most applications to let the kernel choose the address where the mapping will start by setting the addr argument to zero, the caller can request the start address by setting addr to a specific address. If the call to mmap(S) is successful, the mapping is established at the address returned from mmap(S).

The system always rounds up len to the next page boundary. A page is 4096 bytes (4K) on the Intel i386 family of processors so setting len to one byte will always result in a 4Kb page being allocated.

The prot argument specifies the accessibility of the mapping for the mapped pages. The values that prot can take are shown in Table 2.8.

Table 2.8 mmap(S) protection flags

prot values	Description
PROT_READ	Pages are readable.
PROT_WRITE	Pages are writable.
PROT_EXEC	Pages can be executed.
PROT_NONE	Pages cannot be accessed.

If the prot field is constructed as a bit-wise OR of the PROT_READ and PROT_WRITE flags, this provides the same access privileges as calling open(S) with the oflag argument set to O_RDWR. See the open(S) manual page for further details of the arguments to open(S).

By setting the flags argument to PROT_EXEC, applications can provide their own loading mechanisms. The PROT_EXEC flag is used extensively by the dynamic linker which maps dynamic libraries into the process's address space during process creation. The PROT_NONE flag can be used for implementing user level memory management techniques such as distributed shared memory by allowing user processes to determine when memory is accessed.

For most processes, the most effective use of mmap(S) is to have shared access to the contents of a file in a coherent manner in the same way that shared memory allows coherent access to a set of physical pages. Through use of mapping the /dev/zero device, a parent and child can also share memory through the use of mmap(S). For further details of mapping /dev/zero see section 11.4.6.

The flags argument specifies whether the mapping is private to the process or whether writes are visible to other processes mapping the same part of the file. The values that can be taken by flags are shown in Table 2.9.

Table 2.9   Types of mappings

mmap(S) flags	Description
MAP_SHARED	Pages can be shared with other processes.
MAP_PRIVATE	The pages are private to the caller.
MAP_FIXED	The system must establish the mapping at the address specified by the addr argument.

Figure 2.4 illustrates the effect on the process's address space when invoking mmap(S). The off argument specifies the offset into the file and must also be a multiple of the system's page size, for example 0, 4096, 8192 and so on.

mmap(0, 4097, PROT_READ, MAP_PRIVATE, fd, 4096) ;

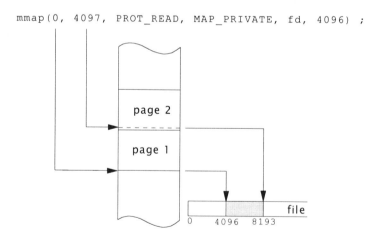

Figure 2.4   Accessing files with mmap(S)

Although the user requested a mapping of 4097 bytes, the kernel rounded this up to 8192 bytes which is equal to two pages. The remainder of the second page will be zero filled when the page is created by the kernel. The application may use this space although the data will not be written back to the disk.

The following two programs demonstrate a simple implementation of the cat (C) command. The first program uses the read(S) system call, buffering data on each read. The second program uses mmap(S), trying to map the whole file into its address space and then outputting it with a single write(S) call.

```
#include <fcntl.h>

#define BUFSZ 4096
char buf[BUFSZ] ;

main(int argc, char *argv[])
{
    int fd ;
    int nread ;

    fd = open(argv[1], O_RDONLY) ;
    while ((nread = read(fd, buf, BUFSZ)) > 0)
        write(1, buf, nread) ;
}
```

In this program, a buffer must be allocated before the data can be read from the file. The buffer allocated is BUFSZ bytes in size. All reads from the file are therefore in units of BUFSZ bytes. It would of course be possible to use the fstat(S) system call to find the size of the file and then to use malloc(S) or sbrk(S) to allocate appropriate storage prior to the read(S) system call.

The version of the program using mmap(S) now follows:

```
#include <sys/types.h>
#include <sys/mman.h>
#include <sys/stat.h>
#include <fcntl.h>

main(int argc, char *argv[])
{
    int         fd ;
    caddr_t     maddr ;
    struct stat st ;

    fd = open(argv[1], O_RDONLY) ;
    fstat(fd, &st) ;
    maddr = mmap(0,(size_t)st.st_size,PROT_READ,MAP_SHARED,fd,0) ;
    write(1, (char *)maddr, (size_t)st.st_size) ;
}
```

In this second example, the fstat(S) library function must be invoked in order to find the size of the file before mmap(S) can be invoked.

There are a number of additional calls supported for managing memory mapped regions. The munmap(S) system call can be used to remove the mapping of pages from a previously established mapping. The msync(S) system call is used to synchronise the memory copy of the data with the file on disk and optionally invalidate parts of the mapping so that subsequent accesses will result in accessing the data from disk again. The mprotect(S) system call is used to alter the access protection previously established by mmap(S) or a previous call to mprotect(S).

For further details on memory mapped files see section 8.7.4.

2.5.5 File permissions

Introduced in section 2.3.3, the user ID and group ID identify the real owner of a process. When a program is executed, it takes on two additional identifiers, the *effective user ID* and *effective group ID*.

The effective user ID and effective group ID of a process determine the process's file access rights during execution. In most circumstances the user ID/group ID and effective user ID/effective group ID are the same. However, the permissions of executable files can be changed so that a user can access privileged commands and resources.

A good example is the passwd command which allows users to change their login password. The access permissions of the passwd command are typically:

```
---x--s--x    1 bin        auth             57852 Apr 13 23:02 /bin/passwd
```

which shows that the file is executable by the user, bin, members of the auth group and others. The group permissions have the set group ID bit set. When a user invokes the passwd command, the process's effective user ID remains the same as the user ID but the effective group ID of the process becomes the group ID of passwd, in this case auth. The following program is used to clarify further the notion of effective group ID:

```
main()
{
    printf("UID  = %d, GID  = %d\n", getuid(), getgid()) ;
    printf("EUID = %d, EGID = %d\n", geteuid(), getegid()) ;
}
```

When run, the program displays the user ID/effective user ID and group ID/effective group ID as follows:

```
$ id
uid=13583(spate) gid=50(group) groups=50(group)
$ ls -l ids
-rwx------    1 spate      group           52699 Jun  1 11:46 ids
$ ids
UID  = 13583, GID  = 50
EUID = 13583, EGID = 50
```

The following root-issued commands change the file's owner and group. This is intended to give the ids program the same access permissions as /bin/passwd.

```
# chown root ids
# chgrp sys ids
# chmod 2111 ids
```

The program is then re-run still as user spate:

```
$ ls -l ids
---x--s--x   1 root      sys         52699 Jun  1 11:47 ids
$ ids
UID  = 13583, GID  = 50
EUID = 13583, EGID = 3
```

2.5.6 Filesystem navigation

Associated with each process, there are two directories, the *root directory* and the *current working directory*. When a file is accessed by a pathname the kernel searches from either the root directory if the pathname is *absolute* or from the current working directory if the pathname is *relative*. An absolute pathname has a forward slash (/) as the first character. All other pathnames are relative, for example /etc/motd is an absolute pathname and misc/file is a relative pathname.

A process may change its root directory using the chroot(S) system call. This creates a restrictive environment in which a process can operate without impacting the surrounding files. An example of where this is necessary is during construction of a large software project, for example UNIX itself, where the master files in the tree need to be protected to avoid being overwritten by possibly invalid copies. For example, a version of the ls(C) command which still contains bugs could overwrite /bin/ls which is in use.

A process may also change its current working directory using the chdir(S) or fchdir(S) system calls. The current working directory can be found using the getcwd(S) system call which returns a character string representing the directory.

The following program prints the current working directory and then changes it to /tmp:

```
#include <unistd.h>
#include <stdlib.h>

main()
{
    char *cwd ;
    cwd = getcwd(0, 64) ;
    if (cwd != NULL)
        printf("current working directory = %s\n", cwd) ;
    else
        pexit("getcwd") ;
    if (chdir("/tmp") == -1)
        pexit("chdir") ;
    else {
        cwd = getcwd(0, 64) ;
        if (cwd != NULL)
            printf("new current working directory = %s\n", cwd) ;
        else
            pexit("getcwd") ;
    }
}
```

The getcwd(S) function will return up to 64 bytes of the pathname. If a 0 is specified as the first argument, space will be allocated dynamically, otherwise the caller must specify a buffer in which to return the pathname. The output of the program is:

```
$ a.out
current working directory = /home/spate/bin
new current working directory = /tmp
```

In addition to moving through the filesystem hierarchy by changing the current working directory, a process may create and remove directories using the `mkdir(S)` and `rmdir(S)` system calls. The prototypes of both functions are:

```
#include <sys/stat.h>

int mkdir(const char *path, mode_t mode) ;
int rmdir(char *path) ;
```

When creating a directory, the `path` argument specifies the directory to be created and the `mode` argument specifies the permissions for the new directory. The `mode` argument should be constructed as a bit-wise OR of the flags shown in Table 2.10.

Table 2.10   File modes passed to `mkdir(S)`

mode	Description
S_IEXEC	Execute (search access) by owner.
S_IREAD	Read by owner.
S_IRGRP	Read by group.
S_IROTH	Read by others.
S_IWRITE	Write by owner.
S_IWGRP	Write by group.
S_IWOTH	Write by other.
S_IXGRP	Execute (search access) by group.
S_IXOTH	Execute (search access) by others.

The flags passed to `mkdir(S)` and their corresponding position in the output displayed by `ls -l` are shown in Figure 2.5. The permissions of the `/etc` directory are shown here by issuing the command `ls -l`.

Note that the same permissions also apply to regular files. The main difference between file and directory permissions concerns the execute bit which is needed to execute a regular file and to read the contents of a directory.

Figure 2.5   Directory permissions

2.5.7 Modifying file and directory owner/permissions

The owner and group of any type of file may be changed with the chown(S) and fchown(S) system calls. The owner and group of a symbolic link can be changed with the lchown(S) system call.

```
#include <unistd.h>
#include <sys/stat.h>

int chown(const char *path, uid_t owner, gid_t group) ;
int lchown(const char *path, uid_t owner, gid_t group) ;
int fchown(int fildes, uid_t owner, gid_t group) ;
```

The chown(S) and fchown(S) system calls change the file specified by the path or fildes arguments. If path or fildes is a symbolic link then only the owner and group of the target file are changed. If the caller wishes to change the owner and group of the symbolic link itself, the lchown(S) system call should be used.

File permissions can be changed by the chmod(S) and fchmod(S) system calls. The prototypes for both functions are:

```
#include <sys/types.h>
#include <sys/stat.h>

int chmod(const char *path, mode_t mode) ;
int fchmod(int fildes, mode_t mode) ;
```

The mode argument is constructed as a bit-wise OR of the fields shown in Table 2.11.

Table 2.11   Mode bit flags used by chmod(S) and fchmod(S)

Field	Bits	Description
S_ISGID	020#0	Set group ID on execution if # is 7, 5, 3, or 1. Enable mandatory file/record locking if # is 6, 4, 2, or 0.
S_ISVTX	01000	Save text image after execution.
S_IRWXU	00700	Read, write, execute by owner.
S_IRUSR	00400	Read by owner.
S_IWUSR	00200	Write by owner.
S_IXUSR	00100	Execute (search if a directory) by owner.
S_IRWXG	00070	Read, write, execute by group.
S_IRGRP	00040	Read by group.
S_IWGRP	00020	Write by group.
S_IXGRP	00010	Execute by group.
S_IRWXO	00007	Read, write, execute (search) by others.
S_IROTH	00004	Read by others.
S_IWOTH	00002	Write by others.
S_IXOTH	00001	Execute by others.

The following program creates a directory called my_dir with read, write and execute access for the owner only. The directory is then modified to allow read access for everyone and finally, the owner and group of the file are changed.

```
#include <sys/stat.h>
#include <stdio.h>
#include <stdlib.h>

main()
{
    mkdir("my_dir", S_IREAD|S_IWRITE|S_IEXEC) ;
    system("ls -ld my_dir") ;
    chmod("my_dir", S_IREAD|S_IWRITE|S_IEXEC|S_IRGRP|S_IROTH) ;
    system("ls -ld my_dir") ;
    chown("my_dir", 0, 3) ;
    system("ls -ld my_dir") ;
}
```

After each of the `mkdir(S)`, `chmod(S)` and `chown(S)` calls, the `system(S)` library function is invoked which issues the specified shell command. This makes it easier to display the effect of the system call. The output of the program is:

```
$ a.out
drwx------   2 spate   group      512 Jun  1 15:43 my_dir
drwxr--r--   2 spate   group      512 Jun  1 15:43 my_dir
drwxr--r--   2 root    sys        512 Jun  1 15:43 my_dir
```

Note that only the superuser may change the owner and group of files owned by others.

2.5.8 File meta-data

In addition to a stream of bytes, files contain additional information called *meta-data* that describes the file's properties, such as owner, access permissions, the type and size of the file and where in the filesystem the data is stored. Some of the meta-data, which is different for each filesystem, can be retrieved using one of the `stat` system calls:

```
#include <sys/types.h>
#include <sys/stat.h>

int stat(char *path, struct stat *buf) ;
int fstat(int fildes, struct stat *buf) ;
int lstat(char *path, struct stat *buf) ;
int statlstat(char *path, struct stat *buf) ;
```

The program below makes use of the `stat(S)` system call to display statistics about the file whose filename is passed as the first parameter to the program:

```
#include <sys/types.h>
#include <sys/stat.h>
#include <sys/sysmacros.h>

main(int argc, char* argv[])
{
    struct stat s ;

    if (argc != 2) {
        printf("Usage: %s filename\n", argv[0]) ;
```

```
          exit(-1) ;
     }

     if (stat(argv[1], &s) != 0) {
          pexit("mstat") ;
          exit(-1) ;
     }
     printf("st_dev   = (%d, %d)\n", major(s.st_dev),
                                   minor(s.st_dev)) ;
     printf("st_ino   = %d\n", s.st_ino) ;
     printf("st_mode  = %o\n", s.st_mode) ;
     printf("st_nlink = %d\n", s.st_nlink) ;
     printf("st_uid   = %d\n", s.st_uid) ;
     printf("st_gid   = %d\n", s.st_gid) ;
     printf("st_rdev  = (%d, %d)\n", major(s.st_rdev),
                                   minor(s.st_rdev)) ;
     printf("st_size  = %d\n", s.st_size) ;
     printf("st_atime = %s", ctime(&s.st_atime)) ;
     printf("st_mtime = %s", ctime(&s.st_mtime)) ;
     printf("st_ctime = %s", ctime(&s.st_ctime)) ;
}
```

The program prints all fields of the `stat` structure returned as shown below:

```
$ mstat mstat
st_dev   = (1, 42)
st_ino   = 22087
st_mode  = 100755
st_nlink = 1
st_uid   = 13583
st_gid   = 50
st_rdev  = (0, 0)
st_size  = 101148
st_atime = Sat Jun  3 04:05:47 1995
st_mtime = Sat Jun  3 04:04:29 1995
st_ctime = Sat Jun  3 04:04:29 1995
$ ls -il mstat
22087 -rwxr-xr-x   1 spate      group        101148 Jun  3 04:04 mstat
```

2.6 Signal management

A signal is a method of communicating an event between one process and another process or between the kernel and a process. It can be viewed as a primitive form of inter-process communication but is more commonly described as a software interrupt, a means by which the normal execution flow of a process is interrupted.

A signal can be *posted* to a process either by the kernel or through use of the `kill(S)` system call. The prototype for `kill(S)` is:

```
#include <sys/types.h>
#include <signal.h>

int kill (pid_t pid, int signo) ;
```

The `pid` argument specifies the process ID of the process to which the signal will be posted. The `signo` argument specifies the type of signal which will be posted.

When the kill(S) system call returns the signal is said to have been posted. When the process receives notification of the signal it is said to have been delivered. As Figure 2.6 shows, there are four methods by which a signal can be sent to a process.

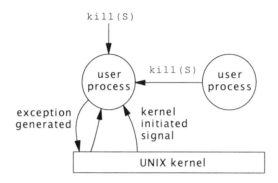

Figure 2.6   Methods of signal delivery

A process may send a signal to itself using the kill(S) system call. It may also post a signal to another process (or process group) by invoking kill(S). In this case, the requesting process must have the same real and effective user IDs as the process to which it wants to post the signal.

A process may receive a signal due to an exception caused by its own execution path, such as a division by zero or accessing an invalid memory address. In both cases the kernel will post the appropriate signal.

The kernel may also post a signal to a process, for example in response to the killall(C) command being invoked during system shutdown, or certain key sequences such as hitting the Delete key.

There are 29 different signal types used by SCO UNIX. Each signal is defined in the <sys/signal.h> header file. The different types of signals are as follows:

SIGHUP   This is posted to the session leader or controlling process associated with a controlling TTY if the kernel detects that the terminal has been disconnected. See section 2.8 for further details.

SIGINT   This is posted by the kernel when the user hits the interrupt key. On SCO UNIX this is usually the Delete key but may also be ^C on other versions of UNIX. The signal is posted to all processes in the foreground process group.

SIGQUIT   This is posted by the kernel when the user hits Control-\. The signal is posted to all processes in the foreground process group.

SIGILL   The kernel posts this if a process tries to execute an illegal instruction.

SIGTRAP   This is used during process debugging. If the running process accesses an address set in one of the i386 debug registers, a SIGTRAP signal will be posted to the process. A controlling process, for example a debugger, has the option of being notified prior to signal delivery. See the ptrace(S) manual page for further details of process debugging.

SIGIOT   This was originally generated when a process called the abort(S) system call. It has now been replaced by the SIGABRT signal and is not used by the SCO UNIX kernel.

SIGABRT   If a process calls the abort(S) system call, a SIGABRT signal will be posted. This allows the process to perform any necessary tidying up following an abnormal termination.

SIGEMT   This is not used by SCO UNIX.

SIGFPE   Floating point exceptions such as division by zero or floating point overflow will result in this signal being posted.

SIGKILL   When this signal is posted, the process will be terminated.

SIGBUS   There are certain circumstances in which a SIGBUS will be generated in place of SIGSEGV. The two main circumstances are when a valid virtual address exists but there is no corresponding physical address and if access is made to a page of memory established during an mmap(S) system call where the page exceeds the length of the file.

SIGSEGV   A segmentation violation occurs when the process accesses either an invalid memory address or an address for which it does not have the correct privileges.

SIGSYS   This is posted when a process calls a system call with an invalid system call number. See section 7.3 for further details on how system calls are handled by the kernel.

SIGPIPE   If a write is made to either a pipe or a socket and the recipient of the data has terminated, a SIGPIPE signal will be posted to the process.

SIGALRM   This is posted when a timer expires after calling the alarm(S) or setitimer(S) system calls.

SIGTERM   This is usually posted as a warning to a process that it is about to be terminated. This allows the process to tidy up and exit cleanly. If the user invokes the kill(C) command, this signal is posted by default to the process.

SIGUSR1   This signal is reserved for application use.

SIGUSR2   This signal is reserved for application use.

SIGCLD   When a process terminates this signal is sent to the parent.

SIGCHLD   This is the same signal as SIGCLD but is the name used by POSIX.1.

SIGPWR   This is generated when power is low and about to be lost. This is usually the result of running on an un-interruptible power supply (UPS) after the main system power has been lost.

SIGWINCH   A process may specify that it be notified if the size of the window changes at which time the SIGWINCH signal will be posted.

SIGPOLL   This is posted when requested events have occurred on a device that is pollable. See section 10.7.6 for further details.

SIGSTOP   This behaves in a similar manner to the SIGSTP signal by stopping the process.

SIGTSTP   This is posted by the kernel when the user hits ^z. It is sent to all processes in the foreground process group.

SIGCONT   When a stopped process is continued, this signal is posted allowing the process to perform any re-initialisation before resuming. This is particularly useful for applications which manipulate the screen such as editors and X windows applications.

SIGTTIN   This is posted if a background process attempts to read from its controlling terminal.

SIGTTOU   If a background process attempts to write to its controlling terminal then this signal will be posted.

SIGVTALRM   This is posted when a process virtual interval timer expires. See section 7.8.6 for details.

SIGPROF   This is also used for interval timers.

In the following example, the basic concepts of signal management are shown using the pre-SVR3, but still supported signal(S) system call. The signal(S) system call specifies how to modify the signal's *disposition*, the action to be taken on receipt of the signal. For each signal, a default behaviour is set up by the kernel. When a new process is created using fork(S) or if the process calls execve(S), the child inherits the set of signal dispositions from the parent.

The prototype for signal(S) is:

```
#include  <signal.h>
void (*signal (int sig, void (*func) (int))) (int);
```

The sig argument specifies the signal whose disposition the caller wishes to modify. The func argument specifies a user function to call if the signal is posted or alternatively, one of the following two values:

SIG_DFL   This specifies that the kernel is to execute the default action taken upon receipt of the signal. For most signals this usually results in termination of the process, possibly with the generation of a core file. The signal(S) or sigsetv(S) system call manual pages describe the default actions for each signal.

SIG_IGN   This specifies that the signal should be ignored. Note however that all
signals cannot be ignored. Again, the details are described by the
signal(S) and sigsetv(S) manual pages.

SIG_DFL and SIG_IGN are defined in <signal.h> as follows:

```
#define __SIG_FTN (void(*)(int))
#define SIG_DFL (__SIG_FTN_0)     /* signal numbers cannot  */
#define SIG_IGN (__SIG_FTN_1)     /* have a value of 0 or 1 */
```

which assumes that no signal handling function will start at address 0 or 1.

The next example alters the disposition of the SIGUSR1, SIGUSR2 and SIGINT
signals. For the SIGUSR1 signal, the kernel is instructed to ignore the signal, that is, there
is no action to perform. For the SIGUSR2 signal, the default behaviour should be taken. If
a SIGINT signal is posted, the kernel is instructed to invoke the user's function
inthdlr().

```
#include <signal.h>

void inthdlr(int sig)
{
    printf("caught SIGINT (%d)\n", sig) ;
    signal(SIGINT,  inthdlr) ;
}

main()
{
    printf("PID=%d\n", getpid()) ;

    signal(SIGUSR1, SIG_IGN) ;
    signal(SIGUSR2, SIG_DFL) ;
    signal(SIGINT,  inthdlr) ;

    while (1)
        pause() ;
}
```

Once all three signal(S) calls have been made, the process loops forever invoking the
pause(S) system call. The prototype for pause(S) is simply:

```
int pause()
```

The process will sleep indefinitely until a signal has been posted. Once the signal has
been caught and the signal handler called, the pause(S) system call returns with a return
value of –1 and with errno set to EINTR.

Figure 2.7 shows an example of the program running in one virtual console and
generating the signals for the process in another.

The kill(C) command is used to post signals to the process. Firstly, a SIGINT is
posted. This is received by the process, the inthdlr() function is called and the
message "caught SIGINT (2)" displayed on standard output.

```
$ a.out
PID=660                        $ kill -s 2 660   #SIGINT
caught SIGINT(2)               $ kill -s 16 660  #SIGUSR1
User signal 2                  $ kill -s 17 660  #SIGUSR2
$
```

Figure 2.7   Example of signal handling

The SIGUSR1 signal is then posted which has no impact on the process since the call to signal(S) specified SIG_IGN.

Finally, the SIGUSR2 signal is generated for which the process has requested the default behaviour. For SIGUSR2, the default behaviour is to display the message "User signal 2" and terminate the process.

Within the inthdlr() signal handler, the signal(S) call is invoked again. When the signal is posted, the kernel resets the signal's disposition back to SIG_DFL. In the example above, if inthdlr() did not call signal(S), a second SIGINT would cause the process to terminate, the default action for SIGINT.

This timing window in which a program may be terminated is one of two main problems with the signal(S) system call. Additionally, if a process does not wish to receive a specific signal for a specific amount of time then it must explicitly ignore the signal, removing the possibility of dealing with the signal at a later date.

2.6.1 SVR3 signal extensions

With the introduction of System V Release 3 came the sigset(S) system call. As the prototype below shows, it has the same interface as the original signal(S) function:

```
void (*sigset (int sig, void (*func) (int))) (int) ;
```

The main difference compared to signal(S) is that in addition to SIG_IGN or SIG_DFL, the disposition specified by func can be set to SIG_HOLD. If specified, the disposition of the signal is unchanged when the signal is posted and the signal is added to the process's *signal mask*, a list of signals that are currently held for the process.

While a signal is held by adding it to the signal mask, if the signal is posted to the process, it will remain pending until the signal is removed from the signal mask. Before calling the signal handler, the signal disposition is set to SIG_HOLD. On normal return from the signal handler, the signal disposition is restored to func and any held signal of this type is released. This removes the timing window introduced with the signal(S) system call.

The increased reliability introduced with sigset(S) can be demonstrated with the following example:

```
#include <unistd.h>
#include <signal.h>
#include <stdio.h>
```

```
void
inthdlr(int sig)
{
    printf("caught SIGINT\n") ;
    sleep(1) ;
}

void
main()
{
    int i = 5 ;

    sigset(SIGINT, inthdlr) ;

    while (i--)
        pause() ;
}
```

In this example sigset(S) is invoked to set the disposition of SIGINT to be the user specified inthdlr() function. When a SIGINT has been posted by the kernel and the inthdlr() function is called, it does not need to call sigset(S) to set the disposition again which would be the case in the previous example when using signal(S).

In addition to sigset(S) four other calls were introduced with SVR3 for signal management. The prototypes for all calls are:

```
#include  <signal.h>

int sighold(int sig) ;
int sigrelse(int sig) ;
int sigignore(int sig) ;
int sigpause(int sig);
```

The sighold(S) and sigrelse(S) calls add and remove the specified signal to and from the process's signal mask. The sigignore(S) call instructs the kernel to set the signal disposition to SIG_IGN. The sigpause(S) call removes the signal from the signal mask and suspends execution until any signal is received.

2.6.2 POSIX signal extensions

The POSIX.1 standard (1990) introduced a new set of signal handling functions based on the 4.2BSD interfaces with the goal of removing the problems of the previous interfaces as described above.

The POSIX signal model is based around the notion of *signal sets* underpinned by the sigset_t type. Currently, sigset_t is implemented as a long and is therefore restricted to 32 bits and thus 32 different signals.

The functions which are used to manipulate signal sets are:

```
#include <signal.h>

int sigemptyset(sigset_t *set) ;
int sigfillset(sigset_t *set) ;
```

```
int sigaddset(sigset_t *set, int signo) ;
int sigdelset(sigset_t *set, int signo) ;
int sigismember(sigset_t, int signo) ;
```

Unlike the `signal(S)` and `sigset(S)` system calls which modify a signal's disposition, these routines only modify the `sigset_t` structure defined by the user process. Additional interfaces which will be described later can be used to modify the signal properties managed by the kernel.

The `sigemptyset(S)` call is used to initialise the set by clearing it. If `sigfillset(S)` is called, the set is initialised to include all of the signals known by the system. The `sigaddset(S)` and `sigdelset(S)` calls are used to add or delete an individual signal to or from the set, while the `sigismember(S)` call tests to see whether the signal specified by the `signo` argument is contained within the set.

In place of the `signal(S)` or `sigset(S)` calls, POSIX.1 defines the `sigaction(S)` call which can be used to set the disposition of the specified signal, obtain the current disposition or perform both simultaneously. The prototype for `sigaction(S)` is:

```
#include <signal.h>

int sigaction(int sig, const struct sigaction *act,
              struct sigaction *oact) ;
```

Instead of specifying a function or constant as in the `signal(S)` and `sigset(S)` calls, `sigaction(S)` requires the caller to pass a pointer to a `sigaction` structure which has the following members:

```
void       (*sa_handler)(int) ;
void       (*sa_sigaction)(int, siginfo_t *, void *) ;
sigset_t   sa_mask ;
int        sa_flags ;
```

The `sa_handler` field specifies the action to be taken and may take the values of `SIG_IGN`, `SIG_DFL` or the address of a user supplied signal handler. If `sa_handler` or `sa_sigaction` are not NULL, `sa_mask` specifies a list of signals which will be added to the process's signal mask before the signal handler is invoked to deal with the signal.

The `sa_flags` specifies a set of flags used to modify the delivery of the signal. The values that `sa_flags` can take are shown below. Note that only `SA_NOCLDSTOP` is defined by the POSIX.1 standard.

SA_ONSTACK   If set and the required signal is caught and an alternative stack used for processing by the signal handler has been specified by use of the `sigaltstack(S)` function, the signal will be delivered on the alternative stack. Otherwise, the normal user stack is used by the handler.

SA_RESETHAND   If set and the signal is caught, the signal's disposition will be set to `SIG_DFL` and will not be blocked on entry to the signal handler. Otherwise, the disposition of the signal is unaltered.

SA_NODEFER   If set and the signal is caught, the signal is only blocked by the kernel while being caught if included in `sa_mask`.

SA_RESTART   If set and the signal is caught, a system call that was interrupted by the signal will be restarted transparently after invocation of the handler. If not set, the kernel call will return `EINTR`.

SA_SIGINFO   If clear and the signal is caught, the signal handler specified by `sa_handler` is invoked with the single argument specifying the signal number. If `SA_SIGINFO` is set, the `sa_sigaction` function is invoked with different arguments. See below for details.

SA_NOCLDWAIT   If set and the specified `sig` is equal to `SIGCHLD`, a zombie process will not be created for one or more of the process's children which exit. If the process then calls the `wait(S)`, `wait3(S)`, `waitid(S)` or `waitpid(S)` functions, it will block until all of the children terminate.

SA_NOCLDSTOP   If set and the specified `sig` argument is equal to `SIGCHLD`, the `SIGCHLD` signal will not be sent to the caller when any of its children stop or terminate.

If `sa_flags` is set to `SA_SIGINFO` and the signal specified by `sig` is caught, the function specified by `sa_sigaction` is called as the signal handler. In addition to being passed the signal number, there are two other arguments passed, a pointer to a `siginfo_t` structure providing information regarding the reason for delivery of the signal and a pointer to a `ucontext_t` structure which specifies the process's context.

The `siginfo_t` structure is defined in the `<siginfo.h>` header file and contains the following fields:

```
int si_signo ;
int si_errno ;
int si_code ;
```

The `si_signo` field contains the signal number. If `si_code` is less than or equal to zero, the signal was generated by a user process. In such circumstances the `siginfo_t` structure will also contains the following fields:

```
pid_t    si_pid ;
uid_t    si_uid ;
```

which identify the process which posted the signal. If the value of `si_code` is greater than zero then there are numerous values that `si_code` can take which allow the process to determine the reason for the signal. The list of values for `si_code` corresponding to the signal number in `si_signo` are shown in Table 2.12.

For each of the signals in Table 2.12 additional supporting information is also supplied as shown in Table 2.13.

Table 2.12   Values of `si_code` returned in the `siginfo_t` structure

si_signo	si_code	Description
SIGILL	ILL_ILLOPC	Illegal opcode.
	ILL_ILLOPN	Illegal operand.
	ILL_ADR	Illegal addressing mode.
	ILL_ILLTRP	Illegal trap.
	ILL_PRVOPC	Privileged opcode.
	ILL_PRVREG	Privileged register.
	ILL_COPROC	Co-processor error.
	ILL_BADSTK	Internal stack error.
SIGFPE	FPE_INTDIV	Integer division by zero.
	FPE_INTOVF	Integer overflow.
	FPE_FLTDIV	Floating point division by zero.
	FPE_FLTOVF	Floating point overflow.
	FPE_FLTUND	Floating point underflow.
	FPE_FLTRES	Floating point inexact result.
	FPE_FLTINV	Invalid floating point operation.
	FPE_FLTSUB	Subscript out of range.
SIGSEGV	SEGV_MAPPER	Address not mapped to object.
	SEGV_ACCERR	Invalid permissions for mapped object.
SIGBUS	BUS_ADRALN	Invalid address alignment.
	BUS_ADRERR	Non-existent physical address.
	BUS_OBJERR	Object specific hardware error.
SIGTRAP	TRAP_BRKPT	Process breakpoint.
	TRAP_TRACE	Process trace trap.
SIGCHLD	CLD_EXITED	Child has exited.
	CLD_KILLED	Child has been killed.
	CLD_DUMPED	Child has terminated abnormally.
	CLD_TRAPPED	Traced child has trapped.
	CLD_STOPPED	Child has stopped.
	CLD_CONTINUED	Stopped child has continued.
SIGPOLL	POLL_IN	Data input available.
	POLL_OUT	Data buffers available.
	POLL_MSG	Input message available.
	POLL_ERR	I/O error.
	POLL_PRI	High priority input available.
	POLL_HUP	Device disconnected.

Table 2.13   Additional data supplied with the `siginfo_t` structure

si_signo	Additional field		Value
SIGILL SIGFPE	caddr_t	si_addr	The address of the faulting instruction.
SIGSEGV	caddr_r	si_addr	The address of the faulty memory reference.
SIGBUS	pid_t	si_pid	The child process ID.
	int	si_status	The exit value or signal.
SIGPOLL	long	si_band	Band error for POLL_IN, POLL_OUT or POLL_MSG

Using the signal set mechanism, the `sigprocmask(S)` function can be used to set the signal mask, retrieve the current signal mask or perform both operations. The prototype for `sigprocmask(S)` is:

```
#include <signal.h>
int sigprocmask(int how, sigset_t *set, sigset_t *oset) ;
```

The signal mask is modified according to the `how` argument which may take one of the following options:

SIG_BLOCK   The resulting signal mask will consist of the union of the set specified by the `set` argument and the current signal mask.

SIG_UNBLOCK   Signals in the set specified by the `set` argument will be removed from the current signal mask.

SIG_SETMASK   The current signal mask is replaced by the signal set specified by the `set` argument.

If the `set` argument is NULL, the `how` argument is ignored. If the `oset` argument is not NULL, the current signal mask is returned in the set specified by `oset`.

The `sigpending(S)` function is used to retrieve the set of signals which are blocked (held in the signal mask) but currently *pending* (ready to be delivered). The prototype for `sigpending(S)` is:

```
#include <signal.h>
int sigpending(sigset_t *set) ;
```

The list of blocked but pending signals is returned in the signal set specified by `set`.

The `sigsuspend(S)` function replaces the current signal mask with the specified set and then suspends the process until it receives a signal whose disposition is either to terminate the process or to invoke a signal handler. If a signal handler exists, it is executed first followed by an immediate return from `sigsuspend(S)`. The signal mask is restored to the mask prior to invoking `sigsuspend(S)`. The prototype for `sigsuspend(S)` is:

```
#include <signal.h>
int sigsuspend(const sigset_t *sigmask) ;
```

In the following example, the signal handler `inthdlr()` (line 6) is installed by invoking the `sigaction(S)` system call (line 25) and will be invoked when a SIGINT signal is posted. A `sigaction` structure is initialised on lines 22 to 24 to specify that the handler should be invoked with any appropriate `siginfo_t` and process context.

Within the main body of the program the process is halted until SIGINT has been posted by invoking the `sigpause(S)` function.

```
 1 #include <signal.h>
 2 #include <stdio.h>
 3 #include <siginfo.h>
 4
 5 void
 6 inthdlr(int signo, siginfo_t *si, void *uctxt)
 7 {
 8     if (si == NULL) {
 9         printf("siginfo_t is NULL!\n") ;
10         return ;
11     }
12
13     if (si->si_code <= 0)
14         printf("SIGINT posted by uid(%d), pid(%d)\n",
15                              si->si_uid, si->si_pid) ;
16 }
17
18 main()
19 {
20     struct sigaction act ;
21
22     act.sa_sigaction = inthdlr ;
23     act.sa_flags = SA_SIGINFO ;
24     sigemptyset(&act.sa_mask) ;
25     sigaction(SIGINT, &act, NULL) ;
26
27     sigpause(SIGINT) ;
28 }
```

When the signal handler is invoked, it first checks to see if a valid `siginfo_t` has been passed and, if so, prints the user ID and process ID of the process which generated the signal. Shown below, the process is run in the background and `kill(C)` is used to post SIGINT:

```
$ a.out &
[1]        478
$ kill -INT 478
SIGINT posted by uid(13583), pid(454)
[1] +  Done(255)          a.out &
```

2.6.3 Additional signal management support

In addition to the signal handling functions described so far, SCO OpenServer Release 5 supports the following signal functions:

```
#include <sys/types.h>      /* for sigsend(S) and sigsendset(S) */
#include <signal.h>
#include <sys/procset.h>    /* for sigsend(S) and sigsendset(S) */
#include <setjmp.h>         /* for sigsetjmp(S) and siglongjmp(S) */

int  sigaltstack(const stack_t *ss, stack_t *oss) ;
int  siginterrupt(int sig, int flag) ;
int  sigsend(idtype_t idtype, id_t id, int sig) ;
int  sigsendset(const procset_t *psp, int sig) ;
int  sigsetjmp(sigjmp_buf env, int savemask) ;
```

```
void siglongjmp(sigjmp_buf env, int val) ;
int  sigstack(struct sigstack *ss, struct sigstack *oss) ;
```

When a signal handler is invoked it typically runs on the user's normal stack. With the `sigaltstack(S)` system call the user can specify an alternative stack on which the signal handler will run. If the `sa_flags` field is set to `SA_ONSTACK` when invoking `sigaction(S)`, the specified signal will be delivered on the alternative stack. The `sigstack(S)` library call is the XPG4.2 version of the same call.

The `siginterrupt(S)` library function is used to change the restart behaviour of a system call when the system call is interrupted by the specified signal `sig`. If the flag is set to 0, system calls will be restarted if they are interrupted by `sig` and no data has yet been transferred.

The `sigsend(S)` and `sigsendset(S)` calls are used to send a signal or group of signals to a process or group of processes.

The `sigsetjmp(S)` and `siglongjmp(S)` library functions are used to provide additional control when performing non-local jumps from within a signal handler. If a process calls `longjmp(S)` from within the handler, the signal may remain in the process's signal mask, preventing further occurrences of the signal from interrupting the signal handler. If the `savemask` argument is non-zero, `sigsetjmp(S)` saves the current process signal mask in `env`. When `siglongjmp(S)` is invoked, if the signal mask was previously saved following a call to `sigsetjmp(S)`, the process signal mask is restored to the signal mask saved in `env`.

2.7 Process creation and control

All of the examples covered so far in this chapter have been single processes run from the shell prompt. There are many instances when it is necessary to create and manage multiple processes. For example, each time a program is requested to be executed by the shell, a new process is created to run the new program. When the process exits, it returns to the shell.

A new process is created using the `fork(S)` system call:

```
int fork() ;
```

The new process, called the *child* process, is a copy of the calling process, the *parent* process, with only a few differences. The child process inherits many attributes from the parent including:

- The environment variables.
- Signal handling settings.
- All attached shared memory segments.
- Process group ID.
- Current working directory for relative pathnames.

- Root directory for absolute pathname.
- File mode creation mask.
- Real, effective and saved user IDs.
- Real, effective and saved group IDs.
- Controlling terminal.

For a full list of inherited attributes, see the fork(S) manual page. There are, however, a number of differences between parent and child processes including:

- The child process has a unique process ID.
- The child process has a different parent process ID.
- The child process has its own copy of the parent's file descriptors.
- No signals are pending in the child.

The following program demonstrates the steps taken when using the fork(S) system call. The value returned from fork(S) differs depending on whether the kernel returns to the parent or to the newly created child. If the value returned from fork(S) is a positive integer, the process is running in the parent's context. If the value returned from fork(S) is zero, the process is running in the child's context.

If the value returned is -1, the fork(S) system call failed and the reason for failure is assigned to the variable errno.

```
main()
{
    int pid ;

    printf("my pid = %d\n", getpid()) ;
    pid = fork() ;

    if (pid == -1)
        pexit("fork")
    else if (pid == 0) {
        printf("I am the child, my pid = %d\n", getpid()) ;
    } else {
        printf("I am the parent, my pid = %d\n", getpid()) ;
    }
}
```

The output of the program for one particular run is shown below. The process ID assigned to the child increases each time fork(S) is invoked. Therefore, repeated runs of this program will almost certainly produce different results.

```
$ a.out
my pid = 701
I am the child, my pid = 702
I am the parent, my pid = 701
```

The process ID of a process, also referred to as the pid, is a number used by the kernel to identify the process uniquely. For more information on how the kernel selects the pid, see section 7.5.

Each time the fork(S) system call is invoked, the kernel ensures that the child process is constructed as a copy of the parent process, that is, the contents of the text, data, stack and other memory objects are copied from the parent to the child.

To execute a new program and therefore replace the parent's program text, data, stack and other memory objects, the process calls one of a number of different exec() functions which are shown below:

```
#include <unistd.h>

int execl(path, arg0, arg1, ..., argn, (char *)0)
     const char *path, *arg0, *arg1, ..., *argn ;

int execle(path, arg0, arg1, ..., argn, (char *)0, envp)
     const char *path, *arg0, *arg1, ..., *argn ;
     char *const envp[] ;

int execlp(file, arg0, arg1, ..., argn, (char *)0)
     const char *file, *arg0, *arg1, ..., *argn ;

int execv(path, argv)
     const char *path ;
     char *const argv[] ;

int execve(path, argv, envp)
     const char *path ;
     char *const argv[], envp[] ;

int execvp(file, argv)
     const char *file ;
     char *const argv[] ;
```

All of these library functions call the execve(S) system call passing the name of the program to execute, a list of pointers to arguments (to become the argv[] array) and a list of pointers to environment variables (to become the environ[] array). Figure 2.8 illustrates the link between the different exec() calls.

The path argument passed to each function specifies the name of the program to execute. This is typically a COFF or ELF executable file but may be one of a number of other different file formats including shell programs, DOS executables and so on.

The type of the executable file is usually invisible when developing applications. Most people are familiar with the concept of an a.out file but the format and content of the file is not usually considered. SCO UNIX supports multiple executable file formats each offering different capabilities. For example, the Common Object File Format (COFF) provided with versions of SCO UNIX prior to OpenServer Release 5 supports static shared libraries while the Executable and Linking Format (ELF) supports static shared libraries and dynamically linked libraries.

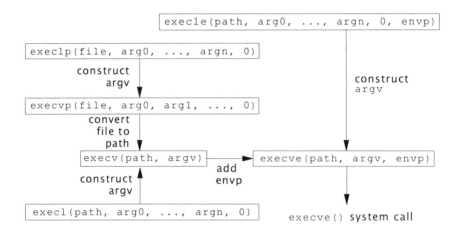

Figure 2.8   The different types of `exec`

At a minimum, an executable file consists of a header describing the layout and content of the file together with text and data from which the process memory image can be constructed.

All executable files created by the C compiler are entered through the user supplied `main()` function. The `argv` and `envp` arguments passed to one of the `exec()` functions are passed to `main()`. Section 2.2.2 describes the handling of environment variables.

Unlike `fork(S)` which inherits most of the parent process attributes, the new process image created by calling `execve(S)` inherits a smaller number of attributes which include:

- The parent process's *nice* value which will be used by the kernel to determine the process's priority during its lifetime.
- The process ID. The process ID changes for the process during `fork(S)` but remains the same across `execve(S)`.
- The same parent process ID.
- The process group ID.
- The TTY group ID.
- The time left until `alarm(S)` expires resulting in a `SIGALRM` signal.
- The current working directory in which files will be opened when specifying a relative pathname and in which the core file is written if the process terminates.
- The root directory which defines the filename space within which the process will operate and to which it has access.
- File mode creation mask. All open files are inherited with the exception of files for which the close-on-exec flag has been set by `fcntl(S)`.
- The maximum size of a file that can be created by the process.

- `utime`, `stime` and `cutime` as defined by `times(S)`.
- File locks which were held by the parent prior to invoking `execve(S)`.

A parent often requires to be informed when a forked child exits. There are two mechanisms for the parent to receive notification. The first method involves signal handling in which the parent will receive a `SIGCHLD` signal and may determine, from information passed to the signal handler, the process that generated the signal plus any other information passed. Signals are discussed in detail in section 2.6.

The second method, which is discussed in detail below, is used when the parent can either glimpse at the status of the child at any moment in time or voluntarily suspend execution until the child's status changes. There are four calls which allow the parent process to receive notification about the child:

```
#include <sys/types.h>
#include <sys/wait.h>

pid_t wait(int *stat_loc) ;
pid_t wait3(int *stat_loc, int options, struct rusage *resource_usage) ;
int   waitid(idtype_t idtype, id_t id, siginfo_t *infop, int options) ;
pid_t waitpid(pid_t pid, int *stat_loc, int options) ;
```

The `wait(S)` system call suspends the caller until one of its immediate children terminates, or until a child that is being traced stops because it has received a signal. If `wait(S)` returns because the status of a child is available, the process ID of the child is returned and the status of the child is stored in the location pointed to by `stat_loc`. If a signal is posted to the calling process which results in a premature return from `wait(S)`, the return value is -1 and `errno` is set to `EINTR`.

The value returned in the location pointed to by `stat_loc` can be evaluated using the following macros:

`WIFEXITED(status)`	The result will be non-zero if the `status` was returned for a child which terminated normally.
`WEXITSTATUS(status)`	If non-zero, the result of this macro evaluates to the exit status of the child, the value passed to `exit(S)` or `_exit(S)`.
`WIFSIGNALLED(status)`	The result is non-zero if `status` was returned for a child that terminated due to receipt of a signal.
`WTERMSIG(status)`	If `WIFSIGNALLED(status)` is non-zero, this macro evaluates to the signal that caused the child process to terminate.
`WCOREDUMP(status)`	If `WIFSIGNALLED(status)` is non-zero, this macro is non-zero if a core file was produced.

The following example shows the most common use of wait(S):

```
 1 #include <sys/types.h>
 2 #include <sys/wait.h>
 3
 4 main()
 5 {
 6     int pid, stat_loc ;
 7
 8     if ((pid = fork()) == -1)
 9         pexit("fork") ;
10
11     if (pid == 0)              // child
12         exit(0x7f) ;
13     else {                     // parent
14         wait(&stat_loc) ;
15         if (WIFEXITED(stat_loc))
16             printf("Child exited normally with status 0x%x\n",
17                                         WEXITSTATUS(stat_loc)) ;
18         else
19             printf("Child did not exit normally\n") ;
20     }
21 }
```

The output of the program is:

```
$ ./wait
Child exited normally with status 0x7f
$
```

The waitid(S) function provides additional control over the child process or group of child processes for which the change in status should be reported. The idtype and id arguments specify which child processes the caller of waitid(S) should await:

idtype = P_PID   waitid(S) waits for a child with process ID equal to id.

idtype = P_PGID   waitid(S) waits for any child with a process group ID equal to id.

idtype = P_ALL   id is ignored and waitid(S) will wait for any children.

The options argument is a bit-wise OR of the following flags:

WEXITED	Wait for processes to exit.
WTRAPPED	Wait for traced processes to become trapped or to reach a breakpoint.
WSTOPPED	Wait for and return the status of any child that has stopped upon receipt of a signal.
WCONTINUED	Return status for a child that was stopped and has been continued.
WNOHANG	Return immediately if no status is available.
WNOWAIT	Keep the process in a waitable state which allows successive calls to waitid(S).

The `infop` argument must point to a `siginfo_t` structure which contains a rich set of information regarding the status of the child. The `siginfo_t` structure is described in section 2.6.2.

The following example uses the `waitid(S)` system call to demonstrate how to access the exit status of a process. The status is obtained from the contents of the `siginfo_t` structure returned from `waitid(S)` if status is available for the child process.

The `waitforchild()` function on lines 8 to 33 calls `waitid(S)` on line 15 for the pid and idtype arguments passed. If status is available, the `si_signo` field is checked to see if the child has died and generated a `SIGCHLD`. If the `si_signo` field is equal to `SIGCHLD`, the exit status is contained in the `si_status` field. This field is then displayed on line 22.

Note, as shown on line 1, that the `waitid(S)` system call requires the variable `_SVID3` to be defined.

```
 1 #define _SVID3 1
 2
 3 #include <sys/types.h>
 4 #include <sys/signal.h>
 5 #include <sys/wait.h>
 6 #include <stdio.h>
 7
 8 waitforchild(int pass, pid_t pid, idtype_t idtype)
 9 {
10     siginfo_t infop ;
11
12     printf("pass %d - ", pass) ;
13     fflush(stdout) ;
14
15     if (waitid(P_PID, pid, &infop, idtype) == -1)
16         perror("waitid") ;
17     else
18         if (infop.si_signo == SIGCHLD) {
19             switch(infop.si_code) {
20                 case(CLD_EXITED)    :
21                     printf("CLD_EXITED ") ;
22                     printf("with status 0x%x\n", infop.si_status) ;
23                     break ;
24                 case(CLD_KILLED)    : printf("CLD_KILLED\n") ; break ;
25                 case(CLD_DUMPED)    : printf("CLD_DUMPED\n") ; break ;
26                 case(CLD_TRAPPED)   : printf("CLD_TRAPPED\n") ; break ;
27                 case(CLD_STOPPED)   : printf("CLD_STOPPED\n") ; break ;
28                 case(CLD_CONTINUED): printf("CLD_CONTINUED\n") ;
29             }
30         }
31         else
32             printf("si_signo = %d\n", infop.si_signo) ;
33 }
34
35 main()
36 {
37     int pid, stat_loc ;
38
39     if ((pid = fork()) == -1)
40         pexit("fork") ;
41
42     if (pid == 0)                // child
43         exit(0x7f) ;
```

```
44      else {                      // parent
45          waitforchild(1, pid, WNOWAIT | WEXITED) ;
46          waitforchild(2, pid, WEXITED) ;
47          waitforchild(3, pid, WEXITED) ;
48      }
49  }
```

The output of the program is shown below. On the first call to `waitforchild()`, the `waitid(S)` system call returns a `siginfo_t` from which the status of the child specifies that it exited normally. Since the `WNOWAIT` flag was specified to `waitid(S)`, the second call to `waitforchild()` returns the same status. This time the kernel removes the state associated with the process and the third call returns `-1` indicating that there are no children from which status can be retrieved.

```
$ waitid
pass 1 - CLD_EXITED with status 0x7f
pass 2 - CLD_EXITED with status 0x7f
pass 3 - waitid: No child processes
```

The `waitpid(S)` function provides functionality similar to both the `wait(S)` and `waitid(S)` functions. The `options` argument is a bit-wise OR of the following flags:

WCONTINUED   The status of any child process which is specified by the `pid` argument that has not been reported since it continued is returned.

WNOHANG   The calling process will not suspend if status is not currently available.

WNOWAIT   Keep the process in a waitable state which allows successive calls to `waitpid(S)`.

WUNTRACED   The status of any child process which is specified by the `pid` argument that is stopped, and whose status has not been reported since it was stopped, is returned.

The value returned in the location pointed to by `stat_loc` can be evaluated using the macros shown when describing the `wait(S)` system call. The following additional macros can also be used:

WIFSTOPPED(status)   The result will be non-zero if the `status` was returned for a child that is currently stopped.

WSTOPSIG(status)   If `WIFSTOPPED(status)` is non-zero, this macro will evaluate to the signal that caused the child process to stop.

WIFCONTINUED(status)   This macro will evaluate to non-zero if the `status` was returned for a child process that has continued from a job control stop signal.

The `wait3(S)` call is equivalent to calling `waitpid(S)` as follows:

```
waitpid((pid_t)-1, stat_loc, options) ;
```

Using `fork(S)`, `exec(S)` and `wait(S)`

In order to illustrate one of the most useful applications of the `fork(S)`, `exec(S)` and `wait(S)` system calls, the following program presents a simple UNIX shell. It loops through the following sequence until the command `logout` is entered:

- Read a command from standard input.
- Fork a new process and execute the command.
- Wait for the child to exit.

The loop in the `main()` function prints the prompt `myshell >` and reads a line from standard input. Input is read from the keyboard and if the string entered is not `logout`, the `process_command()` function is called to process the string. If `logout` is entered, the shell exits and returns control back to its parent (in this case the real shell!).

Within the `process_command()` function, a call is made to `fork(S)` to create the child process in which to run the command. The `execle(S)` function is then called to create the new executable image. The parent (shell) then issues a `wait(S)` system call which will block until the child has exited.

```c
#include <sys/types.h>
#include <sys/wait.h>
#include <unistd.h>
#include <string.h>

#define CMDSIZ 32

extern char **environ ;

process_command(char *cmdbuf)
{
    int pid, sloc ;

    pid = fork() ;
    if (pid < 0)
        write(2, "no more processes\n", 18) ;
    else if (pid == 0) {
        /* child */
        if (execle(cmdbuf, (char *)0, environ) < 0)
        pexit("child") ;
    } else {
        /* parent */
        wait(&sloc) ; /* can determine exit status, see wait(S) */
    }
}

main()
{
    int  logout=0, cmdsiz ;
    char cmdbuf[CMDSIZ] ;

    while(!logout) {
        write(1, "myshell> ", 9) ;
        cmdsiz = read(0, cmdbuf, CMDSIZ) ;
        cmdbuf[cmdsiz-1] = '\0' ;
        if (strcmp("logout", cmdbuf) == 0)
```

```
        ++logout ;
    else
        process_command(cmdbuf) ;
    }
}
```

The output for one run of the simple shell is shown below. The `myfork` program which is entered is present in the current directory. The shell calls `fork(S)` and `execle(S)` to run `myfork` and then calls `wait(S)`.

```
$ myshell
myshell> myfork
my pid = 370
I am the child, my pid = 371
I am the parent, my pid = 370
myshell> testfile
child: No such file or directory
myshell> myshell
myshell> logout
myshell> logout
$
```

The following `myfork` program also calls the `fork(S)` system call. Both the parent and child processes print the values of their process IDs and then exit. At this point the shell returns from `wait(S)` and displays the next prompt.

```
main()
{
    int pid ;

    printf("my pid = %d\n", getpid()) ;
    pid = fork() ;

    if (pid == -1)
        pexit("fork") ;
    else if (pid == 0) {
        printf("I am the child, my pid = %d\n", getpid()) ;
    } else {
        printf("I am the parent, my pid = %d\n", getpid()) ;
    }
}
```

Th next command entered is `testfile` which cannot be found in the current working directory, resulting in a failure of `execle(S)` and thus the message about not being able to locate `testfile`.

The `myshell` program is run again, creating a new shell which requires the two `logout` commands to be entered before return is passed back to the original shell.

2.8 Process group and session management

When a process is created, it can be uniquely identified by its process ID, the value returned from the `fork(S)` system call. In addition to the process ID, the process is also assigned a process group ID by the kernel. A process group consists of one or more processes and exists as long as there is at least one process within the group.

Many system calls can apply to a single process or to a process group. For example, by specifying the P_PGID option to waitpid(S) the process will wait for any child in the specified process group. Another example is the use of the kill(S) system call. A signal can be posted to a single process or to all processes in a specified process group.

Each process is also a member of a *session* which is a collection of one or more process groups. A *login session* is a term often used to describe the set of events between logging in to a system and logging out. The session notation was introduced to group together the set of processes (process groups) created during the login session so that in the event of the terminal being disconnected or the user logging out, the kernel can clean up by removing the remaining processes left in the session.

A process may determine its own process group ID or the process group ID of another process which exists in the same session by invoking the getpgrp(S) and getpgid(S) system calls, respectively.

```
#include <sys/types.h>
#include <unistd.h>

pid_t getpgrp(void) ;
pid_t getpgid(pid_t pid) ;
```

The pid argument passed to getpgid(S) specifies the process ID of the process whose process group ID is required. If the process specified by process ID is not in the same session as the process calling getpgid(S), -1 is returned and errno set to EPERM.

The following example displays the process group ID of a program run from the shell and the process group ID of the shell itself:

```
#include <sys/types.h>
#include <unistd.h>

main(int argc, char *argv[])
{
    printf("process group ID for %s = %d\n", argv[0], getpgrp()) ;
    printf("parent group ID = %d\n", getpgid(getppid())) ;
}
```

The output of the program for one particular run is shown below:

```
$ pgrps
process group ID for pgrps = 251
parent group ID = 250
```

The setpgrp(S) system call allows a process to join an existing process group or to create a new process group within the session with which the calling process is associated.

```
#include <sys/types.h>

int setpgid(pid_t pid, pid_t pgid) ;
```

If the call is successful, the process with a process ID which matches the `pid` argument has its process group ID set to `pgid`. If the value of `pid` is zero, the process ID of the calling process is used.

Each process group can have a *process group leader*, a process whose process ID is the same as the process group ID. The process group leader does not need to remain in existence for the duration of the process group.

The session ID of a process may be obtained by invoking the `getsid(S)` system call which takes a process ID as an argument:

```
#include <unistd.h>

pid_t getsid(pid_t pid) ;
```

As with `getpgrp(S)` and `getpgid(S)`, if the process specified by `pid` is not within the same session or if the calling process does not have root privileges then `getsid(S)` returns −1 and `errno` is set to `EPERM`.

A process can issue the `setsid(S)` system call to create a new session:

```
#include <unistd.h>

pid_t setsid(void) ;
```

A new session is created only if the calling process is not already a process group leader. If the call is successful, the calling process becomes the session leader of the new session, a process group leader of a new process group and has no controlling terminal. This means that it is not possible to generate signals for the process from a terminal by issuing appropriate key sequences, for example hitting the `Delete` key to generate `SIGINT` or `^\` to generate `SIGQUIT`. The new process group ID is set to the process ID of the calling processes.

There are two main uses of the `setsid(S)` system call. The first occurs when the `getty(M)` process calls `execve(S)` to run the `login` program which subsequently invokes the user's shell. Both the shell and all subsequent processes created after logging in, with minor exceptions described below, all have the same session ID. This allows the `SIGHUP` signal to be sent to all processes within the session if the session leader, in this case the shell, is terminated.

The other main use of `setsid(S)` is when creating daemon processes. Described later in section 2.9.1, daemon processes lurk around in the background, usually responding to events asynchronously. Most daemons are started during system initialisation and live for the lifetime of the system. By establishing a new session, the daemon disassociates itself from a terminal and thus becomes immune to `SIGHUP` and keyboard generated signals.

2.8.1 Foreground and background process groups

For each terminal device, whether the system console or a pseudo terminal, there is an associated *foreground* process group and one or more *background* process groups.

Signals such as SIGINT or SIGQUIT generated by the TTY driver are posted to all processes in the foreground process group.

Consider the following command:

```
$ cat | lpr -deng_lw2
```

which reads input from the keyboard and sends the data read to the specified printer. If the shell in which this command pipeline is executed supports job control, the two process created by the shell for cat and lpr run in a separate process group from the shell. A partial ps(C) output shows the two processes with their parent shell.

```
$ ps -f -ouser,pid,ppid,pgid,sess,tty,args
USER    PID   PPID  PGID SESSION    TTY COMMAND
spate   1014   505  1014     505  tty01 -ksh
spate   1053  1014  1053     505  tty01 cat
spate   1054  1014  1053     505  tty01 lpr -deng_lw2
```

All three processes have the same session ID (505) and are associated with the pseudo terminal tty01. The cat and lpr processes have a process group ID of 1053 which is different from the parent ksh which has a process group ID of 1014.

What is not shown in the output is which process group is in the foreground. The Korn shell requires that process group 1053 which contains cat and lpr be placed in the foreground. This allows cat to access stdin to read from the tty01 and stderr to display any errors it may deem appropriate. It also allows the user to terminate both processes by hitting the Delete key to generate SIGINT which, unless a process provides a signal handler or has chosen to ignore the signal, has the default action of terminating the process. Figure 2.9 shows the arrangement of the three processes, two process groups and the session in which they reside.

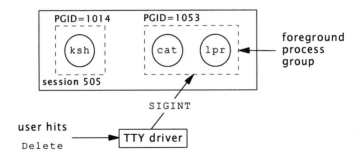

Figure 2.9   Posting a signal to the foreground process group

The shell will call one of the wait() functions and when both processes have terminated, it can display another prompt and start the read-line/fork/exec cycle again.

If the shell does not support job control, cat and lpr will run in the same process group as the parent shell:

```
$ ps -f -ouser,pid,ppid,pgid,sess,tty,args
USER    PID  PPID  PGID SESSION    TTY COMMAND
spate  1110  1014  1110    505   tty01 sh
spate  1111  1110  1110    505   tty01 lpr -deng_lw2
spate  1112  1111  1110    505   tty01 cat
```

This time all three processes share a process group ID of 1110. If the user generates a SIGINT signal then it will be sent to all three processes. The shell must therefore install a signal handler for SIGINT to prevent the login session from terminating due to normal keyboard actions.

For details on how the kernel manages processes see section 7.7.

2.8.2 Per process limits

In order to maximise fairness between multiple processes in terms of how many resources they are allowed to consume, each process is governed by a set of limits. The limits are set on a per process basis. The limits can be viewed through use of the getrlimit(S) system call and altered using the setrlimit(S) system call.

```
#include <sys/time.h>
#include <sys/resource.h>

int getrlimit(int resource, struct rlimit *rlp) ;
int setrlimit(int resource, const struct rlimit *rlp) ;
```

The resource argument identifies a specific resource to query or modify. The rlimit structure consists of a pair of resource limits which has the following members:

```
rlim_t rlim_cur ;
rlim_t rlim_max ;
```

When a process is created, it is given a number of *soft limits* which are specified in the rlim_cur field. After modification of a limit, this field will be set to the value specified to setrlimit(S). The rlim_max field specifies the *hard limit* which is the absolute maximum value that a limit may take. The soft limit is chosen to reflect typical usage of a resource and should be kept as low as possible to avoid wastage of memory, CPU resources and so on.

The hard limit may, in theory, have an infinite value. A caller of setrlimit(S) would in this case set the value of rlim_max to RLIM_INFINITY. In the real world, although rlim_max may be set to RLIM_INFINITY, memory constraints will limit the actual value.

Using the setrlimit(S) system call, a process may set the soft limit to a value that is less than or equal to the hard limit. It may also lower the hard limit to a value that is greater than or equal to the soft limit. If the hard limit is lowered, it is an operation that cannot be reversed at a later date.

The type of resources, their description and the effect that the limit has on the process are shown in Table 2.14.

Table 2.14 Resource limits imposed on a process

Resource type	Description	Effect of limit
RLIMIT_CORE	The maximum size of a core file that will be created. If the size is set to zero, a core file will not be created.	When creating a core file, continued writes to the core file will stop once this limit is reached.
RLIMIT_CPU	The maximum amount of CPU that can be consumed by the process in seconds.	Once exceeded, a SIGXCPU will be posted to the process.
RLIMIT_DATA	The maximum size of the process's heap in bytes.	Once this limit is reached, subsequent calls to brk(S) will return ENOMEM.
RLIMIT_FSIZE	The maximum size of a file that can be created by a process. If RLIMIT_FSIZE is set to zero then files cannot be created.	A SIGXFSZ will be posted to the process. If this signal is held or blocked then continued attempts to increase the file size will fail with errno set to EFBIG.
RLIMIT_NOFILE	This limit specifies the maximum number of open file descriptors that a process can have.	Once this limit is reached, a subsequent attempt to allocate a new file descriptor will return EMFILE.
RLIMIT_STACK	The maximum size in bytes of the process's stack.	SIGSEGV is sent to the process if there is a need to grow the stack beyond this limit. If the process is ignoring SIGSEGV, the disposition is set to SIG_DFL before the signal is posted.
RLIMIT_AS	The maximum size of a process's mapped address space in bytes.	Once this limit is reached, subsequent calls to brk(S) and mmap(S) will fail with errno set to ENOMEM.

The following example uses getrlimit(S) to display the typical set of limits that a process is given. The display_limit() function is repeatedly called for each limit. It displays the soft and hard limits as returned by getrlimit(S).

```
 1 #include <sys/time.h>
 2 #include <sys/resource.h>
 3
 4 void
 5 display_limit(int resource, char *res_name)
 6 {
 7      struct rlimit rlm ;
 8
 9      if (getrlimit(resource, &rlm) == 0) {
10          printf("%-13s - rlim_cur = 0x%x\n",res_name, rlm.rlim_cur) ;
11          printf("%-13s - rlim_max = 0x%x\n",res_name, rlm.rlim_max) ;
12      }
13 }
14
15 main()
16 {
17      display_limit(RLIMIT_CORE, "RLIMIT_CORE") ;
18      display_limit(RLIMIT_CPU, "RLIMIT_CPU") ;
19      display_limit(RLIMIT_DATA, "RLIMIT_DATA") ;
20      display_limit(RLIMIT_FSIZE, "RLIMIT_FSIZE") ;
21      display_limit(RLIMIT_NOFILE, "RLIMIT_NOFILE") ;
22      display_limit(RLIMIT_STACK, "RLIMIT_STACK") ;
23      display_limit(RLIMIT_AS, "RLIMIT_AS") ;
24 }
```

The following output of the program may well come as a surprise! Setting identical soft and hard limits for normal user processes is common practice.

```
$ limits
RLIMIT_CORE    - rlim_cur = 0x3ffffe00
RLIMIT_CORE    - rlim_max = 0x3ffffe00
RLIMIT_CPU     - rlim_cur = 0x7fffffff
RLIMIT_CPU     - rlim_max = 0x7fffffff
RLIMIT_DATA    - rlim_cur = 0x7fffffff
RLIMIT_.DATA   - rlim_max = 0x7fffffff
RLIMIT_FSIZE   - rlim_cur = 0x3ffffe00
RLIMIT_FSIZE   - rlim_max = 0x3ffffe00
RLIMIT_NOFILE  - rlim_cur = 0x6e
RLIMIT_NOFILE  - rlim_max = 0x6e
RLIMIT_STACK   - rlim_cur = 0x7fffffff
RLIMIT_STACK   - rlim_max = 0x7fffffff
RLIMIT_AS      - rlim_cur = 0x7ffff000
RLIMIT_AS      - rlim_max = 0x7ffff000
```

Section 8.2.3 further describes the use of getrlimit(S) and setrlimit(S) system calls to modify the number of available file descriptors together with the implementation of both functions.

2.9 UNIX programming examples

This section concludes the chapter by pulling together many of the functions and system calls so far discussed into three well-known examples.

The first example provides a skeleton for a UNIX daemon showing the type of tasks that need to be performed by a process in order to become a daemon. The two smaller examples provide a simple implementation of grep(C) and the which command used to locate executable files on the caller's search path.

2.9.1 Daemon processes

There are a number of processes which are required to run for the duration of the active system. There are two types of processes which fall into this category:

- *Kernel processes* differ significantly from normal user processes in that the text they execute and the data they access do not come from a normal executable file such as the filename passed to execve(S). The functions that a kernel process can access are those of the kernel text and the data to which it has access is the kernel's protected data which is not usually visible to most user processes.

    Kernel processes cannot be created through the normal execve() system call. They are usually started during kernel initialisation before the init process is created and are distinguishable from other processes when invoking ps(C) by having a parent process ID of zero and no controlling TTY.

- *Daemons* are user processes which are usually created after the kernel has finished initialisation and has created the `init` process. Many daemons have entries in `/etc/inittab`, and others are created when executing the `rc` scripts, although some daemons can be created at any stage in the system's lifetime.

The following `ps(C)` command shows the distinction between kernel processes and daemon processes. The list shown is a subset of the actual processes present on the machine at the time the `ps(C)` command was invoked:

```
$ ps -e -ouser,pid,ppid,tty,sess,args
USER   PID  PPID    TTY SESSION COMMAND
root     0     0      ?       0 sched
root     1     0      ?       0 /etc/init
root     2     0      ?       0 vhand
root     3     0      ?       0 bdflush
root     4     0      ?       0 kmdaemon
root     5     1      ?       0 htepi_daemon /
root     6     0      ?       0 strd
root   198     1  tty01     198 /bin/login spate
root    33     1      ?      33 /etc/ifor_pmd
root    29     1      ?       0 htepi_daemon /stand
root    37    34      ?      33 /etc/ifor_sld
root   199     1  tty02     199 /etc/getty tty02 sc_m
root   200     1  tty03     200 /etc/getty tty03 sc_m
```

The kernel process can be identified as those processes with a session ID of zero. With the exception of the HTFS flushing daemons, the kernel processes all have a parent process ID of 0.

There are two daemons in the `ps(C)` listing above which are both highlighted. Like kernel processes, they have no controlling TTY, making them immune to keyboard generated signals.

The main role of most daemons is to provide a particular type of service. They usually lurk around in the background waiting for an event to occur and respond accordingly. For example, a daemon may get called when a disk fails. By responding to a request from the kernel, a spare disk may be located and brought on-line to replace the disk at fault. Once the disk is operational the daemon will sleep awaiting another failure.

The steps needed to create a daemon process are shown below followed by the skeleton source for a daemon. For completeness, the example shows how to create a daemon which can be started from the shell prompt.

The command executed at the shell prompt to create the daemon must call `exit(S)` in order to allow the shell to continue or, if the command is run in the background, to ensure that a `SIGCHLD` will be generated to inform the parent that it has no outstanding jobs if it needs to exit.

- To achieve the desired effect the process must call `fork(S)` and the parent process should then call the `exit(S)` or `_exit(S)` system calls.

- The child process is now running in a separate process group from the shell and is not a process group leader. This allows the process to call setsid(S) to create a new session in order to divorce itself from its controlling terminal.

  The process then becomes the session leader and sole member of the newly created session. It is also the process group leader of a newly created process group whose process group ID is set to the process ID of the child process.

  The process must take care when opening subsequent files. If a file is a terminal device and the O_NOCTTY flag is not passed to open(S), the kernel sets the terminal to be the controlling terminal of the process. This is not the required behaviour for a daemon.

- For any files created by the daemon, it is important that the daemon creates the files with the permissions it specifies and to ensure that they are not affected by the file mode creation mask it inherited from its parent. The umask(S) system call is used to set the mask to zero.

  It is also useful to assign file descriptors 0, 1 and 2 (stdin, stdout and stderr) to /dev/null to avoid any unexpected results if the daemon forks and execs a process which may make assumptions about the first three file descriptors. However, since daemons run in a very controlled environment, the daemon and any subsequent children should not make such assumptions!

- The current working directory should be changed to the root directory /. If the current working directory inherited by the daemon process is within a filesystem mounted over the root filesystem, presence of the daemon may prevent the filesystem from being un-mounted.

- Many of the file descriptors inherited by the daemon are unlikely to be wanted. Some open files may cause the same problem mentioned in the point above. The usual procedure is then to call close(S) for each file descriptor.

  Since the process is unlikely to know the exact number of open files, it is usual to call close(S) for the whole range of possible file descriptors. The getrlimit(S) system call should be used to determine the maximum number of files that the process can open and therefore the range of possible file descriptors.

- The default action for many signals is to terminate the process to which the signal is to be posted. The daemon should therefore either ignore signals or install handlers for those signals which are of interest to the daemon. The daemon may in fact use signals as a notification or synchronisation mechanism.

  Of course the process cannot ignore SIGTERM and SIGKILL. If the daemon receives SIGTERM, it is usually an indication that the process is shortly to receive SIGKILL and should therefore perform any tidy up functions and exit.

The procedures covered above are sufficient to now build the skeleton daemon. Much of the design of daemons involves elaborate logging and error recovery techniques. Stevens (1992) discusses error logging in detail.

The skeleton daemon is as follows:

```
 1 #include <sys/types.h>
 2 #include <sys/errno.h>
 3 #include <sys/time.h>
 4 #include <sys/resource.h>
 5 #include <signal.h>
 6 #include <fcntl.h>
 7
 8 extern int errno ;
 9
10 main()
11 {
12     int    i, fd ;
13     pid_t  pid ;
14     struct rlimit rlm ;
15
16     /*
17      * fork() so that parent can exit() to keep the shell happy
18      */
19
20     pid = fork() ;
21     if (pid == -1)
22         exit(-1) ;
23     if (pid != 0)              /* parent */
24         exit(0) ;
25
26     /*
27      * Create a new session and process group
28      */
29
30     if (setsid() == -1)
31         exit(-1) ;
32
33     /*
34      * Call getrlimit(S) to obtain maximum number of files
35      */
36
37     if (getrlimit(RLIMIT_NOFILE, &rlm) < 0)
38         exit(-1) ;
39
40     for (i=0 ; i<rlm.rlim_max ; i++)
41         close(i) ;
42     /*
43      * All files will not be open so protect against EBADF
44      */
45
46     errno = 0 ;
47
48     /*
49      * Set process umask to zero
50      */
51
52     umask(0) ;
53
54     /*
55      * Change the current directory to "/"
56      */
57
58     if (chdir("/") < 0)
59         exit(-1) ;
60
61     /*
62      * Setup signal handlers or to to SIG_IGN
63      */
```

```
64
65     /*
66      *   We are now a daemon
67      */
68
69     pause() ;
70 }
```

When the daemon is run, the `ps(C)` command can be called to locate it as shown below. Note that the daemon has a parent process ID of 1, the `init` process, and does not have an associated controlling TTY.

```
$ ps -e -ouser,pid,ppid,tty,sess,args
USER    PID  PPID     TTY SESSION COMMAND
spate   214   198   tty01     198 -ksh
spate   309     1       ?     309 daemon
```

2.9.2 `mgrep` – a simple implementation of `grep`

The following program uses the `open(S)` and `read(S)` system calls to search for the string passed to `argv[1]` in the file `argv[2]` and print each line with the line number where the string is found. This is a simple form of the `grep -n` command.

```
 1 #include <sys/errno.h>
 2 #include <fcntl.h>
 3 #include <stdlib.h>
 4
 5 extern int errno ;
 6
 7 #define BUFSIZ  512
 8
 9 char    buf[BUFSIZ] ;
10 char   *bufptr = buf ;
11 int     linecnt = 0 ;
12
13 main(int argc, char *argv[])
14 {
15     int fd ;
16
17     if (argc != 3) {
18         printf("Usage: %s pattern file\n", argv[0]) ;
19             exit(EINVAL) ;
20     }
21
22     fd = open(argv[2], O_RDONLY) ;
23     if (fd < 0)
24         pexit(argv[2]) ;
25
26     while (read(fd, bufptr, 1) == 1) {
27         if (*bufptr == '\n') {
28             linecnt++ ;
29             *bufptr = '\0' ;
30             if (strstr(buf, argv[1]) != NULL)
31                 printf("%4d %s\n", linecnt, buf) ;
32             bufptr = buf ;
33         }
34         else {
35             if ((++bufptr - buf) == BUFSIZ) {
```

```
36                        printf("%s: line size exceeded\n", argv[0]) ;
37                        exit(-1) ;
38                 }
39            }
40        }
41    return(0) ;
42 }
```

The arguments are checked on lines 17 to 20 and the filename passed to the program (`argv[2]`) is opened read only on line 22. The program then iterates around lines 26 to 40 reading each line of the file and comparing the line with the search string (`argv[1]`).

The characters are read from the file one character at time (line 26) into the buffer pointed to by `buf` until the end of the file is reached when the program terminates. `buf` is declared on line 10 to point to the `buf[]` buffer which can contain at most `BUFSIZ` characters.

The character read is compared with the newline character on line 27. If a match is found, the number of lines read so far is increased (line 28), the line (string) is terminated with the end of string character (line 29) and a check is made to see if the search string is contained within the line read (line 30). If the string comparison succeeds, the line number and line of the file are printed.

If the character read is not a newline character, the position in `buf` to read the next character is incremented and a check is made to see if `buf` can hold any more characters (line 35). If the buffer size is exceeded, an error message is printed and the program will exit (lines 36 to 37).

In the output of the program shown below, a search is made in the program source (passed as an argument) for the string `argv`:

```
$ mgrep argv mgrep.c
 13 main(int argc, char *argv[])
 18            printf("Usage: %s pattern file\n", argv[0]) ;
 22      fd = open(argv[2], O_RDONLY) ;
 24         pexit(argv[2]) ;
 30            if (strstr(buf, argv[1]) != NULL)
 36               printf("%s: line size exceeded\n", argv[0]) ;
```

Although reading the file one character at a time simplifies the program, this does not make the most efficient use of the kernel's I/O mechanisms. Section 8.7.2 and section 9.2 discuss the steps that the kernel follows to read filesystem data from disk. Using this knowledge, the program above can be constructed more efficiently producing greater performance when searching larger files.

2.9.3 `which` – locating files on the search path

One useful program available with some variants of UNIX is `which`. This takes a program name as an argument and displays the pathname where the program resides using the user's search path. This is often used to find programs of the same name but in different places in the UNIX file hierarchy. The program shown here is a variant of `which`. It uses the `PATH` environment variable to search for a specified file, printing each

occurrence in the order in which it is found. The first one displayed will be the program
run if the program name is given to the shell.

The program source is:

```
 1 #include <sys/types.h>
 2 #include <sys/stat.h>
 3 #include <sys/sysmacros.h>
 4 #include <stdlib.h>
 5 #include <stdio.h>
 6
 7 main(int argc, char* argv[])
 8 {
 9     struct stat s ;
10     char        *path, *comp ;
11     char        buf[256] ;
12     int         pathleft = 1 ;
13
14     if (argc != 2) {
15         printf("Usage: which command\n") ;
16         exit(-1) ;
17     }
18
19     path = getenv("PATH") ;
20     if (path == 0) {
21         fprintf(stderr,"which: PATH variable not set\n") ;
22         exit(-1) ;
23     }
24
25     do {
26         comp = strchr(path, ':') ;
27         if (comp != NULL)
28             *comp='\0' ;
29         else
30             pathleft = 0 ;
31         sprintf(buf, "%s/%s", path, argv[1]) ;
32         path = comp + 1 ;
33         if (stat(buf, &s) == 0)
34             printf("%s\n", buf) ;
35     } while (pathleft) ;
36 }
```

After ensuring that a program name is passed to search for on lines 14 to 17, the value of
the environment variable PATH is obtained via the getenv(S) library call. Each
pathname in PATH is separated by a colon (:).

The loop between lines 25 and 35 is repeated for each component of PATH. The
strchr(S) library function is used to extract each pathname from PATH on line 26
which is then joined with the program name requested to form the complete pathname to
be searched for.

The stat(S) system call is invoked on line 33 to obtain details for the file. If the call
returns successfully, the file exists and it is printed with its absolute or relative pathname
on line 34. Note that no check is made to see if the file is executable, a check that can be
made by st_mode field. See section 2.5.8 for further details of the stat(S) system call.

2.10 Summary and suggested reading

This chapter has provided an overview of the UNIX programming environment, the means by which application programs can request services from the UNIX kernel through either system calls or library functions.

It is not possible to describe the complete programming interface to UNIX in a single chapter. Fortunately there are many other sources of information.

The SCO OpenServer Release 5 *Programmer's Reference Manual* (1995) describes each of the system calls and library functions supported by SCO UNIX, including the header files required, errors returned and cross-references to other related functions.

There are numerous books which cover both C and UNIX programming. For many, it is a matter of taste as to which book is preferable over another. Despite the array of publications available there are no better sources than the official and de facto texts.

Kernighan and Ritchie (1978), as well as being the first book to be written about the C language, is still arguably the best text available. It provides good coverage of the standard I/O library showing example implementations of the buffered I/O routines based on the use of the I/O system calls.

The ANSI-C standard (1989) and POSIX.1 (1990) specifications are the standard C and UNIX programming interfaces adopted by many other, non-UNIX environments and provide excellent reference sources.

For UNIX programming, Stevens (1992) provides an in-depth look at the UNIX programming interfaces with many examples.

3

Exploring the UNIX kernel

This chapter describes the different methods used throughout the book to analyse kernel data structures both in the static UNIX kernel image held on disk (/unix) and within the memory image of the kernel while the system is active.

The majority of chapters provide a set of *toolkits*, example programs used to demonstrate practically the subject matter being discussed. There is no set format to the methods used by each toolkit; in fact this is intentional. Different structures are best extracted in different ways and different people have different preferred tools and methods.

3.1 Introduction

Kernel level debuggers, whether using kdb or the better scodb, offer the best means by which a user can gain knowledge of the execution of the kernel. Since this level of support is not available to normal users, it will not be further described here or throughout the remainder of the book. For more information on both kdb and scodb refer to the SCO *Advanced Hardware Developer's Kit* (1995).

This chapter concentrates on what can be achieved with the standard development system and the methods provided with the base installed system which allow the user to access the kernel. By using different tools and methods, understanding the layout of the file hierarchy, the location of header files and other system specific files, an endless amount of information can be obtained. Knowing your system makes the search for information much easier. Learn to find your way around the different manual pages and books; there is a lot of information there!

3.1.1 Who can access kernel structures?

Since the tools and interfaces presented in this chapter allow a user to access and modify kernel structures, they are of course protected, either by explicitly checking for root access or by restricting permissions at the file level. Unfortunately this may limit the opportunity to experiment on a live machine unless the reader has superuser privileges.

For this reason, the examples shown throughout the book demonstrate live sessions to show, as far as is practical, the type of information which can be obtained. Of course, if you can obtain root access to use crash(ADM) or try some of the examples presented throughout the book, experimentation is the best way to learn. Be warned though, modifying kernel structures can have a damaging effect on your system.

3.2 The /usr/include/sys directory

Almost all kernel data structures are defined in header files distributed with the standard SCO OpenServer product and previous releases of SCO UNIX. These header files are used when building the kernel and also by many of the commands and utilities which require access to kernel data structures when the kernel is running.

Access to the header files, for example proc.h, is achieved by including the header file within a program as follows:

```
#include <sys/proc.h>
```

The use of angle brackets instructs the compiler to pre-pend /usr/include to the path sys/proc.h giving the full pathname /usr/include/sys/proc.h.

It is possible to build a good understanding of the kernel from a data structure perspective, from the header files alone. However, using tools such as crash(ADM) and additional methods outlined here, the user can follow the flow of control through the kernel by analysing the change in monitored data structures.

Some of the well-known system header files which are used throughout the book are:

proc.h	Definition of proc, the core kernel structure used to describe a UNIX process.
user.h	The *u_area*, also known as the *u block*, is defined here as type struct user. This contains per process information which is needed only when the process is currently running.
signal.h	Signal types and operations for manipulating signal sets.
siginfo.h	A structure optionally passed to the user level signal handler to pass additional information about the reason for the signal occurring.
buf.h	Definition of struct buf, the buffer header used when reading and writing data through the buffer cache.
inode.h	The inode structure, used to represent an open file in memory regardless of its underlying physical representation.
immu.h	Structures and functions used by the kernel for managing and manipulating page table entries.
fstyp.h	The *File System Switch* (FSS) macros.
file.h	System-wide file table and its appropriate file structure.
elf.h	The header, section, segment and other components of ELF object files.
region.h	The pregion and region structures used to implement the process address space.
pfdat.h	Each page of physical memory has an associated pfdat structure.
sysi86.h	The sysi86(S) system call is used to retrieve a number of different kernel structures and other OS specific related information. This file defines the operations available.
stat.h	The stat structure used to retrieve per file meta-data.
tss.h	Each process is represented by an Intel i386 TSS (*Task State Segment*) for which the structure is defined here.
var.h	The var structure is used to hold system defined limits based on the set of kernel tuneables.

There are many more header files, not just in <sys/...> but throughout the /usr/include directory hierarchy. Take the time to browse this directory. The cscope(CP) utility provides an excellent method of browsing the header files, allowing the user to search for structure fields, variables and links between structures.

3.3 The `kmem` driver

The header files included in `<sys/...>` provide definitions of the structures used by the kernel. The `kmem` driver provides the means to access them from a live kernel.

As its name suggests, the `kmem` driver, commonly referred to as `/dev/kmem` (the device name through which the `kmem` driver can be accessed), provides a means for privileged processes to access the kernel virtual address space. The `kmem` driver provides access to the whole virtual address space; however, accessing the user virtual address space through this mechanism is a little obscure.

Since the device interface offered to user processes is through standard file operations, moving through the kernel address space is therefore achieved through use of the `lseek(S)` system call. The method of accessing structures or variables is as follows:

```
int fd ;
struct kernel_structure ks ;

fd = open("/dev/kmem", O_RDONLY) ;
lseek(fd, KERNEL_STRUCTURE_ADDRESS, SEEK_SET) ;
read(fd, &ks, sizeof(kernel_structure)) ;
```

3.3.1 Accessing symbolic addresses

The only piece of code missing from the above example is how to obtain the address of the kernel structure. Each object file, unless explicitly stripped by the `strip(CP)` command, includes a symbol table specifying the address at which the symbol will be located in memory when the program is running. Thus, given an executable object file and a symbol name, the address of the symbol can be obtained.

There are two main object file formats used in SCO UNIX, the Executable and Linking Format (ELF) which is described in chapter 6 and the Common Object File Format (COFF). The UNIX kernel is linked as a COFF object file. Chapter 5 describes in detail the format of the UNIX kernel and how to extract symbol table entries.

The `nlist(S)` library function hides the work of understanding both ELF and COFF object files by providing a simple interface which takes an object file name and a list of symbol names and returns the corresponding virtual addresses. The prototype for the `nlist(S)` function is:

```
#include <nlist.h>

int nlist(char *filename, struct nlist *nl) ;
```

The fields of the `nlist` structure are described in detail in section 5.3 together with a program which emulates the functionality of `nlist(S)`. The following example program uses `nlist(S)` in conjunction with `/dev/kmem` to retrieve and display the addresses of a number of kernel structures.

Lines 9 to 12 declare and initialise an array of `nlist` structures, one structure for each symbol whose address is required. The null entry indicates to `nlist(S)` the end of the list of symbols to search for.

The example will locate the addresses of a well-known kernel variable and kernel structure and also attempt to access a non-existent kernel variable to show the error values returned from `nlist(S)`.

When `nlist(S)` is called on line 20, it is passed the object file name which contains the symbols in addition to the `nl[]` array. For each symbol which exists, `nlist(S)` will overwrite the `n_value` field of the `nlist` structure with the symbol's address.

```
 1 #include <sys/user.h>
 2 #include <nlist.h>
 3 #include <fcntl.h>
 4
 5 #define LBOLT nl[0].n_value
 6 #define U     nl[1].n_value
 7 #define FAIL  nl[2].n_value
 8
 9 struct nlist nl[] = { { "lbolt", 0 },
10                       { "u", 0 },
11                       { "var_which_does_not_exist", 0 },
12                       { 0 } } ;
13
14 main()
15 {
16     int fd ;
17     long lb ;
18     struct user u ;
19
20     if (nlist("/unix", nl) == -1)
21         pexit("nlist") ;
22
23     fd = open("/dev/kmem", O_RDONLY) ;
24     if (fd < 0)
25         pexit("kmem") ;
26
27     if (LBOLT == -1)
28         printf("lbolt could not be accessed\n") ;
29     else {
30         lseek(fd, LBOLT, SEEK_SET) ;
31         read(fd, &lb, sizeof(long)) ;
32         printf("value of lbolt = %d\n", lb) ;
33     }
34     if (U == -1)
35         printf("u could not be accessed\n") ;
36     else {
37         lseek(fd, U, SEEK_SET) ;
38         read(fd, &u, sizeof(struct user)) ;
39         printf("u.u_psargs = %s\n", u.u_psargs) ;
40         printf("u.u_uid = %d\n", u.u_uid) ;
41         printf("u.u_gid = %d\n", u.u_gid) ;
42     }
43     if (FAIL == -1)
44         printf("couldn't access the var_which_does_not_exist\n") ;
45 }
```

On line 23, `/dev/kmem` is opened for read access, and for each of the symbols in `nl[]`:

- Seek to the virtual address of the symbol.
- Read the contents of the address or a range of contiguous addresses if a structure is required to be read.

The value of lbolt, which contains the number of clock ticks since the system was bootstrapped, is displayed on line 32 and three fields of the u_area are displayed on lines 39 to 41 including u_psargs which holds the name of the program passed to the execve(S) system call. For one particular run of the program the output is:

```
# ./kmem
value of lbolt = 77975653
u.u_psargs = ./kmem
u.u_uid = 13583
u.u_gid = 50
couldn't access the var_which_does_not_exist
```

It is useful to peruse the header files in /usr/include/sys and try the above example to read different variables and structures. Note that some kernel structures may contain pointers to other structures. Examples throughout the book encounter such linked structures which involve multiple reads from /dev/kmem.

3.4 The mem driver

The mem driver, accessed through the /dev/mem special device node, provides a means for user processes to access physical memory addresses using the same lseek(S), read(S) and write(S) interfaces used when accessing /dev/kmem.

There are rarely cases where the mem driver needs to be used. Examples include the eisa(ADM) utility which uses /dev/mem to display boards installed on an EISA bus and the crash(ADM) command. Use of the mem driver is shown in chapter 4.

3.5 The table driver

There are a number of problems with using /dev/kmem for serious system administration or application use. Firstly, there is always a need for synchronisation between the running kernel and the object file from which the name list, and thus the list of virtual addresses, is obtained.

For example, if the kernel which has been bootstrapped is not /unix, the addresses of symbols will more than likely be wrong. An alternative method is for utilities to understand internally the address layout of the kernel. While this may be suitable for commands such as crash(ADM) which are re-issued with each new kernel release, it is not desirable for other commands and utilities.

The table driver, often referred to as /dev/table, provides a means for user processes to access frequently used kernel structures without access to the UNIX kernel name list or access to /dev/kmem. Commands such as ps(C) and killall(C) use /dev/table to access kernel tables.

The tables supported by the table driver are shown in Table 3.1. Each table is accessible by opening and reading the device corresponding to the <name> field shown above. For example, to access the process table, the file /dev/table/proc should be opened.

Table 3.1   Example tables accessible by the `table` driver

`/dev/table/<name>`	Structure	Header file	Description
pregion	pregion	region.h	Per process regions used to establish regions at different virtual addresses per process.
region	region	region.h	Memory regions for constructing a process's address space.
proc	proc	proc.h	Process table entry, one per process.
eproc	eproc	eproc.h	Extended process structure.
file	file	file.h	Open file table entries.
inode	inode	inode.h	Active in-core inodes.

Chapter 7 shows an example which reads `/dev/table/proc` in order to provide a simplified version of `ps(C)`.

There are two methods of reading tables. Either the table can be read element by element or it can be read as a byte stream whereby each read will return the requested number of bytes starting at the current position in the table.

The following example opens the `/dev/table/inode` device file and reads `inode` structures repeatedly for each `inode` returned by the table driver.

```
 1 #include <sys/types.h>
 2 #include <sys/inode.h>
 3 #include <fcntl.h>
 4
 5 main()
 6 {
 7     struct inode in ;
 8     int fd, count = 0 ;
 9
10     fd = open("/dev/table/inode", O_RDONLY) ;
11     if (fd < 0)
12         pexit("/dev/table/inode") ;
13
14     while (read(fd, &in, sizeof(struct inode)) > 0) {
15         if (in.i_count > 0)
16             count++ ;
17     }
18     printf("There are %d active inodes\n", count) ;
19 }
```

For each `inode` structure read, the program increments the `count` variable on line 16 if the inode is currently in use. For an inode to be in use, its reference count is greater than zero (line 15). Once all entries have been read, the program displays the number of active inodes.

The output of the program for one particular run is:

```
There are 295 active inodes
```

Despite providing a much easier and usable interface, the table driver provides only a limited set of structures which can be accessed. Nevertheless, its use is recommended wherever possible.

3.6 The `sysi86` system call

A somewhat unusual system call, `sysi86(S)` provides access to a number of ad hoc and unrelated kernel structures and functionality. The prototype for `sysi86(S)` is:

```
#include <sys/sysi86.h>

long sysi86(int cmd, void *arg) ;
```

Some of the more useful values that `cmd` can take are briefly described below. The example that follows will demonstrate the use of each command.

RTODC   `arg` should be the address of an `rtc_t` structure into which the kernel will copy the contents of the hardware *time of day* clock.

RDUBLK   This reads the u_area for a specified process ID.

SI86FPHW   This returns the method by which floating point computation is supported, for example whether by hardware or software emulation.

SI86MEM   The size of available memory is returned.

SI86SWPI   This is used to add or delete swap areas or to read the existing swap areas.

The following program must be run by root. Whereas many of the programs that use /dev/kmem and /dev/table require only read access to the two devices (/dev/kmem and /dev/table) and the UNIX object file (/unix), the `sysi86(S)` system call will check for a user ID of 0 (root) when invoking it with a cmd type of RTODC.

Line 20 invokes `sysi86(S)` with the RTODC command. This system call reads information from the real-time clock chip and returns it in the structure passed to `sysi86(S)` of type `struct rtc_t`. The time is then printed in hours:minutes:seconds.

Line 29 invokes `sysi86(S)` with the RDUBLK command to read the u_area for the calling process. The user ID of the calling process is displayed together with the u_area u_psargs field which displays the name passed to `execve(S)`.

```
 1 #include <sys/sysi86.h>
 2 #include <sys/fp.h>
 3 #include <sys/user.h>
 4 #include <sys/rtc.h>
 5 #include <sys/swap.h>
 6 #include <sys/sysmacros.h>
 7 #include <stdio.h>
 8
 9 #define rtcTr(T) (((((T)>>4)&0xF)*10)+((T)&0xF))
10
11 main()
12 {
13     struct user    u ;
14     int            fptype, i ;
15     struct rtc_t   rtc ;
16     long           memsz ;
17     struct swapint swb ;
18     swpt_t         swpb[MSFILES] ;
19
```

```
20      if (sysi86(RTODC, &rtc) < 0)
21          pexit("RTODC") ;
22      else {
23          printf("Real time clock details\n") ;
24          printf(" Time - %d:", rtc.rtc_hr) ;
25          printf("%02d:", rtcTr(rtc.rtc_min)) ;
26          printf("%02d\n", rtcTr(rtc.rtc_sec)) ;
27      }
28      if (sysi86(RDUBLK, getpid(), (char *)&u, sizeof(struct user)) <0)
29          pexit("RDUBLK") ;
30      printf("\nu.u_psargs = %s\n", u.u_psargs) ;
31      printf("u.u_uid    = %d\n", u.u_uid) ;
32
33      if (sysi86(SI86FPHW, &fptype) < 0)
34          pexit("SI86FPHW") ;
35
36      printf("\nfloating point support = ") ;
37      switch (fptype & 0xff) {
38          case(FP_NO)  : { printf("FP_NO\n") ; break ; }
39          case(FP_SW)  : { printf("FP_SW\n") ; break ; }
40          case(FP_287) : { printf("FP_287\n") ; break ; }
41          case(FP_387) : { printf("FP_387\n") ; break ; }
42          default      : printf("unrecognized\n") ;
43      }
44
45      memsz = sysi86(SI86MEM) ;
46      printf("\nAmount of memory available = %d bytes\n", memsz) ;
47
48      swb.si_cmd = SI_LIST ;
49      swb.si_buf = (char *)swpb ;
50      if (sysi86(SI86SWPI, &swb) < 0)
51          pexit("SI86SWPI") ;
52
53      for (i=0 ; i<MSFILES ; i++) {
54          if (!swpb[i].st_npgs)
55              continue ;
56          printf("\ndevice (%d %d)", emajor(swpb[i].st_dev),
57                                     eminor(swpb[i].st_dev)) ;
58          printf(" provides %d pages\n", swpb[i].st_npgs) ;
59      }
60  }
```

Line 33 invokes sysi86(S) with the SI86FPHW command to determine the type of floating point support provided on the system. As the following output shows, since the program was run on an 80486 SX/25, floating point is emulated by software.

The next call on line 45 passing the command SI86MEM to sysi86(S) will return the amount of memory available on the system in bytes.

The final call to sysi86(S) on line 50 passes SI86SWPI to return information about the current swap tables. For each valid swap table, the device and the number of pages which the device holds is displayed.

The output of the program for one particular run is:

```
# sysi86
Real time clock details
 Time - 9:31:09

u.u_psargs = sysi86
u.u_uid    = 0
```

```
floating point support = FP_SW

Amount of memory available = 33161216 bytes

device (1 41) provides 12250 pages
```

3.7 Summary and suggested reading

This chapter has introduced a number of different methods used throughout the book for
analysing kernel structures dynamically. The main tool not discussed in this chapter is the
crash(ADM) utility which is fully described in chapter 14.

Since the methods discussed allow a user to access all kernel structures, they are of
course protected either by explicitly checking for root access or by limiting permissions
at the file level. Unfortunately this may limit the opportunity to experiment on a live
machine. For this reason, the examples shown throughout the book demonstrate live
sessions to show, as far as is practical, the type of information which can be obtained.

Chapter 5 describes the format of COFF object files and shows how nlist(S) works
internally.

The main source of reference is the SCO OpenServer Release 5 documentation set,
particularly the following manual pages:

```
nlist(S)
sysi86(S)
mem(FP)
tab(HW)
```

and of course the files residing under /usr/include.

4

Bootstrap and system initialisation

This chapter describes the stages followed from power-on of the machine to the first login prompt being displayed. This covers the state of the CPU following reset, handing control to the BIOS and the subsequent phases of bootstrap followed until the kernel has been loaded into memory and initialised.

The layout of the PC disk is described showing how more than one operating system can occupy the primary disk at any one time. The methods by which SCO UNIX manages the disk and the phases that SCO UNIX based bootstrap programs follow are then described. These show how the bootstrap programs pass information to the kernel about the machine on which it is running, the disk from which it is bootstrapped, the amount of memory available and so on.

The procedures followed when control is passed to the kernel are shown, followed by how the main kernel processes, daemons and application programs are created which are run prior to the login prompt being displayed on the system console.

4.1 Introduction

Most books and published papers on UNIX ignore many of the procedures followed from machine power on to user services becoming available. Bootstrap forms an integral part of kernel startup including initialisation of various machine level structures and hardware based memory management.

SCO bootstrap functions manage a range of complex problems such as handling the numerous PC hardware variants and their often obscure methods of memory management, provision of bootstrap routines for hard disk, the various floppy devices, network boot, and the ability to run diagnostics programs and respond to user supplied options. In order to limit scope and reduce complexity, this chapter covers only the case of bootstrapping from the hard disk with no direct intervention from the user.

In addition to describing kernel initialisation including startup of kernel processes, the chapter describes the procedures followed by `init(ADM)` to take the system to single- or multi-user mode.

4.1.1 The bootstrap and system initialisation toolkit

This chapter includes more theory than practice thus a limited number of toolkit examples are provided. The examples in this chapter are:

Toolkit 4.1   Accessing the `fdisk` partition table, page 101
Toolkit 4.2   Reading the `bootinfo` structure, page 106

Toolkit 4.1 reads and displays the contents of the `fdisk(ADM)` partition table which is used to manage multiple operating systems resident on the same physical disk.

Toolkit 4.2 reads and displays the main structure passed from the final bootstrap program to the kernel, including the amount and layout of physical memory.

4.2 Bootstrapping /unix

The primary purpose of bootstrap is to load the UNIX kernel from disk, floppy or over the network into memory and pass control to it. Despite sounding trivial, this encompasses numerous complicated tasks including taking control of the processor in real mode, sizing memory, understanding disk and filesystem layouts, parsing command line options to be passed to the kernel and finally passing control to the kernel's startup routine.

The different stages of bootstrap are shown in Figure 4.1.

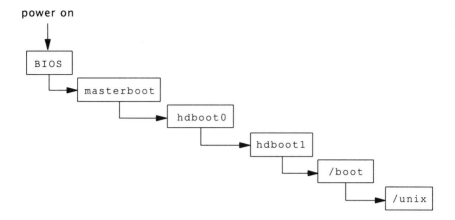

Figure 4.1 The multi-stage SCO UNIX bootstrap

The BIOS loads `masterboot` from the first sector of the primary disk. The `masterboot` program scans the `fdisk(ADM)` partition table looking for the active partition and loads `hdboot0` from the first sector of this partition.

`hdboot0` loads `hdboot1` which is located at sector three of the active partition. `hdboot1` then loads `/boot` from the boot filesystem. `/boot` can then load one of a number of different standalone programs, one of which can be the UNIX kernel.

Each stage of bootstrap is described in more detail throughout the following sections.

4.2.1 The PC-based bootstrap

When the typical PC is switched on, the RESET signal of the CPU is asserted by hardware thus forcing a reset of the CPU. This may also occur at other times, for example when the reset button on many PC front panels is depressed.

Following basic CPU initialisation, the `cs` and `ds` segment registers are set up to allow execution to begin. The base address of the code segment is set to 64K below the top of physical memory allowing room for ROM to hold initialisation code. The data segment is set to the low end of physical memory since RAM is expected to be present!

After processor initialisation, the CPU will start executing in *real mode* therefore the top of physical memory can be viewed as `0xffffff` (1 Mb).

Execution always starts at address `0xffff0`. This points to the ROM-based bootstrap routine. The task of this simple bootstrap routine is to read the first sector off the hard disk or floppy drive into memory and pass control to it. The first sector on disk is generally known as the *boot sector* or the *masterboot block* in SCO terminology.

Figure 4.2 shows the layout of memory on the PC architecture.

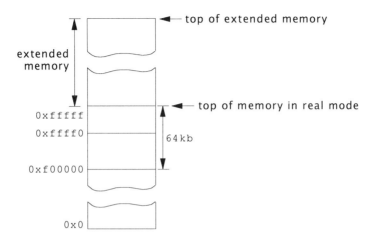

Figure 4.2   PC memory layout

4.2.2 The PC disk layout

Each bootable PC disk consists of between one and four partitions, commonly called *fdisk partitions*. Since each partition can contain a complete bootable operating system, a single disk can contain up to four different operating systems.

Only one partition is active at any one time. When the BIOS bootstrap routine runs, it loads and passes control to the bootstrap routine located in the active partition. At the end of the masterboot block there exists a *partition table* which describes the partitions on the disk, where they are located, what their contents are and so on. Management of partitions is performed using the fdisk(ADM) command.

In the example below, fdisk is run to display the contents of the partition table for the *primary* hard disk. For information about primary and secondary hard disks see the manual page for hd(HW).

```
$ fdisk -p
1 1 25000 25000 UNIX Inactive
2 25001 50000 25000 UNIX Active
3 50001 66600 166000 DOS (32) Inactive
```

This disk contains three partitions (the fourth is empty), two partitions containing UNIX, of which one is active, and another partition containing DOS.

For SCO UNIX, masterboot is only the first phase in a multi-stage bootstrap process which will eventually bootstrap the UNIX kernel. The masterboot program simply locates the partition table, finds the active partition, loads the first sector of the active partition into memory and passes control to it.

The following sections describe the steps taken following execution of masterboot.

Toolkit 4.1   Accessing the `fdisk` partition table

The example demonstrated in this toolkit accesses the `fdisk` partition table and prints out the contents of each non-empty entry. The `<sys/fdisk>` header file defines the structure of the masterboot block and the partition table itself. Figure 4.3 summarises the layout of the masterboot block.

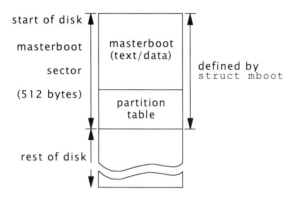

Figure 4.3   Contents of the masterboot block

The masterboot block is described by the `mboot` structure which contains two fields, an array of characters representing the text and data of the masterboot boot program and an array of `ipart` structures. The `ipart` structure defines a single partition table entry. The fields of the structure are shown in Table 4.1.

Table 4.1   Fields of the `ipart` structure

`ipart` structure field	Description
unsigned char bootid	This field indicates whether the partition is bootable.
unsigned char beghead	The starting disk head of the partition.
unsigned char begsect	The starting disk sector of the partition.
unsigned char begcyl	The starting disk cylinder of the partition
unsigned char systid	The operating system type.
unsigned char endhead	The last disk head covering the partition.
unsigned char endsect	The last disk sector of the partition.
unsigned char endcyl	The last disk cylinder.
long relsect	The first sector relative to the start of the disk.
long numsect	The number of sectors in the partition.

On lines 14 to 22, the program opens `/dev/hd00`, the primary disk as defined in `hd(HW)`, and reads the first sector into `mb` which is declared as type `struct mboot`. The address of the partition table is assigned to the `ip` variable on line 24.

The remainder of the program loops through each entry in the `ip[]` array displaying the partition table number, the partition type, the number of sectors and whether the partition is active or inactive. The example here understands only two different partition table entry types (UNIX and DOS). There are of course other possible entries. See the `<sys/fdisk.h>` header file for further information.

Note that the order of the partition table is reversed such that partition table entry number 1 as displayed by `fdisk` is equal to the fourth entry in the array of structures read in the following program.

```
 1 #include <sys/types.h>
 2 #include <sys/fdisk.h>
 3 #include <fcntl.h>
 4
 5 #define PT ip[i]
 6
 7 main()
 8 {
 9     char *pn ;
10     struct mboot mb ;
11     struct ipart *ip ;
12     int i, fd, nread ;
13
14     fd = open("/dev/hd00", O_RDONLY) ;
15     if (fd < 0)
16         pexit("/dev/hd00") ;
17
18     nread = read(fd, (char *)&mb, sizeof(struct mboot)) ;
19     if (nread != sizeof(struct mboot)) {
20         printf("readpt: couldn't read master boot block\n") ;
21         exit(-1) ;
22     }
23
24     ip = (struct ipart *)&mb.parts ;
25
26     for (i=FD_NUMPART-1 ; i>=0 ; i--) {
27         if (PT.systid == 0)
28             continue ;
29         printf("%d ",i) ;
30         if (PT.systid == 99)
31             printf("UNIX ") ;
32         else if (PT.systid == 6)
33             printf("DOS (32) ") ;
34         else
35             printf("NOT KNOWN ") ;
36         printf("%d %s\n",PT.numsect,PT.bootid?"Active":"Inactive") ;
37     }
38 }
```

The output of the program is shown below. For the system on which the program was run, the primary disk has three `fdisk` partitions in use, two by UNIX and one by DOS. One of the UNIX partitions is active.

```
$ readpt
3 UNIX 800000 Inactive
2 UNIX 800000 Active
1 DOS (32) 531200 Inactive
```

4.2.3 SCO UNIX partition format

For each fdisk(ADM) partition that hosts SCO UNIX, the partition is further divided into
a number of *divisions* described by a division table, more commonly known as the *divvy
table*. Each partition can hold between one and eight divisions. The division table and
corresponding divisions are set up for the primary disk during installation. Existing
divisions may be modified or deleted and new divisions created at any stage.

Divisions can be displayed and modified through use of the divvy(ADM) command.
The following example shows a set of divisions for a typical installation of SCO UNIX
with a single root filesystem containing an HTFS filesystem, a separate boot filesystem
containing an EAFS filesystem and a swap division. Note that by default there is no
separate dump partition. If the kernel needs to generate a system dump, it will write the
dump over the swap device and allow it to be saved following the next bootstrap.

```
+-------------+-------------+--------+---+-------------+------------+
| Name        | Type        | New FS | # | First Block | Last Block |
+-------------+-------------+--------+---+-------------+------------+
| boot        | EAFS        |  no    | 0 |           0|       15359|
| swap        | NON FS      |  no    | 1 |       15360|       76799|
| root        | HTFS        |  no    | 2 |       76800|      355956|
|             | NOT USED    |  no    | 3 |          -|          -|
|             | NOT USED    |  no    | 4 |          -|          -|
|             | NOT USED    |  no    | 5 |          -|          -|
| recover     | NON FS      |  no    | 6 |      355957|      355966|
| hd0a        | WHOLE DISK  |  no    | 7 |           0|      356327|
+-------------+-------------+--------+---+-------------+------------+
355968 1K blocks for divisions, 360 1K blocks reserved for the system
```

The first block of the boot division shown here is block 0. This is not the first sector of
the fdisk(ADM) partition but the first block of the area defined within the partition for
holding divisions. Figure 4.4 shows in more detail the layout of the disk containing the
active UNIX partition shown in the divvy(ADM) output above.

The masterboot and partition table reside in sector 0 followed by an inactive UNIX
partition. This is followed by an active UNIX partition which is then followed by an
inactive DOS partition.

Within the active UNIX partition, the first sector is occupied by hdboot0, the
program loaded by masterboot. There is a one sector gap after hdboot0 followed by
hdboot1 which is twenty sectors in size.

hdboot0 loads hdboot1 which is the first boot program that understands the layout
of the boot (EAFS) filesystem, the location of which can be found in the divvy table. The
boot program which loads the kernel, /boot, which is located in the root directory of the
boot filesystem, is loaded by hdboot1. It is /boot which prompts the user to press
Return to boot the default kernel or to specify the kernel which will be bootstrapped.

The *bad track table* is set up during installation and administered thereafter by the
badtrk(ADM) command. This is used in conjunction with a set of *alias tracks*. When a
request is made for data on a bad track the disk driver redirects the request to one of the
alias tracks without the knowledge of the user.

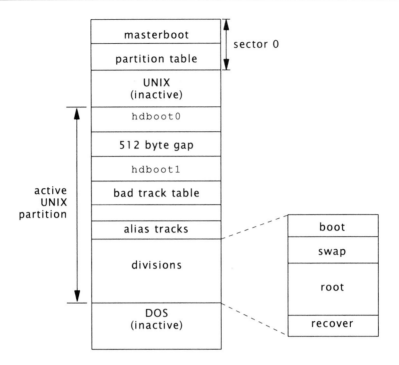

Figure 4.4   Format of an SCO UNIX partition

Following the set of alias tracks is a contiguous area of the disk set aside for holding the divisions. In Figure 4.4, there are four divisions holding boot, swap, root and a recover division used by `fsck(ADM)`.

The `/dev/hd00` device which was used in the previous program allows access to the whole partition.

4.2.4 Booting the UNIX kernel

The UNIX kernel is loaded by `/boot`. This represents the final stage of bootstrap. The functionality provided by `/boot` is richer than the previous bootstrap phases which follow the same sequence of events each time.

`/boot` works from either a set of defaults or options passed on the command line after it displays the prompt as follows:

```
SCO OpenServer(TM) Release 5

Boot
:
```

The set of defaults are stored in the file `/etc/default/boot`. A set of typical default parameters is:

```
DEFBOOTSTR=hd(40)unix swap=hd(41) dump=hd(41) root=hd(42)
AUTOBOOT=YES
FSCKFIX=YES
MULTIUSER=YES
PANICBOOT=NO
MAPKEY=YES
SERIAL8=NO
SLEEPTIME=NO
BOOTMNT=RO
```

The DEFBOOTSTR parameter specifies that the file to be loaded is called unix and it should be loaded from the primary hard disk. The number 40 represents the *minor* number of the device from which unix should be loaded. The device numbers used by /boot are identical to the device numbers used by the running kernel.

Each minor number can be interpreted using Table 4.2.

Table 4.2   Encoding of the minor device field

			Bit number					
7	6	5	4	3	2	1	0	Description
X	X	–	–	–	–	–	–	Disk number (0 to 3).
–	–	X	X	X	–	–	–	Partition number (1 to 4).
–	–	–	–	–	X	X	X	Division number (0 to 6).
–	–	X	X	X	1	1	1	Whole partition.
–	–	0	0	0	0	0	0	Whole physical disk.
–	–	1	0	1	–	–	–	Active partition.
–	–	1	1	0	–	–	–	DOS partition.
–	–	1	1	1	X	X	X	DOS drive (C–J).

The minor number 40 can be broken down as shown in Figure 4.5. Thus, minor number zero points to division 0 on the active partition which corresponds to the information returned by divvy(ADM) as shown in section 4.2.3. Similarly, device minors 41 and 42 correspond to the swap and root divisions respectively.

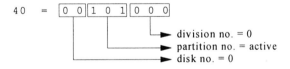

Figure 4.5   Interpreting DEFBOOTSTR minor numbers

The position in memory that /boot loads the kernel is dependent on how the kernel has been compiled and linked. For further details on the format of the UNIX kernel image see chapter 5.

Since the kernel is not a normal C program and therefore does not have the concept of argc and argv[], information captured by /boot, such as the amount of physical memory and the ranges in the address space at which memory is valid, is passed to the kernel through a number of structures placed in well-known memory locations.

One of the structures passed to the kernel is the `bootinfo` structure. The fields of this structure are shown in Table 4.3.

Table 4.3   Fields in the `bootinfo` structure

`bootinfo` structure field		Description
ulong	checksum	Checksum data.
ulong	bootflags	Miscellaneous flags.
ulong	basemem	The size of base memory (below 1Mb).
ulong	extmem	The size of extended memory.
long	memavailcnt	Number of slots in `memavail[]`.
struct	bootmem memavail[]	An array specifying the ranges of available memory. The `bootmem` structure has three fields. The `base` field represents the base address of the slot, the `extent` field specifies the size of the extent in bytes and the `flags` field defines the properties of the slot.
long	memusedcnt	Number of slots in `memused[]`.
struct	bootmem memused[]	Ranges of memory which are already used.
ulong	magic	The hex value `0xfeedbac`.
ulong	pad2[2]	Padding.
long	bootstrlen	The size of data used by `bootstr`.
char	bootstr[1]	A list of strings to be passed to the kernel.

The `bootinfo` structure is accessed by the kernel early in its initialisation, primarily to understand how much memory it has available and where.

Toolkit 4.2   Reading the `bootinfo` structure

The `bootinfo` structure is defined in the header file `<sys/bootinfo.h>`. The same header file also specifies the location at which `/boot` will place the `bootinfo` structure in memory. Note that this address is a physical address and therefore to read the contents of `bootinfo`, the `/dev/mem` device must be used.

The source of the program is as follows:

```
 1 #include <sys/types.h>
 2 #include <sys/bootinfo.h>
 3 #include <fcntl.h>
 4
 5 #define M 1048576
 6
 7 prsz(long sz)
 8 {
 9     if (sz >= M)
10         printf("%3dM", sz/M) ;
11     else
12         printf("%3dk", sz/1024) ;
13 }
14
```

```
15 main()
16 {
17     int fd, n, i ;
18     struct bootinfo bi ;
19
20     fd = open("/dev/mem", O_RDONLY) ;
21     if (fd < 0)
22         pexit("/dev/mem") ;
23
24     lseek(fd, BOOTINFO_LOC, SEEK_SET) ;
25
26     n = read(fd, (char *)&bi, sizeof(struct bootinfo)) ;
27     if (n != sizeof(struct bootinfo)) {
28         printf("couldn't read bootinof\n") ;
29         exit(-1) ;
30     }
31
32     printf("bootinfo structure fields\n") ;
33     printf("   basemem     = ") ; prsz(bi.basemem) ;
34     printf("\n   extmem      = ") ; prsz(bi.extmem) ;
35     printf("\n   magic       = %x\n", bi.magic) ;
36     printf("   memory ranges...\n") ;
37
38     for (i=0 ; i<bi.memavailcnt ; i++) {
39         printf("     base = ") ; prsz(bi.memavail[i].base) ;
40         printf(" extent = ") ; prsz(bi.memavail[i].extent) ;
41         printf("  flags = %x", bi.memavail[i].flags) ;
42         printf("\n") ;
43     }
44 }
```

The program starts by opening the mem driver on line 20. The location of bootinfo is defined in <sys/bootinfo.h> by the constant BOOTINFO_LOC. Line 24 involves a seek to this address and the structure is read on line 26.

The remainder of the program involves printing out various fields of the structure including the range of valid memory addresses.

In the output of the program shown below there is 640 kb of base memory and an additional 31 Mb of extended memory. The layout of physical memory and the flags corresponding to each entry are displayed. The interpretation of the flags is shown for each memory range shown.

```
$ prbootinfo
bootinfo structure fields
   basemem     = 640k
   extmem      =  31M
   magic       = feedbac
   memory ranges...
     base =    0k extent =  32k  flags = 1        # reserved memory
     base =  32k extent = 608k  flags = 0        # available memory
     base =   1M extent =  14M  flags = 0        # available (DMA'able)
     base =  15M extent = 740k  flags = 8        # Kernel BSS
     base =  15M extent = 140k  flags = 4        # Kernel Data
     base =  16M extent =  14M  flags = 500      # >16M (non-DMA)
     base =  30M extent =   1M  flags = 502      # Kernel text
     base =  31M extent =   4k  flags = d00      # EISA BIOS, >16M
```

/boot also initialises the page directory and a limited number of page tables which are used by the kernel once loaded. For more information on how the i386 handles paging see section 6.4.7 and chapter 12.

4.3 Kernel initialisation

Once the kernel has been loaded, /boot jumps to the kernel entry point which is located in the kernel object file *header*. The format of the kernel is described in chapter 5 which shows the format of the kernel object file header including the location of the kernel text and data and the address at which the kernel should be entered.

The first function executed by the kernel is pstart(), also called _start(). Entered in protected mode established by /boot, pstart() is responsible for low level initialisation of descriptor tables and switching on paging using the page directory created by /boot.

Once low level initialisation has been performed, pstart() jumps into the kernel TSS emerging at vstart(). At this stage the processor will be running in protected mode with paging enabled. When vstart() is entered, it calls two kernel functions to perform the majority of kernel initialisation, namely mlsetup() and main(). For further details on the TSS see section 7.9.4.

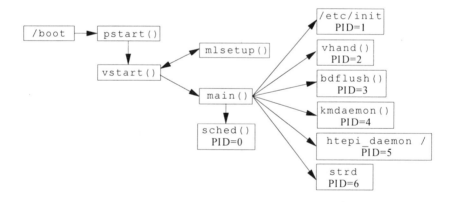

Figure 4.6   Basic phases of kernel initialisation

The main paths through kernel initialisation following /boot are shown in Figure 4.6. The phases following vstart() are described throughout the remainder of the chapter.

4.3.1 Machine level setup

When mlsetup() (machine level setup) is called the kernel is executing its first function which is not coded in assembler. Most kernel subsystems which require sparse address spaces including the kernel memory allocator (kma) are called from `mlsetup()` to allocate the space they require in memory and initialise appropriate data structures.

At this stage of initialisation the kernel has no concept of a process. One of the main tasks performed by `mlsetup()` is to establish a user area (u_area) which will be used by the first UNIX process (`sched`) and copied to subsequent UNIX processes which are created. The main steps performed by `mlsetup()` are:

- Initialise the page directory `kpd0[]` passed by `/boot`. This involves ensuring that any entries in the table which have not yet been used are zeroed.
- Initialise memory which the kernel will use dynamically.
- Call `p0u()` to create the first u_area.
- Call `binit()` to initialise the buffer cache.
- Initialise the general kernel memory allocator (kma).
- Initialise the region tables `region[]`.
- Initialise the process table `proc[]`.
- Initialise the file table `file[]`.
- Call `p0init()` to initialise the first process `proc[0]`.

Many of the initialisation routines covered here involve basic allocation of memory based upon appropriate kernel tuneables and the amount of physical memory available. Before such tables and functionality can be offered by these subsystems, for example the file table, additional setup routines will be called later during kernel initialisation.

The `p0u()` and `p0init()` functions are called to create the u_area for the first process and initialise various fields of the `proc` structure. Note that all processes created in the system inherit many properties from these two initial structures. For further details on the `user` and `proc` structures see chapter 7.

After `mlsetup()` has completed initialisation it returns to `vstart()` which then calls `main()`, the final stage in kernel initialisation, where some of the more familiar UNIX processes are created.

4.3.2 Entering kernel `main()`

When `main()` is entered it can be viewed as running in the *context* of process 0. The u_area and process table entry have been created and initialised at this stage so fields of the u_area can be accessed via the kernel variable `u` and fields of the `proc` structure for process 0, at this stage the current process, can be accessed via the `curproc` kernel variable.

However, there are a number of additional initialisation functions which need to be executed prior to completion and hand-over to the `init(M)` process. The main tasks performed by `main()` are:

- Call `clkstart()` to initialise and start the clock.
- Call `disp_init()` to initialise the process scheduler.

- Call all functions in the `io_init[]`, `init_tbl[]` and `io_start[]` arrays, allowing device drivers to initialise.

- Initialise the swap devices and structures.

- Call `newproc()` to create process ID 1, the `init(M)` process.

- Call `newproc()` to create process ID 2, `vhand()`, the pageout daemon.

- Call `newproc()` to create process ID 3, `bdflush()`, which is responsible for periodically flushing dirty buffers in the buffer cache to disk.

- Call `kmstartdaemon()` which creates process ID 4, `kmdaemon`, for managing memory owned by kma.

- Call `htepi_daemon()` which creates a kernel process for the root filesystem which is responsible for processing transactions and maintaining the intent log.

- Call `newproc()` to create process ID 6, `strd()`, a kernel process for managing STREAMS memory allocated at interrupt time.

- Set up `u_psargs` to contain the string "sched". The `u_psargs` field is used by `ps(C)` when displaying the names of active processes.

- Call `sched()`, the swapper, which is invoked when the amount of free memory reaches zero. Thus, the main flow of control through kernel initialisation emerges as process ID 0 which loops indefinitely around the `sched()` function.

The `io_init[]` array contains the entry points of device driver initialisation functions. This allows device drivers to perform any required initialisation prior to the first open. The entries in the `io_start[]` array contain initialisation routines for network support and management.

The `io_tbl[]` array holds the entry points of functions which further initialise many of the main tables and structures used by the kernel. For example, this is where `finit()` is called to initialise the file table and where `inoinit()` is called to initialise the inode table. The `iinit()` kernel function is called from here which calls `srmountfun()` to mount the root filesystem whose device number is found in the `rootdev` kernel variable.

Running the `ps(C)` command displays the seven kernel processes created:

```
$ ps -ef | head -10
     UID   PID  PPID  C    STIME     TTY        TIME CMD
    root     0     0  0  22:28:36       ?    00:00:00 sched
    root     1     0  0  22:28:36       ?    00:00:01 /etc/init
    root     2     0  0  22:28:36       ?    00:00:00 vhand
    root     3     0  0  22:28:36       ?    00:00:00 bdflush
    root     4     0  0  22:28:36       ?    00:00:00 kmdaemon
    root     5     1  0  22:28:36       ?    00:00:01 htepi_daemon /
    root     6     0  0  22:28:36       ?    00:00:00 strd
    root   204     1  0  22:31:29   tty01    00:00:03 /bin/login spate
    root    33     1  0  22:29:39       ?    00:00:00 /etc/ifor_pmd
```

Most of the processes created are called kernel processes, that is they occupy no memory in user space. Their text and data reside purely within the kernel address space.

One of the exceptions is the `init` process. The procedures followed for creation of `init` are different to the creation of any other UNIX process as the following steps show:

- Set up fields in u and `proc[1]` accordingly.

- Allocate a text region.

- Copy out to the text region a predefined array of bytes corresponding to the following program:

```
for (;;) {
        (void) exec("/etc/init", "/etc/init", [ "-a", ] 0) ;
        _exit(errno) ;
        _asm("hlt") ;
}
```

- Allocate a stack region.

- Continue with the remainder of the `main()` function.

At this stage, the `init` process is ready to run and will be scheduled to run at the end of kernel initialisation.

4.3.3 `init` processing

The `init(ADM)` process is the first UNIX process created and is always given a process ID of 1. All UNIX processes in the system with the exception of the kernel processes described in the previous section are descendants of `init`. The `init` process is often referred to as a *general process spawner*. Its primary role in life is repeatedly to read and execute commands from the file `/etc/inittab` which is fully described in `inittab(F)`.

The live system can be in one of eight possible *run levels*. When moving from one run level to another, `init` executes commands found in `inittab(F)` corresponding to that run level. Each entry in `inittab(F)` contains four fields, each separated by a colon:

```
id:rstate:action:process
```

The interpretation of each field is shown below. For a more comprehensive description of `init(M)` and `inittab(F)` see the appropriate manual pages.

id This field contains up to four characters and is used to identify an entry in `inittab(F)` uniquely.

rstate The `rstate` field identifies the run level at which this entry will be processed. The values that `rstate` can take range between 0 and 6 or can be letters S or s. If no run level is specified, the entry will be processed whenever a switch is made between one run level and another.

    The exception to this rule is when `init` first processes `inittab` after boot. In this case, `init` only processes entries with a specified `action` of sysinit.

`action`	Based on this field, there are a number of possible actions that `init` will perform. The values which `action` can take are:

`boot`	The entry is processed only during `init`'s boot time read of `inittab(F)`.
`bootwait`	The entry is processed the first time that `init` goes from single user to multi-user.
`initdefault`	This field is used by `init` to determine which run state to go to automatically after the system is bootstrapped.
`off`	This field is used to terminate processes running when this run level is entered.
`once`	The entry is processed only once when entering the specified run level. If the process terminates then it is not restarted.
`ondemand`	See `respawn`.
`powerfail`	This entry is processed only when `init` receives a `SIGPWR` signal.
`powerwait`	As for `powerfail` but wait for completion of the specified `process`.
`respawn`	Start the process, do not wait for its completion and if it dies, restart it.
`sysinit`	Execute these entries when the system first goes to single user mode after reboot but not on a subsequent move to single user mode.
`wait`	Start the entry and wait for its completion.

`process`	This field contains the command to be executed. It will be passed to a forked `sh(C)` and may therefore contain any valid shell syntax.

A cut-down version of the `inittab(F)` is shown for information:

```
bchk::sysinit:/etc/bcheckrc </dev/console >/dev/console 2>&1
is:S:initdefault:
r0:056:wait:/etc/rc0  1> /dev/console 2>&1 </dev/console
r1:1:wait:/etc/rc1  1> /dev/console 2>&1 </dev/console
r2:2:wait:/etc/rc2 1> /dev/console 2>&1 </dev/console
r3:3:wait:/etc/rc3  1> /dev/console 2>&1 </dev/console
co:2345:respawn:/etc/getty tty01 sc_m
co1:1:respawn:/bin/sh -c "sleep 20; exec /etc/getty tty01 sc_m"
c02:234:off:/etc/getty tty02 sc_m
c03:234:respawn:/etc/getty tty03 sc_m
c04:234:respawn:/etc/getty tty04 sc_m
c05:234:respawn:/etc/getty tty05 sc_m
```

The shell scripts `rc0`, `rc1` and `rc2` execute further scripts in the directories `/etc/rc0.d`, `/etc/rc1.d` and `/etc/rc2.d`. Users wishing to add their own scripts can either add them to `inittab(F)` directly or place them in one of the `rc` directories.

4.3.4 Getting to a login prompt

A number of entries in `inittab(F)` result in `init` running `getty(M)`, a program used to set the type, mode, speed and line discipline of the terminal device passed as an argument. The `getty` program is the second part of a chain of events that ultimately allow a user to login to the system. The chain of events is shown in Figure 4.7.

The first argument passed to `getty` is the name of a TTY line which is located in `/dev`. The `getty` process opens the TTY line establishing `stdin` and calls `fdup(S)` twice to establish `stdout` and `stderr`. It then prints the message located in the `/etc/default/issue` file, for example:

```
SCO OpenServer(TM) Release 5 (xian.london.sco.com) (tty01)
```

`getty` then displays the login message, reads the username entered and calls `execve(S)` to run `login(M)` passing the username entered as an argument.

When `login` runs, it prompts the user for a password. The password is encrypted by `login` and compared against the encrypted password for the user located in `/etc/shadow`. If the encrypted password entered and the entry in `/etc/shadow` match, `login` calls `execve(S)` with the name of the shell found in `/etc/passwd`.

For example, consider the entries in `/etc/passwd` and `/etc/shadow`:

```
spate:x:13583:50:Steve Pate:/home/spate:/bin/ksh        # /etc/passwd
spate:DXmcjhUmk:9432::                                   # /etc/shadow
```

Once it has both the user name (`spate`) and the encrypted password (`DXmcjhUmk`), `login` will compare the encrypted password with the entry in `/etc/shadow` which is highlighted above. If the comparison fails, `login` will call `exit(S)`. The `exit(S)`

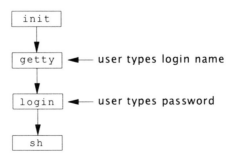

Figure 4.7   The steps followed from `init` running to the user's shell running

system call will result in a SIGCHLD signal being posted to init which will call fork() and exec(S) to create another getty(M). The login process is then repeated.

If the comparison succeeds, login will set up a number of environment variables and exec the shell specified in the /etc/passwd entry, in this case /bin/ksh.

4.4 Summary and suggested reading

This chapter has described the phases followed from powering on the machine to the user login prompt being displayed in multi-user mode.

Further detail on the various phases of kernel initialisation will be described throughout the remainder of the book, with particular attention to the initialisation of kernel tables used for file I/O, process management and so on.

The I/O subsystem described in section 9.7 describes in more detail the tasks performed by getty(M) to allow users to login to UNIX.

The SCO OpenServer manual set provides further information on bootstrap, the init(M) process and the procedures followed during system initialisation. Of particular interested are the init(M), inittab(F), boot(HW), boot(F), rc0(ADM) and rc2(ADM) manual pages.

5

Inside /unix

The format of the kernel file on disk (/unix) conforms to the Common Object File Format (COFF), the file format used for application programs in SCO OpenDesktop and supported alongside the Extensible and Linking Format (ELF) in SCO OpenServer Release 5. The COFF format is described in this chapter in sufficient detail to analyse both the /unix file format and standard COFF executable files.

Using the toolkits provided in the chapter for analysing COFF object files, a function mlist() is shown which provides functionality similar to nlist(S).

5.1 Introduction

This chapter concentrates on the format of the UNIX kernel held on disk: its structure, the location of text and data within the file and the location and structure of symbolic information used for debugging and analysis. The purpose of this is threefold:

- To describe the underlying file format in order to enable the reader to understand the basic principles behind the nlist(S) and kmem mechanisms on which tools such as crash(ADM), dump(CP) and many of the examples used throughout the book are based.

- To understand how the kernel is linked which is essential for both device driver writers and system administrators wishing to tune the kernel.

- The format of application programs defines how support for execve(S) is provided by the kernel. Understanding the format of binary files is essential to gaining a full understanding of many UNIX kernel principles. The UNIX kernel is compiled as a COFF file and therefore the principles described in this chapter are also applicable to application programs.

A function, mlist(), is shown at the end of the chapter which builds on the COFF based toolkits presented in the earlier sections of the chapter. This allows callers to extract the addresses of symbol names from the kernel object file which can then be used to retrieve information from the kernel while it is active.

5.1.1 The /unix toolkit

The toolkit programs presented in this chapter are:

Toolkit 5.1 Displaying COFF headers, page 119
Toolkit 5.2 Displaying COFF sections, page 123
Toolkit 5.3 Displaying the COFF string table, page 125
Toolkit 5.4 Displaying COFF symbols, page 126
Toolkit 5.5 Locating symbols with mlist(), page 128

Toolkit 5.1 through Toolkit 5.4 display the various components of COFF object files. Toolkit 5.5 builds on these toolkits to show a function which provides similar functionality to the nlist(S) library function.

5.2 The Common Object File Format (COFF)

COFF was developed to define the format used for binary programs and intermediate object files for UNIX System V. In releases of SCO UNIX prior to OpenServer Release 5, COFF was used for both the kernel and application binaries. In OpenServer Release 5 the kernel (/unix) still remains COFF based.

Applications developed using the OpenServer Release 5 development system can be constructed using either the COFF or ELF object formats. ELF provides newer features such as dynamic libraries, enhanced portability between different processor architectures and greater flexibility in program placement in memory. The ELF format is discussed in more detail in chapter 6.

SCO, Intel, USL and others standardised on the COFF format to produce iBCS-2, the UNIX binary compatibility standard for Intel based processors. The iBCS-2 standard (1991) extends the notion of binary formats by including a specification of the system call interface, header and library file formats, packaging and so on.

This section describes the basic principles of COFF in order to explain the format of the UNIX kernel on disk. For a complete description of COFF see Gircys (1988). For a description of the tools used to construct a new kernel see chapter 9.

5.2.1 COFF principles

While it may seem unnecessary to describe the format of application binaries in a book about UNIX internals, the format of an executable file and the functionality provided by COFF and ELF have an impact not only on the development system for constructing and debugging application programs but also on many parts of the kernel such as:

- Loading the program into main memory: which parts need loading, how does the un-initialised data (BSS) get created, can the file contents be demand paged or do they need to be copied into memory?

- Where the program's text and data segments should reside in memory.

- Which libraries are needed by the program.

- For shared and dynamically linked (ELF only) libraries, how the libraries should be shared and where they should be mapped in memory.

- The relationship between the disk-based binary file, the memory image and the swap device for paging and swapping purposes.

The specific areas of functionality listed above are described throughout the book.

As shown in Figure 5.1, COFF executable files comprise two file headers, a generic COFF file header and an a.out header present only in executable files. There are also sections holding the program's text and data and symbolic information used for debugging purposes.

The program text contains the instructions to be executed by the program. The program data section holds the initialised data. Since all un-initialised data is guaranteed to be set to zero when the program starts, it is only necessary to hold information within the COFF file on how much space needs to be zero filled and at which location in memory.

The symbol table, as the name suggests, holds the program symbols, their addresses and types; for example, the program symbol tblptr may be a pointer and its address may be 0x4ebc0.

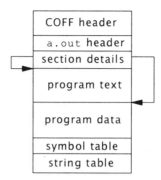

Figure 5.1   Format of a COFF executable file

   Symbol table entries have a fixed size. If a symbol name exceeds eight characters, the name is held in the string table instead of the symbol table. The symbol table and string table are normally present in the object file unless the -s option is passed to ld (or cc) or the strip(CP) command has been run on the binary.

   There are additional parts of COFF files not shown here including line numbers, relocation information and archive file information used for producing archive libraries. While such information is essential for writing debuggers and linkers and gaining a solid understanding of program construction, it is beyond the scope of this book. See Gircys (1988) for further information.

5.2.2 COFF headers

In addition to a magic number used to identify a COFF file, the COFF header contains enough information to locate the other COFF components in the file. The contents of the COFF header are defined by the filehdr structure as shown in Table 5.1.

Table 5.1   The COFF filehdr structure

struct filehdr field		Description
unsigned long	f_magic	Identifies the type of architecture needed by the object file, i.e. the machine on which the file is executable.
unsigned short	f_nscns	The number of sections contained in the file. In the example shown in Figure 5.1 there are two sections, one for text and one for data.
long	f_timdat	The time and date the object file was created.
long	f_symptr	An offset within the file to the start of the symbol table.
long	f_nsyms	The number of symbol table entries.
unsigned short	f_opthdr	The size of the UNIX system header, also known as the a.out header. If no system header is present, this field is set to zero. If the header is present, it immediately follows the filehdr.
unsigned short	f_flags	Flags indicating whether symbols have been stripped, the file is executable or if relocation information is present.

The COFF header is always present in an object file whether it is an executable file, intermediate object file or library archive. The COFF header provides all the information required to analyse the structure of a COFF file including the location and size of the file's sections where the text and data is stored, the number of symbols in the program and their location in the file and so on.

For each executable file, a UNIX system header immediately follows the `filehdr` and contains information needed by the UNIX kernel in order to load and execute the program or for `/boot` to load and pass control to the UNIX kernel. The fields of this structure are defined by the `aouthdr` structure and are shown in Table 5.2.

Table 5.2   The COFF `aouthdr` structure

struct aouthdr field		Description
short	magic	System specific information to aid memory allocation and paging policies.
short	vstamp	The version number of the a.out header.
long	tsize	Text size in bytes.
long	dsize	Initialised data size in bytes.
long	bsize	Size of un-initialised data in bytes.
long	entry	The program's entry point.
long	text_start	The base address in memory of the text segment.
long	data_start	The base address in memory of the data segment.

The starting address of the program, `entry`, is rarely the same address as the start of the text section, `text_start`. It is set by the linker to a well-known symbol, for example `_start` or `_main`.

Toolkit 5.1   Displaying COFF headers

The program presented in this toolkit reads the `/unix` file and prints out the contents of both the COFF `filehdr` and the UNIX system header.

The header files shown on lines 1 to 7 and the global variables shown on lines 9 to 15 are also used by other toolkits throughout the remainder of the chapter. They are shown only once to avoid duplication.

The source for the program is as follows:

```
 1   #include <aouthdr.h>
 2   #include <filehdr.h>
 3   #include <scnhdr.h>
 4   #include <linenum.h>
 5   #include <reloc.h>
 6   #include <syms.h>
 7   #include <stdio.h>
 8
 9   int    nsects ;         /* total number of sections */
10   int    nsyms ;          /* total number of symbols */
11   long   secoff ;         /* fseek() ptr to the first COFF section */
12   long   symptr ;         /* fseek() ptr to the symbol table */
```

```
13   char   secnames[64][8] ; /* section names for associating symbols */
14   char   *str_tab ;          /* string table - allocated dynamically */
15   FILE   *fp ;               /* file pointer for object file */
16
17   print_headers()
18   {
19       struct filehdr f_hdr ;
20       struct aouthdr a_hdr ;
21
22       fread(&f_hdr, sizeof(FILHDR), 1, fp) ;
23       printf("\nfilehdr:\n") ;
24       printf("    f_magic     - 0%o\n",f_hdr.f_magic) ;
25       printf("    f_nscns     - %d\n",f_hdr.f_nscns) ;
26       printf("    f_timdat    - %s",ctime(&f_hdr.f_timdat)) ;
27       printf("    f_symptr    - %d\n",f_hdr.f_symptr) ;
28       printf("    f_nsyms     - %d\n",f_hdr.f_nsyms) ;
29       printf("    f_opthdr    - %d\n",f_hdr.f_opthdr) ;
30       printf("    f_flags     - 0%o\n\n",f_hdr.f_flags) ;
31
32       nsects = f_hdr.f_nscns ;
33       nsyms  = f_hdr.f_nsyms ;
34       secoff = FILHSZ + f_hdr.f_opthdr ;
35       symptr = f_hdr.f_symptr ;
36
37       if (f_hdr.f_opthdr) {
38           fread(&a_hdr, sizeof(AOUTHDR), 1, fp) ;
39           printf("aouthdr:\n") ;
40           printf("    magic       - 0%o\n",a_hdr.magic) ;
41           printf("    vstamp      - %d\n",a_hdr.vstamp) ;
42           printf("    tsize       - %d\n",a_hdr.tsize) ;
43           printf("    dsize       - %d\n",a_hdr.dsize) ;
44           printf("    bsize       - %d\n",a_hdr.bsize) ;
45           printf("    entry       - 0x%x\n",a_hdr.entry) ;
46           printf("    text_start  - 0x%x\n",a_hdr.text_start) ;
47           printf("    data_start  - 0x%x\n",a_hdr.data_start) ;
48       }
49   }
50
51   main(argc, argv)
52       int   argc ;
53       char  **argv ;
54   {
55       fp = fopen(argv[1], "r") ;
56
57       print_headers() ;
58       print_sections() ;
59       print_strings() ;
60       print_symbols() ;
61   }
```

The program opens the file passed as its first argument (line 55) and can therefore be used to examine any COFF object file.

The `print_headers()` function (lines 17 to 49) starts by reading the COFF header on line 22 and printing its contents (lines 23 to 30) using the `ctime(S)` library call for the file's time and date stamp.

The COFF header provides all the information that is needed to locate the structures and contents of the rest of the file including:

- The number of sections present in the file (line 32).
- The number of symbols in the symbol table (line 33).
- An offset within the file where the sections are described (line 34).
- An offset within the file to where the symbol table is located (line 35).
- Whether the UNIX system header is present (line 37). If the header is present then it is read and its contents printed as shown on lines 39 to 47.

If only the `print_headers()` function is invoked from `main()`, the output from one run of the program is as follows:

```
# a.out /unix
filehdr:
      f_magic     - 0514
      f_nscns     - 14
      f_timdat    - Mon Apr 17 09:26:37 1995
      f_symptr    - 1620824
      f_nsyms     - 13677
      f_opthdr    - 28
      f_flags     - 0403

aouthdr:
      magic       - 0413
      vstamp      - 0
      tsize       - 1434196
      dsize       - 152408
      bsize       - 744660
      entry       - 0xf0010000
      text_start  - 0xf0010000
      data_start  - 0xf016f000
```

The file header shows the magic number, the number of sections, the date when the file was created, the offset within the file of the symbol table, the number of symbols and the size of the `aouthdr` which follows.

Application programs will typically have a smaller number of sections. In this example the UNIX kernel has 14 sections and a total of 13 677 symbols.

The address at which the kernel is entered when loaded by `/boot` is `0xf0010000`. The other fields show the size of the text and data and the locations in which they will reside in memory when loaded.

5.2.3 COFF sections

All COFF object files have one or more sections each described by a section header.

The fields of the section header are defined by the `scnhdr` structure for which the fields are shown in Table 5.3.

Table 5.3   The COFF `scnhdr` structure

scnhdr structure field	Description
char s_name[]	Section name which is either is either .text, .data, .bss or can be set to a different name by using assembler directives.
long s_paddr	The section's physical address in memory when the program is loaded. This is usually the same as s_vaddr.
long s_vaddr	The section's virtual address in memory when the program is loaded.
long s_size	Size of the section in bytes rounded up to the next 4 byte boundary.
long s_scnptr	The offset within the file where the section's contents can be found.
long s_relptr	Offset within the file to the section's relocation information.
long s_lnnoptr	Offset within the file where the line number structures can be found.
short s_nreloc	Number of section's relocation entries.
short s_nlnno	Number of section's line number structures.
long s_flags	Flags which determine the type of the section.

The section headers always start immediately after either the COFF header or the UNIX system header if one is present. The position of the section headers and their respective contents within a COFF file are shown in Figure 5.2.

The section pointer s_scnhdr can be used to fseek() into the file to locate the section's data as shown in the diagram. Many of the fields present in the scnhdr structure are beyond the scope of this book.

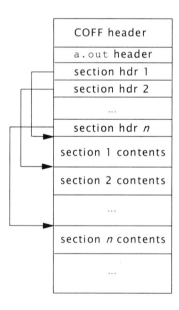

Figure 5.2   The position of COFF section headers and contents

Toolkit 5.2   Displaying COFF sections

Continuing from the program introduced in Toolkit 5.1, the `print_sections()` function is shown below. This relies only on the `secoff` variable set during the `print_headers()` function to allow `print_sections()` to `fseek()` to the first section header.

```
 1  print_sections()
 2  {
 3       int    x ;
 4       SCNHDR s_hdr ;
 5       char nm[9]; nm[8] = '\0' ;
 6
 7       for (x=0 ; x<nsects ; x++) {
 8            fseek(fp, secoff, 0) ;
 9            fread(&s_hdr, sizeof(SCNHDR), 1, fp) ;
10            secoff += sizeof(SCNHDR) ;
11            strncpy(nm, s_hdr.s_name, 8) ;
12
13            printf("\nSection: %8s\n", nm) ;
14            printf("    s_paddr    - 0x%x\n", s_hdr.s_paddr) ;
15            printf("    s_vaddr    - 0x%x\n", s_hdr.s_vaddr) ;
16            printf("    s_size     - %d\n", s_hdr.s_size) ;
17            printf("    s_scnptr   - %d\n", s_hdr.s_scnptr) ;
18            printf("    s_relptr   - %d\n", s_hdr.s_relptr) ;
19            printf("    s_lnnoptr  - %d\n", s_hdr.s_lnnoptr) ;
20            printf("    s_nreloc   - %d\n", s_hdr.s_nreloc) ;
21            printf("    s_nlnno    - %d\n", s_hdr.s_nlnno) ;
22            printf("    s_flags    - %x\n", s_hdr.s_flags) ;
23       }
24  }
```

The function loops for each section header between lines 7 and 23. For each iteration the appropriate `fseek()` is performed on line 8 and the header is then read (line 9). Since the name of the section may not be null terminated, it is first copied to a null terminated buffer (line 11). The section contents are then displayed (lines 13 to 22).

Since the output of `print_sections()` for 14 sections would be too lengthy to display here, the output of the function is piped through `fgrep` to display only the section name and the virtual address at which the section contents will reside in memory. The output for one particular run is:

```
$ a.out unix | fgrep 'Section
> s_vaddr'
Section: uv_stack
    s_vaddr    - 0x7ffffffc
Section: kv_windo
    s_vaddr    - 0xdffea000
Section: kv_crllr
    s_vaddr    - 0xdfffc000
Section: kv_stack
    s_vaddr    - 0xdfffe000
Section: uv_ubloc
    s_vaddr    - 0xe0000000
Section:    page0
    s_vaddr    - 0xf0000000
Section: dft_stac
```

```
       s_vaddr    - 0xf0000000
Section:    .text
       s_vaddr    - 0xf0010000
Section:    .data
       s_vaddr    - 0xf016f000
Section:    .bss
       s_vaddr    - 0xf0195000
Section: kv_sysse
       s_vaddr    - 0xf0800000
Section: kv_table
       s_vaddr    - 0xfa000000
Section:    BKI
       s_vaddr    - 0x0
Section: .comment
       s_vaddr    - 0x0
```

Note that not all sections shown here will occupy memory when the kernel is loaded as the s_vaddr field of 0x0 indicates.

5.2.4 The COFF symbolic system

The symbol table is the centre of the COFF debugging system; only the basics of the symbol table will be presented here.

All symbols present in a COFF object file are located in the symbol table. The symbol table is an array of syment structures for which the fields of the structure are shown in Table 5.4. The number of symbol table entries is defined in the COFF header by the f_nsyms field.

Table 5.4 The COFF syment structure

syment struct field	Description
union {	The symbol name or an offset into the string table if
char _n_name[SYMNMLEN]	the symbol's name is greater than eight characters.
struct {	
long _n_zeroes	
long _n_offset	
} _n_n	
char *_n_nptr[2]	
} _n	
long n_value	The symbol's value.
short n_scnum	The section number in which the symbol is located.
unsigned short n_type	The type and derived type of the symbol.
char n_sclass	The storage class.
char n_numaux	Number of auxiliary entries.

The _n field is used to hold the symbol's name. If the name is less than or equal to eight characters, it is held in _n._n_name[]. If the name is greater than eight characters, _n._n_n._n_zeroes is set to zero and _n._n_n._n_offset is an offset into the string table where the name is held. Since these field names are somewhat difficult to remember, the following macros are available:

```
#define n_name              _n._n_name
#define n_nptr              _n._n_nptr[1]
#define n_zeroes      _n._n_n._n_zeroes
#define n_offset      _n._n_n._n_offset
```

so that the following expressions refer to the same field:

```
_n._n_n._n_offset    and      n_offset
```

The value of the symbol is held in the `n_value` field. If the symbol's value requires additional space, one or more auxiliary entries follow the symbol table entry. For example, pointers and base C language types will require only the `n_value` field to hold their value while structures and arrays will generally require auxiliary entries. Each auxiliary entry is the same number of bytes as the `syment` structure.

The `n_sclass` field is used to determine how to read the `n_value` field, for example whether the symbol is an automatic variable, register variable, union tag-name and so on.

The string table is located immediately after the symbol table in the COFF file. In order to scan the symbol table and display symbolic information it is necessary to read the string table first to locate symbol names of greater than eight characters.

Toolkit 5.3   Displaying the COFF string table

The function to read the string table and print its contents, `print_strings()`, is shown below. The location of the string table is calculated on line 7 using the start of the symbol table, the number of symbol table entries and the size of `syment`, defined by `SYMESZ`.

The first 4 bytes of the string table give the total size of the string table. The 4 bytes are read on line 9 and the amount of memory required to hold the string table is allocated on line 14. The string table is then read on line 16.

The string table consists of null-terminated strings which are printed on lines 18 to 22.

```
1   print_strings()
2   {
3       int strings ;
4       char *str_ptr ;
5       long strlength ;
6
7       strings = symptr + (SYMESZ * nsyms) ;
8       fseek(fp, strings, 0) ;
9       fread(&strlength, 4, 1, fp) ;
10
11      if (strlength) {
12          printf("\nSTRING TABLE\n") ;
13          strlength -= 4 ;
14          str_tab = (char *)malloc(strlength) ;
15          fseek(fp, (strings+4), 0) ;
16          fread(str_tab, strlength, 1, fp) ;
17          str_ptr = str_tab ;
18          do {
19              printf("    %s\n", str_ptr) ;
20              while (*str_ptr++ != '\0') ;
21          }
```

```
22                while (str_ptr < (str_tab + strlength)) ;
23          }
24       else
25            printf("\nNo strings found!\n") ;
26    }
```

The following first few entries of the string table are printed when the program is run.
The output shown is only from the print_strings() function.

```
$ a.out unix | head -10
STRING TABLE
     Idt2_dscr
     munge_table
     moretable
     donetable
     kentry_done
     kentry_loop
     kexit_done
     kexit_neg
     kexit_loop
```

Toolkit 5.4   Displaying COFF symbols

This example shows the print_symbols() function. The only functionality provided
here is to list the symbol names either directly from the symbol table entry (lines 11 to
18) or from the string table (line 20).

```
1   print_symbols()
2   {
3        SYMENT se ;
4        int x, ncs=0 ;
5
6        fseek(fp, symptr, 0) ;
7        printf("\nSYMBOLS: ") ;
8        while (ncs++ != nsyms) {
9             fread(&se, SYMESZ, 1, fp) ;
10            printf("\n       ") ;
11            if (se.n_zeroes) {
12                 for (x=0 ; x<8 ; x++) {
13                      if ((se.n_name[x] > 0x1f) && (se.n_name[x] < 0x7f))
14                           printf("%c", se.n_name[x]) ;
15                      else
16                           printf(" ") ; ;
17                 }
18            }
19            else
20                 printf("%s", &str_tab[se.n_offset-4]) ;
21            for (x=0 ; x < se.n_numaux ; x++)
22                 fseek(fp, AUXESZ, SEEK_CUR) ;
23       }
24   }
```

If a symbol has auxiliary entries, they are skipped (lines 21 to 22). The output for one
particular run showing the first 9 symbols is:

```
$ a.out unix | head -10
SYMBOLS:
        .text
        .data
        Gdt_dscr
        Idt_dscr
        Idt2_dscr
        kvseip
        munge_table
        moretable
        donetable
```

The following sections which describe how to emulate the nlist(S) library function return the other fields of the syment structure.

5.3 Emulating nlist() functionality

Using the information presented so far in this chapter, this section describes the environment in which the following toolkit program, which emulates the functionality provided by the nlist(S) library function, can be used. Together with the kmem driver, nlist(S) provides the means to access kernel data structures by their symbolic names. These mechanisms are used extensively throughout the remainder of the book.

The flow of control through programs which use nlist(S) and /dev/kmem is shown in Figure 5.3.

The nlist(S) library function is used to locate symbol table entries given an array of nlist structures and a COFF object file. The user program passes a list of names to nlist(S) which retrieves their symbol table values. This is shown in steps 1 and 2. The user process then opens /dev/kmem, performs an lseek(S) to one of the addresses returned from nlist(S) and reads from or writes to the kernel virtual address space using the kmem driver as shown in steps 3 and 4.

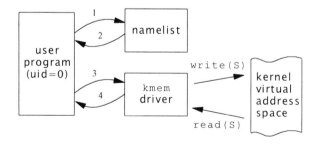

Figure 5.3   Using nlist() and /dev/kmem

The fields of the nlist structure are shown in Table 5.5.

Table 5.5   The `nlist` structure

`nlist` structure field		Description
char	*n_name	The symbol's name.
long	n_value	The symbol's value.
short	n_scnum	Section number in which the symbol belongs.
unsigned short	n_type	Symbol's type and derived type.
char	n_sclass	Storage class.
char	n_numaux	Number of auxiliary entries.

The prototype for the `nlist(S)` library function is:

```
int nlist(char *filename, struct nlist *nl) ;
```

The caller passes a filename and a pointer to an array of `nlist` structures. Each element of the array needs only the symbol name initialised; `nlist()` will fill in the remaining fields. The array is terminated by having a null `nlist` structure as the last element:

```
struct nlist n[] = { { "sym1", 0, 0, 0, 0, 0},
                     { "sym2", 0, 0, 0, 0, 0},
                     { 0 },
                   } ;
```

Toolkit 5.5   Locating symbols with `mlist()`

This toolkit demonstrates the function `mlist()` which mimics the functionality of `nlist(S)`, used in many of the toolkit programs presented throughout the book. The prototype for `mlist()` is similar to `nlist(S)` as follows:

```
void mlist(char *filename, struct mlist *ml) ;
```

Since the toolkit presented here is only to show how `nlist(S)` works, no error checking is performed. This is sufficient for demonstration purposes although a more complete implementation would return either an error if one or more of the symbols cannot be found or the number of symbols found.

This toolkit presents a complete program built around `mlist()`. This will be presented gradually throughout this section. Shown first are the header files required, the declaration of the `mlist` structure and global variables used.

```
 1  #include <filehdr.h>
 2  #include <syms.h>
 3  #include <stdio.h>
 4
 5  struct mlist {
 6      char*            m_name ;
 7      long             m_value ;
 8      short            m_scnum ;
 9      unsigned short   m_type ;
10      char             m_sclass ;
```

```
11      char            m_numaux ;
12   } ;
13
14   char* string_table ;
15   int   nsyms ;
16   long  symptr ;
17   FILE* fp ;
```

The `mlist` structure defined on lines 5 to 12 contains the same fields as the `nlist` structure and most of the information found within a symbol table entry.

Space for the string table is allocated dynamically and pointed to by the `string_table` variable. Both `nsyms` and `symptr` hold information about the symbol table extracted from the COFF file header. The following function for allocating the string table, `read_string_table()`, is similar to the `print_strings()` function shown in Toolkit 5.3.

```
1   read_string_table()
2   {
3       long  strings ;
4       long  strlength ;
5
6       strings = symptr + (SYMESZ * nsyms) ;
7       fseek(fp, strings, SEEK_SET) ;
8       fread(&strlength, 4, 1, fp) ;
9       if (strlength) {
10          string_table = (char *)malloc(strlength) ;
11          fseek(fp, strings, SEEK_SET) ;
12          fread(string_table, strlength, 1, fp) ;
13      }
14  }
```

The `mlist()` function is shown next. After the file is opened on line 7, `mlist()` analyses how many `mlist` structures have been passed (lines 9 to 12). The COFF file header is then read (line 13) and the size of the symbol table and number of entries read (lines 14 to 15). This information is passed to `read_string_table()`.

```
1   mlist(char* obj_file, struct mlist ml[])
2   {
3       struct filehdr  f_hdr ;
4       SYMENT          se ;
5       int x, ncs=0, sizelst=0, nsrch=0 ;
6
7       fp = fopen(obj_file, "r") ;
8
9       while (ml[sizelst].m_name != '\0') {
10          sizelst++ ;
11          nsrch++ ;
12      }
13      fread(&f_hdr, sizeof(FILHDR), 1, fp) ;
14      nsyms  = f_hdr.f_nsyms ;
15      symptr = f_hdr.f_symptr ;
16
17      read_string_table() ;
18
19      while ((ncs++ != nsyms) || (sizelst == 0)) {
10          fseek(fp, symptr, SEEK_SET) ;
21          fread(&se, SYMESZ, 1, fp) ;
```

```
22              symptr += SYMESZ ;
23              eval_sym(&se, ml, nsrch, &sizelst) ;
24              for (x=0 ; x<se.n_numaux ; x++)
25                  symptr += SYMESZ ;
26      }
27  }
```

The `mlist()` function then starts reading symbol table entries and calling `eval_sym()` to check whether the symbol matches any of the requested symbols. Note that on lines 24 to 25 of `mlist()`, all auxiliary entries are skipped.

The `eval_sym()` function is as follows:

```
1   eval_sym(SYMENT*       se,
2               struct mlist ml[],
3               int          nsrch,
4               int*         sizelst)
5   {
6       int x, found=0 ;
7
8       for (x=0 ; x<nsrch; x++) {
9           if (se->n_zeroes) {
10              if (strncmp(ml[x].m_name, se->n_name, 8) == 0)
11                  found=1 ;
12          }
13          else {
14              if (strcmp(ml[x].m_name,&string_table[se->n_offset])== 0)
15                  found=1 ;
16          }
17
18          if (found) {
19              ml[x].m_value  = se->n_value;
20              ml[x].m_scnum  = se->n_scnum ;
21              ml[x].m_type   = se->n_type ;
22              ml[x].m_sclass = se->n_sclass ;
23              ml[x].m_numaux = se->n_numaux ;
24              found = 0 ;
25              *sizelst-- ;
26          }
27      }
28  }
```

The `eval_sym()` function loops through each requested `mlist` structure on lines 8 to 27 and compares each `mlist m_name` field to the name of the symbol table entry read. There are two possible options:

1. The symbol name is less than eight characters (lines 9 to 12).

2. The name is located in the string table (lines 13 to 16).

If a match is found, the fields of the particular `mlist` field are filled in on lines 18 to 26 from the symbol table entry.

The following `main()` function is used to test `mlist()`.

```
 1   main()
 2   {
 3
 4       struct mlist ml[] = { { "u",0,0,0,0,0 },
 5                             { "proc",0,0,0,0,0 },
 6                             { 0 }
 7                           } ;
 8
 9       mlist("/unix", ml) ;
10
11       printf("m_name   = %s\n",ml[0].m_name) ;
12       printf("m_value  = %x\n",ml[0].m_value) ;
13       printf("m_scnum  = %d\n",ml[0].m_scnum) ;
14       printf("m_type   = %d\n",ml[0].m_type) ;
15       printf("m_sclass = %d\n",ml[0].m_sclass) ;
16       printf("m_numaux = %d\n\n",ml[0].m_numaux) ;
17
18       printf("m_name   = %s\n",ml[1].m_name) ;
19       printf("m_value  = %x\n",ml[1].m_value) ;
20       printf("m_scnum  = %d\n",ml[1].m_scnum) ;
21       printf("m_type   = %d\n",ml[1].m_type) ;
22       printf("m_sclass = %d\n",ml[1].m_sclass) ;
23       printf("m_numaux = %d\n",ml[1].m_numaux) ;
24   }
```

The main() function simply calls mlist() with an array of mlist structures and prints
the contents returned. Running the program gives the following output:

```
$ a.out
m_name   = u
m_value  = e0000000
m_scnum  = 5
m_type   = 0
m_sclass = 2
m_numaux = 0

m_name   = proc
m_value  = fb117000
m_scnum  = 12
m_type   = 4
m_sclass = 2
m_numaux = 0
```

When running a similar program which used nlist(S) in place of mlist() the
program which used nlist(S) ran in the order of 12 times faster. It is left to the reader
as an exercise to determine to what the difference in speed can be attributed and how the
performance of mlist() can be improved.

5.4 Summary and suggested reading

This chapter described the Common Object File Format (COFF), the file format which is
used for the on-disk image of the UNIX kernel and for many applications.

A number of toolkits for extracting information from COFF object files were introduced. These toolkits provided the basis for `mlist()`, a function which provides functionality similar to the `nlist(S)` library function.

Gircys (1988) provides an in-depth look at COFF. Intel (1991) provides the specification of iBCS2, the Intel binary standard for UNIX applications developed for the i386 family of Intel processors. It also provides a good description of setting up stack frames prior to calling functions, handling parameters across the UNIX system call interface and other topics.

6

Memory management principles

This chapter describes the principles of memory management, mapping the memory requirements of a UNIX process onto the memory management mechanisms supported by the i386 family of processors.

The chapter first concentrates on the creation of ELF binary programs produced by the SCO development system together with a description of their memory based requirements during program execution. This includes a description of how multiple user processes and the UNIX kernel share memory simultaneously.

The memory management support provided by the i386 processor is described to show how the kernel and user processes utilise the underlying physical hardware. This leads to a description of the protection and multitasking features provided by the processor.

6.1 Introduction

Memory management is often greeted by programmers, even experienced kernel engineers, with some degree of fear. Although the manuals of most common CPUs describe in detail the mechanisms by which they perform memory management, the use of such features by operating systems is usually poorly documented.

This chapter describes how the i386 processor is used to satisfy the memory requirements that application programs place on the kernel. By first describing the format of an ELF file, it is possible to understand how the kernel loader creates the memory image of the process from the file contents.

The memory management features of the i386 family of processors are explained, including segmentation, paging and how protection is achieved both between individual UNIX processes and between user processes and the kernel. Examples show the memory management based kernel structures of processes including their mapping onto the i386 hardware abstractions.

6.1.1 The memory management toolkit

In chapter 5, COFF files were analysed by directly manipulating the COFF header in order to extract the appropriate COFF object file structures. To demonstrate the use of existing tools, the ELF object files described in this chapter are analysed by a combination of the `dump(CP)` utility and system debugging utilities such as `crash(ADM)` and `adb(CP)`.

Many of the kernel structures used for memory management, which are described later in the chapter, are analysed using the `crash(ADM)` utility.

The following toolkit programs are presented in this chapter:

Toolkit 6.1 through Toolkit 6.3 analyse the various structures and contents of ELF object files. Toolkit 6.4 shows how to display the Local Descriptor Table which contains the memory objects that each process can reference.

Toolkit 6.5 and Toolkit 6.6 show the memory state of a UNIX process during execution and display some of the kernel structures used to implement the address space of the process.

6.2 The Executable and Linking Format (ELF)

This section introduces the Executable and Linking Format (ELF), which, with COFF, the Common Object File Format, is one of the two main types of binary file formats supported by SCO UNIX.

Following the approach used when describing the COFF format introduced in chapter 5, this section covers the components of the ELF format that describe an executable file and is therefore not an exhaustive description of ELF itself. By concentrating on the format of ELF files it is possible to understand the demands that ELF places on the kernel's memory management subsystem, how a program is loaded, how memory is shared between multiple UNIX processes and the kernel and how the memory management capabilities of the i386 processor are utilised.

6.2.1 ELF basics

There are many terms used to describe an executable file ranging from 'program' to 'executable program' to 'object file'. All of these terms are in fact correct. The published ELF documentation clearly classifies the different types of object files as follows:

- A *relocatable file* holds code and data that can be linked with other object files to produce an executable file or a shared object file.

- A *shared object file* also holds code and data but is used in two different contexts. Firstly, it can be linked with other relocatable object files and shared object files to produce another object file. Secondly, it can be used by the system when a program is run to link its contents dynamically with an executable file to create the running process image. The latter case covers program libraries.

- An *executable file* contains a complete description of how the system can create a process image. It includes text and data, the specification of which shared object files are needed and appropriate symbolic and debugging information needed by the system's debuggers.

The ELF file format has two views, the program *linking view* and the *execution view*. Shown in Figure 6.1, the linking view is used during construction of a relocatable, shared object or executable file. The execution view can be seen as the finished product, the file from which the system can create a process image and thus run the program.

The program header is the only part of an ELF file that is guaranteed to start at a specific offset within the file. The other components are placed according to information that can be found in the ELF header or other control structures. The ELF header therefore describes the overall organisation of the file, the offset of various structures and their sizes.

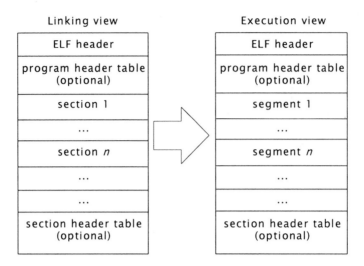

Figure 6.1   The two views of an ELF object file

The *program header table* informs the kernel how to construct the process image from the file's contents or more specifically from the file's *segments*. Most segments are copied into memory or mapped from the disk file when the process image is created. The section header table describes the file's *sections*. The file sections hold most of the information associated with an object file during program linking, such as text, data, symbols and relocation information.

A segment usually consists of more than one section. Toolkit 6.3 shows the mapping between segments and sections.

6.2.2 The ELF header

The ELF header provides all the information needed to identify a file as an ELF object and includes other information such as the machine type on which the file can run, the version of the ELF format used and the location of the other components within the file. ELF headers are described by the Elf32_Ehdr structure as shown in Table 6.1.

The ELF header is similar in both function and content to the COFF header described in section 5.2.2.

To check if a file is an ELF object file, the first four bytes of the file, that is, the first four bytes of the e_ident[] array will be set as follows:

```
e_ident[E_MAG0]    =    0x7f
e_ident[E_MAG0]    =    'E'
e_ident[E_MAG0]    =    'L'
e_ident[E_MAG0]    =    'F'
```

Table 6.1   File header for ELF object files

`Elf32_Ehdr` structure field	Description
`unsigned char  e_ident[]`	This array of `EI_NIDENT` bytes identifies the file as an ELF object file, provides the version number of the ELF format used and specifies whether the file contains data for 32- or 64-bit architectures.
`Elf32_Half    e_type`	There are multiple object file types from relocatable object files to core files. This chapter covers only `e_type` of `ET_EXEC`, the executable file format.
`Elf32_Half    e_machine`	The machine architecture on which this ELF object file was produced. For i386 platforms this will be `EM_386`.
`Elf32_Word    e_version`	The version number of the ELF format. This will be set to `EV_CURRENT` for the most recent version of the format. `e_version=1` represents the original format.
`Elf32_Addr    e_entry`	The virtual address to which the system transfers control when the program is loaded.
`Elf32_Off     e_phoff`	The offset from the start of the file in bytes of the program header table. Program headers are always present in ELF files of type `ET_EXEC`.
`Elf32_Off     e_shoff`	The offset from the start of the file in bytes of the section header table. Section headers may or may not be present in `ET_EXEC` type files.
`Elf32_Word    e_flags`	Processor specific flags.
`Elf32_Half    e_ehsize`	The size in bytes of the ELF header.
`Elf32_Half    e_phentsize`	The size in bytes of each program header.
`Elf32_Half    e_phnum`	The number of program headers.
`Elf32_Half    e_shentsize`	The size in bytes of each section header.
`Elf32_Half    e_shnum`	The number of section headers.
`Elf32_Half    e_shstrndx`	Used to locate the section containing the string table.

Displaying the header in hex and ASCII format can be done using `hd(C)` as follows:

```
$ hd a.out | head -1
0000  7f 45 4c 46 01 01 01 00  00 00 00 00 00 00 00 00   .ELF...........
```

The other fields of the ELF header can be determined by analysing the output above in conjunction with the ELF header file `<sys/elf.h>`, or by using the mechanisms employed by the following toolkit.

Toolkit 6.1   Analysing the ELF header

The ELF header can be displayed with the `dump(CP)` command. Consider the following well-known program which will be used throughout the chapter:

```
$ cat hello.c
main()
{
    printf("hello world\n") ;
}
$ cc -o hello -dy -belf hello.c
```

The command line shown here compiles the source file `hello.c`, specifying that the output file, `hello`, should be an ELF binary (`-belf`) and that it should use dynamically linked libraries (`-dy`).

The following `dump(CP)` command displays the fields of the ELF header:

```
$ dump -fv hello
hello:

                    **** ELF HEADER ****
Class       Data      Type       Machine    Version
Entry       Phoff     Shoff      Flags      Ehsize
Phentsize   Phnum     Shentsz    Shnum      Shstrndx

32-bit      2LSB      Exec       80386      Current
0x8048408   0x34      0xcc0      0          0x34
0x20        6         0x28       19         17
```

The mapping between the names displayed by `dump(C)` and the individual `Elf32_Ehdr` structure fields is:

```
Class      →   e_ident[EI_CLASS]
Data       →   e_ident[EI_DATA]
Type       →   e_type
Machine    →   e_machine
Version    →   e_version
Entry      →   e_entry
Phoff      →   e_phoff
Shoff      →   e_shoff
Flags      →   e_flags
Ehsize     →   e_ehsize
Phentsize  →   e_phentsize
Phnum      →   e_phnum
Shentsz    →   e_shentsize
Shnum      →   e_shnum
Shstrndx   →   e_shstrndx
```

Many of the fields within the header present a roadmap of the rest of the file. For example, shown in bold font, the first program header starts at offset `0x34` within the file, there are 6 of them and each is `0x20` bytes in size. The entry point of the program once it is loaded into memory is the virtual address `0x8048408`. The actual function which will be executed first can be seen from within `adb(CP)` as follows:

```
$ adb hello
* $v
variables
```

```
b = 0x1f:0x0
d = 0x10
e = 0x17:0x8048408        # <e represents the starting virtual address
m = 0x464c457f
t = 0x70
* <e,4?ia
_start:        push    0x0
_start+0x2: push    0x0
_start+0x4: mov     ebp,esp
_start+0x6: call    near 0x17:0x80483a8
_start+0xb:
```

The $v command displays the current set of internal adb variables. The value held in the adb variable e represents the segment selector and offset within the segment at which control is transferred when the program is executed. Note that the segment base address is zero. Segmentation is discussed in more detail in section 6.3.2.

All C programs start executing the routine _start provided by the standard C library unless specifically told otherwise by passing options to ld(CP).

Toolkit 6.6 shows how the memory regions allocated by the kernel when the process is loaded correspond to the addresses shown above.

6.2.3 Program headers

Each executable ELF file contains a number of segments whose contents are used to form part of the memory image of the process during program loading and execution. Each segment is described by its own program header which can be located in the program header table. The location of the program header table, the number of entries within the table and the size of each program header is found in the ELF header.

Each program header is described by an Elf32_Phdr structure. The fields of the Elf32_Phdr structure are shown in Table 6.2.

Table 6.2   The ELF program header structure

Elf32_Phdr field		Description
Elf32_Word	p_type	The type of the segment or how the contents should be interpreted.
Elf32_Off	p_offset	The offset of the segment in bytes from the start of the file.
Elf32_Addr	p_vaddr	The starting virtual address in memory of the segment when the program is to be executed.
Elf32_Addr	p_paddr	The physical address of the segment. This is ignored on the i386 family of processors.
Elf32_Word	p_filesz	The number of bytes that the segment occupies within the file.
Elf32_Word	p_memsz	The number of bytes in memory that the segment will occupy.
Elf32_Word	p_flags	Flags specifying the accessibility of the segment, for example whether it is readable, writeable or executable.
Elf32_Word	p_align	The alignment of the segment in memory.

Segments usually consist of multiple sections (see section 6.2.4) although this is not reflected within the segment header as shown later. Some segments are copied or mapped into memory during process creation. Other segments, although not part of the memory image, provide additional control information needed during program loading.

Toolkit 6.2   Displaying program segment headers

Using the *hello world* program presented in Toolkit 6.1, the dump(ADM) utility can be used to display the fields of each program header within the file as follows:

```
$ dump -ov hello
hello:
***** PROGRAM EXECUTION HEADER *****
Type            Offset      Vaddr          Paddr
Filesz          Memsz       Flags          Align

PHDR            0x34        0x8048034      0
0xc0            0xc0        r-x            0

INTERP          0xf4        0              0
0x13            0           r--            0

LOAD            0x34        0x8048034      0
0x444           0x444       r-x            0x1000

LOAD            0x478       0x8049478      0
0xa4            0xa8        rwx            0x1000

DYN             0x4bc       0x80494bc      0
0x60            0           rwx            0

NOTE            0x51c       0              0
0x1c            0           ---            0
```

Note that the segment headers displayed will vary depending on the program being compiled. The mapping between the names displayed by dump(ADM) and the appropriate fields of the Elf32_Phdr structure is:

```
Type      ➜   p_type
Offset    ➜   p_offset
Vaddr     ➜   p_vaddr
Paddr     ➜   p_paddr
Filesz    ➜   p_filesz
Memsz     ➜   p_memsz
Flags     ➜   p_flags
Align     ➜   p_align
```

The segment of type PHDR marks the program header itself. The program header is copied into memory so that the dynamic linker can understand the location and content of the program's segments to ensure that any necessary libraries can be linked and made available to the program. Section 7.6 describes the steps taken during program loading, including dynamic linking, in more detail.

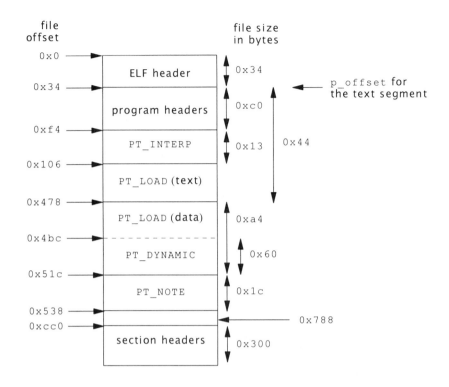

Figure 6.2   The ELF layout for *hello world*

For sections marked LOAD, a kernel region structure which defines a contiguous area of memory will be created when the program is loaded. The memory region will be created at the virtual address specified by p_vaddr and occupy p_memsz bytes. The memory region maps the portion of the file located at p_offset of p_filesz bytes.

For a loadable segment, the memory size may exceed the number of bytes within the file. In this case, the additional bytes in memory may be zero filled. This mechanism is used during program loading to create the program's un-initialised data (BSS).

A segment of type INTERP specifies a program interpreter. This segment type is used for programs that require dynamic linking. The pathname of the dynamic linker is obtained from the INTERP segment. Instead of creating the program image of the file requested to be run, the kernel creates the process image from the contents of the interpreter's segments. The dynamic linker used in conjunction with the kernel creates the executable file's memory image. It adds shared object memory segments, the pathnames of which are located in a separate segment, to the process image corresponding to the required libraries and performs any outstanding relocations. Finally, control is passed from the dynamic linker to the original program.

Figure 6.2 shows the layout of the segments within the file based on the information displayed by dump(ADM).

Although the text segment starts at offset `0x106` within the file, the kernel must map not only the text segment but also the program header and `PT_INTERP` segment owing to alignment constraints – see the `mmap(S)` manual page for further details. This gives the dynamic linker easy access to each of the program headers so that it can determine where the appropriate dynamic information and shared library data can be found.

There is a gap of `0x788` (1928) bytes from the end of the `PT_NOTE` segment to the start of the section header table. This includes additional section data which will not be part of the memory image of the process, for example symbolic debugging information.

6.2.4 Section headers and contents

Although the inclusion of a section header table in an ELF executable file is not mandatory, executable files constructed by the SCO development system comprise a number of different sections for both stripped and non-stripped executable files. Stripped files have certain sections removed, such as those specifying symbolic and debugging information, but the majority of sections are contained within one segment or another.

Sections are described by a section header defined by the `Elf32_Shdr` structure. Each section header is held in the section header table located by the `e_shoff` member of the ELF header. The `Elf32_Shdr` structure is shown in Table 6.3.

Table 6.3   The ELF section header structure

Elf32_Phdr field		Description
Elf32_Word	sh_name	The name of the section. This field is an offset into the string table where the name is held.
Elf32_Word	sh_type	Section's type and how the contents should be interpreted.
Elf32_Word	sh_flags	Attributes such as whether the contents can be written to during execution, whether the section holds executable instructions and indeed whether any memory is occupied by the section during program execution.
Elf32_Addr	sh_addr	The address in memory where the section should reside.
Elf32_Off	sh_offset	The offset within the file to the first byte in the section.
Elf32_Word	sh_size	The size of the section in bytes.
Elf32_Word	sh_link	A means to locate the string table or symbol table for entries in this section dependent on sh_type.
Elf32_Word	sh_info	Additional information depending on the section type.
Elf32_Word	sh_addralign	This field determines address alignment constraints.
Elf32_Word	sh_entsize	For sections which include structured data such as a symbol table, the section contains fixed size entries. This field specifies the size of such entries if appropriate.

The format and content of many of the sections is beyond the scope of this book. The following toolkit example will demonstrate the relationship between sections and segments and show which section types are applicable to an executable program.

Toolkit 6.3   Displaying section headers and contents

Continuing with the *hello world* program used in the previous two toolkits, the section headers can be displayed with the dump(ADM) command as follows:

```
$ dump -hv hello | grep -v "^$"
hello:
         **** SECTION HEADER TABLE ****
[No] Type  Flags  Addr        Offset    Size    Name
     Link  Info   Adralgn     Entsize
[1]  PBIT  -A-    0x80480f4   0xf4      0x13    .interp
     0     0      0x1         0
[2]  HASH  -A-    0x8048108   0x108     0x90    .hash
     3     0      0x4         0x4
[3]  DYNS  -A-    0x8048198   0x198     0x110   .dynsym
     4     1      0x4         0x10
[4]  STRT  -A-    0x80482a8   0x2a8     0xba    .dynstr
     0     0      0x1         0
[5]  REL   -A-    0x8048364   0x364     0x30    .rel.plt
     3     7      0x4         0x8
[6]  PBIT  -AI    0x8048394   0x394     0x4     .init
     0     0      0x4         0
[7]  PBIT  -AI    0x8048398   0x398     0x70    .plt
     0     0      0x4         0x4
[8]  PBIT  -AI    0x8048408   0x408     0x70    .text
     0     0      0x4         0
[9]  PBIT  WA-    0x8049478   0x478     0x10    .data
     0     0      0x4         0
[10] PBIT  WA-    0x8049488   0x488     0xd     .data1
     0     0      0x4         0
[11] PBIT  WA-    0x8049498   0x498     0x24    .got
     0     0      0x4         0x4
[12] DYNM  WA-    0x80494bc   0x4bc     0x60    .dynamic
     4     0      0x4         0x8
[13] NOBI  WA-    0x804951c   0x51c     0x4     .bss
     0     0      0x4         0
[14] NOTE  ---    0           0x51c     0x1c    .note
     0     0      0x1         0
[15] SYMT  ---    0           0x538     0x3e0   .symtab
     16    41     0x4         0x10
[16] STRT  ---    0           0x918     0x168   .strtab
     0     0      0x1         0
[17] STRT  ---    0           0xa80     0x82    .shstrtab
     0     0      0x1         0
[18] PBIT  ---    0           0xb04     0x1b9   .comment
     0     0      0x4         0
```

Note that the sections displayed will vary depending on the method by which the program is compiled. The field names displayed by dump(ADM) and their equivalent names in the Elf32_Shdr structure are as follows:

```
Name     ➔    sh_name
Type     ➔    sh_type
Flags    ➔    sh_flags
Addr     ➔    sh_addr
Offset   ➔    sh_offset
Size     ➔    sh_size
Link     ➔    sh_link
```

Info	→	sh_info
Adralgn	→	sh_addralign
Entsize	→	sh_entsize

Although the ELF header indicated that there were 19 section headers, only 18 are shown here. The first one, which is not displayed above, is reserved and not used by the system.

Using the data displayed by dump(ADM) it is possible to show the composition of segments as a number of sections. For the text segment, Figure 6.3 shows the mapping. The part of the file holding the text segment is shown on the left while the same area of the file divided into its appropriate sections is shown on the right.

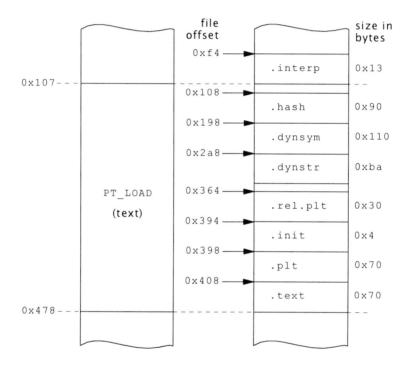

Figure 6.3   Mapping the text segment to its corresponding sections in the ELF file

The gap between the .dynstr and .rel.plt sections allows the .rel.plt section to be aligned on a word boundary.

All of the section types which constitute the text segment are termed *special sections* since they are reserved by the system to have specified types and semantics. The text related sections shown in Figure 6.3 are:

.hash   This is a hash table for holding symbol name indexes. There is a hash function which takes a symbol name and allows the caller to calculate the offset into the symbol table where the symbol is located.

.dynsym	The dynamic linking symbol table used to locate and relocate symbolic definitions and references.
.dynstr	Strings that are needed for dynamic linking.
.rel.plt	Relocation information allowing symbolic references to be associated with their appropriate symbolic definitions.
.init	Executable instructions that are part of the process initialisation code. Instructions within this section are executed prior to calling the program's _start () function.
.plt	The procedure linkage table used by the dynamic linker.
.text	The executable instructions of the program.

Using the same section header information displayed by the dump (ADM) program above, Figure 6.4 shows the mapping between the data segment and its corresponding sections. The portion of the file containing the data segment is shown on the left and its appropriate sections are shown on the right.

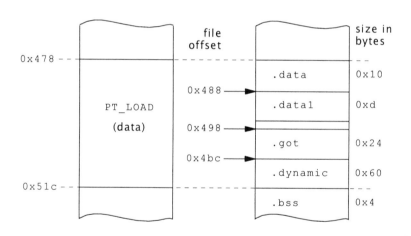

Figure 6.4   Mapping the data segment to corresponding sections within the ELF file

As with the text segment, a gap is introduced between two of the sections to ensure correct data alignment. The sections within the data segment are:

.data .data1	The program's initialised data.
.got	The global offset table used by the dynamic linker.
.dynamic	A section holding the virtual addresses of symbol names.

.bss   The program's un-initialised data. This section holds no data within
                  the file although it forms part of the memory image of the process.
                  The file offset of this section is therefore conceptual. When the
                  process is created, this part of memory will be zero filled.

The dump(CP) utility also provides the ability to dump section contents. For example, the
pathname of the dynamic linker is stored as a null-terminated string in the .interp
section. The contents of the section can be displayed as follows. Note that the -d option
specifies which section to dump:

```
$ dump -sv -d1 hello
hello:

.interp:
        2f75  7372  2f6c  6962  2f6c  6962  632e  736f  2e31  00
```

This represents the null-terminated pathname "/usr/lib/libc.so.1". For further
information on the mechanisms employed by the dynamic linker refer to SCO
OpenServer Release 5 *Developer's Topics* (1995) and see also section 7.6.6.

Finally, the .data section, which holds initialised data, is displayed below:

```
$ dump -sv -d10 hello
hello:

.data1:
        6865  6c6c  6f20  776f  726c  640a  00
```

No prizes for guessing what is contained in the section! (Hint: see the ASCII(M) manual
page for interpretation of this null-terminated string.)

6.2.5 ELF summary and usage

The ELF format contains enough features to warrant a book of its own. The previous
sections have concentrated on those aspects of ELF which are used by the kernel when an
execve(S) system call has been made.

Section 7.6 describes the phases followed by the kernel loader in order to create an
executable process.

Toolkit 6.6 (Analysis of the process memory image, page 169) shows how to use
crash(ADM) to analyse the memory image of the *hello world* program shown throughout
the previous sections.

6.3 Intel i386 memory management

Memory management is a complex area with implications for many aspects of kernel and
application construction. This section provides a description of the memory management

capabilities provided by the i386 family of processors showing which features are used by SCO UNIX.

Section 6.4.2 (Per process memory management, page 159) introduces the main memory management structures used by the kernel and shows how these kernel structures map onto the hardware features of the processor.

Chapters 7 and 12 build on the material presented in this chapter to describe process construction and management and how the kernel uses the memory management capabilities of the hardware to support paging and swapping.

6.3.1 Virtual and physical memory

Memory is and always has been expensive! Even in systems with large amounts of memory, the memory that is required by both user processes and the kernel will at times exceed the amount of memory that is physically available. Many methods have been previously used both in hardware and software to best manage the limited amount of memory that is available.

Figure 6.5 shows a basic hardware configuration where requests to read from or write to locations in memory are sent from the CPU over the system bus to the memory. The addresses sent by the CPU are physical addresses; as such, only memory that is physically available can be addressed. Physical memory is organised as a sequence of bytes where each byte has its own unique physical address.

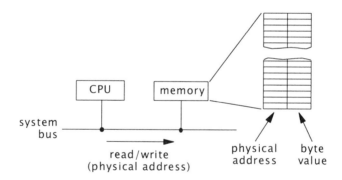

Figure 6.5   Accessing physical memory

This type of configuration suffers from two problems. Firstly, the amount of memory available is limited by both cost and properties such as the physical size of the memory and the maximum address that can be sent by the CPU across the system bus.

Secondly, if the instruction set of the processor can access only physical addresses, there may be little or no protection between one user application and another or between user applications and the kernel. In this case the instructions, data and stack of one program may be overwritten by another program or, more importantly, kernel structures may be damaged by user programs, resulting in possible irreversible damage.

Before long, systems became available which went a long way forward to solve these problems by supporting *virtual memory* underpinned by the introduction of additional memory management hardware. The idea behind virtual memory is to create the illusion that there is a large amount of memory available even though the amount of physical memory present may be quite small.

With virtual memory, addresses used by applications and the kernel do not necessarily match the physical addresses sent to the memory. Virtual addresses are translated into physical addresses by a combination of hardware and kernel software support.

On the i386 family of processors addresses are grouped together into variable sized quantities called *segments* or fixed size quantities called *pages*. A segment or page may or may not be present in physical memory at any one moment in time. For example, if access is made to a virtual address for which the corresponding page is present in physical memory, the read or write will be successful. If the page is not present in physical memory, the kernel is called to locate the page, set up the mapping between the virtual address and the page in physical memory and inform the processor to retry the operation. The application does not see this undercover work.

The amount of physical memory available can be logically extended by use of one or more swap devices which are usually separate divisions on disk. When pages are not present in memory, the kernel copies them from the swap device into physical memory. This usually involves creating space by copying the contents of a page already present in memory out to the swap device.

As Figure 6.6 shows, the amount of virtual memory usually exceeds both the amount of physical memory and the amount of swap space available. Additional support from the kernel must carefully control the allocation of memory so that the amount of memory used does not exceed the total amount of physical memory and swap space available.

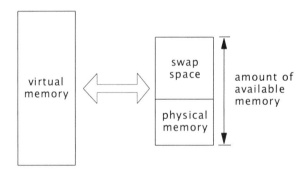

Figure 6.6   The relationship between virtual memory, physical memory and swap space

The type of virtual memory that will be used by the operating system on the i386 family of processors is a system designer's choice and can be implemented using a combination of segmentation and paging, both of which are described in the following sections.

SCO UNIX uses both segmentation and paging.

6.3.2 Segmented memory

The i386 processor provides the ability to divide the system's physical memory into a number of logical segments, not to be confused with ELF segments, where each segment consists of a range of contiguous addresses. The addresses within a segment are referenced using a combination of a segment selector and one of the i386 general purpose registers. There are six segment registers, namely `cs`, `ss`, `ds`, `es`, `fs` and `gs`, and eight general purpose registers are also available called `eax`, `edx`, `ecx`, `ebx`, `ebp`, `esi`, `edi` and `esp`. Each general purpose register is 32 bits in size.

The segment containing instructions currently being executed by the processor is called a code segment and is referenced by the segment selector held in the `cs` register. The address within the segment that holds the instruction to be executed is held in the `eip` register.

Figure 6.7 shows an address in memory accessed using segmentation. In this case the segment being accessed contains program code. Use of different segment selectors, for example `ds`, allows access to different types of data.

Section 6.3.3 shows how the different segments are used by the kernel to represent different parts of a user process and what the user actually sees in terms of segmentation when writing and running programs.

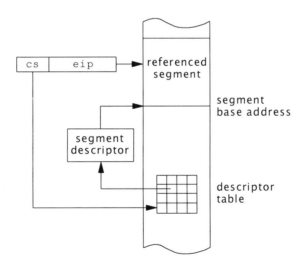

Figure 6.7   Segmented memory access

Each segment selector, which is 16 bits in size, references a *segment descriptor*. The segment descriptor describes the properties of the segment such as its location in memory, size and access rights. Segment descriptors are held in one of two tables, the *Local Descriptor Table* (LDT) or the *Global Descriptor Table* (GDT). In SCO UNIX there is a single GDT containing descriptors used by the whole system and there is one

LDT per process. The table to be referenced given a specific segment selector is dependent on the contents of the selector as shown in Figure 6.8.

Figure 6.8   Segment selectors

The TI bit indicates which of the descriptor tables the hardware segmentation unit will reference. If TI=0, the GDT is accessed, otherwise the LDT is accessed. The location in memory of the GDT is referenced by the gdtr register, while the LDT is referenced by the ldtr register.

The RPL (*Requester Privilege Level*) field is one of the mechanisms used by hardware to provide protection between different segments in memory. For example, if a user process attempts to access a segment owned by the kernel, an exception will be generated by the processor and caught by the kernel which will subsequently terminate the process by posting a SIGSEGV signal. For further details on the Intel CPU protection mechanisms, including a description of the different privilege levels, see the Intel486 *Programmer's Reference Manual* (1992).

Each entry in the GDT or LDT is called a segment descriptor. There are a number of different types of descriptors, for example code, data and stack, and a number of descriptors used for supporting multitasking and protected mode transfers between a lower priority i386 task, for example a UNIX process, and a higher priority i386 task, for example the kernel.

Section 7.3 shows the descriptor type used to implement UNIX system calls. For code, data and stack segments, the segment descriptor contains a number of different fields including:

Base address   This field contains a 32-bit address to which the contents of the segment offset are added. For code segments, the offset is the value in the eip register; for data segments it may be one of the general purpose registers, for example eax.

Limit   This field is used to define the size of the segment. If the offset added to the base address falls outside of the bounds of the segment defined by the limit field, the processor generates an exception.

DPL   This field, called the *Descriptor Privilege Level*, defines the privilege level of the segment and is used in conjunction with the RPL field of the segment selector to determine whether access to the segment is permitted.

Present bit   The present bit provides the kernel with one of the mechanisms for implementing virtual memory. If this bit is not set, the processor will generate a *segment not present* exception allowing the kernel to load the segment from a secondary device, for example disk, and then retry the operation without the knowledge of the user process. In SCO UNIX segments are always present, only pages move in and out of memory.

Type   This field indicates the type of the segment.

The combination of the segment selector and the offset (general purpose register) is called the *logical address*. Shown in Figure 6.9, the segmentation unit, which is part of the CPU, uses the selector to locate the segment descriptor. The base address found in the segment descriptor is then added to the offset to obtain the *linear address*.

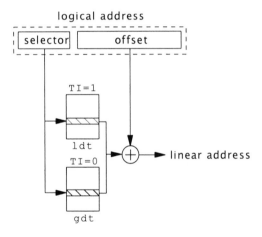

Figure 6.9   Address translation using segmentation

If paging is not enabled, the linear address is used as the physical address and is sent by the processor to memory as shown in Figure 6.5 on page 147.

The index field of the segment selector references one of 8192 possible segment descriptors. Since the size of a descriptor is eight bytes, the index is multiplied by 8 to locate the actual address of the descriptor. The following example shows a possible segment selector:

15		3	2 1	0
0000000010100		1	11	

The TI bit is 1 thus the LDT is referenced. The RPL is 3, representing least privilege. The index into the LDT is 20.

Toolkit 6.4   Displaying per process LDTs

The following crash(ADM) session displays the contents of the LDT for the *hello world* program used throughout the chapter. The LDT for each process is referenced from a kernel proc structure using the following proc structure field:

```
caddr_t      p_ldt ;
```

There is a single proc structure for each active UNIX process in the system. Chapter 7 describes the proc structure and other process related structures in greater detail.

The crash command is used to enter a crash session as follows:

```
# crash
dumpfile = /dev/mem, namelist = /unix, outfile = stdout
> proc ! grep hello
  25 p    251    250    250 13583  51  0                 hello        load trc
> ldt 25
iAPX386 LDT for process 25
SLOT      BASE/SEL LIM/OFF  TYPE        DPL   ACCESSBITS
    0         0158 f00d3888 CGATE386     3    CNT=1
    1         0158 f00102e8 CGATE386     3    CNT=1
    2     00000000 bffff000 XSEG         3    ACCS'D R&X DFLT G4096
    3     00000000 ffc0f000 DSEG         3    ACCS'D R&W BIG  G4096
    4     00000000 ffc0f000 DSEG         3    R&W BIG   G4096
    5     e0000e80 00000180 DSEG         3    ACCS'D R&W BIG
    7         0158 f0010394 CGATE386     3    CNT=1
```

To display the *hello world* program, a break point is set in the program and crash(ADM) is run from another virtual console or window. The *hello world* process is located by using the proc command to display the process table and grep(C) is used to search for hello, the name of the program. The LDT for the hello process, which is found in process slot 25, is then displayed using the ldt command.

There are four LDT entries representing the memory regions of the hello process for which there are three data (DSEG) segments and one text (XSEG) segment. Note that all four segments overlap in their virtual address ranges although, as section 6.4.2 shows, each UNIX process is composed of non-overlapping regions. The following section describes in more detail how segmentation is used for UNIX processes.

The other three entries are *call gates*. They are used by UNIX processes to gain access to kernel functions at higher levels of privilege. The functions accessed through the call gates are used for system calls, signal handling and extended support for databases. Section 7.3 shows how call gates are used by the kernel to implement UNIX system calls and return from signal handlers.

Although there is an LDT per process there is a single GDT used by the kernel. Chapter 14 shows how to display the GDT.

6.3.3 The kernel use of segmentation

The kernel uses segmentation in a limited manner, allowing management of memory to be based on the use of the paging aspects of the CPU. As the previous toolkit highlighted, the segments used to implement the process's text, data and stack all have a base address of zero and a limit which covers the 3 Gbytes of virtual address space that is available to user processes – the division of virtual memory between the kernel and user processes is described in section 6.4.1.

The adb(CP) debugger can be used to display the code segment attributes and current data segment attributes of the *hello world* program using the $m internal variable:

```
$ adb hello
* $m

Text Segments              File - 'hello'
Seg #          File Pos    Vir Size       Phys Size       Reloc Base
0x17           0x0         0x68b4         0x68b4          0x0

Data Segments              File - 'hello'
Seg #          File Pos    Vir Size       Phys Size       Reloc Base
0x1f           0x6000      0x1c28         0x1a70          0x400000
*
```

The Seg fields highlighted are the segment selectors of the code and data segments. Using the format of segment selectors shown in Figure 6.8 (page 150) the selectors can be decomposed as shown in Figure 6.10.

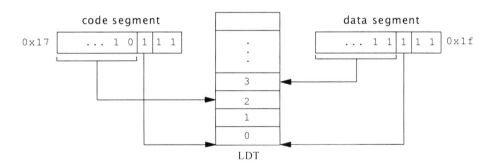

Figure 6.10   User application code and data segments

The entries in the LDT correspond to the executable segment and one of the data segments which were displayed by the ldt command shown in Toolkit 6.4 (Displaying per process LDTs, page 152). Recall that once the segments are established by the kernel, they are never altered when the process is running. Only the offset within the segment changes as the program counter (eip) executes instructions, one of the general purpose registers is used to access data within the data segment or the esp and ebp registers are changed when accessing the process's stack.

6.3.4 Paged memory

In addition to segmented memory, the i386 processor supports paging. If only segmentation is used, either the whole of the segment is present in memory or it is held elsewhere, for example within the file from which the process was created or on the swap device if the amount of memory available becomes low.

When using paging, the complete 4 Gbytes of virtual address space supported by the kernel is divided into a number of fixed sized pages. Each page is 4 kbytes in size. As with segmentation, a page is either present in memory or held elsewhere, for example on the swap device or in the file with which it is associated.

Paging is enabled during kernel initialisation by setting the PG bit (bit 31) of the cr0 control register. If this bit is clear, the linear address generated by the segmentation unit is the physical address used to access memory. If the PG bit is set, the paging unit is invoked to continue the address translation process using the linear address produced by the segmentation unit.

The linear address generated by the segmentation unit is divided by the paging unit into three distinct fields as shown in Figure 6.11.

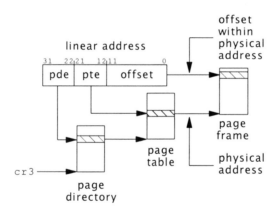

Figure 6.11   The i386 has two levels of page tables

Bits 22 to 31 of the linear address point to a page directory entry (pde) which is located in the page directory. The base physical address of the page directory is located in the cr3 register. The 1024 page directory entries each point to the base physical address of a different page table.

Bits 12 to 21 of the linear address point to a page table entry (pte) within the page table referenced by the pde. The page table entry contains the base physical address of a 4 kbyte page frame. The offset within the page frame and thus the required physical address is obtained by taking bits 0 to 11 of the linear address.

The page directory and 1024 page tables allow access to 1024 * 1024 * 4096 possible physical addresses giving a maximum of 4 Gbytes of physical memory.

To describe the relationship between segmentation and paging consider the 1 Mbyte segment shown in Figure 6.12.

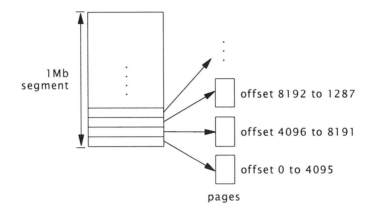

Figure 6.12   A 1 Mbyte segment and corresponding pages

Recall from section 6.3.2 that there is a single bit in the segment descriptor indicating whether the segment is present in physical memory or not. Using segmentation as the sole method of implementing virtual memory, segments would need to be provided which matched the size of the process text, data and stack.

To swap various sized segments in and out of memory would involve complex allocation algorithms for both the segments in memory and those segments which are temporarily on secondary storage. The chance of fragmenting memory would be high, resulting in wastage of memory and therefore reducing one of the main benefits of virtual memory, to make better use of the limited amount of physical memory available.

Dividing a segment into a number of pages allows part of the segment to be in memory and part swapped out. This gives the kernel the option of having only those pages of the segment that are currently in use, the *working set*, to be present in memory, leaving space for other pages belonging to other processes. Another advantage of paging is that the pages of a segment do not need to be contiguous in physical memory.

Each page table contains a number of appropriately named page table entries which describe the properties of the page. For example, bit 0 of the page table entry indicates whether the page is present in physical memory or not. If the page is present, other bits indicate whether it can be read from or written to or whether it has been accessed. Each page table entry is 4 bytes in size and the format of each page table entry is shown in Table 6.4.

Table 6.4   Page table entry format

Bit	Mnemonic	Description
0	P	If this bit is set to 1, the page is present in physical memory. Accessing a physical address within a page which does not have the present bit set results in a page fault, an exception raised by the processor and handled by the kernel.
1	R/W	If set to 0, only read access is permitted to the page, otherwise read and write access is allowed.
2	U/S	If set to 0, only protection ring 0 tasks (the kernel) can access the page, otherwise all tasks have access.
3	PWT	If set to 1, only write through caching is permitted.
4	PCD	If set to 1, the page will not be cached.
5	A	The page directory or page table has been accessed.
6	D	The page directory or page table has been written to.
7	0	Page size which can be 4 Mbytes on Pentium processors.
8	0	Intel reserved.
9–11	AVAIL	Available for use by system programmers.
12–31	–	The base physical address of the page frame.

Chapter 12 shows how the kernel handles page faults and uses the bits in the page table entry to construct paging policies.

For completeness, the total address translation process performed by the segmentation and paging units is shown in Figure 6.13.

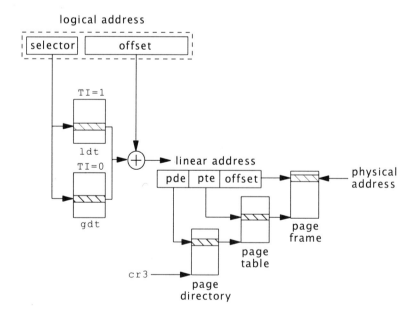

Figure 6.13   Combined segmentation and paging

The use of paging techniques within the kernel is described in chapter 7, which shows how processes are created by the kernel, and chapter 12, which shows how the kernel handles page faults and implements paging and swapping policies.

6.4 The UNIX process address space

Each UNIX process resides in its own virtual address space protected from other processes with support from the i386 processor. The hardware state or *context* of the process, including the general purpose registers, segment registers and control registers, are referenced by a specific segment, the *Task State Segment* (TSS).

For each process supported by the kernel there is a separate TSS. When a process is not running, the hardware state of the process is saved in its TSS which is pointed to from the process's u_area.

In a multitasking operating systems such as UNIX, the method of transferring control from one process to another is called a *context switch* or *task switch*. The data structures used to perform the context switch are shown in Figure 6.14.

The complete hardware state of the process currently executing must be saved in its TSS in memory prior to a context switch. The state of the next process to run is then copied from memory into the hardware registers including the new program counter (eip), ldtr, page directory pointer (cr3) and other registers.

Control is then passed to the new process which carries on running from the exact position it was in when it ran previously. The mechanics of the context switch are described in section 7.9.

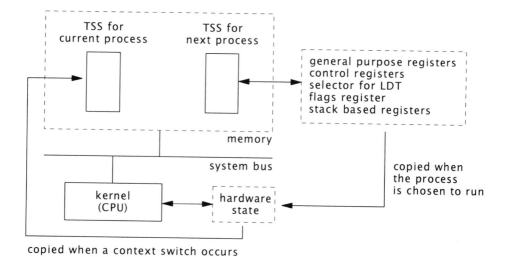

Figure 6.14   The TSS structures used when performing a context switch

6.4.1 The 4 Gbyte address space layout

The kernel shares the 4 Gbytes of available virtual address space it supports with each UNIX process as shown in Figure 6.15. The kernel is said to reside in the same *context* as each process. Each time a process is scheduled to be run by the CPU, the appropriate context must be set up so that the general purpose registers, segment registers, pdbr and page tables represent the context of the new process.

The page directory base register located in the cr3 control register points to the current process's page directory. SCO UNIX uses only a single page directory regardless of which process is running. Since the kernel text and data are part of every process, page tables describing the top 1 Gbyte of memory are common to all processes. This covers 256 page tables, the top quarter entries in the page directory.

The page tables representing the user process, entries 0 to 767 in the page directory, are changed on each context switch, so following the context switch, the image of the new process is visible and the old process context is hidden, even though pages of the old process will still be present in memory.

The division of the user virtual address space is dependent on a number of factors including the type of binary run, for example COFF or ELF. Figure 6.16 shows the layout of both COFF and ELF executable files in virtual memory.

The memory layouts for both COFF and ELF executable files shown here are using default addresses.

In the ELF memory layout, the stack is limited to approximately 128 Mbytes of memory. Programmers should never make assumptions about where the kernel will place library text, data or memory mapped files. The COFF memory layout is more strict on the layout of memory, for example the placement of static shared libraries, but allows a larger stack size. Whether this is an advantage or not depends on the application program.

Both COFF and ELF support the ability for the programmer to specify more precisely where in memory each component will start. However, in both formats user addresses cannot exceed the 3 Gbyte limit.

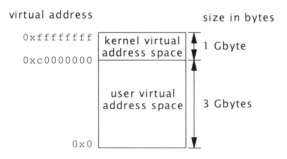

Figure 6.15   User and kernel virtual address space

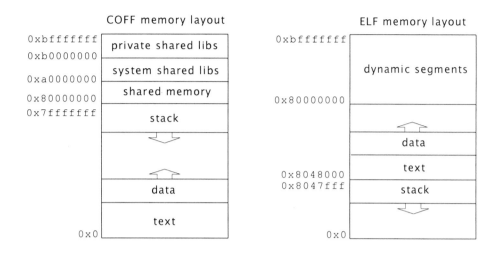

Figure 6.16   Format of the user virtual address space

6.4.2 Per process memory management

The address space used by each UNIX process is divided into a number of *regions*. Each region is a kernel structure used to represent a contiguous area of non-overlapping virtual addresses and is governed by its own set of attributes defining the region type and additional properties such as whether the region can be read from, written to or executed. A region can be used to hold many different types of data including text, data, shared memory, library text and memory mapped files.

Figure 6.17 shows mapping between a UNIX region structure and an i386 segment with corresponding pages.

Since the region is represented by an i386 segment, and therefore a number of pages, only those pages of the region which are required need to be present in physical memory when the process is running. For example, a large program may require a large number of Mbytes of text. If the program is repeatedly looping within a small function, there may only be a need to have one or two pages of the region in memory at that time. When a context switch occurs to another process, the likelihood of the pages of the new process still being resident in memory are therefore increased.

Regions are not accessed directly from the process `proc` structure but by an intermediate structure called a *pregion* which is short for per process region. Since processes may share regions through either shared memory, memory mapped files or libraries, the starting virtual address of the region may be different in each process. The virtual address of the region is therefore held in the `pregion` structure.

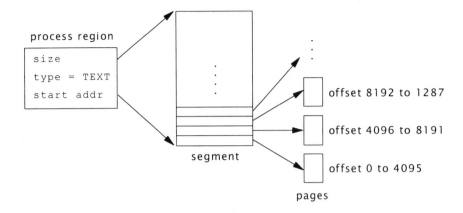

Figure 6.17   Mapping kernel regions to segments and pages

The relationship between the `proc`, `pregion` and `region` structures for a single process is shown in Figure 6.18. The example here shows three regions corresponding to the process's text, data and stack.

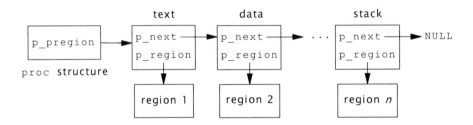

Figure 6.18   Kernel structures for implementing a process's address space

Each process's `pregion` structures are held in a linked list and referenced from the `p_pregion` field of the `proc` structure. The fields of the `pregion` structure are shown in Table 6.5.

Table 6.5   The `pregion` structure

`pregion` structure field		Description
struct region	*p_reg	A pointer to the region structure.
caddr_t	p_regva	The region's virtual address within the process's address space.
short	p_flags	Flags describing the region properties for this process.
short	p_type	The type of the region such as text, data or stack.
struct pregion	*p_next	pregion structures are connected via a linked list.

The type of the region is described by the p_type field. Some of the pregion types are as follows:

PT_UNUSED   The region is not currently used.

PT_TEXT   The region holds program text.

PT_DATA   The region holds program data.

PT_STACK   This region is used to hold the process stack.

PT_SHMEM   The region holds shared memory.

PT_LIBTXT   The region holds library text.

PT_LIBDAT   The region holds library data.

PT_SHFIL   A memory mapped file region.

The p_flags field describes the access properties of the region, for example whether the process has read, write or execute access or whether the region is locked in memory. The complete list of flags for the pregion structure can be found in the <sys/region.h> header file.

The region structure contains many fields some of which are shown in Table 6.6.

Table 6.6   The region structure

region structure field		Description
short	r_flags	Flags describing the properties of the region.
long	r_pgsz	The size of the region in pages.
long	r_nvalid	The number of valid pages in the region.
ushort	r_refcnt	The number of processes pointing at the region.
char	r_type	Type of the region providing additional information to the p_type field of the pregion structure.
pde_t	*r_list	A pointer to list of page directory entries for page tables used to locate the page tables of the region.
pde_t	r_pde	A page directory entry used for regions which are smaller than 4 Mbytes.
long	r_gpoff	An offset within the region used by the page stealer, vhand, to resume stealing.
struct region	*r_ancr	MAP_INHERIT ancestor/anchor region used when sharing memory between related processes as an effect of mapping /dev/zero.
struct inode	*r_iptr	A pointer to the inode where the page/blocks of the region reside.
struct region	*r_forw	A link used when the region is on the free list.
struct region	*r_back	A link used when the region is on the free list.

The first notable field is the reference count r_refcnt. Each time a process acquires access to an existing region, the reference count is increased. If the count falls to zero, the region may be freed. The fields of the region structure are described throughout the remainder of this chapter and in chapter 7.

The complete range of possible values that the `r_flags` and `r_type` field can take are described in the `<sys/region.h>` header file.

6.4.3 Kernel region management

Region structures can be either allocated from a static pool or allocated dynamically. The number of regions available in the system is governed by the `MAX_REGION` kernel tuneable defined in `/etc/conf/cf.d/mtune` and modified by the `configure(ADM)` utility.

Regions are initialised during system startup by the routine `reginit()` which is called from `mlsetup()`. The tasks performed by `reginit()` are as follows:

- The number of regions is calculated based on `MAX_REGION`.
- The `table_setup()`, `table_alloc()` and `table_grow()` functions used for dynamically allocating tables are called to allocate memory for the `region[]` array which points to each valid region in the system. The `region[]` array is also referred to as the region table.
- The `rfree` region, which heads the free list, is set to point to `region[0]` using the `r_forw` field. The `r_forw` field of each region structure in the `region[]` array is then set to point to the next region in the array, building a linked list of free regions.
- The `ractive` region which is used to link active regions is set to NULL.

Once `reginit()` has completed, the kernel variable `regcnt` holds the number of regions available for allocation. Each `region` structure is linked on a doubly linked list to the previous and next elements of the `region[]` array. The linked list of `region` structures following `reginit()` is shown in Figure 6.19.

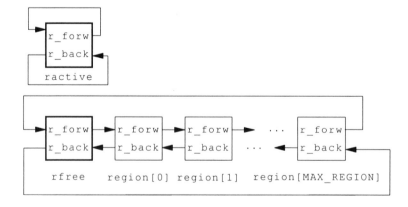

Figure 6.19   The kernel `region` structures following `reginit()`

At this stage, all `region` structures are linked to the region free list headed by `rfree`. The list of active regions, that is, those regions currently being used by one process or another, are held on another doubly linked list headed by `ractive`. Following `reginit()` the `ractive` list is empty.

The following sections describe the kernel functions use to allocate, de-allocate and duplicate regions.

6.4.4 Region allocation

The memory image of each process is constructed using a number of different regions. At a minimum, text, data and stack regions are allocated for the process following a call to `execve(S)`. Regions are also allocated to hold library text and data, mapped files and shared memory segments.

Each region is allocated by the kernel function `allocreg()`. The main tasks performed by the `allocreg()` function are:

- If the region free list headed by `rfree` is empty, the `grow_region()` function is called to grow the region table dynamically by allocating new free `region` structures.

- The `region` structure at the head of the free list is removed, the pointers of `rfree` adjusted to reference the next `region` structure on the list and the `regcnt` variable is decremented.

- The fields of the `region` structure are initialised to arguments passed to `allocreg()`, including the inode which points to the file where the region's data will be read from and the region type.

- The region is linked to the active list headed by `ractive`.

If there are no free regions available, the kernel will dynamically grow the region table up to the maximum limit defined by the MAX_REGION kernel tuneable. The limits for MAX_REGION can be found in `/etc/conf/cf.d/mtune` and are described in detail in the SCO OpenServer *Performance Guide* (1995).

Figure 6.20 shows the effects of the very first call to `allocreg()` following the initialisation of the `region` structures by `reginit()`. The first element of the free list referenced by `rfree` (`region[0]`) is unlinked and added to the start of the active list headed by `ractive`.

After a call to `allocreg()` has been made, the region will not have yet been attached to a process. This is performed using the `attachreg()` kernel function, for which the main tasks are as follows:

- The `kmem_alloc()` function is called to allocate memory (virtual and physical) to hold the `pregion` structure which describes the region to be attached.

- The `p_reg` field of the `pregion` structure is set to point to the region to be attached and the `p_regva` field is set to the starting virtual address.

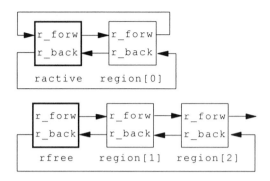

Figure 6.20 Region allocation

- The `chkgrowth()` function is called to ensure that the memory limits of the process will not be exceeded if the new process is attached.
- Since the region may also be attached to one or more other processes, the region reference count, the `r_refcnt` field, is incremented.
- The `pregion` structure is inserted into the linked list of `pregion` structures that are already attached to the process and accessed via the `p_pregion` field of the `proc` structure.
- The sizes of the process's memory resources are incremented.
- The `pdgrow()` function is called to add appropriate page directory entries to cover the new region.

Figure 6.21 shows the effects of invoking `attachreg()`.

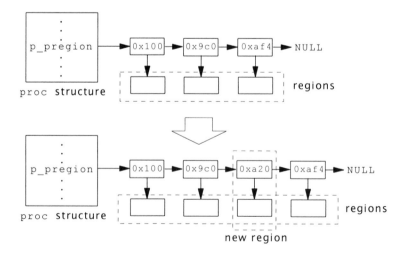

Figure 6.21 Attaching a region to a process's address space

In this example, the virtual address of the new region to be added is `0xa20` which results in the region being inserted between the process's second and third existing regions.

6.4.5 Duplicating a region

Duplicating a region involves invoking `allocreg()` and copying all of the page table entries from the old region to the new region. There are two places in the kernel where a process region needs to be duplicated:

- A process is forked. Following the `fork(S)` system call the parent and child need to have an identical address space with both parent and child sharing the same pages.

- A process is being debugged and the debugger needs to modify part of the process's memory image. The region covering the area to be modified needs to be duplicated such that any modifications made to the process being debugged are not visible to other processes which are sharing the region.

One major modification that `dupreg()` makes is to set each page table entry of the region as read only. This allows the kernel to implement *copy on write* semantics for data and stack regions whereby the kernel maximises usage of memory by only allocating physical pages when required, for example when the parent or child process writes to a page. Copy on write regions are described in detail in section 7.5. The use of memory management support from the i386 processor to aid in copy on write is described in chapter 12.

The main tasks performed by `dupreg()` are as follows:

- The kernel checks to make sure that by duplicating a region, the address space limits of the process will not be exceeded.
- `allocreg()` is called to allocate a new region.
- The `uptgrow()` function is called to allocate page table entries for the new region.
- All relevant fields of the original `region` structure are copied to the new `region` structure.
- For each page of the parent region, the page table entry is copied to the child region and the write access bit of both page table entries is turned off to force a page fault if a write occurs, allowing a new page to be allocated.

6.4.6 Region de-allocation

Regions are de-allocated for a number of reasons, including termination of a process, detaching a shared memory segment, or when a mapped file region is no longer required by the process, for example following a call to `munmap(S)`.

Removal of a region from the process's address space is performed using `dettachreg()`. The main tasks performed by `detachreg()` are as follows:

- If the region is used for a shared memory segment, appropriate reference counts are decremented and any dirty pages that exist in the address range covered by the region are written to disk. For example, the region may map a portion of a file as writeable. The `mmfsync()` function is called to write out any pages of the region that have been modified.

- The `pregion` structure associated with the region is unlinked from the process's `pregion` list.

- The `pdgrow()` function is called to remove the appropriate entries from the process's page directory and `flushtlb()` is called to ensure that all page table entries that are cached in the *Translation Lookaside Buffer* (TLB) are flushed. For further details of the TLB refer to the *Intel486 Programmer's Reference Manual* (1992).

- The `update_usizes()` function is then called to update the size of the process.

- Finally, the `pregion` structure is set to `PT_UNUSED` or freed by `kmem_free()`, depending on whether the region is referenced solely by this process.

As an example of detaching a region, consider Figure 6.22. The region to be detached is referenced by a pointer from its associated `pregion` structure. In this example the region to be detached is accessed by the second `pregion` structure in the list.

Once the region has been detached, any references by the process to addresses in the range of virtual addresses which were covered by the region will cause a segmentation violation, resulting in `SIGSEGV` being posted to the process.

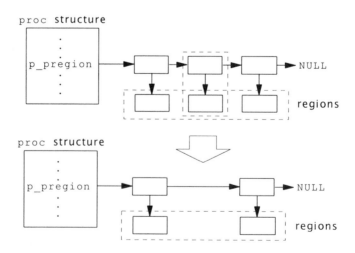

Figure 6.22   Detaching a process region

There are times when all of the regions need to be detached from a process. For example, when the execve(S) system call is invoked which requires that a new process be created or when a process is about to terminate. The function to remove all regions is detachregs(), which consists of a set of calls to detachreg() for each pregion attached to the process. Once all regions have been detached, the process size, accessed from the p_size field of the proc structure, is set to zero.

Toolkit 6.5   Accessing memory following detachreg()

This toolkit program shows the use of the mmap(S) and munmap(S) system calls to demonstrate the use of the attachreg() and detachreg() functions.

The program opens the file specified by argv[1], maps the entire file into its address space and writes the value 0xff to the first byte of the mapping. The entire file is then unmapped and an attempt is made to write to the same address.

```
#include <sys/types.h>
#include <sys/mman.h>
#include <sys/stat.h>
#include <sys/signal.h>
#include <fcntl.h>

main(int argc, char *argv[])
{
    int         fd ;
    caddr_t     maddr ;
    struct stat st ;

    fd = open(argv[1], O_RDWR) ;
    fstat(fd, &st) ;

    maddr = mmap(0, (size_t)st.st_size, PROT_WRITE, MAP_SHARED, fd, 0) ;
    *maddr = 0xff ;
    printf("First write okay at address 0x%x\n", maddr) ;

    munmap(maddr, (size_t)st.st_size) ;
    *maddr = 0xff ;
}
```

When the program is run it generates a segmentation violation on the second attempt to write to the address specified by maddr.

```
$ map filex
First write okay at address 0x80001000
Memory fault(coredump)
```

By inserting the following line into the program after the printf(C) call and before the call to munmap(S):

```
getc(stdin) ;
```

the memory image of the process can be analysed from within crash(ADM) (on a separate virtual console or xterm) to display the region tables following the call to mmap(S) and following the call to munmap(S). The output at both stages is as follows:

```
# crash          # "map filex" has been run in a separate virtual console
dumpfile = /dev/mem, namelist = /unix, outfile = stdout
> proc ! grep map
  20 s    411    239    411 13583   75    0 cn_tty+0xd0        map        load
> pregion 20    # "First write okay..." has already been written
SLOT PREG REG#        REGVA    TYPE FLAGS
  20    0   94             0    text rd ex cm
        1  145    0x400000    data rd wr cm
        2  128  0x7fffe000   stack rd wr cm
        3  140  0x80001000   shfil rd wr wa
> pregion 20    # Return has been pressed to execute munmap(S)
SLOT PREG REG#        REGVA    TYPE FLAGS
  20    0   94             0    text rd ex cm
        1  145    0x400000    data rd wr cm
        2  128  0x7fffe000   stack rd wr cm
```

The process, called map, is located in slot 20 of the proc table. The pregion structures for the process are first displayed after the message "First write okay at address 0x80001000" has been displayed by the map program. This shows that the process has four regions. The final data region starting at address 0x80001000 and of type shfil is used for the mapped file.

Following the munmap(S) call, the pregion structures are displayed once more. This time, the region has been removed from the process following a call to detachreg().

6.4.7 The principles of paging

This section provides an overview of the steps taken to fault pages into memory on demand. The details of the paging mechanisms employed by the kernel to handle page faults can be found in chapter 12. Chapter 7 further describes copy on write.

When a region is created to be filled with the contents of a regular file for the purpose of process execution, the region is associated with the inode of the file. This is referenced by the r_ip field of the region structure.

When the region is created, it is not necessary to fill the entire region with its appropriate section of the file. As the process runs it may only ever access a subset of the text or data and therefore any underlying physical pages that may have been allocated to the region may be allocated unnecessarily.

Therefore, when the region is created, it is created empty. When the process accesses any one of the addresses in the region, the CPU detects that the virtual address accessed does not point to a valid physical address and generates a page fault. For example, consider a hypothetical process whose text region is shown in Figure 6.23.

The memory image of the process shows the text segment covering the first four pages of the virtual address space from 0x0 to 0x3fff. When the region was created, the appropriate entry in the page directory was set up by pdgrow(). In this example, the first four pages of the virtual address space are covered by entry zero in the page directory. For the page table referenced by the page directory entry, the corresponding page table entries covering the first four pages have bit zero set to 0 indicating that the pages are not present in physical memory.

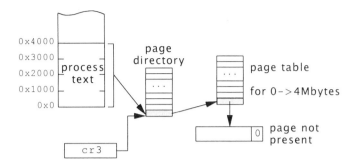

Figure 6.23   Mapping the text region onto its page directory and page table entries

Assume that the process is just about to run for the first time and that the `eip` register references address `0x0`. Since the page covering this address, as shown in Figure 6.23, is not present, the processor will generate a page fault and pass control to a kernel supplied fault handler.

The page of text required is held in the executable file on disk which is referenced by the `r_ip` pointer in the `region` structure. The kernel will allocate a new page, read the data from disk into the new page, alter the page table entry to indicate that the page is present and inform the CPU that the instruction can be restarted.

Toolkit 6.6   Analysis of the process memory image

This section combines the previous toolkits presented in this chapter and the description of i386 memory management hardware support to analyse a process part way through execution. This will make use of `adb(CP)`, `crash(ADM)` and multiple virtual consoles. The program to be analysed is the same *hello world* program used throughout the previous sections of the chapter.

Shown below, `adb(CP)` is entered and a breakpoint is set at `main()`. The program is then run and the breakpoint quickly reached. Control returns to `adb(CP)` which awaits further instructions:

```
$ adb hello
* main:br
* :r
hello: running
breakpoint      main:           jmp       near main+0xf
```

Switching virtual consoles and entering `crash(ADM)`, the process can be located using the `proc` command to display each entry in the kernel's process table. The `grep(C)` command is used to search for the program name:

```
# crash
dumpfile = /dev/mem, namelist = /unix, outfile = stdout
> proc ! grep hello
  23 t    254    245    245 13583  51    0              hello  load   trc
```

This locates the `hello` process in slot `23` of the `proc[]` table. For this process, each of the `pregion` structures can be displayed using the `pregion` command which takes a process slot as an argument:

```
> pregion 23
SLOT PREG REG#      REGVA   TYPE FLAGS
  23    0  136  0x8046000 stack rd wr cm
        1  138  0x8048000  text rd ex cm
        2  130  0x8049000  data rd wr cm
        3   73 0x80001000 lbtxt rd ex pr
        4  137 0x80051000 lbdat rd wr ex pr
```

There are five pregions linked to the process. Pregions 0, 1 and 2 represent the process stack, text and data, respectively. Regions 3 and 4 are used for library text and data. The `REG#` field shows the position in the region table where the region is located although note that the `p_region` field of the `pregion` structure is actually a pointer and not an index. The `REGVA` gives the virtual address of the region in this process.

The `region` structures can be displayed in greater detail using the `region` command:

```
> region 138
REGION TABLE SIZE = 170
Region-list:

SLOT PGSZ VLD SMEM NONE SOFF REF SWP NSW FORW BACK INOX TYPE FLAGS
 138    1   0    1    0   72   1   0   0  114  130   55 stxt nosh nosmem
```

The `region` structure displayed here is one page in size (`PGSZ`), is a text region (`TYPE`) and the contents of the region will be created by reading from the inode in slot `55` of the inode table. The `FORW` and `BACK` fields are used to link the region with other regions that are on the active list.

Using the `INOX` field it is possible to determine from which file the contents of the region are loaded. The inode in slot `55` of the inode table can be displayed as follows:

```
> inode 55
INODE TABLE SIZE = 204
SLOT MAJ/MIN FS INUMB RCNT LINK   UID  GID   SIZE   MODE MNT M/ST FLAGS
  55    1,42  2 22374    4    1 13583   50   4024 f---755   0 R130 tx
```

The fields to notice here are `MAJ/MIN` and `INUMB` which represent the device on which the inode resides and its inode number. The file can be located using `ncheck(ADM)` as follows:

```
> ! ncheck -i 22374
/dev/root:
22374       /home/spate/book/mem/hello
```

Section 7.5 provides a similar example but shows the allocation of pages to the region as the process accesses them.

6.5 Summary and suggested reading

This chapter provided an introduction to ELF showing how the different components of the file are analysed by the kernel when creating an in-core image of the program.

The i386 memory management capabilities were then described to show the distinction between virtual and physical memory and how SCO UNIX uses the i386 memory management mechanisms.

The latter part of the chapter described the basic kernel structures which are used to construct a user process. Chapter 7 describes how the kernel uses the information contained within an ELF object file together with the `pregion` and `region` structures and algorithms described in this chapter to construct an executable process.

The ELF format is described in detail in the SCO OpenServer *Developer's Topics* (1995). This describes all aspects of ELF including the phases of the compilation and linking process. Nohr (1994) contains a similar description of ELF but also includes information on use of the `elf` library functions available for analysing and manipulating ELF files and other useful tools and utilities.

The Intel processor manuals, for example the *Intel486 Programmer's Reference Manual* (1992), provides the definitive description of the memory management capabilities of the processor.

7

Process management

This chapter describes the process subsystem, the component of the kernel which deals with the creation and management of user processes.

The actions taken to create a process from the executable image on disk, the provision of services by the kernel throughout the lifetime of the process and the actions taken by the kernel to terminate the process and free process resources are described together with the structures and functions used to implement process groups and sessions.

7.1 Introduction

The chapter starts by introducing the basic concepts and structures that are used to implement UNIX processes. The UNIX system call interface is then described showing how user processes move between user mode and kernel mode when invoking system calls. This section is followed by a detailed look at signal handling within the kernel.

The main part of the chapter describes how process are created, the relationship between different processes, scheduling, context switching and the actions taken when processes terminate, including the creation of core dumps.

7.1.1 The process management toolkit

This chapter provides a large number of different examples. Many of these use crash(ADM) and adb(CP) to display various process structures as the process issues system calls and performs other actions.

The examples also make use of the kmem and table drivers described in chapter 3.

7.2 Process management fundamentals

At the heart of the UNIX kernel is the process management subsystem. Almost all activity within the kernel is process related, whether servicing system calls, generating signals in response to internal or external events, allocation of memory, handling of exceptions due to process related errors or providing I/O services in response to the user requests.

This section describes the principal structures which are used by the kernel to represent a UNIX process and the possible states that the process can move between throughout its lifetime.

The section concludes by bringing together the information presented with a simple implementation of the ps (C) command in Toolkit 7.1.

7.2.1 From program to process

A UNIX process can be viewed as the executable image of the program, that is the memory image of the disk based program generated by the compilation system together with a stack, library text and data and a number of kernel and CPU-related structures. Figure 7.1 shows the steps taken from source program to running process.

The process consists of both *user mode* and *kernel mode* components. The user mode of a process consists of the text, data, stack, libraries and any structures that the process can directly access in memory.

The kernel mode component consists of all the structures which the process cannot directly access but which are used by the kernel to provide services to the process, implement and manage its address space and interface with the hardware. For example, hardware related structures such as the TSS (Task State Segment) and LDT (Local Descriptor Table) are held in kernel mode. Although they are used by the process they cannot be accessed directly by the process.

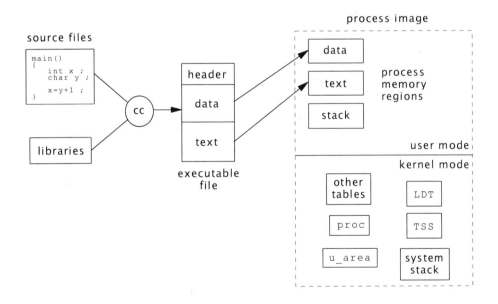

Figure 7.1   Constructing the process memory image

During execution of the process in user mode, the process does not generally have read or write access to any of the structures in the kernel. While executing in kernel mode, the process can access any part of memory. In order to access kernel data structures and services the process switches from user mode to kernel mode through the system call interface using mechanisms provided by the i386 processor. The method by which this transfer is achieved is described in section 7.3.

7.2.2 Process related structures

Each process in the system is represented by two main structures, the `proc` and `user` structures defined in `<sys/proc.h>` and `<sys/user.h>`, respectively.

Table 7.1 shows some of the fields of the `proc` structure. Other fields not shown in this table are described throughout the remainder of the book where relevant.

Table 7.1   Fields of the `proc` structure

proc structure field		Description
char	p_stat	The status of the process (running, sleeping, etc.).
char	p_pri	The priority of the process.
unsigned int	p_flag	Flags used in conjunction with the process status (p_stat) to determine process specific actions or actions which may affect the process.
unsigned short	p_uid	The user ID of the process.
unsigned short	p_suid	The effective user ID of the process.
int	p_sid	The process session ID.
short	p_pgrp	ID of the process group leader.
short	p_pid	The process ID.
short	p_ppid	The parent's process ID.
sigset_t	p_sig	The current signal which the kernel is processing.
unsigned int	p_size	Process size in pages.
time_t	p_utime	Time spent in user mode in seconds.
time_t	p_stime	Time spent in system mode in seconds.
caddr_t	p_ldt	A pointer to the process's LDT.
struct pregion	*p_region	List of per process memory regions.
short	p_xstat	Exit status to be returned to the parent.
unsigned int	p_uptbl[]	An array of page table entries for the u_area.

Each time a `fork(S)` system call is made, the kernel returns an identifier for the process called the process ID or PID which is held in the `p_pid` field. When a system call is made which passes the PID as an argument, the kernel examines each `proc` structure in turn until a process is found where the PID matches the `p_pid` field.

Since the number of processes available in the kernel is usually a relatively small number and the `proc` structures occupy consecutive memory locations, such a search is quick enough not to warrant any additional structures such as a hash queue.

Some of the basic process related system calls use fields in the `proc` structure to return information to the user process, for example:

`getpid(S)`	Return the contents of the `p_pid` field.
`getppid(S)`	Return the contents of the `p_ppid` field.
`wait(S)`	Return the contents of the `p_pid` and `p_xstat` field.

At any stage while the system is running, all `proc` structures must be present in memory even though most of the other kernel structures and user mode image of the process may be swapped out (see chapter 12). This allows the kernel to determine from a minimal amount of process related information the location of other process kernel structures and data if the process has been swapped out.

Each `proc` structure is contained in an array called `proc[]`, also called the `proc` table, which can grow dynamically as the number of processes increases. The `proc` table is initialised by the `mkproc()` function called during kernel initialisation. There is little work to perform during `mkproc()` other than to call `table_setup()`, `table_alloc()` and `table_grow()` to set up the `proc[]` table and allocate the required amount of memory.

At any stage during execution, the contents of the `proc` structure for the process which is currently running are accessed through the `curproc` kernel variable as shown in Figure 7.2. Each time a context switch occurs, `curproc` is set to the `proc` structure of the new process to run.

The process `user` structure, called the u_area or u block, contains additional, per process information which is required only when the process is running. Unlike the `proc` structure of the currently running process which is accessed through `curproc`, the u_area is located at a fixed virtual address in memory and is accessed through the variable `u`. Figure 7.3 shows the u_area at its fixed location in memory.

The u_area contains a number of fields used by most kernel subsystems, including open file descriptors, signal state, I/O transfer sizes and process statistics. The fields of the u_area are described throughout the remainder of the book when describing the subsystems that use them.

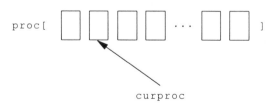

Figure 7.2   Accessing process data for the currently executing process

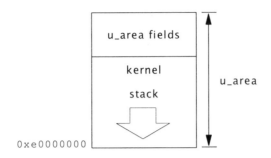

Figure 7.3   The user area (u_area) including the kernel stack

As shown in Figure 7.3, the u_area also contains a fixed size stack. When executing in kernel mode, the kernel uses this stack and not the stack in the user's address space. Section 7.3 shows how the kernel switches between the user and kernel stacks when a system call is invoked.

7.2.3 Process states

During its lifetime the process can move between many different states whether it is running, sleeping, swapped out and so on. The state of the process is held in the p_stat field of the proc structure, and can be one of the following values:

SSLEEP   The process is sleeping awaiting an event, for example when a read(S) system call has been invoked on standard input and no data is currently available.

SRUN   The process is on the run queue. In this case the process is eligible to run and is awaiting its time-slice.

SZOMB   The process has terminated but the parent has not yet issued a wait(S) system call to retrieve the child's exit status. A process in this state is called a zombie.

SSTOP   The process has stopped or is being traced by a debugger. A process may enter the SSTOP state due to job control signals.

SIDL   An intermediate state set during process creation. After the process has been fully created the state will be set to SRUN.

SONPROC   The process is currently executing on the processor.

SXBRK   This state is used to indicate that the process is waiting for memory to become available. When a process enters this state the swapper should be called to free up memory by swapping out one or more processes.

Figure 7.4 shows the transition in process states from creation to termination.

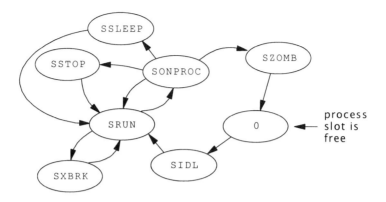

Figure 7.4   Process state transition

The kernel uses the `p_stat` field in conjunction with the `p_flag` to determine the complete state of the process. The `p_flag` field contains additional status information and consists of a bit-wise OR of the following flags:

`SSYS`	This is a kernel process, whose text and data reside in kernel space.
`STRC`	The process is being traced.
`SNWAKE`	The process cannot be awakened by a signal.
`SULOAD`	The process's u_area is in memory.
`SUSWAP`	The u_area is currently being swapped out.
`SLOCK`	The process is locked in memory.
`SSEXEC`	Stop the process on `exec()`.
`SASLEEP`	The process is stopped in a call to sleep.
`SNOTRC`	Only root can `ptrace(S)` the process.

Toolkit 7.1   `mps` – an implementation of `ps (C)`

This toolkit example uses the `table` driver in order to read each `proc` structure in turn. By displaying some of the fields of the `proc` structure a simple version of the `ps(C)` command can be easily implemented. For further information on the `table` driver see chapter 3 and the `tab(HW)` manual page.

In order to display the `p_stat` field an array of strings is declared on lines 8 and 9 which is initialised with the different process states. The ordering of each string is important and matches the values held in `p_stat` as defined in the `<sys/proc.h>` header file. For example, if `p_stat` equals 2, the process is in the SRUN state.

```
1 #include <sys/proc.h>
2 #include <sys/user.h>
3 #include <sys/sysi86.h>
4 #include <fcntl.h>
```

```
 5 #include <errno.h>
 6 #include <pwd.h>
 7
 8 char *Pstat[] = { "", "SSLEEP", "SRUN", "SZOMB",
 9                    "SSTOP", "SIDL", "SONPROC", "SXBRK" } ;
10
11 main()
12 {
13     int i, pslot=0, fd ;
14     struct proc p ;
15     struct passwd *pswd ;
16     struct user u ;
17
18     fd = open("/dev/table/proc", O_RDONLY) ;
19     if (fd < 0) {
20         perror("Couldn't access /dev/table/proc") ;
21         exit(errno) ;
22     }
23
24     printf("PSLOT STATUS   PID PPID USER    COMMAND\n") ;
25
26     while (read(fd, (char *)&p, sizeof(struct proc)) > 0) {
27         if (p.p_stat != 0) {
28             pswd = getpwuid(p.p_uid) ;
29             printf("%3d   %-7s %4d %4d %-6s ",pslot, Pstat[p.p_stat],
30                             p.p_pid, p.p_ppid, pswd->pw_name) ;
31             sysi86(RDUBLK, p.p_pid, &u, sizeof(struct user)) ;
32             printf("%s\n",u.u_psargs);
33         }
34         pslot++ ;
35     }
36 }
```

The program begins by opening /dev/table/proc on line 18. The first read from this device will return the first element of the proc table, proc[0], the next read will return proc[1] and so on until no further elements remain, when the number of bytes read will equal zero. The program loops around lines 26 to 35 until no more proc structures are returned by the table driver.

A check is made on line 27 to ensure that the process slot is currently being used and, if so, various fields of the proc structure are displayed. The getpwuid(S) library function is called on line 28 to locate the name of the process owner.

Finally, a call is made to sysi86(S) on line 31 to read the u_area for process read. This allows access to the u_psargs[] field which holds the command line passed to the execve(S) system call.

The output of the program for one particular run is as follows:

```
$ ./mps
PSLOT STATUS   PID PPID USER    COMMAND
    0 SSLEEP     0    0 root    sched
    1 SSLEEP     1    0 root    /etc/init
    2 SSLEEP     2    0 root    vhand
    3 SSLEEP     3    0 root    bdflush
    4 SSLEEP     4    0 root    kmdaemon
    5 SSLEEP     5    1 root    htepi_daemon /
    6 SSLEEP     6    0 root    strd
```

```
 7    SSLEEP   204    1 root    /bin/login spate
 8    SSLEEP    33    1 root    /etc/ifor_pmd
 9    SSLEEP    34   33 root    /etc/ifor_pmd
10    SSLEEP    35   34 root    /etc/sco_cpd
11    SSLEEP    29    1 root    htepi_daemon /stand
12    SSLEEP    37   34 root    /etc/ifor_sld
13    SSLEEP   205    1 root    /etc/getty tty02 sc_m
14    SSLEEP   206    1 root    /etc/getty tty03 sc_m
15    SSLEEP   188    1 root    /var/scohttp/scohttpd -d /var/scohttp
16    SSLEEP   207    1 root    /etc/getty tty04 sc_m
17    SSLEEP   208    1 root    /etc/getty tty05 sc_m
18    SSLEEP   209    1 root    /tcb/files/no_luid/sdd
19    SSLEEP   220  204 spate   -ksh
20    SONPROC  333  220 spate   ./mps
```

Since there was no activity on the system on which the process was run only the mps process (slot 20) was either running or ready to run. An exercise for readers would be to modify the program to display further fields and run in an environment with greater system activity.

7.3 System call handling

The system call interface is the mechanism by which user processes request services from the UNIX kernel either directly through system calls or indirectly via library calls.

This section describes the steps taken when invoking a system call, how access to the kernel is achieved, the steps taken by the kernel to determine which *system call handler* to call to process the system call and how data and results are transferred across the boundary between user mode and kernel mode.

This section also demonstrates system call handling by using a simple user program which invokes the open(S) system call as an example, together with adb(CP) and crash(ADM) to demonstrate the transition between user mode and kernel mode.

7.3.1 User/kernel address spaces

As explained in chapter 6, a user process and the kernel share the same virtual address space. The user address space consists of the process's text, data, stack and bss as well as any shared libraries, shared memory segments and file mappings created with the mmap(S) system call.

The kernel address space contains data applicable to all user processes, for example proc structures and open file tables. It also contains CPU specific structures such as the TSS, LDT and GDT. The kernel address space must therefore be protected from each user process in order to secure these vital resources.

Since access to kernel protected resources is required by user processes, for example to open a file, there must exist a mechanism by which control of execution can be passed from user mode to kernel mode. This mechanism is referred to as the system call interface. Figure 7.5 shows the two mechanisms by which a user process will access system calls.

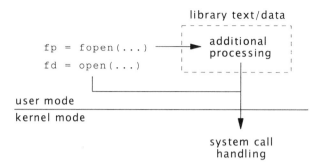

Figure 7.5   Accessing the kernel directly or through additional library code

- *System calls* – Calls such as `open(S)` and `read(S)` are system calls. They provide the mechanism for the transition from user mode to kernel mode in a controlled manner which allows the kernel to access the system call arguments passed and perform the requested function.

- *Library calls* – A library call is often a wrapper around a system call which presents the user program with a different interface and set of results from a system call. For example, the `fopen(S)` library call invokes the `open(S)` system call and returns a file pointer corresponding to the file descriptor returned from `open(S)`.

To the C programmer there is no difference in programming to either interface, both of which offer standard C language function calls. Section (S) of the SCO OpenServer *Programmer's Reference Manual* (1995) lists all library functions and system calls.

7.3.2 Protected mode transition

In order to demonstrate how the Intel protection mechanism is used by SCO UNIX to provide system calls, the following user program will be analysed which invokes the `open(S)` system call:

```
#include <fcntl.h>

int fd ;
main()
{
    fd = open("/etc/motd", O_RDONLY) ;
}
```

The program should be compiled as follows:

```
cc -O -o sys_open sys_open.c
```

The -o (optimise) flag is used to reduce the number of instructions generated. As an exercise, recompile without the -o flag and observe the effects on the following examples.

For each system call there is a small library stub contained within the standard C library which provides the necessary instructions to set up arguments for the system call on the user's stack and then enter the kernel. Using adb to analyse the executable image, it is possible to:

- Single-step the program instruction by instruction to show how the arguments to the system call are set up on the user's stack.

- Disassemble the instructions which allow control to pass from user mode to kernel mode and to see how the result and error values are set up on return from the kernel.

Within adb, information about the program's text and data segment can be displayed with the $m command as follows:

```
*  $m

Text Segments        File - 'sys_open'
Seg #   File Pos  Vir Size       Phys Size    Reloc Base
0x17    0x0       0x12b0         0x12b0       0x0

Data Segments        File - 'sys_open'
Seg #   File Pos  Vir Size       Phys Size    Reloc Base
0x1f    0x1000    0x1134         0xf20        0x400000
```

There are two segments, one for text and one for data. The text segment is identified by the selector 0x17 while the data segment is identified by the selector 0x1f. For information on the interpretation of these numbers see section 6.3.3.

During the link editing phase of compilation, the small number of instructions needed to perform the transition to kernel mode for all system calls are linked with the program's text. These instructions are often called *system call stubs* since their only purpose is to pass control to the kernel with the appropriate system call arguments and return the result or error code; they perform no other role in system call processing.

Since open() is called directly from main(), disassembly of main() within adb shows the open() system call stub being called:

```
1   *  main?i
2   main:          push    ebp            # Establish the stack frame
3   main+0x1:      mov     ebp,esp        # for the main() function
4   main+0x3:      push    0x0            # The oflag argument of open
5   main+0x5:      push    0x4002c0       # The address of the pathname
6   main+0xa:      call    near open      # Call the syscall stub
7   main+0xf:      add     esp,0x8        # Reset stack pointer
8   main+0x12:     mov     fd,eax         # Store the result from open
9   main+0x17:     mov     esp,ebp        # Reset previous stack ptr
```

```
10   main+0x19:      pop     ebp        # Reset previous stack frame
11   main+0x1a:      ret                # Return from main()
12   * 1f:0x4002c0/s
13   /etc/motd
14   * fd=X
15   0x401a54
```

Lines 2 to 3 establish a stack frame for main() by saving the old ebp (base pointer) register and assigning to ebp the current stack pointer esp.

Lines 4 to 5 push the arguments to open(S) onto the stack which are the open flag 0x0 (O_RDONLY) and the address 1f:0x4002c0 which points to the string "/etc/motd". The filename is displayed on lines 12 to 13. Note that the arguments are pushed onto the stack in reverse order.

Line 6 calls the open() function (assembler stub). The result of the open() call and therefore the result of the system call is returned in the eax register which is assigned to fd. The address of fd can be obtained as shown on lines 14 to 15. Finally, on lines 9 to 10, the old stack frame is restored before returning from the main() function on line 11.

The open() function is responsible for copying the system call number into the eax register and executing a call instruction with the address 0x7:0x0.

The selector (0x7) part of the address references an entry in the LDT which contains a *gate descriptor*. This allows the protected mode transfer into kernel mode. Using the description of selectors in section 6.3.2, the selector can be broken down as shown in Table 7.2.

Table 7.2   Call gate selector used for system calls

INDEX	TI	CPL
0000000000000	1	11

For call gate selectors, the offset component of the address, i.e. 0x0, is not used. The Current Privilege Level (CPL) is equal to 11 (3) representing protection ring 3 (user mode), which confirms that the user process is currently running at the expected privilege level.

The Table Indicator (TI) is equal to 1 indicating that the LDT should be used to locate the required descriptor. The descriptor referenced is the first entry in the table as specified by the index of 0.

The crash(ADM) command can be used to display the LDT for this process. First, however, the process must be currently running. crash(ADM) can therefore be run on one virtual console while the process can be started on another virtual console with a breakpoint set on return from open(). Within adb(CP) this is achieved as follows:

```
1   * main+0xf:br
2   * :r
3   sys_open: running
4   breakpoint     main+0xf:    mov     fd,eax
5   * <eax=x
6              0x3
```

Line 1 sets the breakpoint. This address is obtained from disassembly of main() (line 7 in the previous example). The process is set to start running on line 2 until it hits the breakpoint and returns to adb on line 4. Since this is the first instruction after return to main() from open(), the result of the open() call can be found in the eax register as shown on lines 5 to 6.

Switching to another virtual console at this point, the sys_open process can be located from within crash(ADM) using the proc as follows:

```
> proc ! grep sys_open

  32 t  1605  1595  1595  0  51  0  sys_open  load  trc
```

All processes are searched for the string sys_open. On this run of the program, the process is located in process table slot 32. Still within crash, the LDT for the process is displayed as follows:

```
> ldt 32
iAPX386 LDT for process 32
SLOT BASE/SEL LIM/OFF  TYPE      DPL ACCESSBITS
   0       0158 f00fdc7c CGATE386  3 CNT=1
   1       0158 f00102e8 CGATE386  3 CNT=1
   2 00000000 bffff000 XSEG       3 ACCS'D R&X DFLT G4096
   3 00000000 ffc0f000 DSEG       3 ACCS'D R&W BIG  G4096
   4 00000000 ffc0f000 DSEG       3 R&W BIG    G4096
   5 e0000e84 0000017c DSEG       3 R&W BIG
   7       0158 f0010394 CGATE386  3 CNT=1
```

The selector (0x7) specifies the 0th entry in the table for which crash unbundles the descriptor before printing out the gate address, f00fdc7c, shown under the LIM/OFF field. The gate address, f00fdc7c, is the address at which the kernel is entered after passing through the call gate. The kernel routine sys_call(), located at this address, is invoked for every system call. The crash command dis can be used to disassemble this address.

Figure 7.6 summarises the steps taken when transferring from user mode to kernel mode to execute a system call.

After copying the arguments required by open(S) onto the user stack, the system call number is placed in eax and a call is made through a call gate. The next instruction to be executed after the call instruction in open() is the first instruction in the kernel's sys_call() function.

7.3.3 Confirming the return value

The result returned from open() is the file descriptor 0x3. Using crash(ADM), the file descriptor can be checked to verify that it does indeed reference the file /etc/motd.

Each file descriptor is an index into an array of file table pointers held in the process's u_area. For further details see section 8.2.1.

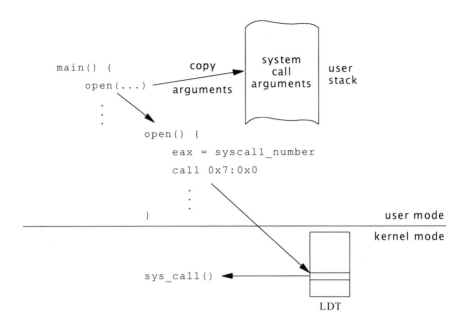

Figure 7.6   Transferring from user mode to kernel mode

Continuing the previous `crash` session where the `sys_open` process resides in process slot 32, the u_area, and therefore the list of open files for the process, can be displayed as follows:

```
> user 32
<other u_area fields not shown>
OPEN FILES AND POFILE FLAGS:
    [ 0]: F#16   r   [ 1]: F#16   w   [ 2]: F#16   w
    [ 3]: F#8    r
<other u_area fields not shown>
```

The process in this example has four open files, the first three specifying file table slot 16. The fourth, highlighted entry is the file descriptor (3) returned from `open(S)`. This references file table slot 8.

The file table entry, which is described in detail in section 8.3, can be displayed from within `crash` as follows. The `I/FL` field displayed is an index into the inode table for slot 139.

```
> file 8
FILE TABLE SIZE = 341
SLOT   RCNT    I/FL       OFFSET   FLAGS
   8      1 I# 139            0 read
```

Displaying the inode entry from within `crash`, the fields of interest are MAJ/MIN which specifies the device on which the file resides and INUMB which is the file's inode number:

```
> inode 139
INODE TABLE SIZE = 485
SLOT MAJ/MIN FS INUMB RCNT LINK UID GID SIZE    MODE   ...
 139   1,42   4  4353    1     1    0   3  111 f---644  ...
```

Finally, using the ncheck(ADM) utility, both device and file can be confirmed:

```
# ncheck -i 4353
/dev/root:
4353 /etc/motd
# ls -l /dev/root
br--r-----  1 root  backup  1,42 Aug 12 15:48 /dev/root
```

The ncheck(ADM) utility is used to locate the file corresponding to the inode number displayed by crash. The file resides in the root filesystem (/dev/root) as expected.

7.3.4 The system call table

Since the same call gate is used to enter the kernel for all system calls, the kernel must be able to determine which system call is requested and how many parameters are expected.

The kernel maintains a table, sysent[], which holds information about each of the system calls. Each element in the table is defined in <sys/systm.h> and contains the fields shown in Table 7.3.

Table 7.3   The format of each entry in sysent[]

sysent structure field	Description
char sy_narg	The number of 32 bit arguments required.
char sy_setjmp	The sy_setjmp field indicates whether the system call is interruptible; for example, a user may wish to hit control-C if the call does not return when expected.
char sy_mthread	The sy_mthread fields indicates whether the system call can be executed in parallel by more than one processor.
int (*sy_call)()	The sy_call field is a pointer to a kernel function which will be called to process the system call request.

Using the nlist(S) library function and /dev/kmem, the following program is used to display each entry in the sysent[] table.

The data types used in the program are:

```
1   #include <fcntl.h>
2   #include <nlist.h>
3
4   typedef struct Ssysent {
5           char    sy_narg ;
6           char    sy_setjmp ;
7           char    sy_mthread ;
8           int     (*sy_call)() ;
9   } Ssysent ;
10
11  int Ssize = sizeof(struct Ssysent) ;
```

```
12
13    extern char *addr_to_symbol() ;
14
15    struct nlist nl[] = {
16         { "sysent", 0 },
17         { "nsysent", 0 },
18         { 0 },
19    } ;
20
21    #define SYSENT  nl[0]
22    #define NSYSENT nl[1]
23    #define Bsize (Ssize * n_ent)
```

Since the sysent[] table is declared as extern in <sys/systm.h>, an equivalent
structure is defined on lines 4 to 9 to use within the program. Note that this is not usual
practice. Most structures are generally defined in full within their respective header files.

The nlist[] array on lines 15 to 19 indicates which symbol addresses are required
when calling nlist(S). The value of Bsize on line 23 is used later in the program to
specify the size of the buffer needed to read the entire sysent[] table.

The main body of the program is as follows:

```
24    main()
25    {
26         int     x, fd, s_ent, n_ent ;
27         char    *sym, *buf ;
28         struct  Ssysent *s ;
29
30         nlist("/unix", nl) ;
31
32         fd = open("/dev/kmem", O_RDONLY) ;
33
34         lseek(fd, NSYSENT.n_value, SEEK_SET) ;
35         read(fd, &n_ent, sizeof(n_ent)) ;
```

The nlist(S) library function is called on line 30 to retrieve the symbol address for the
entries specified in the nl[] array. The lseek(S) system call is invoked on line 34 to
seek within /dev/kmem to the address of nsysent which is then read on line 35. Note
that the caller must have read access to both /dev/kmem and /unix.

The remainder of the program is:

```
36         printf("\nSCO UNIX System Call Table\n") ;
37         printf("nsysent[%x] entries[%x] sysent[%x]\n\n",
38                 NSYSENT.n_value, n_ent, SYSENT.n_value) ;
39
40         buf = (char *)malloc(Bsize) ;
41
42         lseek(fd, SYSENT.n_value, SEEK_SET) ;
43         read(fd, buf, Bsize) ;
44
45         printf("entry    call              args") ;
46         printf("  mp-safe  intr\n") ;
47         for (x = 0 ; x < n_ent ; x++) {
48             s = (struct Ssysent *)(buf + (x*Ssize)) ;
49             sym = (char *)addr_to_sym(s->sy_call) ;
50             printf(" %3d    %-12s  %d      %d      %d\n",
```

```
51                             x, sym, s->sy_narg, s->sy_mthread,
52                             s->sy_setjmp)  ;
53      }
54  }
```

Lines 36 to 53 print the heading and data read through the `nlist(S)` call as shown. A buffer is allocated using `malloc(S)` on line 40 in order to read the entire `sysent[]` table on lines 42 to 43.

Lines 47 to 53 loop through each entry in the buffer. Since the `sy_call` entry is the address of a kernel function, a function `addr_to_sym()`, which is based on the examples demonstrated in chapter 5, is used to locate the symbol table in `/unix` to match the address to the required symbol.

The output of the program showing the first 12 entries in the `sysent[]` table is as follows:

```
SCO UNIX System Call Table (sysent)
nsysent[f012aa00] entries[c1] sysent[f012a3f8]

entry   call        args  mp-safe  intr
  0     nosys         0      1       1
  1     rexit         1      1       1
  2     fork          0      1       1
  3     read          3      1       0
  4     write         3      1       0
  5     open          3      1       0
  6     close         1      1       0
  7     wait          3      1       0
  8     creat         2      1       0
  9     link          2      1       1
 10     unlink        1      1       1
 11     exec          2      1       1
 12     chdir         1      1       1
<the output continues up to system call 192(c1)>
```

7.3.5 Kernel handling of system calls

There is little work performed by the `sys_call()` function other than to save the current registers on the kernel stack in a well-defined order and call the `systrap()` function.

Throughout processing of `systrap()` the following fields of the u_area are used:

u_syscall   The `eax` register is used to pass the system call number from user to kernel mode. The `u_syscall` field is set to the system call number passed through `eax`.

u_arg   The arguments to the system call are on the user's stack when the transition to kernel mode is made. These arguments are copied into the u_area field `u_arg` prior to execution of the system call handler.

u_ap   The `u_ap` field is set to point to the `u_arg` array and is used by each system call handler to construct a pointer to a structure containing the arguments passed.

u_ar0   Points to the system stack which is contained within the u_area. The
               user registers are copied here so that once the system call is
               completed, program execution can be restarted at the instruction
               immediately after the call through the call gate.

u_r   The u_r field is used by the system call handlers to return values
               which will be copied out to user mode prior to returning from the
               system call. This structure is a union for which the two sub-fields,
               r_val1 and r_val2, are mainly used.

u_error   In the case of an error occurring during system call processing, the
               u_error field is used to record the error value which is passed back
               from kernel to user mode. If an error occurs, the carry flag of the
               eflags register is set. On return from the system call, if the carry flag
               is set, errno is set to the returned value and the eax register is set to
               –1.

u_qsav   If the sy_setjmp field of the sysent[] table entry is not set for the
               system call in operation, the system call is interruptible. For example,
               read(S) and write(S) can suspend indefinitely (for example when
               reading from an empty pipe), therefore users may wish to interrupt the
               process by sending it a signal.
                   The kernel invokes a setjmp() call, saving the stack environment
               in u.u_qsav to be used if an interrupt to the normal flow of the
               system call occurs, for which a longjmpval() will be invoked. See
               section 7.9.3 for details on how the kernel handles the case where a
               process wakes up from a sleep() call due to a signal.

The tasks performed by systrap() are as follows:

- Set the u_error field to zero to ensure that no previous error value will be used.

- Set the u_ar0 field to point to the registers on the kernel stack.

- The system call number held in the eax register is copied to u_syscall.

- A check is made on the validity of the system call number by ensuring that it falls
  within the bounds of the sysent[] table. If the system call requested is not
  known, the u_error field is set to ENOSYS and psignal() is called to post a
  SIGSYS signal to the process.

- The arguments saved on the user stack are copied into the u_arg[] array which
  is referenced by the u_ap field.

- Using the system call number stored in u_syscall the system call handler is
  located in the sysent[] array. The system call handler is then called which can
  locate any required arguments via the u_ap field.

- After the handler has returned, a check is made to see if the system call should be restarted if it was interrupted by a signal. If not, the values returned in the u_rval1 and u_rval2 fields are stored on the stack together with the contents of u_error. This allows the system call stub in user mode to ensure that the correct error is returned from the system call.

- After a return is made from systrap(), the registers are restored by sys_call() from the u_area and a return is made to the system call stub in user mode, emerging at the instruction following the call made through the call gate.

Flow of control through the kernel for system call handling is summarised in Figure 7.7.

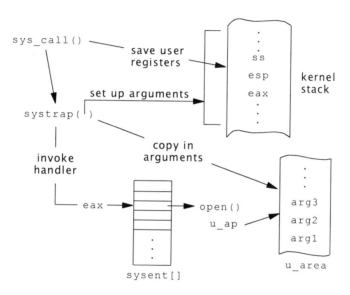

Figure 7.7   Invoking the system call handler

For system calls that can be restarted refer to section 7.4.6. Section 7.6 shows how the arguments are passed to the execve() system call on the kernel stack.

7.3.6 Xenix system calls

Xenix system calls are handled slightly differently from UNIX system calls in that there is only one entry in sysent[], cxenix() found in entry number 40. The Xenix specific system calls are located in the cxentry[] array.

The low 8 bits of the eax register value set up by the Xenix system call stubs contain the appropriate entry in the cxentry[] table. Shifting the value in eax by 8 bits to the right gives the appropriate entry.

Using the program demonstrated earlier to display the `sysent[]` table, the equivalent Xenix system call table can be displayed by:

- Searching for the `cxentry[]` table in place of `sysent[]`.

- Searching for the `ncxentry` variable in place of `nsysent` to obtain the size of the `cxenix[]` table.

Making the appropriate modifications and running the program gives the list of Xenix system calls. The first 12 entries are displayed:

```
SCO UNIX System Call Table (cxentry)
ncxentry = f012ac8c (entries = 3e), cxentry = f012aa9c

entry    call       args   mp-safe   intr
   0     nosys       0        1        1
   1     locking     3        1        0
   2     creatsem    2        0        0
   3     opensem     1        0        0
   4     sigsem      1        0        0
   5     waitsem     1        0        0
   6     nbwaitsem   1        0        0
   7     rdchk       1        1        0
   8     nosys       0        1        1
   9     nosys       0        1        1
  10     chsize      2        1        0
  11     ftime       1        1        0
  12     nap         1        1        0
```

7.4 Signal handling

Chapter 2 introduced the signal handling functions available in SCO UNIX from the programmer's perspective. This section concentrates on the main signal handling functions, how they alter the signal disposition, modify the process signal mask (block signals) and how the kernel manages per process signal information internally.

As section 2.6 explained, the UNIX signal architecture has evolved considerably over its history but still encompasses the original interfaces and semantics.

7.4.1 Signal based system calls

Although there are numerous signal management functions, there are only four signal system call entry points into the kernel. The mapping between each library call and its corresponding system call is shown in Figure 7.8.

The `ssig()` kernel function handles all six callers by analysing the arguments passed on the user's stack. The `cxenix()` kernel function merely invokes one of five other functions corresponding to `siginterrupt(S)`, `sigaction(S)` and so on. There are also kernel functions underpinning `sigsendset(S)` and `sigstack(S)`, each of which deals with `sigsend(S)` and `sigstack(S)`, respectively.

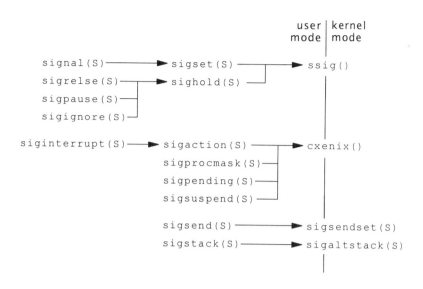

Figure 7.8   Mapping signal calls to system calls

7.4.2 Basic signal management

Before trying to explain the subtle differences in how the kernel deals with the different semantics of the varying signal models, the next few sections and toolkits describe the effect that the `signal(S)` and `sigset(S)` signal functions have on kernel structures and how the kernel deals with any signals that arrive.

Both `signal(S)` and `sigset(S)` alter the disposition of the specified signal. With `signal(S)`, the disposition of the signal can be set to `SIG_IGN` (ignore the signal), `SIG_DFL` (take the default action) or the address of a user defined signal handler to be invoked on receipt of the signal. The `sigset(S)` function has the same interface but also allows the caller to set the disposition to `SIG_HOLD`. The effect of specifying `SIG_HOLD` is described later.

The disposition of process signals is held in the `u_signal[]` array in the u_area. The disposition specified by `signal(S)` and `sigset(S)` is stored in the appropriate element of `u_signal[]`. For example, setting the disposition of `SIGUSR1` to `SIG_IGN` would involve assigning the constant `SIG_IGN` to `u_signal[SIGUSR - 1]`. Each signal's entry in the array is one less than its actual value. For example, `SIGABRT` has a signal number of 1 and its disposition is stored in `u_signal[0]`.

If a signal handler is installed using `signal(S)`, the disposition is set to `SIG_DFL` prior to calling the handler if the specified signal is delivered. If `SIG_HOLD` is specified to `sigset(S)`, the current disposition is unchanged and the signal is added to the process's signal mask. The signal mask is held in the `p_hold` field of the `proc` structure and is declared as type `sigset_t`. Note that for manipulating signal sets (type `sigset_t`), the kernel also uses the macros defined in `<sys/signal.h>`:

```
sigemptyset(sigset_t *set)
sigismember(sigset_t *set, int signo)
sigaddset(sigset_t *set, int signo)
sigdelset sigset_t *set, int signo)
sigfillset(sigset_t *set)
```

There exists a kernel signal set for supporting the difference between `signal(S)` and `sigset(S)`. When `sigset(S)` is invoked, the signal is added to the `p_chold` field of the `proc` structure. This is used prior to invoking the handler to allow the kernel to differentiate between the two different semantics.

Toolkit 7.2   Accessing per process signal dispositions

This example provides the basis for all signal based toolkits in this chapter. It centres around the `read_ks()` function defined on line 51. This takes a process ID and returns the u_area and `proc` structure associated with the process ID in the structure defined by `kern_struct` which is declared on lines 45 to 48.

The `read_ks()` function uses the `table` driver and successively reads process table entries. For each valid entry read, the process ID passed to `read_ks()` is checked against the `p_pid` field (line 60). If a match is found, `sysi86(S)` is invoked on line 61 to read the u_area.

An array of strings (`signm`) is defined on lines 9 to 41 which allows the signal's symbolic name to be displayed using its signal number. As with `u_signal[]`, the signal is stored such that its position in the array is one less than its signal number. This array of symbolic signals will be used throughout the remainder of the chapter.

```
 1 #include <sys/proc.h>
 1 #include <sys/proc.h>
 2 #include <sys/user.h>
 3 #include <sys/sysi86.h>
 4 #include <sys/signal.h>
 5 #include <fcntl.h>
 6 #include <errno.h>
 7 #include <pwd.h>
 8
 9 char *signm[] = {
10     "SIGHUP",      /* hangup */
11     "SIGINT",      /* interrupt (DEL key - see stty intr) */
12     "SIGQUIT",     /* quit (^\) */
13     "SIGILL",      /* illegal instruction */
14     "SIGTRAP",     /* trace trap */
15     "SIGABRT",     /* used by abort */
16     "SIGEMT",      /* EMT instruction */
17     "SIGFPE",      /* floating point exception */
18     "SIGKILL",     /* kill (cannot be caught or ignored) */
19     "SIGBUS",      /* bus error */
20     "SIGSEGV",     /* segmentation violation */
21     "SIGSYS",      /* bad argument to system call */
22     "SIGPIPE",     /* write on a pipe with no one to read it */
23     "SIGALRM",     /* alarm clock */
24     "SIGTERM",     /* software termination */
25     "SIGUSR1",     /* user defined signal 1 */
```

```
26          "SIGUSR2",     /* user defined signal 2 */
27          "SIGCHLD",     /* death of a child */
28          "SIGPWR",      /* power-fail */
29          "SIGWINCH",    /* window change */
30          "NOT_USED",
31          "SIGPOLL",     /* pollable event */
32          "SIGSTOP",     /* sendable stop signal not from tty */
33          "SIGTSTP",     /* stop signal from tty */
34          "SIGCONT",     /* continue a stopped process */
35          "SIGTTIN",     /* to readers pgrp upon background tty read */
36          "SIGTTOU",     /* like TTIN but for output */
37          "SIGVTALRM",   /* virtual timer alarm */
38          "SIGPROF",     /* profile alarm */
39          "SIGXCPU",     /* CPU time limit exceeded */
40          "SIGXFSZ"      /* File size limit exceeded */
41 } ;
42
43 /* SIGIOT covered by SIGABRT, SIGCLD covered by SIGCHLD */
44
45 struct kern_struct {
46      struct user k_user ;
47      struct proc k_proc ;
48 } ;
49
50 int
51 read_ks(pid_t pid, struct kern_struct *ks)
52 {
53      int i, fd ;
54
55      fd = open("/dev/table/proc", O_RDONLY) ;
56      if (fd < 0)
57          return(0) ;
58
59      while (read(fd, (char *)&ks->k_proc, sizeof(struct proc)) > 0)
60          if ((ks->k_proc.p_stat != 0) && (ks->k_proc.p_pid == pid)) {
61              sysi86(RDUBLK, ks->k_proc.p_pid, &ks->k_user,
62                                              sizeof(struct user)) ;
63              return(1) ;
64          }
65      return(0) ;
66 }
67
68 main()
69 {
70      int i ;
71      struct kern_struct ks ;
72
73      if (!read_ks(getpid(), &ks))
74          exit(-1) ;
75
76      for (i=0 ; i<MAXSIG-1 ; i++) {
77          printf("u_signal[%2d] = ", i) ;
78          if (ks.k_user.u_signal[i] == SIG_IGN)
79              printf("SIG_IGN  ") ;
80          else if (ks.k_user.u_signal[i] == SIG_DFL)
81              printf("SIG_DFL  ") ;
82          else
83              printf("0x%7-x", ks.k_user.u_signal[i]) ;
84          printf("signo[%2d] %s\n", i+1, signm[i]) ;
85      }
86 }
```

The purpose of `main()` is to print the value of each signal disposition when the process is first created. The only two signals for which the kernel does not specify the default action are SIGUSR1 and SIGUSR2; the kernel explicitly ignores them if posted.

Although `fork()` and `exec()` will be described later in the chapter it is worth noting here that a child process will inherit all signal dispositions from its parent across fork(S). For exec(S) the process will inherit all dispositions which are set to SIG_DFL, SIG_IGN and SIG_HOLD dispositions. If a signal handler has been installed, the disposition will be set to SIG_DFL since the image of the process will change and the handler will no longer be present in the process's address space.

The output of the above program is as follows:

```
$ a.out
u_signal[ 0] = SIG_DFL  signo[ 1] SIGHUP
u_signal[ 1] = SIG_DFL  signo[ 2] SIGINT
u_signal[ 2] = SIG_DFL  signo[ 3] SIGQUIT
u_signal[ 3] = SIG_DFL  signo[ 4] SIGILL
u_signal[ 4] = SIG_DFL  signo[ 5] SIGTRAP
u_signal[ 5] = SIG_DFL  signo[ 6] SIGABRT
u_signal[ 6] = SIG_DFL  signo[ 7] SIGEMT
u_signal[ 7] = SIG_DFL  signo[ 8] SIGFPE
u_signal[ 8] = SIG_DFL  signo[ 9] SIGKILL
u_signal[ 9] = SIG_DFL  signo[10] SIGBUS
u_signal[10] = SIG_DFL  signo[11] SIGSEGV
u_signal[11] = SIG_DFL  signo[12] SIGSYS
u_signal[12] = SIG_DFL  signo[13] SIGPIPE
u_signal[13] = SIG_DFL  signo[14] SIGALRM
u_signal[14] = SIG_DFL  signo[15] SIGTERM
u_signal[15] = SIG_IGN  signo[16] SIGUSR1
u_signal[16] = SIG_IGN  signo[17] SIGUSR2
u_signal[17] = SIG_DFL  signo[18] SIGCHLD
u_signal[18] = SIG_DFL  signo[19] SIGPWR
u_signal[19] = SIG_DFL  signo[20] SIGWINCH
u_signal[20] = SIG_DFL  signo[21] NOT_USED
u_signal[21] = SIG_DFL  signo[22] SIGPOLL
u_signal[22] = SIG_DFL  signo[23] SIGSTOP
u_signal[23] = SIG_DFL  signo[24] SIGTSTP
u_signal[24] = SIG_DFL  signo[25] SIGCONT
u_signal[25] = SIG_DFL  signo[26] SIGTTIN
u_signal[26] = SIG_DFL  signo[27] SIGTTOU
u_signal[27] = SIG_DFL  signo[28] SIGVTALRM
u_signal[28] = SIG_DFL  signo[29] SIGPROF
u_signal[29] = SIG_DFL  signo[30] SIGXCPU
u_signal[30] = SIG_DFL  signo[31] SIGXFSZ
```

7.4.3 Signal set management

POSIX.1 introduced the notion of signal sets represented by the `sigset_t` structure and introduced the signal set operations described above.

Since SCO UNIX defines a `sigset_t` as a long int, the number of signals that can be supported by the operating system is limited to the number of bits in a long which on the Intel 386 to P6 range of processors is 32 bits.

If a signal is a member of a signal set then the bit position corresponding to the signal is set to 1. See `<sys/signal.h>` to see how the bit manipulations are performed by the signal set functions.

Toolkit 7.3   Analysing signal sets

This toolkit shows the use of the signal set manipulation operations in order to display which signals the kernel holds in its structures based on the type `sigset_t`. The first example shows the function `prsigset()` (lines 5 to 12) which takes a pointer to a `sigset_t` and prints out all signals which are members. Signal members can be found by invoking the `sigismember(S)` function. The signal name is then displayed using the `signm[]` array of signal names introduced in Toolkit 7.2.

```
 1 #include <sys/signal.h>
 2
 3 extern char *signm[] ;
 4
 5 prsigset(sigset_t *st)
 6 {
 7     int i ;
 8
 9     for (i=1 ; i < MAXSIG ; i++)
10         if (sigismember(st, i))
11             printf(" %s\n", signm[i-1]) ;
12 }
13
14 main()
15 {
16     sigset_t t ;
17
18     sigemptyset(&t) ;
19     sigaddset(&t, SIGHUP) ;
20     sigaddset(&t, SIGINT) ;
21     sigaddset(&t, SIGUSR1) ;
22
23     prsigset(&t) ;
24 }
```

The main body of the program calls `sigemptyset(S)` to ensure that the signal set is empty and then invokes `sigaddset(S)` three times to add the signals SIGHUP, SIGINT and SIGUSR1. The output of the program is as follows:

```
$ a.out
  SIGHUP
  SIGINT
  SIGUSR1
```

The next example demonstrates the differences in semantics between the `signal(S)` and `sigset(S)` system calls by showing their effect on the kernel structures described earlier. In this example, the `prsignaldisp()` function (lines 13 to 25) displays the signal disposition for a specified signal. The function takes a pointer to a `kern_struct` structure and a signal number. The contents of `kern_struct` must have been filled with a call to `read_ks()`. The function displays the contents of the `u_signal[]` field for the specified signal and the signal's symbolic name.

```
 1 #include <sys/signal.h>
 2 #include "sigstruct.h"
 3 #include "pexit.h"
```

```
 4
 5 extern char *signm[] ;
 6
 7 int
 8 sighdlr(int signo)
 9 {
10     printf("--Caught %s\n", signm[signo - 1]) ;
11 }
12
13 prsignaldisp(struct kern_struct *ks, int signo)
14 {
15     printf("u_signal[%2d] = ", signo-1) ;
16
17     if (ks->k_user.u_signal[signo - 1] == SIG_IGN)
18         printf("SIG_IGN  ") ;
19     else if (ks->k_user.u_signal[signo - 1] == SIG_DFL)
20         printf("SIG_DFL  ") ;
21     else
22         printf("0x%7-x", ks->k_user.u_signal[signo-1]) ;
23
24     printf("signo[%2d] %s\n", signo, signm[signo - 1]) ;
25 }
26
27 main()
28 {
29     struct kern_struct ks ;
30
31     sigset(SIGINT, sighdlr) ;
32
33     signal(SIGUSR1, sighdlr) ;
34     sighold(SIGUSR1) ;
35     printf("Address of sighdlr() = 0x%x\n",sighdlr) ;
36
37     kill(getpid(), SIGUSR1) ;
38
39     if (!read_ks(getpid(), &ks))
40         pexit("read_ks") ;
41
42     prsignaldisp(&ks, SIGINT) ;
43     prsignaldisp(&ks, SIGUSR1) ;
44
45     printf("signal set, p_hold\n") ;
46     prsigset(&ks.k_proc.p_hold) ;
47
48     printf("signal set, p_chold\n") ;
49     prsigset(&ks.k_proc.p_chold) ;
50
51     printf("\n") ;
52     pause() ;
53
54     sigrelse(SIGUSR1) ;
55
56     printf("\n") ;
57     if (!read_ks(getpid(), &ks))
58         pexit("read_ks") ;
59
60     prsignaldisp(&ks, SIGINT) ;
61     prsignaldisp(&ks, SIGUSR1) ;
62
63     printf("signal set, p_hold\n") ;
64     prsigset(&ks.k_proc.p_hold) ;
65
66     printf("signal set, p_chold\n") ;
```

```
67      prsigset(&ks.k_proc.p_chold) ;
68 }
```

In the main body of the program the following actions are taken. The output displayed following this description is annotated so that the output shown can be traced to these actions:

line 31	The disposition for SIGINT is set to the handler sighdlr() using sigset(S). This ensures that when the handler is called the disposition is set to SIG_HOLD and when the handler returns the disposition is set back to sighdlr().
lines 33 to 35	The disposition for SIGUSR1 is set by calling signal(S). Before the handler is called the disposition will be reset back to SIG_DFL. The sighold(S) function is then called to add the signal to the signal mask, the list of signals which are blocked.
	The address of the signal handler is then printed so that it can be checked against the signal disposition displayed by a call to prsignaldisp().
line 37	The process then invokes the kill(S) system call to send the SIGUSR1 signal to itself. Since the signal is blocked, the signal should be held until explicitly released.
lines 39 to 43	The read_ks() function is then invoked to read the user and proc structures for calling process. The signal disposition of both SIGINT and SIGUSR1 are then displayed.
lines 45 to 49	The prsigset() function is called to display the set of signals which have been added to p_hold, the signal mask, and p_chold, the list of signals for which the disposition has been set by sigset(S).
line 52	The pause(S) system call is then invoked which will put the process to sleep until a signal is posted. At this stage, the program is waiting for the user to generate SIGINT by hitting the interrupt key, for example Delete or ^C.
line 54	The sigrelse(S) system call is then invoked to unblock SIGUSR1 for which the signal was posted on line 37. The signal handler should now be called for SIGUSR1.
lines 60 to 67	The actions taken on lines 39 to 49 are repeated to display the signal disposition for SIGINT and SIGUSR1 and to display which signals are members of the p_hold and p_chold signal sets.

```
# a.out
Address of sighdlr() = 0x130                            # line 35
u_signal[ 1] = 0x130      signo[ 2] SIGINT              # line 42
u_signal[15] = 0x130      signo[16] SIGUSR1             # line 43
signal set, p_hold                                     # lines 45 to 46
  SIGUSR1
```

```
signal set, p_chold                          # lines 48 to 49
  SIGINT

--Caught SIGINT                              # Delete pressed
--Caught SIGUSR1                             # SIGUSR1 unblocked

u_signal[ 1] = 0x130     signo[ 2] SIGINT    # line 60
u_signal[15] = SIG_DFL   signo[16] SIGUSR1   # line 61
signal set, p_hold                           # lines 63 to 64
signal set, p_chold                          # lines 66 to 67
  SIGINT
```

7.4.4 Posting signals

Signals are sent from one process to another using the `kill(S)` system call or by the kernel as the result of one of a number of different events. For example, signals can be generated by the console driver when users hit various keys or key sequences, when child processes terminate, or when a process executes an illegal instruction or attempts to access an invalid memory address.

This section looks at the explicit case when the `kill(S)` system call is invoked. Later sections discuss some of the other places where signals are generated.

The `kill(S)` system call is underpinned by the `kill()` kernel function. The tasks performed by `kill()` are as follows:

- A check is made to ensure that the specified signal number is valid.
- For each `proc` structure in the `proc[]` table, `kill()` performs the following:
  - ⇨ Check the process to see if it is a target for posting the signal to, for example if the `p_pid` field matches the `pid` argument passed to `kill(S)` or the `pid` argument is 0 and the process is a member of the same process group as the caller.
  - ⇨ If a match is found, a `sigqueue_t` structure is allocated and filled with the signal number and the caller's process ID and session ID. The `psignalinfo()` function is then called to post the signal.

The majority of the work performed by `kill()` is in checking the relationship between the process ID specified to `kill(S)` and the individual `proc` structures. For example, consider the prototype for `kill(S)`:

```
#include <sys/types.h>
#include <signal.h>

int kill(pid_t pid, int signo) ;
```

The target process or group of processes differs depending on the value of `pid`. The possible values that `pid` can take and their individual semantics are shown in Table 7.4.

Table 7.4   Posting a signal with `kill(S)`

pid value	Semantics
`pid > 0`	Send the signal to the process whose process ID is equal to `pid`.
`pid = 0`	The signal is sent to all processes (except `sched` and `init`) whose process group ID is equal to `pid`.
`pid = -1`	If the effective user ID of the calling process is 0 (superuser), the signal is sent to all processes except `sched` and `init`. If the effective user ID is not 0, the signal is sent to all processes (except `sched` and `init`) whose real user ID is equal to the effective user ID of the caller.
`pid < -1`	The signal is posted to all processes whose process group ID is equal to the absolute value of `pid`.

Once the process has been confirmed as a target process and the various permission checks have been performed, `kill()` calls the `psignalinfo()` function to post the signal and the appropriate `sigqueue_t` structure. The `sigqueue_t` structure contains two fields declared as follows:

```
struct sigqueue *sq_next ;
struct ksiginfo  sq_info ;
```

The `ksiginfo` structure is identical to the `siginfo_t` structure declared in the `<sys/siginfo.h>` header file with the exception of some padding added to `siginfo_t` for future growth. The `sq_next` field is used to implement a linked list of `sigqueue_t` structures with the constraint that there is a maximum of one `sigqueue_t` structure per signal type. This list is allocated dynamically and attached to the process's `eproc` structure field `ep_sqp`. This is shown in Figure 7.9.

There is an `eproc` structure per `proc` structure which holds additional per process information. The fields of the `eproc` structure are described throughout the book.

The `psignalinfo()` function performs two main actions, namely to post the signal (adding it to the `proc` structure's `p_sig` field) and to add any supplied `siginfo_t` structure to the linked list of `sigqueue_t` structures accessed from the `ep_sqp` field.

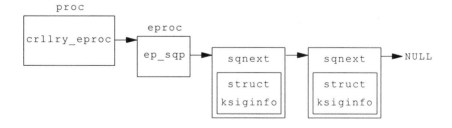

Figure 7.9   `siginfo_t` structures held for posted signals

Toolkit 7.4   Accessing kernel `siginfo_t` structures

In the example that follows, the POSIX signal based functions are used to demonstrate how the signal disposition and signal masks are effected by the POSIX signal based system calls.

This toolkit builds on Toolkit 7.3 but using `sigaction(S)` in place of `signal(S)` and `sigset(S)` to allow retrieval of the two additional arguments to the signal handler, a `siginfo_t` structure and the user context.

The signal handler (lines 10 to 19) is thus extended to include the additional parameters. Line 14 checks to see if the `siginfo_t` `si_code` field <= 0. If so, the user ID and process ID of the process which posted the signal are displayed (lines 15 to 16).

Since the `sigqueue_t` structures which contain the data used to pass the `siginfo_t` structures to the user handler are allocated dynamically by the kernel and attached to the `eproc` structure, the `read_eproc()` function on lines 21 to 34 is introduced to read an `eproc` structure given a specified address. This function simply opens `/dev/kmem`, seeks to the specified address and reads the `eproc` structure located at the address.

```
 1 #include <sys/signal.h>
 2 #include <sys/siginfo.h>
 3 #include <sys/eproc.h>
 4 #include <fcntl.h>
 5 #include "sigstruct.h"
 6 #include "pexit.h"
 7
 8 extern char *signm[] ;
 9
10 void
11 sighdlr(int signo, siginfo_t *si, void *uctxt)
12 {
13     printf("--Caught %s", signm[signo - 1]) ;
14     if (si->si_code <= 0)
15         printf(" - posted by: UID(%d) PID(%d)\n",si->si_uid,
16                                                 si->si_pid) ;
17     else
18         printf("\n") ;
19 }
20
21 int
22 read_eproc(struct eproc *ep, void *address)
23 {
24     int fd = open("/dev/kmem", O_RDONLY) ;
25     if (fd < 0) {
26         close(fd) ;
27         return(0) ;
28     }
29
30     lseek(fd, address, SEEK_SET) ;
31     read(fd, (char *)ep, sizeof(struct eproc)) ;
32     close(fd) ;
33     return(1) ;
34 }
35
36 void
37 prsigq(sigqueue_t *sqp)
38 {
39     sigqueue_t sq ;
```

```
40      int fd = open("/dev/kmem", O_RDONLY) ;
41
42      while (sqp != NULL) {
43          printf("sigqueue_t at address %x\n", sqp) ;
44          lseek(fd, sqp, SEEK_SET) ;
45          read(fd, &sq, sizeof(sigqueue_t)) ;
46          printf("  si_signo = %s\n", signm[sq.sq_info.si_signo-1]) ;
47          if (sq.sq_info.si_code <= 0) {
48              printf("  si_uid = %d\n", sq.sq_info.si_uid) ;
49              printf("  si_pid = %d\n", sq.sq_info.si_pid) ;
50          }
51          sqp = sq.sq_next ;
52      }
53 }
54
55 main()
56 {
57      struct kern_struct ks ;
58      struct sigaction act ;
59      sigset_t set ;
60      struct eproc ep ;
61
62      act.sa_flags = SA_SIGINFO | SA_RESETHAND ;
63      act.sa_sigaction = sighdlr ;
64      sigemptyset(&act.sa_mask) ;
65      sigaction(SIGUSR1, &act, NULL) ;
66
67      sigemptyset(&set) ;
68      sigaddset(&set, SIGUSR1) ;
69      sigprocmask(SIG_SETMASK, &set, (sigset_t *)0) ;
70
71      act.sa_flags = SA_SIGINFO ;
72      act.sa_sigaction = sighdlr ;
73      sigemptyset(&act.sa_mask) ;
74      sigaction(SIGUSR2, &act, NULL) ;
75      printf("Address of sighdlr() = 0x%x\n",sighdlr) ;
76
77      kill(getpid(), SIGUSR1) ;
78
79      if (!read_ks(getpid(), &ks))
80          pexit("read_ks") ;
81
82      if (!read_eproc(&ep, ks.k_proc.crllry_eproc))
83          pexit("eproc") ;
84
85      printf("ep_sqp = %x\n", ep.ep_sqp) ;
86      if (ep.ep_sqp)
87          prsigq(ep.ep_sqp) ;
88
89      prsignaldisp(&ks, SIGUSR2) ;
90      prsignaldisp(&ks, SIGUSR1) ;
91
92      printf("signal set, p_hold\n") ;
93      prsigset(&ks.k_proc.p_hold) ;
94
95      printf("signal set, p_chold\n") ;
96      prsigset(&ks.k_proc.p_chold) ;
97
98      printf("\n") ;
99      kill(getpid(), SIGUSR2) ;
100
101     sigrelse(SIGUSR1) ;
102
```

```
103        printf("\n") ;
104        if (!read_ks(getpid(), &ks))
105            pexit("read_ks") ;
106
107        if (!read_eproc(&ep, ks.k_proc.crllry_eproc))
108            pexit("eproc") ;
109
110        printf("ep_sqp = %x\n", ep.ep_sqp) ;
111
112        prsignaldisp(&ks, SIGUSR2) ;
113        prsignaldisp(&ks, SIGUSR1) ;
114
115        printf("signal set, p_hold\n") ;
116        prsigset(&ks.k_proc.p_hold) ;
117
118        printf("signal set, p_chold\n") ;
119        prsigset(&ks.k_proc.p_chold) ;
120  }
```

Within main(), the following actions are taken:

lines 36 to 53   When an eproc structure has been read with a call to read_proc(), the ep_sqp field of the eproc structure points to a linked list of sigqueue_t structures. The prsigq() function takes this address and prints out each of the elements in the list.

This involves reading each structure through /dev/kmem. The address of the first sigqueue_t is held in the eproc structure. The next structure's address is held in the sq_next field of the first sigqueue_t and so on. For each sigqueue_t structure read, the si_signo, si_uid and si_pid fields are displayed (lines 46 to 49) which correspond to the same fields passed to the signal handler.

lines 62 to 65   The sigaction structure referenced by act is initialised prior to invoking sigaction(S) for the SIGUSR1 signal. The sa_flags field is set to SA_SIGINFO so that the signal handler will be passed the additional siginfo_t and user context.

The sa_flags field is also set to SA_RESETHAND to mimic the behaviour of signal(S). This ensures that the signal disposition is set to SIG_DFL before the signal handler is invoked.

The sa_mask signal set is cleared. This field specifies the set of additional signals which will be blocked while the signal handler is active.

lines 67 to 69   The sigprocmask(S) call is invoked to specify a list of signals to be added to the signal mask. By emptying the set and adding SIGUSR1, this has the same behaviour as the sighold(S) call in Toolkit 7.3.

lines 71 to 75   sigaction(S) is used again to set up sighdlr() as the signal handler for SIGUSR2. Again, the SA_SIGINFO field is set to retrieve the additional parameters to be passed to the signal handler.

The address of `sighdlr()` is then output so that the disposition displayed for both `SIGUSR1` and `SIGUSR2` can be verified.

line 77   `kill(S)` is invoked to send `SIGUSR1` to the same process as specified by a call to `getpid(S)`.

lines 79 to 87   The `read_ks()` function is called to read the `proc` and `user` structures for the calling process. The associated `eproc` structure is then read whose address is contained in the `crllry_eproc` field of the `proc` structure. If there is at least one `sigqueue_t` structure associated with the process, i.e. the `ep.ep_sqp` field is not `NULL`, `prsigq()` is called to display the contents of each structure. Since a `SIGUSR1` signal has been posted then at least one `sigqueue_t` structure should exist since `SIGUSR1` has been blocked.

lines 89 to 90   `prsignaldisp()` is called twice to display the signal disposition for `SIGUSR1` and `SIGUSR2`.

lines 92 to 96   The `prsigset()` function is called to display the contents of `p_hold` (signal mask) and `p_chold` (mask used by `sigset(S)`).

line 99   The `kill(S)` system call is now called to send `SIGUSR2` which should be handled immediately on return from the system call.

line 101   The `sigrelse(S)` system call is invoked to release `SIGUSR1` and allow the previously posted signal to be delivered.

lines 104 to 119   Some of the previous actions taken are repeated to display the `ep_sqp` field, the signal dispositions for `SIGUSR1` and `SIGUSR2` and the contents of `p_hold` and `p_chold`.

The output of the program is displayed below. Again the output is annotated so that information displayed can be traced back to the program and the description of the actions.

```
# a.out
Address of sighdlr() = 0x130                          # line 75
ep_sqp = fb659054                                     # line 85
sigqueue_t at address fb659054                        # line 43
  si_signo = SIGUSR1                                  # line 46
  si_uid = 13583                                      # line 48
  si_pid = 4477                                       # line 49
u_signal[16] = 0x130     signo[17] SIGUSR2            # line 89
u_signal[15] = 0x130     signo[16] SIGUSR1            # line 90
signal set, p_hold                                    # line 92
  SIGUSR1                                             # line 93
signal set, p_chold                                   # line 95

--Caught SIGUSR2 - posted by: UID(13583) PID(4477)    # lines 77/11
--Caught SIGUSR1 - posted by: UID(13583) PID(4477)    # lines 99/11
```

```
ep_sqp = 0                                        # line 110
u_signal[16] = 0x130     signo[17] SIGUSR2        # line 112
u_signal[15] = SIG_DFL   signo[16] SIGUSR1        # line 113
signal set, p_hold                                # line 115
signal set, p_chold                               # line 118
```

7.4.5 Signal delivery

Signals are posted immediately, either through invocation of the kill(S) system call, the psignal(K) kernel call or some other event such as an exception, for example division by zero, access to an invalid memory address and so on.

However, signals are not delivered to the process as soon as they are posted. The signal may remain pending for some unspecified time before the default action is taken or the signal handler is called. For example, a process may have recently completed its time-slice and may not run again for some time.

There are four main places where the kernel checks for pending signals and decides to take action:

- After a previous signal handler has been called and the kernel is re-entered.
- After handling a processor exception.
- After a system call has been made, just before the return to user mode.
- When a process goes to sleep, waiting for an event to occur.

The kernel issig() function is called to check if signals are pending. The kernel actually invokes a macro ISSIG() which can often detect if a signal is pending without always invoking issig().

If a signal is pending, the kernel calls psig() to handle the signal, for example by calling the user's signal handler or by performing the default action. The psig() function is responsible for handling the varying semantics of the different signal functions. When psig() is entered, the signal which will be delivered to the process is held in the p_cursig field of the proc structure. The tasks performed by psig() are as follows:

- If the disposition of the signal is set to SIG_DFL, a core file will be created for signals of type SIGQUIT, SIGILL, SIGTRAP, SIGIOT, SIGEMT, SIGFPE, SIGBUS, SIGSEGV, SIGSYS, SIGXCPU and SIGXFSZ prior to terminating the process. For other signal types the process will be terminated without a core file being created.
- If the disposition of the signal has been set to a user level signal handler, the following set of tasks are performed:
  - ⇨ If the signal handler was installed using sigset(S), the signal is added to the process's signal mask.

⇨   If the handler was installed using `signal(S)`, the disposition of the signal is set to `SIG_DFL`.

⇨   Call `sendsig()` with the signal handler address and the signal number.

Figure 7.10 shows the flow of control through the kernel if a signal is pending and a signal handler needs to be invoked. All of this functionality is performed in the context of the user process for which the signal is pending. For example, `issig()` is never called to check for pending signals in a process which is not currently running.

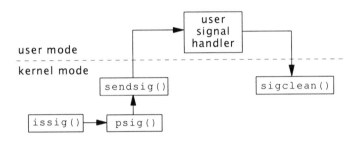

Figure 7.10   Steps followed for invoking signal handlers

The work performed by the `sendsig()` and `sigclean()` functions is highly dependent on the processor architecture since both routines involve a great deal of manipulation of the user's stack. The `sendsig()` function must set up the process's stack frame before the return is made to user mode to call the signal handler. There are a number of tasks which `sendsig()` must perform, including:

- Calculate which stack will be used. The `sigaltstack(S)` system call allows the user to specify an alternative stack to be used by signal handlers. The alternative stack is used if the `p_sigflags[]` element for the signal is set to SA_ONSTACK.

- Set up the user process's stack frame. The signal handler will be either the old style handler (`signal(S)`) where only the signal number is passed to the signal handler or the POSIX style handler (`sigaction(S)`) which takes the additional `siginfo_t` and user context arguments. In the latter case an appropriate `siginfo_t` must be retrieved from the `eproc` structure if one exists.

- Save the current user context so that when `sigclean()` is entered on return from the handler, it can be restored.

The `sigclean()` function is entered when the signal handler returns to kernel mode. It must reset the user context to the position it was in prior to invoking `issig()`. In addition to resetting the user's context, the `sigclean()` function also checks to see if any other signals are pending and invokes their appropriate handlers.

Toolkit 7.5   Using the alternative signal stack

The following example demonstrates a number of different signal principles that further tie together the mechanisms by which signal handlers are invoked and how the kernel is re-entered once the handler has completed.

The sigaltstack(S) system call is called to demonstrate the switch from the user's normal stack to the alternative stack. sigaltstack(S) expects two arguments, both of type struct sigaltstack or stack_t, as the prototype shows:

```
#include <signal.h>

int sigaltstack(const stack_t *ss, stack_t *oss) ;
```

The stack_t structure includes the following members:

```
void    *ss_sp
size_t  ss_size
int     ss_flags
```

The ss_sp field specifies the base address of the area of memory to be used for the stack. The ss_size field specifies the size of the stack in bytes. If the ss_flags field is set to SS_DISABLE, the alternative stack will be disabled and both ss_sp and ss_size are ignored. If the oss argument passed to sigaltstack(S) is not NULL, the stack_t that was used prior to the call to sigaltstack(S) is returned.

On line 17 of the following program the stack is allocated by invoking the malloc(S) library function requesting SIGSTKSZ bytes, the recommended stack size for signal handlers. The address returned by malloc(S) is assigned to the ss_sp field and displayed with the value of SIGSTKSZ on line 20. The ss_size field is set to SIGSTKSZ on line 22 and the ss_flags field is set to 0 to ensure that the alternative stack will be enabled.

The sigaltstack(S) system call is then invoked on line 25.

```
1 #include <signal.h>
2 #include <stdio.h>
3
4 extern char *signm[] ;
5
6 void
7 sighdlr(int signo, siginfo_t *si, void *uctxt)
8 {
9       return ;
10 }
11
12 main()
13 {
14      stack_t us ;
15      struct sigaction act ;
16
17      if ((us.ss_sp = (void *)malloc(SIGSTKSZ)) == NULL)
18          pexit("malloc") ;
19
20      printf("Stack at 0x%x for %d bytes\n", us.ss_sp, SIGSTKSZ) ;
21
```

```
22      us.ss_size = SIGSTKSZ ;
23      us.ss_flags = 0 ;
24
25      if (sigaltstack(&us, (stack_t *)0) < 0)
26          pexit("sigaltstack") ;
27
28      act.sa_sigaction = sighdlr ;
29      act.sa_flags = SA_SIGINFO | SA_ONSTACK;
30      sigemptyset(&act.sa_mask) ;
31
32      sigaction(SIGUSR1, &act, (struct sigaction *)0) ;
33
34      kill(getpid(), SIGUSR1) ;
35
36      pause() ;
37 }
```

The sigaction(S) system call is invoked on line 32 to set up the handler for SIGUSR1 to be the function sighdlr(). The sa_flags field is set to SA_ONSTACK. This ensures that the alternative stack will be used to execute sighdlr().

adb(CP) is used to control the flow through the program so that the switch between stacks can be shown and to show how the kernel is re-entered after the signal handler has completed. The program is started from within adb as follows:

```
$ adb sigalt
* main:br
* sighdlr:br
* :r
sigalt:         running
breakpoint   main:           jmp     near main+0xa5
* $r
eax  0x1                      efl     0x206
ebx  0x8005828c              eip     0x13c
ecx  0x80058dec              cs      0x17
edx  0x7ffffa08              ds      0x1f
esi  0x8047470               es      0x1f
edi  0x80474ec               fs      0x0
ebp  0x7ffff9fc              gs      0x0
esp  0x7ffff9ec              ss      0x1f
main:            jmp     near main+0xa5
```

The main() and sighdlr() functions both have breakpoints set. When executing main() the process should be using the normal process stack and when sighdlr() is invoked, the alternative stack should be in use.

When the program is run, it hits the breakpoint at main(). The current set of registers for the process is displayed. This shows the position of the current stack frame pointer (ebp) and stack pointer (esp). The stack is located by the ss selector.

Execution is then continued until the next breakpoint is hit. Note that adb stops the process prior to invocation of sighdlr(). A further :co command must then be invoked to reach the breakpoint set in sighdlr().

```
* :co
sigalt:         running
Stack at 0x403b7c for 8192 bytes
```

```
      user defined signal 1
stopped        at        kill+0xc:        jb        _cerror
* :co
sigalt:        running
breakpoint  sighdlr:        jmp        near sighdlr+0x6
* $r
eax  0x0                      efl        0x212
ebx  0x8005828c               eip        0x130
ecx  0x7ffff9d0               cs         0x17
edx  0x161c                   ds         0x1f
esi  0x8047470                es         0x1f
edi  0x80474ec                fs         0x0
ebp  0x7ffff9e8               gs         0x0
esp  0x405898                 ss         0x1f
sighdlr:     jmp       near sighdlr+0x6
```

At this stage the registers are displayed again. Figure 7.11 shows the difference between the two stacks. At the higher end of memory the ebp and esp registers point to the normal user stack. At the lower end of memory, the area of memory returned by malloc(S) is located between 0x403b7c and 0x405b7b. When sighdlr() is entered the frame pointer still points to an address in the normal user stack but esp points within the alternative stack specified to sigaltstack(S).

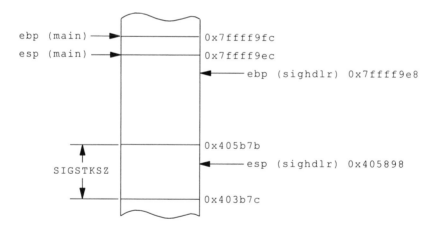

Figure 7.11   Switching to the alternative stack

Continuing within adb, sighdlr() is then single stepped as follows:

```
* :s
sigalt:        running
stopped        at        sighdlr+0x7:     mov        ebp,esp
* :s
sigalt:        running
stopped        at        sighdlr+0x9:     jmp        near sighdlr+0x2
* :s
sigalt:        running
```

```
stopped      at      sighdlr+0x2:    jmp     near sighdlr+0x4
* :s
sigalt:      running
stopped      at      sighdlr+0x4:    leave
* :s
sigalt:      running
stopped      at      sighdlr+0x5:    ret
* :s
sigalt:      running
stopped      at      _sigreturn:     add     esp,0x4
* :s
sigalt:      running
stopped      at      _sigreturn+0x3:    call    far 0xf:0x0
*
```

The `sendsig()` kernel function set up the stack so that once the signal handler has returned, it returns to the function `sigalt()`. The purpose of `sigalt()` is to pass control back to the kernel. This `far call` references a gate descriptor allowing the protected mode transfer into kernel mode.

The selector can be broken down as shown in Table 7.5.

Table 7.5   Call gate selector used to return from signal handlers

INDEX	TI	CPL
0000000000001	1	11

The Current Privilege Level (CPL) is equal to 11 (3) representing protection ring 3 (user mode). The Table Indicator (TI) is set to 1 which indicates that the Local Descriptor Table (LDT) should be used. Finally, the index of 1 references the second descriptor in the LDT. The first descriptor is used by user processes to invoke system calls. This is described in detail in section 7.3.

Using `crash`, the LDT for the `sigalt` process can be displayed as follows:

```
# crash
dumpfile = /dev/mem, namelist = /unix, outfile = stdout
> proc ! grep sigalt
  64 t  5607  5582  5582 13583  45   0     sigalt        load trc
> ldt 64
iAPX386 LDT for process 64
SLOT    BASE/SEL LIM/OFF  TYPE       DPL  ACCESSBITS
   0         0158 f014e7d4 CGATE386    3   CNT=1 AVL
   1         0158 f00102e8 CGATE386    3   CNT=1
   2     00000000 bffff000 XSEG        3   ACCS'D R&X DFLT G4096
   3     00000000 ffc0f000 DSEG        3   ACCS'D R&W BIG   G4096
   4     00000000 ffc0f000 DSEG        3   R&W BIG   G4096
   5     e0000e84 0000017c DSEG        3   R&W BIG
   7         0158 f0010394 CGATE386    3   CNT=1
> dis f00102e8
  sig_clean            subl    $0x8,%esp
```

The second descriptor in the LDT (slot 1) is highlighted. The address at which the process will execute following the jump through the call gate is `0xf00102e8`. The function at this address is `sig_clean()`. After performing some machine dependent initialisation, `sig_clean()` invokes the `sigclean()` kernel function.

7.4.6 Restartable system calls

Signals can be posted at any time. If a process is sleeping, `psignalinfo()` will wake up the process if the `p_stat` field is set to `SSLEEP` and the `p_flag` field is not set to `SNWAKE`. If the `p_flag` field is set to `SNWAKE`, signals are not allowed to wake up a sleeping process.

If the process is sleeping and `p_flag` is not set to `SNWAKE`, `setrun()` is called to place the process on the run queue. In this case `p_stat` is set to `SRUN`.

The usual action to be taken in response to an interrupted sleep is to return `EINTR` to the user, indicating that the system call was interrupted. This potentially causes problems to application programmers who then have to try to determine the cause of the interruption and invoke the system call for a second time.

By setting the `sa_flags` field of the `sigaction` structure to `SA_RESTART`, system calls that were interrupted and return `EINTR` will be restarted. Figure 7.12 shows the paths through the kernel for handling restartable system calls.

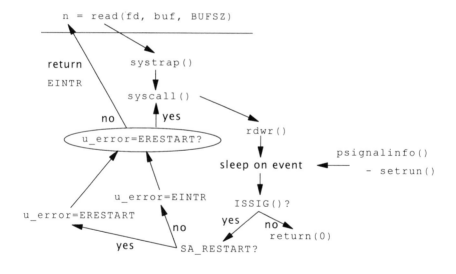

Figure 7.12   Kernel paths followed for restartable system calls

Figure 7.12 describes the paths followed for the `read(S)` system call. The kernel `systrap()` function is invoked initially to determine which system call handler to call. In the example shown here it is the `rdwr()` function. An assumption is made here that the `read(S)` system call will sleep awaiting data. At this stage a signal is posted by `psignalinfo()` which detects that the process is sleeping so invokes `setrun()`.

When the process wakes up, it calls ISSIG() to determine if the reason for being woken up is a signal. If not, the system call continues as normal.

If a signal did interrupt the sleep, the u_error field of the u_area is either set to ERESTART if the p_sigflags field for the signal is set to SA_RESTART or set to EINTR if the system call has not been specified as being restartable.

The systrap() function checks the return value of the system call handler. If u_error is set to ERESTART, the system call is restarted, otherwise u_error is returned to the user process. Once the system call has been re-issued, the signal will be processed before the system call returns.

Toolkit 7.6   Demonstrating restartable system calls

The example shown in this toolkit demonstrates the effect of using sigaction(S) to set system calls to be restarted if a SIGINT occurs part way through system call processing.

Lines 19 to 22 install sighdlr() as the signal handler for SIGINT. If the user passes the argument r to the program, the sa_flags field of the sigaction structure is set to SA_RESTART and SA_SIGINFO, otherwise sa_flags is only set to SA_SIGINFO.

```
 1 #include <signal.h>
 2
 3 extern char *signm[] ;
 4
 5 void
 6 sighdlr(int signo, siginfo_t *si, void *uctxt)
 7 {
 8       printf("caught %s\n", signm[signo - 1]) ;
 9 }
10
11 main(int argc, char *argv[])
12 {
13      struct sigaction act ;
14      char buf[256] ;
15      int n ;
16
17      int restart = (argc == 2 && argv[1][0] == 'r') ? 1 : 0 ;
18
19      act.sa_flags = (restart) ? (SA_SIGINFO|SA_RESTART) : SA_SIGINFO ;
20      sigemptyset(&act.sa_mask) ;
21      act.sa_sigaction = sighdlr ;
22      sigaction(SIGINT, &act, (struct sigaction *)0) ;
23
24      printf("PID = %d\n", getpid()) ;
25
26      n = read(0, buf, 256) ;
27      if (n == -1)
28          pexit("read") ;
29      else {
30          buf[n] = '\0' ;
31          printf("DATA = %s", buf) ;
32      }
33 }
```

Input is expected from stdin on line 26 which is read into the buffer pointed to by buf. If the read(S) system call fails, pexit() is called to display the error and exit. If the read(S) call is successful, the data read into buf is output.

The output of the program is as follows:

```
$ restart
PID = 5847
hello world                      # data entered
DATA = hello world
$ restart
PID = 5848                       # SIGINT generated during read()
caught SIGINT
read: Interrupted system call
$ restart r
PID = 5849                       # SIGINT generated during read()
caught SIGINT
hello world                      # data entered
DATA = hello world
```

When the program is initially run, the signal handler is installed without the
sa_flags field being set to SA_RESTART and is run without interruption. The data read
from standard input is then displayed.

On the second invocation, the signal handler is again installed without the sa_flags
field being set to SA_RESTART. This time the Delete key is pressed which results in a
SIGINT signal being posted to the process. The read(S) system call is interrupted and
returns EINTR to the user. This corresponds to the message: Interrupted system
call.

Finally, the program is called with the r argument. This installs the signal handler,
setting sa_flags to SA_RESTART. The Delete key is pressed while the read(S)
system call is sleeping awaiting input. The signal handler is called but the system call is
restarted. Thus, the data is entered and displayed.

7.5 Process creation

Processes are created with the fork(S) system call whose prototype is:

```
int fork()
```

The fork(S) system call makes a copy of the calling process such that when the system
call returns, a *child* process has been created which starts executing. The calling process
is referred to as the *parent process* or simply the *parent*.

The child process executes in a separate context from the parent. For example, it has
its own registers and memory regions which are protected from the parent such that a
change to data, by either the parent or the child, will not affect the other.

Consider the process shown in Figure 7.13 which is about to execute the fork(S)
system call. On return from fork(S) it checks to see the return value assigned to the
variable pid. If pid is equal to 0, the check is executing in the context of the child. If the
value of pid is greater than 0, the check is made in the context of the parent.

Figure 7.14 shows the effect of calling fork(S). The parent obtains the process ID of
the child and will execute the do_parent() function. The child receives the value of 0
from fork(S) and therefore executes the do_child() function.

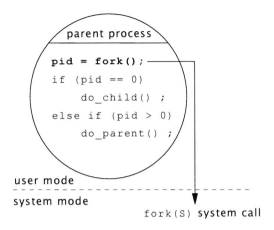

Figure 7.13   Process invoking the fork(S) system call

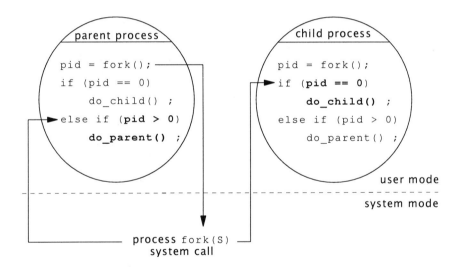

Figure 7.14   Creation of the child process with fork(S)

The fork(S) manual page states that the child is an exact copy of the calling process. This is certainly true regarding the memory image of both processes. The fork(S) manual page lists the attributes that the child inherits from the parent.

However, there are a number of differences between parent and child. These differences are:

- The child is given a unique process ID such that a call to getpid(S) will be different between the parent and child.

- Similarly, the process ID returned by `getppid(S)` is also different.

- The child receives its own file descriptors although the file table entries for each file descriptor are shared. See chapter 8 for further information on file descriptors and the system file table.

- There are no pending signals in the child process.

- Memory locks acquired by the parent using the `lock(S)` or `plock(S)` system calls are not inherited.

- The amount of time spent executing in user mode and system mode is reset to zero in the child process.

- The time left until an alarm or interval timer expires is reset to zero.

- Record locks set by the parent are not inherited.

The `vfork(S)` system call is a variation of the `fork(S)` system call which was originally provided in BSD UNIX. The declaration of `vfork(S)` is:

```
#include <unistd.h>
pid_t vfork(void) ;
```

Since many calls to `fork(S)` will be followed by a call to `execve(S)` to execute a new program, `vfork(S)` was introduced to remove the need for copying the full address space of the parent since it will almost always be removed by the child when `execve(S)` is invoked. Another difference between `fork(S)` and `vfork(S)` is that the parent sleeps until the child either calls `execve(S)` or exits. Originally introduced in the BSD version of UNIX, `vfork(S)` provided enhanced performance but was claimed as being architecturally inelegant. The details of `vfork(S)` will be covered in Toolkit 7.8.

Figure 7.15 shows the main paths followed through the kernel for both the `fork(S)` and `vfork(S)` system calls.

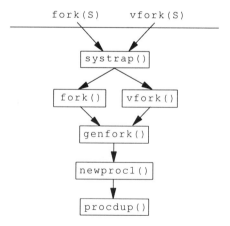

Figure 7.15   Paths followed to fork a process

The `systrap()` function is called for each system call. Described in detail in section 7.3, the main task of `systrap()` is to invoke the appropriate system call handler responsible for implementing the system call.

`fork(S)` and `vfork(S)` have different system call numbers. The kernel functions for `fork()` and `vfork()` do little else other than invoke `genfork()`, specifying which type of fork should be followed.

Most of the work performed for `fork(S)` is carried out by `newproc1()` and `procdup()`. Since the child process is created before control is returned back to `genfork()`, `genfork()` is actually returned to twice, once for the parent and once for the child. Figure 7.16 illustrates the transition back to user mode.

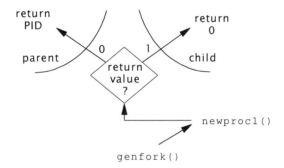

Figure 7.16   Returning from `fork()` to user mode

The steps taken by `newproc1()` are as follows:

- If the number of free process slots falls below the process table water mark, `grow_proc()` is called to grow the `proc[]` table by an additional page.

- The variable `mpid` is incremented which will be the next process ID to allocate.

- For each element in `proc[]`, if the slot is free (`p_stat` is equal to 0), the `proc[]` table entry is a candidate for allocation to the new process. If the process at this slot has a process ID of `mpid`, `mpid` is incremented and the next element in the table is tried.

- At this stage an empty slot has been found so the `proc` structure is allocated to the process by setting the `p_flag` field to `SLOCK`.

- The `p_stat` field is set to `SIDL` to indicate that the process is currently being created.

- The fields of the new `proc` structure are initialised.

- The fields of its associated `eproc` structure are initialised.

- `procdup()` is called to duplicate the process.

- Zero is returned for parent and 1 for child.

The `mpid` variable is used to allocate a process ID for the next new process. Since `mpid` can wrap around (exceed its maximum value and return to zero on the next increment), checking for the first free slot in the `proc` table is not sufficient.

A process slot is free if the `p_stat` field is 0. When a slot is located for the child, the `p_stat` field is set to `SIDL`, indicating that the process is currently being created.

The `procdup()` function is responsible for creating a duplicate of the parent process using the process slot found in `newproc1()`. The tasks followed by `procdup()` are:

- Call `uballoc()` to allocate a u_area for the child process and copy the fields of the parent's u_area to it.

- Call `dupreg()` to duplicate all of the parent's regions.

- Call `attachreg()` to attach each region to the child's address space.

- Set up the child's registers and initial stack frame used on return from `fork(S)`.

Many of the `proc` structure fields for the child are initialised by `newproc1()`. Within `procdup()`, the child's u_area is created by calling `uballoc()` and then initialised from the parent's copy.

The next stage is to ensure that the child process obtains the same memory image as the parent process. For regions which are not shareable, this involves copying all of the parent's regions by calling `dupreg()` and attaching them to the child's address space with `attachreg()`. For regions which can be shared directly, for example the process text, the region is used directly by the child without a call to `dupreg()`.

Figure 7.17 illustrates the shared regions which are manipulated directly by `procdup()` and the non-shared regions which must be copied by a call to `dupreg()`. In the case of shared regions the reference count of the region will be incremented.

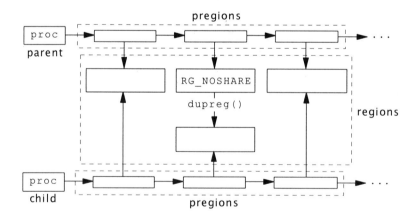

Figure 7.17   Shared and non-shared regions across `fork(S)`

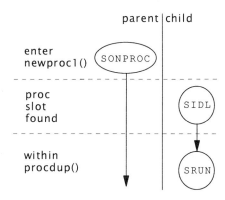

Figure 7.18   Transition between process states

In order to avoid wasting memory by copying the contents of the physical pages from the parent to the child, pages are generally shared between the two processes. Recall that a process may call execve(S) almost immediately or may only access a subset of the data that is present in the parent's address space.

Toolkit 7.7 illustrates in detail the sharing of regions and page tables and demonstrates copy on write semantics. To implement copy on write semantics for a page, the kernel marks the page read only. If the parent or child attempts to write to the page, the CPU generates a page fault allowing the kernel to allocate a new page for the process which attempted the write, to copy the contents of the page to the new page and to instruct the CPU to retry the write instruction.

Figure 7.18 shows the transition between different states of the child process when initially created. When the proc slot is found, the p_stat field is set to SIDL to indicate the process is currently being created. It is only when the initialisation of the process is fully complete that the state is changed to SRUN and the process is placed on the run queue.

Toolkit 7.7   Shared pages and copy on write

The example provided in this toolkit demonstrates the level of memory sharing between a parent and child process following the fork(S) system call. The example goes further to demonstrate copy on write semantics to show how shared pages are handled when one process attempts to write to a memory location within a shared page. Figure 7.19 shows the steps followed through the program.

The parent process calls fork(S) to create the child. The child calls pause(S) which will return after any signal is posted, while the parent installs a signal handler for SIGUSR1 and, using sigpause(S), explicitly waits until this signal arrives.

The signal handler invoked will write a message to the screen. Since printf(S) is used, the data will be written into a file stream before the kernel is entered, using the write(S) system call. This guarantees that the parent process will write to its data region. The child process, however, will not touch the data region at all.

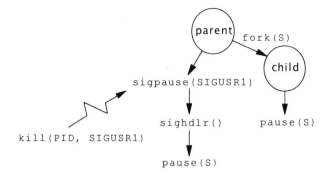

Figure 7.19   Toolkit code paths for demonstrating copy on write

The following program is relatively straightforward. For details on signal handling see section 7.4.

```
 1 #include <signal.h>
 2
 3 void
 4 sighdlr(int signo)
 5 {
 6     printf("process %d caught signal\n", getpid()) ;
 7 }
 8
 9 main()
10 {
11     int pid, ppid ;
12
13     printf("Parent PID = %d\n", getpid()) ;
14
15     sigset(SIGUSR1, sighdlr) ;
16
17     if ((pid = fork()) < 0)
18         pexit("fork") ;
19     else if (pid == 0) {        /* child */
20         pause() ;
21     }
22     else {                  /* parent */
23         sigpause(SIGUSR1) ;
24         pause() ;
25     }
26 }
```

The crash(ADM) command is used to monitor the program from another virtual console or window. Initially the program is run as follows:

```
$ fork
parent PID = 1804
```

Both processes are now suspended awaiting a signal. When crash(ADM) is entered the processes are located and their pregion structures are displayed:

```
# crash
dumpfile = /dev/mem, namelist = /unix, outfile = stdout
> proc ! grep fork
   71 s  1804   450  1804 13583  66   0 u    fork   load        # parent
   74 s  1805  1804  1804 13583  66   0 u    fork   load nxec   # child
> pregion 71 74
SLOT PREG REG#       REGVA   TYPE FLAGS
   71   0   686           0  text rd ex cm
        1   682   0x400000  data rd wr cm
        2   712 0x7fffe000  stack rd wr cm
   74   0   686           0  text rd ex cm
        1   680   0x400000  data rd wr cm
        2   703 0x7fffe000  stack rd wr cm
```

The parent process (`PID 1804`) is located in process slot 71 and the child in slot 74
(`PID 1805`). At this stage, both processes share `region 686` as highlighted, which
represents the text of the program they are both executing. However, they both have
separate data and stack regions. Looking more closely at the data regions (`682` and `680`)
for both processes:

```
> region -f 682 680
REGION TABLE SIZE = 768
Region-list:

SLOT  PGSZ VALID  SMEM NONE SOFF  REF SWP NSW FORW BACK INOX TYPE FLAGS
 682     6     6     5    0    0    1   0   0  692  680   74 priv nosh

Page-tables:

LIST fa00ffe0  3231 01125000 pres rw us                        none     -
SLOT    OFFSET PFDAT PHYSADDR ---------- FLAGS ----------- TYPE    BLKNO
   0 00000000  3434 011f0000 pres     us ref                none     -
   1 00001000  2397 00a9d000 pres     us ref                none     -
   2 00002000  4312 0155e000 pres     us ref                none     -
   3 00003000  3048 0106e000 pres     us ref                file    96
   4 00004000   270 0024e000 pres     us ref                none     -
   5 00005000  3089 01097000 pres     us ref                none     -

Region-list:

SLOT  PGSZ VALID  SMEM NONE SOFF  REF SWP NSW FORW BACK INOX TYPE FLAGS
 680     6     6     5    0    0    1   0   0  682  686   74 priv nosh

Page-tables:

LIST fa00ff20  3453 01203000 pres rw us                        none     -
SLOT    OFFSET PFDAT PHYSADDR ---------- FLAGS ----------- TYPE    BLKNO
   0 00000000  3434 011f0000 pres     us ref                none     -
   1 00001000  2397 00a9d000 pres     us ref                none     -
   2 00002000  4312 0155e000 pres     us ref                none     -
   3 00003000  3048 0106e000 pres     us ref                file    96
   4 00004000   270 0024e000 pres     us ref                none     -
   5 00005000  3089 01097000 pres     us ref                none     -
```

At this stage, the parent has returned from `fork(S)` and immediately executed
`sigpause(S)`. When the child starts running, it immediately executes `pause(S)`.

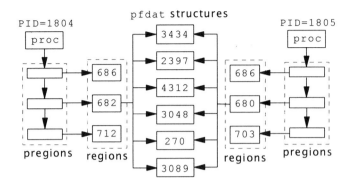

Figure 7.20   Sharing of page tables after `fork(S)`

In the `region` structures listed above, both regions consist of six pages which are identified by the `PFDAT` column. Each page in the parent process is the same page in the child process. At this stage in execution no pages have been modified by either process. Figure 7.20 illustrates the shared and non-shared objects.

Still within `crash`, the parent is sent a `SIGUSR` signal by invoking `kill(C)`:

```
> !kill -USR1 1804
```

The parent process executes the signal handler displaying the following message:

```
process 1804 caught signal
```

Using `crash` again to display the region tables for both processes shows that they no longer access all the same pages for the data region. Where pages are still shared, they are highlighted.

```
> region -f 682 680
REGION TABLE SIZE = 768
Region-list:

SLOT  PGSZ VALID  SMEM NONE SOFF  REF SWP NSW FORW BACK INOX TYPE FLAGS
682    6     6     5    0    0     1   0   0   692  680   74 priv nosh

Page-tables:

LIST fa00ffe0  3231 01125000 pres rw us                          none     -
SLOT    OFFSET PFDAT PHYSADDR ----------- FLAGS ----------- TYPE     BLKNO
   0 00000000  3455 01205000 pres rw us ref mod              none     -
   1 00001000  2397 00a9d000 pres    us ref                  none     -
   2 00002000  4312 0155e000 pres    us ref                  none     -
   3 00003000  3048 0106e000 pres    us ref                  file    96
   4 00004000  2261 00a15000 pres rw us ref mod              none     -
   5 00005000  3089 01097000 pres    us ref                  none     -

Region-list:

SLOT  PGSZ VALID  SMEM NONE SOFF  REF SWP NSW FORW BACK INOX TYPE FLAGS
680    6     6     5    0    0     1   0   0   682  686   74 priv nosh
```

```
Page-tables:

LIST fa00ff20  3453 01203000 pres rw us                        none       -
SLOT    OFFSET PFDAT PHYSADDR ---------- FLAGS ---------- TYPE       BLKNO
   0 00000000  3434 011f0000 pres      us ref              none       -
   1 00001000  2397 00a9d000 pres      us ref              none       -
   2 00002000  4312 0155e000 pres      us ref              none       -
   3 00003000  3048 0106e000 pres      us ref              file      96
   4 00004000   270 0024e000 pres      us ref              none       -
   5 00005000  3089 01097000 pres      us ref              none       -
```

As a consequence of issuing the `printf(S)` statement in the signal handler, two pages in the parent's address space were modified. As part of the `fork(S)` operation the kernel modifies the attributes of the pages so that any attempt to write to an address within one of the pages will result in a page fault. This allows the kernel to allocate a new page for the process, copy the contents to it, mark the page as read/write and retry the instruction.

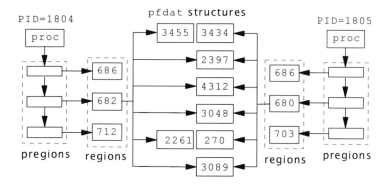

Figure 7.21   New pages allocated for copy on write

Figure 7.21 shows the two pages, identified by `pfdat` structures `3455` and `2261` which have been allocated to the parent. The contents of the pages are copied before the write takes place. The fields of the `pfdat` structure are described in section 12.3.

Toolkit 7.8   Process creation with `vfork(S)`

This example demonstrates the differences between `fork(S)` and `vfork(S)` and explains in more detail how `vfork(S)` is implemented in SCO UNIX.

First, consider the following simple usage of `fork(S)`:

```
1 main()
2 {
3     int pid ;
4
5     pid = fork() ;
6
7     if (pid == 0) {
8         printf("I am the child\n") ;
```

```
 9          pause() ;
10      }
11      else
12          printf("I am the parent\n") ;
13 }
```

Here, the parent calls `fork(S)`, prints a message and exits. The child prints a message and then calls `pause(S)`. Running the example gives the following output:

```
$ nfork
I am the child
I am the parent
$ ps -ef | grep nfork
    spate    527    1   0 10:30:43    ttyp4    00:00:00 nfork
    spate    529  521   3 10:30:47    ttyp4    00:00:00 grep nfork
```

The parent process returns from `fork(S)`, displays the message and exits. The child, however, displays its message and then pauses awaiting a signal. The `ps(C)` command shows the child process still in existence but now orphaned; the parent process ID field indicates that the process is inherited by the `init` process which is standard practice for processes which outlive their parents.

In the following example, the parent calls `vfork(S)` in place of `fork(S)`. The semantics of `vfork(S)` state that the parent will sleep until the child either exits or calls one of the `exec(S)` functions. In this example, the child calls `pause(S)`, which should result in the child and, therefore, parent both sleeping until the child receives a signal or the parent is terminated directly.

```
 1 #include <signal.h>
 2
 3 extern char *signm[] ;
 4
 5 void
 6 sighdlr(int signo)
 7 {
 8      printf("Signal caught = %s\n", signm[signo - 1]) ;
 9 }
10
11 main()
12 {
13      int pid ;
14
15      sigset(SIGCHLD, sighdlr) ;
16
17      if ((pid = vfork()) < 0)
18          pexit("vfork") ;
19      else if (pid == 0) {              /* child */
20          pause() ;
21      }
22      else {                            /* parent */
23          printf("I am the parent\n") ;
24      }
25 }
```

As the following output of the program shows, both the parent and child are sleeping. By sending `SIGKILL` to the child, the child terminates, resulting in a `SIGCHLD` signal being sent to the parent. The parent's signal handler is then invoked, followed by normal execution of the parent process.

```
$ vfork &
[1]  683
$ ps -ef | grep vfork
   spate   683   678  0 10:46:51   ttyp5   00:00:00 vfork
   spate   684   683  0 10:46:51   ttyp5   00:00:00 vfork
   spate   686   678  3 10:46:56   ttyp5   00:00:00 grep vfork
$ kill -KILL 684
Signal caught = SIGCHLD
I am the parent
[1] +  Done(16)                 vfork &
```

The goal of vfork(S) is to reduce memory footprint and speed up creation of a new process which will invoke execve(S). Since the amount of physical memory consumed by the child is minimal, as it shares most data with the parent, and the performance increases are minimal, the implementation of vfork(S) in SCO UNIX uses the standard implementation of fork(S) to duplicate the process, but with the extensions shown in Figure 7.22.

When newproc1() is called, both the child and parent processes have the SVFORK flag set in the p_flag field of their proc structures. When returning to genfork(), the parent sleeps on the address of its own proc structure while the child continues as normal.

Later on, the parent can be woken up by two different events. Firstly, when the child issues one of the exec(S) system calls the kernel checks to see if the SVFORK flag is set

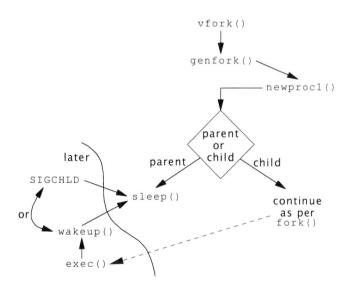

Figure 7.22 Handling vfork(S) in the kernel

in p_flag. If set, the kernel will issue an explicit wakeup() to put the parent on the run queue. If the child exits, the parent will be woken up as a consequence of receiving a SIGCHLD signal for which the default action is to ignore the signal.

7.6 Calling exec to start a new program

One of the main reasons for calling fork(S) is for the child to issue one of the exec(S) functions to start running from a new executable file. This is one of the main tasks of the UNIX shells as Figure 7.23 shows.

The different exec library functions were discussed in section 2.7. All of these library functions enter the kernel through the execve() system call.

The arguments passed to execve(S) are the name of the file to be executed, a list of arguments to the program (argv[]) and a list of environment variables (envp[]).

After passing through systrap(), the system call handler for execve(S) is the kernel function exece(). The length of the pathname passed to exece() together with the size of argv[] and envp[] could be substantial. Because of this, they should not be copied from user space onto the kernel stack, the normal behaviour of system call handlers, since this would increase the chance of overflowing the kernel stack which is of fixed size.

One of the initial tasks performed by exece() is to set up a table defined by the execa structure which is used to point to the filename, argv[] array and envp[] array on the user's stack. The initial setup is shown in Figure 7.24.

The uap variable within the exece() function is assigned the contents of the u_ap field of the u_area. This field points to the u_arg[] array which holds the arguments passed to the system call. For all of the exec() functions, pointers to the three arguments

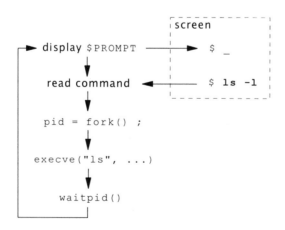

Figure 7.23   The basic skeleton of a UNIX shell

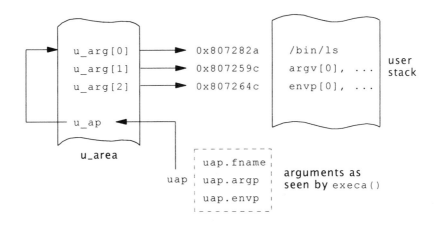

Figure 7.24   Handling arguments passed to execve(S)

will be passed through the system call interface with the appropriate data on the user stack. Thus u_arg[0] points to the first argument, the name of the file to be exec'ed and so on.

However, at some stage during the processing of exece(), the kernel will need to copy all arguments from the user stack in order to process the pathname and copy the arguments onto the stack which is allocated for the new process. To achieve this, exece() calls table_setup() to initialise a table of type "exec data". This table will be grown dynamically in order to read the user arguments and other dynamic components used by exece(), such as the number of shared libraries. The table_setup() call is then followed by a call to table_alloc() to allocate the requested amount of virtual address space. At this point no physical pages are allocated to the table which avoids potential wastage if all parts of the table are not used.

7.6.1 Analysing the binary type

The namei() function is invoked by exece() to resolve the pathname of the program to execute. If the file exists, a pointer to an in-core inode will be returned. For details of how namei() works see section 8.4.3.

The gethead() function is then called to read the header of the file to allow exece() to determine what type of binary the file is and therefore how to set up the appropriate environment in which it can run. There are numerous binary formats supported by SCO UNIX including COFF, ELF, Intel x.out format, System V 286 executables, DOS executables and shell interpreted files.

The first task performed by gethead() is to call the filesystem access routine to ensure that the file is executable.

Since the header types of binaries are different, gethead() must be able to distinguish between the various types. The kernel defines a union consisting of the different object file headers. For example, the following structure is a union of three different object file headers:

```
union fileheader {
    Elf32_Ehdr     elf ;
    struct xexec   xout ;
    struct filehdr coff ;
} ;
```

The distinguishing factor between the different header types usually lies in the first few characters of the file which represent a specific magic number. For example, in the ELF format, which is described in section 6.2.2, the first character is the value 0x7f. The next three characters are 'E', 'L' and 'F' respectively.

After reading the header, gethead() checks the magic number against the range of executable file types it recognises. If the file is of type COFF, the getcoffhdr() function is called to read additional information from the file that is COFF specific. If the file is an ELF object file, getelfhdr() is called to read ELF specific information.

Toolkit 7.9   Calculating the object file type

The example shown here demonstrates the type of processing that is performed by gethead(). On lines 8 to 11 the filhdr union is defined containing two types, one which defines an ELF header and the other which defines a COFF header. The first byte of each structure is used for identification purposes.

```
 1 #include <sys/elf.h>
 2 #include <filehdr.h>
 3 #include <sys/errno.h>
 4 #include <fcntl.h>
 5
 6 extern int errno ;
 7
 8 union fileheader {
 9         Elf32_Ehdr     elf ;
10         struct filehdr coff ;
11 } filhdr;
12
13 main(int argc, char *argv[])
14 {
15     int fd ;
16     char *hashpling = (char *)&filhdr ;
17
18     if (argc != 2) {
19         errno = EINVAL ;
20         pexit("fileheader") ;
21     }
22
23     fd = open(argv[1], O_RDONLY) ;
24     if (fd < 0)
25         pexit(argv[1]) ;
```

```
26
27      read(fd, (char *)&filhdr, sizeof(filhdr)) ;
28
29      if (filhdr.coff.f_magic == I386MAGIC)
30          printf("This is a COFF object file\n") ;
31      else
32          if (filhdr.elf.e_ident[0] == 0x7f &&
33                      filhdr.elf.e_ident[1] == 'E')
34              printf("This is an ELF object file\n") ;
35          else if (hashpling[0] == '#' && hashpling[1] == '!')
36                  printf("This looks like a shell file\n") ;
37              else
38                  printf("Bad magic number!\n") ;
39  }
```

The program expects to receive a filename as its only argument. The file is opened on line 23 and a read(S) system call is issued on line 27. This will read the first few bytes from the file, the size of which depends on the largest structure in the filhdr union.

The program then checks whether the file is of type COFF or ELF. If both checks fail, a further check is made to see if the program starts with the characters #!, indicating that the file may be a shell script. In this case, further processing would have to be performed to extract the name of the shell interpreter. In the example here it is the Bourne shell.

In the following output a program is first compiled. By default the output file is of type COFF which the filehdr program confirms. Next the program is re-compiled. The -b option specifies that the object file should be ELF.

```
$ cc -o hello hello.c
$ filehdr hello
This is a COFF object file
$ cc -o hello -belf hello.c
$ filehdr hello
This is an ELF object file
$ cat shell
#!/bin/sh
echo "hello world"
$ filehdr shell
This looks like a shell file
```

In the final example, filehdr is run on the shell script found in the file shell. The program recognises the first two characters and indicates that it may have found a shell.

7.6.2 Object file generic data

One of the arguments passed to getheader() is a pointer to the u_exdata field in the u_area. This specifies file information from which the kernel can construct the appropriate executable image. The u_exdata field is a structure of type struct exdata which is defined in the <sys/user.h> header file. Some of the fields of exdata structure are shown in Table 7.6.

The goal of the getcoffhdr() and getelfhdr() functions is to populate this structure. Since the same structure is used for both file types, the kernel can construct the appropriate memory image without knowledge of what the file type is.

Table 7.6   exdata structure fields

exdata fields		Description
struct inode	*ip	Inode with which the executable data is associated.
long	ux_tsize	Size of the process text.
long	ux_dsize	The data size.
long	ux_bsize	The BSS size.
long	ux_lsize	The library size.
long	ux_nshlibs	The number of shared libraries needed.
long	ux_toffset	File offset to the text.
long	ux_doffset	File offset to the data.
long	ux_loffset	File offset to the section containing the library names.
long	ux_txtorg	The start address of text in memory.
long	ux_datorg	Start address of data in memory.
long	ux_entloc	The address at which the program should be entered.

7.6.3 Managing shared libraries

Once gethead() returns to exece(), all of the data needed to create the memory image
is available. The next task performed by exece() is to call getshlibs() to validate
each shared library for accessibility and suitability. All of the information needed to
access the contents of the shared library in order to complete the memory image of the
process is obtained from this call.

The number of shared libraries is stored in the u_exdata.ux_nshlibs field of the
u_area. For each shared library, getshlibs() will also call gethead(). It must be
noted that each shared library must be a COFF object file. Dynamically linked libraries
are discussed in section 7.6.6.

7.6.4 Building the executable image

At this stage, the kernel has all the information it needs to create the executable image.
Figure 7.25 shows the stages followed by exece() to remove the memory image of the
calling process and replace it with the image of the new executable file together with any
appropriate shared libraries. In Figure 7.25, the program requires access to a single shared
library.

Since the arguments to be passed to the new process image have been copied into
kernel mode, the user mode memory image of the process is no longer required. The
detachregs() function is called to remove all the regions currently attached to the
process. The detachregs() function and other associated region management functions
are described in section 6.4.

The getxfile() function is called to create regions for an executable file and either
load the contents of the region from the file or map a portion of the file into the process's
virtual address space managed by the region. getxfile() is passed a pointer to an
exdata structure which describes the properties of the file from which the region image

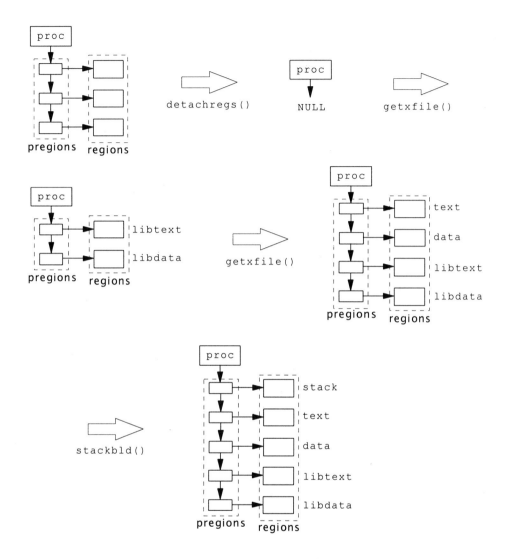

Figure 7.25   Memory image transition through execе()

will be created. For both text and data, arguments are also passed to getxfile() indicating the type of the region.

The following example shows the difference in memory image between the crash process and the shell from which it originated. The shell calls fork(S) and then calls execve() to run crash. Analysis within crash on a per region basis will show the executable file image and libraries which both processes use.

```
# crash
dumpfile = /dev/mem, namelist = /unix, outfile = stdout
> proc ! grep crash
   75 p    731    726    731     0  36  16                      crash  load
> proc #726          # parent's process ID
PROC TABLE SIZE = 83
SLOT ST  PID   PPID  PGRP  UID PRI CPU EVENT                NAME   FLAGS
   74 s   726   725   726    0  73   0   region_end+0x6370  ksh    load
> pregion 74
SLOT PREG REG#       REGVA   TYPE  FLAGS
   74   0   706  0x8046000  stack rd wr cm
        1   712  0x8048000   text rd ex cm
        2   702  0x8069000   data rd wr cm
        3   705  0x80001000 lbtxt rd ex pr
        4   710  0x80051000 lbdat rd wr ex pr
        5   711  0x8005c000 shfil rd
        6   708  0x8005e000 lbtxt rd ex pr
        7   700  0x80084000 lbdat rd wr ex pr
> pregion 75
SLOT PREG REG#       REGVA   TYPE  FLAGS
   75   0   703  0x8046000  stack rd wr cm
        1   699  0x8048000   text rd ex cm
        2   698  0x8062000   data rd wr cm
        3   701  0x80001000 lbtxt rd ex pr
        4   709  0x80051000 lbdat rd wr ex pr
```

The tasks performed by `getxfile()` are shown in Figure 7.26. The `xalloc()` function is called to allocate the text region. If a region is already associated with the file, this region can be shared by the new process if the region is a text region and is marked as shareable. In this case, `attachreg()` is called to attach the region to the new process's address space. If no region is associated with the file, `allocreg()` is called to allocate a new region which is then attached. For the data region a new region is always allocated.

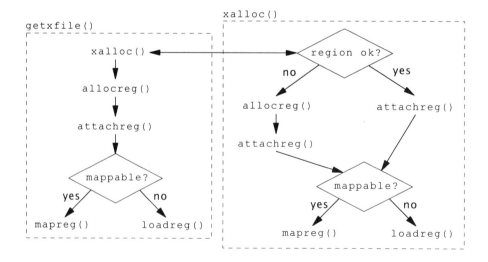

Figure 7.26   Allocating memory for an executable file

In both cases, a check is made to see if the file can be mapped by the region and therefore paged in on demand. In this case a call is made to mapreg(). If the file cannot be mapped, loadreg() is called to fill the contents of the region with the appropriate file contents.

Under most circumstances the file can be mapped. Exceptions include when the executable image must be loaded and locked into core or where the file is currently mapped by a process but with different protections.

Since the region is associated with an inode, a page fault which occurs once the process starts executing over the mapped region can be easily resolved by the kernel.

The main task performed by the mapreg() function is to call the FS_ALLOCMAP() function to build the file's block list map. This is a list of the file's blocks which are attached to the inode such that satisfying reads following a page fault can be performed with the minimal number of read operations. For further details on mapped files see section 8.7.4.

7.6.5 Returning to user space

When systrap() is entered to handle the system call the set of process registers which existed prior to jumping through the call gate is saved on the process's kernel stack held in the u_area as shown in Figure 7.27. Despite the fact the process image has completely changed as a consequence of invoking exece(), the user process returns to user mode just like any other system call.

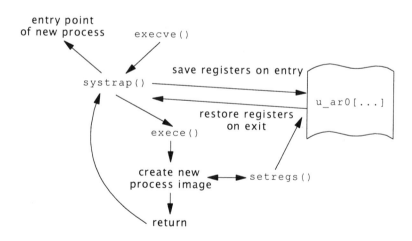

Figure 7.27   Saving and restoring registers across execve(S)

When exece() has created the memory image of the new process it calls setregs() to update the registers saved in the u_area to point to the entry address within the new text region and to reset the stack frame and stack pointer. When control returns to user mode, the process will start executing the new program.

7.6.6 Invoking the dynamic linker

Chapter 6 described the format of ELF executable files and dynamically linked libraries. If an executable ELF file has a segment of type INTERP, the segment contents typically specify the pathname of the dynamic linker. In this case the dynamic linker must be run prior to the file specified to execve(S) in order to link the appropriate DLLs (*Dynamically Linked Libraries*).

If the executable file has a segment of type INTERP the value returned by gethead() indicates that the ELF file has been dynamically linked. With both dynamically linked and statically linked ELF executables, exece() invokes getxfile() to load the text and data of the process specified to execve(S).

After stackbld() is called to set up the user's stack, getelfhdr() is called again in the case of a dynamically linked ELF executable. The text and data of the dynamic linker are mapped into the address space of the user process and the entry point of the program set to the entry point of the dynamic linker and not the program specified to execve(S). Figure 7.28 shows an example of the memory layout of a dynamically linked program after return to user space.

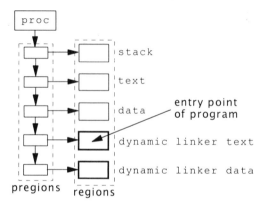

Figure 7.28   Returning from execve() to the dynamic linker

Before returning to user space, exece() needs to set up appropriate information on the user's stack including envp[] and the arguments to main(). In the case of dynamically linked binaries, the dynamic linker needs access to the ELF program header information for the file it will control. This information is also passed to the dynamic linker on the user's stack.

7.7 Process relationships

With the exception of the init process which is hand-crafted by the kernel, all processes in UNIX are created by a parent process using fork(S), building a parent/child relationship which lasts until either the parent or the child process terminates. Each process may call `fork(S)` multiple times to create many children. Each child may then call `fork(S)` to create its own children and so on, building a hierarchy of processes.

There are a number of features provided by UNIX for which the basic parent/child `fork(S)`, `exec(S)`, `wait(S)` relationship is not sufficient alone. The following sections build on the description of process groups and sessions in section 2.8, showing how they are implemented in the kernel.

7.7.1 Process group management

The process group model allows processes to be grouped together and under certain circumstances be treated as a single entity. For example, consider the following shell command:

```
$ cat | lp -deng_lw2
```

This command sequence will sit indefinitely waiting for input from the keyboard. To terminate such a sequence usually involves hitting the `Delete` key. This sends a `SIGINT` signal to both processes and unless `SIGINT` is caught, the default action is to terminate the processes.

The shell creates two processes and connects the standard output of `cat` to the standard input of `lp`. By generating a `SIGINT` with the `Delete` key, the signal must be posted to the `cat` and `lp` processes only and not to the shell which created the processes. This involves creation of a new process group by the shell in which both `cat` and `lp` will run. The `SIGINT` signal will be delivered to the process group and thus to both processes.

7.7.2 Session management

A session is a collection of process groups with one process designated as the session leader. Sessions are used to group a set of processes together which are associated with a specific terminal, whether the system console, a virtual console, modem and so on.

Under certain circumstances this grouping allows the kernel to treat the session as a single entity. For example, if a modem disconnect is detected, all processes which belong to the session should be terminated. In this case the kernel will post a `SIGHUP` signal to each process in the session.

Session management is best described by considering the relationship between the `init` process, `getty` and `login` processes and the user interaction with the system. Consider the following abbreviated output from `ps(C)`:

```
$ ps -ef -ouser,pid,ppid,pgid,sess,tty,args
USER       PID  PPID  PGID SESSION     TTY COMMAND
root         0     0     0       0      ? sched
root         1     0     0       0      ? /etc/init -a
root         2     0     0       0      ? vhand
root         3     0     0       0      ? bdflush
root         4     0     0       0      ? kmdaemon
root         5     1     0       0      ? htepi_daemon /
root         6     0     0       0      ? strd
```

```
root       425       1     425       425    tty05 /etc/getty tty05 sc_m
root       426       1     426       426    tty06 /etc/getty tty06 sc_m
root       427       1     427       427    tty07 /etc/getty tty07 sc_m
root       428       1     428       428    tty08 /etc/getty tty08 sc_m
root       429       1     429       429    tty09 /etc/getty tty09 sc_m
root       430       1     430       430    tty10 /etc/getty tty10 sc_m
root       431       1     431       431    tty11 /etc/getty tty11 sc_m
root       432       1     432       432    tty12 /etc/getty tty12 sc_m

root      1821       1    1821      1821    tty01 /bin/login spate
spate     3590    1821    3590      1821    tty01 -ksh
spate     3665    3590    3665      1821    tty01 ps -e -ouser,pid,ppid,pgid ...

root      1120       1    1120      1120    tty03 /bin/login sam
sam       3547    1120    1120      1120    tty03 -sh

root       424       1     424       424    tty04 /bin/login ashley
ashley    3555     424     424       424    tty04 -sh
```

The output shows a system with a number of kernel processes, the `init` process, a number of dormant `getty` processes and three users logged in. With the exception of the dormant `getty` processes, the processes are grouped together by their session ID. The `init` process and kernel processes all have a session ID of 0. There are three other sessions, all corresponding to the users logged into the system. The data displayed by `ps(C)` is shown in Figure 7.29.

If user `sam` logs off the system, the session 1120 will be terminated. The shell exits causing `login` also to exit. This is detected by `init` and another `getty` is spawned for the terminal device whose entry in a `ps(C)` output is:

```
root   3703   3703      1     3703    tty03 /etc/getty tty03 sc_m
```

The new `getty` process runs within a new session and also within a new process group.

7.7.3 Kernel support for process groups and sessions

This section describes the relationship between the different kernel structures designed to handle parent, child and sibling relationships, together with support for process groups and sessions.

There are numerous fields used to hold process, process group and session related information. The more important fields are listed in Table 7.7 and the places where the kernel accesses these fields are described throughout this section. Those structure fields starting with p_ are from the `proc` structure while those fields starting with u_ are fields within the u_area.

Since the p_pid field is the handle on a process from a user perspective it is used extensively throughout the kernel.

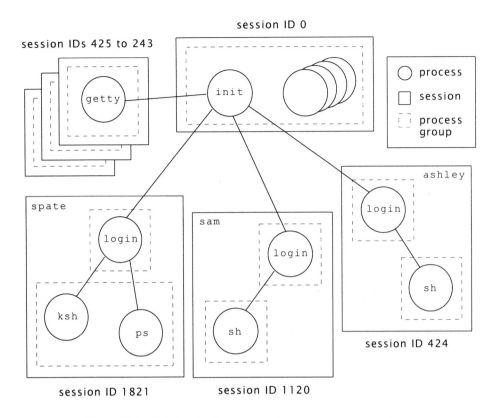

Figure 7.29   Relationship between sessions, process groups and processes

Table 7.7   Process, process group and session fields in the `user` and `proc` structures

Field		Description
short	p_pid	Process ID.
short	p_pgrp	ID of the process group leader.
short	p_ppid	Process ID of the parent process.
int	p_sid	Session ID.
struct proc	*p_parent	Pointer to the parent's `proc` structure.
struct proc	*p_child	Pointer to the first child process.
struct proc	*p_sibling	Pointer to the next sibling process on the list.
struct proc	*p_ptracep	Which process is tracing me?
struct proc	*p_controlp	First process that the process controls (for debugging).
struct proc	*p_controllink	List of processes with the same controller.
struct inode	*u_ttyip	Pointer to inode for controlling TTY.
short	*u_ttyp	Pointer to the t_pgrp field in the controlling TTY.
dev_t	*u_ttyd	The device ID of the process's controlling TTY.

The process group ID which is held in the `p_pgrp` field has more limited use and is primarily used for signal management. The `kill(S)` system call allows a signal to be sent to a process group as well as to individual processes. The other use, discussed previously, concerns posting of the SIGINT, SIGQUIT and job control signals by the console driver in response to various key sequences.

If the `p_pgrp` field is identical to the `p_pid` field, the process is a process group leader. All processes within the same process group will have the same value stored in their `p_pgrp` fields.

The `p_sid` field, which stores the session ID of the process, is used in a similar manner. If the `p_sid` field is identical to the `p_pid` field, the process is a session leader. Also discussed previously, if the session leader terminates, SIGHUP is sent to all processes in the same session, that is, all processes with the same `p_sid` field.

In many respects, the `p_ppid` field is redundant. Although it stores the process ID of the parent process, the `p_parent` field points to the parent's `proc` structure from which the same information can be obtained.

For each process created by `fork(S)`, the `p_parent` field of the child is set to point to the parent process's `proc` structure. If a process calls `fork(S)`, the `p_child` field is set to point to the child. If the same parent then calls `fork(S)` to create another child, the parent's `p_child` field is set to point to the newly created child's `proc` structure whose `p_sibling` field is set to point to the first child process created. Figure 7.30 illustrates the establishment of parent and child relationships across multiple `fork(S)` system calls.

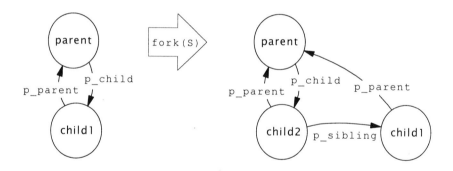

Figure 7.30 Process sibling relationships

The `p_tracep`, `p_controlp` and `p_controllink` fields are used to establish links between a process which is tracing one or more other processes, for example, the `ptrace(S)` system call is used by debuggers to trace a process. The use of these links allows the connection to be broken in a tidy manner following termination of the process controlling the tracing or to inform the controller when the status of a child changes.

TTY management is described in detail in section 9.7. The `u_ttyip`, `u_ttyp` and `u_ttyd` fields of the u_area are used to associate a process or process group with a specific terminal driver. When key sequences that should result in signals are generated, the driver uses the process group ID stored in its `tty` structure in a call to `psignal(K)` to deliver the signal.

Toolkit 7.10   Extracting process relationship state

The program shown in this toolkit extracts fields from the `proc` structure for a given process ID. This shows the relationship between the specified process, its parent and siblings and any relationships established as part of debugging.

The toolkit program uses the `table` driver to extract each `proc` structure in turn from `/dev/table/proc` until either a match is found with the specified process ID or the end of the process table is reached. The `/dev/table/proc` device is opened on line 49 and `proc` entries are read and checked against the specified process ID on lines 53 to 59. A check is made to see if a match is found on line 61. If the process cannot be found, the program will exit.

```
 1 #include <sys/proc.h>
 2 #include <sys/user.h>
 3 #include <sys/sysi86.h>
 4 #include <sys/errno.h>
 5 #include <sys/types.h>
 6 #include <fcntl.h>
 7 #include <unistd.h>
 8
 9 extern int errno ;
10
11 int
12 read_proc(off_t addr, struct proc *pr)
13 {
14      int fd ;
15      fd = open("/dev/kmem", O_RDONLY) ;
16      if (fd == -1)
17          return(0) ;
18      lseek(fd, addr, SEEK_SET) ;
19      read(fd, (char *)pr, sizeof(struct proc)) ;
20          return(1) ;
21 }
22
23 void
24 pr_pid(off_t address)
25 {
26      struct proc pr ;
27      if (address) {
28          read_proc(address, &pr) ;
29          printf("    PID %d\n", pr.p_pid) ;
30      }
31      else
32          printf("\n") ;
33 }
34
35 main(int argc, char *argv[])
36 {
37      int fd, nread, found=0 ;
38      struct proc p ;
39      struct user u ;
40      pid_t pid ;
41
```

```
42    if (argc != 2) {
43        errno = EINVAL ;
44        pexit("pstate") ;
45    }
46
47    pid = atoi(argv[1]) ;
48
49    fd = open("/dev/table/proc", O_RDONLY) ;
50    if (fd < 0)
51        pexit("/dev/table/proc") ;
52
53    do {
54        nread = read(fd, (char *)&p, sizeof(struct proc)) ;
55        if (p.p_pid == pid) {
56            found = 1 ;
57            break ;
58        }
59    } while (nread == sizeof(struct proc)) ;
60
61    if (!found) {
62        printf("Process (PID=%d) not found\n", pid) ;
63        exit(-1) ;
64    }
65    printf("p_pid        = %d\n", p.p_pid) ;
66    printf("p_pgrp       = %d\n", p.p_pgrp) ;
67    printf("p_ppid       = %d\n", p.p_ppid) ;
68    printf("p_sid        = %d\n", p.p_sid) ;
69    printf("p_parent     = %x", p.p_parent) ;
70        pr_pid(p.p_parent) ;
71    printf("p_child      = %x", p.p_child) ;
72        pr_pid(p.p_child) ;
73    printf("p_sibling    = %x", p.p_sibling) ;
74        pr_pid(p.p_sibling) ;
75    printf("p_ptracep    = %x", p.p_ptracep) ;
76        pr_pid(p.p_ptracep) ;
77    printf("p_controlp   = %x", p.p_controlp) ;
78        pr_pid(p.p_controlp) ;
79    printf("p_controllink = %x", p.p_controllink) ;
80        pr_pid(p.p_controllink) ;
81 }
```

Lines 65 to 80 display the fields of the `proc` structure covered in Table 7.7 (page 237). For fields which hold a pointer to another `proc` structure, the `pr_pid()` function (lines 23 to 33) is called. This function calls the `read_proc()` function (lines 11 to 21) which opens `/dev/kmem`, calls `lseek(S)` with the address specified and reads the appropriate `proc` table entry. `pr_pid()` then displays the `p_pid` field.

Consider again the process group created by the following two commands:

```
$ cat | lpr -deng_lw2
```

The modified output given by `ps(C)` is:

```
$ ps -ef
  UID    PID  PPID  C    STIME      TTY        TIME CMD
  root     1     0  0    Nov-27       ?     00:00:11 /etc/init -a
  root  3794     1  0    Nov-30    tty01    00:00:00 /bin/login spate
  spate 6349  3794  0 08:36:21    tty01    00:00:00 -ksh
  spate 6355  6349  0 08:36:35    tty01    00:00:00 cat
  spate 6356  6349  0 08:36:35    tty01    00:00:00 lp -deng_lw2
```

The following program is run, passing the process IDs for processes shown with the exception of the `init` process. The process group and session relationships mirror those shown previously in Figure 7.29. Of course the actual values will change each time the program runs.

```
$ pstate 6355
p_pid        = 6355
p_pgrp       = 6355
p_ppid       = 6349
p_sid        = 3794
p_parent     = fb11b5e0    PID 6349
p_child      = 0
p_sibling    = 0
p_ptracep    = 0
p_controlp   = 0
p_controllink = 0
$ pstate 6356
p_pid        = 6356
p_pgrp       = 6355
p_ppid       = 6349
p_sid        = 3794
p_parent     = fb11b5e0    PID 6349
p_child      = 0
p_sibling    = fb11b738    PID 6355
p_ptracep    = 0
p_controlp   = 0
p_controllink = 0
$ pstate 6349
p_pid        = 6349
p_pgrp       = 6349
p_ppid       = 3794
p_sid        = 3794
p_parent     = fb117968    PID 3794
p_child      = fb11b890    PID 6356
p_sibling    = 0
p_ptracep    = 0
p_controlp   = 0
p_controllink = 0
$ pstate 3794
p_pid        = 3794
p_pgrp       = 3794
p_ppid       = 1
p_sid        = 3794
p_parent     = fb117158    PID 1
p_child      = fb11b5e0    PID 6349
p_sibling    = fb118178    PID 3703
p_ptracep    = 0
p_controlp   = 0
p_controllink = 0
```

Figure 7.31 shows the information presented when running the program. The main observation that can be made here is that the immediate child of the `ksh` process is not `cat` but `lp`. Although the process for `cat` is created first, subsequent invocations of `fork(S)` always attach the newly created child to `p_child` and the process which was previously pointed to by `p_child` is referenced by the `p_sibling` field of the newly created process.

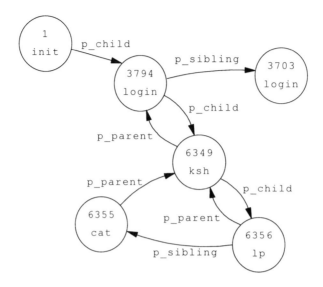

Figure 7.31   Parent, child and sibling relationships

To demonstrate the use of two of the `proc` structure control links, consider the following example. The program shown invokes the `fork(S)` system call. This is followed by both the parent and child processes invoking `pause(S)` and therefore suspending themselves until a signal is received.

```
main()
{
    int pid ;

    pid = fork() ;
    pause() ;
}
```

The process can be set running within `adb` as follows:

```
$ adb debug
* :r
debug: running
```

The following output from `ps(C)` run from another virtual console highlights the parent/child relationships between the different processes:

```
$ ps -ef | grep spate
  UID    PID  PPID  C    STIME     TTY        TIME CMD
 root   3794     1  0   Nov-30   tty01    00:00:00 /bin/login spate
spate   6349  3794  0 08:36:21   tty01    00:00:00 -ksh
```

```
spate  6578  6349  0 16:46:34  tty01  00:00:00 adb debug
spate  6579  6578  0 16:46:35  tty01  00:00:00 debug
spate  6580  6579  0 16:46:35  tty01  00:00:00 debug
```

Using the `pstate` program to analyse the `adb` and both `debug` processes, the output is as follows:

```
$ pstate 6578
p_pid          = 6578
p_pgrp         = 6578
p_ppid         = 6349
p_sid          = 3794
p_parent       = fb11b5e0      PID 6349
p_child        = fb11b890      PID 6579
p_sibling      = 0
p_ptracep      = 0
p_controlp     = fb11b890      PID 6579
p_controllink  = 0
$ pstate 6579
p_pid          = 6579
p_pgrp         = 6578
p_ppid         = 6578
p_sid          = 3794
p_parent       = fb11b738      PID 6578
p_child        = fb11bb40      PID 6580
p_sibling      = 0
p_ptracep      = fb11b738      PID 6578
p_controlp     = 0
p_controllink  = 0
$ pstate 6580
p_pid          = 6580
p_pgrp         = 6578
p_ppid         = 6579
p_sid          = 3794
p_parent       = fb11b890      PID 6579
p_child        = 0
p_sibling      = 0
p_ptracep      = 0
p_controlp     = 0
p_controllink  = 0
```

The `adb` process has its `p_controlp` field set to point to the first `debug` process. In the child debug process, the `p_tracep` field is set to point back to the `adb` (parent) process. Note, however, that the second `debug` process forked is not under control of `adb` and therefore simply has the `p_parent` field set to point to the first `debug` process. The example is shown in Figure 7.32.

7.7.4 Process group and session related system calls

Figure 7.33 shows how the different process group and session management related functions are multiplexed onto the `setpgrp(S)` system call. The `getpgrp(S)`, `setpgid(S)` and `setpgrp(S)` functions enter the kernel by jumping through a call gate while the `getpgid(S)`, `getsid(S)` and `setsid(S)` functions enter the kernel by first calling `setpgid(S)`.

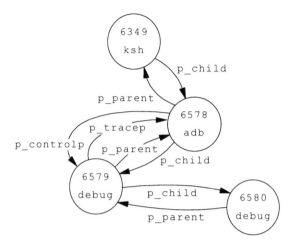

Figure 7.32   Debugged process control links

Prior to invoking the setpgrp() kernel function, each system call or library function places a specific flag on the user stack in order to allow setpgrp() to distinguish between the different functions. The following tasks are performed by setpgrp():

- If the flag is set to GETSID, the contents of p_sid are returned.
- If the flag is set to SETSID, if the process is a group leader (p_pid = p_pgrp) return EPERM to the caller, otherwise set the p_sid field to p_pid and return the contents of p_pgrp.

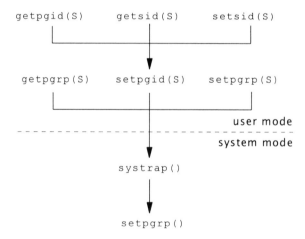

Figure 7.33   System call handling for process group and session management functions

- If the flag is set to SETPGRP, the p_sid and p_pgrp fields are set to p_pid and the contents of p_pgrp are returned.

- If the flag is set to GETPGRP, the contents of the p_pgrp field are returned.

- If the flag is set to SETPGID, the setpgid() function is called.

Many of the kernel functions which take a process ID as an argument call the prfind() function which takes a process ID as an argument and returns a pointer to the process table entry in which the process is located.

The setpgid() kernel function is invoked to handle the setpgid(S) system call and must perform additional checking above the other calls. For example, it must ensure that the process ID requested by the caller resides in the same session, that the process specified is not a session leader and that the child matched has not invoked one of the execve(S) system calls.

7.8 Time management

The kernel relies on the use of a hardware clock to generate interrupts at a specified and regular interval. This allows the kernel to manage the time and date, provide user level alarms and high resolution timers, timeout capabilities for kernel subsystems and device drivers and provide other time related accounting statistics and tasks.

For example, to implement a time-shared multitasking environment, the kernel must keep a record of how long the current process has been running on the CPU in order to switch to another process when the time-slice of the process expires.

PC-based hardware utilises the i8253/8254 Programmable Interval Timer (PIT). Shown in Figure 7.34, the PIT is connected to the CPU's INTR pin via the first Peripheral Interrupt Controller (PIC).

The PIT generates programmable time intervals from an external clock based on a crystal oscillator and provides three separately programmable counters. The PIT is programmed by writing to the PIT's control port followed by one or two bytes to the port of the intended counter.

The individual counters can be read directly or the PIT can be programmed to generate an interrupt when a counter reaches 0 or 1.

7.8.1 PIT initialisation

The clkstart() function is called by the kernel main() function. Its role is to initialise the PIT. SCO UNIX uses only one of the three PIT counters (counter 0). The counter is initialised so that the PIT will generate an interrupt at a frequency of Hz (100) times per second.

On return to main(), clock interrupts are enabled and will arrive at the rate of 100 per second. The routine called at each interrupt is clock().

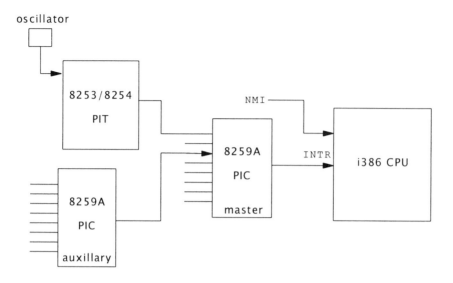

Figure 7.34   Schematic showing connection of the PIT, PICs and CPU

7.8.2 Per clock interrupt processing

The interrupt generated on each clock tick is a maskable interrupt. The clock interrupt line is vectored according to its ID through the Interrupt Descriptor Table (IDT) which contains a number of task, interrupt and gate descriptors. The i386 processor selects the descriptor from the IDT which matches the interrupt vector ID for the clock.

The descriptor contains a selector pointing to the GDT and an offset which specifies the address of a function in the kernel. The function calls the common interrupt handler cmnint() which in turn calls the device interrupt handler for the clock, the kernel function clock().

The clock() function needs to perform a number of different tasks including:

- Call each driver's poll() function if registered.

- Perform processing for the *callout* table.

- Update the u_utime or u_stime fields of the u_area depending on whether the process is running in user mode (u_utime) or kernel mode (u_stime). If there is a limit on the time that the process can execute, the process will be sent a SIGXCPU signal. See getrlimit(S) and setrlimit(S) for further details.

- Process any outstanding interval timers.

- If swapping is required, run sched() which is located in proc[0].

- If memory is low, wake up vhand().

- Call DISP_TICK() to perform per process scheduler time accounting.

- Increment `lbolt` and decrement `one_sec`. The `lbolt` variable is a signed integer which contains the number of clock ticks since the system was booted. It can be used by device drivers to keep track of short delays. The `one_sec` variable is used to allow additional processing every clock second.

When `one_sec` reaches zero, the following additional tasks are performed by `clock()`:

- Increment the `time` variable which counts the number of seconds since the system was booted.
- For each process in the `proc[]` table perform the following tasks:
  - ⇨ Increment `p_time` up to a maximum of 127. The `p_time` field of the `proc` structure is used to record how long the process has been resident in memory since it was last swapped in or how long it has been swapped out.
  - ⇨ Decrement the `p_clktim` field of the `proc` structure which is used to implement the `alarm(S)` system call. If it reaches zero, `psignalinfo()` is called to post a `SIGALRM` signal to the process.
  - ⇨ Call each process's `DISP_ONESEC()` scheduler function. This allows the class schedulers, described in section 7.10.2, to monitor activity on the system and re-schedule processes if necessary.
- Decrement the `bdflushcnt` variable and if it reaches zero, wake up the buffer cache flushing daemon `bdflush`. See section 9.2.7 for further details.

7.8.3 Time of day and time related system calls

UNIX maintains the notion of time and date and provides a number of system calls for reading and modifying the time. The time is maintained internally by the variable `time` which is incremented by the `clock()` interrupt routine each second. The value held in `time` is the number of seconds since 1 January 1970, called *Universal Coordinated Time* or *UCT*. It is also termed the Epoch and the phrase 'time since the Epoch' is often used.

PC-based hardware usually includes a battery backed *real-time clock*. Shown in Figure 7.35, the real-time clock is usually a Motorola MC146818 device which contains 64 bytes of RAM; it is usually called the CMOS RAM or just CMOS.

The CMOS RAM is used for holding information about the types of devices present, the amount of memory, and the time and date. The contents of the CMOS are read and written by a kernel device driver using `inb` and `outb` instructions. The time and date can be read by invoking `cat(C)` on the device itself:

```
# cat /dev/rtc
1217083896
```

which represents 8:38 a.m. on 17 December 1996. The `cat(C)` command opens the device, reads from it and then closes the device.

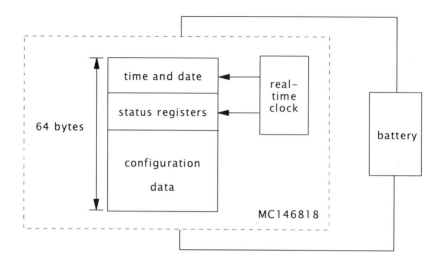

Figure 7.35   Contents of the MC146818 real-time clock

Shown in Figure 7.36, when the `clock()` interrupt handler runs it increments `lbolt` and decrements `one_sec`. After each second, `one_sec` reaches zero and the `do_clock_one_sec()` function is called which increments the `time` variable.

There is a period of time where the value in `time` is invalid. When the kernel is booted, the value of `time` is equal to zero so when the kernel starts servicing clock interrupts, `time` represents the number of seconds since initialisation of the PIT.

Once the `init` process starts running, it processes entries in `/etc/inittab`. One of the first entries run is `/etc/bcheckrc` which invokes the `setclk(ADM)` function. This calls the `sysi86(S)` system call with the `RTODC` argument to read the value of the real-time clock. It then passes the time read to `sysi86(S)` with the `STIME` argument which will set the value of `time` to be the value passed to `sysi86(S)`. The value of `time` is now set to seconds since UCT.

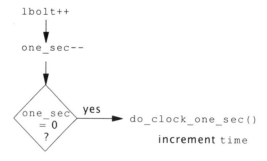

Figure 7.36   Incrementing `time` after each `Hz` clock ticks

There are five main system calls available for reading and setting the time. The first two, described in detail, are time(S) and stime(S):

```
#include <sys/types.h>
#include <time.h>

time_t time(time_t *tloc) ;
int stime(long *tp) ;
```

The time(S) system call returns the time in seconds since the Epoch both as a return value and in the location pointed to by tloc. This involves simply returning the value held in the time kernel variable.

The stime(S) system call takes the time in seconds since the Epoch. This sets the kernel time variable and also updates the time held on the real-time clock.

Three other system calls are provided which allow a finer level of control when reading or setting the time:

```
#include <sys/time.h>

int gettimeofday(struct timeval *tp) ;
int settimeofday(struct timeval *tp) ;
int adjtime(struct timeval *delta, struct timeval *olddelta) ;
```

As with time(S) and stime(S), both the gettimeofday(S) and settimeofday(S) system calls work in time since the Epoch. The timeval structure, however, specifies the time in seconds and microseconds. In addition to reading or writing the value held in time, both calls access one_sec which, when added to time, gives the time value in seconds and milliseconds. Note that the granularity of clock ticks is restricted by the value of Hz which is set to 100.

The adjtime(S) system call allows the caller to specify a delta to the existing time. The delta can be either positive or negative so the time will be either incremented or decremented depending on the second and microsecond values passed in the timeval structure. The modifications performed to the system time and the real-time clock are also dependent on a number of kernel tuneables:

update_rtc	If this value is set to 1 (default), the real-time clock is set to the system time after adjtime(S) has completed.
clock_drift	This tuneable specifies the rate at which the adjustment is made in nanoseconds per second.
track_rtc	This keeps the system clock accurate which involves binding it to the real-time clock.

7.8.4 Callout management

Both the kernel and device drivers need the ability to execute a function at some designated time without explicitly using the sleep(K) and wakeup(K) functions, for example a device driver that is waiting for an event which is not guaranteed to happen.

Rather than just poll or wait indefinitely, the driver would typically set up a function to run after a specified amount of time to cancel the request or perform some other clean-up function.

The `timeout(K)` kernel function is used to register a function which will be called after the specified period of time has elapsed and passes the specified argument:

```
int timeout(int (*routine)(), caddr_t arg, int clock_ticks) ;
int untimeout(int id) ;
```

An identifier is returned from `timeout(K)` which can be used as the argument to the `untimeout(K)` function which the kernel provides to cancel a previously instantiated timeout request.

The kernel maintains each routine to be invoked in the *callout table*, a linked list of `callo` structures pointed to by the `callout` kernel variable. The fields of the `callo` structure are shown in Table 7.8.

Table 7.8   The `callo` structure used to implement the callout table

callo structure field		Description
int	c_time	The time before expiry, incremental to the previous `callo` structure in the list in clock ticks.
int	c_id	The timeout ID returned by `timeout(K)` and used on a subsequent call to `untimeout(K)`.
caddr_t	c_arg	The argument to be passed to the function when the timeout expires.
int	(*c_func)()	The function to be invoked when the timeout expires.
struct callo	next	A pointer to the next entry in the callout table or NULL if this is the last element.

The `callo` structures are held, as shown in Figure 7.37, in a list linked using the `next` field. For the last element in the list, the `next` field is set to NULL.

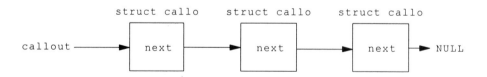

Figure 7.37   The callout table as a linked list of `callo` structures

The list is headed by the kernel variable `callout`. If `callout` is NULL, the list is empty. The entries in the list are kept in chronological order such that the value held in the `c_time` field is relative to the previous element in the list. For example, consider the list shown in Figure 7.38.

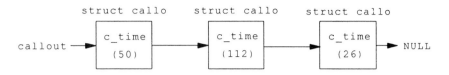

Figure 7.38   Example callout table

If all three timeouts were entered into the callout table between one clock tick and another, the three `timeout(K)` calls invoked would be:

```
timeout(funcA, arg1, 50) ;
timeout(funcB, arg2, 162) ;   # 50 + 112 = 162
timeout(funcC, arg3, 188) ;   # 162 + 26 = 188
```

If a further `timeout(K)` call was invoked as follows:

```
timeout(funcD, arg4, 65) ;
```

the callout table would be altered as shown in Figure 7.39.

Figure 7.39   Inserting a `callo` structure into the callout table

Each time `timeout(K)` is called the kernel calls `kmem_zalloc()` to allocated a zero filled area of memory large enough to hold a `callo` structure. When the timeout expires, the structure is freed by a call to `kmem_free()`.

When the `clock()` interrupt handler is called, it checks to see if there are any elements in the callout table (`callout` is not `NULL`) and decrements the `c_time` field of the first element in the list. If it reaches zero, the `timein()` function is called which performs the following tasks:

- Remove and free all elements on the list for which the value of `c_time` has reached zero.
- Set `callout` to point to the first element with a non-zero value in `c_time`.
- Invoke the function of each expired timeout.

Toolkit 7.11   Displaying the callout table

The example presented here displays the contents of the callout table by printing the elements of each `callo` structure. In order to locate the table, the contents of the `callout` kernel variable must be read to obtain the value of the pointer to the first element in the list.

The `nlist(S)` function is called on line 30 which returns the virtual address of `callout`. Lines 34 to 38 then read the contents of this address by opening `/dev/kmem`, seeking to the address and reading four bytes. The value is read into the variable `crp`.

```
 1 #include <sys/types.h>
 2 #include <sys/callo.h>
 3 #include <fcntl.h>
 4 #include <errno.h>
 5 #include <nlist.h>
 6
 7 struct nlist nl[] = { { "callout", 0, 0, 0, 0, 0 },
 8                       { 0 }
 9                     } ;
10
11 int
12 read_callout(long addr, struct callo *cr)
13 {
14     int fd ;
15     fd = open("/dev/kmem", O_RDONLY) ;
16     if (fd == -1)
17         return(0) ;
18     lseek(fd, addr, SEEK_SET) ;
19     read(fd, (char *)cr, sizeof(struct callo)) ;
20     close(fd) ;
21 }
22
23 main()
24 {
25     caddr_t callout_addr ;
26     struct callo cr ;
27     long crp ;
28     int fd ;
29
30     if (nlist("/unix", nl) == -1)
31         pexit("nlist") ;
32
33     callout_addr = nl[0].n_value ;
34     fd = open("/dev/kmem", O_RDONLY) ;
35     if (fd == -1)
36         pexit("kmem") ;
37     lseek(fd, callout_addr, SEEK_SET) ;
38     read(fd, (char *)&crp, sizeof(long)) ;
39
40     printf("callo addr    c_id   c_time     c_func    c_next\n") ;
41     while (crp) {
42         printf("%10x", crp) ;
43         read_callout(crp, &cr) ;
44         printf(" %7d", cr.c_id) ;
45         printf(" %8d", cr.c_time) ;
46         printf(" %9x", cr.c_func) ;
47         printf(" %9x\n", cr.next) ;
48         crp=(long)cr.next;
49     }
50 }
```

The program then loops around lines 41 to 49 reading the `callo` structure at the address pointed to by `crp`, displaying the contents of the structure, reassigning `crp` to the value of the `next` field until `next` is equal to `NULL` at which time there are no further elements.

The `read_callout()` function on lines 11 to 21 is used to read the contents of each `callo` structure. This involves opening `/dev/kmem`, seeking to the address specified and reading the contents of the structure.

The output of the program is shown below. The actual callout functions to be executed can be seen from within `crash(ADM)` by using the `dis` command.

```
$ callout
callo addr     c_id    c_time     c_func    c_next
  f08009a0   575439        18    f007c03c   f08009c0
  f08009c0   575413        50    f00a31f0   f0800720
  f0800720   575403        40    f00d2254   f08008a0
  f08008a0   575107       914    f0145824   f0800860
  f0800860   575091      2262    f0145824   f08007c0
  f08007c0   575101       706    f0145824   f0800960
  f0800960   575350      1497    f0078224   f0800940
  f0800940   573219     11131    f006d3c8   f0800740
  f0800740   575449     43381    f0145824   f0800820
  f0800820   479612      7450    f0145824   f0800900
  f0800900   573203      9052    f0125ef8   f0800880
  f0800880   240350   1623094    f0145824          0
```

The callout table can also be displayed from `crash(ADM)` with the `callout` command:

```
> callout
FUNCTION         ARGUMENT        TIME          ID      PROC
epi_poker        0xc0160000         8     1124739         0
in_fasttimo               0         7     1124782         0
in_slowtimo               0         4     1124780         0
wd_hang_check    0xf02059a4        36     1124766         0
unselect         0xfb117ac0      1018     1124488         0
unselect         0xfb117d70      2894     1124560         0
unselect         0xfb118178       712     1124582         0
ip_pmtu_age               0         8     1124584         0
kmwakeup                  0      3947     1118384         0
arptimer                  0       275     1123035         0
unselect         0xfb1199a8     51098     1124796         0
unselect         0xfb11a468    739820     1109451         0
unselect         0xfb1182d0   2272206      932904         0
```

The `crash` command cannot always display the full callout table between two clock ticks and therefore the values read may be not be completely accurate. However, the `callout` command is particularly useful for analysing system dumps where the table will be accurate at the time that the panic occurred.

7.8.5 Supporting alarms

The `alarm(S)` system call informs the kernel to post the `SIGALRM` signal to the process after the number of seconds specified to `alarm(S)` has elapsed:

```
#include <unistd.h>
unsigned int alarm(unsigned int seconds) ;
```

The actual `alarm()` kernel function has little functionality to perform. The time left until an alarm expires is held in the `p_clktim` field of the `proc` structure. The field is checked and decremented by the `clock()` interrupt handler. Thus, the `alarm()` function sets `p_clktim` to the value passed to `alarm(S)`, returning the old value to the caller.

For each clock interrupt, the `clock()` interrupt handler checks for one second intervals. After each second it walks through the `proc` table looking for active processes which have a `p_clktim` field greater than zero. If a matching process is found, the `p_clktim` field is decremented. If the value reaches zero, `psignalinfo()` is called to post `SIGALRM` to the process.

Toolkit 7.12   Watching the alarm clock!

The program presented in this toolkit makes use of the `alarm(S)` system call to trigger a `SIGALRM` signal after five seconds. The program then constantly reads the value in `p_clktim` and, if it changes, prints out its value until the signal handler, installed to receive the `SIGALRM` signal, is called.

```
 1 #include <sys/proc.h>
 2 #include <sys/user.h>
 3 #include <sys/sysi86.h>
 4 #include <fcntl.h>
 5 #include <errno.h>
 6 #include <pwd.h>
 7
 8 int
 9 sighdlr(int signo)
10 {
11     printf("Signal arrived\n") ;
12     exit(0) ;
13 }
14
15 int
16 read_proc(struct proc *addr, struct proc *pr)
17 {
18     int fd ;
19     fd = open("/dev/kmem", O_RDONLY) ;
20     if (fd == -1)
21         return(0) ;
22     lseek(fd, (long)addr, SEEK_SET) ;
23     read(fd, (char *)pr, sizeof(struct proc)) ;
24     close(fd) ;
25 }
26
27 main()
28 {
29     struct proc p ;
30     struct user u ;
31     int old_time = -1 ;
32
33     sigset(SIGALRM, sighdlr) ;
34
35     alarm(5) ;
36
37     sysi86(RDUBLK, getpid(), (char *)&u, sizeof(struct user)) ;
38
39     while (old_time != 0) {
40         read_proc(u.u_procp, &p) ;
```

```
41              if (old_time != p.p_clktim) {
42                  printf("p_clktim = %d\n", p.p_clktim) ;
43                  old_time = p.p_clktim ;
44              }
45          }
46
47      while (1) ;    // let signal handler terminate the process
48  }
```

The program starts by establishing a signal handler for SIGALRM on line 33 and then calls alarm(S) on line 35 to set a five second alarm. In order to pass the address of the proc structure for this process to the read_proc() function on line 16, the sysi86(S) system call is invoked on line 37. The u_procp pointer in the u_area contains the appropriate address.

Lines 39 to 45 of the program then loop repeatedly calling read_proc() to read the proc structure in order to access the p_clktim field. A check is made to see if the value is different to the last time it was read and, if so, it is printed out on line 42.

The following output shows p_clktim ticking down. What cannot be seen from this output is the one second delay between each printf() call, since although read_proc() is called many times each second, the value of p_clktim is updated only every second.

```
$ alarm
p_clktim = 5
p_clktim = 4
p_clktim = 3
p_clktim = 2
p_clktim = 1
p_clktim = 0
Signal arrived
```

7.8.6 High resolution timers

Each process has three interval timers, also called *itimers*, associated with it. An itimer is a value which is decremented at each clock tick. If it reaches zero, the itimer expires and a signal is sent to the process. The itimer is optionally reset after expiring so that the process can receive the signal at programmed intervals.

Itimers are similar in concept to alarms but offer much finer control over their operation as the following definitions show:

ITIMER_REAL	This itimer is used to count in real time, also called wall-clock time. When the itimer expires, a SIGALRM is sent to the process. A process may have an alarm specified by the alarm(S) system call or an ITIMER_REAL itimer but not both.
ITIMER_VIRT	This itimer counts only when processing in user mode. When the itimer expires it send a SIGVTALRM signal to the process.
ITIMER_PROF	This itimer counts when executing in user mode and when the system is executing on behalf of the process. When it expires the process is sent a SIGPROF signal.

Itimers are manipulated using the setitimer(S) and getitimer(S) system calls which are defined as follows:

```
#include <sys/select.h>
#include <sys/itimer.h>

int getitimer(int which, struct itimerval *value) ;
int setitimer(int which, struct itimerval *value,
                         struct itimerval *ovalue) ;
```

For both system calls the which argument specifies the itimer to set or retrieve and takes the value ITIMER_REAL, ITIMER_VIRT or ITIMER_PROF.

The getitimer(S) system call returns the current value of the itimer specified by the which argument into the itimerval structure specified by value.

The setitimer(S) system call is used to set the itimer specified by the which argument to the value specified in the value argument. If the ovalue field is not NULL, the previous value of the itimer is returned.

Each itimer is defined by the itimerval structure as follows:

```
struct itimerval {
    struct timeval   it_interval ;
    struct timeval   it_value ;
} ;

struct timeval {
    long tv_sec ;    // seconds
    long tv_usec ;   // microseconds
} ;
```

If the it_value field is non-zero it specifies the time until the next itimer expiration. As time advances, this field is decremented. When the itimer expires and the signal is delivered, if the value of it_interval is non-zero, it is assigned to it_value and the process is repeated. For example, an itimer could be set to expire after 10 seconds. After the signal has been delivered it could be set to expire after each 10 millisecond interval.

Time values greater than the resolution of the system clock, i.e. 100 Hz, are rounded up to the resolution of the system clock which can be obtained by calling the gethz(S) function or sysconf(S).

The following example demonstrates the use of itimers. As the example shows, the accuracy of the itimer as seen by the user process is heavily dependent on the system load.

The program loops around lines 53 to 63. For each loop, the parent calls fork(S). The child executes the test_itimer() function with the value specified by res on line 56. Thus after the first fork(S), test_itimer() is called with an argument of 1, the second time with 10, then 100, 1000, 10 000 and so on up 10 000 000.

The child then calls setitimer(S) to establish the ITIMER_REAL itimer with the value passed to test_itimer() to send a SIGALRM repeatedly. Each time the signal arrives the child increments the timer_expired variable.

The parent allows the child to run for 10 seconds which will give an indication of how many SIGALRM signals the child will receive in a single second. Once the parent's 10 second alarm expires it sends a SIGUSR1 to the child. The child then prints the value of timer_expired and terminates.

```
 1 #include <sys/select.h>
 2 #include <sys/itimer.h>
 3 #include <signal.h>
 4
 5 int timer_expired ;
 6
 7 int
 8 usrhdlr(int signo)
 9 {
10     printf("SIGUSR1:itimerhdlr() called %d times\n", timer_expired) ;
11     exit(0) ;
12 }
13
14 int
15 itimerhdlr(int signo)
16 {
17     ++timer_expired ;
18 }
19
20 test_itimer(int resolution)
21 {
22     long tm ;
23     struct itimerval ival ;
24
25     timer_expired = 0 ;
26
27     sigset(SIGALRM, itimerhdlr) ;
28     sigset(SIGUSR1, usrhdlr) ;
29
30     ival.it_value.tv_sec = 0 ;
31     ival.it_value.tv_usec = resolution ;
32
33     ival.it_interval.tv_sec = 0 ;
34     ival.it_interval.tv_usec = resolution ;
35
36     setitimei(ITIMER_REAL, &ival, (struct itimerval *)0) ;
37
38     while(1) ;
39 }
40
41 int
42 palrm(int signo)
43 {
44     return ;
45 }
46
47 main(int argc, char *argv[])
48 {
49     int pid, res, x ;
50
51     sigset(SIGALRM, palrm) ;
52
53     for (res=1 ; res<10000000 ; res *= 10) {
54         pid = fork() ;
55         if (pid == 0) {
56             test_itimer(res) ;
57         }
58         else {
59             alarm(10) ;
```

```
60              pause() ;
61              kill(pid, SIGUSR1) ;
62          }
63      }
64      sleep(1) ;
65  }
```

In the run of the program, the number of SIGALRM signal handler calls is reported over a 10 second period:

```
$ itimer
SIGUSR1: itimerhdlr() called 550 times   # 1 usecs
SIGUSR1: itimerhdlr() called 551 times   # 10 usecs
SIGUSR1: itimerhdlr() called 550 times   # 100 usecs
SIGUSR1: itimerhdlr() called 543 times   # 1000 usecs
SIGUSR1: itimerhdlr() called 551 times   # 10000 usecs
SIGUSR1: itimerhdlr() called 110 times   # 100000 usecs
SIGUSR1: itimerhdlr() called 0 times     # 1000000 usecs
```

Since the resolution of the clock is 100 Hz, the value passed to setitimer(S) is rounded up to this resolution which results in the similar number of SIGALRMs generated for an itimer value ranging from one microsecond up to 10 000 microseconds.

In the following output the same program is run but with a CPU-bound program running in the background. This highlights the degraded accuracy in itimers when the system is heavily loaded.

```
$ itimer
SIGUSR1: itimerhdlr() called 237 times
SIGUSR1: itimerhdlr() called 284 times
SIGUSR1: itimerhdlr() called 315 times
SIGUSR1: itimerhdlr() called 284 times
SIGUSR1: itimerhdlr() called 280 times
SIGUSR1: itimerhdlr() called 63 times
SIGUSR1: itimerhdlr() called 0 times
```

Alongside the proc[] table is a corresponding proc_itimer[] array which is used to hold itimer information per process. Each element of the proc_itimer[] array contains an itimer structure which holds information about all three process itimers. The fields of the itimer structure are shown in Table 7.9.

Table 7.9   Per process itimer management with the itimer structure

itimer structure field	Description
short it_pid	The process ID that the itimers are for.
time_t it_rset	Time when the ITIMER_REAL itimer was set.

struct itimer_tics {
    time_t value
    time_t interval
} timer[NITIMERS]
	For each itimer type, this array holds the value and interval fields that were passed to setitimer(S).

int to_id	ITIMER_REAL itimer timeout ID.

Processing of timeouts differs depending on the itimer type. The ITIMER_VIRT and ITIMER_PROF are manipulated only when the process is currently running. When the clock() interrupt handler is called it locates the proc_itimer[] entry for the current process. If the process is running in user mode when the clock interrupt arrives, clock() decrements the value field for both ITIMER_VIRT and ITIMER_PROF itimers. If either value reaches zero, psignal() is called to post either the SIGVTALRM or the SIGPROF signal to the process.

If the process is running in kernel mode when the clock interrupt arrives, the value field for the ITIMER_PROF itimer is decremented. If it reaches zero, psignal() is called to post a SIGPROF signal to the process.

The ITIMER_REAL itimer is handled differently. A timeout(K) is invoked during processing of the setitimer(S) system call. The ID returned from timeout(K) is stored in the to_id of the process's itimer structure in proc_itimer[]. This is used on calls to setitimer(S) which might cancel the itimer. In this case, the to_id value is used as an argument to untimeout(K).

Toolkit 7.13   Accessing per process CPU times

Associated with each process are a number of time-related fields which allow the process to determine for how long both it and its children have been running. The fields can be read by issuing the times(S) system call:

```
#include <sys/types.h>
#include <sys/times.h>

clock_t times(struct tms *buffer) ;
```

The tms structure contains four fields of type clock_t as shown in Table 7.10.

Table 7.10   Fields of the tms structure

tms struct field	Description
tms_utime	The time in clock ticks that the process has been executing in user mode.
tms_stime	The time in clock ticks that the process has been executing in kernel mode.
tms_cutime	Sum of clock ticks of the process's children while executing in user mode.
tms_cstime	Sum of clock ticks of the process's children while executing in kernel mode.

The times returned here are not representative of the elapsed time that the process has been running since these values are incremented only while the process is running.

The following example implements a version of the times(S) system call in a function called mtimes(), which is shown on lines 9 to 19. Since all of the fields used to update the tms structure are located in the u_area, the sysi86(S) system call is invoked with the RDUBLK command. The various fields are then copied to the tms structure passed as an argument.

```
 1 #include <sys/types.h>
 2 #include <sys/times.h>
 3 #include <sys/user.h>
 4 #include <sys/sysi86.h>
 5 #include <signal.h>
 6
 7 int alarm_count = 0 ;
 8
 9 void
10 mtimes(struct tms *tms)
11 {
12     struct user u ;
13
14     sysi86(RDUBLK, getpid(), (char *)&u, sizeof(struct user)) ;
15     tms->tms_utime  = u.u_utime ;
16     tms->tms_stime  = u.u_stime ;
17     tms->tms_cutime = u.u_cutime ;
18     tms->tms_cstime = u.u_cstime ;
19 }
20
21 void
22 alarmhdlr(int signo)
23 {
24     struct tms buffer ;
25
26     if (++alarm_count == 10) {
27         mtimes(&buffer) ;
28         printf("tms_utime = %d\n",  buffer.tms_utime) ;
29         printf("tms_stime = %d\n",  buffer.tms_stime) ;
30         printf("tms_cutime = %d\n", buffer.tms_cutime) ;
31         printf("tms_cstime = %d\n", buffer.tms_cstime) ;
32         exit(0) ;
33     }
34     else
35         alarm(1) ;
36 }
37
38 main()
39 {
40     sigset(SIGALRM, alarmhdlr) ;
41
42     alarm(1) ;
43
44     while(1)
45         getpid() ;
46 }
```

The program sets up a signal handler for SIGALRM on line 40 and establishes an alarm call for 1 second on line 42.

The program then loops repeatedly invoking the getpid(S) system call. After 10 calls to alarmhdlr() the program calls mtimes(), displays the values returned and then terminates.

The output when the program is run is:

```
# mtimes
tms_utime = 135
tms_stime = 885
tms_cutime = 0
tms_cstime = 0
```

In this example the only times that the process is actually executing in kernel mode are when the process is created, when it terminates and when it returns from processing the SIGALRM signal.

If the call to getpid(S) is removed and the program simply executes a null while() loop, the time returned for tms_stime will be either zero or a number of clock ticks very close to zero.

Generating the SIGALRM is performed directly by the clock() interrupt service routine for which the time taken to deliver the signal is not attributed to the process.

7.9 Context switching

As UNIX is a multitasking operating system, the kernel frequently needs to switch between one process and another, creating the concept of a virtual machine for each user of the system. Since the work needed to switch to the new process involves modifying the processor state to recognise the memory context of the process, the term *context switch* is usually used in place of task or process switch.

Processes cannot be automatically context switched when executing in kernel mode since there are a number of places in the kernel that prohibit immediate pre-emption. In fact, pre-emption may occur only if the process executing in kernel mode has no further work to do, resulting in a sleep() call, or if the process is about to return to user space. There are five cases in the kernel where a context switch can actually occur:

- The process terminates voluntarily by invoking the exit(S) or _exit(S) system calls.

- A process which is currently executing in kernel mode relinquishes control of the processor by going to sleep on a specific resource, for example, a process may require a buffer to perform I/O and no buffers may be currently available.

- A process is about to return from kernel mode to user mode following an exception, an interrupt, a trap or a system call. At this stage all locks have been released and it is safe to relinquish control of the processor.

- The process invokes the sched_yield(S) system call which forces the caller to give up the CPU. If no other processes are eligible to run, the calling process will stay on the processor.

- A process attempts to allocate memory while executing in kernel mode and the amount of memory available reaches zero. The process's p_stat field is set to SXBRK and the swapper is invoked to free space by swapping processes out. The tasks performed by the swapper are described in chapter 12.

The main paths through the kernel when performing a context switch are shown in Figure 7.40. Since context switching is closely related to process scheduling there will be a number of references to scheduling routines and functionality. Process scheduling is described in section 7.10. However, where scheduling routines are mentioned in the following sections, their functionality is described in enough detail to avoid constantly switching between this section and section 7.10.

The following sections describe in detail the first four conditions under which a context switch will occur. Swapping is described in chapter 12. It is useful when reading these sections to refer to Figure 7.40.

7.9.1 Returning from kernel to user mode

Although there are numerous places throughout the kernel where a decision is made to perform a context switch, under many circumstances the actual switch is delayed until the process is about to return to user mode. As an example, consider Figure 7.41 where a process invokes the fork(S) system call. The systrap() function is called after kernel mode is entered which calls genfork() to handle the fork(S) system call. The newproc1() function is then called to create the child process.

It is normal practice to run the child process before the parent returns from the fork(S) system call therefore a context switch should be made.

The procdup() function is called to duplicate the child process image from that of its parent. The DISP_FORK() scheduler call is made to place the child process on the run queue. On return from procdup() the DISP_POSTFORK() scheduler function is called. If the parent process, and therefore the child due to inheritance, is associated with the TS (*Time Sharing*) scheduling class, the runrun flag is set to indicate that a context switch should occur before returning to user space.

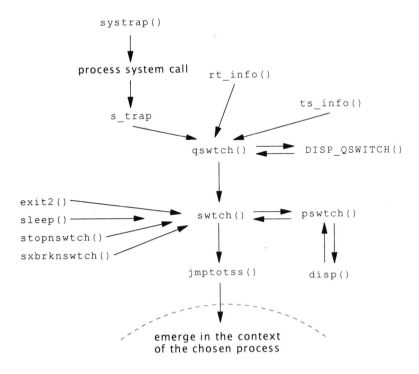

Figure 7.40   The kernel paths followed to perform a context switch

After `systrap()` has returned, and just before returning to user space, the `s_trap()` function checks the `runrun` flag. If `runrun` is not zero, the kernel must perform a context switch. In this case, the `s_trap()` calls `qswtch()` to perform the context switch and therefore to start running the child process before the parent returns from the `fork(S)` system call.

When the parent eventually resumes, it is still running in kernel mode within `s_trap()`. It then returns to user mode and thus exits the `fork(S)` system call.

For processes associated with the RT (*Real Time*) scheduling class there is no operation to perform since the parent will always run first. The child will sleep until the parent relinquishes control of the CPU.

7.9.2 Voluntary process termination

A process will be terminated when the `exit(S)` system call is invoked. Once resources held by the process are released and the process becomes a zombie, the `swtch()` function is called to perform a context switch, allowing another process to run. Only the child's exit status and `siginfo` structure will remain.

The tasks performed by issuing `exit(S)` or `_exit(S)` are described in section 7.11.

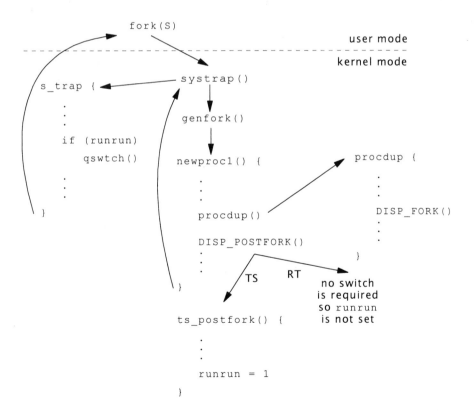

Figure 7.41   Setting `runrun` to force a context switch before returning to user mode

7.9.3 The kernel `sleep()` and `wakeup()` functions

There are numerous times when executing in kernel mode that a process may voluntarily issue the kernel `sleep()` function. The need for a process to sleep can occur for a number of reasons, for example if the process requires a resource which is temporarily unavailable, if it calls one of the `wait()` functions to receive a child status, if it is waiting for I/O completion and so on. The prototype of `sleep()` is:

```
int sleep(caddr_t wchan, int disp)
```

The `sleep()` function takes two parameters. The first argument is a pointer to an *event* for which the process should wait. This event is usually called a *wait channel* and is stored in the `p_wchan` field of the `proc` structure. The terms 'event' and 'wait channel' are often used interchangeably. The second argument is the priority at which the process will run when it is woken again. The wait channel can be seen by issuing the `ps(C)` command using the `-o` option as the following example shows:

```
$ ps -a -ouser,pid,ppid,wchan,args
USER    PID  PPID    WCHAN COMMAND
root   6344  6341  fc1f3310 vbiosd 0
spate  6349  3794  f0185ea0 -ksh
root   6357  3703  f0185f70 -sh
root   7028  6636  f019166c xterm
spate  9226  7029  f019166c rlogin scopilot -1 spate
spate  9769  6637         - ps -a -ouser,pid,ppid,wchan,args
```

Processes which are not currently sleeping do not have an address in the `WCHAN` of the `ps(C)` output. In the output shown above, only process ID `9769` is not sleeping.

All processes sleeping on an event are linked together using the `p_link` field of the `proc` structure. Linking all processes on a single list would require potentially large search times to locate a specified process. In order to reduce the amount of time required to search for a required process, the `p_wchan` field is hashed and the processes are linked together on one of 64 hash queues pointed to by the `hsque[]` array.

`hsque[]` is an array of 64 pointers to `proc` structures. Each element of the `hsque[]` array contains a linked list of all processes whose `p_wchan` field hashes to the same value and therefore the same element of the `hsque[]` array. Figure 7.42 shows the `hsque[]` array and a number of processes residing on different hash queues. If there are no processes whose `p_wchan` field hashes to an element of `hsque[]`, the element contains a `NULL` pointer. Element 1 in Figure 7.42 is such an element.

The `sqhash()` function, which is passed the wait channel as an argument, is used to locate the array position at which the process should be inserted. The algorithm used by `sqhash()` is:

```
#define sqhash(X) (&hsque[((int)X >> 3) & (NHSQUE - 1)])
```

The `NHSQUE` variable represents the size of the queue which is usually 64.

The tasks performed by the `sleep()` function are shown below. These tasks show in more detail how the `hsque[]` array and `sqhash()` macro are used.

- The `p_stat` field of the `proc` structure is set to `SSLEEP`.

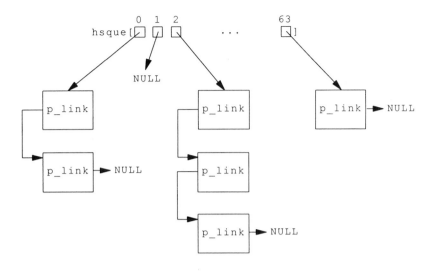

Figure 7.42   Hash queues for managing sleeping processes

- The p_wchan field of the proc structure is set to the wchan argument passed to sleep().

- sqhash() is called, passing wchan as an argument to locate the position in hsque[] where the process will be linked while sleeping. The process is then inserted at the head of the queue.

- The DISP_SLEEP() function is called to determine the priority at which the process will run when it wakes up.

- The swtch() function is called to force a context switch.

- Once the process has woken up as a consequence of the wakeup() function being called, if the priority specified to sleep() was less than or equal to PZERO, sleep() will return with a value of zero.

- If the priority specified to sleep() was greater than PZERO, the ISSIG() macro is invoked to see if the process was awoken by a signal. If so, sleep() will issue a longjmpval() call to return to the address held in the u_qsav field of the u_area, otherwise sleep() will return 0.

If the priority passed to sleep() is greater than PZERO, the process can be awoken by signals, otherwise signals will not affect the sleeping process. A process which called sleep() with priority > PZERO which is interrupted by a signal will call longjmpval() to return to the address held in the u_qsav field of the u_area. The usual effect of this is to return EINTR to the user.

Alternatively, if the sleep() occurred as a result of processing a system call, the system call may be retried. Section 7.4.6 describes restartable system calls in more detail.

Used in conjunction with the sleep() function, the kernel provides a corresponding wakeup() function which can be called to wake up all processes which are sleeping on a specific wait channel.

```
int wakeup(caddr_t wchan)
```

The argument specified to `wakeup()` is the address of a wait channel. If a process is sleeping on the same wait channel, the process will be woken up. If there are multiple processes sleeping on the same wait channel, they will all be woken up by the single call to `wakeup()`.

The actual processing of `wakeup()` is performed by the `wakeupn()` function. The tasks performed by `wakeupn()` are:

- Call `sqhash(wchan)` to locate the appropriate hash queue on which processes may be sleeping.
- Walk through the list of processes on the hash queue. If the `p_wchan` field of the process is equal to the `wchan` argument passed to `wakeup()`, the `w_chan` field is set to zero, the `p_stat` field is set to SRUN and `DISP_WAKEUP()` is called to add the process to the run queue.

As an example of where `sleep()` and `wakeup()` are used, if a process issues the `wait(S)` system call for a child process which has not yet terminated, the parent process may sleep until the child terminates and an exit status is available. The order of events taken to handle the `wait(S)` and `exit(S)` of parent and child are shown in Figure 7.43.

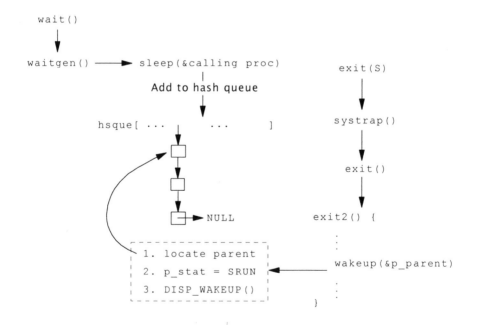

Figure 7.43   `sleep()`, `wakeup()` and wait channel hash queues

The wait channel passed to `sleep()` is the address of the `proc` structure of the caller. When the child terminates the kernel issues a `wakeup()` call, passing the address of the parent's `proc` structure which is located in the `p_parent` field of the child's `proc` structure.

Toolkit 7.14   Analysing the kernel wait channel queues

In the example shown here, the contents of the `hsque[]` array are read from the kernel to display which processes are currently sleeping, the wait channel on which each sleeping process is waiting and on which hash queue the process is currently residing.

The data read is stored in the equivalent `hsque[]` array declared on line 9. Since the address of the kernel `hsque[]` array is unknown, `nlist(S)` must be called to locate the symbol's virtual address. The `nlist(S)` function is called on line 33 with a pointer to the `nl[]` array declared on lines 11 to 13. If the `nlist(S)` call is successful, the address can be accessed via the `nl[0].n_value` field.

```
 1 #include <sys/proc.h>
 2 #include <sys/user.h>
 3 #include <sys/sysi86.h>
 4 #include <nlist.h>
 5 #include <fcntl.h>
 6
 7 #define WCHANSZ 64
 8
 9 struct proc *hsque[WCHANSZ] ;
10
11 struct nlist nl[] = { { "hsque", 0, 0, 0, 0, 0 },
12                       { 0 }
13                     } ;
14
15 int
16 read_proc(struct proc *addr, struct proc *pr)
17 {
18       int fd ;
19       fd = open("/dev/kmem", O_RDONLY) ;
20       if (fd == -1)
21           return(0) ;
22       lseek(fd, (long)addr, SEEK_SET) ;
23       read(fd, (char *)pr, sizeof(struct proc)) ;
24           return(1) ;
25 }
26
27 main()
28 {
29       int i, fd, hd ;
30       struct proc p, *pos ;
31       struct user u ;
32
33       if (nlist("/unix", nl) == -1)
34           pexit("nlist") ;
35
36       printf("hsque located at %x\n", nl[0].n_value) ;
37
38       fd = open("/dev/kmem", O_RDONLY) ;
39       if (fd < 0)
40           pexit("/dev/kmem") ;
41
```

```
42      lseek(fd, nl[0].n_value, SEEK_SET) ;
43      read(fd, &hsque, (WCHANSZ * sizeof(struct proc *))) ;
44
45      for (i = 0 ; i<WCHANSZ ; i++) {
46          hd=1 ;
47          pos = hsque[i] ;
48          while (pos != NULL) {
49              if (hd) {
50                  printf("hsque[%2d]\n", i) ;
51                  hd = 0 ;
52              }
53              read_proc(pos, &p) ;
54              printf("   PID = %4d, wchan = %x, ", p.p_pid,p.p_wchan);
55              sysi86(RDUBLK, p.p_pid, (char *)&u, sizeof(struct user));
56              printf("%s\n", u.u_psargs) ;
57              pos = p.p_link ;
58          }
59      }
60  }
```

Lines 38 to 43 of the main body of the program open /dev/kmem, call lseek(S) to seek to the address of hsque[] returned by nlist(S) and then call read(S) to read the contents of the hsque[] array into the locally defined hsque[] array.

Once the contents of hsque[] have been read, each element is a pointer to either a proc structure or NULL if there are no elements on that particular hash queue. Lines 45 to 59 implement two loops. The outer loop is for each element in hsque[]. If the element is not NULL, the inner loop is executed which walks through each proc structure in the list and performs the following tasks:

- Calls read_proc() on line 53 to read the contents of proc structure using the kmem driver. The read_proc() function can be found on lines 16 to 25. The process ID and wait channel are then displayed on line 54.

- The sysi86(S) system call is invoked to read the u_psargs[] field which contains the name of the process and arguments which were passed to execve(S). The contents of this structure are used by ps(C).

- The current process used in the inner loop is set to point to the next process in the list by accessing the p_link field.

An abbreviated output of the hsque program for one particular run follows; some of the entries have been removed to reduce the amount of output displayed. Running this program on a system with a large number of processes will produce a large amount of output!

```
# hsque
hsque located at f02be84c
hsque[ 0]
    PID =   319, wchan = e0000000, /usr/mmdf/bin/deliver -b
    PID =     1, wchan = e0000000, /etc/init
hsque[ 1]
    PID =    37, wchan = f0220808, /etc/syslogd
    PID =   450, wchan = f0220808, rlogin scompost -1 spate
hsque[ 3]
    PID =    41, wchan = fb117c18, /etc/ifor_pmd
```

```
hsque[ 4]
    PID =   411, wchan = f020b824, /etc/getty tty07 sc_m
hsque[ 5]
    PID =   416, wchan = f020ba2c, /etc/getty tty12 sc_m
hsque[ 6]
    PID =   329, wchan = fb118830, /usr/bin/X11/scologin
hsque[ 9]
    PID =   361, wchan = fcee7648, lockd
hsque[10]
    PID =     4, wchan = f020ae54, kmdaemon
hsque[12]
    PID =   417, wchan = fc3b7860, /tcb/files/no_luid/sdd
hsque[13]
    PID =   338, wchan = fc1f3268, vbiosd 0
hsque[16]
    PID =   407, wchan = f020b684, /etc/getty tty03 sc_m
hsque[17]
    PID =   412, wchan = f020b88c, /etc/getty tty08 sc_m
hsque[18]
    PID =   363, wchan = fcee7690, lockd
    PID =     0, wchan = f02bd294, sched
hsque[29]
    PID =   408, wchan = f020b6ec, /etc/getty tty04 sc_m
hsque[30]
    PID =   413, wchan = f020b8f4, /etc/getty tty09 sc_m
    PID =   351, wchan = f0837af0, biod 4
hsque[32]
    PID =   398, wchan = fc3b6f06, /usr/lib/scosh/caldaemon
    PID =   352, wchan = f0837b00, biod 4
hsque[33]
    PID =   394, wchan = fc3ad30e, /usr/lib/scosh/calserver
hsque[34]
    PID =   349, wchan = f0837b10, biod 4
hsque[36]
    PID =   350, wchan = f0837b20, biod 4
hsque[39]
    PID =   442, wchan = fb11b738, /bin/sh /home/spate/.startxrc
hsque[42]
    PID =    34, wchan = c0164150, htepi_daemon /stand
    PID =   409, wchan = f020b754, /etc/getty tty05 sc_m
hsque[43]
    PID =   227, wchan = fc3aa95e, /etc/cron
    PID =   414, wchan = f020b95c, /etc/getty tty10 sc_m
hsque[50]
    PID =     3, wchan = f0134394, bdflush
hsque[54]
    PID =   406, wchan = f020b5b4, /etc/getty tty01 sc_m
hsque[55]
    PID = 1023, wchan = f020d1bc, vi hsxxx
    PID =   410, wchan = f020b7bc, /etc/getty tty06 sc_m
hsque[56]
    PID =   415, wchan = f020b9c4, /etc/getty tty11 sc_m
hsque[58]
    PID =     2, wchan = f01445d4, vhand
hsque[62]
    PID =    68, wchan = fcee43f0, strerr
```

7.9.4 Task switching on the i386 processor

Since a context switch relies heavily on the underlying processor, this section describes how a context switch is made on the i386 range of processors. The following section describes how SCO UNIX builds on these hardware mechanisms to perform a context switch between UNIX processes.

In this section the term 'task' is used to represent a context. Switching between tasks is the same as switching context or switching between processes. Intel terminology describes a task as a program which is running or waiting to run. This could be thought of in terms of a UNIX process. However, there are processes which are currently sleeping and therefore fall outside of this strict definition.

The term 'task' in this section will refer to a program which runs in its own memory context and has its own set of registers, Local Descriptor Table (LDT) and page tables.

There are a number of hardware registers and structures implemented in hardware that support multitasking which are described below.

The Task State Segment (TSS)

The Task State Segment (TSS) is a data structure held in memory referenced by the `u_tss` field in the process's u_area. It is used to hold all the processor state associated with a task. It contains the following registers and structures:

- The general registers `eax`, `ebx`, `ecx`, `edx`, `esp`, `ebp`, `esi`, and `edi`.

- The segment registers `es`, `cs`, `ss`, `ds`, `fs` and `gs`.

- The `eflags` register.

- The `cr3` (page directory) register.

- The instruction pointer `eip`.

- A selector for the task's LDT.

- A selector for the TSS of the previous task.

- The logical address of the stacks for privilege levels 0, 1 and 2. Note that UNIX uses only privilege levels 0 and 3.

- A debug bit trap which, when set, causes the processor to raise a debug exception when a task switch occurs.

- The base address of the I/O permission bit map.

Before a task switch occurs the state associated with the task is stored in its TSS and the state of the new task to run is restored from its TSS.

The TSS descriptor

The TSS, like other segments, is accessed through a descriptor. The TSS descriptor for the currently running task is stored in the Global Descriptor Table (GDT).

Setting the busy bit in the type field of the descriptor indicates that the task is either running or ready to run. The processor may use this bit to prevent invocation of a task whose execution has been interrupted.

The base, limit and DPL fields and the granularity and present bits are used in a similar way to data segment descriptors as described in chapter 6. However, the limit field must be greater than 0x67, the minimum size of a TSS. If the I/O permission bit map is used then this will increase the size above 0x67 bytes.

If a task has access to a TSS descriptor it can cause a task switch. Note, however, that TSS descriptors can reside only in the GDT and are therefore only accessible by the kernel.

The Task Register (TR) and TSS descriptor

The TR references the current TSS, that is the TSS for the task which is currently running on the processor. Shown in Figure 7.44, the selector component of the TR references the TSS selector stored in the GDT. The TSS descriptor gives the base address and the limit of the TSS. The limit is added to the base address to give the maximum address of the TSS.

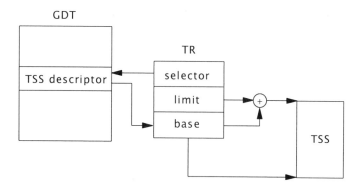

Figure 7.44   Accessing the TSS with the TR and TSS descriptor

Performing the task switch

There are four cases where the processor will perform a task switch. Note, however, that jmp, call and iret are ordinary instructions that do not usually result in a task switch. Only by referencing specific objects do they cause a task switch.

- A jmp or call instruction is made to a TSS descriptor.
- A jmp or call instruction is made to a task gate.
- An interrupt or exception indexes into a task gate located in the IDT (Interrupt Descriptor Table).
- An iret instruction is invoked and the NT (Nested Task) flag is set in eflags.

The type of switch invoked by SCO UNIX during processing of the `swtch()` function is a `jmp` to a TSS descriptor and therefore this section will concentrate on that particular case. A task switch involves four main steps which are performed by the processor:

- A check is made to ensure that the task requesting the switch has appropriate privileges. The data access privileges apply to the `jmp` and `call` instructions. The DPL (Descriptor Privilege Level) of the TSS descriptor and the task gate must be numerically greater (lower privilege) than or equal to both the CPL (Current Privilege Level) and RPL (Requester Privilege Level) of the gate selector.

- The state of the current task is saved in its TSS. The base address of the TSS is located in the TR. The `eax`, `ebx`, `ecx`, `edx`, `esp`, `ebp`, `esi`, `edi`, `es`, `cs`, `ss`, `ds`, `fs`, `gs` and `eflags` registers are all saved.

- The TR is loaded with a selector to the new task's `TSS` descriptor. The selector of the new task is passed as an argument to the `jmp` or `call` instruction. The task busy bit is set in the TSS descriptor and the TS bit is set in the `cr0` register to indicate that a task switch has occurred. This is useful when co-ordinating operations between the integer unit of the CPU and the floating point unit or co-processor.

- The state of the new task is loaded from its TSS. This is an inverse of the register save operation performed above. The next instruction executed is performed in the context of the new task.

Address space management

Separate memory contexts are implemented by having a separate LDT and `pdbr` (Page Directory Base Register) per task underpinned by separate page tables per process. SCO UNIX provides per process page tables and a per process LDT but maintains the same page directory for all processes. Thus when a context switch is performed, the kernel is responsible for removing the entries in the page directory for the old task and replacing them with the page directory entries for the new task.

This switch of page directory entries is described in more detail in the next section.

7.9.5 Performing a context switch in SCO UNIX

A context switch will occur when the `swtch()` function is invoked. Figure 7.40 showed the places in the kernel from where the `swtch()` function is invoked.

The first task performed by `swtch()` is to call `DISP_SWTCH()`, the scheduler class switch function associated with the process, which is called to place the process back on its appropriate scheduling queue. It must be noted here that when a process is currently running (`p_stat` has the value `SONPROC`), the process is not on the run queue. When the process is runnable but not currently running (`p_stat` has the value `SRUN`) it resides on the run queue.

The `pswtch()` function is then called by `swtch()` to perform most of the work for the context switch. The tasks performed by `pswtch()` are as follows:

- If the process which is currently running has not just entered a zombie state, that is, the process is currently being terminated, `p_stat` is set to SRUN.
- The `runrun` variable is reset to zero.
- The `disp()` function is called to get the next process to run.
- If the process to run identified by `disp()` is not the process currently running, call `mapnewtss()`.

The `disp()` function is used to identify the next process to run. In many circumstances, particularly on a machine with little activity, the process identified by `disp()` will be the process that is currently running. In this scenario there is little work to do.

If the `idle()` process is returned from `disp()`, the kernel will ensure that interrupts are enabled and will then halt the CPU until another process needs to be scheduled. By enabling interrupts the run queue will be checked during clock interrupt processing.

The final task performed by `pswtch()` is to call `mapnewtss()`. This sets the LDT selector in the GDT to point to the new process's LDT which is located in the `p_ldt` field of its `proc` structure. Note that at this stage in the switch the u_area of the new process to run is not mapped into the address space referenced by the variable u but is mapped temporarily at the address specified by nu. The new process's TSS can be accessed via the `u_tss` field of the u_area. The GDT is updated to reference this new TSS.

When `pswtch()` returns to `swtch()` a check is made to see if a new process has actually been selected by `disp()`. If the process identified by `disp()` is the same process as the caller then `swtch()` simply returns.

If a new process is returned by `disp()` then `swtch()` calls `jmptotss()` which invokes a jump to a TSS selector, for which the TSS descriptor of the new process was set up in the GDT by `mapnewtss()`.

When the new process resumes from the task switch it starts execution in the kernel `resume()` function. This has responsibility for performing low level initialisation of the new process and kernel state. It initialises the kernel `curproc`, `cur_eproc` and `cur_sched` variables and sets up the page table entries for the new process's u_area. The page table entries for u_area of each process are stored in the `p_ubptbl[]` array located in each process's `proc` structure. Figure 7.45 shows how the page directory and therefore the page tables are accessed from the TSS.

The virtual address space is divided between the user process and the kernel. This means that certain entries in the page directory reference page tables for the kernel text and data. Since this arrangement is the same for all UNIX processes, it would be wasteful duplicating the page directory for each process. Instead of switching page directories there is a single page directory used by all processes and accessed via the kernel array `kpd0[]`. The page table pointers for the old process are cleared in the page directory and the page tables for the new process are then inserted.

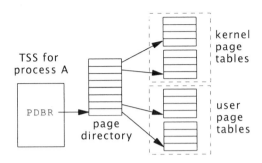

Figure 7.45   Accessing the page directory from the TSS

The other tasks performed by `resume()` are:

- Flush the Translation Lookaside Buffer (TLB) so that any references to the u_area use the page tables of the new process and do not locate any cached page table entries of the old process.

- Set up the stack pointer (`esp`), the value of which can be found in the `TSS`.

- Push the `eax`, `edi`, `esi` and `ebx` registers onto the stack. Again, these registers were saved in the TSS prior to the process being switched out.

- The TR is then loaded to point to the `TSS` for the new process.

Finally, `resume()` returns to the system stack of the new process.

7.10 Process scheduling

At any moment in time, the process that is currently running on the CPU is the process with the highest priority of the set of runnable processes. Processes which are eligible to run but which have a lower priority than the running process, `curproc`, are placed on the *run queue*. The run queue can be viewed as an array of lists where each element of the array represents a specific priority and all processes on the run queue at that priority are linked together.

The position that a process occupies on the run queue is a function of its priority and the scheduling class with which it is associated. SCO UNIX follows the POSIX 1003.1b-1993 (1993), formerly POSIX.4, model of scheduling which supports three distinct scheduling classes and a number of functions to help processes control their own scheduling. The three scheduling classes are:

SCHED_FIFO   All processes of type SCHED_FIFO for a specific priority will be at a position on the list in the order of how long they have been on it. Thus, the process at the head of the list for its priority is the process that has been on the list longest while the process at the tail is the one that has been on the list for the shortest amount of time.

When manipulating a priority list for processes of type SCHED_FIFO, the following rules apply. These are the only conditions under which the priority of a SCHED_FIFO process can be altered:

- If the current running process is pre-empted it is placed at the head of the list for its priority.

- If a blocked process becomes runnable it is placed at the end of the list for its priority.

- If the sched_setscheduler(S) function is invoked, the process which is specified takes on the specified scheduling policy and priority. If the specified process is either running or runnable it is placed at the tail of the list for its priority.

- If the sched_setparam(S) function is invoked, the process specified receives the specified priority. If the specified process is either running or runnable it is placed at the tail of the list for its priority.

- If the process currently running invokes the sched_yield(S) function, it is placed at the end of the list for its priority.

SCHED_RR   The SCHED_RR class implements a round-robin scheduling policy. The actions taken when manipulating SCHED_RR priority lists are identical to SCHED_FIFO with the following exception. When a process runs for the time interval given by a call to the sched_get_rr_interval(S) system call, the process is placed at the end of its priority list and, if there are no processes of higher priority to run, the process at the head of this list will run.

SCHED_OTHER   POSIX.1b specifies SCHED_OTHER as an implementation-defined policy which allows system designers to implement a non-real-time scheduling policy in a portable manner. The SCHED_OTHER policy is used to implement the time-sharing policy supported by SCO in releases of UNIX prior to OpenServer Release 5.

7.10.1 POSIX scheduling APIs

POSIX.1b-1993 specifies a number of functions which can be used to control the scheduling properties of either the calling process or another specified process. The list of POSIX.1b functions which are supported by SCO UNIX is:

```
#include <sched.h>

int sched_getparam(pid_t pid, struct sched_param *param) ;
int sched_getscheduler(pid_t pid) ;
```

```
int sched_get_priority_max(int policy) ;
int sched_get_priority_min(int policy) ;
int sched_rr_get_interval(pid_t pid, struct timespec *min) ;
int sched_setparam(pid_t pid, const struct sched_param *param) ;
int sched_setscheduler(pid_t pid, int policy,
                       const struct sched_param *param) ;
int sched_yield(void) ;
```

The following example program makes use of the sched_getscheduler(S), sched_get_priority_max(S) and sched_get_priority_min(S) functions to find the scheduling class of the caller and to display the minimum and maximum priority ranges for each scheduling class.

```
 1 #include <sched.h>
 2
 3 main()
 4 {
 5     int pid = getpid() ;
 6
 7     switch(sched_getscheduler(pid)) {
 8         case(SCHED_OTHER) : printf("class = SCHED_OTHER\n") ; break ;
 9         case(SCHED_FIFO)  : printf("class = SCHED_FIFO\n") ; break ;
10         case(SCHED_RR)    : printf("class = SCHED_RR\n") ; break ;
11         case(-1)          : printf("call failed\n") ;
12         default : printf("unknown class\n") ; break ;
13     }
14
15     printf("SCHED_OTHER max = %d\n",
16             sched_get_priority_max(SCHED_OTHER)) ;
17     printf("SCHED_OTHER min = %d\n",
18             sched_get_priority_min(SCHED_OTHER)) ;
19
20     printf("SCHED_FIFO max = %d\n",
21             sched_get_priority_max(SCHED_FIFO)) ;
22     printf("SCHED_FIFO min = %d\n",
23             sched_get_priority_min(SCHED_FIFO)) ;
24
25     printf("SCHED_RR max = %d\n",
26             sched_get_priority_max(SCHED_RR)) ;
27     printf("SCHED_RR min = %d\n",
28             sched_get_priority_min(SCHED_RR)) ;
29 }
```

If the program is run by a normal UNIX process executed from the shell prompt, this should result in the following output:

```
$ sched
class = SCHED_OTHER
SCHED_OTHER max = 95
SCHED_OTHER min = 0
SCHED_FIFO max = 127
SCHED_FIFO min = 0
SCHED_RR max = 127
SCHED_RR min = 0
```

Note that higher numbers correspond to higher priorities. Since the use of real-time scheduling offers the capabilities to disrupt a system badly or even halt completely all other activity, functions to modify the scheduling class or priority of a process are available only to a process with user ID of zero.

Gallmeister (1995) describes how to use real-time scheduling and compares it with the traditional time-sharing schedulers of UNIX.

7.10.2 Class specific schedulers

Associated with each scheduling class is a *class scheduler*. Since the placement of processes on the scheduling queues is dependent on the type of class to which a process belongs, a set of generic scheduling interfaces are called which map the call onto the per class scheduler call for the process in question.

A process scheduler is defined by the `disp_reg_t` structure. Each process scheduler provides class specific data structures and a list of functions that can be called by the kernel in order to schedule processes in the class or classes that they control. The functions provided by the scheduling classes are described later.

The schedulers are stored in the `sched_list[]` array. The first entry is the scheduler corresponding to `SCHED_OTHER` and is used by default by all processes in the system.

The `ep_dispreg` field of each process's `eproc` structure is used to locate the scheduler which is currently used by the process. Before a new process starts running on the processor the kernel variable `cur_sched` is assigned to the scheduler associated with the process which is held in `ep_dispreg`.

Each of the scheduler functions is invoked by the kernel through macros. Consider the macro used for invoking the scheduler `disp_fork()` function as defined in `<sys/disp.h>`:

```
#define DISP_FORK(p, c) \
     if (cur_sched->disp_fork) \
          cur_sched->disp_fork(p, c)
```

A check is made to see if the current scheduler has a `disp_fork()` function defined and, if so, calls it with the address of the parent and child processes.

7.10.3 The scheduler run queues

There are 128 possible priorities in the system. Unlike versions of SCO UNIX prior to SCO OpenServer Release 5 where there was a single run queue for all runnable processes regardless of their priorities, there is now a queue per priority. The range of priorities and the coverage of priority levels by each scheduling class is shown in Figure 7.46.

The run queues are held in the `hrunq[]` array which contains `NHASHPROC` (128) entries of type struct `rqchain`. Each `rqchain` structure is used to indicate whether any processes are available to run, to point to the first and last process on the list and to point to the next `rqchain` where processes exist on the run queue.

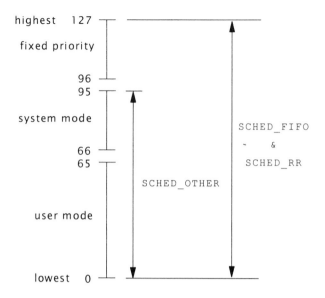

Figure 7.46   The range of scheduling priorities and class coverage

The fields of the rqchain structure are shown in Table 7.11.

Table 7.11   The rqchain structure used for implementing the scheduler run queues

rqchain field		Description
struct proc	*headp	The first process on the queue to run.
struct proc	*tailp	The last process on the queue to run.
char	bmask	The mask value used to check the brunq[] entry.
char	*pmask	Pointer to the brunq[] mask covering the range of eight queues of which this queue is a member.
struct rqchain	*ngrp	Pointer to the next queue when pmask is 0.

Searching the rqchain structures corresponding to each priority to locate a process to run could be a time consuming task. In order to minimise this search time, a bit mask, external to hrunq[], is used to locate quickly which queue has runnable processes attached. The bit mask is contained in the brunq[] array. Figure 7.47 shows the relationship between the brunq[] array and hrunq[].

The brunq[] array which contains 16 bytes can be viewed as a 128 bit mask where each bit references a particular entry in the hrunq[] array. If the bit is set, there are processes on the run queue at that particular priority.

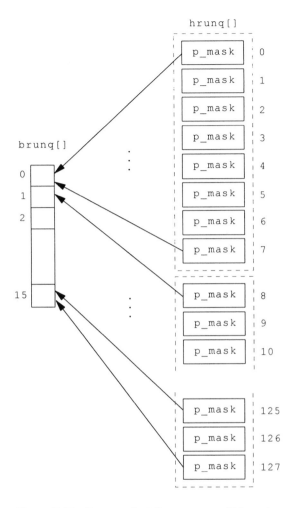

Figure 7.47 Process scheduling queues and bit masks

7.10.4 Initialising the run queue and class schedulers

The run queue and each class scheduler are initialised by the `disp_init()` function invoked from `main()` during kernel initialisation. `disp_init()` performs the following tasks:

- Set the class scheduler of `curproc` to the TS class located in `sched_list[0]`. Note that when `disp_init()` is called only `proc[0]`, the swapper, is in existence. The scheduler class of each subsequent process will be inherited from its parent when the process is forked.

- Call the `disp_init()` function for each scheduler.

- Initialise each of the run queues. This involves setting the `bmask` field of each `rqchain` structure so that it references the appropriate bit position in `brunq[]`. The `bmask` field for `hrunq[0]` is 1, `hrunq[1]` is 2, `hrunq[7]` is 8, `hrunq[8]` is 1 and so on.

  The `pmask` field is set so that it references the correct byte in `brunq[]`. Elements 0 to 7 of `hrunq[]` point to `brunq[0]`, elements 8 to 15 of `hrunq[]` point to `brunq[1]` and so on.

- Finally, the `ngrp` field of each `rqchain` structure is set to point to the `rqchain` of the next group of queues. `hrunq[0]` to `hrunq[7]` point to the `rqchain` of `hrunq[8]` while `hrunq[8]` to `hrunq[15]` point to the `rqchain` of `hrunq[16]`. If there are no processes ready to run for a particular group then moving to the next group is simplified.

Figure 7.48 shows the run queues and bit mask following `disp_init()`.

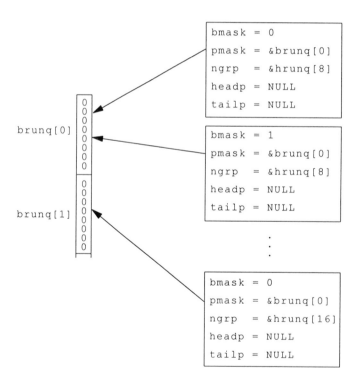

Figure 7.48   The scheduler run queues following `disp_init()`

7.10.5 Scheduler operations

This section describes the operations for each scheduler defined in a per scheduler disp_reg_t structure and the places in the kernel from where they are invoked.

disp_fork()

A child inherits the same scheduling class as the parent process when it invokes the fork(S) system call. The DISP_FORK() macro is invoked during procdup() which will invoke either the ts_fork() or rt_fork() scheduler function depending on the scheduling class of the parent and therefore of the child.

For the TS class, the ts_fork() function calculates the priority for the child, sets the p_pri field of the child's proc structure to the priority calculated and invokes disp_puttail() to add the child process to the end of its priority queue.

disp_postfork()

After a child process has been created by newproc1(), the DISP_POSTFORK() macro is invoked which calls the postfork operation defined by the scheduling class of the child. In the case of the TS class, this is ts_postfork() and for the RT class it is a null operation.

For the TS class, the child process is required to run before the parent. To satisfy the standard fork(S) semantics the ts_postfork() function sets runrun equal to 1 which will force a context switch before the parent returns to user mode. Figure 7.41 shows the steps taken when switching processes on runrun.

disp_qswtch()

The scheduler specific qswtch functions are called from the qswtch() kernel function to put the process on the run queue and to select another process to run.

The position on the queue at which the process is placed depends on its scheduling class. For processes in the TS class, the process is always placed on the end of its priority queue. For processes in the RT class it is placed on the head of the queue.

disp_sleep()

The sleep() kernel function is passed the priority at which the process should run when it wakes up. For processes in the TS class the ts_sleep() function is called. This maps the priority passed to sleep() by calling map_real() to convert the traditional priority, used in versions of SCO UNIX prior to OpenServer Release 5, to its appropriate value in the OpenServer Release 5 environment.

disp_comppri()

This function is used to determine the new priority of a process. It is called from s_trap() and u_trap() when a processor exception occurs or when the process is about to return to user mode from systrap(). The priority returned by DISP_COMPPRI() is assigned to the p_pri field of the proc structure. In s_trap(), if runrun is set, a context switch will be made.

For processes in the TS class the ts_comppri() function is called which calculates the new priority based on the p_cpu and p_nice fields of the proc structure. For processes in the RT class, the rt_comppri() function returns the current priority since the only way that a real-time process will change priority is through a direct user level request.

disp_attr()

The disp_info scheduler functions are used to return information requested by the priocntl(S) system call in response to a PC_GETCLINFO command. The information returned by both the ts_info() (TS class) and rt_info() (RT class) functions is the maximum priority that a user process can have within the class.

disp_normpri()

Since priorities were reversed in SCO OpenServer Release 5, the disp_normpri() function is called to return a priority value that can be compared with the p_pri field of the proc structure.

disp_secure()

The rt_secure() and ts_secure() functions are invoked when performing the priocntl(S) system call to ensure that the caller has sufficient privileges to perform the PC_SETPARMS command.

disp_setrun()

Called from setrun() when a specific process is chosen to run on the processor, this function involves calling rt_setrq() for the RT class and ts_setrq() for the TS class. For both functions, the disp_puttail() function is called to add the process to the end of the list of processes for its priority.

disp_wakeup()

When a wakeup() call has been invoked, the wakeupn() function calls DISP_WAKEUP() to place the process on the run queue. For the TS class the ts_setrq() function is called and for the RT class the rt_setrq() function is called. Both functions are described above under disp_setrun().

disp_cwakeup()

This function can be invoked to add a number of processes of the same priority to the run queue simultaneously.

disp_donice()

This function is called when invoking the nice(S) system call to recalculate the process's priority.

disp_init()

This is called from the kernel disp_init() function during kernel initialisation. There is no function to perform for the RT class. For the TS class, the ts_init()

function is invoked to build a table of re-mapped priorities to be used when an old style priority needs to be mapped to a new style priority and vice versa.

disp_setslice()

When pswtch() calls disp() to locate a process to run, the scheduler queues must be searched to locate the first non-empty queue. If a non-empty queue is found then disp_scan() is invoked to remove the process from the queue and set the p_stat field to SONPROC. The last task performed by disp_scan() is to call DISP_SETSLICE() to set the time-slice for which the process can run.

For the RT class, no work is performed by the rt_slice() function. For the TS class the ts_setslice() function sets the global variable lticks to the number of clock ticks for which the process can run.

disp_tick()

During processing of the clock interrupt handler, the DISP_TICK() function is called for the current process. This allows each scheduler to perform its own time accounting on the process, for example to check whether the process has exceeded its time-slice.

For processes in the TS class the ts_tick() function is called which decrements the lticks global variable set up during a call to ts_setslice() when the process is selected to run on the processor. If the value of lticks reaches zero then ts_ticks() sets the runrun variable to force a context switch. Section 7.9.1 describes the procedures followed when runrun is set.

For processes in the RT class each process maintains its own lticks variable in the eproc structure. This variable is set on a call to rt_fork() and reset each time a SCHED_RR process reaches the end of its time-slice. As with ts_tick(), when the lticks variable associated with a SCHED_RR process reaches zero the runrun variable is set to indicate that a context switch is required.

disp_onesec()

DISP_ONESEC() is called from clock() each time one second processing is performed. For both the RT and TS classes there is no additional work to perform since time accounting is performed by their respective disp_tick() functions.

disp_sched()

The swapper (sched) calls DISP_SCHED() when a process that was previously in the SXBRK state is once again available to run. This ensures that the process is placed back on its appropriate run queue.

For the TS class the ts_setrq() function is called and for the RT class the rt_setrq() function is called. Both functions are described earlier under disp_setrun().

disp_setpri()

The disp_setpri() function is called to set the priority of the currently running process. For processes in the TS class the ts_setpri() is called only from ts_init(). Priorities are then inherited across fork(S).

For processes in the RT class no function is defined since the priority of the process can be altered only by a user level call.

7.11 Process termination

There are three methods by which a process can terminate:

- The process voluntarily terminates itself by calling the _exit(S) or exit(S) system calls, passing an exit status back to the kernel which the parent process can retrieve using one of the wait() system calls.
- A signal is posted which results in termination of the process. Many signal types have a default action of terminating the process for which some will generate a core file. Signal handling is described in detail in section 7.4 with particular emphasis on how the kernel invokes user specified signal handlers. This section describes how the kernel deals with signals where the default action is to terminate the process.
- As a result of an illegal operation, the kernel terminates the process. To terminate the process the kernel posts a signal such as SIGSEGV when the process accesses an invalid memory address or SIGILL if the process attempts to execute an invalid instruction.

The system call handler invoked to handle the exit(S) system call is the rexit() function which performs no other function than to call the internally used exit2() function with the value passed to exit(S). The exit2() function is also called from the following places:

sigclean()   If the user overwrites the stack during execution of a signal handler and the kernel cannot restore the user's context when the kernel is re-entered after the signal handler exits, the process will be terminated.

psig()   When a signal is posted to the process and the default disposition of the signal is to terminate the process.

The steps followed by exit2() are:

- The p_flag field of the proc structure is set to SEXIT, indicating that the process is about to exit.
- All itimers that may have been established are cancelled.
- The disposition of all signals, held in the u_signal[] array in the u_area, is set to SIG_IGN.
- All signal state information is cleared, such as pending and masked signals.
- The closef() function is invoked to close each open file.
- detachregs() is called to detach all memory regions.

- For each process that is being controlled by this process, if the `p_stat` field of the process is set to `SSTOP`, `setrun()` is called to put the process on the run queue.

- For each child process the `p_ppid` field is set to 1 and the `p_parent` field to `&proc[1]` so that the child will have the `init` process as its parent.

- Send a single `SIGCLD` signal to `init` and call `setrun()` to put `init` on the run queue. The `init` process will then issue a `wait(S)` system call to avoid having process slots filled with zombie processes.

- The `p_stat` field of the process is set to `SZOMB`, indicating that the process is now a zombie. Section 7.11.1 further describes zombie processes.

- `psignalinfo()` is called to send a `SIGCLD` signal to the parent, specifying a `siginfo_t` structure to indicate the reason for exit.

- The `swtch()` function is called to force a context switch.

Figure 7.49 shows the effect on children of the process to be terminated after `exit2()` has completed. One of the children is accessed from the parent by the `p_child` field of the `proc` structure. The remaining siblings are accessed via the `p_sibling` field of the `proc` structure of the child referenced by the parent.

While the parent process is active, each of the children points to the parent via the `p_parent` field. After `exit2()` is complete this process is no longer valid and only holds zombie state. All of the valid children are then orphaned and adopted by the `init` process located in `proc[1]` to which their `p_parent` fields are modified.

Section 7.7 describes the relationships between processes in more detail.

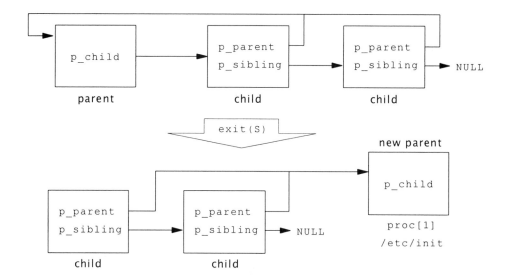

Figure 7.49   Parent and child relationships during process termination

7.11.1 Zombie processes

Consider the parent/child relationship shown in Figure 7.50. Initially the parent performs a fork(S) system call. Following the fork(S) call, the child runs and the parent receives the process ID of the child. The parent then calls waitpid(S) with the process ID of the child process, requesting that it be awoken when the child has changed status.

This change in status occurs as a result of the process either stopping or being terminated.

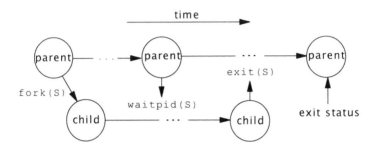

Figure 7.50   Waiting for a child to exit

Once the child has stopped or terminated the kernel wakes the suspended parent process, passing back the exit status of the child.

If the child terminates before the parent calls waitpid(S), the parent is not interrupted unless it installs a signal handler for SIGCHLD.

Since the parent may request the exit status of the child some time later, the child process becomes a *zombie* process. Its regions, u_area, file state and all other kernel structures with the exception of its proc table entry are deleted. The p_stat field of the process's proc structure is set to SZOMB and the p_xstat field is set to the exit status of the process. The process will remain in this state until the parent process issues one of the wait(S) system calls so that the exit status can always be retrieved.

Toolkit 7.15   Analysing a zombie process

This example demonstrates the scenario in which a zombie is created. Firstly, a process is forked on line 8 and the parent issues a waitpid(S) system call (line 14). To ensure that the waitpid(S) call is executed before the child issues exit(S) on line 11, the child sleeps for five seconds.

```
1 #include <sys/types.h>
2 #include <sys/wait.h>
3
4 main()
5 {
6     int pid, stat_loc ;
7
```

```
 8      pid = fork() ;
 9      if (pid == 0) { /* child */
10          sleep(5) ;
11          exit(0x7f) ;
12      }
13      else {
14          waitpid(pid, &stat_loc, 0) ;
15          printf("child returned 0x%x\n",WEXITSTATUS(stat_loc)) ;
16      }
17 }
```

As expected from the following results, the exit status returned to the parent is equal to the value passed to exit(S) by the child. The times for running the parent confirm the five seconds waiting.

```
$ time a.out
child returns 0x7f

real    0m5.05s
user    0m0.01s
sys     0m0.025
```

However, in the following example, the program is modified so that the child sleeps for 20 seconds and the parent sleeps for a considerable amount of time before issuing the waitpid(S) system call. The purpose of the 20 second delay is to allow the two processes to be analysed with crash(ADM), both before the child exits and after.

```
 1 #include <sys/types.h>
 2 #include <sys/wait.h>
 3
 4 main()
 5 {
 6     int pid, stat_loc ;
 7
 8     pid = fork() ;
 9     if (pid == 0) { /* child */
10         sleep(20) ;
11         exit(0x7f) ;
12     }
13     else {
14         sleep(100000000) ;
15         waitpid(pid, &stat_loc, 0) ;
16         printf("child returned 0x%x\n",WEXITSTATUS(stat_loc)) ;
17     }
18 }
```

After starting the program, crash(ADM) is run immediately on a separate virtual console. The first invocation of the proc command shows the two processes.

```
# crash
dumpfile = /dev/mem, namelist = /unix, outfile = stdout
> proc ! grep a.out
  74 s    955   447   955 13853  66   0 u       a.out  load omsk
  75 s    956   955   955 13853  66   0 u       a.out  load omsk nxec
```

```
> proc 74 75 # after 20 seconds
SLOT ST PID    PPID PGRP    UID PRI CPU EVENT   NAME    FLAGS
  74 s   955   447   955 13853  66   0 u        a.out   load omsk
  75 z   956   955   955 13853  45   0          zombie  nou nxec exit
> pregion 75
SLOT PREG REG#      REGVA  TYPE FLAGS
```

After waiting for longer than 20 seconds, allowing the sleep(20) to complete in the child process, the proc command is invoked again. This time, the parent is displayed as before but there are considerable differences with the child. The name has been changed to reflect the state of this zombie process.

The pregion crash command, which is used to display the process's memory regions, is then invoked. Since the process is now a zombie, all memory associated with the process has been removed.

Finally, the following example illustrates the case when the parent terminates before the child. In this example the parent sleeps for 20 seconds and then calls exit(0). The child sleeps considerably longer and will therefore outlive the parent.

```
 1 main()
 2 {
 3     int pid, stat_loc ;
 4
 5     pid = fork() ;
 6     if (pid == 0) { /* child */
 7         sleep(1000000) ;
 8         exit(0x7f) ;
 9     }
10     else {
11         sleep(20) ;
12         exit(0) ;
13     }
14 }
```

As before, the two processes can be located within crash(ADM). This shows the parent process with PID=413 (slot 24) and the child process with PID=414 (slot 25).

```
$ crash
dumpfile = /dev/mem, namelist = /unix, outfile = stdout
> p ! grep a.out
  23 s   413   220   413 13583  66   0 u      a.out   load omsk
  25 s   414   413   413 13583  66   0 u      a.out   load omsk nxec
> proc 23 25 # after 20 seconds
PROC TABLE SIZE = 47
SLOT ST PID    PPID PGRP    UID PRI CPU EVENT NAME     FLAGS
  23     0     0     0 13583  51   0
  25 s   414     1   413 13583  66   0 u      a.out    load omsk nxec
```

After waiting for the parent process to exit, the two process slots are displayed again. This time slot 23 is empty. The child process still continues to run. The only difference is that the PPID field has changed to 1, the init process. By default, whenever a process with children terminates, all of the children become children of the init process.

7.11.2 Waiting for a child to exit

Both `waitpid(S)` and `wait(S)` enter the kernel through the same system call with `waitpid(S)` performing additional functionality in user space. The main functions carried out by the kernel when `wait(S)` is called are shown in Figure 7.51.

The `wait()` kernel function call is invoked for both `wait(S)` and `waitpid(S)`. The `waitid(S)` system call has its own system call entry point. The system call handler for both `wait(S)` and `waitid(S)` is `waitgen()` which performs the wait on behalf of both system calls.

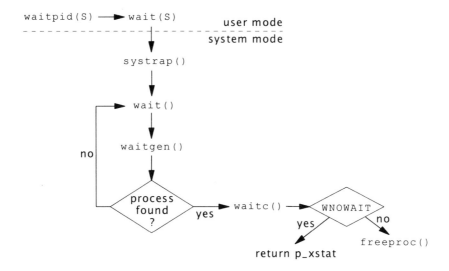

Figure 7.51   Kernel handling of `wait(S)`

The main task performed by `waitgen()` is to locate a child process which has changed state and meets the specified constraints, such as matching the process ID specified by `waitpid()`, the process was stopped but has continued, and so on. If a match is found, `waitc()` is called to determine the action to be taken and return the process status. The functionality performed by `waitc()` is as follows:

- If the process's p_stat field is set to SZOMB, the return value is set to the contents of p_xstat, the process exit status. If the option passed to `waitid(S)` or `waitpid(S)` was set to WNOWAIT, the process should be left in a wait state (as a zombie), otherwise `freeproc()` is called to free the process slot.
- If the process's p_stat field is set to SSTOP, a siginfo_t structure is created to indicate the reason for stoppage and is returned to the caller.

- If neither of the above conditions is true, for example the process has continued from a job control stop signal, a `siginfo_t` structure is also created to indicate that the process has resumed. The `siginfo_t` structure is returned to the caller.

When the process called `exit(S)` or `_exit(S)` all resources associated with the process were freed with the exception of the `proc` structure which remained purely for holding the exit status. When the `freeproc()` function is called, the `proc` structure becomes free for allocation by `newproc1()` which is called when processing the `fork(S)` system call.

The main tasks performed by `freeproc()` is to remove the process from its sibling chain and to set the `p_stat` field to 0.

Toolkit 7.16   Analysing zombie state

The example shown here provides the mechanisms for a process to determine whether a process is in a zombie state and, if so, what the exit status of the process is. This mimics part of the behaviour of the `wait(S)` and `waitpid(S)` system calls and does not modify the process state in any way.

The `pwait()` function (lines 6 to 24) takes the process ID of interest and a pointer to an integer in which the exit status of the process will be returned if found. The function opens the `table` driver (lines 12 to 14) and searches through each `proc` structure trying to match the specified process ID against the `p_pid` field of the `proc` structure read. If a match is found and the process is a zombie (line 17), the exit status of the process can be found in the `p_xstat` field of the `proc` structure. This is assigned to the `loc` variable passed to `pwait()` and the process ID of the process is returned.

```
 1 #include <sys/types.h>
 2 #include <sys/wait.h>
 3 #include <sys/proc.h>
 4 #include <fcntl.h>
 5
 6 int
 7 pwait(int pid, int *loc)
 8 {
 9      int fd ;
10      struct proc proc ;
11
12      fd = open("/dev/table/proc", O_RDONLY) ;
13      if (fd < 0)
14          pexit("/dev/table/proc") ;
15
16      while (read(fd, (char *)&proc, sizeof(struct proc)) != 0)
17          if (proc.p_pid == pid && proc.p_stat == SZOMB) {
18              close(fd) ;
19              *loc = proc.p_xstat ;
20              return(proc.p_pid) ;
21          }
22      close(fd) ;
23      return(-1) ;
24 }
25
26 main()
27 {
```

```
28      int pid, sloc = 0, waitloc ;
29      struct sigaction sa ;
30
31      pid = fork() ;
32
33      if (pid == 0)                    // child
34          exit(0x7f) ;
35      else {                           // parent
36          sleep(2) ;
37          if (pwait(pid, &sloc) < 0)
38              printf("Could not access the child process\n") ;
39          else {
40              printf("p_xstat status = %x\n", WEXITSTATUS(sloc)) ;
41
42              wait(&waitloc) ;
43              printf("wait exit status = %x\n", WEXITSTATUS(waitloc)) ;
44
45              if (pwait(pid, &sloc) < 0)
46                  printf("Zombified child is no longer there!\n") ;
47          }
48      }
49 }
```

In the main body of the program the parent calls fork(S) on line 31 and the child immediately exits with a status of 0x7f (line 34). In order to allow the child time to exit, the parent sleeps and then calls pwait() (line 37) to see if the child has terminated and been left in a zombie state. If the child is found, the parent outputs the exit status that was found by pwait() in p_xstat.

The parent then calls the wait(S) system call to obtain the exit status of the child. At this stage the parent knows that the child has exited. The exit status returned by wait(S) is then displayed. Finally, the parent re-issues another pwait() call which should fail to locate the child.

The output of the program is as follows:

```
$ pwait
p_xstat status = 7f
wait exit status = 7f
Zombified child is no longer there!
```

7.11.3 Core dumps

There are certain signals for which the default action is to terminate the process and generate a core file. The signals which result in a core file being generated are SIGQUIT, SIGILL, SIGTRAP, SIGIOT, SIBABRT, SIGEMT, SIGBUS, SIGSEGV and SIGSYS.

The name of the core file which is generated is core and it will be written to the process's current working directory, assuming the process has write access on the directory, otherwise no core file will be generated. The main purpose of generating a core file is to save enough information to be able to diagnose the fault at a later date. The core file therefore contains all relevant portions of the process's virtual address space plus system specific information about the process.

The core file is divided into a number of sections which describe the core file itself, the contents of kernel data structures or a copy of the process's memory contents at the time at which the core file was generated.

Each section in the file contains a section header, some optional supporting information and the actual contents. The headers are chained together and defined by the coresecthead structure, the fields of which are shown in Table 7.12. The core file starts with a coresecthead structure and subsequent headers can be accessed via the cs_hseek field.

Table 7.12 Core file section header contents

coresecthead structure field		Description
uchar_t	cs_stype	The type of section. See below for details.
uchar_t	cs_hsize	Size in bytes of this section header.
ushort	cs_osize	Size in bytes of the optional header which will follow the coresecthead if present.
union	cs_x	This field depends on the type of section. See below for details.
ulong_t	cs_vaddr	The virtual address of the contents in the process address space.
ulong_t	cs_vsize	The size in bytes of this section's contents.
long	cs_sseek	The offset within the core file that applications must seek to in order to locate the section contents.
long	cs_hseek	The offset from the start of the file that the next section header can be found. If this field is 0 then there are no further sections.

There are numerous different types of possible sections within the core file. The type of sections and their contents are as follows:

CORES_MAGIC   This section always appears first and is used by core analysis tools to determine whether the core file contains valid data or may potentially be corrupt.

CORES_UAREA   The process's u_area is held in this section. This provides access to the user registers and kernel stack together with other useful information about the process.

CORES_PREGION   Sections of this type contain the process's valid memory regions. The cs_x field of coresecthead contains the pregion's p_type and p_flags fields which can be used to identify the type of memory dumped. See the <sys/paccess.h> header file for further details.

CORES_PROC   This section holds the process's proc structure.

CORES_ITIMER   Interval timer values which were valid for the process prior to the crash are held as an array in this section.

CORES_SCOUTSNAME   This section holds the scoutsname structure as defined in the <sys/utsname.h> header file. This structure provides information about the kernel and system on which the core file was generated. This section is particularly useful for core files which may be analysed on a different machine from that on which the core file was generated.

CORES_OFFSETS   This section holds the process's coreoffsets structure which holds the offset within specific sections of the most often used variables. For example, the u_stack field provides the offset in the core file of the user's stack. For further details of this structure see the core(FP) manual page.

Although the core file contains sufficient data to analyse the cause of failure, it is best used in conjunction with the original un-stripped executable file to provide symbolic representation of the data found in the core file.

This approach is supported by most debuggers including dbxtra(CP) and adb(CP).

Toolkit 7.17   Analysing a core file

The example shown in this toolkit takes a core file as an argument and displays each of the file's section types together with a statement as to whether the core file is valid or not. The core(FP) manual page describes in detail the format of each section type.

The program provided here can be used as the basis for detailed analysis and to determine why the program produced the core file.

```
 1 #include <sys/types.h>
 2 #include <sys/paccess.h>
 3 #include <sys/errno.h>
 4 #include <fcntl.h>
 5
 6 section_name(uchar_t stype)
 7 {
 8     switch(stype) {
 9         case(CORES_MAGIC)      : printf("CORES_MAGIC      ") ; break ;
10         case(CORES_UAREA)      : printf("CORES_UAREA      ") ; break ;
11         case(CORES_PREGION)    : printf("CORES_PREGION    ") ; break ;
12         case(CORES_PROC)       : printf("CORES_PROC       ") ; break ;
13         case(CORES_ITIMER)     : printf("CORES_ITIMER     ") ; break ;
14         case(CORES_SCOUTSNAME): printf("CORES_SCOUTSNAME ") ; break ;
15         case(CORES_OFFSETS)    : printf("CORES_OFFSETS    ") ; break ;
16         default                : printf("invalid section  ") ; break ;
17     }
18 }
19
20 main(int argc, char *argv[])
21 {
22     struct coresecthead ch ;
23     int fd, n, nsects = 0 ;
24
25     if (argc != 2) {
26         printf("Usage: core <corefile>\n") ;
27         exit(EINVAL) ;
28     }
```

```
29
30        fd = open(argv[1], O_RDONLY) ;
31        if (fd < 0)
32            pexit(argv[1]) ;
33
34        printf("SNO  SNAME              SIZE\n") ;
35
36        while(1) {
37            n = read(fd, (char *)&ch, sizeof (struct coresecthead)) ;
38
39            ++nsects ;
40            printf("%d    ", nsects) ;
41            section_name(ch.cs_stype) ;
42            printf("%d  ", ch.cs_vsize) ;
43
44            if (ch.cs_stype == CORES_MAGIC)
45                if (ch.cs_x.csx_magic == COREMAGIC_NUMBER)
46                    printf("    valid corefile\n") ;
47                else
48                    printf("    invalid corefile\n") ;
49            else
50                printf("\n") ;
51
52            if (n != sizeof(struct coresecthead))
53                break ;
54
55            if (ch.cs_hseek <= 0)
56                break ;
57            lseek(fd, ch.cs_hseek, SEEK_SET) ;
58        }
59 }
```

The program begins by opening the core file for read access on line 30. The main body of the program (lines 36 to 58) loop repeatedly, reading each `coresecthead` structure. Since the first section header is at offset zero, it is read immediately on line 37.

The `section_name()` function is called for each section header read and is passed the section type which is held in the `cs_stype` field. The section name is then displayed by name. On return from `section_name()` the section size which is held in the `cs_vsize` field is displayed.

If the section is of type `CORES_MAGIC`, the `csx_magic` field is checked on line 45 to determine whether the core file is valid or whether it may be corrupt. Line 57 uses the `ch_hseek` field to seek to the next section header in the core file and the loop repeats.

The following program is run and passed a core file which resulted from a program which tried to perform division by zero.

```
$ acore core
SNO  SNAME              SIZE
1    CORES_MAGIC        5        valid corefile
2    CORES_OFFSETS      108
3    CORES_SCOUTSNAME   98
4    CORES_ITIMER       48
5    CORES_PROC         344
6    CORES_PREGION      8192
7    CORES_PREGION      5948
8    CORES_UAREA        8192
```

The core file is marked valid and contains eight sections. A useful exercise would be to use the section contents to determine the type of failure. For example, the process registers are held in the CORES_UAREA section. Together with the user stack and knowledge of how stack frames are constructed, it is possible to print a stack backtrace for the process.

7.11.4 Kernel handling of core dumps

Figure 7.52 shows the places in the kernel that may call core() to produce a core file. The psig() function is responsible for processing a signal and will call core() if the disposition of the signal is SIG_DFL and the default action is to produce a core file.

Both sigclean() and kern_gpfault() invoke core() if the user has corrupted the user stack during execution of a signal handler.

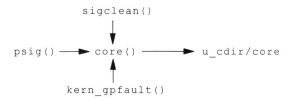

Figure 7.52   Kernel calls to produce a core file

The core() function is responsible for producing the core file. Other routines in the kernel such as exit2() and freeproc() are responsible for terminating the process and returning it to the free list.

The following tasks are performed by the core() function. It must be noted that the size of the core file is limited and therefore core() must prioritise which data can and cannot be written. The getrlimit(S) and setrlimit(S) system calls can be used to get and set the maximum size of the core file. This limit is set on a per process basis.

- Set the u_dirp field of the u_area to point to the string "core".
- If the effective user ID and group ID do not equal the real user ID and group ID, the core file cannot be dumped so core() returns.
- Ensure that the core file can be written and truncate if necessary.
- Call findpreg() to obtain the sizes for the text, data and stack regions.
- Determine how much data can be written. If the complete core file cannot be written, the stack takes precedence over the data region which takes precedence over the text.
- Create a CORES_UAREA section header and call dumpcorecontents() to write out the u_area.
- Create a CORES_PREGION section header and call dumpcorecontents() to write out the data region.

- Create a `CORES_PREGION` section header and call `dumpcorecontents()` to write out the stack region.

- Call `dumpcoreheader()` to write out section headers for the u_area, data and stack.

- For each other region, call `dumpcorecontents()` and `dumpcoreheader()`.

- Create a `CORES_PROC` section header and call `dumpcorecontents()` to write out the `proc` structure. Call `dumpcoreheader()` to write out the section header for `CORES_PROC`.

- Create a `CORES_ITIMERS` section header and call `dumpcorecontents()` to write out the itimer array. Call `dumpcoreheader()` to write out the section header for `CORES_ITIMERS`.

- Create the `coreoffsets` structure and write at the end of the file.

The core file is always written, access permitting, to the current working directory which is held in the `u_cdir` field of the u_area and set by the `chdir(S)` system call.

7.12 Summary and suggested reading

This chapter described the components in the kernel which collectively form the process management subsystem.

The process management related topics described in Bach (1986) still provide useful background material. Leffler *et al.* (1989) provide an historical view of `vfork(S)` and also describe the BSD UNIX implementation of `vfork()`.

The Intel 80486 *Programmer's Reference Manual* (1992) and books describing the other i386 family of processors contain a wealth of information on the CPU, how memory is managed, how multitasking is performed, how the processor deals with interrupts and exceptions and of course acts as a detailed reference for the instruction set of the processor.

The POSIX.1b standard (1993) is the definitive reference for real-time extensions to the POSIX.1 standard and serves as excellent reference material.

Gallmeister (1995) was written just before publication of the POSIX.1b standard (1993) but is an excellent source of information on POSIX.1b, providing many examples of how and where the real-time APIs should be used.

Messmer (1995) provides what is arguably the most comprehensive book on the internals of the PC from the early 8086 based PCs to today's Pentium processors. It covers in detail all of the PC components from the Programmable Interval Timer (PIT) to the Peripheral Interrupt Controller (PIC) to the different bus types used.

8

File management

This chapter explores the UNIX file subsystem, the part of the kernel which is responsible for the storage of files and for providing the mechanisms to create, retrieve and modify files and their contents.

Since SCO UNIX supports many different filesystem types, the first part of the chapter introduces the mechanisms provided by the kernel to separate filesystem independent and filesystem dependent layers of the kernel and concentrates on the filesystem independent structures and functions.

The structures used for separating different mounted filesystems within the kernel are then explained, together with the main paths executed by the kernel for the common file-based system calls. This includes the handling of memory mapped files.

The chapter concludes by providing a brief introduction to `fsdb(ADM)`, the filesystem debugger.

8.1 Introduction

UNIX kernels usually support many different filesystems, each offering their own unique features, different on-disk formats and internal functions. SCO UNIX supports the simultaneous operation of multiple filesystems. Co-ordination of these filesystems and the presentation to the rest of the kernel of a single common entry point for file access is achieved through an interface inside the kernel called the *File System Switch* (FSS). Figure 8.1 shows the position of the FSS in the kernel.

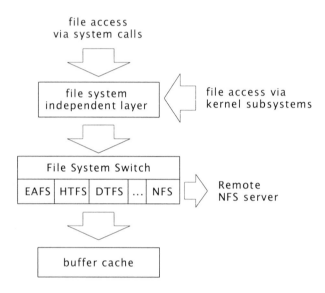

Figure 8.1   The filesystem independent and filesystem dependent layers of the kernel

The first part of the chapter discusses the structures and algorithms used by the kernel above the FSS. This is followed by a description of how the FSS is implemented, the routines performed by individual filesystems and how multiple filesystems co-exist concurrently.

8.1.1 The file management toolkit

The following toolkit programs are presented in this chapter:

Toolkit 8.1 Accessing file descriptors, page 302
Toolkit 8.2 Extending open file limits, page 305
Toolkit 8.3 Locating file table entries, page 308
Toolkit 8.4 Accessing and displaying `file_t` flags, page 311
Toolkit 8.5 Reading an in-core inode, page 321

Most of the examples presented build on earlier examples as the chapter progresses to show how many of the file related structures are linked. For example, Toolkit 8.2 which displays file table entries must use Toolkit 8.1, Toolkit 8.3 uses Toolkit 8.2 and so on.

8.2 The filesystem independent layer

This section describes the structures and interfaces used by the kernel above the FSS shown in Figure 8.1, particularly with reference to how processes access files.

Figure 8.2 summarises the main file related structures used above the FSS which are described in more detail throughout the following sections.

Each file descriptor used to access a file is an index into a per process *open file table* for which there are two open file tables shown in Figure 8.2. Each entry in the open file table for an active (open) file references an entry in the *system file table* which holds the offset within the file used for reading and writing as well as a pointer to an entry in the in-core *inode table*.

Although there may be multiple file table entries referencing the same file there will be a single inode table entry as Figure 8.2 highlights. Each entry in the inode table contains general information about the file, including its size and type as well as a

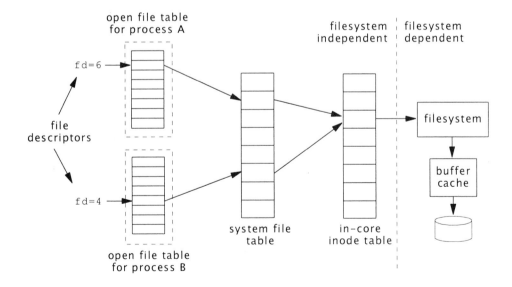

Figure 8.2   Structures in the filesystem independent layer of the kernel used for file access

reference to the filesystem which owns the file and therefore is a means of accessing the file contents.

8.2.1 Introducing file descriptors

A *file descriptor* is a non-negative integer or pair of non-negative integers returned from the system calls open(S), fcntl(S), pipe(S) or dup(S). Once obtained, a process can use the file descriptor for subsequent system calls that manipulate a file such as read(S), write(S) and close(S).

The kernel structures used to manage user file access start in the process's u_area. There are three fields shown in Table 8.1 which are used to manage file descriptors on behalf of each user process.

Table 8.1   The u_area fields used for file descriptor management

u_area field		Description
ushort	u_nofiles	The number of file descriptor slots available for allocation.
struct file	*u_ofile[1]	An array holding pointers to entries in the system file table.
char	*u_pofile	A pointer to an array of per file descriptor flags.

A file descriptor is nothing more than an index into the u_ofile[] array. Each entry in u_ofile[] is a pointer to a file structure which holds information such as the flags passed to open(S) and the file offset used when reading and writing. If an entry in u_ofile[] is not used, it is set to NULL. Each file descriptor has a set of flags which are held in the u_pofile[] array.

For example, consider the following program which opens the file /etc/motd and prints the value of the file descriptor returned:

```
#include'<fcntl.h>

main()
{
    int fd ;
    fd = open("/etc/motd", O_RDONLY) ;
    printf("fd=%d\n", fd) ;
}
```

In this example whose output is shown below, the file descriptor returned from open(S) is used by the kernel to access u_ofile[3] and its flags held in u_pofile[3]:

```
$ a.out
fd=3
```

File descriptors 0, 1 and 2 are inherited from the shell and reference the process's standard input, output and error streams.

Figure 8.3 shows the location of u_nofiles, u_ofile[] and u_pofile in the process's u_area in memory.

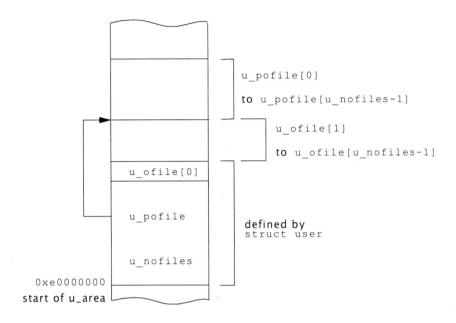

Figure 8.3   u_area management of per process file descriptors

The u_ofile[] array is placed at the end of the u_area and is declared only with one element despite the real number of file descriptors initially available being defined by the kernel tuneable NOFILES. This allows successful compilation of kernel structures, permitting the real size of the u_area to be modified at a later date.

The u_nofiles field indicates how many file descriptors can be allocated and therefore holds the size of the u_ofile[] and u_pofile[] arrays.

8.2.2 Open file flags

Currently, there is only one flag that can be assigned to each u_pofile[] element, the FD_CLOEXEC flag. If this flag is set, the file descriptor is closed when the exec(S) system call is invoked. There are two places where this can be set:

- The user calls the fcntl(S) system call with the F_SETFD command and argument of FD_CLOEXEC.

- A process calls opendir(S). In this case the kernel will set the flag for POSIX.1 compliance. Since directory manipulation is done via user level libraries, a file descriptor associated with a directory will have little meaning following an execve() system call. This also applies to other library calls.

The value of the open file flags field can be retrieved by calling the fcntl(S) system call with the F_GETFD command.

Toolkit 8.1   Accessing file descriptors

Since the area of memory used to hold file descriptors and their associated flags lies outside of the static boundaries of the u_area, defined by `sizeof()`, reading the u_area alone is not sufficient to be able to access the contents of u_ofile[] or u_pofile[].

The example in this toolkit provides a function, `read_userf()`, which will read the u_area together with the additional space allocated for the u_ofile[] and u_pofile[] arrays. It returns a pointer to a `struct user` so the caller need not be aware that the data referenced is greater than `sizeof(struct user)`.

The `read_userf()` function (lines 13 to 37) is used to read both the u_area and the additional space used by u_ofile[] and u_pofile[].

`read_userf()` first opens /dev/kmem and then invokes `nlist(S)` on line 25 to obtain the address of the u_area. This is done in order to extract the value of u_nofiles, without which the full size of data to be read would not be known.

A buffer is then allocated with a call to `malloc(S)` on line 31 to allocate space to hold the u_area, together with the u_ofile[] and u_pofile[] arrays. On the second call to read from /dev/kmem, the required amount of data is read. On line 36, `read_userf()` returns a pointer to the buffer allocated.

```
 1 #include <sys/types.h>
 2 #include <sys/user.h>
 3 #include <fcntl.h>
 4 #include <unistd.h>
 5 #include <nlist.h>
 6
 7 #define EUSER(u) (sizeof(struct user) + \
 8                 ((sizeof(struct file *)) * (u.u_nofiles-1)) + \
 9                 ((sizeof(char)) * u.u_nofiles))
10
11 struct nlist nl[] = { { "u", 0 }, { 0 } } ;
12
13 struct user *
14 read_userf()
15 {
16      struct user  utp ;
17      char         *buf ;
18      ushort       nofiles ;
19      int          fd ;
20
21      fd = open("/dev/kmem", O_RDONLY) ;
22      if (fd < 0)
23          pexit("kmem") ;
24
25      if (nlist("/unix", nl) < 0)
26          pexit("nlist") ; ;
27
28      lseek(fd, nl[0].n_value, SEEK_SET) ;
29      read(fd, (char *)&utp, sizeof(struct user)) ;
30
31      buf = (char *)malloc(EUSER(utp)) ;
32
33      lseek(fd, nl[0].n_value, SEEK_SET) ;
34      read(fd, buf, EUSER(utp)) ;
35
36      return((struct user *)buf) ;
```

```
37  }
38
39  main()
40  {
41       int             fd, i ;
42       struct user *ua ;
43
44       ua = read_userf() ;
45       for (i=0 ; i<ua->u_nofiles ; i++) {
46            if (ua->u_ofile[i] != NULL)
47                 printf("u_ofile[%d] = 0x%x\n", i, ua->u_ofile[i]) ;
48       }
49  }
```

The EUSER macro (lines 7 to 9) defines the size of the required u_area which is calculated as the size of the u_area plus the size of the u_ofile[] array minus one element (u_ofile[0] is contained within the u_area) plus the size of the u_pofile[] array. The sizeof() call is required since both arrays have elements of different sizes. This also increases the portability of the program since no assumptions are made about the basic type sizes. The output of the program for one particular run is:

```
# a.out
u_ofile[0] = 0xf00e87c0
u_ofile[1] = 0xf00e87c0
u_ofile[2] = 0xf00e87c0
u_ofile[3] = 0xf00e864c
```

The first three file descriptors (u_ofile[0] to u_ofile[2]) are used to represent the stdin, stdout and stderr streams. The fourth file descriptor (u_ofile[3]) points to the file /dev/kmem which is used by read_userf().

Figure 8.4 summarises how the first three file descriptors are created. During execution of the getty process, the TTY line which getty has been set to monitor is opened, producing stdin. The fdup(S) library call is then invoked twice, yielding stdout and stderr. Following execution of getty, the login process ensures that there are no more than these three file descriptors open before creation of the shell.

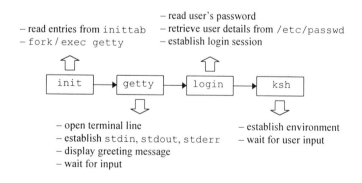

Figure 8.4 The login process

The file descriptors associated with a process can also be displayed from within a
crash(ADM) session as follows:

```
$ crash
dumpfile = /dev/mem, namelist = /unix, outfile = stdout
> proc ! grep crash
  24 p    445    443    445 13583   40   29          crash              load ntrc
> user 24
PER PROCESS USER AREA FOR PROCESS 24
USER ID's:   uid: 13583, gid: 50, real uid: 13583, real gid: 50
      supplementary gids: 50
PROCESS TIMES:      user: 225, sys: 40, child user: 10, child sys: 26
PROCESS MISC:
      command: crash, psargs: /etc/crash
      proc: P#24, cntrl tty:   58,1
      start: Mon Jun 12 07:09:04 1995
      mem: 0xb7ee, type: exec
      proc/text lock: none
      current directory: I#101
OPEN FILES AND POFILE FLAGS:
      [ 0]: F#49   r    [ 1]: F#49     w   [ 2]: F#49     w
      [ 3]: F#58   r
FILE I/O:
      u_base: 0x80a6644, file offset: 6730136, bytes: 4096
      segment: data, cmask: 0022, ulimit: 2097151
      file mode(s): read
SIGNAL DISPOSITION:
      sig#       signal oldmask sigmask
        2:   0x805eb50    -     2 13
       13:   0x805eb50    -     2 13
       16: ignore         -
       17: ignore         -
```

In this example the proc command is used to locate the crash process. The user
command is then used to display the u_area for the process. Those files which the process
has open are displayed in addition to other information stored in the u_area. There are
four open files, as highlighted, the first three representing stdin, stdout and stderr
and the fourth for /dev/mem which crash uses to read and write kernel structures.

8.2.3 Open file limits

The number of files that a process can open at any one time is restricted by the kernel.
There are two limits which govern the total number of available file descriptors: a soft
limit which represents the initial size of u_ofile[] and a hard limit which defines the
absolute maximum number of file descriptors that can be allocated.

The value of both limits can be retrieved using the getrlimit(S) system call.
Initially u_nofiles is set to the soft limit although it can be increased up to the hard
limit by invoking the setrlimit(S) system call.

The hard limit can be lowered although it must be noted that this is a non-reversible
operation. Only a process with superuser privileges can increase the hard limit.

Toolkit 8.2   Extending open file limits

The following toolkit program demonstrates reading and modifying the soft and hard limits for the number of per process open files.

The program starts by calling the getrlimit(S) system call on line 11. The hard and soft limits are returned in the rlimit structure passed and the contents displayed on lines 12 and 13.

```
 1 #include <sys/select.h>
 2 #include <sys/resource.h>
 3 #include <sys/errno.h>
 4 #include <fcntl.h>
 5
 6 main()
 7 {
 8     int    i, x, *fd ;
 9     struct rlimit lim ;      /* lim.rlim_cur & lim.rlim_max */
10
11     getrlimit(RLIMIT_NOFILE, &lim) ;
12     printf("soft limit = %d\n", lim.rlim_cur) ;
13     printf("hard limit = %d\n", lim.rlim_max) ;
14     fd = (int *)malloc(lim.rlim_max * sizeof(int)) ;
15
16     for (i=0 ; i<lim.rlim_max ; i++) {
17         fd[i] = open("/etc/motd", O_RDONLY) ;
18         if (fd[i] < 0) {
19             printf("%d file descriptors allocated\n", i+3) ;
20             break ;
21         }
22     }
23     lim.rlim_max += 50 ;
24     setrlimit(RLIMIT_NOFILE, &lim) ;
25
26     getrlimit(RLIMIT_NOFILE, &lim) ;
27     printf("soft limit = %d\n", lim.rlim_cur) ;
28     printf("hard limit = %d\n", lim.rlim_max) ;
29     x = open("/etc/motd", O_RDONLY) ;
30     if (x > 0)
31         printf("x=%d\n", x) ;
32 }
```

When getrlimit(S) returns, an array is allocated to hold the maximum number of possible file descriptors. The loop on lines 16 to 22 then attempts to open as many files as possible. When open(S) eventually returns –1, the number of open files is displayed.

On line 23 the soft limit is increased by 50 and a call is made to setrlimit(S) on line 24 to try and increase the hard limit. When the program is run by root the expected results are shown below:

```
# a.out
soft limit = 110
hard limit = 110
110 file descriptors allocated
soft limit = 110
hard limit = 160
```

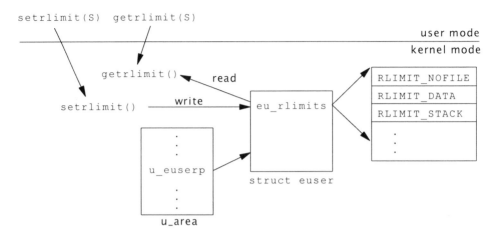

Figure 8.5   Retrieving and setting per process limits

The `eu_rlimits[]` array in the extended u_area structure contains a number of `rlimit` structures, each corresponding to one of the limits that can be retrieved or set by `getrlimit(S)` and `setrlimit(S)`. After the `setrlimit()` kernel function has validated the limits passed to `setrlimit(S)`, the `rlimit` structure passed is copied to its appropriate position in the `eu_rlimits[]` array.

Figure 8.5 shows the paths followed through the kernel for `getrlimit(S)` and `setrlimit(S)`.

The `getrlimit()` kernel function simply locates the appropriate position in the array and copies the data out to the user supplied `rlimit` structure.

8.2.4 File descriptor allocation and de-allocation

File descriptors are allocated by the kernel routine `ufalloc()`. The tasks performed by `ufalloc()` are as follows:

- A search is made through the `u_ofile[]` array in the u_area starting at element 0 and not exceeding (`u_nofiles - 1`). If an empty slot is found, i.e. its pointer value is `NULL`, the value held in its corresponding `u_pofile[]` entry is reset and the position in `u_ofile[]` is returned.

- If the number of allocated file descriptors will exceed the soft limit, the system call will fail and `errno` will be set to `EMFILE`.

- If an entry in `u_ofile[]` could not be found and the number of file descriptors currently open does not exceed the soft limit, `expand_upage()` is called to allocate further space for the `u_ofile[]` and `u_pofile[]` arrays, allowing more file descriptors to be allocated. If this call is successful, the first free entry in the newly allocated space for `u_ofile[]` is returned.

The assignment of a file table pointer to the appropriate entry in u_ofile[] is described in the following section. If the u_area needs to be increased, space is allocated dynamically above the area occupied by u_pofile[]. The u_pofile[] array is then moved to allow u_ofile[] to expand.

There are generally two methods by which a file descriptor is de-allocated. Firstly, the entry in u_ofile[] may be set to NULL if, for example, an error occurs part way through a file open. Secondly, to close an already open file, the kernel invokes the closef() routine. The tasks performed by closef() are:

- Call plock() to lock the inode. Inode locking is described in section 8.4.5.
- Call the filesystem dependent close() function. This allows any underlying device, for example a STREAMS device, to de-allocate any resources which may have been created when the STREAM was opened.
- If the reference count in the file structure (see next section) is greater than 1, it is decremented and closef() returns.
- The file structure reference count is set to zero. If the file is open for writing, the inode write count is decremented. The file structure is added to the free list.

8.3 The system file table

Although the u_ofile[] and u_pofile[] arrays hold the initial information that the process needs to access the file, most of the information required by the kernel is held in the *system file table* and *inode table*. This section describes the system file table (usually simply called the *file table*).

The file table is an array of file structures. Each entry in u_ofile[] points to a file structure. The file structure (or file_t as it is commonly called) is used to hold further information about the file on behalf of a single user process. A reference to the same file by a different process usually results in allocation of a different file structure.

The fields of the file structure are shown in Table 8.2.

Table 8.2   The fields of the file structure

Field		Usage
ushort	f_flag	Flags passed to open()/creat().
cnt_t	f_count	The file structure reference count.
f_up		A union of following two types:
struct inode	*f_uinode	Pointer to filesystem independent inode.
struct file	*f_unext	Pointer to the next free file structure if not used.
f_un		A union of following two types:
off_t	f_off	The current offset in the file for reading/writing.
struct file	*f_slnk	Xenix semaphore queue (no longer used).

If a file structure is currently being used, the f_up.f_inode field will point to an in-core inode which describes in more detail the properties of the file being accessed. If a file structure is not being used, it is stored on a free list headed by the kernel variable ffreelist. Each element in the free list is chained via the f_up.f_unext field. If the free list becomes empty then an attempt is made to allocate additional space.

The f_off field is used to hold the current offset within the file for reading and writing. The use of the f_off field is demonstrated in Toolkit 8.3.

8.3.1 System file table organisation

The system file table is initially held in an array of file structures appropriately named file[]. The size of the array is determined by the kernel tuneable MAX_FILE.

During kernel initialisation, the routine finit() is called to initialise the file table. The tasks performed by finit() are:

- Link together all elements in the file[] array using the f_next field.
- The f_next field of the last element is set to NULL.
- The ffreelist is set to point to the first element in the list.
- The kernel variable filecnt which contains a count of the number of free file table entries is set to the number of elements in file[].

After completion of finit(), the file table forms a list of file structures linked by the f_next field. This is shown in Figure 8.6. The kernel variable filecnt holds the number of free file structures available at any one time.

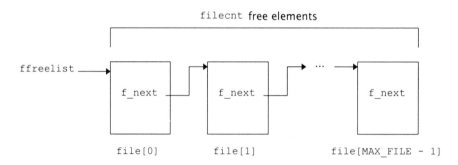

Figure 8.6   The system file table following a call to finit()

Toolkit 8.3   Locating file table entries

The following toolkit program builds on Toolkit 8.1 to locate a file_t entry from a specified file descriptor.

The read_userf() function is called on line 26 to read the u_area. Using the file descriptor returned from the open() call (line 24), read_file_t() is called on line 27 to read the contents of the appropriate file structure.

The `read_file_t()` function on lines 11 to 16 is called with the address of the `file_t` structure requested and its operation involves seeking `/dev/kmem` and reading the structure's contents.

The `dup(S)` system call is then invoked (line 33) to demonstrate sharing of the `file` structure. Note that the `f_inode` field shown on lines 31 and 40 is a macro used to reference `f_up.f_uinode`. See the `<sys/file.h>` header file for further details.

```
 1 #include <sys/types.h>
 2 #include <sys/dir.h>
 3 #include <sys/user.h>
 4 #include <sys/file.h>
 5 #include <fcntl.h>
 6 #include <unistd.h>
 7 #include "ksym.h"
 8
 9 extern struct user *read_userf() ;
10
11 read_file_t(file_t *ftp, long fta)
12 {
13      int kfd = open("/dev/kmem", O_RDONLY) ;
14      lseek(kfd, fta, SEEK_SET) ;
15      read(kfd, ftp, sizeof(file_t)) ;
16 }
17
18 main()
19 {
20      struct user *ua ;
21      file_t      ft ;
22      int         fd, dfd ;
23
24      fd = open("/etc/motd", O_RDONLY) ;
25
26      ua = read_userf() ;
27      read_file_t(&ft, (long)ua->u_ofile[fd]) ;
28      printf("u_ofile[%d] = %x\n", fd, ua->u_ofile[fd]) ;
29      printf("  f_count  = %d\n", ft.f_count) ;
30      printf("  f_offset = %d\n", ft.f_offset) ;
31      printf("  f_uinode = %x\n\n", ft.f_inode) ;
32
33      dfd = dup(fd) ;
34      lseek(dfd, 16, SEEK_SET) ;
35      free(ua) ; ua = read_userf() ;
36      read_file_t(&ft, (long)ua->u_ofile[dfd]) ;
37      printf("u_ofile[%d] = %x\n", dfd, ua->u_ofile[dfd]) ;
38      printf("  f_count  = %d\n", ft.f_count) ;
39      printf("  f_offset = %d\n", ft.f_offset) ;
40      printf("  f_uinode = %x\n", ft.f_inode) ;
41 }
```

The output for one particular run of the program is:

```
u_ofile[4] = f00d0760
  f_count  = 1
  f_offset = 0
  f_uinode = f0129794

u_ofile[5] = f00d0760
  f_count  = 2
  f_offset = 16                 # 16 (hex) = 17 (decimal)
  f_uinode = f0129794
```

The first open(S) returns file descriptor 4 which is used by the kernel to access u_ofile[4]. This points to the file_t structure at address f00d0760 which has a reference count of 1. The offset is at byte 0 since no file access has yet taken place.

Following the call to dup(S), a new file descriptor (5) is returned which points to the same file_t structure as the original file descriptor returned by the open(S) system call. Since the same file structure is used, the kernel has incremented the reference count to 2.

The lseek(S) system call on line 34 moves the file pointer (f_offset) forward to the 17th byte (note that reading/writing starts at byte 0). The next read(S) or write(S) call will start at this offset. Following the call to lseek(S), file access via either file descriptor will modify f_offset, allowing data be to read or written in sequence (but not shared) between the two file descriptors (4 and 5).

The output of this example is shown in Figure 8.7.

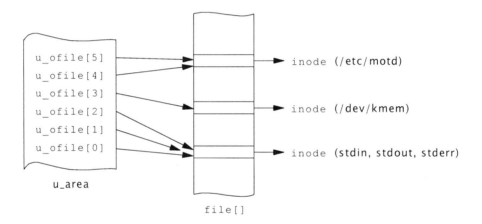

Figure 8.7   Connection between file descriptors and the system file table

Individual file table entries can be displayed in crash(ADM) using the file command. The following example displays the entry in slot 3, file[2]:

```
$ crash
dumpfile = /dev/mem, namelist = /unix, outfile = stdout
> file 3
FILE TABLE SIZE = 341
SLOT  RCNT   I/FL      OFFSET  FLAGS
   3     3 I#    5           0  read
```

This output shows the position in the table being displayed, the reference count, the entry in the inode table to which the file_t points, the file offset used for reading or writing and the file flags passed to open(S).

8.3.2 File table flags

The `f_flag` field contains flags that are set by the user process calling the `open(S)` or `creat(S)` system calls, modified by the `fcntl(S)` system call and maintained by the kernel. Table 8.3 shows the possible flags that can be set. Note that the flag names shown here are the names used by the kernel which differ from the flag names used by user processes; for example, `FSYNC` is used in placed of `O_SYNC`.

Table 8.3   System file table flags

Flag	Set by	Description
FREAD	open(O_RDONLY) open(O_WRONLY)	Permits read access to the file.
FWRITE	open(O_WRONLY) open(O_RDWR) creat()	Permits write access to the file.
FCREAT	Kernel	Used during file creation and then reset before returning to user space following `creat()`.
FTRUNC	Kernel	Used only when file is first opened and then reset before returning to user space.
FEXCL	Kernel	Used only when file is first opened and then reset before returning to user space.
FNOCTTY	open(O_NOCTTY)	Used to stop an open of a TTY from becoming the controlling TTY of the process and therefore making it a candidate for TTY-generated signals.
FAPPEND	open(O_APPEND) fcntl(O_APPEND)	All writes will be appended to the file.
FSYNC	open(O_SYNC) fcntl(O_SYNC)	All writes will be committed before returning.
FNONBLOCK	open(O_NONBLOCK) fcntl(O_NONBLOCK)	Non-blocking I/O for FIFOs.
FSTOPIO	Kernel	Used for C2 security to prevent further file access.
FBMODE	Kernel	Used for >2 Gb filesystem support.

In older versions of SCO UNIX, the `O_NDELAY` flag was used in place of the newer `O_NONBLOCK`. Both are supported in SCO UNIX today although their semantics differ slightly. The `O_NONBLOCK` flag should always be used when writing applications.

Toolkit 8.4   Accessing and displaying `file_t` flags

The following toolkit program reads the `file` structure for a specified file descriptor and displays its flags. This builds on the previous two toolkits for reading the u_area and reading a `file_t` structure corresponding to a specified file descriptor.

The `prflags()` function shown on lines 11 to 31 takes the `f_flag` field of the `file_t` structure and displays the flags that are set.

```
 1 #include <sys/types.h>
 2 #include <sys/stat.h>
 3 #include <sys/file.h>
 4 #include <sys/dir.h>
 5 #include <sys/user.h>
 6 #include <fcntl.h>
 7
 8 extern struct user *read_userf() ;
 9 extern struct user *read_file_t() ;
10
11 prflags(ushort flags)
12 {
13     ushort rfl = (flags + FOPEN) & O_ACCMODE ;
14     printf("flags = %x ( ", flags) ;
15     if (flags & FREAD)   printf("(FREAD) ") ;
16     if (flags & FWRITE)   printf("(FWRITE) ") ;
17
18     if (rfl == O_RDONLY)   printf("O_RDONLY ") ;
19     else
20         if (rfl == O_WRONLY)   printf("O_WRONLY ") ;
21         else
22             if (rfl == O_RDWR)      printf("O_RDWR ") ;
23     if (flags & O_CREAT)  printf("O_CREAT ") ;
24     if (flags & O_TRUNC)  printf("O_TRUNC ") ;
25     if (flags & O_EXCL)   printf("O_EXCL ") ;
26     if (flags & O_NOCTTY) printf("O_NOCTTY ") ;
27     if (flags & O_NDELAY) printf("O_NDELAY ") ;
28     if (flags & O_APPEND) printf("O_APPEND ") ;
29     if (flags & O_SYNC)   printf("O_SYNC ") ;
30     printf(")\n") ;
31 }
32
33 main()
34 {
35     struct user   *ua ;
36     file_t        ft ;
37     int           fd1, fd2 ;
38
39     fd1 = open("foo", O_RDWR) ;
40     fd2 = open("bar", O_WRONLY|O_SYNC|O_APPEND) ;
41     ua = read_userf() ;
42     read_file_t(&ft, (long)ua->u_ofile[fd1]) ;
43     prflags(ft.f_flag) ;
44     read_file_t(&ft, (long)ua->u_ofile[fd2]) ;
45     prflags(ft.f_flag) ;
46 }
```

The `main()` function opens two files (`foo` and `bar`) and calls `read_userf()` to read the u_area followed by two calls to `read_file_t()` to read the contents of the `file_t` structures corresponding to the open file.

For each `file_t` read the `prflags()` function is called. The output for one particular run of the program is:

```
flags = 3 ( (FREAD) (FWRITE) O_RDWR )
flags = 1a ( (FWRITE) O_WRONLY O_APPEND O_SYNC )
```

It must be noted, however, that the results shown may vary depending on whether the file already exists or not and what permissions it has set. It is useful to repeat the example on different types of files with varying permissions.

Building on previous toolkits presented in this chapter, the `read_userf()` function is called (line 41) following the two `open(S)` calls. For each `file_t` the contents are read and the appropriate flags are displayed (lines 43 and 45).

The `prflags()` function (line 11) takes the flags field as an argument, masks it to make the field more easily readable (line 13) and then displays which flags are set.

8.3.3 File structure allocation and de-allocation

The system file table consists of an array of `file` structures. During kernel initialisation the elements are linked together via the `f_up.f_unext` field and pointed to by the `ffreelist` kernel variable as shown earlier. The tasks performed when allocating a single `file` structure through the `falloc()` function are as follows:

- The `ufalloc()` function is called to allocate a file descriptor. If a file descriptor cannot be allocated, `u_error` will have been set by `ufalloc()` so `falloc()` simply returns `NULL` indicating that a file table entry could not be allocated.

- If the file table is empty, `grow_file()` is called to grow the file table.

- The first free element is taken from the list headed by `ffreelist` and the `u_ofile[]` entry set to point to it. The flags passed to `open(S)` or `creat(S)` are stored in the `f_flags` field and the `f_inode` field is set to point to the inode table entry passed as an argument to `falloc()`.

- The value in `filecnt` is decremented and the file table entry address is returned.

Many kernel routines executed both on behalf of system call processing and internally use the kernel routine `getf()` which takes a file descriptor as its argument and returns the corresponding `file` structure in the u_area if available.

The tasks performed for freeing a `file` structure by the `unfalloc()` function are as follows:

- The reference count held in the `f_count` field is decremented.

- If the reference count reaches zero, there are no processes referencing the file table entry. In this case the `file` structure can then be added to the free list headed by `ffreelist` and the number of free file structures (`filecnt`) can be incremented.

8.4 The filesystem independent inode

Files stored on disk or other types of physical media are usually described by an `inode` structure. One exception to this general rule are DOS files for which the structure of file data and meta-data is very different to traditional UNIX file formats. All filesystems supported under SCO UNIX maintain their own inode structures. While each inode provides information common to all file types, such as the file's size, owner and access rights, it also contains additional attributes which are dependent on the particular filesystem to which it belongs.

When a file is currently being accessed it is represented in memory by an *in-core* inode defined by the `inode` structure (or `inode_t`). From here on we use the term `inode` to refer to the in-core inode and explicitly state if the on-disk inode is referenced.

The fields of the `inode` are identical for each file regardless of the underlying physical file it represents. For open files, the inode is pointed to by one or more `file` structures. However, unlike `file` structures for which there may be multiple entries for accessing the same physical file, there is only `inode` entry representing the file.

8.4.1 Basic file properties

The basic inode fields that describe the more well-known properties of the file are shown in Table 8.4. These fields are also used as a basis for the `stat` structure following invocation of the `stat(S)`, `fstat(S)`, `xstat(S)` and `fxstat(S)` system calls.

Table 8.4   `inode` structure fields

inode field		Description
ino32_t	i_number	The filesystem dependent inode number of the file.
ushort	i_ftype	The type of the inode (regular file, directory etc.).
off_t	i_size	The size of the file in bytes.
ushort	i_uid	The file's owner.
ushort	i_gid	The file's group.
short	i_nlink	Number of hard links to the file.
dev_t	i_rdev	Device number used for raw I/O.
dev_t	i_dev	The device where the inode resides.

The type of file can be determined by issuing one of the `stat(S)` system calls and then checking the file type using one of the following macros:

S_ISREG()	Regular file
S_ISBLK()	Block special file
S_ISCHR()	Character special file
S_ISDIR()	Directory file
S_ISFIFO()	Named pipe or FIFO
S_ISLNK()	Symbolic link
S_ISNAM()	Special named file

There are a number of different `stat` calls that can be made. For example, `stat(S)` takes a pathname while `fstat(S)` takes a file descriptor. The contents of the `stat` structure are filled by the kernel from two different sources. Some of the fields are copied from the `inode` structure, while the remaining fields are filled by the filesystem to which the file belongs. Figure 8.8 shows the separation of the two field types.

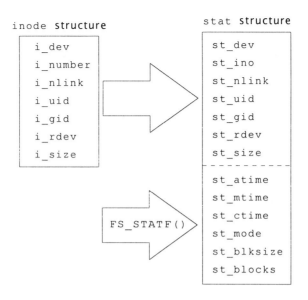

Figure 8.8   Construction of the stat structure

The FS_STATF() macro used to retrieve per file attributes is described in section 8.6.

8.4.2 Inode table organisation

All inodes available for use following system initialisation are held in the inode[] table. The size of the table is determined by the kernel tuneable MAX_INODE. The inode[] array is initialised during kernel startup by the routine inoinit(). An inode can be in one of two lists:

- Linked on the inode free list. This is headed by the kernel variable ifreelist and contains ifreecnt elements. After system initialisation ifreecnt will be set to MAX_INODE.

- Linked on one of NHINODE hash queues allowing a fast lookup. The kernel tuneable NHINODE must be a multiple of 2 within the range 64 to 8192. The default value of NHINODE is 128.

The hash queues are used to locate an in-core inode quickly rather than perform a linear search through the whole inode[] table. The details of the inode hash queues are discussed later in this section.

The fields used to link inodes on to either the free list or one of the hash queues are shown in Table 8.5.

Table 8.5   Inode fields for free list and hash queue management

inode field		Description
struct inode	*i_forw	Link for inode hash chain if the inode is in use.
struct inode	*i_back	Link for inode hash chain if the inode is in use.
struct inode	*av_forw	Link for the inode free list if the inode is not being used.
struct inode	*av_back	Link for the inode free list if the inode is not being used.

The free list is headed by `ifreelist` which, although declared as an inode, is not part of the `inode[]` table itself. The hash queues are formed by the array `hinode[]` containing NHINODE elements of type `struct hinode`. The elements of the `hinode` structure are shown in Table 8.6.

Table 8.6   Hash queue fields for the `hinode` structure

hinode field		Description
struct inode	*i_forw	Pointer to the first inode on this hash queue.
struct inode	*i_back	Pointer to the last inode on this hash queue.

The `inoinit()` kernel function is called early during system initialisation prior to any filesystems being mounted. The tasks performed by `inoinit()` are as follows:

- For the head of each element of `hinode[]` set the `i_forw` and `i_back` fields to point to itself indicating that the list is empty.
- For each element in the `inode[]` table set the `i_forw` pointer of `ifreelist` to point to the inode and set the `i_forw` field of the inode to point to the inode currently at the head of the list.
- The `ifreelist` inode actually points to the last element in the `inode[]` array when `inoinit()` has completed.
- The `ifreecnt` variable is set to the number of elements in `inode[]`.

Following the call to `inoinit()` the free list pointed to by `ifreelist` forms a doubly linked list as shown in Figure 8.9.

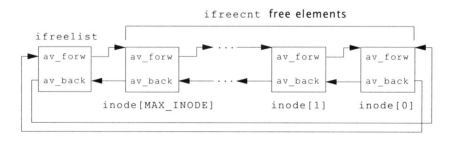

Figure 8.9   The inode table following `inoinit()`

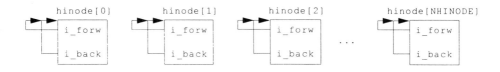

Figure 8.10   The inode hash queues following inoinit()

The inode hash queues will be empty following the call to inoinit(). The format of the hash queues at this stage are shown in Figure 8.10.

The construction and management of the hash queues needs to be kept simple to allow efficiency of management and access. Inodes are hashed using their inode number by the following hash algorithm:

```
#define ihash(ino)    (&hinode[(int)ino & (MAXINODE - 1)])
```

For example, consider the size of MAX_INODE to be 2048 and two inodes with inode numbers 32 and 2080:

```
MAX_INODE = 2048    = 100000000000       # note this is binary
MAX_INODE - 1       = 011111111111

inumber of 32       = 000000100000
hash queue          = 011111111111 & 000000100000 = hinode[32]

inumber of 2080     = 100000100000
hash queue          = 011111111111 & 100000100000 = hinode[32]
```

This shows an example where two different inode numbers hash to the same value and will therefore be placed on the same hash queue. Determining the optimum value of both MAX_INODE and NHINODE is not an easy task since it depends on the workload of the particular machine in question. Generally speaking the following equation can be used to calculate the best values:

$$\frac{MAX\_INODE}{NHINODE} = 4$$

where NHINODE is a power of 2.

8.4.3 Pathname resolution

The user process usually only deals with a file's pathname and the file descriptor returned by the kernel used to access the file. The structures presented so far (file descriptors, file_t and inode_t) must be created before file access can take place.

In order to allocate the necessary chain of structures to represent the file in memory, the kernel must first translate the pathname given to system calls such as open(S) and convert it into the file's corresponding inode number. This process is called *pathname resolution* or *pathname translation*. To aid pathname resolution two u_area fields are used as shown in Table 8.7.

Table 8.7   u_area fields used during pathname resolution

inode Field		Description
struct inode	*u_cdir	inode of the current working directory.
struct inode	*u_rdir	inode of the root directory.

A pathname is a string of filenames, each separated by a single / character. Each component in the pathname must be either a directory or a symbolic link with the exception of the last component which references the target file.

The two u_area fields dictate from where to start the pathname translation which depends on whether the pathname given is *absolute* (it starts from root directory and therefore has a / as the first character) or *relative*, in which case it starts from the current working directory. For example:

/etc/motd   Example of an absolute pathname
bin/mygrep   Example of a relative pathname

Each time open(S) or creat(S) is called, a file descriptor is returned for the requested file. To locate the requested file, the kernel must translate the pathname into an in-core inode. This involves the co-ordination of both filesystem independent and filesystem dependent layers of the kernel.

The kernel function that performs pathname resolution is called namei(). In addition to pathname translation, namei() can be called to perform various operations on the last component of the pathname as shown in Figure 8.11.

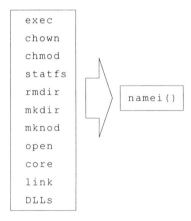

Figure 8.11   Some of the users of namei()

Two parameters are passed to `namei()`, a function to read the pathname from either user or supervisor space and a pointer to an `argnamei` structure. The fields of the `argnamei` structure are shown in Table 8.8.

Table 8.8 `struct argnamei` fields used by `namei()`

argnamei field		Description
ushort	cmd	Command to be performed. See Table 8.9 for details.
short	rcode	Return code from `namei()`.
long	inode	Inode number of the field to be linked.
long	mode	File mode for file/directory creation or mode change.
ushort	ftype	File type used by `mknod()`.
ushort	uid	Caller's user ID.
ushort	gid	Caller's group ID.
dev_t	idev	Device number for `link()` and `creat()`.
struct inode	*ip	Inode used by `rename(S)`.

The basic operation performed by `namei()` for all commands is to resolve the pathname as far as possible, working on each component in turn. If `namei()` is called with a NULL `argnamei` structure, the pathname will be resolved to an inode for the last component. If a pointer to an `argnamei` structure is passed to `namei()`, the operation will depend on the `argnamei` cmd field. The possible values of cmd are shown in Table 8.9.

Table 8.9 Command types for `namei()` processing

cmd type	Description
NI_DEL	Delete a file if creation failed due to an overflow of the file table.
NI_CREAT	Create a file.
NI_XCREAT	Create a file exclusively (O_EXCL).
NI_LINK	Increase a file's link count.
NI_MKDIR	Make a directory.
NI_RMDIR	Remove a directory.
NI_MKNOD	Make a special file.
NI_NOFOLLOW	Do not follow symbolic links.
NI_SYMLINK	Create a symbolic link.
NI_RELNAMEI	Rename a file.

The tasks performed by `namei()` are shown below. In practice, the actual work performed by `namei()` is considerably more complex!

- Copy the pathname into a `namei` provided buffer.
- If the pathname is absolute, set the current working directory to `u.u_rdir`, otherwise set the current working directory to `u.u_cdir`.
- Repeat the following tasks until the last component is resolved:

⇨ Lock the current working inode.

⇨ Test for read/write/execute access.

⇨ Select the next component.

⇨ Call the filesystem dependent `namei()` routine via `FS_NAMEI()`.

⇨ Set the current working inode to the inode returned by `FS_NAMEI()`.

8.4.4 General access flags

The `inode` structure fields shown in Table 8.10 are used to manage access to the file in one way or another by multiple processes. Some fields are used to serialise access to the inode during read and write operations and some provide user level locking, while the remaining fields are used for traditional file services.

8.4.5 Inode locking and synchronisation

When accessing the `inode`, a process must first obtain the `inode` lock. The inode is locked if the `i_flag` has the `ILOCK` bit set. SCO UNIX supports both exclusive and non-exclusive access to individual files. Only one process can access the file when writing, while there may be multiple readers. Table 8.11 lists the kernel routines used to manage inode locks.

Table 8.10   Additional `inode` structure fields

inode field		Description
ushort	i_flag	Inode flags describing the state of the inode.
ushort	i_want	Set by a process requiring access to the inode after detecting that the inode is currently locked.
ushort	i_count	Number of references to the inode.
i_u		Union of the following types:
struct mount	*i_mton	Pointer to mount structure covering this inode.
struct region	*i_rp	Associated region for used for mapped files.
struct stdata	*i_sp	Pointer to the STREAM head.
struct iisem	*i_sem	Used for Xenix semaphores.
struct iisd	*isd	Used for Xenix shared data.
long	*i_filocks	Used for file and record locking.
unsigned long	i_mappages	Used to check if the file is mapped and has pages in the page cache.
unsigned long	i_vcode	Read ahead block used by NFS.
short	i_wcnt	Write open count or ITEXT count.
struct lockb	i_cilock	Lock to synchronise i_flag changes.
ushort	i_rdlocks	Count of non-exclusive locks.

If a process needs to obtain the inode lock, it calls `plock()`, `prdlock()` or `prelock()`. If the lock cannot be obtained, for example a read lock is required while another process holds the write lock, the process will set the i_want field to one of the following values and sleep until the inode becomes available:

IWANT   For exclusive access
IRDWANT   For non-exclusive access
IREWANT   If a lock upgrade is required

Since any process may wish to test and/or modify the i_flag and i_want fields simultaneously on a multi-processor platform, the i_cilock field is used further to synchronise access to the inode by allowing only a single process to hold the i_cilock at any one time.

Table 8.11   Kernel routines for manipulating inode locks

Lock function	Description
plock()	Lock the inode for write access.
prdlock()	Lock the inode for read access.
prelock()	Upgrade a lock from read to write access.
prele()	Unlock the inode and wake up any processes sleeping on the lock.

Toolkit 8.5   Reading an in-core inode

The example provided here builds on Toolkit 8.1 and Toolkit 8.3 to read the contents of an inode corresponding to a specified file descriptor.

The source of the program is as follows:

```
 1 #include <sys/types.h>
 2 #include <sys/dir.h>
 3 #include <sys/user.h>
 4 #include <sys/file.h>
 5 #include <sys/inode.h>
 6 #include <fcntl.h>
 7 #include unistd.h>
 8 #include "ksym.h"
 9
10 extern struct user *read_userf() ;
11 extern struct user *read_file_t() ;
12
13 read_inode(inode_t *ip, long ia)
14 {
15     int kfd = open("/dev/kmem", O_RDONLY) ;
16     lseek(kfd, ia, SEEK_SET) ;
17     read(kfd, ip, sizeof(inode_t)) ;
18 }
19
20 main()
21 {
22     struct user  *ua ;
23     struct inode i ;
24     file_t       ft ;
25     int          fd, dfd ;
26
27     fd = open("/etc/motd", O_RDONLY) ;
28
```

```
29        ua = read_userf() ;
30        read_file_t(&ft, (long)ua->u_ofile[fd]) ;
31        printf("u_ofile[%d] = %x\n", fd, ua->u_ofile[fd]) ;
32        printf("  f_count   = %d\n", ft.f_count) ;
33        printf("  f_offset  = %d\n", ft.f_offset) ;
34        printf("  f_uinode  = %x\n\n", ft.f_inode) ;
35
36        read_inode(&i, (long)ft.f_inode) ;
37        printf("  i_number = %d\n", i.i_number) ;
38        printf("  i_size   = %d\n", i.i_size) ;
39        printf("  i_uid    = %d\n", i.i_uid) ;
40        printf("  i_gid    = %d\n", i.i_gid) ;
41  }
```

For the file opened on line 27, the read_userf() (Toolkit 8.1) and read_file_t() (Toolkit 8.3) functions are called to locate and read the u_area for the process and the file structure for the file opened. This provides access to the inode address which is passed to the read_inode() function (called on line 36).

Since the address of the inode is known at this point, the read_inode() function only needs to lseek(S) into /dev/kmem and read the inode.

The output for one particular run of the program is:

```
# a.out
u_ofile[4] = f00d07f0
  f_count  = 1
  f_offset = 0
  f_uinode = f01305b8

  i_number = 468
  i_size   = 114
  i_uid    = 0
  i_gid    = 3
# ncheck -i 468
/dev/root:
468       /etc/motd
# ls -inl /etc/motd
  468 -rw-r--r--   1 0        3            114 Mar 24  1993 /etc/motd
```

The inode number is scanned by the ncheck(ADM) utility to confirm that the entry read corresponds to the file opened.

The same information obtained in this toolkit can be retrieved using crash(ADM). The following example displays the first few entries of the inode[] table and then selects an arbitrary entry to display in more detail.

```
# crash
dumpfile = /dev/mem, namelist = /unix, outfile = stdout
> inode ! more
INODE TABLE SIZE = 1280
SLOT MAJ/MIN FS INUMB RCNT LINK UID GID    SIZE    MODE MNT M/ST FLAGS
   1   1,42   6   193    2    1    2   2   56308 f--t711   0 R515 ac tx
   3   1,42   6 17587    2    1    0   0   38367 f---644   0  -
   6   1,42   6 17566    1    2    2  16     512 d---770   0  -
  16   1,42   6  8563    2    1    2   2   19464 f---755   0 R 88 tx
  17   1,42   6   701    1    1    0   0       0 f---644   0  -
  19 255,255  0     0    1    0    0   0       0 c------   -  -
  22   1,42   6   247   27    1    2   2  187208 f---555   0 R116 tx
```

```
24    1,42   6 17570     1     1     2     2       756 f---664    0    -
26    1,42   6   376    86     1     2     2    359652 f---555    0 R186 ac tx
27    1,42   6   308   108     1     2     2    170132 f---555    0 R207 tx
30    1,42   6    73     1     1     0     3         0 c---666    0    -
31 255,255   4     4     2     0     0     0         0 p---000    -    -
32    1,42   6  2334     2     2     2     2     45772 f---100    0 R  0 tx
36    1,42   6  2478     2     1     0     3      4484 f---100    0 R 19 tx
38    1,42   6 19036     1     1     7    21       433 f---664    0    -
40    1,42   6 18003     2     1     0     0     21844 f---711    0 R 83 tx
41 255,255   0    -1     1     0     0     0         0 b------    -    -    sw
42 255,255   0     0     1     0     0     0         0 c------    - S  7
43    1,42   6     2    36    20     0     2      1024 d---755    0    - at rt
44 255,255   0     0     1     0     0     0         0 c------    - S  5
45 255,255   0     0     1     0     0     0         0 c------    - S  4
46 255,255   0     0     1     0     0     0         0 c------    - S  3
> inode -f 6
INODE TABLE SIZE = 1280
SLOT MAJ/MIN FS INUMB RCNT LINK   UID   GID  SIZE      MODE MNT M/ST FLAGS
   6   1,42   6 17566     1    2     2    16   512 d---770    0    -
        FORW    BACK AFOR ABCK    MAPPAGES              RDLOCKS         WANT
      { 158}    1086   -    -            0                    0
        RMAJ/MIN     FSTYPP       FSPTR      FILOCKS     VCODE WCNT FS
        0,0     0xf0156620 0xfc3aa9e0           0           0    0 HTFS
HTFS INODE:
    FLAGS: used
        LASTREAD      MAP/DOFF            DADDRS
        0xffffffff           0            [ 0] 167996      [ 1] 0
          EPIPTR    DIRBLKPTR
               0            0
> q
# ncheck -i 17566
/dev/root:
17566      /var/opt/K/SCO/Unix/5.0.0Cl/usr/spool/cron/atjobs/.
```

The crash(ADM) utility can also be used in conjunction with adb to analyse further the toolkit example as it runs. This technique is used throughout the book.

8.5 File record locking

There are two functions available for locking a range of bytes of a specified file, namely lockf(S) and fcntl(S). The lockf(S) function is described briefly below since it is supported by a number of different versions of UNIX. The section then concentrates on the semantics and implementation of fcntl(S) locking, which is the method chosen by POSIX.1. In fact, lockf(S) is built on top of fcntl(S).

The prototype for lockf(S) is:

```
#include <unistd.h>

int lockf(int fildes, int function, long size) ;
```

The function argument passed to lockf(S) can take one of the following values:

F_LOCK   A section of the file is locked for exclusive access.

F_ULOCK   A previously locked section is unlocked.

| F_TLOCK | A section of a file is tested to see if it is locked and if not locked, the section is locked for exclusive access. |
| F_TEST | A test is made to see if a section of a file is locked. |

The file section is specified as a range of bytes given by the size argument which can be negative or positive. The section is relative to the current file offset.

The fcntl(S) system call provides a more complete interface:

```
#include <fcntl.h>

int fcntl(int fildes, int cmd, (void *)arg) ;
```

There are three values that the cmd argument can take:

F_GETLK	This gets the first lock that blocks the lock description described in the flock structure passed in the arg argument of fcntl(S).
F_SETLK	This command is used to set or clear a file segment lock using the lock description described in the flock structure passed in the arg argument. It can be used to establish a read or write lock.
F_SETLKW	This command performs the same actions as F_SETLK except that if a read or write lock is blocked by an existing read or write lock on the file, the process will sleep until the segment is free to be locked.

The flock structure describes the properties of the lock such as the size and starting offset and whether it is a read or write lock. For details of the flock structure see the fcntl(S) manual page.

For most fcntl(S) operations including file locking the system call arguments are passed through to the filesystem to which the file belongs as shown in Figure 8.12.

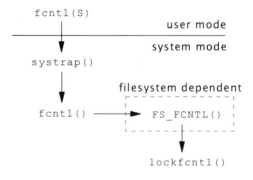

Figure 8.12   Kernel handling of fcntl(S) for file locking

Since file locking mechanisms are generic to most filesystems, the filesystems supported by SCO UNIX call the generic `lockfcntl()` function to establish any required locks and return lock information to the caller.

Each lock established is represented in the kernel by a `filock` structure. The `i_filocks` field of the inode structure is used to point to a linked list of `filock` structures as shown in Figure 8.13. Each `filock` structure represents a separate segment of the file.

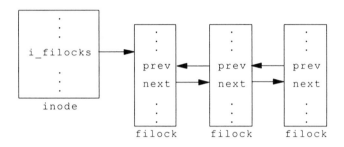

Figure 8.13   `filock` structures linked from the inode used for record locking

Calling `fcntl(S)` with the `F_GETLK` command involves searching the list of `filock` structures, looking for the first `filock` structure which blocks the segment specified by the `flock` structure.

Calling `fcntl(S)` with the `F_SETLK` command for a previously unlocked segment will involve allocation of a new `filock` structure which will be inserted into the correct position within the current list of `filock` structures.

Toolkit 8.6   Displaying file record locks

This example uses `fcntl(S)` to provide a read and write lock on different segments of a file and then uses the `crash(ADM)` `lck` command to display the current list of locks.

In the following program, an `flock` structure is initialised on lines 8 to 11 to set a read lock which is then set by a call to `fcntl(S)` on line 13. The read lock starts at byte 0 and covers 32 bytes.

The `flock` structure is then initialised to set a write lock on lines 16 to 19 which is then set by a call to `fcntl(S)` on line 21. The write lock starts at byte 64 and covers 5 bytes.

```
1 #include <fcntl.h>
2
3 main()
4 {
5     struct flock fl ;
6     int fd = open("my_passwd", O_RDWR);
7
8     fl.l_type    = F_RDLCK ;
```

```
 9     fl.l_start  = 0 ;
10     fl.l_whence = SEEK_SET ;
11     fl.l_len    = 32 ;
12
13     if (fcntl(fd, F_SETLK, &fl) < 0)
14         pexit("fcntl") ;
15
16     fl.l_type   = F_WRLCK ;
17     fl.l_start  = 64 ;
18     fl.l_whence = SEEK_SET ;
19     fl.l_len    = 5 ;
20
21     if (fcntl(fd, F_SETLK, &fl) < 0)
22         pexit("fcntl") ;
23
24     pause() ;
25 }
```

When both locks have been set, the program calls pause(S) so that the process will stop until it receives a signal. This allows the process to be analysed by crash(ADM).

The program can either run in the background or crash(ADM) can be run from another virtual console or window. The lck command is run which displays the following output. Note that all file locks are displayed.

```
> lck
ACTIVE LOCKS:
   INO TYP W       START       LEN PROC  EPID  SYSID      WAIT PREV NEXT
    41  W  0           0         1   18   214      0         0   -    -
   185  R  0           0        31   21   266      0         0   -    -
   185  W  0          64        68   21   266      0         0   -    -

SLEEP LOCKS:
TYP W        START       LEN LPRC   EPID   SYSID BPRC   EPID   SYSID PREV
NEXT

CONFIGURED RECORD LOCKS:
RECS  RECCNT  RECOVF  RECTOT
 128       3       0      34

ACTUAL RECORD LOCKS:
TOTAL  ACTIVE  FREE  SLEEP
  128       3   125      0
```

The locks set by the program are displayed in bold. Note that the LEN field is a little misleading since it actually specifies the byte offset where the lock ends.

8.5.1 Advisory and mandatory locking

The file locks described above are all called *advisory locks*. Each process must check to see if locks exist on the file and, if so, wait until the appropriate locks are released before accessing the file. There is nothing to prevent a process that is not co-operating in the locking protocol from reading from or writing to the file directly, that is, advisory locks do not prevent a process from reading or writing over a locked segment.

Mandatory locking can be set on a file using the chmod(S) system call. By turning off group execute and turning on the set group ID on execution bit, mandatory locking is enabled for the file. All subsequent calls to open(S), read(S) and write(S) will check to ensure that the caller is not violating an existing lock on the file.

8.6 The File System Switch

All of the structures and kernel functions described so far in this chapter are part of the filesystem independent layer of the kernel. All structures and functions present a common set of fields and interfaces regardless of the underlying filesystem type.

As seen in some of the functions presented, there is usually a need to cross the boundary from the filesystem independent to filesystem dependent layer to invoke per filesystem specific routines, for example to translate part of a pathname, fill in part of a stat structure and perform file I/O. At this stage, a call must be made through the File System Switch (FSS) table to pass control to the appropriate filesystem which owns the file being operated on.

There are some fields of the inode structure not covered so far that are used for accessing the underlying filesystem. These fields are shown in Table 8.12 and described in greater detail throughout this section.

Table 8.12   inode fields used for filesystem management

inode field		Description
int	*i_fsptr	Pointer to filesystem dependent data (e.g. disk inode).
short	i_fstyp	Identifies the filesystem type.
struct mount	*i_mntdev	Pointer to the owning mount structure.
i_u		A union of:
struct mount	*i_mton	Pointer to mount structure covering the inode.
struct stdata	*i_sp	Pointer to the STREAM head if accessing a STREAM.
struct region	*i_rp	Pointer to a region structure for shared regions.
struct fstypsw	*i_fstypp	Pointer to FSS table for filesystem specific functions.

The FSS table is an array of fstypsw structures appropriately named fstypsw[]. Each field of the fstypsw structure is a pointer to a filesystem specific function. The fields of the fstypsw structure are shown in Table 8.13. Instead of indexing by hand to access one of the filesystem calls, each function is accessed by macros which take an inode pointer and additional arguments and perform the indirection required.

There are two inode fields which are used to describe the relationship between the inode and the FSS. Each filesystem has a unique identifier which is used to locate its position in the fstypsw[] table. This identifier is held in the i_fstyp field and is used by filesystem dependent layers of the kernel to access the FSS table.

The other inode field used, i_fstypp, is a pointer to an fstypsw structure held within the fstypsw[] table which identifies the set of filesystem operations available for that inode. As an example, to access the itrunc function for a specified inode, the macro FS_ITRUNC is defined as follows:

```
#define FS_ITRUNC(ip)  (*(ip)->i_fstypp->fs_itrunc)(ip)
```

Table 8.13   The `fstypsw` (FSS) functions

function	macro(s)	Description
init	–	Called to initialise the filesystem.
iput	FS_IPUT & IPUT	Decrement the inode reference count and release the inode to free list.
iread	FS_IREAD	Read the inode (associated with `namei`).
iupdat	FS_IUPDAT	Updates the inode with current time.
readi	FS_READI	Read from file identified by inode.
writei	FS_WRITEI & WRITEI	Write to file identified by inode.
itrunc	FS_ITRUNC & ITRUNC	Free all blocks associated with inode.
statf	FS_STATF	Return file statistics to caller.
namei	FS_NAMEI	Called to resolve a pathname lookup.
mount	–	Mount a filesystem.
umount	–	Unmount a filesystem.
getinode	–	Allocate a file for an anonymous pipe.
openi	FS_OPENI & OPENI	Call device open for special files.
closei	FS_CLOSEI & CLOSEI	Call device close for special files.
update	–	Update the superblock on disk.
statfs	–	Return filesystem statistics to caller.
access	FS_ACCESS	Determine accessibility of file.
getdents	FS_GETDENTS	Read directory entries.
allocmap	FS_ALLOCMAP	Build block list map for demand paging.
freemap	FS_FREEMAP	Free the above map.
readmap	FS_READMAP	Read a page (usually from page fault).
setattr	FS_SETATTR	Set a file's specified attributes.
notify	FS_NOTIFY	Inform filesystem of specific events.
fcntl	FS_FCNTL & FREESP	Change various 'states' of the file.
ioctl	FS_IOCTL	Device specific `ioctl`.
security	FS_SECURITY	Interrogate/set security mode for file.
rename	FS_RENAME	Rename the file.
fsync	FS_FSYNC	Flush file in-core buffers to disk.

The macros available for accessing the `fstypsw` functions are defined in the header file `<sys/fstyp.h>` and also shown in Table 8.13.

Figure 8.14 shows two different inodes for which the underlying files are from separate filesystems.

8.6.1 FSS initialisation

The FSS is constructed by the `idtoolset`, a number of utilities used to configure and link the UNIX kernel. Each filesystem type specifies whether it should be linked into the kernel by default through its `mfsys(FP)` file. For example, see the per filesystem `mfsys` files in `/etc/conf/mfsys.d`.

The `mfsys` files specify which filesystem operations are supported and are therefore accessible by the kernel through the FSS. The `idbuild(ADM)` command then constructs the `fstypsw[]` array prior to linking the kernel.

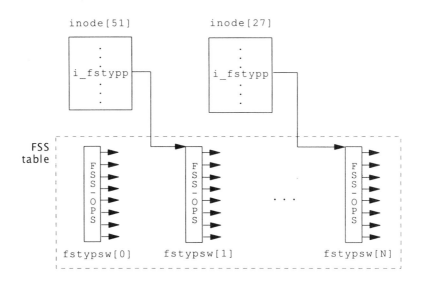

Figure 8.14   Accessing filesystem dependent functions

8.6.2 Filesystem mounting

Since the primary purpose of the FSS is to support multiple filesystems which can be mounted throughout the lifetime of the running system, the kernel must maintain structures which distinguish one filesystem from another. Multiple filesystems are managed by the kernel by placing a reference to each mounted filesystem in the appropriately named mount table. The mount table is an array of mount structures held in the array mount[]. The fields of the mount structure are shown in Table 8.14.

Table 8.14   mount structure fields

mount structure field		Description
ushort_t	m_flags	Status for this mount structure.
short	m_fstyp	The filesystem type.
long	m_bsize	The filesystem's block size.
dev_t	m_dev	The device the filesystem is mounted from.
caddr_t	m_bufp	Pointer to a buffer to hold the superblock.
struct inode	*m_inodp	Pointer to the inode that this filesystem covers.
struct inode	*m_mount	Pointer to the root inode for this filesystem.
char	*m_name	The filesystem name.

Figure 8.15 shows two mount structures used for the root filesystem and the boot filesystem which is mounted on /stand. There are three inodes shown in Figure 8.15:

- The inode of the root directory in the root filesystem is shown on the left-hand side of Figure 8.15. The i_flag field is set to IISROOT to indicate that it is the root inode of a mounted filesystem.

- The inode in the centre of Figure 8.15 is the inode for the /stand directory in the root filesystem. Since it is marked IMOUNT, this indicates that a filesystem is mounted on top. The i_mnton field points to the mount structure of the filesystem which is mounted on top of /stand. This field is used during pathname traversal to avoid accessing files in the /stand directory of the root filesystem and use files in the boot filesystem mounted on top of /stand instead.

- The root inode of the boot filesystem is shown on the right-hand side of Figure 8.15. The i_flag field is set to IISROOT to indicate that it is the root inode of a mounted filesystem.

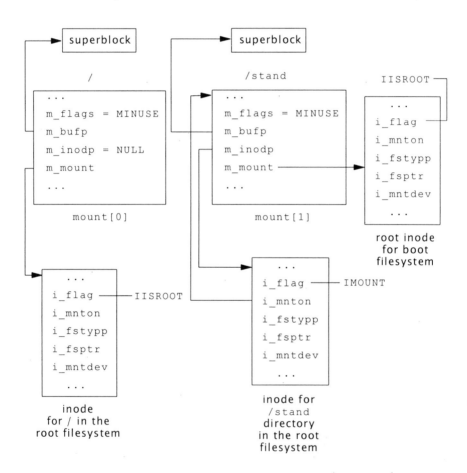

Figure 8.15   The use of the mount structure for the root filesystem and /stand

Toolkit 8.7   Accessing `mount` table structures

The example presented in this toolkit reads the contents of the `mount[]` table and displays various fields of the `mount` structures in use, that is, the current set of mounted filesystems. The type of information displayed can be easily altered to display similar information to the `mount(ADM)` command.

The program starts by calling `nlist(S)` on line 46 to locate the virtual addresses for v and `mount`. The `v_mount` field of the `v` (var) structure holds the size of the `mount[]` table. The contents of `v` and `mount[]` are then read using `/dev/kmem` on lines 54 and 58, respectively.

```
 1 #include <sys/types.h>
 2 #include <sys/dir.h>
 3 #include <sys/var.h>
 4 #include <sys/mount.h>
 5 #include <sys/sysmacros.h>
 6 #include <sys/user.h>
 7 #include <sys/file.h>
 8 #include <sys/inode.h>
 9 #include <sys/fstyp.h>
10 #include <sys/fsid.h>
11 #include <fcntl.h>
12 #include <unistd.h>
13 #include <nlist.h>
14
15 #define MSIZE (sizeof(struct mount) * v.v_mount)
16
17 struct nlist nl[] = { { "v", 0 },
18                       { "mount", 0 },
19                       { 0 } } ;
20
21 read_inode(inode_t *ip, long ia)
22 {
23     int kfd = open("/dev/kmem", O_RDONLY) ;
24     lseek(kfd, ia, SEEK_SET) ;
25     read(kfd, (char *)ip, sizeof(inode_t)) ;
26 }
27
28 pr_inode(struct inode *ip, char *type)
29 {
30     char fsname[16] ;
31
32     printf("  %s> inumber = %3d, ", type, ip->i_number) ;
33     printf("i_fstypp = %x, ", ip->i_fstypp) ;
34     printf("i_fstyp = %d, (", ip->i_fstyp) ;
35     sysfs(GETFSTYP, ip->i_fstyp, fsname) ;
36     printf("%s)\n", fsname) ;
37 }
38
39 main()
40 {
41     struct var     v ;
42     struct mount   *m ;
43     int            i, fd ;
44     struct inode ip ;
45
46     if (nlist("/unix", nl) < 0)
47         pexit("nlist") ;
48
```

```
49      fd = open("/dev/kmem", O_RDONLY) ;
50      if (fd < 0)
51          pexit("kmem") ;
52
53      lseek(fd, nl[0].n_value, SEEK_SET) ;
54      read(fd, (char *)&v, sizeof(struct var)) ;
55
56      m = (struct mount *)malloc(MSIZE) ;
57      lseek(fd, nl[1].n_value, SEEK_SET) ;
58      read(fd, (char *)m, MSIZE) ;
59
60      for (i=0 ; i<v.v_mount ; i++)
61          if (m[i].m_flags & MINUSE) {
62              printf("\nmount[%d] device (%d, %d), ", i,
63                  major(m[i].m_dev), minor(m[i].m_dev)) ;
64              printf("m_mount @ %x\n", m[i].m_mount) ;
65              read_inode(&ip, (long)m[i].m_mount) ;
66              pr_inode(&ip, "m_mount") ;
67              if (m[i].m_inodp == NULL)
68                  printf("  m_inodp> NULL\n") ;
69              else {
70                  read_inode(&ip, (long)m[i].m_inodp) ;
71                  pr_inode(&ip, "m_inodp") ;
72              }
73          }
74  }
```

The loop on lines 60 to 73 walks through the list of mount structures read. If the m_flags field has the MINUSE bit set, the mount structure is in use and contains details about the mounted filesystem.

For the root directory inode of each mounted filesystem, accessed via the m_mount field, the read_inode() function is called on line 65 to read the contents of the inode from /dev/kmem and pr_inode() is called on line 66 to display various inode fields.

If the m_inodp field of the mount structure is not NULL (line 67), this field points to the inode covered by the mounted filesystem. If m_inodp is not NULL, pr_inode() is called on line 71 to display various inode fields.

The output of the program for one particular run is:

```
# a.out

mount[0] device (1, 42), m_mount @ fb8f8fa0
  m_mount> inumber =    2, i_fstypp = f00e0060, i_fstyp = 3, (HTFS)
  m_inodp> NULL

mount[1] device (1, 40), m_mount @ fb8f8730
  m_mount> inumber =    2, i_fstypp = f00e0060, i_fstyp = 3, (HTFS)
  m_inodp> inumber =   14, i_fstypp = f00e0060, i_fstyp = 3, (HTFS)

mount[2] device (2, 60), m_mount @ fb8f82d0
  m_mount> inumber =    2, i_fstypp = f00dffe0, i_fstyp = 2, (DOS)
  m_inodp> inumber =   20, i_fstypp = f00e0060, i_fstyp = 3, (HTFS)
```

In this example, there are three filesystems mounted, two of type HTFS and one DOS filesystem. For each mounted filesystem, the root directory inode (m_mount) and mounted-on inode (m_inodp) are shown. Note that the root inode for each filesystem type has an inode number of 2 which has been common practice in UNIX for many years.

The only filesystem for which m_inodp is NULL is the root filesystem since, in this case, the root filesystem does not cover any other inode.

The output of the mount(ADM) command is shown below together with a series of ls(C) commands so that the fields displayed above can be checked.

```
# mount
/ on /dev/root read/write on Mon Jun 12 09:29:30 1995
/stand on /dev/boot read only on Mon Jun 12 09:29:32 1995
/mnt on /dev/fd0 read/write/trunc on Mon Jun 12 09:39:06 1995
# ls -l /dev/root
br--r-----   1 root      backup     1, 42 Apr 25 21:23 /dev/root
# ls -l /dev/boot
br--r-----   1 root      backup     1, 40 Apr 25 21:22 /dev/boot
# ls -l /dev/fd0
brw-rw-rw-   2 bin       bin        2, 64 Apr 23 09:03 /dev/fd0
```

Similar information to the output displayed by the program can be accessed using the mount command within crash(ADM) as follows:

```
> mount
MOUNT TABLE SIZE = 8
SLOT FS  BSZ MAJ/MIN BUFPTR BCOUNT IPTR MPTR RFLAG RD FLAGS NAME
   0  3 1024   1,42 0xc0139000 0    -     50  ---- rw inuse notrunc HTFS
   1  3 1024   1,40 0xc0140000 0   19     23  ---- ro inuse notrunc EAFS
   2  2  512   2,60 0xf012ea70 0    8    181  ---- rw inuse
```

The mount command displays each mount structure which is marked MINUSE. Note the differences between the results obtained by hand above and the output displayed by crash(ADM). For the boot filesystem mounted on /stand, crash has reported a filesystem of type EAFS. For the boot filesystem, the on-disk layout is identical to the old EAFS format used in versions of SCO UNIX prior to SCO OpenServer Release 5 although the filesystem is managed by the HTFS filesystem driver.

This is confirmed by the FS field which is equal to 3.

8.7 File based system calls

This section describes how the kernel handles the basic file-related system calls for regular files. It first concentrates on the open, read/write and close paths and then describes how files which are mapped into the address space of the process using the mmap(S) system call are accessed.

Chapter 9 describes how character and block devices are accessed and chapter 10 describes how STREAMS devices are accessed. The interface between the filesystem and the buffer cache is described in section 9.2.6.

8.7.1 Opening a file

The steps taken by the kernel in response to the open(S) system call are shown in Figure 8.16. The copen() routine shown is used by the open(S) and creat(S) system calls.

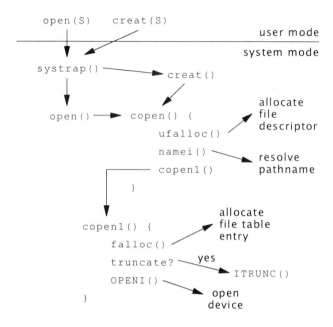

Figure 8.16   Paths followed by the kernel when opening a file

The main tasks performed by copen() and copen1() are as follows:

- The ufalloc() function is called to locate a file descriptor by looking through the u_ofile[] array in the u_area for the first empty slot.

- namei() is then called to resolve the pathname given by the user. If successful, an inode pointer is returned.

- copen1() is then called which performs the following tasks:

  ⇨ falloc() is called to locate a free slot in the file[] table. The file descriptor and inode pointer are passed as arguments. The entry in the u_ofile[] array is set to point to the allocated file structure and the f_inode field of the file structure is set to point to the inode returned by the call to namei().

  ⇨ If the oflag argument passed to open(S) has the O_TRUNC bit set, ITRUNC() is called to truncate (free all blocks) of the file.

  ⇨ The OPENI() macro is called for which the filesystem will invoke a device open routine if the file references a device.

When opening a device, the devfs filesystem is used in place of the filesystem where the device special file resides. For details of devfs refer to chapter 9.

8.7.2 Reading and writing from and to a file

The steps performed by the kernel in the filesystem independent layer of the kernel are similar for both read(S) and write(S). This involves validating arguments, setting up the fields in the u_area which specify the I/O properties and then calling the filesystem to perform the read/write. Figure 8.17 shows the main steps performed for both system calls. The tasks performed by the rdwr() function are shown below:

- The file table entry is located by indexing into the u_ofile[] array using the file descriptor passed to read(S) or write(S). The inode[] table can then be accessed from the f_inode field of the file structure.

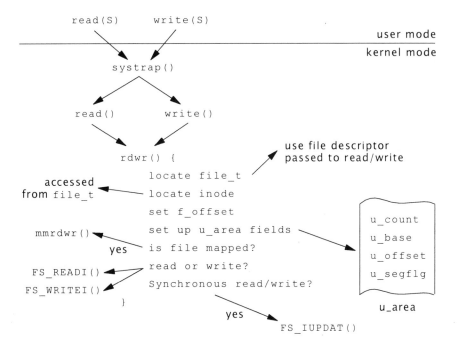

Figure 8.17 Flow control through the kernel for read(S) and write(S) system calls

- If the O_APPEND flag is set on open(S) and the write(S) system call is invoked, the f_offset field is set to the size of the file given in the i_size field of the inode. This ensures that writes will always be appended to the file.

- The following fields of the u_area are set up to specify the transfer properties. These fields will be read and updated by the filesystem:

  u_offset   This specifies the offset within the file from where the read or write will start.

u_base   This specifies the user's data address where the data to be written resides or where the data to be read should be copied to. This address is specified to read(S) and write(S).

u_count   The transfer size in bytes passed to read(S) and write(S).

u_segflg   This specifies whether the transfer will be between user mode and kernel mode or entirely within the kernel address space. This allows an optimal form of copy if both addresses are within the kernel.

- If the i_mappages field of the inode is not zero, the file has been mapped with a call to mmap(S). In this case the mmrdwr() function will be called to satisfy the read or write. Memory mapped files are described in section 8.7.4.

- If a read(S) system call is being invoked, the FS_READI() macro is called to allow the underlying filesystem to read the data. For the write(S) system call, FS_WRITEI() is called.

- Since fields of the inode will be updated, change the appropriate access or modification time-stamp. If the file is opened O_SYNC, FS_IUPDAT() will be called to write the file meta-data back to disk.

- Finally, the f_offset field of the file structure is updated by the number of bytes read or written which is also returned to the calling process.

Chapter 9 describes the type of actions that the filesystem takes when reading and writing data through the buffer cache. The mmrdwr() function called for files which have been mapped is described in section 8.7.4.

Chapter 10 shows the different steps followed by the read(S) and write(S) system calls when accessing a STREAMS device.

8.7.3 Closing a file

The close(S) system call is handled by the close() and closef() kernel functions as shown in Figure 8.18. The closef() function is also used by kernel subsystems that open and close files internally within the kernel.

The main tasks performed by the kernel when closing a file are as follows:

- The getf() function is called to locate the file table entry that is referenced by the file descriptor passed to close(S).

- The u_ofile[] entry that the file descriptor refers to is set to NULL, allowing the file descriptor to be re-used on a subsequent call to ufalloc().

- The closef() function, which is also used by kernel subsystems that open and close files, is then called which performs the following tasks:

    - CLOSEI() is called to allow the close to be propagated to the device if the file to be closed is a device.

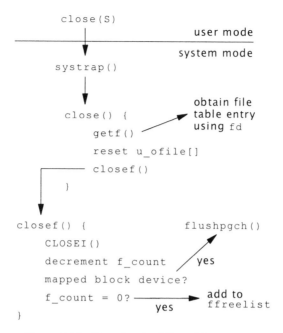

Figure 8.18   Kernel paths followed for closing a file

- The f_count field of the file structure is decremented. If it reaches zero, it will be added to the free list headed by ffreelist and the number of free file structures (filecnt) is incremented.

- If the file is a block device which has been mapped (mmap(S)) and this is the last reference to the device, the flushpgch() function is called to write out any pages that are cached in the page cache.

For details of device access see chapter 9.

8.7.4 Memory mapped files

Section 2.5.4 described the mmap(S) system call that allows a process to map part of a file into its address space. Reading from and writing to the file can then be achieved by accessing the region of memory in which the mapping is established.

The mmap(S) prototype is shown once again:

```
#include <sys/types.h>
#include <sys/mman.h>

caddr_t mmap(caddr_t addr, size_t len, int prot, int flags,
                                        int fd, off_t off) ;
```

The addr argument specifies the address at which the mapping, of len bytes, will start. If set to zero, the kernel will choose the address at which the mapping will start. The prot argument, which can be PROT_READ, PROT_WRITE, PROT_EXEC or PROT_NONE, specifies whether the mapped pages have read, write, execute access or, in the case of PROT_NONE, have no access rights.

The flags argument specifies additional attributes of the mapping. If set to MAP_SHARED, changes to pages of the mapping will change the file being mapped. If the flags argument is set to MAP_PRIVATE then any changes to the mapping are visible only to the process which established the mapping. If MAP_FIXED is specified, the addr argument must be used as the address at which the mapping should start.

The fd argument specifies the open file descriptor and the off argument specifies the offset within the file at which the mapping should start. The value specified in off must be aligned to a page (4K) boundary.

As an example of how mmap(S) is called, Figure 8.19 shows the effect of issuing an mmap(S) system call to establish a read only mapping of 8 kbytes of a file to a system chosen address starting at byte offset 4096 within the file.

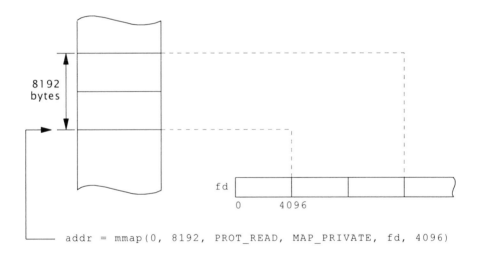

Figure 8.19   Establishing a read only mapping

To allocate the mapping the kernel establishes a new region within the process's address space. Since the address space of processes may differ depending on the size of process text and data, libraries used and any shared memory segments, the addr argument should be set to zero to allow the kernel to choose the most appropriate address. This also makes the code more portable between different UNIX platforms where address space layouts may differ substantially.

The processing of arguments, establishing which devices can be accessed and the other main tasks performed by mmap() are as follows:

- The getf() function, using the file descriptor passed to mmap(S), is called to locate the file table entry and therefore the inode of the file to be mapped.

- The arguments passed to mmap(S) are then validated. This includes checking that the address specified falls within the boundaries of the user address space, that the access of the mapping specified by the prot argument corresponds to the mode in which the file was opened and so on.

- Once all arguments have been validated, the mmapfile() function, which is also used by other kernel subsystems, is called to create the appropriate region. The tasks performed by mmapfile() are:

    ⇨ If the MAP_FIXED flag is passed to mmap(S), existing mappings covering the area of memory addr to (addr+len) must be removed.

    ⇨ If MAP_FIXED is not set, chkpgrowth() is called to ensure that by creating the mapping, the size of the process does not exceed the process's memory limits.

    ⇨ The mmfindhole() function is called to locate a slot in the address range of the process where the region can be created. mmfindhole() walks through the list of pregion structures and returns the address at which the region can be created.

    ⇨ The allocreg() and attachreg() functions are called to allocate a region and attach the region to the process's address space.

    ⇨ If the PROT_EXEC flag is set, the FS_ALLOCMAP() filesystem function is called to allocate a block list map used for demand paging.

Once the mapping is established there are two routes by which data from the file can be read by this process and others. Data can be read through the read(S) and write(S) system calls or by accessing the memory region created by the call to mmap(S).

When the region is created there are no physical pages associated with the region. As the process touches a page within the mapping, the page fault handler will allocate a page and read the data from disk. When a page fault is satisfied, the page of memory is associated with the region created for the mapping. The page is said to be in the page cache. It is used by the process or by a candidate for paging if memory becomes scarce. The details of paging are described in chapter 12.

The block list map is a list of the file's on-disk block numbers. When a page fault occurs by accessing a page within the mapping, the page fault handling code issues an FS_READMAP() call to locate and read the required blocks to satisfy the page fault. By use of the block list map, the speed of demand paging can be increased by avoiding the need to perform multiple reads from disk to locate the required blocks.

Section 8.7.2 showed that the rdwr() function checks the i_mappages field of the inode to see if the file is mapped and has pages held in the page cache. If the value of i_mappages is zero, the FS_READI() or FS_WRITEI() macros are called to request the filesystem to read or write the data through the buffer cache.

If the value of i_mappages is not zero, the mmrdwr() function is called to try and locate the data through the page cache before going through the filesystem to read or write the data from or to disk. For example, consider the situation in Figure 8.20 where a file is mapped in the address space of one program and an attempt is made to access the file using the read(S) system call from another process.

When the rdwr() function is entered it checks whether there are any pages associated with the file in the page cache. In the example here the first two pages of the file have been mapped into the address space of process B.

The mmrdwr() function can then be called to read the data from the page cache which removes the need to call the FS_READI() routine of the filesystem.

If pages in the page cache do not cover the range of bytes of the file required by read(S), mmrdwr() will call FS_READI() to read the data through the filesystem.

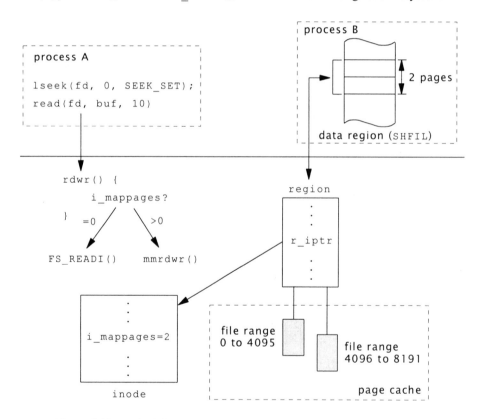

Figure 8.20   Paths followed through the kernel when reading a file that is mapped

8.7.5 Additional mapped file operations

There are a number of other system calls that are available for managing mapped files. The munmap(S) system call allows an area of memory that was previously established during a call to mmap(S) to be unmapped. The area requested can be a subset of the original mapping.

The mprotect(S) system call allows the caller to alter the access protection of a mapping previously set by a call to mmap(S) or another mprotect(S) system call. For example, an area of the mapping can be changed from PROT_READ to PROT_WRITE.

The msync(S) system call allows a specified range of pages within an existing mapping to be flushed to the file from which the mapping was created.

The device file /dev/zero can be used for creating a region within the process's address space which will be zero filled when read. Mappings from this device can also provide a means to share memory between a parent and child. For details of mapping /dev/zero refer to chapter 11.

Toolkit 8.8   Analysing mapped files

This toolkit example describes how to use crash(ADM) to analyse the various process and file related structures used to implement and manage memory mapped files. The analysis is performed using the following program.

```
 1 #include <sys/types.h>
 2 #include <sys/mman.h>
 3 #include <sys/stat.h>
 4 #include <fcntl.h>
 5 #include <signal.h>
 6
 7 void
 8 sighdlr(int sig)
 9 {
10     /* no action, just return */
11 }
12
13 main(int argc, char *argv[])
14 {
15     int         fd ;
16     caddr_t     maddr ;
17     struct stat st ;
18
19     sigset(SIGUSR1, sighdlr) ;
20
21     fd = open(argv[1], O_RDWR) ;
22     fstat(fd, &st) ;
23     maddr = mmap(0, (size_t)st.st_size, PROT_READ|PROT_WRITE,
24                                     MAP_SHARED, fd, 0) ;
25     pause() ;
26
27     *maddr = 0x58 ;              /* character=X */
28     *(maddr + 4096) = 0x58 ;
29     *(maddr + 8192) = 0x58 ;
30
31     pause() ;
32 }
```

The program maps the file passed as an argument into its address space at a kernel generated address and then pauses on line 25. This allows the state of the process to be analysed before any of the pages associated with the mapping are modified.

The program assumes that the file is greater than 8 kbytes and will therefore require at least three pages to be created in the user's address space. The file to be mapped is as follows:

```
-rw-------   1 spate    group      11429 Mar  4 15:35 my_passwd
```

The process then writes to the first byte of each of the first three pages of the file. It then calls pause(S) for a second time so that the process state can be analysed once more.

The process can be run in the foreground or background and crash(ADM) entered to locate the process using the proc command as follows:

```
> proc ! grep mmap
  64 s  6553  5111  6553 13583  66   0 u           mmap          load
```

As highlighted above, the process is found in slot 64 of the proc[] table and has a process ID of 6553. The user command can be invoked to display the process's open files as follows:

```
> user 64
PER PROCESS USER AREA FOR PROCESS 64
...
OPEN FILES AND POFILE FLAGS:
      [ 0]: F#239   r   [ 1]: F#239    w  [ 2]: F#239    w
      [ 3]: F#186
...
```

The first three file descriptors reference the process's standard input, output and error. The fourth entry refers to the file which has been opened and mapped. Using the file command followed by the inode command, the fields of the inode structure can be displayed in order to find the i_mappages field:

```
> file 186
FILE TABLE SIZE = 341
SLOT  RCNT   I/FL       OFFSET  FLAGS
 186     2 I# 975            0 read write
> inode -f 975
...
      FORW   BACK AFOR ABCK   MAPPAGES          RDLOCKS          WANT
      1108 {  80}  -    -         0                0
...
```

Although the file has been mapped, no access has yet been made to the file which is reflected in the zero count in the i_mappages field identified by the MAPPAGES column. This can be confirmed by locating the region created within the process's address space to map the file.

The pregion command is first used to display the pregion structure associated with the process. The process ID is passed as an argument to pregion.

```
> pregion #6553
SLOT PREG REG#      REGVA   TYPE FLAGS
  64   0  403           0   text rd ex cm
       1  439    0x400000   data rd wr cm
       2  454 0x7fffe000   stack rd wr cm
       3  517 0x80001000   shfil rd wr wa
```

Regions which are used for mapped files have the p_type field of the pregion structure set to shfil as highlighted above.

The region command can be used to display the contents of the region in more detail. As shown, the region occupies three pages for which there are currently no physical pages associated:

```
> region -f 517
REGION TABLE SIZE = 768
Region-list:
SLOT PGSZ VALID  SMEM NONE SOFF  REF SWP NSW FORW BACK INOX TYPE FLAGS
 517    3     0     0    0    1    1   0   0  454  446  975 map  nosh...
Page-tables:
LIST fa00c200  3859 013fd000 pres rw us                        none      -
SLOT    OFFSET PFDAT PHYSADDR ---------- FLAGS ---------- TYPE      BLKNO
   1 00000000    -        -   nval rw                     file         0
   2 00001000    -        -   nval rw                     file         8
   3 00002000    -        -   nval rw                     file        16
```

By sending a SIGUSR1 signal to the process, all three pages will be modified before the second call to pause(S). This involves reading the data from the file and then allowing the write to take place.

Since no physical pages are currently allocated for the region, each reference to the page will result in a page fault allowing the kernel to allocate a page, read in the data and retry the write instruction.

The kill(C) command is issued to post the signal:

```
> !kill -USR1 6553    # See proc command above for the process ID
```

Running the inode command again shows that the number of pages associated with the inode in the page cache is now equal to 3. This allows the close() paths followed by the kernel to determine that the page cache must be flushed before all links to the file can be relinquished.

```
> inode -f 975
...
     FORW   BACK AFOR ABCK   MAPPAGES        RDLOCKS      WANT
     1108 {  80}  -    -         3              0
...
```

Running the region command again shows the region now associated with three physical pages. For details of page related structures see chapter 12.

```
> region -f 517
REGION TABLE SIZE = 768
Region-list:
```

```
SLOT PGSZ VALID SMEM NONE SOFF  REF SWP NSW FORW BACK INOX TYPE FLAGS
 517    3     3    0    0    1    1   0   0  454  446  975 map  nosh...
Page-tables:
LIST fa00c200  3859 013fd000 pres rw us                       none      -
SLOT   OFFSET PFDAT PHYSADDR ---------- FLAGS ---------- TYPE    BLKNO
   1 00000000   144 001d0000 pres rw us ref                file      0
   2 00001000  2861 01017000 pres rw us ref                file      8
   3 00002000  1543 00747000 pres rw us ref                file     16
```

Located at address 0xc0000000 in the kernel address space is a range of virtual addresses used to map physical memory such that accessing 0xc0000000 accesses physical address 0, 0xc0000001 accesses physical address 1 and so on.

Using the od command and converting the physical address of the first page displayed (0x001d0000), the contents of the physical page can be displayed using the corresponding virtual address at location 0xc01d0000 as follows:

```
> od -c c01d0000 20
c01d0000:   X   o   o   t   :   x   :   0   :   3   :   S   u   p   e   r
c01d0010:   u   s   e   r
```

This shows the first page of the my_passwd file with the X character written to the first byte of the page.

8.8 An overview of fsdb (ADM)

Filesystems can be analysed and modified using the fsdb(ADM) command. If a filesystem is corrupt, fsdb(ADM) can be used to repair the filesystem in conjunction with the fsck(ADM) command.

This section provides a brief overview of the facilities offered by fsdb. Be warned, though, it is possible to damage a filesystem irreversibly through incorrect use! When experimenting with the features of fsdb, use a filesystem mounted on a floppy disk before using it on one of the main filesystems. Nevertheless, once familiarity is obtained with the terse syntax used by fsdb, walking through the filesystem can be fun.

To demonstrate using fsdb, a filesystem is created on a floppy disk, two directories are created and /etc/passwd is copied to the filesystem as follows:

```
# mkfs -f HTFS /dev/rfd0135ds18
bytes per logical block = 1024
total logical blocks = 1440
total inodes = 360
gap (physical blocks) = 1
cylinder size (physical blocks) = 400
setting cluster to default size (16)
mkfs: Available blocks = 1388
# mount /dev/fd0135ds18 /mnt
# mkdir /mnt/dira
# mkdir /mnt/dira/dirb
# cp /etc/passwd /mnt
# umount /mnt
```

The filesystem should be un-mounted before fsdb is run.

When `fsdb` is entered the `i` command is used to display the root inode; recall that an inode number of 2 is traditionally used for the root inode. Note that `fsdb` does not display a prompt:

```
# fsdb /dev/fd0
/dev/fd0(): HTFS File System
FSIZE = 1440, ISIZE = 360
2i
i#:   2  md: d---rwxrwxrwx  ln:    3  uid:    0  gid:    0  sz:      512
a0: 51  a1:    0  a2:    0  a3:    0  a4:    0  a5:    0  a6:    0
a7:  0  a8:    0  a9:    0  a10:   0  a11:   0  a12:   0
at: Sun Jun 25 23:50:09 1995
mt: Sun Jun 25 23:28:32 1995
ct: Sun Jun 25 23:28:32 1995
2i.a0b.p80d
d    0:        2  v0   12     1 .
d   12:        2  v0   12     2 ..
d   24:        3  v0   20     9 .ilog0000
d   44:        4  v0   16     4 dira
d   60:        6  v0  452     6 passwd
```

Most of the fields displayed for the root inode will be familiar. Fields marked `a0` to `a9` are the first 10 blocks of the file, `a10` to `a12` are indirect block addresses. Only the first block of the root directory (`a0`) is in use and it contains the disk block number accessed.

The second command entered selects inode 2, converts the block number specified in the `a0` field (`b`) to a filesystem block address and displays the first 80 bytes of the block in directory format.

In the following example the name of the `passwd` file is changed to `new_name`. This is achieved by specifying inode 2, the block specified by `a0` and the directory entry at an offset of 60 bytes from the start of the block.

```
2i.a0b.d60.nm="new_name"
d   60:        6  v0  452     8 new_name
6i
i#:   6  md: f---rw-rw-r--  ln:    1  uid:    0  gid:    3  sz:     1104
a0: 64  a1:   65  a2:    0  a3:    0  a4:    0  a5:    0  a6:    0
a7:  0  a8:    0  a9:    0  a10:   0  a11:   0  a12:   0
at: Sun Jun 25 23:28:32 1995
mt: Sun Jun 25 23:28:32 1995
ct: Sun Jun 25 23:28:32 1995
6i.a0b.p40c

200000: root:O0y360iTk8e
200020: Ow,..jI:0:3:Supe
200040: ruser:/:
```

The second command displays the first 20 bytes of the file (`new_name`) specified by the first block (`a0`) of inode 6.

The access modes of the file can be changed using the `md` command as follows:

```
6i.md=000700
005200: 000700 (448)
6i
i#:   6  md: ----rwx------  ln:    1  uid:    0  gid:    3  sz:     1104
```

```
a0: 64  a1:    65  a2:     0  a3:     0  a4:     0  a5:     0  a6:     0
a7:  0  a8:     0  a9:     0  a10:    0  a11:    0  a12:    0
at: Sun Jun 25 23:28:32 1995
mt: Sun Jun 25 23:28:32 1995
ct: Sun Jun 25 23:28:32 1995
```

As a final example, the link count of `new_name` is set to 0:

```
6i.ln=0
005202: 000000 (0)
6i
i#:   6  md: ----rwx------  ln:    0  uid:    0  gid:    3  sz:    1104
a0: 64  a1:    65  a2:     0  a3:     0  a4:     0  a5:     0  a6:     0
a7:  0  a8:     0  a9:     0  a10:    0  a11:    0  a12:    0
at: Sun Jun 25 23:28:32 1995
mt: Sun Jun 25 23:28:32 1995
ct: Sun Jun 25 23:28:32 1995
```

This example demonstrates how to lose a file easily! As shown below, although a directory entry still exists, the file cannot be accessed since it does not have a valid link count:

```
# mount /dev/fd0 /mnt
# ls /mnt
dira
new_name
# cat /mnt/new_name
cat: cannot open /mnt/new_name: No such file or directory (error 2)
```

Although the examples presented here have been brief, they demonstrate the power of `fsdb` for repairing filesystems. Further details of the commands and options available to `fsdb` can be found in the `fsdb`(ADM) manual page.

The `fsdb`(ADM) command should be used in conjunction with the header files associated with the filesystem found in `/usr/include/sys/fs`. The superblock and inode structures differ greatly between one filesystem and another.

8.9 Summary and suggested reading

This chapter has described the file subsystem within the kernel. The first part of the chapter concentrated on the structures and functions used to represent files in memory. The File System Switch (FSS) used to support multiple different filesystems in the kernel simultaneously was then described, showing how the filesystem independent layers of the kernel communicate with the individual filesystems.

The chapter then described the main paths through the kernel for open, read/write and close routines followed by a description of how memory mapped files are supported.

It concluded with a brief description of the `fsdb`(ADM) filesystem debugger used for analysing and repairing filesystems.

Chapter 9 describes the I/O paths taken when accessing physical devices and includes a description of the buffer cache which is used by all filesystems in SCO UNIX. This includes a description of how `read(S)` and `write(S)` access devices directly without going through the filesystem.

Chapter 10 describes the I/O paths followed by the kernel when accessing STREAMS devices. This includes the mechanisms used for issuing standard `read(S)` and `write(S)` system calls to STREAMS devices.

9

I/O management

This chapter describes the I/O management subsystem, the part of the kernel that handles the buffering of data between the user and hardware, the transfer of data between the kernel and devices in response to user requests and the services available to device drivers.

The chapter first describes the buffer cache, an important kernel subsystem which is used to buffer data between filesystems and device drivers, to reduce disk I/O and therefore to improve performance for many applications.

Character and block device drivers are then described with practical examples of drivers commonly in use. Hardware specific features are covered including Direct Memory Access (DMA) and interrupt management.

The final part of the chapter covers the TTY subsystem and is based on the user's interaction with the system. This shows the flow of control between the user, keyboard, monitor and kernel together with the procedures and structures used for managing virtual consoles.

9.1 Introduction

The I/O subsystem contains all of the kernel components that deal with the management of hardware, buffering techniques used to reduce access times when performing I/O and pseudo devices which access no physical hardware but are implemented as device drivers and provide services to users and kernel alike.

The buffer cache is first described. This kernel subsystem is used to read and write blocks of data between memory and hardware devices such as disk drives. The buffer cache provides a significant performance increase by cacheing data and therefore reducing the number of I/O operations that are needed.

The chapter then describes the role that device drivers play in UNIX, covering their location in the kernel, the kernel services to which they have access and the procedures required for adding new device drivers to the kernel.

The PC hardware architecture relating to device management is briefly described, showing how interrupts are generated by the hardware and handled by the kernel.

The chapter describes both character and block device drivers, providing examples of each type. The TTY subsystem is explained showing the interaction between the console driver, the TTY line discipline, the use of buffering and the flow of control through the kernel.

9.1.1 The I/O toolkit

There are a number of toolkit examples presented in this chapter. For device driver examples, wherever possible the toolkits provide working examples of device drivers that are in everyday use.

The toolkits provided in the chapter are shown below:

Toolkit 9.1 Locating per file buffers, page 369
Toolkit 9.2 Which drivers are present?, page 377
Toolkit 9.3 Adding a device driver to the kernel, page 383
Toolkit 9.4 Accessing kernel virtual memory, page 393
Toolkit 9.5 A simple pipe driver using clists, page 398
Toolkit 9.6 Analysing flow control through /dev/tty01, page 416
Toolkit 9.7 mscript – an implementation of script(TC), page 422
Toolkit 9.8 An example block device driver, page 433

9.2 The system buffer cache

All data that is read from a filesystem is first copied into the system buffer cache before being copied into the user or kernel address space. Similarly, all data that is written to a filesystem is written through the buffer cache.

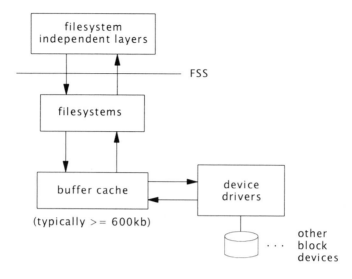

Figure 9.1   Position of the buffer cache in the kernel

The buffer cache is a collection of variable sized buffers used to hold or cache data copied from disk or about to be written to disk. The buffers cache data, producing an increase in performance when a process accesses data that has previously been read into the cache. On a typical system, up to 85% of disk I/O can be avoided.

When a process issues a read request from a filesystem, the buffer cache is first searched to see if the data is available. If the data is found, it is copied to the user supplied address. If the data is not available, an I/O request is made and the process will sleep until its completion. Since many I/O patterns tend to be sequential, filesystems will generally perform read-ahead so that subsequent reads are likely to achieve a cache hit.

For normal write operations, the data is not written directly to disk but written from the user address space into the buffer cache, at which point the write returns. This increases performance from the user's perspective. The actual physical write to disk will take place at a later date based on a number of factors which are described throughout this section. By specifying the O_SYNC flag to the open(S) system call the data will be written to the file synchronously.

By delaying such a write it is possible to lose recently written data in the event of a power failure. This allows the application writer to make a trade-off between maximum performance and maximum data integrity.

Figure 9.1 shows the position of the buffer cache in relation to other kernel components. The buffer cache is primarily used by filesystems. However, some of the interfaces exported by the buffer cache can also be used by device drivers directly.

To demonstrate the effect of cacheing data consider the following example. This program opens a file, reads all of the file's data in 512 byte chunks and then exits.

```
 1 #include <fcntl.h>
 2
 3 char buffer[512]
 4 main()
 5 {
 6     int fd
 7
 8     fd = open("bigfile", O_RDONLY)
 9     if (fd < 0)
10         pexit("bigfile")
11
12     while (read(fd, buffer, 512) > 0)
13         ;
14 }
```

The file to be read is just over 330 kbytes, as shown below by running ls(C). The program is run three times. On the second and third runs, the time taken is half the time taken for the first invocation. When the program is first run, the data must be copied from disk into the buffer cache and then copied into the user supplied buffer. When the program is run again, some or all of the data is still held in the buffer cache and therefore significantly less disk I/O will be required.

```
$ ls -l bigfile
-rw-r--r--  1 spate    group       335616 Jun 14 19:48 bigfile
$ time bread

real 0m0.93s
user 0m0.03s
sys 0m0.85s
$ time bread

real 0m0.52s
user 0m0.01s
sys 0m0.51s
$ time bread

real 0m0.51s
user 0m0.02s
sys 0m0.49s
```

The buffer cache can be increased or decreased in size based on kernel tuneables. It cannot, however, vary in size dynamically, thus if there is contention for buffers, the cache will be less effective. To increase or decrease the size of the buffer cache the kernel needs to be re-linked and a reboot must be performed.

9.2.1 Buffer cache structures

The buffer cache consists of a number of buffer headers and for each buffer header there is an associated data buffer as shown in Figure 9.2. The data buffers hold the data that has been read from the device or the data which is to be written to the device. The buffer headers describe the state of the buffer, for example the data in the buffer is valid or I/O is pending and the buffer is therefore busy. They also hold additional information such as the process which initiated the I/O, the number of bytes read or written and so on.

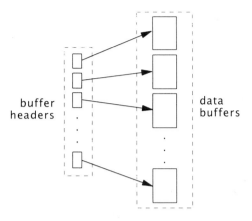

Figure 9.2   Each data buffer is referenced from and described by a buffer header

Each buffer header is described by a `buf` structure which is found in the `<sys/buf.h>` header file. The main fields of the `buf` structure are shown in Table 9.1.

Table 9.1   Fields of the `buf` structure

buf structure field		Description
`int`	`b_flags`	A mask of bits which describe the state of the buffer. The values that `b_flags` can take are shown below.
`struct buf` `struct buf`	`*b_forw` `*b_back`	When a buffer is in use it is linked onto one of a number of hash queues using these two fields.
`struct buf` `struct buf`	`*av_forw` `*av_back`	These two fields link buffers together when they are on the free list.
`dev_t`	`b_dev`	The `b_dev` field holds the major and minor numbers of the device from which data will be read or written.
`short`	`b_want`	This field is used internally within the buffer cache subsystem to indicate that the buffer, which is currently busy, is wanted by another process.
`unsigned`	`b_bcount`	This field specifies the transfer count, the number of bytes to be read from or written to the device.
`caddr_t`	`b_un.b_addr`	The `b_addr` field specifies the address where the buffer data is located.
`daddr_t`	`b_blkno`	This field specifies the block number on the device.
`char`	`b_error`	If I/O is unsuccessful, device drivers set the `b_error` field to indicate the reason for failure.
`unsigned int`	`b_resid`	If all bytes requested in `b_bcount` cannot be transferred, the number of bytes not transferred is stored here by the device driver.
`daddr_t`	`b_sector`	This field is the physical offset into the drive of the start of the I/O transfer.
`struct proc`	`*b_proc`	The process which has requested the I/O transfer.
`long`	`b_inum`	The inode number with which the buffer data is associated.
`unsigned long`	`b_bufsize`	The size of the underlying data buffer which ranges from 1024 bytes to 4 kbytes in multiples of 1 kbyte.

The `b_flags` contains a bit-wise OR of flags which are used to describe the state of the buffer at any moment in time. The most commonly used flags are:

B_WRITE	This indicates that a transaction pending on this buffer does not correspond to a read operation. B_WRITE traditionally has the value zero so a check is made to see if B_READ is set; if not then B_WRITE can be assumed.
B_READ	Data will be read into the buffer during an I/O operation.
B_DONE	This is set when an I/O operation has completed.
B_ERROR	If there is a failure during an I/O operation, this flag is set.
B_BUSY	This indicates that the buffer is currently in use.
B_PHYS	This marks a multi-physical buffer header.
B_DELWRI	A delayed write has been initiated. The actual write will not take place until the buffer is required at a later date.
B_AGE	This is set when issuing a delayed write for correct ageing.
B_ASYNC	This indicates a delayed write, therefore the process should not wait for I/O completion.
B_AIO	An asynchronous I/O request is pending.
B_STALE	The data in the buffer is no longer valid.
B_INODE	The buffer contains inode meta-data.
B_FAIO	The buffer is being used for fast asynchronous I/O.

The `crash(ADM)` command `bufhdr` displays the contents of an individual buffer header or a summary of all buffer headers. The first five buffer headers, which are held in consecutive memory locations, are shown here in summary format:

```
> bufhdr ! head -8
BUFFER HEADER TABLE SIZE = 3084
 SLOT MAJ/MIN  BLOCK     ADDRESS    FOR   BCK    AVF    AVB FLAGS
    0   1,40   13658 0xc009f000   2445    -    2295    392 read  done
    1   1,42   21116 0xc009f400   3053    -    2713   3082 read  done
    2   1,42    5926 0xc009f800    -    356    3021    811 write done 0x1000
    3   1,42  346650 0xc009fc00   1399    -    2254    448 read  done
    4   1,42  154782 0xc009e000    -      -    2662   2233 read  done
    5   1,42    4488 0xc009e400   2245    -    2688   2838 write done 0x1000
```

The MAJ/MIN column corresponds to the `b_dev` field and the ADDRESS column corresponds to the `b_un.b_addr` field.

Each buffer header can also be displayed in full format as the following example shows for the buffer header in slot 5:

```
> bufhdr -f 5
BUFFER HEADER TABLE SIZE = 3084
 SLOT MAJ/MIN BLOCK    ADDRESS    FOR   BCK    AVF    AVB FLAGS
    5   1,42   4488 0xc009e400   2245    -    2688   2838 write done 0x1000
```

```
BCNT ERR RESI     START PROC  RELTIME       INUM WANT
1024  0      0 0x4ee5be     -  0x4ef42f         -
BSIZ    IODONE   BWRITE DWFOR DWBCK FFORW FBACK  FSDATA
1024       -         -      -     -     -     -       -
```

The contents of the actual buffers can be displayed using the buffer command. Toolkit 9.1 provides an example of its usage.

Since there are potentially many buffers, searching for a buffer which contains the correct device and block number could be a time consuming task which could reduce the performance benefits of the buffer cache.

To help alleviate this problem, buffers are linked on hash queues held in the hbuf[] array. Each buffer is hashed using its b_dev and b_blkno fields using the following algorithm:

```
#define bhash(d, b)
    ((buf_t *)((int *)&hbuf[((int )d+(int )(b>>1))&v.v_hmask]-1))
```

The number of hash queues is dependent on the NHBUF kernel tuneable. Increasing the value of NHBUF decreases the length of each queue and therefore the time to search for a specified buffer. If NHBUF is set to zero, the system will automatically configure the number of hash queues to be the nearest power of two that is greater than or equal to half the value of NBUF, the number of buffers.

Figure 9.3 shows the arrangement of the hash queues. Each element of the hbuf[] array is a structure of type hbuf which contains two elements, b_forw and b_back, which are used to link those buffers which are on the particular hash queue.

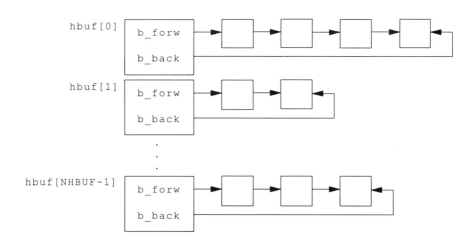

Figure 9.3   Buffers queued on hash buckets

9.2.2 Multi-physical buffers

Part of the buffer cache is used to provide multi-physical buffers. This area of memory, typically between 160 kbytes and 256 kbytes, is used for three different types of I/O:

- 16 kbyte *scatter/gather buffers* are used to transfer contiguous blocks of data between the buffer cache and disk. This operation is usually performed only if the underlying hardware does not support scatter/gather capabilities.

- *Transfers buffers* of 4 kbytes are used for moving data between memory and devices where the user's data may reside in memory above 16 Mbytes. These buffers are necessary only when performing DMA with a peripheral controller that can address up to only 16 Mbytes of memory.

- As with the previous point, transfers of 1 kbyte are performed using *copy buffers* whereby buffer cache data to be transferred resides above 16 Mbytes and peripheral controllers can address only 16 Mbytes of memory.

The NMPBUF kernel tuneable controls the number of 4 kbyte pages which are used for scatter/gather, transfer and copy/request buffers. The kernel will automatically select appropriate values if the values of NMPBUF is set to zero.

9.2.3 Buffer cache initialisation

The buffer cache is initialised early on during kernel initialisation by invocation of the binit() function when the kernel is executing mlsetup(). The binit() function must initialise the buffer headers, hash queues and multi-physical buffer headers as well as allocate data buffers which are associated with the buffer headers.

The tasks performed by binit() are as follows:

- Allocate headers and buffer space for the multi-physical buffers. The list of buffers is headed by the mpheadbuf variable. The number of multi-physical buffers is obtained from the NMPBUF kernel tuneable. If NMPBUF is zero the kernel chooses an appropriate value. The data space allocated is located within the first 16 Mbytes of physical memory.

- If the value of the NBUF kernel tuneable, which specifies the number of buffer headers, is zero, the kernel must choose an appropriate value.

- The imemget() kernel function is called to allocate space for the buffer headers. The amount of space allocated is calculated as NBUF multiplied by sizeof(struct buf). The buf kernel variable is set to point to the start of the space allocated.

- Space is allocated for the hash queues headed by the NHBUF kernel variable. The amount of space allocated is NHBUF multiplied by the sizeof(struct hbuf).

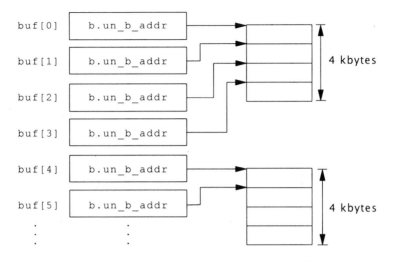

Figure 9.4   Arrangement of buffers and buffer headers

- The percentage of buffers which will reside in DMA'able memory is then calculated and assigned to the kernel variable `allocdma`.

- The delayed write free list headed by `dwfreelist` and the free list headed by `bfreelist` are initialised.

- `binit()` then loops through each buffer header starting at `buf` and performs the following tasks:

  ⇨ For each fourth buffer, if `allocdma` is greater than zero, `imemget()` is called to allocate a DMA'able 4 kbyte buffer, otherwise `imemget()` is called to allocate a 4 kbyte buffer above 16 Mbytes. The `allocdma` variable is then decremented.

  ⇨ The `b_un.b_addr` field is set to point within the 4 kb buffer associated with each group of four buffer headers. This is shown in Figure 9.4.

  ⇨ The `brelse()` function is called to add the buffer to the free list headed by the `bfreelist` kernel variable.

- The hash queue heads are initialised.

- The list of multi-physical buffers is initialised.

Once the `binit()` function has completed, the buffer cache routines described later in section 9.2.4 for allocating and using buffers can be used.

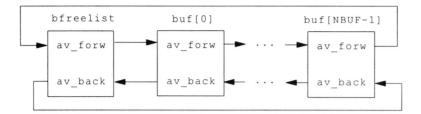

Figure 9.5   Arrangement of buffers on the free list following `binit()`

For each buffer header, `binit()` calls `brelse()` which, among other things, adds the buffer to the free list. The free list is headed by `bfreelist` as shown in Figure 9.5.

When buffers are currently in use or have valid data but have not yet been freed, they will be removed from the free list and placed on one of the hash queues.

The hash queues are initialised such that each head will point to itself. The next section shows how buffers are linked onto the hash queues.

9.2.4 Buffer retrieval and allocation routines

There are numerous routines provided by the buffer cache subsystem for allocating buffers, reading and writing data, freeing buffers and so on.

Listed below are some of the common operations for retrieving a buffer:

```
buf_t *getblk(dev_t dev, daddr_t blkno, long bsize) ;
buf_t *ngetblk(dev_t dev, daddr_t blkno, long bsize) ;
buf_t *getablk(int flag) ;
buf_t *geteblk() ;
buf_t *geteblk_any() ;
buf_t *ngetblkw(dev_t dev, daddr_t blkno, long bufsize,
                              bio_wait_spec_t wait_spec) ;
buf_t *ngeteblk(long bufsize) ;
buf_t *ngeteblk_any(long bufsize) ;
```

Some functions are provided for compatibility reasons with earlier releases of UNIX and many of the functions use common buffer cache internal routines.

Most of the functions are used only by internal kernel subsystems including filesystems. The only two functions which should be accessed by device drivers are the `getablk(K)` and `geteblk(K)` functions.

The return value for all of these functions is a pointer to a `struct buf` (`buf_t`). The buffer returned may match the device and block number specified and contain valid data, it may contain invalid (stale) data or simply be a freely available buffer.

The `getblk()` function is as old as the buffer cache itself! It is included for compatibility reasons since many of the older filesystems still use it. The `dev` argument specifies the device on which the block resides. The major number is used to select the appropriate device driver. The blkno argument specifies the logical block number on this device and the bsize argument specifies the size of the buffer required.

The only processing performed by getblk() is to convert the logical block number into a physical block number used by the device driver and call ngetblk(). The translation is performed using the LTOPBLK() macro which is defined in <sys/buf.h> as follows:

```
#define LTOPBLK(blkno, bsize) ((blkno) * (((bsize)>>SCTRSHFT)))
```

The blkno argument is the logical block number used by the filesystem and the bsize argument is the block size of the filesystem. The value of SCTRSHFT is equal to 9. Toolkit 9.1 demonstrates how the translation is performed to locate per file blocks within the buffer cache.

The ngetblk() function has the same interface as getblk() with the exception of taking a physical versus logical block number. It will always wait until a buffer is available before returning. This will involve sleeping if the buffer requested is busy, that is, I/O is pending, or no buffers are currently available. Very little processing is performed by ngetblk() other than to call the internal function getblkh() specifying that the hash queues should be searched and that it is acceptable to sleep if required.

The ngetblkw() function differs from ngetblk() by calling getblkh() specifying that, should the process be required to sleep on an event, the sleep should not occur and getblkh() should return. This is used by kernel subsystems which must not sleep and are prepared for the fact that no buffer may be returned.

Figure 9.6 summarises the relationship between getblk(), ngetblk(), ngetblkw() and the internal buffer cache routine getblkh(). The state of the buffer once it is returned is described later when getblkh() is discussed. Note that these are the only three interfaces where the device and block number are specified.

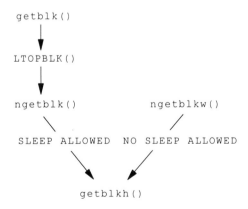

Figure 9.6   Buffer retrieval when specifying a device and block number

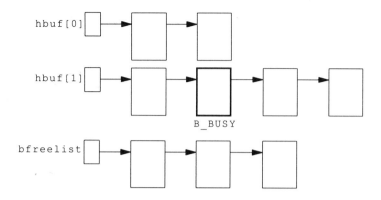

Figure 9.7   The requested buffer is on the hash queue but busy

getblkh() is the internal function used for obtaining a buffer. The first task performed by getblkh() is to call bhash() to locate the hash queue on which the buffer may reside. If a buffer has been used previously for the same device and block number, it will always be held on one of the hash queues. If the buffer is not marked B_BUSY, it will also be held on the free list.

Either way, if the buffer exists, getblkh() can locate the buffer through its hash queue. Figure 9.7 shows the case where the buffer is located on the hash queue. It is marked B_BUSY so is not part of the free list.

In Figure 9.8, the buffer is not marked B_BUSY so it is linked onto the hash queue and the free list. Either way, getblkh() can locate the buffer by calling bhash() and searching the resulting hash queue.

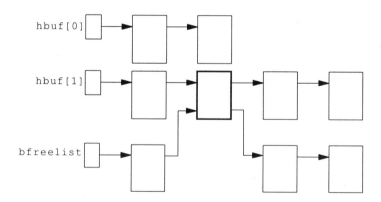

Figure 9.8   The requested buffer is not busy so it can also be found on the free list

Buffers are linked on the hash queues using the b_forw and b_back fields of the buf structure, while buffers which are on the free list are linked using the av_forw and av_back fields.

Once getblkh() locates the hash queue, it walks through the list using the b_forw field and tests each buffer to see if the b_dev and b_blkno fields match the requested device and block number. If the buffer is found, a check is made to see if the buffer is busy. If the b_flags field is set to B_BUSY, the following tasks are performed:

- The b_want field is set to B_WANTED to indicate that the buffer is wanted.
- The kernel calls sleep() with the address of the buffer header.

When the buffer becomes available, for example an I/O transaction has completed, or if B_BUSY was not set, getblkh() calls the internal notavail() function which:

- Marks the buffer as busy by setting B_BUSY in the b_flags field.
- Sets the b_proc field of the buf structure to curproc, which points to the current process's proc structure.
- Unlinks the buffer from the free list if necessary.

Once notavail() has been called, getblkh() returns the address of the buffer header. It is the responsibility of the caller to check the b_flags field to determine the status of the buffer, for example whether it contains valid data.

If the buffer is not found on the hash queue, a buffer must be taken from the free list. In this case, the following tasks are performed:

- If the free list headed by bfreelist is empty, call sleep() with the address of bfreelist. When a buffer becomes available, the process will be woken up.
- Take the first buffer off the free list and call notavail().
- If the buffer is a delayed write buffer (b_flags is set to B_DELWRI), b_flags is set to B_ASYNC and B_AGE. A write request using bwritem_bio() is then invoked. The process then continues to check the free list.
- The buffer is unlinked from the hash queue it was previously on and b_forw and b_back are set to point to the buffer header itself.
- The buffer is marked B_BUSY.
- The buffer is linked onto the hash queue which was determined when getblkh() was first called.
- The b_dev and b_blkno fields are set to the arguments passed to getblkh().
- The address of the buffer is returned.

The getablk(K) and geteblk(K) functions, which are available to device driver writers, both call ngetblk(SBUFSIZE) where SBUFSIZE is equal to 1024. The flag argument passed to getablk() is historical and no longer used.

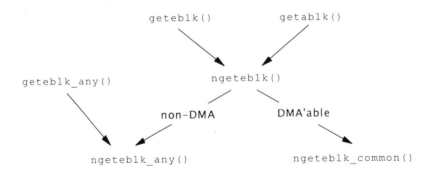

Figure 9.9   Routines for allocating buffers

On return from both functions, the b_flags field of the buffer header is OR'ed with B_BUSY and B_AGE, the b_back and b_forw fields are set to point to the buffer header itself, b_dev is set to NODEV and b_bcount is set to SBUFSIZE.

Since neither geteblk() nor getablk() specify a device or block number, the kernel must choose a suitable buffer header. The buffer chosen may lie above the range of buffers which can be used for DMA. The geteblk_any() function is available for use by filesystems which then call ngeteblk_any(SBUFSIZE).

The ngeteblk() function checks to see if any non DMA'able buffers are available. If so, ngeteblk_any() is called, otherwise ngeteblk_common() is called.

The relationship between the different functions is shown in Figure 9.9.

The functionality of ngeteblk_any() is similar to the functionality of getblkh() when the buffer to be obtained is from the free list and not on one of the hash queues. This includes potential processing of delayed write buffers. Before returning the address of the buffer, the b_dev field is set to NODEV.

The functionality performed by ngeteblk_common() allows for both DMA'able and non-DMA'able buffers and requires more complex processing for space allocation.

9.2.5 Performing I/O through the buffer cache

There are a number of functions available for reading and writing buffers. The functions available for reading buffers are as follows:

```
buf_t *bread(dev_t dev, daddr_t lblkno, long bsize) ;
buf_t *breada(dev_t dev, daddr_t lblkno, daddr_t rablkno, long bsize) ;
buf_t *breadn(dev_t dev, daddr_t lblkno, long bsize) ;
buf_t *nbreadw(dev_t dev, daddr_t lblkno, long bsize,
                                  bio_wait_spec_t wait_spec) ;
```

The bread() function is available for compatibility with older versions of UNIX. Similar to getblk(), the only processing to be performed is to convert the logical block number to a physical block number using LTOPBLK() and to call the nbreadw()

function. It is allowable for bread() to sleep awaiting completion of an I/O transaction. This is specified when nbreadw() is called.

The tasks performed by nbreadw() are:

- Call getblkh() to see if the buffer already exists in the cache.

- If the buffer returned is in the cache and is marked B_DONE, a check is made to see if any errors occurred during the last I/O operation.

- If the buffer is not in the cache then for the buffer returned:

    ⇨ Set the b_flags field to B_READ.

    ⇨ Call issue_strat() to call the device driver specified by the b_dev field of the buffer header. If the buffer retrieved lies above DMA'able space and the underlying hardware can support physical addresses only below 16 Mbytes memory, copyprep() is called prior to issue_strat() to ensure that copy buffers are used to perform the I/O. This involves using a buffer which resides within the first 16 Mbytes of memory to perform the I/O and copying the data to the buffer supplied by getblkh().

    ⇨ Call iowait() with the address of the buffer to wait for completion of the I/O transaction.

- Return a pointer to the buffer.

The iowait() function, which is covered in greater detail in section 9.2.8, will call sleep() with the address of the buffer and will be woken when the I/O transaction completes.

The breada() function was introduced to increase performance by reading the specified block and starting an asynchronous read of the next adjacent block. Thus, if a process is reading through the file sequentially, which is a common operation, either the next block to read will be available when requested or the I/O to read it will have already been scheduled, reducing work in the buffer cache subsystem. The tasks performed by breada() are:

- Call LTOPBLK() to convert the specified logical block number into a physical block number.

- Call incoreh() to see if the block is already in the cache. If the block is not found, breada() will call breadh() specifying that the I/O should be initiated but the buffer will be waited on at a later date.

- For the read-ahead block, LTOPBLK() is called to convert the logical block number to a physical block number. The incoreh() function is called to see if the buffer is in the cache and, if not found, breadh() is called to initiate an asynchronous read.

- `breadh()` is then called again. This time the initial buffer is awaited.
- The address of the buffer read is returned.

The `breadh()` function is only used internally within the buffer cache subsystem and provides various methods of accessing buffers including synchronous and asynchronous reads as described. Internally, it uses `getblkh()` to retrieve either the specified buffer or a buffer from the free list.

The `breadn()` function reads in the requested block and may also initiate read-ahead or multi-block reads. This uses the following four fields from the u_area in addition to the arguments passed:

`u_rablock`	This specifies the next block to read in the same manner as the `breada()` function.
`u_ahead`	This field specifies the block number where the current cluster finishes.
`u_nxtstart`	This field specifies the starting block number of the next cluster.
`u_nxtend`	This field specifies the block number where the next cluster finishes.

Filesystem blocks are allocated to files in clusters in order to try to minimise fragmentation. By grouping blocks together, the filesystem and buffer cache can work together to read multiple blocks with minimal disk head movement.

There are two scenarios under which clustered reads will be performed:

- If the requested block is part of a cluster and the block is not found in the cache, a multi-block read is initiated.
- If the block is found in the cache and is part of a cluster, `breadn()` will initiate a multi-block read of the next cluster.

The functions provided by the buffer cache subsystem for writing buffers are shown below. This list shows functions which are used by other kernel subsystems and functions which are used internally within the buffer cache subsystem:

```
void bwrite(struct buf *bp) ;
int  bwritem(struct buf *bp) ;
void bawrite(struct buf *bp) ;
void bdwrite(struct buf *bp) ;
void bdwrite_store(struct buf *bp, long i_number) ;
void bwrite_bio(struct buf *bp, int caller_type) ;
int  bwritem_bio(struct buf *bp, int caller_type) ;
```

The `bwrite()` function is accessible outside of the buffer cache subsystem. Its only task is to call `bwrite_bio()` which is also used internally within the buffer cache. `bwrite()`

specifies, using the `caller_type` argument, that the write has come from outside the buffer cache.

Unless the `B_ASYNC` flag is set in the `b_flags` field, the buffer will be written synchronously so that when the call has completed, the data has been committed to disk.

The `bdwrite()` function, which relies on `bdwrite_store()`, can be called to issue a delayed write. To delay the write simply involves freeing the buffer. When another function, such as `getblkh()`, requires a buffer and finds the delayed write buffer, it writes the contents to the device.

To issue an asynchronous write, the `bawrite()` function is called. This sets the `b_flags` field to `B_ASYNC` and calls `bdwrite_store()`.

The processing of `bwrite()`, `bawrite()` and `bdwrite()` is performed by the `bdwrite_store()` internal function which handles both asynchronous and delayed writes by performing the following tasks:

- If the buffer is not already on the delayed write list headed by the `dwfreelist` variable, the buffer is added to this list. The `b_start` field of the buffer header is set to the current value of `lbolt`. This is used by the `bdflush` kernel process to determine when the buffer needs to be written.

- If the device indicates that delayed writes should be avoided, the buffer is marked `B_ASYNC` in order to perform an asynchronous write.

- If an asynchronous write needs to be performed, `bwrite_bio()` is invoked with the address of the buffer.

- If a delayed write needs to be performed, the buffer is marked `B_DELWRI` and `B_DONE`. The `brelse()` function is then called to add the buffer to the free list.

The `bwritem()` function writes the specified block asynchronously and looks for any adjacent blocks that may be written concurrently. It calls the internal function `bwritem_bio()` to perform the work.

`bwritem_bio()` writes the requested block and adjacent blocks asynchronously and returns the number of buffers that it has started to write. If no suitable adjacent blocks are found, `bwrite_bio()` is called to write the specified buffer.

If there are multiple blocks to be written, `bwritem_bio()` calls `getmbuf()` to obtain a multi-physical buffer, initialises it with the buffers to be written and calls the `issue_strat()` function to call the driver using its capabilities for scatter/gather.

As shown in Figure 9.10, all of the write functions so far mentioned make use of the `bwrite_bio()` function.

The tasks performed by `bwrite_bio()` are:

- Call `issue_strat()` to enter the device driver's `xxstrategy()` routine and start the I/O. If the buffer resides outside of the 16 Mbyte DMA'able space and the underlying hardware cannot support DMA above 16 Mbytes, `copyprep()` is called which will copy the data into a temporary DMA'able buffer which is used in the call to `issue_strat()`.

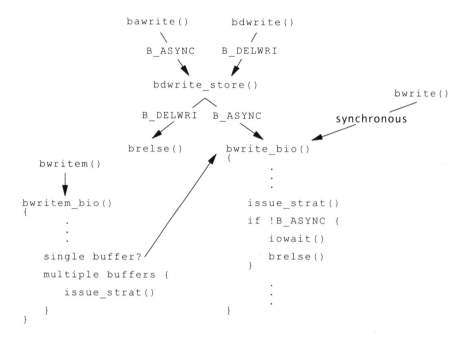

Figure 9.10   Flow control through the buffer cache for writes

- If the write is not asynchronous, the `iowait()` function is called to wait for completion of the I/O.

- Finally, `brelse()` is called to add the buffer to the free list.

9.2.6 Filesystem I/O

The following pseudo code provides a simplified example of how a filesystem will read a block through the buffer cache. The I/O paths through the filesystem are described in more detail in chapter 8.

```
xxreadi(inode *ip)
{
    ...

    if the file is a regular file {
        blkno = xxbmap(ip)
        bp = breadn(u.u_pdev, blkno, u.u_bsize)
        biomove(bp, bp->b_un.b_addr, nbytes, user_address)
    }

    ...

}
```

The filesystem's `xxreadi()` routine is called with the address of the inode for which data should be read. The `xxbmap()` routine is called to calculate the logical block number to be read. This uses the file offset which is located in the `u.u_offset` field of the u_area. The `breadn()` function is then called to read the block. Either the block may already be in the cache or the driver's `xxstrategy()` routine must be called to read the block from disk.

The `biomove()` function is then called which copies the data from the buffer to the address requested by the user.

9.2.7 Flushing buffer cache data

Since not all writes through the buffer cache are synchronous, there are times when the filesystem and other kernel subsystems need to flush data that was written either asynchronously or as a delayed write. There are a number of functions available for flushing buffers, most of which use `bflush_common()` which is also used by the `bdflush` kernel process:

```
bflush(dev_t dev) ;
bflush_wait(dev_t dev) ;
bfsync(dev_t dev, long inumber) ;
bfsync_nowait(dev_t dev, long inumber) ;
blkflush(dev_t dev, daddr_t lblkno) ;
nblkflush(dev_t dev, daddr_t blkno) ;
bflush_common(dev_t dev, long i_number, time_t age, int waitflg) ;
```

The `bflush()` function is called from `update()`, the kernel function called to handle the `sync(S)` system call. When calling `bflush_common()`, `bflush()` specifies that it will not sleep until all buffers have been written. Once the I/O transactions have been initiated `bflush()` returns.

The `bflush_wait()` function, unlike `bflush()`, will wait until all buffer data associated with the specified device has been committed to the device. The `bflush_wait()` function is called by filesystems when un-mounting a filesystem.

The `bfsync()` and `bfsync_nowait()` functions are used to write out all buffers which are associated with the specified inode number. This allows finer control over flushing by allowing the flush to be performed on a per file basis. This is used by the `msync(S)`, `memcntl(S)` and `fsync(S)` system calls. The `bfsync()` function sleeps until all buffers have been written while the `bfsync_nowait()` initiates the I/O and then returns.

The `bflush_common()` function is responsible for flushing all buffers associated with the specified device with the option of selecting buffers associated with a particular inode. This involves searching through the delayed write list headed by `dwfreelist` and constructing a list of all buffers to be written. The `bwritem_bio()` function is called for each buffer in the list. If the `waitflg` flag is set, `bflush_common()` will call `sleep()` for each buffer written.

The `blkflush()` and `nblkflush()` functions are called to write synchronously a specific buffer. The `lblkno` argument passed to `blkflush()` is a logical block number and must be converted to a physical block number using the LTOPBLK() macro described in section 9.2.4. After the conversion, blkflush() calls nblkflush().

The tasks performed by nblkflush() are:

- Call incoreh() to see if the buffer is in the cache. If found and the buffer is marked B_BUSY, the process sets the b_flags field to B_WANTED and calls sleep() with the address of the buffer header.

- If the buffer is not in the cache, it must be a delayed write (it is on the free list). In this case the notavail() function is called to take the buffer off the free list, the buffer is marked B_ASYNC, and bwritem_bio() is called to write the buffer to the device.

9.2.8 Completing I/O on a buffer

When an I/O transaction is scheduled by invoking issue_strat() to call the device driver's xxstrategy() routine, the parent calls iowait() with the address of the buffer. The iowait() function will then call sleep() with the same address to await completion of the I/O transaction.

When the device driver completes the I/O operation, it calls iodone() which issues a wakeup() call on the specified buffer address. The flow of control through the write paths including scheduling and completion of the I/O are shown in Figure 9.11 following a call to nbreadw().

When the process which issued iowait() is awoken, it checks to see if the b_flags field is set to B_ERROR which indicates that an error occurred. The u_error field of the u_area is then set up so that the error code can be returned to the user.

```
nbreadw()
{
    . . .
        issue_strat(dev,bp)
        iowait(bp)  ◄──────────────── iowait()
        return(bp)                    {
}                                         sleep(bp, ...) ◄──┐
                                          check for B_ERROR  │
                                      }                      │
                                                             │
       ──► xxstrategy(bp, ...)                               │
           {                                    wakeup(bp)   │
                schedule I/O     xxintr()                    │
           }                     {                           │
                                      iodone(bp) ────────────┘
                                 }
```

Figure 9.11   Issuing the I/O transfer and waiting for completion

Toolkit 9.1   Locating per file buffers

One operation which would be useful in `crash(ADM)` would be to locate buffers which are in the buffer cache and correspond to a particular file. The following example shows how this can be performed using standard `crash(ADM)` commands.

The effectiveness of this example depends on the load of the system and the size of the buffer cache. Buffers in the cache for a particular file are transient, so although I/O for a particular file block has been performed, by the time it is scanned for within `crash(ADM)` it may have been re-used and overwritten.

The first task is to make sure that an I/O operation has been performed on a file. Using the `more(C)` command, the file will be opened and blocks read:

```
# more /etc/passwd
```

Using another window or virtual console, the `crash(ADM)` command is entered and the open file can be searched for as follows:

```
# crash
dumpfile = /dev/mem, namelist = /unix, outfile = stdout
> !ls -i /etc/passwd
22345 /etc/passwd
> inode ! grep 22345
 143   1,42   3 22345   5   1   2   21     1104 f---664   0    -
```

The `ls(C)` command is used to display the inode number of the `/etc/passwd` file. By invoking the `inode` command, a search is made for the entry in the inode table which has an inode number of `22345`. An entry is found in slot number `143` as highlighted.

The `inode` command is then re-issued requesting full information in order to extract the file's logical block numbers which will be used to locate any valid buffers:

```
> inode -f 143
INODE TABLE SIZE = 204
SLOT MAJ/MIN FS INUMB RCNT LINK    UID    GID  SIZE     MODE MNT M/ST FLAGS
 143   1,42  3 22345    5    1      2     21  1104 f---664   0    -
       FORW   BACK AFOR ABCK    MAPPAGES           RDLOCKS            WANT
     {  73}    193   -    -             0                 0
       RMAJ/MIN     FSTYPP       FSPTR    FILOCKS      VCODE WCNT FS
        0,0     0xf00e0060 0xfc1f7898         0           0    0 HTFS
HTFS INODE:
     FLAGS: used
       LASTREAD     MAP/DOFF         DADDRS
          0x0            0        [ 0] 160252      [ 1] 160262
```

The on-disk inode is an HTFS inode for which the block numbers corresponding to the file are highlighted. The last block read into the buffer cache was block number `0x0` of the file. The block numbers displayed are logical block numbers and therefore the `LTOPBLK()` macro must be used to convert them into physical block numbers to locate any valid buffers via the `b_blkno` field of the `buf` structure. Recall that the macro is defined as follows:

```
#define LTOPBLK(blkno, bsize) ((blkno) * (((bsize)>>SCTRSHFT)))
```

Since HTFS requests I/O for read operations in 1024 byte quantities, the physical block number corresponding to the first file block is:

```
160252 * (1024 >> 9)
```

which is equal to `320504`. The `bufhdr` command can then be used within `crash` to scan for a buffer which may hold this block as follows:

```
> bufhdr ! grep 320504
  251   1,42       320504 0xc0060c00   568   300   376   183 read  done
```

A buffer for this block is found in slot number `251`. The other fields of the `buf` structure are described in section 9.2.1.

Finally, the contents of the buffer can be displayed using the `buffer` command. The `-c` option is used to display the buffer in ASCII format:

```
> buffer -c 251 ! head -8
BUFFER 251:

00000:    r  o  o  t  :  O  0  y  3  6  0  i  T  k  8  e
00010:    O  w  ,  .  .  j  I  :  0  :  3  :  S  u  p  e
00020:    r  u  s  e  r  :  /  :\n  d  a  e  m  o  n  :
00030:    *  ,  .  .  :  1  :  1  :  S  y  s  t  e  m
00040:    d  a  e  m  o  n  s  :  /  e  t  c  :\n  b  i
00050:    n  :  *  ,  .  .  :  2  :  2  :  O  w  n  e  r
```

9.2.9 Flushing delayed writes

When a user process issues the `write(S)` system call and if the file is not opened with the `O_SYNC` flag, the data is not usually written immediately to disk but written asynchronously by the filesystem. This involves calling buffer cache routines to schedule the write for completion at a later date. This asynchronous write is also known as a delayed write.

When an asynchronous write is issued, the buffer is marked dirty. The data must first be written to disk before the buffer can be re-used. Once the buffer has aged in memory for a set time interval, it will be flushed to disk by the `bdflush` kernel process.

The kernel tuneable `BDFLUSHR` specifies the interval in seconds between invocations of `bdflush`. The default value of `BDFLUSHR` is 30 seconds.

An additional kernel tuneable, `NAUTOUP`, specifies how long the buffer must be dirty for before it can be written to disk for which the default is 10 seconds.

The `bdflush` kernel process is started during kernel initialisation from within `main()` as described in section 4.3.2. The `bdflush` process loops indefinitely calling `bflush_common()` followed by a call to `sleep()` with the address of the `bdflush()` function.

During processing of a clock interrupt, when `clock()` performs one second processing it decrements the `bdflushcnt` variable which is initialised to the value of `BDFLUSHR`. If this value reaches zero, it is reset to `BDFLUSHR` and `bdflush()` is called.

9.3 Device drivers

Device drivers represent a large and very significant part of the kernel. They interact with a number of different kernel components including the buffer cache, the paging and swapping subsystems, the TTY subsystem and, most importantly, the hardware.

It is a difficult task to do justice to the complex world of device drivers in a short amount of space. Kettle and Statler (1992) provide an excellent and in-depth view of device drivers written for SCO UNIX, providing many practical examples. While this chapter does not cover the subject in the same depth as Kettle and Statler, it attempts to cover device drivers in sufficient detail so that programmers can start writing drivers, build a new kernel incorporating their driver and understand where to look for kernel interfaces and other information.

Within this section, STREAMS based drivers are not discussed to aid clarity. The STREAMS subsystem is described in chapter 10.

9.3.1 Device driver fundamentals

Device drivers provide an interface between the kernel and the physical hardware, hiding the underlying low level details such as device registers, interrupts and DMA (Direct Memory Access), and also a uniform interface to the kernel which is easy to access.

The UNIX kernel contains a large number of device drivers. Some drivers access physical hardware such as disks, tapes and CD-ROMs, while others provide hardware independent services, such as the `/dev/kmem` and `/dev/null` drivers.

During initialisation, the kernel will call any registered device driver initialisation routines. Many drivers that control hardware print a message during initialisation to specify details about the device found, any configuration parameters and the capabilities of the hardware. An example output displayed during initialisation is:

```
device     address         vector dma comment
----------------------------------------------------------------------
%fpu       -               13     -   type=80387
%serial    0x03F8-0x03FF   4      -   unit=0 type=Standard nports=1
%floppy    0x03F2-0x03F7   6      2   unit=0 type=135ds18
%console   -               -      -   unit=vga type=0 12 screens=68k
%adapter   0x0330-0x0332   11     5   type=ad rev=E0 ha=0 id=7 fts=s
%pci       0xC000-0xCFFF   -      -   am=2 sc=0 buses=1
%eisarom   -               -      -   eisa (1.3.0)
%smc/wdn   0x0220-0x023F   9      -   type=8013EPC addr=00:00:c0:08:ad:a3
%tape      -               -      -   type=S ha=0 id=2 lun=0 bus=0 ht=ad
%disk      -               -      -   type=S ha=0 id=0 lun=0 bus=0 ht=ad
%Sdsk      -               -      -   cyls=1042 hds=64 secs=32 fts=sb
mem: total = 32384k, kernel = 6832k, user = 25552k
swapdev = 1/41, swplo = 0, nswap = 98000, swapmem = 49000k
Autoboot from rootdev = 1/42, pipedev = 1/42, dumpdev = 1/41
kernel: Hz = 100, i/o bufs = 3084k
```

This information can be obtained by running `tail(C)` on `/usr/adm/messages` or by using the `hwconfig(ADM)` command.

The `device` field specifies the name of the device driver. The `address` field specifies the start and end addresses in I/O space used by the driver solely for this device. The `vector` field is the interrupt vector number, the `dma` field is the DMA channel number and the `comment` field provides additional information specific to the device. All of these fields are described in more detail later.

For device-specific information, consider the host bus adapter highlighted. The `comment` field indicates, by specifying `fts=s`, that 32 bit DMA addresses are supported which removes the need for copy buffers. See the SCO OpenServer *Performance Guide* (1995) for further information.

9.3.2 Device driver types

Hardware devices differ greatly in terms of the capabilities they offer and also the manner in which they are accessed and controlled. This requires different behaviour in the device driver which controls it. As such, device drivers fall into three different categories:

Character drivers   This type of driver exists for devices where the method of access is character by character. Such devices include modems, communication lines, terminals and printers.

   When the kernel needs to access character devices, the buffer cache is not used although, if required, buffering can be performed using *clists* which will be described in detail later. Other buffering techniques may also be used by character device drivers.

Block drivers   Some devices allow access only in multiple byte sized units. For example, hard disks and floppy disks are addressable only in sector size units where the size of the sector is usually 512 bytes. For block devices, the buffer cache is used as the interface between the user or filesystem and the device.

   A filesystem will allow access in sizes which are smaller or larger than the block size of the device. For both reads and writes of non-block sized units, this may involve reading blocks from disk, updating the part of the block that is written by the user and then writing the whole block back.

Raw I/O support   Although block device drivers are limited to transferring blocks of a fixed size, it is useful to be able to address the device in units smaller or larger than the device block size.

   Such transfers are performed independently of the filesystem or buffer cache and allow the kernel, and thus the user process, to transfer data directly to or from the underlying device without copying the data to a kernel buffer first. Such a transfer is typically called *raw I/O*. It has often been called *direct I/O* but the latter term is now commonly used to describe a transfer which still passes through the filesystem but avoids the additional copy.

Support for raw I/O is provided by an extension to the interface offered by block device drivers and supported by kernel routines. The raw I/O interface is described in section 9.11.

Figure 9.12 shows the position of device drivers in the kernel in relation to other kernel subsystems. The flow of control has been simplified in order to demonstrate some major differences that exist when accessing device drivers.

Each device is represented by a unique number called the device major number.

The buffer cache acts as a buffer between the filesystem and the block devices which are accessed through the bdevsw[] array, whereby the major number of the device represents the position in this array. An example of this is shown later. The buffer cache can be bypassed by using the raw I/O interface if offered by a block device driver.

Character device drivers are accessed through the cdevsw[] array. As with block devices, the major number represents the position of the device driver in the table. There also exists a buffering technique which may or may not be used by character drivers underpinned by clists which are described later.

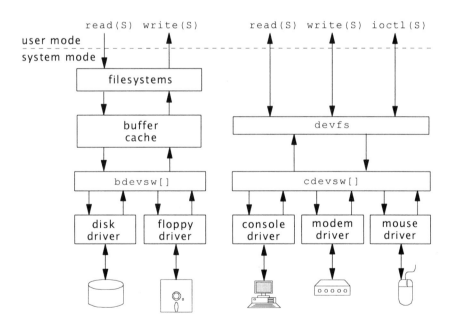

Figure 9.12   The position of device drivers in the UNIX kernel

Block and character drivers differ not just in their location in one of the two switch tables but also in the interfaces they present to the rest of the kernel. Table 9.2 shows the different driver functions (entry points) which are accessed through the cdevsw[] and bdevsw[] tables.

Table 9.2   Device driver entry points

Driver entry point	Character drivers	Block drivers	Block drivers with raw interface
XXinit()	✓	✓	✓
XXopen()	✓	✓	✓
XXclose()	✓	✓	✓
XXread()	✓	-	✓
XXwrite()	✓	-	✓
XXioctl()	✓	-	✓
XXintr()	✓	✓	✓
XXpoll()	✓	-	✓
XXhalt()	✓	✓	✓
XXstrategy()	-	✓	✓
XXprint()	-	✓	✓

The XX characters at the start of each function name indicate a unique driver prefix. Since there are many device drivers in the kernel at any one time, there needs to be a way of distinguishing one driver open routine from another to avoid linkage problems. How the prefix is specified is shown later.

The driver entry point called is dependent on a number of factors. For example, when the user invokes the read(S), write(S) or ioctl(S) system calls on a character device, the driver's xxread(), xxwrite() and xxioctl() entry points will be called. When a process issues a read or write on a regular file, the filesystem invokes routines in the buffer cache which will call the driver's xxstrategy() entry point.

9.3.3 Hardware versus software (pseudo) drivers

Not all device drivers access hardware. There are many character and block drivers which provide services to the kernel or user without controlling any physical devices. Such drivers are called *software drivers* or *pseudo drivers*. Examples include:

/dev/null   The bottomless sink used to discard unwanted data.

/dev/zero   Returns a stream of zeros when read and can be used with mmap(S) to provide shared memory between a parent and child. See section 11.4.6 for further details.

/dev/kmem   Access to kernel virtual memory.

/dev/mem   Access to the machine's physical memory.

Toolkit examples provided later demonstrate an implementation of a /dev/kmem equivalent character driver and show a block driver implementing a RAM disk on which filesystems can be created and mounted.

9.3.4 Kernel tables used for accessing device drivers

There are a number of tables in the kernel which are used to access a device driver. The bdevsw[] and cdevsw[] tables are used to access the main entry points of the driver in response to requests by the kernel on behalf of the user or by internal kernel subsystems. The bdevsw and cdevsw structures are described in detail in the next section.

The io_init[] array is used to call driver initialisation routines soon after the system boots. When the kernel is executing main(), it calls all driver XXinit() routines which are present in the io_init[] table. This allows the driver to perform any initialisation routines such as memory allocation, resetting the device and so on. It is here that the driver initialisation messages are displayed as shown earlier in section 9.3.1.

The io_init[] array is constructed during kernel link-time. It is declared in /etc/conf/cf.d/conf.c as follows:

```
int (*io_init[])() = {
    firstinit,
    audinit,
    itiminit,
    nmi_init,
    sioinit,
    ...
} ;
```

The io_halt[] array, also constructed during kernel link-time and held in the /etc/conf/cf.d/conf.c file, contains XXhalt() driver functions which are invoked by the kernel dhalt() function late during kernel shutdown. This allows drivers to perform any device shutdown routines that may be required.

The ivect[] and intvect[] arrays are used to access a driver's interrupt service routine when an interrupt is received from the device. Interrupt handling is described in section 9.4. See /etc/conf/cf.d/vector.c for a definition of the ivect[] and intvect[] arrays.

The io_poll[] array contains entry points for driver XXpoll() functions. This allows a driver function to be invoked on each clock tick (Hz times a second). The io_poll[] array is also constructed during kernel link-time and held in the /etc/conf/cf.d/conf.c file. Polling is described in section 9.6.

9.3.5 Accessing drivers

The addresses of the device driver entry points are held in their respective positions in the bdevsw[] and cdevsw[] arrays. The bdevsw[] array contains elements of type struct bdevsw for which the elements are shown in Table 9.3. The cdevsw[] array contains elements of type `struct cdevsw` for which the elements are shown in Table 9.4. Both structures are declared in the `<sys/conf.h>` header file.

Table 9.3   Elements of the `bdevsw` structure

bdevsw structure field		Description
`int`	`(*d_open)()`	The address of the driver's open routine.
`int`	`(*d_close)()`	The address of the driver's close routine.
`int`	`(*d_strategy)()`	The address of the driver's strategy routine.
`int`	`(*d_print)()`	The address of the driver's print routine.
`char`	`*d_name`	This string, which can contain up to five characters, is the driver prefix. It should be added to the driver entry points to identify driver routines uniquely.
`struct iobuf`	`*d_tab`	This field is used by the driver to link multiple buffers passed through an `XXstrategy()` call. The buffers are usually linked in order of their physical position on the device. The driver will work its way through this list, reading or writing the data specified by the `buf` structures.

Note that the block driver `XXread()` and `XXwrite()` routines are not covered by the `bdevsw` structure. These are part of the raw interface which is described in section 9.11.

Table 9.4   Elements of the `cdevsw` structure

cdevsw structure field		Description
`int`	`(*d_open)()`	The address of the driver's open routine.
`int`	`(*d_close)()`	The address of the driver's close routine.
`int`	`(*d_read)()`	The address of the driver's read routine.
`int`	`(*d_write)()`	The address of the driver's write routine.
`int`	`(*d_ioctl)()`	The address of the driver's `ioctl` routine.
`struct tty`	`*d_ttys`	The `tty` structure associated with a device.
`struct streamtab`	`*d_str`	If this entry refers to a STREAMS device, this field points to the STREAM head.
`char`	`*d_name`	This string, which can contain up to five characters, is the driver prefix. It should be added to the driver entry points to identify driver routines uniquely.

The contents of both the `bdevsw[]` and `cdevsw[]` arrays for the running kernel can be found in `/etc/conf/cf.d/conf.c`. For example, the first few entries of the `cdevsw[]` structure are:

```
struct cdevsw cdevsw[] = {
/*  0*/ cnopen, cnclose, cnread, cnwrite, cnioctl, cn_tty, 0, "cn",
/*  1*/ hdopen, hdclose, nodev,  nodev,   nodev,   0,      0, "hd",
```

```
/*  2*/ flopen,   flclose, flread,  flwrite, flioctl, 0,     0, "fd",
/*  3*/ syopen,   nulldev, syread,  sywrite, syioctl, 0,     0, "sy",
/*  4*/ nulldev,  nulldev, mmread,  mmwrite, nodev,   0,     0, "mm",
```

Consider the kmem driver whose device major and minor are:

```
$ ls -l /dev/kmem
cr--r-----   1 root       mem        4,  1 Apr 26  1995 /dev/kmem
```

The file represents a character device as the highlighted c shows. The major number of the device referenced is 4 which means that the driver entry points can be accessed in cdevsw[4]. Looking at the list of cdevsw[] entries, the driver prefix is mm. The mm driver is used for /dev/kmem, /dev/mem and /dev/null. The minor number allows the driver to determine whether kmem, mem or null is being accessed. A minor number of 1 is used for kmem, 0 for mem and 2 for null.

The kernel calls the driver entry points by accessing the appropriate field in the cdevsw structure. For example, for the kernel to call the kmem driver's read function, it issues the following call:

```
(*cdevsw[4].d_read)(...args...) ;
```

To avoid this complicated usage, many calls are hidden behind other functions, some of which perform additional error handling. For example, all calls from the buffer cache to the driver's strategy routine are invoked as follows:

```
issue_strat(dev, bp) ;
```

This function checks that the device major number is within valid boundaries. It then uses the major number to index the bdevsw[] table and calls the strategy routine passing bp as an argument.

Toolkit 9.2   Which drivers are present?

Viewing the /etc/conf/cf.d/conf.c file will show whether a driver will be linked into the kernel or not. Some drivers have an XXinit() routine and print messages during initialisation and others do not.

The conf.c file does not specify whether a driver is present in the booted kernel. The program presented here is used to take a driver prefix and determine whether the driver is present in the cdevsw[] table, bdevsw[] table or both. Note that this program, like many others which require access to the UNIX name list, cannot determine whether the booted kernel is, in fact, the same as the kernel found in /unix.

The source of the program is as follows:

```
1 #include <sys/conf.h>
2 #include <sys/errno.h>
3 #include <fcntl.h>
4 #include <nlist.h>
```

```
 5
 6 #define CDEVSZ (cdevcnt * sizeof(struct cdevsw))
 7 #define BDEVSZ (bdevcnt * sizeof(struct bdevsw))
 8
 9 int          fd ;
10 int          cdevcnt ;
11 int          bdevcnt ;
12 struct cdevsw *cdevsw ;
13 struct bdevsw *bdevsw ;
14
15 struct nlist nl[] = {   { "cdevcnt", 0, 0, 0, 0, 0 },
16                         { "bdevcnt", 0, 0, 0, 0, 0 },
17                         { "cdevsw",  0, 0, 0, 0, 0 },
18                         { "bdevsw",  0, 0, 0, 0, 0 },
19                         { 0 }
20                     } ;
21
22 read_tables()
23 {
24     cdevsw = (struct cdevsw *)malloc(CDEVSZ) ;
25     lseek(fd, nl[2].n_value, SEEK_SET) ;
26     read(fd, (char *)cdevsw, CDEVSZ) ;
27
28     bdevsw = (struct bdevsw *)malloc(BDEVSZ) ;
29     lseek(fd, nl[3].n_value, SEEK_SET) ;
30     read(fd, (char *)bdevsw, BDEVSZ) ;
31
32     return(1) ;
33 }
34
35 read_counts()
36 {
37     if (nlist("/unix", nl) < 0)
38         return(0) ;
39
40     lseek(fd, nl[0].n_value, SEEK_SET) ;
41     read(fd, (char *)&cdevcnt, sizeof(int)) ;
42
43     lseek(fd, nl[0].n_value, SEEK_SET) ;
44     read(fd, (char *)&bdevcnt, sizeof(int)) ;
45
46     return(1) ;
47 }
48
49 drvnam(long addr, char *name)
50 {
51     lseek(fd, addr, SEEK_SET) ;
52     read(fd, name, 8) ;
53 }
54
55 main(int argc, char *argv[])
56 {
57     int i, flag = 0 ;
58     char name[8] ;
59
60     if (argc != 2) {
61         printf("usage: driver prefix\n") ;
62         exit(EINVAL) ;
63     }
64
```

```
65      fd = open("/dev/kmem", O_RDONLY) ;
66      if (fd < 0)
67          pexit("/dev/kmem") ;
68
69      if (read_counts())
70          printf("cdevcnt = %d, bdevcnt = %d\n", cdevcnt, bdevcnt) ;
71      else
72          pexit("nlist") ;
73
74      read_tables() ;
75
76      for (i=0 ; i<cdevcnt ; i++){
77          drvnam((long)cdevsw[i].d_name, name) ;
78          if (strcmp(name, argv[1]) == 0) {
79              flag++ ;
80              printf("cdevsw[%d] = %s\n", i, name) ;
81          }
82      }
83
84      for (i=0 ; i<bdevcnt ; i++){
85          drvnam((long)bdevsw[i].d_name, name) ;
86          if (strcmp(name, argv[1]) == 0) {
87              flag++ ;
88              printf("bdevsw[%d] = %s\n", i, name) ;
89          }
90      }
91
92      if (!flag)
93          printf("Driver with the prefix \"%s\" not found\n",argv[1]) ;
94 }
```

The program starts by opening /dev/kmem on line 65 for which the file descriptor is assigned to a global variable accessible by all functions.

The size of the cdevsw[] and bdevsw[] arrays are defined by the cdevcnt and bdevcnt kernel variables, respectively. The read_counts() function is called from main() on line 69 to read the values of both variables which, if successful, are displayed on line 70.

read_counts(), which is defined on lines 35 to 47, first calls nlist(S) to obtain the symbol addresses for cdevcnt, bdevcnt and the cdevsw[] and bdevsw[] arrays. The structure passed to nlist(S) is defined on lines 15 to 20.

Once the addresses have been obtained, read_counts() calls lseek(S) and read(S) for cdevcnt and bdevcnt. The value for each variable is read from /dev/kmem and stored in a global variable of the same name.

Now that the size of each table is known, main() calls read_tables() (defined on lines 22 to 33) to read in both the cdevsw[] and bdevsw[] arrays. Since the addresses were obtained from read_counts(), read_tables() calls malloc(S) to allocate space for the tables which it subsequently reads through /dev/kmem.

Each table is then searched on lines 76 to 90 to see if the specified prefix matches the prefix pointed to by the d_name field of the cdevsw or bdevsw structures. Since d_name is a pointer, drvnam() is called to read each name from /dev/kmem.

The output from the program, for a number of different prefixes, is as follows:

```
# driver mem
cdevcnt = 101, bdevcnt = 101
Driver with the prefix "mem" not found
# driver hd
cdevcnt = 101, bdevcnt = 101
cdevsw[1] = hd
bdevsw[1] = hd
# driver sio
cdevcnt = 101, bdevcnt = 101
cdevsw[5] = sio
# driver ram
cdevcnt = 101, bdevcnt = 101
Driver with the prefix "ram" not found
```

The program can be used by driver writers as a sanity check to ensure that their drivers have been linked into the kernel in the correct place in cdevsw[] and bdevsw[].

9.3.6 Linking new device drivers into the kernel

There are a number of files and commands used to link device drivers into the kernel. Both commands and files are usually referred to as the *link kit*. The commands by themselves are generally referred to as the *idtoolset* or simply *idtools*.

The following files need to be provided by the driver writer to be able to link a driver into the kernel:

Driver.o   This is the driver's object file. It must be a COFF based file. For example, the following command can be used to create Driver.o from driver source implemented in a single file called mydriver.c:

cc -o Driver.o -c -bcoff mydriver.c

By default, a COFF object will actually be generated if the -b option is missing.

Master   This file contains information that will be added to the mdevice(F) file located in the conf/cf.d directory in the link kit.
An example Master file is shown later in Toolkit 9.3.

System   This file contains information that will be added to the sdevice(F) file located in the conf/cf.d directory in the link kit.
An example System file is shown later in Toolkit 9.3.

Both the Master and System files are optional since the information they provide can be configured by hand as the examples in this chapter will show.

The idtoolset can be used to configure drivers by hand although using Master and System reduces the likelihood of errors. The arrangement of files and the idtools under /etc/conf are shown in Figure 9.13.

Many of the files and directories shown have manual pages or can often be found by using the -k option to man(C). The purpose of each directory and their contents are as follows:

```
bin/

        idaddld      idbuild      idcheck      idconfig     iddeftune
        idinstall    idmaster     idmkenv      idmkinit     idmknod
        idmkreg      idmkunix     idreboot     idscsi       idspace
        idtune       idvbuild     idvidi

cf.d/

        conf.c       link_unix    mscsi        sfsys
        config.h     mtune        stune        majorsinuse
        configure    mdevice      sdevice      vector.c
        fsconf.c     mfsys        vuifile

init.d/

        scohttp      scologin     sio

mfsys.d/

        devfs_ dos dt hpps hs ht lmcfs namefs_ xx znfs

node.d/

        fd   hd   marry   mm   prf   tcp   ...

pack.d/

        kernel/

                os.a        space.c      locore.o    ...

        mm/

                Driver.o

        sio/

                Driver.o   space.c      stubs.c

rc.d/

sd.d/

sdevice.d/

        fd   hd   udp   vx   sio   ...

sfsys.d/

        devfs_ dos dt hpps hs ht lmcfs namefs_ xx znfs
```

Figure 9.13   Layout of files in the link kit

bin   All of the binaries and utilities (idtools) needed to configure and link a new kernel, copy it to the boot filesystem and build the device environment are located in this directory.

cf.d   This set of files describes the devices which will be linked into the kernel. The switch tables and other device tables are also found in this directory. Many of the source files held in this directory are constructed by the idtoolset.

init.d   The set of files found in this directory will be appended to cf.d/init.base which is used to create /etc/inittab.

mfsys.d   Described by mfsys(F), the per filesystem files in this directory describe the filesystem name and a specification of valid filesystem driver entry points.

node.d   The idmknod(ADM) utility uses the files in this directory to construct the kernel environment. This includes creation of any necessary special files in /dev.

pack.d   Each driver, whether linked into the kernel or not, has its own directory under pack.d in which is stored the driver object file, any tuneable parameters and stubs to be used if the driver is not linked into the kernel.

rc.d   No longer used.

sd.d   No longer used.

sdevice.d   This directory contains driver entries which describe the hardware specific properties of the driver, for example the Interrupt Priority Level (IPL), register addresses and whether the driver should be included in the next kernel link performed.

sfsys.d   For each filesystem type in mfsys.d there is a file in this directory which specifies whether the filesystem should be linked into the kernel or not.

Once the driver and the files needed to link the driver into the kernel have been created, the idinstall(ADM) utility can be called to add the driver to the link kit. This requires that the current directory has the driver object called Driver.o, files called Master and System and some optional, additional files. See the idinstall(ADM) manual page for further details.

Many driver writers manually perform the tasks undertaken by idinstall(ADM) using the configure(ADM) utility. The steps involved here are shown in Toolkit 9.4.

To create a bootable kernel, the link_unix(ADM) command is used. Once the kernel is created, the caller is prompted to specify whether the kernel built will be bootable by default. When creating new device drivers it is recommended not to boot the new kernel by default even though the existing kernel, /unix, will be copied to /unix.old.

When the link_unix(ADM) command is run, it prompts the caller to answer some questions as the following example shows:

```
# cd /etc/conf/cf.d
# ./link_unix

        The UNIX Operating System will now be rebuilt.
        This will take a few minutes.  Please wait.

        Root for this system build is /

        The UNIX Kernel has been rebuilt.
```

```
Do you want this kernel to boot by default? (y/n) y
Backing up unix to unix.old
Installing new unix on the boot file system

The kernel environment includes device node files and /etc/inittab.
The new kernel may require changes to /etc/inittab or device nodes.


Do you want the kernel environment rebuilt? (y/n) y

The kernel has been successfully linked and installed.
        To activate it, reboot your system.

Setting up new kernel environment
```

It is not necessary to rebuild the kernel environment unless new device nodes need to be created. However, it is usually recommended to rebuild the environment since the permissions of device files will be verified.

Toolkit 9.3   Adding a device driver to the kernel

This example creates a skeleton character device driver which prints a message whenever the kernel calls one of its entry points. The steps shown to link the driver into the kernel are described. The source of the driver is as follows:

```
 1 #include <sys/types.h>
 2 #include <sys/cmn_err.h>
 3
 4 dmopen(dev_t dev, int flag, int id)
 5 {
 6     printf("dmopen() called") ;
 7 }
 8
 9 dmclose(dev_t dev, int flag, int id)
10 {
11     printf("dmclose() called") ;
12 }
13
14 dmread(dev_t dev)
15 {
16     printf("dmread() called") ;
17 }
18
19 dminit()
20 {
21     printcfg("dummy", 0,0,-1,-1, "Dummy device driver", (char *)0) ;
22 }
```

The driver should be compiled as follows:

```
cc -c -o Driver.o -bcoff dummy.c
```

Since the UNIX kernel is built as a COFF object, the driver object file created must also be a COFF object file. If an ELF object is produced link_unix(ADM) will fail, reporting the incompatibility. Since the Driver.o object is not executable there will be a number of unresolved symbols in the object file. These symbols may be checked with the `nm(CP)` command out of interest.

The contents of the `Master` file for the driver are:

```
dm   Iocr   irc   dm   0   0   0   1   -1
```

The first field is the driver's name which is stored in the `d_name` field of the `bdevsw` or `cdevsw` structure. The second field specifies the entry points of the driver which are used to populate the entries in the appropriate position of the `cdevsw[]` or `bdevsw[]` arrays.

The third field specifies that the driver is installable (`i`), should be linked in every kernel (`r`) and is a character device (`c`).

The next field specifies the driver prefix which is added to the init, open, close, read and write routines to generate the symbolic names used to compile the contents of the switch tables.

The next two fields are the driver's block and character major numbers. By setting both to zero, the system will choose appropriate free slots.

The remaining three fields specify the number of devices that can be supported by the controller and the DMA channel if used. For more details of these fields and the fields discussed above, see the `mdevice(F)` manual page.

The `System` file created for the dummy driver is:

```
dm   Y   1   0   0   0   0   0   0   0
```

The first field is the driver prefix as specified in the `Master` file. By setting `Y` in the second field, this informs the idtoolset that the driver should be linked into the kernel.

The third field specifies how many devices are attached to the controller if the driver supports hardware and is used in conjunction with the values specified in the `Master` file. For details of the remaining fields see the `sdevice(F)` manual page.

Once the files have been created, `idinstall(ADM)` should be invoked as follows:

```
# /etc/conf/bin/idinstall -ak dm
```

This installs the driver and its configuration files into the link kit. See the `idinstall(ADM)` manual page for the options available.

The final stage is to link the new kernel and specify that it should be booted by default at the next system bootstrap:

```
# cd /etc/conf/cf.d
# ./link_unix
```

When the system is rebooted, the `dminit()` function should be called which will display the following output:

```
device     address           vector dma comment
-------------------------------------------------------------------
%fpu       -                 13     -   type=80387
%serial    0x03F8-0x03FF     4      -   unit=0 type=Standard nports=1
```

```
%floppy    0x03F2-0x03F7   6       2    unit=0 type=135ds18
%console   -               -       -    unit=vga type=0 12 screens=68k
%adapter   0x0330-0x0332   11      5    type=ad rev=E0 ha=0 id=7 fts=s
%pci       0xC000-0xCFFF   -       -    am=2 sc=0 buses=1
%eisarom   -               -       -    eisa (1.3.0)
%smc/wdn   0x0220-0x023F   9       -    type=8013EPC addr=00:00:c0:08:ad:a3
%dummy     -               -       -    Dummy device driver
%tape      -               -       -    type=S ha=0 id=2 lun=0 bus=0 ht=ad
%disk      -               -       -    type=S ha=0 id=0 lun=0 bus=0 ht=ad
%Sdsk      -               -       -    cyls=1042 hds=64 secs=32 fts=sb
mem: total = 32384k, kernel = 6832k, user = 25552k
swapdev = 1/41, swplo = 0, nswap = 98000, swapmem = 49000k
Autoboot from rootdev = 1/42, pipedev = 1/42, dumpdev = 1/41
kernel: Hz = 100, i/o bufs = 3084k
```

Before the driver can be accessed, a special file needs to be created using the mknod(ADM) utility. The name of the file is passed to mknod(C) together with the special file type, in this case c for character device, and the major/minor numbers:

```
# mknod /dev/dummy c 81 0        # idinstall chose major number 81
# ls -l /dev/dummy
crw-rw-rw-   1 root     sys       81,  0 Jan 11 12:20 /dev/dummy
```

Device files can also be created by the link kit by supplying a Node file when idinstall(ADM) is invoked.

The device driver can now be invoked. To access the dmread(), dmwrite() and dmclose() routines, the cat(C) command can be run on the device as follows:

```
# cat /dev/dummy
dmopen() called
dmread() called
dmclose() called
```

cat(C) opens the specified file, reads from it and then closes it. Since the dmread() function does not return any data, nothing is displayed by cat(C).

9.4 Hardware management

Despite the fact that most PCs are compatible in the sense that they contain an Intel x86 CPU or equivalent CPU from another manufacturer, that is where the compatibility ends. There are numerous hardware differences between PCs and even where two PCs look identical or very similar when analysing the individual components, programs which work on one system may not work on another.

This is where the fun starts for device driver writers who need to compensate for hardware peculiarities, provide support for the numerous different buses, disk adapters, graphics cards and so on.

This section briefly describes the CPU specific support for I/O and I/O management together with some of the more well-known support chips.

Most device drivers do not talk directly to individual devices such as disks or tape drives but to hardware controllers or adapters which control the individual devices

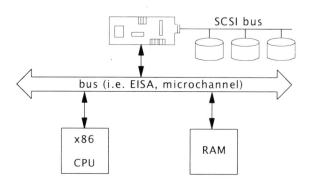

Figure 9.14   Accessing an EISA/MCA SCSI host bus
adapter

themselves. For example, Figure 9.14 shows the CPU accessing a SCSI host bus adapter
which in turn communicates with the SCSI devices. Control signals are sent to the adapter
which will often read and write data directly from and to the system's memory using
DMA.

Most I/O transfers are asynchronous. The CPU sends controller specific commands
and other control signals to the hardware adapter but does not wait until the transfer is
complete. Some time later, which may be significant compared with the speed of the
CPU, the transfer will be complete. Either the data will have been transferred to memory
directly using DMA or the data will be in hardware buffers on the controller card.

For some devices, the device driver must determine when the I/O operation has
completed. This is usually accomplished by reading status registers on the controller card.
The device driver must poll the controller, usually at a fixed rate using either the
XXpoll() function which is called on every clock tick or by issuing a timeout using the
timeout(K) function. Timeouts are described in section 7.8.4.

For non-polled devices, when the I/O operation is complete, the device notifies the
CPU by raising an *interrupt*. Shown in Figure 9.15, this involves asserting one of the
interrupt request lines on the PIC (Peripheral Interrupt Controller) which raises the INTR
(Interrupt Request) line on the CPU. This results in the processor finishing the instruction
it is currently executing and jumping to an *interrupt handler*, provided by the kernel, after
it has finished. This type of interrupt is called a *maskable interrupt* since the processor
can block out the interrupt until the processor, or more appropriately the kernel, is ready
to receive another interrupt.

There are also non-maskable interrupts which cannot be blocked by the CPU. Such
interrupts cannot always be generated by PC hardware. EISA-based machines provide a
watchdog timer whereby a counter is set to a specific value by software. If a specified
amount of time has been exceeded without the kernel resetting the timer, the NMI pin is
asserted. This allows the kernel to detect endless loops that may occur, perhaps owing to
interrupts being masked.

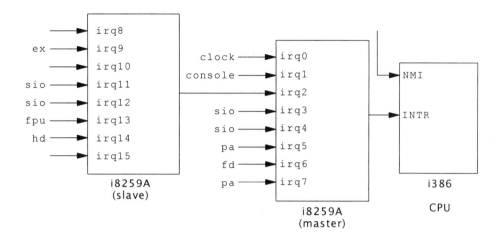

Figure 9.15   The i8259A PIC used to generate maskable interrupts

9.4.1 Interrupt handling

Recall from section 7.8.2 that the `clock()` function is called `Hz` (100) times per second in response to a clock interrupt.

The kernel programs the PIC so that it will generate a range of interrupt vectors that correspond to different entries in the i386 Interrupt Descriptor Table (IDT). For example, if a clock interrupt occurs, the PIC asserts the `INTR` pin of the CPU. After each instruction, the CPU checks the `INTR` pin. If asserted, a protocol between the CPU and the PIC results in the PIC placing the programmed ID matching the IRQ to the IDT entry on the data bus. This allows the CPU to jump through the IDT to the appropriate interrupt handler. For the clock interrupt on IRQ0 of the master PIC, this corresponds to entry 64 in the IDT as shown in Figure 9.16.

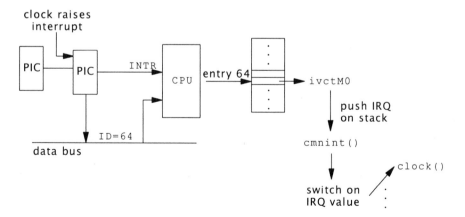

Figure 9.16   Interrupt handling between the PIC and CPU

The routine referenced by entry 64 of the IDT is ivctM0 which pushes the IRQ onto the stack and calls cmnint(). Similarly for IRQ1, the ivectM1 handler pushes the value for IRQ1 onto the stack and calls cmnint() and so on.

Entries in the IDT can be displayed from within crash(ADM) using the idt command as shown. The address contained in the IDT descriptor is shown using the dis command.

```
> idt 64
iAPX386 IDT
CPU SLOT      SELECTOR OFFSET    TYPE       DPL  ACCESSBITS
   0    64            0158 f0011168 IGATE386    0  CNT=0
> dis f0011168
ivctM0                   pushl   $0x0
```

cmnint() performs a number of low level operations before using the argument passed on the stack to call the appropriate interrupt handler in ivect[]. For a clock interrupt it is the function clock(). For details of the tasks performed by clock() see section 7.8.2.

9.4.2 Masking interrupts

The PIC allows the interrupt request lines to be ordered in priority value such that IRQ0 has the highest priority. The kernel programs the PIC early during kernel initialisation so that when each interrupt occurs, the PIC automatically disables interrupts of the same or lower priority. Since the clock is attached to IRQ0 of the master PIC, a clock interrupt has the highest priority so no other interrupts will be generated until the interrupt handler returns.

If two devices were attached to the same IRQ line of the PIC, and if an interrupt were raised by one of the devices, an interrupt from the other device would be blocked until the interrupt handler of the first device driver completed.

This hardware restriction can be removed when executing interrupt handlers by using *software priority levels* accessible through the functions shown in Table 9.5. Software priority levels, which are supported by most versions of UNIX, allow device drivers to modify the hardware priority levels imposed by the PIC. The spl(K) routines manipulate the PIC to set the software priority level specified and return the current software priority level.

An additional use of software priority levels is for drivers to protect data structures they are currently accessing from damage by the driver's interrupt handler which may also need to access the same data structure at interrupt time. The driver can set a software priority level to mask interrupts from occurring until it has finished its critical section.

It is usual to save the current software priority level when masking interrupts and to restore this level when the critical section of code has been executed as follows:

```
s = spl5() ;
    {
        critical section
    }
splx(s) ;
```

Table 9.5 Software priority levels

spl function	Description
spl0()	Permit all interrupts.
spl1()	Prevent priority level 1 interrupts.
spl2()	Prevent priority level 2 interrupts.
spl3()	Prevent priority level 3 interrupts.
spl4()	Prevent priority level 4 interrupts.
spl5(), splstr(), spltty()	Prevent interrupts from parallel and serial ports, STREAMS and clist processing.
spl6()	Prevent interrupts from the clock, block devices and network devices.
spl7(), splhi()	Prevent all interrupts.
splx()	Restore a former interrupt level.

For further details on how to use software priority levels within device drivers see Kettle and Statler (1992).

9.5 Support for writing device drivers

Since device drivers are linked into the kernel, they can in theory use any of the functions located in the kernel address space and access kernel variables or the fields of any kernel structures. However, for the next and subsequent releases of the kernel, such functions may have interface changes, may change in semantics or may not even be provided at all.

To alleviate this problem while still providing a rich set of support functions for device driver writers, a set of functions and variables are provided as part of the SCO OpenServer *Advanced Hardware Developer's Kit* (AHDK) (1995). They will be maintained in subsequent releases of the operating system and are the only functions that should be used by device driver writers.

The manual pages for these functions appear in section (K); for example, the printcfg(K) function used in the dummy device driver earlier can be accessed via

```
$ man K printcfg
```

Multi-threaded device drivers which have been written for SCO MPX, the *symmetric multi-processing* (SMP) version of SCO UNIX, have access to an additional set of routines which can be found in section (MPX).

Device drivers, as part of the kernel, cannot be debugged with traditional UNIX debuggers such as adb(CP) and dbx(CP). The crash(ADM) tool is useful for analysing kernel structures, printing stack back traces, analysing crash dumps and so on.

Included with the AHDK is a kernel debugger, scodb, which provides many features for debugging kernel code including structure dumping, stack traces, signal generation, single stepping, the ability to stop or display messages only when specified conditions are met and much more.

9.6 Character devices

Character devices represent the majority of hardware devices with which the kernel has to deal. Most character device drivers, for example those managing keyboards, mice, serial lines, modems and parallel printers, differ from block device drivers in that they handle small volumes of data, either a byte at a time or a few bytes at a time.

9.6.1 Accessing character device drivers

Data that is passed to and from a character device does not pass through the buffer cache. All system calls that would normally be routed by the kernel through a filesystem such as read(S) and write(S) pass through the devfs filesystem before they reach the character device driver. The devfs filesystem was introduced to provide a common interface for device access regardless of the filesystem which is managing the device special file.

When namei() is called to resolve a pathname on behalf of an open(S) request which corresponds to a device special file, the inode returned by the filesystem managing the special file will be shadowed by a devfs inode, and thus the devfs inode is returned from namei(). This allows all device I/O to be performed independently of the filesystem in which the special file resides.

Following the device open, calls to read(S) and write(S) result in the kernel calling FS_READI(ip) or FS_WRITEI(ip) as shown in Figure 9.17.

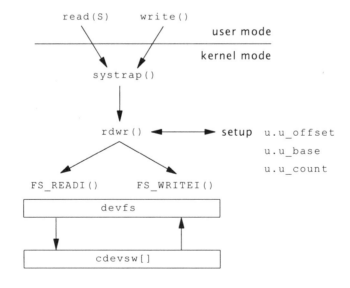

Figure 9.17   Kernel flow control using devfs

The u_area fields which are used by character drivers to perform an I/O transfer are set up by `rdwr()` before calling the filesystem. The following section describes which u_area fields are used.

When accessing character devices, `devfs` performs little work other than to call the `XXread()` or `XXwrite()` driver call. The device major number used to access the device is stored in the `devfs` inode which was created during pathname resolution.

9.6.2 u_area manipulation

Prior to calling the driver, the kernel sets up a number of fields in the u_area to specify the offset within the device from where the transfer will start, the user address where the data will be written to or read from and so on.

The device driver must follow certain protocols when accessing the u_area to ensure that the higher layers of the kernel can determine whether the transfer was successful and how much data was transferred.

The following fields of the u_area are of particular importance to character drivers:

unchar	u_error	If an I/O transfer fails, or the arguments contained in the other fields of the u_area are invalid, the `seterror(k)` function should be called to set an appropriate error value in this field. The list of possible errors can be found in the header file `<sys/errno.h>`. If set to anything other than zero, the system call will return an error with `errno` set to `u_error`.
off_t	u_offset	This field specifies the offset into the device from where the read or write should take place. This field is not relevant for some device types.
caddr_t	u_base	This field specifies the virtual address in user space or kernel space to or from which the data transfer should take place.
unsigned	u_count	This field specifies the size of the transfer in bytes.
short	u_fmode	If the FBMODE flag is turned on in the `u_fmode` field of the `file` structure, the driver should interpret `u_offset` as a block offset and not as a byte offset. This is used to allow access to large device spaces.

After a transfer has been successfully completed, the driver should decrement `u.u_count` by the number of bytes that have been transferred and increment `u.u_offset` by the same amount.

9.6.3 Copying data between the driver and the caller

There are a number of different functions available to driver writers for copying data to and from user space. The functions available are shown below. For functions that should manipulate u.u_offset, u.u_base and u.u_count, the actions to be taken are shown.

fubyte(K)   These two routines copy a single byte and a single word from a
fuword(K)   user virtual address. If the required address has been set up above
            the driver in u.u_base, cpass(K) should be used.
            These routines are usually called from XXwrite().

subyte(K)   These two routines copy a single byte and single word to a user
suword(K)   virtual address. If the required address has been set up above the
            driver in u.u_base, passc(K) should be used.
            These routines are usually called from XXread().

cpass(K)   This function is usually called from XXwrite() to read a byte
            from user mode to kernel mode. The cpass(K) function calls
            fubyte(K) and automatically updates u.u_offset, u.u_base
            and u.u_count. It also returns an error in u.u_error.

passc(K)   This function is usually called from XXread() to copy a byte from
            kernel mode to user mode. The passc(K) function calls
            subyte(K) and automatically updates u.u_offset, u.u_base
            and u.u_count. It also returns an error in u.u_error.

bcopy(K)   This function copies a specified number of bytes from one kernel
            virtual address to another.

copyin(K)   These two routines copy a specified number of bytes from user
copyout(K) mode into kernel mode or from kernel mode out to user mode.
            If the call is successful, u.u_offset will be increased by the
            number of bytes copied and u.u_count will be decremented by
            the number of bytes copied.

copyio(K)   The copyio(K) function performs a number of different types of
            copy – kernel to kernel, user to kernel or kernel to user. It uses
            bcopy(K), copyin(K) or copyout(K) depending on the type of
            transfer which is specified as an argument.
            The copyio(K) function takes two addresses. The first address
            is a physical address while the second address is a virtual address.
            If copyio(K) returns successfully, u.u_base should be
            incremented by the number of bytes transferred and u.u_count
            should be decremented by the number of bytes transferred.

As an example, consider the following read from a character driver:

```
fd = open("/dev/device", O_RDONLY) ;
n = read (fd, buff, 1024) ;                    # assume buf address = 0x403bd0
```

Before the driver's `XXread()` function is called, the kernel sets up the u_area fields as shown:

```
u.u_offset = 0              # This is the first read
u.u_base = 0x403bd0
u.u_count = 1024
```

If the I/O transfer is successful, 1024 will be added to `u.u_offset` and decremented from `u.u_count`. This is analysed by the kernel once the driver has returned to ensure that the correct number of bytes transferred is returned to the user.

Toolkit 9.4   Accessing kernel virtual memory

This example presents a simple character driver which provides the same behaviour as `/dev/kmem`, allowing a process to read the contents of kernel memory by specifying kernel virtual addresses.

The driver provides only `XXread()` and `XXwrite()` interfaces. Since an `open(S)` actually opens the special file used to access the device, the driver open is not required unless there is some specific task for the driver to perform.

The source for the driver is as follows:

```
 1 #include <sys/param.h>
 2 #include <sys/types.h>
 3 #include <sys/immu.h>
 4 #include <sys/cmn_err.h>
 5 #include <sys/errno.h>
 6 #include <sys/user.h>
 7 #include <sys/sysmacros.h>
 8
 9 extern struct user u ;
10
11 #define READ  0
12 #define WRITE 1
13
14 mem_rdwr(int in_out)
15 {
16     switch(in_out) {
17         case(READ) :
18             if (copyout(u.u_offset, u.u_base, u.u_count) == -1) {
19                 seterror(EFAULT) ;
20                 return ;
21             }
22             break ;
23
24         case(WRITE) :
25             if (copyin(u.u_base, u.u_offset, u.u_count) == -1) {
26                 seterror(EFAULT) ;
27                 return ;
28             }
29             break ;
30     }
31     u.u_offset += u.u_count ;
32     u.u_count   = 0 ;
33 }
34
35 memread(dev_t dev)
```

```
36 {
37      mem_rdwr(READ) ;
38 }
39
40 memwrite(dev_t dev)
41 {
42      mem_rdwr(WRITE) ;
43 }
```

The read and write operations are both performed by mem_rdwr() shown on lines 14 to 33. The in_out parameter specifies whether a read or write should be performed.

The copyin(K) and copyout(K) functions are used to copy data into and out of the kernel. If copyin(K) or copyout(K) is successful, the number of bytes requested is subtracted from u.u_count and added to u.u_offset. If either call returns −1 indicating a failure, seterror(K) is called to set the value of u.u_error to EFAULT and the driver returns without modifying u.u_count or u.u_offset.

Figure 9.18 shows the flow of control from user mode to the driver and the establishment of the u_area fields needed by the driver to perform the I/O.

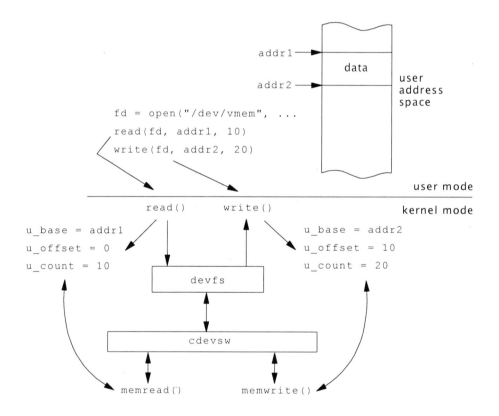

Figure 9.18 Flow control for accessing /dev/vmem

The steps taken to link the driver into the kernel are:

```
# cd /etc/conf/pack.d
# mkdir mem
# cp /tmp/Driver.o mem/.
# cd ../cf.d
# ./configure -j NEXTMAJOR
83
# ./configure -a memread memwrite -c -m 83
# ./link_unix
```

Before invoking these steps, a check should be made to ensure that a directory called mem does not exist and that there is no other driver with a prefix of mem. Most drivers are stored in a directory under /etc/conf/pack.d which has the same name as the prefix.

The Driver.o object is copied to the directory created under pack.d. The configure(ADM) utility is then run with the -j NEXTMAJOR option to locate the lowest available device major number.

The configure(ADM) utility is then run again to add the driver to the link kit configuration files. The -a option is followed by the driver entry points, the -c option specifies that a character driver is being configured and the -m option is used to specify the device major number. link_unix(ADM) is finally called to create a new kernel including the driver.

A device special file must be created to allow access to the driver. This is achieved using mknod(C) as follows:

```
# mknod /dev/vmem c 83 0
```

The driver is tested using a modified version of the driver program presented in Toolkit 9.2. All references to /dev/kmem in the original program have been changed to reference /dev/vmem:

```
$ ls -l /dev/vmem
crw-r--r--   1 root      sys        83,  0 Jan 14 07:29 /dev/vmem
$ ddriver sio
cdevcnt = 101, bdevcnt = 101
cdevsw[5] = sio
$ ddriver mem
cdevcnt = 101, bdevcnt = 101
cdevsw[83] = mem
$ ddriver hd
cdevcnt = 101, bdevcnt = 101
cdevsw[1] = hd
bdevsw[1] = hd
$ ddriver xxx
cdevcnt = 101, bdevcnt = 101
Driver with the prefix "xxx" not found
```

9.6.4 Accessing the hardware

There are six functions available for accessing the I/O address space, allowing transfers of byte, word or double word quantities. The prototypes for these functions are:

```
int inb(int read_addr) ;
int outb(int write_addr, char value) ;
int ind(int read_addr) ;
int outd(int write_addr, int value) ;
int inw(int read_addr) ;
int outw(int write_addr, int value) ;
```

For all functions, the `read_addr` or `write_addr` argument specifies the I/O address from or to which the transfer should take place.

The `inb(K)` and `outb(K)` functions are used to read and write 8 bit quantities from and to the device, the `inw(K)` and `outw(K)` functions are used to read and write 16 bit quantities and the `ind(K)` and `outd(K)` functions are used to read and write 32 bit quantities from and to the device.

9.6.5 Buffering support for character drivers

Transferring data between a user process and a character device one character at a time is inefficient. A character must be transferred from user space; it is then written to the device; the device driver may have to wait for a period of time before transferring another character and so on. When a character needs to be written and the device is busy, the user process must sleep, perhaps resulting in a context switch.

If the device is capable of generating interrupts, performance could be greatly improved if the next character were available when the interrupt occurred, since the driver's `XXwrite()` function can read characters into a buffer independently of the `XXintr()` function which continues writing characters until the buffer becomes empty.

For those devices that do not support interrupts, the `XXpoll()` routine can be used in conjunction with a software interrupt handler. The `XXpoll()` routine is called on each clock tick by the `clock()` interrupt handler. `XXpoll()` is usually written to call an `XXintr()` function based on some set of heuristics. For example, for each tenth call to `XXpoll()` it will call `XXintr()` allowing ten invocations per second. The `XXintr()` function could then check the device status and transfer the next character if available. Toolkit 9.5 shows how the `XXpoll()` and `XXintr()` routines work together.

To support buffering for character drivers, the kernel provides a character buffer called a `clist` with an easy-to-use interface for adding and removing characters to and from the buffers. Each `clist` structure contains three fields as follows:

```
int             c_cc ;
struct cblock  *c_cf ;
struct cblock  *c_cl ;
```

The `c_cc` field contains a count of the number of characters in the buffer. The `c_cf` and `c_cl` fields each point to the first and last elements of a linked list of `cblock` structures which are used to hold the characters in the buffer:

```
struct cblock  *c_next ;
unsigned char   c_first ;
unsigned char   c_last ;
unsigned char   c_data[CLSIZE] ;        // 64
```

The cblock structure can hold up to CLSIZE (64) characters. When one cblock becomes full another is automatically allocated by kernel support routines. Figure 9.19 shows the relationship between the clist and cblock structures.

Characters are read from the cblock referenced by the c_cf field of the clist structure and the c_next element of the c_data[] array in the cblock. Characters are added to the c_last element of the c_data[] array of the cblock referenced by the c_cl field of the clist.

The NCLIST kernel tuneable defines the maximum number of cblock structures that the system can allocate. The number of free cblocks is governed by high and low water marks. When the number of free cblocks reaches the high water mark, processes writing characters are put to sleep to allow the driver to write characters to the device and thus to free up existing, in-use cblock structures.

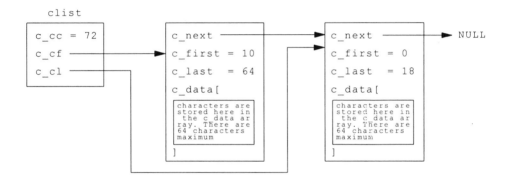

Figure 9.19   Mapping between the clist and cblock structures

Characters can be stored and retrieved using the following routines:

```
int              getc(struct clist *cp) ;
struct cblock    *getcb(struct clist *cp) ;
int              getcbp(struct clist *cp, char *buf, int n) ;
struct cblock    *getcf() ;
int              putc(int c, struct clist *cp) ;
int              *putcb(struct cblock *cbp, struct clist *cp) ;
int              putcbp(struct clist *cp, char *buf, int n) ;
int              *putcf(struct cblock *cp) ;
```

The getc(K) function gets a single character from the specified clist. The getcb(K) function removes the first cblock referenced by the c_cf field of the requested clist. The getcbp(K) function removes n characters from the clist and copies them to the buffer specified by buf. The getcf(K) function returns a pointer to the first cblock structure on the free list.

The putc(K) function adds the character c to the specified clist. The putcb(K) function adds a cblock structure to the end of the specified clist. If the clist is not empty the specified cblock will then be referenced by the c_cl field of the clist. The putcbp(K) function adds n characters from the buffer specified by buf to the specified clist. Finally, the putcf(K) function returns the specified cblock to the free list.

To use any of the above functions, the driver simply declares a clist structure and then starts to use it. The following toolkit provides an example of how clists are accessed. Section 9.7.6 describes how clists are used for terminal I/O.

Toolkit 9.5   A simple pipe driver using clists

This example provides a character driver which makes use of clists for buffering data and the XXpoll() routine to call a software interrupt handler to manage the data buffers.

The example implements a simple pipe mechanism where one process can write data into the pipe and another process can read the data written to the pipe.

The pipe can be accessed by reading from and writing to /dev/pip. The flow of data through the kernel from writer to reader is shown in Figure 9.20.

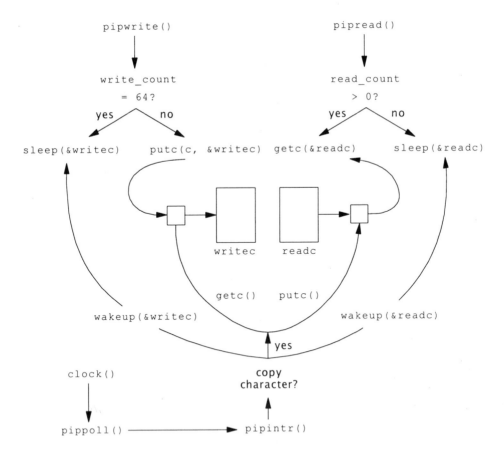

Figure 9.20   Flow control through the clist pipe

The driver maintains two `clist` structures each pointing to a single `cblock` structure. The writer can write up to 64 characters into the `clist` referenced by `writec` before the driver will invoke `sleep()`. If the reader does not find any data in the `clist` referenced by `readc` the driver will also call `sleep()`. If there is no data in `readc` or `writec`, the `pipread()` function will return.

The `pippoll()` function is called on each clock interrupt by `clock()`. It checks to see if there is space in the read buffer (`readc`). If there is space and there is data available in the write buffer (`writec`), a character is copied, the count of characters in each buffer is adjusted accordingly and any process sleeping on either of the buffers will be woken up by a call to `wakeup()`.

```
 1 #include <sys/types.h>
 2 #include <sys/user.h>
 3 #include <sys/tty.h>
 4
 5 struct clist readc ;
 6 struct clist writec ;
 7
 8 int read_count ;
 9 int write_count ;
10
11 extern struct user u ;
12
13 pipinit()
14 {
15     read_count  = 0 ;
16     write_count = 0 ;
17 }
18
19 pipintr()
20 {
21     char c ;
22     if (read_count < 64) {
23         if (write_count > 0) {
24             c = getc(&writec) ;
25             putc(c, &readc) ;
26             read_count++ ;
27             wakeup(&readc) ;
28             write_count-- ;
29             wakeup(&writec) ;
30         }
31     }
32     wakeup(&readc) ;
33     wakeup(&writec) ;
34 }
35
36 pipread()
37 {
38     int c ;
39
40     while (u.u_count) {
41         if (read_count == 0 && write_count == 0) /* pipe empty */
42             return ;
43         while (read_count == 0)
44             sleep(&readc, PZERO+1) ;
45         c = getc(&readc) ;
46         passc(c) ;
47         read_count-- ;
```

```
48      }
49  }
50
51  pipwrite()
52  {
53      int c ;
54
55      while (u.u_count) {
56          c = cpass() ;
57          putc(c, &writec) ;
58          write_count++ ;
59          if (write_count == 64)
60              sleep(&writec, PZERO+1) ;
61      }
62  }
63
64  pippoll()
65  {
66      pipintr() ;
67  }
```

When the `pipwrite()` function, shown on lines 51 to 62, is entered, it loops on
`u.u_count`, the number of characters to be written. The `cpass(K)` function is called to
read in a character from user space and adjust the u_area fields accordingly. The
`putc(K)` function is then called to add the character to the `clist`. After incrementing
`write_count`, it checks `write_count` on line 59 to see if there is space in the `cblock`
to write another character. If no space exists `sleep(K)` is called.

The `pipread()` function shown on lines 36 to 49 also loops around `u.u_count`. If
`read_count` and `write_count` are both zero the pipe is empty and `pipread()` returns.
This check could in fact be removed. In this case, the reader would wait indefinitely until
data was written into the pipe.

If the `read_count` is zero, `pipread()` invokes `sleep(K)`, otherwise `getc(K)` is
called to read a character from the `clist` and `passc(K)` is called to write the character
to user space.

The `pippoll()` function is called on each clock interrupt. It calls `pipintr()` (lines
19 to 34) to copy a character from the write buffer to the read buffer and wake any
processes which may be sleeping on either. It first checks to see if any space exists in the
read buffer and then to see if any data exists in the write buffer. To copy a character,
`pipintr()` calls `getc(K)` followed by `putc(K)`, adjusts `read_count` and
`write_count` and issues a `wakeup(K)` call on the address of both clists.

Since `pipintr()` is only called `Hz` (100) times each second, the maximum transfer
rate through the pipe is `Hz` characters per second.

The following example shows data being written into the pipe from standard input.
The contents of the pipe are then read and written to standard output.

The contents of the `/etc/passwd` are then written to the pipe. This file is greater
than 64 characters so the process will sleep. Data is then read from the pipe and written to
standard output again.

```
$ cat > /dev/pip
hello world                    # followed by a ^D
$ cat < /dev/pip
```

```
hello world
$ cat /etc/passwd > /dev/pip &
[1]  238
$ cat < /dev/pip
root:OOy160XTk8eOw,..jI:0:3:Superuser:/:
daemon:*,..:1:1:System daemons:/etc:
bin:*,..:2:2:Owner of system commands:/bin:
sys:*,..:3:3:Owner of system files:/usr/sys:
adm:*,..:4:4:System accounting:/usr/adm:
uucp:*,..:5:5:UUCP administrator:/usr/lib/uucp:

... some lines removed

spate:jA6qWCZJPPg36,..cI:13583:50:Steve Pate:/home/spate:/bin/ksh
ashley:KCawrtxjVryb2,..iI:13584:50:Ashley:/home/ashley:/tmp/msh
sam::13585:50:Sam:/home/sam:/tmp/ssh
[1] +  Done                        cat /etc/passwd > /dev/pip &
```

For the /etc/passwd example, it takes about ten seconds to read the data from the pipe even on a system with 90 MHz Pentium, 32 Mb RAM and no other system activity!

The pipintr() routine is called 100 times each second, therefore the pipe has a throughput of 100 characters per second. The /etc/passwd file is 1038 bytes in size.

In the next example, crash(ADM) is used to locate and display the readc clist and corresponding cblock. First of all, data is written to the pipe as follows:

```
$ cat /etc/passwd > /dev/pip      # the process will now sleep
```

Within crash(ADM), run from another virtual console or window, the read_count and write_count variables can be displayed with the od command. As shown, both buffers are currently full:

```
> od read_count
f0289d54:  00000040
> od write_count
f0289d58:  00000040
```

Each clist structure is three (32 bit) words in size. The contents of both the readc and writec clist structures are displayed below with od. The second word points to the first cblock used and the third word points to the last cblock used.

```
> od readc 3
f0289d68:  00000040   fc0d0910   fc0d0910
> od writec 3
f0289d5c:  00000040   fc0d0ac0   fc0d0ac0
```

Since only 64 characters can be written, each clist is associated with one cblock. Both cblock structures are displayed using the cblock command in crash(ADM) as follows:

```
> cblock -f @fc0d0910      # readc
SLOT     ADDRESS          NEXT  FIRST  LAST
 -     0xfc0d0910           0     0    64
  72 6f 6f 74 3a 78 3a 30 3a 33 3a 53 75 70 65 72      root:x:0:3:Super
  75 73 65 72 3a 2f 3a 0a 64 61 65 6d 6f 6e 3a 78      user:/:.daemon:x
```

```
3a 31 3a 31 3a 53 79 73 74 65 6d 20 64 61 65 6d          :1:1:System.daem
6f 6e 73 3a 2f 65 74 63 3a 0a 62 69 6e 3a 78 3a          ons:/etc:.bin:x:

> cblock -f @fc0d0ac0          # writec
SLOT      ADDRESS          NEXT FIRST LAST
  -       0xfc0d0ac0          0    0    64
32 3a 32 3a 4f 77 6e 65 72 20 6f 66 20 73 79 73          2:2:Owner.of.sys
74 65 6d 20 63 6f 6d 6d 61 6e 64 73 3a 2f 62 69          tem.commands:/bi
6e 3a 0a 73 79 73 3a 78 3a 33 3a 33 3a 4f 77 6e          n:.sys:x:3:3:Own
65 72 20 6f 66 20 73 79 73 74 65 6d 20 66 69 6c          er.of.system.fil
```

There are a number of flaws with this driver, including an unnecessary call to sleep(K).
A number of methods could be used to increase performance although still using clists.
Are read_count and write_count required, for example?

Readers may wish to spend time with this driver to see what benefits can be achieved.
It is also interesting to add printf(K) statements to pipread() and pipwrite() and
run different utilities such as cat(C), more(C), dd(C) and so on to see how much data
they request in single reads or writes.

9.7 The TTY (teletype) subsystem

Rather than diving straight into the complex world of serial I/O drivers, line disciplines,
canonical and raw mode and other such terminology, terminal I/O is best understood by
describing what the user sees: the keyboard and the screen.

This section concentrates on the user interface to the machine, the keyboard and
monitor. The console driver, the structures used to manage virtual consoles and the flow
control through the kernel in response to user generated actions is described.

Kettle and Statler (1992) provide a complete serial driver for SCO UNIX which
makes use of line discipline 0, the TTY line discipline described in this chapter.

9.7.1 TTY access following kernel initialisation

All UNIX systems require a system console, often simply called the console and referred
to by its device name, /dev/console. This is the device which is used by the system
administrator for system maintenance operations. It is also the TTY to which the first
shell is attached when in single user mode.

One of the first tasks performed by init is to process the sysinit entries in
/etc/inittab. If the default init level is single user, init will fork(S) and
exec(S) the sulogin(ADM) program. This displays the familiar message:

```
Type CONTROL-d to proceed with normal startup.
(or give root password for system maintenance):
```

The sulogin(ADM) process opens /dev/tty for reading which is also established as the
process's controlling TTY. If the root password is entered, sulogin will call exec(S) to
create a shell which calls dup(S) to allocate file descriptors for stdout and stderr.

The example shows this shell process:

```
# ps -ef
    UID    PID  PPID  C    STIME     TTY        TIME CMD
    root     1     0  0 09:26:21       ?    00:00:00 /etc/init
    root    83     1  0 09:27:44 console    00:00:00 -
    root   108    83  6 09:32:10 console    00:00:00 ps -ef
```

The TTY field shows the controlling TTY which can be seen from within crash(ADM) by analysing the shell process. The user command is used to display part of the u_area for the process.

```
> user #83 ! head -15
PER PROCESS USER AREA FOR PROCESS 7
USER ID's:  uid: 0, gid: 3, real uid: 0, real gid: 3
    supplementary gids:
PROCESS TIMES:      user: 6, sys: 11, child user: 55, child sys: 100
PROCESS MISC:
    command: sh, psargs: -
    proc: P#7, cntrl tty:   3,1
    start: Sat Jan 20 09:27:44 1996
    mem: 0x85f, type: exec su-user
    proc/text lock: none
    current directory: I#42
OPEN FILES AND POFILE FLAGS:
    [ 0]: F#10   r   [ 1]: F#10      w  [ 2]: F#10      w
FILE I/O:
    u_base: 0xe0000d3d, file offset: 284, bytes: 16
```

This shows the process's open file descriptors and the device number of the controlling TTY, all of which are highlighted.

The file and inode commands can be used to see which file is accessed by all three file descriptors as follows:

```
> file 10
FILE TABLE SIZE = 341
SLOT  RCNT   I/FL       OFFSET  FLAGS
  10      8 I# 136       26779 read write
> inode 136
INODE TABLE SIZE = 204
SLOT MAJ/MIN FS INUMB RCNT LINK UID  GID  SIZE    MODE MNT M/ST FLAGS
 136   1,42  1    70    2    1   2   15     0 c---000   0   -  up ac ch
> q
# ls -li /dev/console
   70 crw-------   3 bin     terminal   3,  1 Jan 20 09:32 /dev/console
```

As shown, the open files correspond to the device, /dev/console. The /dev/tty device which was opened by sulogin(ADM) is used to establish connection to the controlling TTY. This is shown in section 9.7.5.

9.7.2 Multi-user TTY access

When the system goes to multi-user mode, the following lines in the inittab(F) file are processed by init, each of which creates a getty process to control the TTY devices

tty01 up to tty12. This establishes 12 virtual consoles which are accessible by the
<Control-Alt-Fn> key sequence.

```
co:2345:respawn:/etc/getty tty01 sc_m
co2:2345:respawn:/etc/getty tty02 sc_m
co3:2345:respawn:/etc/getty tty03 sc_m
     .
     .
     .
co11:2345:respawn:/etc/getty tty11 sc_m
co12:2345:respawn:/etc/getty tty12 sc_m
```

Each getty will sit waiting for input after which it will invoke login(M) to request and
then validate the password entered which in turn exec's the user's shell.

All 12 virtual consoles are handled by a single console driver which is responsible for
driving the keyboard and display adapter. Figure 9.21 shows the relationship between the
virtual and physical consoles.

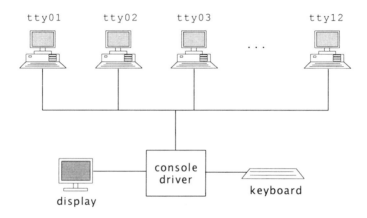

Figure 9.21   The console driver supporting 12 virtual consoles

Only one virtual console is active at any one time. The internal operations performed
by the console driver are described in section 9.7.6.

9.7.3 Logging in to UNIX

Consider the getty process that is run and passed the tty01 argument. At this stage
there is no concept of stdin, stdout or stderr. When the getty process is started it
opens the device passed as an argument, in this case /dev/tty01.

The getty process displays the familiar login: prompt and waits for input. Using
crash(ADM) on another virtual console, the process's files, controlling TTY and the
event on which the process is sleeping can be displayed.

The getty process must be first located using the proc command as follows:

```
> proc ! grep getty
    7 s    772    1    772    0   75    0 cn_tty                getty        load
   11 s    675    1    675    0   75    0 cn_tty+0x68           getty        load
   14 s    676    1    676    0   75    0 cn_tty+0xd0           getty        load
   18 s    679    1    679    0   75    0 cn_tty+0x138          getty        load
```

There are four `getty`s, each corresponding to the four multiscreens that have been spawned on the machine used. Since the `getty` that is being examined is the first entry processed in /etc/inittab, the process in slot 7 is assumed to be correct. The process is currently sleeping, having specified the address of cn_tty as the argument to sleep().

The user command is then invoked within crash(ADM) to display the per process open files. Those fields of the u_area which are of interest are highlighted:

```
> user 7 ! head -15
PER PROCESS USER AREA FOR PROCESS 7
USER ID's:  uid: 0, gid: 0, real uid: 0, real gid: 0
     supplementary gids:
PROCESS TIMES:     user: 73, sys: 47, child user: 58, child sys: 30
PROCESS MISC:
     command: getty, psargs: /etc/getty tty01 sc_m
     proc: P#7, cntrl tty:   0,0
     start: Fri Jun 16 12:42:35 1995
     mem: 0x456c, type: exec
     proc/text lock: none
     current directory: I#196
OPEN FILES AND POFILE FLAGS:
     [ 0]: F#38    r    [ 1]: F#38        [ 2]: F#38        w
FILE I/O:
     u_base: 0x8056136, file offset: 59, bytes: 1
```

The psargs field confirms that the correct process has been found.

At this stage, getty has opened the specified TTY device passed as an argument and established the file descriptors which will be used to form stdin, stdout and stderr. Since the file opened is a device file, it is established as a controlling terminal as displayed in the cntrl tty field.

The file table and inode table entries for the process are:

```
> file 38
FILE TABLE SIZE = 341
SLOT  RCNT   I/FL        OFFSET  FLAGS
   38    3 I# 141            59 read write
> inode 141
INODE TABLE SIZE = 204
SLOT MAJ/MIN FS INUMB RCNT LINK    UID   GID  SIZE    MODE MNT M/ST FLAGS
 141  1,42  1    28    1    1      2    15     0 c---000   0   -
> !ncheck -i 28
/dev/root:
28   /dev/tty01
```

Performing the same set of operations for each of the other getty processes will yield similar results; each getty will be waiting for input on the device passed.

9.7.4 The controlling TTY

Section 7.7 described the associations between sessions, process groups and the controlling TTY which are established when a user logs into the system. The device driver corresponding to the controlling TTY plays an important role in a login session. It must be capable of generating signals corresponding to certain key sequences. For example, control-C (or the Delete key) generates SIGINT and control-\ generates SIGQUIT.

Information describing the relationship between the process and its controlling TTY is held in three fields in the u_area:

short	*u_ttyp	Pointer to the t_pgrp field in the device's tty structure.
inode_t	*u_ttyip	Inode of the controlling TTY.
dev_t	u_ttyd	The controlling TTY device.

The u_ttyp field is used by the terminal driver to send signals to all processes in the foreground process group. The u_ttyd field contains the device number of the controlling TTY. It is used when accessing /dev/tty to determine the real driver that should be called to perform I/O.

9.7.5 The indirect terminal driver

There are times when a process may wish to determine its controlling TTY, whether to set specific terminal characteristics or simply to read or write characters. When a process is invoked, file descriptors 0, 1 and 2 may not reference the controlling TTY and the process may wish to write an error message. A typical example of where this occurs is when using redirection. For example, consider the following command:

```
$ cat fileA > fileB
```

The standard output of cat(C) is set to point to fileB. Writing an error message to file descriptor 1 will result in the message being written to fileB.

The isatty(S) and ttyname(S) system calls can be used to determine whether the specified file descriptor is associated with a TTY and the name of the TTY, respectively. For example, consider the following program:

```
#include <unistd.h>

main()
{
    if (isatty(0) == 1) {
        printf("fd 0 is a tty [%s]\n", ttyname(0)) ;

    }
}
```

If file descriptor 0, traditionally `stdin`, is a TTY, the TTY name is printed. The output of the program for one particular run is:

```
fd 0 is a tty [/dev/tty04]
```

The device file `/dev/tty` can be opened by any process to obtain a file descriptor corresponding to the controlling TTY. This allows the `cat(C)` command to write an appropriate error message.

The driver used when accessing `/dev/tty` is the `sy` character driver which has a major number of 3 and is also accessed when any of the following devices are opened:

```
crw-------    3 bin      terminal   3,   1 Jun 16 17:14 console
crw-------    3 bin      terminal   3,   1 Jun 16 17:14 syscon
crw-------    3 bin      terminal   3,   1 Jun 16 17:14 systty
crw-rw-rw-    1 bin      terminal   3,   0 Jun 16 17:10 tty
```

When `syopen()` is invoked as a result of opening any one of the four devices listed, it checks to see if the minor device number corresponds to either `console`, `syscon` or `systty`. In this case the driver whose major number corresponds to the major number of the kernel `systty` variable is invoked. This is set to zero during kernel initialisation to reference the console driver which is described in the next section.

When `/dev/tty` is opened, `syopen()` ensures that the process issuing the `open(S)` has an associated controlling terminal by looking at the `u_ttyp` field of the u_area. If there is no controlling TTY associated with the process, `EIO` is returned.

If the process has an associated controlling TTY, the driver whose major number is held in `u.u_ttyd` has its `XXopen()` function invoked. All reads and writes are then routed to the correct device.

9.7.6 The console driver

The console driver manages the keyboard and display adapter and is multiplexed between a number of different virtual consoles or multiscreens.

The characters read from the keyboard are said to be read in *raw mode*. The keyboard driver component of the console driver sees all key depresses, shift keys, the control key, function keys and so on. Raw mode is also called *non-canonical mode*.

The data which is read by most programs, and indeed by the user, has been processed into *cooked* or *canonical mode*. Processes issuing read requests when the console driver is operating in canonical mode will always receive one line of data at a time. Canonical mode processing is set by default.

Associated with most serial drivers, including the console, are a *line discipline* and `tty` structure which are used to provide a set of common operations to be performed on data being read or written, for example:

- Handling of the backspace character.
- Enabling and disabling echo.

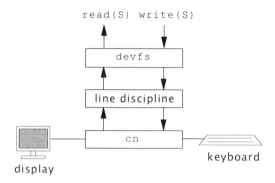

Figure 9.22   Logical position of the line discipline and console driver (cn)

- Flow control with XON and XOFF.
- Signal generation.

These are some of the common options that are applicable to most serial line drivers. To provide this common, shared set of services that are available to device driver writers, a number of different *line discipline modules* are available in the kernel. Each line discipline logically sits between the user and the device driver as shown in Figure 9.22.

A process has the option of controlling the characteristics of the console driver. For example, editors such as vi(C) require that characters are read in raw mode. This allows vi(C) to interpret various control and escape sequences as part of its command set.

Each line discipline is described by a linesw structure which is shown in Table 9.6. The details of each function will be described later when discussing *line discipline 0* which is used by the console driver.

Table 9.6   Entry points exported by line discipline modules

linesw structure field	Description
int (*l_open)()	This function is called from XXopen() each time a device is opened.
int (*l_close)()	Called by XXclose() on the last close of the device.
int (*l_read)()	Data is transferred to the user in response to a read(S) request. The data can be in either raw or canonical form.
int (*l_write)()	This function is called to copy characters from user space.
int (*l_ioctl)()	Called in response to an ioctl(S) system call to specify characteristics of the line, flush data and so on.
int (*l_input)()	This function is called on input to remove characters read from the device to a queue of raw characters.
int (*l_output)()	Called to move characters into the buffer of characters ready to be written to the device.

There are a total of `linecnt` different line disciplines in the released operating system although more line disciplines may be added as needed.

Each line discipline is held in the `linesw[]` array. An open of line discipline 0 is performed by indexing the 0th element of the `linesw[]` array and calling `l_open()`. The line discipline names are held in the `line_names[]` array declared in `pack.d/kernel/space.c` as follows:

```
char line_names[][LDNAMEMAX] = {
        "tty",              /* 0 */
        "sxt",              /* 1 */
        "evld",             /* 2 */
        "xt",               /* 3 */
        "slip",             /* 4 */
        "ppp",              /* 5 */
        "svid",             /* 6 */
};
```

Most line disciplines communicate with the underlying character driver through a set of interfaces and a `tty` structure which is used for buffering raw and canonical data to be read from and written to the device. The fields of the `tty` structure are used by both the driver and the line discipline although many fields in the `tty` structure are used only by the line discipline.

Some fields are formed as a bit-wise OR of various flags, describing properties such as how the input characters should be transformed, whether echoing is enabled and which control sequences generate signals. For a full description of each flag see the `termio(M)` and `stty(C)` manual pages.

Some of the fields of the `tty` structure are as follows:

struct clist t_rawq

When data is read from the device it is often placed in a temporary buffer used internally by the driver at interrupt time, usually the `t_rbuf clist`. The driver moves data from `t_rbuf` to the `t_rawq clist` by invoking the line discipline's `l_input()` function. Characters are not processed, with the exception of removing parity and so on. If raw mode is requested, the characters stored in the `t_rawq clist` will be returned to the user when the user calls `read(S)`.

struct clist t_canq

If characters are being read in canonical mode they will be moved from the `t_rawq clist` onto `t_canq` with various transformations applied which depend on the line discipline used.

struct clist t_outq

The `t_outq clist` holds the characters to be output to the device. Characters are placed on the queue by the line discipline. The driver will read characters from `t_outq` to output them to the device. If echoing is enabled, the driver will also add characters to this list during interrupt processing when characters are read.

`struct ccblock t_tbuf`

> Characters are copied into this buffer from `t_outq`. The driver calls the line discipline's `l_output()` function to perform the transfer.

`struct ccblock t_rbuf`

> This is an intermediate buffer used by the driver's interrupt routine when reading characters from the device. The characters will be copied from here to `t_rawq` by `l_input` as described above.

`int (* t_proc)()`

> A serial driver must provide an `XXproc()` entry point which is stored in this field. This function is used by the line discipline to call the driver when it needs to alter the control flow. For example, if characters are being received from the device quicker than they can be stored in `t_rawq`, `XXproc()` will be invoked to ask the driver to suspend input.

`ushort t_iflag`

> This field specifies the input modes of the line. There are a number of flags which specify properties such as checking of parity, using only the first 7 bits of each character and transforming upper case to lower case.

`ushort t_oflag`

> This field specifies the output modes of the line, for example mapping a carriage return and newline to a newline character. This field is managed by the line discipline.

`ushort t_cflag`

> This field specifies the status of the line, for example the baud rate, character size, parity generation and so on.

`ushort t_lflag`

> This field is used internally by the line discipline to hold status flags such as whether echoing is enabled, data read should be in raw or canonical mode and so on.

`short t_state`

> The status of the driver is described by this field, for example whether the line is open, output is in progress, output has been stopped by `control-s` and so on.

`short t_pgrp`

> This field is used to record the foreground process group. It can be checked by the line discipline to determine whether a background process is trying to read from or write to the TTY, and generate `SIGTTIN` or `SIGTTOU` as appropriate.

`char t_line`

> This field is used by the driver to specify which line discipline is being used.

```
unsigned char t_cc[NCC+5]
```

This field contains the current values of the settable control characters. For example, which control sequence will generate SIGINT, SIGQUIT and the job control signals.

The tty structure for a particular type of device can be displayed from within crash(ADM) using the tty command. By default, the tty structures for the console multiscreens are displayed.

In the following example, the -t option is used to specify that the tty structures associated with the console driver (cn) should be displayed. On the system where the example was run, the entries in /etc/inittab corresponding to tty06 to tty12 have been removed. For the five active virtual consoles, the process group associated with each one is displayed.

```
> tty -tcn
cn TABLE SIZE = 12
SLOT OUT RAW CAN DEL   PGRP STATE
   0   0   0   0   0    214 isop carr islp
   1   0   0   0   0    199 isop carr islp
   2   0   0   0   0    200 isop carr islp
   3   0   0   0   0    223 isop carr islp
   4   0   0   0   0    297 isop carr islp
   5   0   0   0   0      0 carr
   6   0   0   0   0      0 carr
   7   0   0   0   0      0 carr
   8   0   0   0   0      0 carr
   9   0   0   0   0      0 carr
  10   0   0   0   0      0 carr
  11   0   0   0   0      0 carr
```

In the next example, the -f option and -p option are used to display one entry in full. The tty structure for /dev/tty01 is displayed here:

```
> tty -f -tcn -p 0
cn TABLE SIZE = 12
SLOT OUT RAW CAN DEL   PGRP STATE
   0   0   0   0   0    214 isop carr islp
     rawq.cf:          0, rawq.cl:        0
     canq.cf:          0, canq.cl:        0
     outq.cf:          0, outq.cl:        0
                 c_ptr   count   size
     tbuf:   0xfc0d0efe      0      0
     rbuf:   0xfc0d0f8e     64     64
             proc line term    termflag col row vrow lrow hqcnt dstat
            cnproc   0    0          0   7   0    0    0     0     0
     intr:     ^C    quit:     ^\    erase:    ^H   kill:    ^U
     eof:      ^[    eol:      ^M    eol2:     ^D   swtch:   ^@
     susp:     ^Z    start:    ^Q    stop:     ^S   ceof:    ^@
     ceol:     ^@
     iflag: brkint ignpar inlcr ixon ixany
     oflag: opost onlcr nl0 cr0 tab0 bs0 vt0 ff0
     cflag: b9600 cs8 cread hupcl
     lflag: isig icanon echo echoe echok
```

Toolkit 9.6 shows how the fields of the tty structure can be changed by simple operations and subsequently displayed from within crash(ADM).

9.7.7 Flow control through the console driver

To illustrate how the `tty` structure is used between the console (`cn`) driver and the line discipline, this section describes the flow of control between the user and the driver, and how the console driver interacts with both the hardware and the line discipline 0.

Opening `/dev/tty`

An `open(S)` system call specifying `/dev/tty` will involve a call to `namei()` to resolve the pathname. Since this is a device file, a `devfs` inode will be returned such that all further operations will be directed through `devfs` rather than through the filesystem owning the namespace where the device name resides.

Following resolution of the pathname, the device open function, `cnopen()`, is called to perform device specific initialisation. The `cnopen()` function uses the minor device number passed to determine which multiscreen the open has been called for. Associated with each multiscreen is an `mscrn` structure which holds a pointer to a per multiscreen `tty` structure. This is shown in Figure 9.23.

`cnopen()` uses the minor number held in the `u_ttyd` field of the u_area to locate the `tty` structure and examines the `t_state` field to see if the device is already open (`ISOPEN`). For a first open, `cnopen()` calls the kernel routine `ttinit(K)` passing a `tty` structure as an argument. `ttinit(K)` initialises the `tty` structure for use with line discipline 0. For details of the functions performed by `ttinit(K)` see `tty(K_TTY)`. The `t_line` field of the `tty` structure is set to 0 to ensure that subsequent calls through the `linesw[]` array will invoke the correct line discipline.

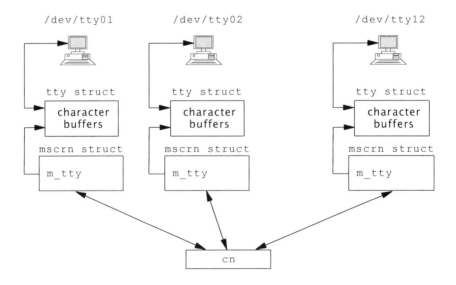

Figure 9.23   Data structures used by the cn driver for each multiscreen

Following initialisation, or if the device is already open, cnopen() calls the l_open() function as follows:

```
(*linesw[tp->t_line].l_open)(tp)
```

This calls the ttopen(K_TTY) function of line discipline 0 which sets the t_pgrp field of the tty structure to the process group ID of the process which is opening the device. Any subsequent key sequences which will generate signals will be sent to this process group. The t_state field is then set to ISOPEN.

Reading from /dev/tty

A read(S) system call will be routed through devfs into the cnread() entry point of the console driver. This performs a call through linesw[] to the ttread() function.

The first task performed is a check to ensure that the process can read from the device. Processes running in the background which attempt to read from the device will be sent a SIGTTIN signal.

The data to be read can be either raw or canonical. If there is no data on the t_canq clist, ttread() invokes the kernel canon(K_TTY) routine to copy characters from the t_rawq clist to the t_canq clist. The canon(K_TTY) function will continue to copy characters until a delimiter (end of line character) is received.

If the ICANON flag is set in the t_lflag field of the tty structure, the data should be read in canonical mode. In this case, canon() must process characters such as backspace and delete before returning them to the user.

The control flow from cnread() through ttread() is summarised in Figure 9.24.

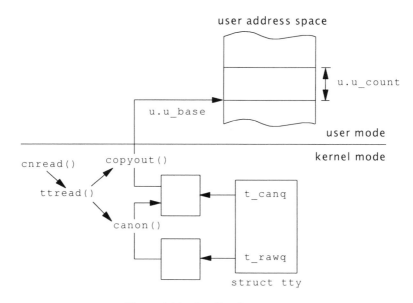

Figure 9.24   Reading from /dev/tty

Writing to /dev/tty

A write(S) system call will be routed through devfs into the cnwrite() entry point of the console driver. This performs a call through linesw[] to the ttwrite() function.

The first task performed is to check to ensure that the process can write to the device. Processes which are running in the background which attempt to write to the device will be sent a SIGTTOU signal.

If there is no space left on the t_outq clist, ttwrite() will call the console driver's cnproc() function, accessible via the t_proc field of the tty structure, with the T_OUTPUT command. The cnproc() function calls ttout() through the line switch l_output field. This copies data from t_outq to the output buffer t_tbuf before writing the data to the device.

Once space is available on t_outq, ttwrite() will copy the data from user space to temporarily allocated cblocks. The ttxput(K_TTY) function is then called to copy the characters from the temporary buffer to t_outq.

The flow of control from cnwrite() through the ttwrite() function is summarised in Figure 9.25.

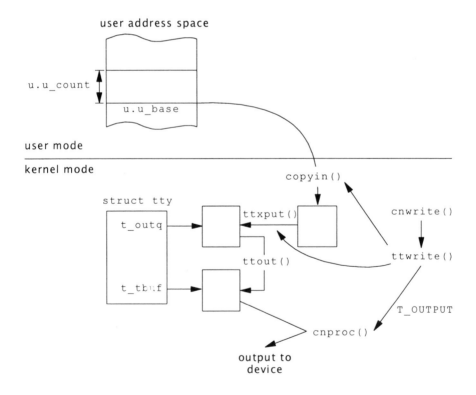

Figure 9.25   Writing to /dev/tty

Ioctl operations on `/dev/tty`

User processes can alter a large number of characteristics of the TTY line. Some of these characteristics are specific to the console driver such as the setting of display modes and fonts, or reading keyboard or display specific information.

Some of the characteristics are handled by the line discipline such as the ability to determine whether data can be read from the device without blocking, checking whether data is waiting to be read, setting or retrieving attributes such as the input and output modes and altering control sequences.

The `ioctl(S)` system call is routed through `devfs` to the `cnioctl()` driver entry point. A check is made to see if the ioctl is specific to the console driver and if so, it is processed internally within the driver.

For ioctl commands that are general purpose terminal I/O controls, `cnioctl()` will call the `ttiocom(K_TTY)` kernel function to handle the command.

Some of the ioctls supported by `ttiocom(K_TTY)` are:

`IOC_SELECT`	This determines whether a character can be read from or written to the TTY device without blocking. The `ttselect(K_TTY)` function is invoked by `ttiocom(K_TTY)` to perform the check.
`TCSETA` `TCGETA`	These two commands set or retrieve TTY attributes such as the input and output modes, control modes and control characters. `ttiocom(K_TTY)` calls `cnproc()` to process the commands.
`TCXONC`	This is used to suspend output or restart suspended output. It is usually invoked in response to ^S and ^Q. `ttiocom(K_TTY)` calls `cnproc()` to process these commands.

For a complete list of supported ioctl commands see `ttiocom(K_TTY)`.

Reading and writing from and to the device

Keystrokes will result in a keyboard interrupt which is handled by the `cnintr()` function which calls `kbintr()` to process the interrupt.

Characters are copied onto the `t_rbuf` clist in the `tty` structure by the interrupt handler at the time the interrupt is being processed.

If the device is open, the `l_input()` line discipline function is called to transfer any characters from `t_rbuf` to `t_rawq`. The line discipline routine called is `ttin(K_TTY)`. If the characters need to generate signals, `ttin()` will post the signals. If echoing is enabled, `ttin()` will call `ttxput(K_TTY)` to add the character to the `t_outq` clist ready to be output.

If the number of characters in the `t_rawq` buffer exceeds a high water mark, `cnproc()` is called with the `T_BLOCK` command to suspend input. The `cnproc()` function is then called with the `T_OUTPUT` command to request that the driver starts I/O. This ensures that any characters to be echoed will be output immediately.

Figure 9.26 summarises the flow of control through the various buffers.

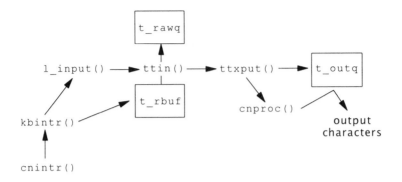

Figure 9.26   Handling keyboard interrupts in the console driver

Toolkit 9.6   Analysing flow control through /dev/tty01

The examples provided in this toolkit use the `tty` and `cblock` commands in `crash(ADM)` to show the effects on the `tty` structure associated with tty01 by invoking simple operations including `cat(C)` to display a file and hitting the space bar a few times to move the cursor!

The intention behind the toolkit is to encourage the reader to try different combinations of key sequences, `stty(C)` commands and so on to observe their effect.

First of all, the `tty` structure associated with tty01 is displayed in full. Note that `crash` should be run on another virtual console.

```
> tty -f -tcn -p 0
cn TABLE SIZE = 12
SLOT OUT RAW CAN DEL  PGRP STATE
   0   0   0   0   0    214 isop carr islp
   rawq.cf:          0, rawq.cl:       0
   canq.cf:          0, canq.cl:       0
   outq.cf:          0, outq.cl:       0
               c_ptr  count  size
   tbuf:  0xfc0d0efe     0      0
   rbuf:  0xfc0d0f8e    64     64
        proc line term   termflag col row vrow lrow hqcnt dstat
        cnproc   0    0          0   2   0    0    0     0     0
   intr:    ^C   quit:     ^\    erase:   ^H   kill:    ^U
   eof:     ^[   eol:      ^M    eol2:    ^D   swtch:   ^@
   susp:    ^Z   start:    ^Q    stop:    ^S   ceof:    ^@
   ceol:    ^@
   iflag: brkint ignpar inlcr ixon ixany
   oflag: opost onlcr nl0 cr0 tab0 bs0 vt0 ff0
   cflag: b9600 cs8 cread hupcl
   lflag: isig icanon echo echoe echok
```

At this stage there is no activity on tty01. The $ prompt is displayed and the cursor is blinking in column 2 as shown in the line highlighted in the `crash` output.

Switching temporarily to `tty01` and hitting the space bar eight times shows the alteration in the column number in the `tty` structure:

```
> tty -f -tcn -p 0 ! grep cnproc
        cnproc   0    0           0  10   0    0    0    0    0
```

Running `vi(C)` in `tty01` produces a number of changes. Where lines differ from the full `tty` structure listing shown above they are listed below:

```
>    intr:   ^C   quit:   none   erase:   ^H   kill:   ^U
>    min=    1    time=   1      eol2:    ^@   swtch:  ^@
>    susp:   none start:  ^Q     stop:    ^S   ceof:   ^@
>    iflag: brkint ignpar ixon ixany
>    oflag: opost nl0 cr0 tab0 bs0 vt0 ff0
>    lflag: isig echoe echok
```

Note the removal of canonical mode processing, allowing `vi(C)` to interpret various escape and control sequences which it uses as commands.

The final example requires displaying a file on `tty01` using `cat(C)` and hitting the stop key, usually `control-S`. This allows the `cblock` command to be used to display the contents of the `t_outq` clist.

Displaying part of the `tty` structure after the output has been stopped shows that the state of the line has been changed to `stop` and the `t_outq` clist references a linked list of `cblock` structures which contain characters to be output when output is restarted:

```
> tty -f -tcn -p 0 ! head -6
cn TABLE SIZE = 12
SLOT OUT RAW CAN DEL  PGRP STATE
   0 261   0   0   0   345 isop carr oslp stop
     rawq.cf:           0, rawq.cl:          0
     canq.cf:           0, canq.cl:          0
     outq.cf: 0xfc0d0e68, outq.cl: 0xfc0d0d90
```

The `outq.cf` field contains a pointer to the first `cblock` containing data to be displayed. The `outq.cl` contains a pointer to the last `cblock` in the list. For details of how the `cblock` structures are linked together see Figure 9.19.

The contents of the first `cblock` referenced are displayed using the `cblock` command as follows:

```
> cblock -f @fc0d0e68
SLOT      ADDRESS           NEXT   FIRST  LAST
  -     0xfc0d0e68   0xfc0d0be0      0     64
  6c 65 67 65 73 3a 2f 3a 2f 62 69 6e 2f 66 61 6c  leges:/:/bin/fal
  73 65 0d 0a 6c 69 73 74 65 6e 3a 2a 3a 33 37 3a  se..listen:*:37:
  34 3a 4e 65 74 77 6f 72 6b 20 64 61 65 6d 6f 6e  4:Network.daemon
  73 3a 2f 75 73 72 2f 6e 65 74 2f 6e 6c 73 3a 0d  s:/usr/net/nls:.
```

The NEXT field specifies the address of the next `cblock` on the list. Since this differs from `outq.cl`, there are at least three `cblock` structures containing data to be displayed. The chain can be followed by repeated calls to `cblock`.

The following section covers the functions available to a user process for providing control over a TTY line.

9.7.8 Process control of /dev/tty

The termios(S) manual page lists a number of functions which can be used by user programs to control serial ports and in particular the TTY device with which they are associated.

The tcgetattr(S) and tcsetattr(S) functions are used to get and set the terminal attributes for the device corresponding to the file descriptor passed. Both functions use the termios structure as shown in Table 9.7.

Table 9.7   The termios structure used for setting and retrieving TTY attributes

Fields of the termios structure		Description
tcflag_t	c_iflag	The TTY's input modes corresponding to the t_iflag field of the tty structure.
tcflag_t	c_oflag	The TTY's output modes corresponding to the t_oflag field of the tty structure.
tcflag_t	c_cflag	The TTY's control modes corresponding to the t_cflag field of the tty structure.
tcflag_t	c_lflag	The local (line discipline) modes which correspond to the t_lflag field of the tty structure.
char	c_line	The line discipline associated with the TTY device or a new line discipline for the TTY device to use.
cc_t	c_cc[NCCS]	The TTY's settable control characters which correspond to the t_cc field of the tty structure.

Each of the fields of the termios structure corresponds to the line discipline fields described earlier. Shown below is a skeleton program for retrieving terminal attributes.

```
#include <termios.h>
#include <fcntl.h>

main()
{
    int fd ;
    struct termios gattr ;

    fd = open("/dev/tty", O_RDONLY) ;
    if (fd < 0)
        pexit("/dev/tty") ;

    if (tcgetattr(fd, &gattr) != 0)
        pexit("tcgetattr") ;
}
```

Both the tcgetattr(S) and tcsetattr(S) functions work by calling the ioctl(S) system call which ends up in the console driver. Figure 9.27 shows the flow control from the user process.

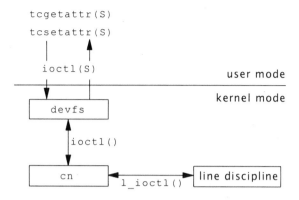

Figure 9.27   Setting and retrieving TTY attributes

The console driver performs little else other than to invoke the line discipline `l_ioctl()` function. The setting and retrieving of attributes is then dealt with by the line discipline.

A number of other general terminal interface functions are available for setting attributes of the TTY line. Some of these functions are listed below. See `termios(M)` and `stty(C)` for further information.

`tcdrain(S)`	The `tcdrain(S)` function waits until all output written to the specified file descriptor has been transmitted.
`tcflow(S)`	The flow of control of data can be stopped and started by `tcflow(S)`.
`tcflush(S)`	Any data that has been written to the specified TTY but has not yet been transmitted is discarded by `tcflush(S)`.
`tcgetpgrp(S)`	This function returns the foreground process group ID of the TTY specified by the file descriptor passed.
`tcsetpgrp(S)`	This function sets the foreground process group ID of the TTY specified by the file descriptor. The TTY must be the controlling terminal of the calling process and must also be currently associated with the session of the calling process.

9.8 Pseudo TTYs

A *pseudo TTY* is a special device which behaves in a similar manner to a pipe. Although it is used as a mechanism to communicate between two processes, its main use is in simulating a TTY device, including mode setting, interrupts and multiple end of files, all of which are not possible on a pipe. Pseudo TTYs are an often used but mysterious feature of the operating system in that they are neither well documented nor well understood. This section provides an insight into their operation.

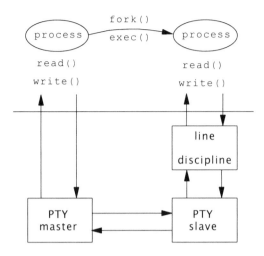

Figure 9.28 Logical flow control through a pseudo TTY

The previous sections described the case where the user is sitting in front of a physical terminal. Input and output are directed through the console driver with support from the TTY line discipline.

When a user logs into the system over the network, pseudo TTYs are used to simulate a TTY device such that to the user there appears to be no difference between a real terminal and the pseudo terminal created for the network login. For example, control over line discipline settings described earlier are supported, signals will be generated in response to certain key sequences and so on.

The pseudo TTY driver can be viewed as two separate drivers. One driver is the device which looks like a TTY, called the *slave device*, and has routines which are prefixed with spt (*slave pseudo TTY*). The other driver is called the *master device*, and its routines are prefixed by mpt (*master pseudo TTY*). Details of the driver interfaces and internals are described later.

Figure 9.28 shows the logical flow of control using a pseudo TTY. The process created on the right-hand side of the figure has control over the line discipline settings as per a normal TTY connection.

Pseudo TTYs are used for a number of purposes including the ability to login from another machine using telnet(TC) and rlogin(TC), X Windows xterms and the script(TC) command, for which a similar program will be presented later in Toolkit 9.7.

In order to show a practical use of pseudo TTYs, consider the case where a user logs in from another machine as shown in Figure 9.29. This command involves a message sent over TCP/IP which is received by the rlogind daemon which processes the request and establishes the login session.

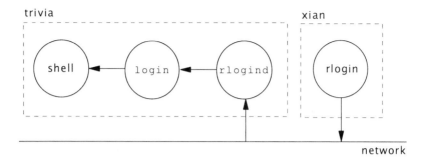

Figure 9.29   Invocation of the `rlogin(TC)` command

Using `ps(C)`, the two processes which are in existence once the connection has been established can be examined as shown below. The `login` process is run to prompt for a password and validate the password typed. The shell is then created.

```
$ ps -ef -ouser,pid,ppid,tty,args

root   694 693 ttyp5 login -r xian.london.sco.COM spate spate -c xterm
spate  695 694 ttyp5 -ksh
```

Using `crash(ADM)`, more information can be obtained about the process. The relevant fields of the u_area displayed below show the process's controlling TTY and open file descriptors:

```
> user #695
PER PROCESS USER AREA FOR PROCESS 69
...
        proc: P#69, cntrl tty:  58,5
...
OPEN FILES AND POFILE FLAGS:
        [ 0]: F#289   r    [ 1]: F#289      w  [ 2]: F#289      w
        [31]: F#301 c r w
```

When the shell is exec'd the file descriptors assigned to `stdin`, `stdout` and `stderr` correspond to the pseudo TTY as the following output from `crash` shows:

```
> file 289
FILE TABLE SIZE = 341
SLOT  RCNT   I/FL      OFFSET  FLAGS
 289     6 I# 273       5952 read write
> inode -f 273
INODE TABLE SIZE = 665
SLOT MAJ/MIN FS INUMB RCNT LINK   UID   GID  SIZE    MODE MNT M/ST FLAGS
 273   1,42  1    70    1    1 13853    15     0 c---000   0    -
           FORW    BACK AFOR ABCK   MAPPAGES        RDLOCKS           WANT
           273     273    -    -          0               0
           RMAJ/MIN    FSTYPP       FSPTR   FILOCKS      VCODE WCNT FS
             58,5  0xf018d560 0xf0897e00         0           0    1 DEVFS
```

The in-core inode is owned by `devfs`. The major and minor numbers of the device are `58,5` which correspond to the controlling TTY shown. The device name can be found in `/dev` as follows:

```
crw-------   1 spate     terminal  58,  5 Jan 29 08:50 /dev/ttyp5
```

The `spt` driver is used to implement pseudo TTYs and interacts with the TTY line discipline to provide terminal emulation including signal handling.

9.8.1 Accessing pseudo TTYs

To allocate a pseudo TTY, a process must first locate an unused master device entry in `/dev`. The number of pseudo TTYs is configurable. Each master device is accessed by the name `ptypX` where `X` is the same as the minor number of the device. For example:

```
crw-------   1 root      root       59,  5 Jan 29 08:50 /dev/ptyp5
```

A process must iterate through the list of `ptyp` entries invoking the `open(S)` system call on each successive device until an open is successful.

The next step is for the process to `fork(S)` and for the child to open the slave half of the device. If the parent was successful in opening `/dev/ptyp5`, the child should open the slave device `/dev/ttyp5`. There is no guarantee that the open will succeed other than an undocumented protocol between applications using pseudo TTYs that the master half of the device will always be opened first.

Once the open is complete, the pseudo TTY can be used by both processes. Data written to the master device can be read by the process which opened the slave and so on.

Toolkit 9.7   `mscript` – an implementation of `script(TC)`

This toolkit example demonstrates the use of pseudo TTYs by providing an implementation of the `script(TC)` program which can be used to make a typescript of everything that will be output to the terminal.

The example presented here saves all output to the file called `script` in the current working directory of the process. The program is invoked by typing `mscript`. A Korn shell will be created by `mscript` and all output will be captured until the Korn shell is terminated.

There are a number of small but fairly complex steps followed to establish the pseudo session. Figure 9.30 illustrates the first few steps performed by the `mscript` program.

When `mscript` is run, the shell has established `stdin`, `stdout` and `stderr` to reference the console on which the shell is running.

An unallocated master PTY is searched for by scanning the `/dev/ptypX` entries and if successful, `mscript` will read the attributes of the console through file descriptor 0 using `tcgetattr(S)`. These attributes will be used later and restored when the program exits. The attributes of the console are modified so that the line discipline will pass characters to `mscript` in raw mode.

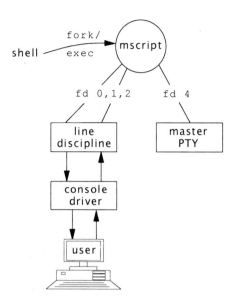

Figure 9.30   Opening the master half of the pseudo TTY

The tasks next performed by mscript are to establish the slave half of the pseudo terminal, establish the line discipline with the attributes obtained from the terminal and create the shell. This is shown in Figure 9.31.

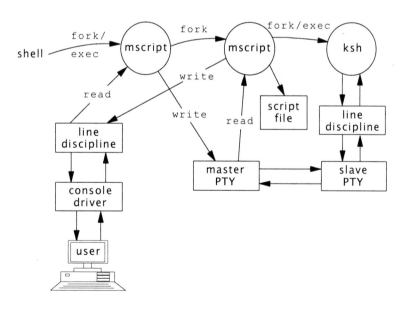

Figure 9.31   Flow control between the console and the PTY

Consider the case when the user process reads from the keyboard. Characters read through the console driver are received by the first `mscript` process in raw mode. All characters are written through the master PTY. The line discipline attached to the slave PTY which has been set to the same characteristics as the original terminal will perform canonical mode processing on the characters before they are returned to the user.

Any write calls will result in data being read by the second `mscript` process which writes the data to the console and also writes the data to the script file.

```
 1 #include <sys/types.h>
 2 #include <sys/stat.h>
 3 #include <sys/wait.h>
 4 #include <stdio.h>
 5 #include <termios.h>
 6 #include <signal.h>
 7 #include <termio.h>
 8 #include <fcntl.h>
 9
10 #define BUFSZ 1024
11
12 int     master ;              /* File descriptor for master PTY */
13 int     slave ;              /* File descriptor for slave PTY */
14 pid_t   mscript_child ;      /* mscript child's process id */
15 pid_t   shell_pid ;          /* pid of the shell created */
16 FILE    *script ;            /* The mscript typescript file */
17
18 struct  termio ttyattr ;     /* "real" TTY attributes */
19 char    ptynam[16] ;         /* used to locate master and slave */
20
21 set_tty()
22 {
23     struct termio st ;
24
25     st = ttyattr ;                 /* copy attributes and modify */
26     st.c_cc[VMIN] = 1;
27     st.c_lflag &= ~(ISIG|ECHO|ICANON) ;
28     st.c_oflag &= ~OCRNL ;
29     tcsetattr(0, &st) ;
30 }
31
32 terminate()
33 {
34     kill(0, SIGTERM) ;
35     finished() ;
36 }
37
38 pty_master()
39 {
40     struct stat st ;
41     int minor = 0 ;
42
43     while (1) {
44         sprintf(ptynam, "/dev/ptyp%d", minor) ;
45         if (stat(ptynam, &st) < 0)
46             break ;
47         master = open(ptynam, O_RDWR) ;
48         if (master > 0) {
49             tcgetattr(0, &ttyattr) ;
50             return ;
51         }
52         minor++ ;
```

```
53          }
54          fprintf(stderr, "mscript: Could not allocate a pty\n") ;
55          terminate() ;
56  }
57
58  pty_slave()
59  {
60          struct termio ti ;
61
62          ptynam[5] = 't' ;    /* eg /dev/ptyp5 -> /dev/ttyp5 */
63          stopio(ptynam) ;
64          slave = open(ptynam, O_RDWR) ;
65          if (slave < 0) {
66              perror(ptynam) ;
67              terminate() ;
68          }
69
70          ti = ttyattr ;
71          ti.c_lflag &= ~ICANON ;
72          ti.c_line = 0 ;
73          ti.c_cc[VMIN] = 0 ;
74          ti.c_cc[VTIME] = 0 ;
75          tcsetattr(slave, &ti) ;
76          tcflush(slave, TCIFLUSH) ;
77  }
78
79  void
80  stop_script(int signo)
81  {
82          int    status ;
83          pid_t pid ;
84
85          while ((pid = wait3(&status, WNOHANG, NULL)) > 0)
86              if (pid == mscript_child)
87                  finished() ;
88  }
89
90  finished()
91  {
92          if (shell_pid) {
93              fclose(script) ;
94              close(master) ;
95          } else {
96              tcsetattr(0, &ttyattr) ;
97              printf("Script done, file is \"script\"\n") ;
98              {
99                  ptynam[5] = 't' ;
100                 stopio(ptynam);
101             }
102         }
103         exit(0) ;
104 }
105
106 pty_read()
107 {
108         char buf[BUFSZ] ;
109         int c ;
110
111         fclose(script) ;
112         while ((c = read(0, buf, BUFSZ)) > 0)
113             write(master, buf, c) ;
114         finished() ;
115 }
```

```
116
117 pty_write()
118 {
119     char buf[BUFSZ] ;
120     int c ;
121
122     close(0) ;
123     while(1) {
124         c = read(master, buf, sizeof (buf)) ;
125         if (c <= 0)
126             break ;
127         write(1, buf, c) ;
128         fwrite(buf, 1, c, script) ;
129     }
130     finished() ;
131 }
132
133 exec_shell()
134 {
135     setpgrp() ;
136     pty_slave() ;
137     close(master) ;
138     fclose(script) ;
139     dup2(slave, 0) ;                    /* create pseudo stdin */
140     dup2(slave, 1) ;                    /* create pseudo stdout */
141     dup2(slave, 2) ;                    /* create pseudo stderr */
142     close(slave) ;
143     execl("/bin/ksh", "ksh", "-i", 0) ;
144     terminate() ;                       /* shouldn't get here! */
145 }
146
147 main()
148 {
149     if ((script = fopen("script", "w")) == NULL)
150         pexit("script") ;
151
152     pty_master() ;
153
154     printf("mscript started, output file is \"script\"\n") ;
155     set_tty() ;
156
157     signal(SIGCHLD, stop_script) ;
158
159     mscript_child = fork() ;
160     if (mscript_child < 0)
161         pexit("mscript:fork") ;
162
163     if (mscript_child == 0) {
164         shell_pid = mscript_child = fork() ;
165         if (mscript_child < 0) {
166             perror("mscript:fork") ;
167             terminate() ;
168         }
169         if (mscript_child)
170             pty_write() ;       /* mscript - output*/
171         else
172             exec_shell() ;      /* the user shell */
173     }
174     pty_read() ;                /* mscript - input*/
175 }
```

The program starts by creating the script file on line 149 and follows this with a call to `pty_master()` on line 152 to open the master half of the PTY.

The `pty_master()` function (lines 38 to 56) locates a PTY master in `/dev/ptypX`, calls `stat(S)` to see if the entry exists and if so, attempts to open it. If the open is successful, `tcgetattr(S)` is called on line 49 to retrieve the TTY attributes. The attributes are copied to the `ttyattr` variable.

On return to `main()`, the `set_tty()` function is called to change the attributes of the terminal so that the line discipline attached to the console driver will not perform any canonical mode processing of characters. The `ttyattr` structure is copied to the `st` structure on line 25 for which the following fields of the `termio` structure are changed:

`c_lflag`	The `ISIG` flag is turned off to disable checking against the control characters that will generate signals. This ensures that signal handling will be managed by the line discipline associated with the slave PTY.
	The `ECHO` flag is switched off since echoing will be handled by the slave PTY line discipline. Similarly, the `ICANON` flag is also turned off to ensure that the console driver works in raw mode.
`c_cc[VMIN]`	Setting this control flag to 1 ensures that a `read(S)` will not return until a character has been read.
`c_oflag`	Switch off processing a carriage return character as a newline character since this will be handled by the slave PTY line discipline.

On return to `main()` the `mscript` process forks to create the second `mscript` process which will be responsible for reading characters generated by the user and writing them to the console and to the script file.

The second `mscript` process forks again. The original `mscript` process calls `pty_read()` to process characters read from the console while the second `mscript` process calls `pty_write()` to handle characters to be written to the console.

The third process calls `exec_shell()` on lines 133 to 145. It calls `setpgrp(S)` to create a new process group. It then calls `pty_slave()` to open the slave half of the PTY. The master PTY file and script files are closed and `dup2(S)` is called to set `stdin`, `stdout` and `stderr` to the slave PTY followed by a close of the slave PTY to ensure that the shell, which is exec'd on line 143, will start with three file descriptors allocated.

The `pty_slave()` function on lines 58 to 77 opens the slave half of the PTY, sets the terminal attributes to the console attributes retrieved by `pty_master()` and sets the line discipline to reference line discipline 0.

Line 62 opens the slave device corresponding to the master PTY opened. For example, if `/dev/ptyp5` is opened the `/dev/ttyp5` slave half should be opened. The `stopio(S)` system call is first invoked to block any I/O that may be pending on the slave before the `open(S)` is invoked on line 64. The attributes of the slave PTY are then set with a call to `tcsetattr(S)`. For details of the various attributes that can be set, see the `termio(M)` manual page.

A signal handler is installed by the first `mscript` process such that if a `SIGCHLD` signal is received, `stop_script()` will be called. If a `SIGCHLD` is received from the second `mscript` process, the `finished()` function is called to close the PTY device pair and close the script file before terminating.

The `finished()` function is also called by `pty_read()` and `pty_write()` if a `read(S)` call on either the console or the master PTY fails.

When `finished()` is called it must close the PTY and reset the attributes of the console back to the attributes first read by `pty_master()`.

An example run of the `mscript` program is as follows:

```
$ mscript
mscript started, output file is "script"
$ ls
makefile      mscript.c    mscript.o    pexit.h      script
mscript*      mscript.cs   pexit.c      pexit.o      typescript
$ head -6 mscript.c
#include <sys/types.h>
#include <sys/stat.h>
#include <sys/wait.h>
#include <stdio.h>
#include <signal.h>
#include <termio.h>
$ exit
Script done, file is "script"
$ cat script
$ ls
makefile      mscript.c    mscript.o    pexit.h      script
mscript*      mscript.cs   pexit.c      pexit.o      typescript
$ head -6 mscript.c
#include <sys/types.h>
#include <sys/stat.h>
#include <sys/wait.h>
#include <stdio.h>
#include <signal.h>
#include <termio.h>
$ exit
```

The `mscript` program can be easily modified to add the extra capabilities supported by `script(TC)` or to have additional functionality added. Superuser access is not required to use `mscript`.

9.8.2 The kernel pseudo TTY driver

The `spt` driver provides two device interfaces as shown in Figure 9.32. Access through a major device number of 58 will access the slave half of the driver while access through device major 59 will access the master half of the driver.

Associated with each master/slave is a `tty` structure. There is an array of `tty` structures held in the `spt_tty[]` array which is indexed by the minor number of the master or slave device.

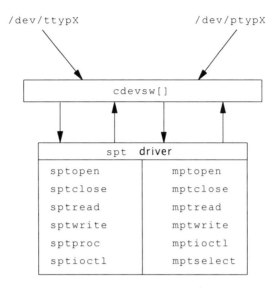

Figure 9.32   The pseudo TTY driver

To understand how the master and slave devices are connected consider the actions taken by mptopen() and sptopen().

The tasks performed by mptopen() are:

- Locate the tty structure in spt_tty[] using the minor number passed.
- Using the minor number as an index, examine the flags in the mptflags[] array. If the master PTY is already open (MPT_OPEN) or if there is already an association with the master established when the slave is opened (MPT_SPT_ASSOC), EIO is returned to the caller.
- Initialise the tty structure so that t_proc points to sptproc().
- Set the flags in mptflags[] to MPT_OPEN | MPT_SPT_ASSOC.

The tasks performed by sptopen() are:

- Locate the tty structure in spt_tty[] using the minor number passed.
- If the flags in mptflags[] are set to MPT_SPT_ASSOC but not MPT_OPEN, the slave is already open. In this case EIO is returned to the caller.
- If t_state does not have the ISOPEN flag set, ttinit(K_TTY) is called to initialise the tty structure for use with line discipline 0.
- Initialise the tty structure so that t_proc points to sptproc().
- Invoke the line discipline's open routine through linesw[].

When reading from the slave device, the line discipline read routine is called to perform the read and similarly for writing data.

The `mptread()` function invoked on the master half of the device involves copying the characters from the `t_outq` field of the `tty` structure and performing a `copyout(K)` to the process issuing the `read(S)` system call. The `mptwrite()` function involves copying characters from user space to the `t_rbuf` field of the `tty` structure and calling the line discipline's `l_input()` function to process the characters.

The flow of control through the pseudo TTY is very similar to the flow control through the console driver. See section 9.7.7 for further details.

9.9 Block drivers

Block device drivers represent only a few of the total number of drivers in the kernel. Their main purpose is to support devices for which the transfer rate must be performed in units greater than a single character and which are usually in fixed size quantities or *blocks*. Their main use is to support filesystems and swap files where allocation is performed in multiples of the block size of the underlying device. For example, a swap device is used for reading and writing page size (4 kbytes) quantities from and to the device. Filesystems usually read and write in multiple sized units but always in units greater than or equal to the device block size.

The two main block device drivers in the kernel are for hard disks and floppy drives. Both device drivers must provide a method of translating logical block offsets within a division to device specific parameters such as the cylinder and sector number.

For filesystem access to a device, all requests pass through the buffer cache, with the exception of operations such as `mkfs(ADM)` and `fsck(ADM)` where the raw interface supported by the device is accessed.

When paging and swapping is performed, the kernel talks directly to the driver through the `bdevsw[]` table. Figure 9.33 shows the main paths through the kernel to access block drivers supporting filesystems and swapping/paging.

9.9.1 Block driver entry points

Block device drivers are accessible using three basic entry points, the `XXopen()`, `XXclose()` and `XXstrategy()` functions.

After issuing the `open(S)` system call on a block device, all subsequent operations will involve accessing the `devfs` filesystem such that all subsequent reads and writes will go through `devfs` directly to the driver.

Before a filesystem can be accessed it must first be mounted. An `open(S)` system call on a regular file will involve pathname resolution performed by the filesystem which owns the file. Subsequent reads from and writes to this file will be translated by the filesystem into buffer cache calls. When the buffer cache needs to issue a request to the driver, for example when a cache miss has occurred, it will invoke the `XXstrategy()` routine.

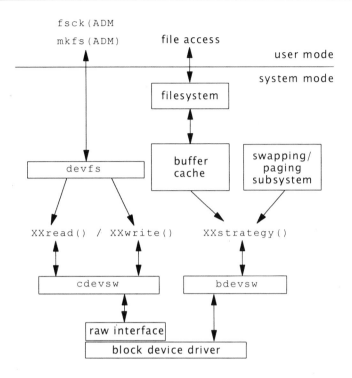

Figure 9.33   Filesystem and paging access to block device drivers

9.9.2 Data transfer properties

Unlike character drivers where the offset, size and number of bytes to transfer are stored in the u_area, the equivalent information for XXstrategy() calls is passed to the driver in the buffer header structure passed as XXstrategy()'s only argument.

Figure 9.34 shows the fields of the buffer header (struct buf) used to specify the properties of the transfer.

The b_flags field specifies whether a read (B_READ) or write (B_WRITE) should be performed. The b_addr and b_bcount fields specify the location and size of the buffer to or from where the data should be copied.

The b_dev field is used for two purposes. The major number selects the entry in the bdevsw[] array and thus the driver to be called, and the minor number is used to determine in which partition and division the block specified by b_blkno resides. Section 4.2.3 describes the method of encoding this information in the minor number for disk access.

9.9.3 Performing I/O through the buffer cache

The method of copying data depends on whether the buffer address is in user mode or kernel mode. Before issuing a call to the driver's XXstrategy() routine, the caller

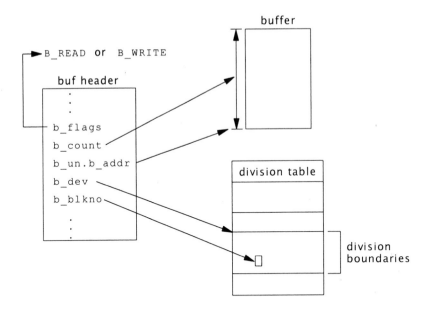

Figure 9.34   Buffer header fields used to specify data transfer properties

should set the `u_segflg` field in the u_area to `0` if the address is in the user's address space or `1` if the address is a kernel address.

If the address is in kernel space the `bcopy(K)` function is used. Since it does not expect to generate errors, the `bcopy(K)` function is not suitable for copying to and from user space.

When a transfer needs to take place between kernel mode and user mode, the `copyout(K)`, `copyin(K)` or `copyio(K)` functions are used. All three functions will return errors to the caller such as:

- The transfer generated a page fault.
- Part of the address range specified is invalid.
- The transfer would result in data being copied to the u_area.

When data is to be transferred between the buffer cache and the driver or the transfer is requested by the paging/swapping subsystem, `bcopy(K)` will be used.

Once I/O has completed, if the request for transfer came from a call to the driver's `XXstrategy()` routine, the driver must set the `B_DONE` bit in the buffer header's `b_flags` field and call `iodone(K)` with the address of the buffer header. This involves issuing a `wakeup(K)` call to any processes that are currently sleeping awaiting I/O completion on the buffer. Section 9.2.8 shows the invocation of the driver from the buffer cache followed by the call to `iodone(K)` once the I/O transfer has completed.

Toolkit 9.8   An example block device driver

This example presents a block device driver which implements a RAM disk on which filesystems can be created, mounted and so on or can be used for other purposes such as a fast log buffer. The driver is also extended to provide a character interface which is the basis for raw I/O which will be discussed in section 9.11.

The driver provides an initialisation routine, `ramdinit()`, shown on lines 18 to 29. This function gets called from the kernel `main()` function during kernel initialisation. It invokes `kmem_zalloc()` to allocate a zero-filled, 100 kbyte area of contiguous virtual address space.

The base of the RAM disk is the address returned from `kmem_zalloc(K)` and assigned to the `ramd` variable. If the memory is allocated successfully, the `ramd_valid` flag is set, which can be checked on subsequent read and write calls. The `ramd_end` variable is set to point at the address following the last byte of the allocated memory. Figure 9.35 shows the layout of the RAM disk in memory.

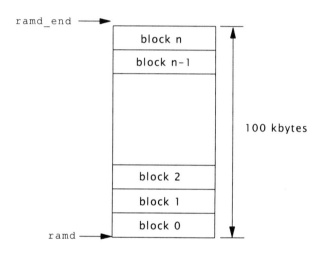

Figure 9.35   Layout of the RAM disk in memory

The message displayed by the call to `printcfg(K)` is as follows:

```
%ramd        -                 -      -    Size 100 KB
```

The driver has no work to do on `ramdopen()` or `ramdclose()`. By providing an empty function body, an open or close of the device will not fail.

```
1 #include <sys/types.h>
2 #include <sys/param.h>
3 #include <sys/kmem.h>
4 #include <sys/errno.h>
```

```
 5 #include <sys/user.h>
 6 #include <sys/buf.h>
 7
 8 extern struct user u ;
 9
10 /* set size of RAM disk to 100K */
11
12 #define ramd_sz 102400
13
14 static char *ramd ;
15 static char *ramd_end ;
16 static int   ramd_valid = 0 ;
17
18 ramdinit()
19 {
20     ramd = (char *)kmem_zalloc(ramd_sz, KM_NOSLEEP) ;
21
22     if (ramd != (char *)0) {
23         ramd_valid = 1 ;
24         ramd_end = ramd + ramd_sz ;
25         printcfg("ramd", 0, 0, -1, -1, "Size %d KB",ramd_sz / 1024) ;
26     }
27     else
28         printcfg("ramd", 0, 0, -1, -1, "kmem_zalloc failed") ;
29 }
30
31 ramdopen(dev_t dev, int flags, int id)
32 {
33 }
34
35 ramdclose(dev_t dev, int flags, int id)
36 {
37 }
38
39 ramdread(dev_t dev)
40 {
41     char *addr;
42     int   count;
43
44     if (u.u_offset < 0 || (int)ramd + u.u_offset >= (int)ramd_end) {
45         return ;
46     }
47
48     addr = ramd + u.u_offset ;
49     count = (u.u_count > (ramd_end - addr))
50                     ? (int)(ramd_end - u.u_offset) : u.u_count ;
51
52     if (count > 0) {
53         if (copyout(addr, u.u_base, count) < 0)
54             seterror(EFAULT) ;
55         else
56             u.u_count -= count ;
57     }
58     else if (count < 0)
59         seterror(ENXIO) ;
60 }
61
62 ramdwrite(dev_t dev)
63 {
64     char *addr ;
65     int   count ;
66
67     if (u.u_count == 0)
```

```
68          return ;
69
70      if (u.u_offset < 0 || (int)ramd + u.u_offset >= (int)ramd_end) {
71          return ;
72      }
73
74      addr = ramd + u.u_offset ;
75      count = (u.u_count > (ramd_end - addr))
76                          ? (int)(ramd_end - u.u_offset) : u.u_count ;
77
78      if (count > 0) {
79          if (copyin(u.u_base, addr, count) < 0)
80              seterror(EFAULT) ;
81          else
82              u.u_count -= count ;
83      }
84      else if (count < 0)
85          seterror(ENXIO) ;
86 }
87
88 ramdstrategy(struct buf *bp)
89 {
90      char *addr ;
91      int count ;
92      int offset = (bp->b_blkno << SCTRSHFT) ;
93
94      if (offset < 0 || offset >= (ramd_end - ramd)) {
95          bp->b_resid = bp->b_bcount ;
96          iodone(bp) ;
97          return ;
98      }
99
100      addr = ramd + (bp->b_blkno << SCTRSHFT) ;
101      if (bp->b_bcount > (ramd_end - addr))
102          count = (ramd_end - addr) ;
103      else
104          count = bp->b_bcount ;
105
106      if (count > 0) {
107          if (bp->b_flags & B_READ)
108              bcopy(addr, bp->b_un.b_addr, count) ;
109          else
110              bcopy(bp->b_un.b_addr, addr, count) ;
111      }
112      else if (count < 0 || (bp->b_flags & B_READ) == 0) {
113          count = 0 ;
114          bp->b_error = ENXIO ;
115          bp->b_flags |= B_ERROR ;
116      }
117      bp->b_resid = bp->b_bcount - count ;
118      iodone(bp) ;
119 }
120
121 ramdprint(dev_t dev, char *str)
122 {
123 }
```

The driver provides the `ramdstrategy()` function which will be called from the buffer cache subsystem and `ramdread()` and `ramdwrite()` functions which are accessed from the `devfs` filesystem.

The `ramdstrategy()` function which is shown on lines 88 to 199 performs the following tasks:

lines 92 to 98	The value of `bp->b_blkno` is the block number requested from the buffer cache in units of 512 bytes. This is converted to a byte offset into the RAM disk on line 93 by shifting the value of `b_blkno` by `SCTRSHFT`. The value of `offset` is checked on line 94 to ensure it falls within the bounds of the RAM disk. If the check fails, the `b_resid` field is assigned the value of `b_bcount`. This indicates that no bytes have been transferred. The `iodone(K)` function is then invoked on the buffer to wake up any processes that are sleeping on the address of the buffer supplied.
lines 100 to 104	The starting address in the RAM disk of the transfer is calculated on line 100. This is simply the offset calculated earlier plus the start address of the RAM disk in memory. The number of bytes to transfer is then calculated. If the offset within the RAM disk plus the number of bytes to read is less than the value of `ram_end`, all `b_bcount` bytes will be transferred. If the offset plus `b_bcount` stretches beyond the RAM disk, only the valid bytes will be copied.
lines 106 to 111	On line 107 a check is made to see if the data should be read or written. For both types of transfer the `bcopy(K)` function is called to read or write the data.
lines 112 to 116	If there are no bytes to transfer and a write is being performed, the `b_error` field of the buffer is set to `ENXIO` and the buffer is marked with `B_ERROR`.
lines 117 to 118	The final task performed is to set `b_resid` to the number of bytes not transferred and call `iodone(K)` to wake up processes sleeping on the buffer address.

The `ramdread()` and `ramdwrite()` functions shown on lines 39 to 60 and 62 to 86 are invoked via the `devfs` filesystem and have not been passed a buffer header.

For each function, the offset within the RAM disk is held in `u.u_offset`. The base address to copy data to (`ramdread()`) or copy data from (`ramdwrite()`) is stored in `u.u_base`. The number of bytes to transfer is stored in `u.u_count`.

The first step performed by both functions is to validate the offset and count. For the `ramdread()` function, this check is made on lines 44 to 50. The offset passed to `ramdread()` and `ramdwrite()` is an offset in bytes, whereas the offset passed to `ramdstrategy()` is in units of 512 bytes.

Once the number of bytes to transfer has been calculated, the data is copied to or from user space using `copyout(K)` for `ramdread()` and `copyin(K)` for `ramdwrite()`. If the copy is successful, the number of bytes transferred is decremented from u.u_count and the function returns. If the copyin(K) or copyout(K) fails, seterror(K) is called to set u.u_error to EFAULT.

The driver is linked into the kernel using the configure(ADM) utility using the following steps:

```
# mkdir /etc/conf/pack.d/ramd
# cp Driver.o /etc/conf/pack.d/ramd/.     # Driver.o in current directory
# cd /etc/conf/cf.d
# ./configure -J NEXTMAJOR
82
#  ./configure  -a  ramdinit  ramdopen  ramdclose  ramdread  ramdwrite
ramdstrategy -b -c -m 82
# ./link_unix
```

Two device special files must be established prior to the RAM disk being used, one for the block interface and one for the character interface. In both calls to mknod(C), the minor number could be set to any number since it is not used by this particular driver.

```
# mknod /dev/rramd c 82 0
# mknod /dev/ramd b 82 0
```

In the following output, mkfs(ADM) is called to create a filesystem using the character device. Since no arguments are specified, the default filesystem is used together with the whole device. The HTFS mkfs utility reports that there are 100 1-kbyte blocks and that there are 89 1-kbyte blocks available for use by users.

```
# mkfs /dev/rramd
mkfs: default type (HTFS) used
bytes per logical block = 1024
total logical blocks = 100
total inodes = 32
gap (physical blocks) = 1
cylinder size (physical blocks) = 400
setting cluster to default size (16)
mkfs: Available blocks = 89
# mount /dev/ramd /mnt
# cp /etc/passwd /mnt
# umount /mnt
```

Once the filesystem has been created, it is mounted, by specifying the block device, on /mnt, the /etc/passwd file is copied to its root directory and it is then un-mounted.

To show further that the RAM disk functions correctly, the dd(C) utility is used to copy the data from the raw device to the raw floppy device. The transfer size is left to dd(C) to calculate. The number of 512 byte blocks transferred is 200.

```
# dd if=/dev/rramd of=/dev/rfd0135ds18
200+0 records in
200+0 records out
# mount /dev/fd0135ds18 /mnt
# head -4 /mnt/passwd
root:x:0:3:Superuser:/:
```

```
daemon:x:1:1:System daemons:/etc:
bin:x:2:2:Owner of system commands:/bin:
sys:x:3:3:Owner of system files:/usr/sys:
# umount /mnt
```

Once copied, the floppy block device is used to mount the filesystem. The first four lines of the `passwd` file copied are then displayed.

9.10 Direct Memory Access (DMA)

Once a device driver has queued or initiated an I/O transaction in response to an `XXstrategy()` call, it returns to the caller. When the I/O transaction is complete an interrupt is raised and the driver can analyse device registers to determine the status of the transfer. Transferring the data from the device can be performed in one of two ways:

- The data must be transferred between hardware buffers on the controller to the appropriate location in memory. The transfer is performed using `inb` (or similar) instructions repeatedly until the data is transferred. This model of I/O is called *programmed I/O*.

- Data can be transferred to and from physical memory directly without CPU intervention and while the CPU is performing other tasks. This type of transfer is called *Direct Memory Access* (DMA).

9.10.1 Hardware support for DMA

Some peripheral controllers rely on use of the i8237 DMA support chip which can only support DMA for the first 16 Mbytes of physical memory. Newer peripheral controllers bypass the i8237 completely and can therefore provide support for DMA beyond this restrictive 16 Mbyte limit.

The capabilities of the hardware have a direct effect on the performance of the buffer cache and therefore on the overall performance of the machine. If a 16 Mbyte limit is imposed and buffers to be read or written lie above 16 Mbytes, the buffer cache must use copy buffers which lie in the first 16 Mbytes of memory thus allowing DMA to be performed. This will involve an additional copy for many transfers.

9.10.2 Kernel support for DMA

There are a number of functions available to device drivers that require the use of the capabilities of the i8237 DMA controller:

```
#include <sys/dma.h>

int  dma_alloc(unsigned chan, unsigned mod) ;
int  dma_param(unsigned chan, unsigned mode, paddr_t addr, long cnt) ;
int  dma_enable(unsigned chan) ;
```

```
int   dma_start(struct dmareq *arg) ;
long dma_resid(unsigned chan) ;
int   dma_relse(unsigned chan) ;
int   dma_breakup(int (*xxstrategy, bp)(), struct buf *bp) ;
```

A driver should call the dma_alloc(K) routine to allocate a DMA channel. The chan argument specifies the channel that should be allocated:

8 bit channels	DMA_CH0, DMA_CH1, DMA_CH2, DMA_CH3
16 bit channels	DMA_CH5, DMA_CH6, DMA_CH7

The mod argument specifies whether the call should block until the channel becomes free or whether the call should return immediately.

The dma_param(K) function is used to set the registers of the controller chip in preparation for performing the DMA transfer. The chan field specifies the channel number as described above, the mode argument specifies whether a read or a write will be performed, the addr argument specifies the starting address in physical memory to or from which the transfer will take place and cnt specifies the number of bytes to transfer. The dma_enable(K) function can then be called to start a DMA transfer on the specified channel.

The dma_start(K) function is used to queue a DMA request for later execution when the specified channel becomes available. The dmareq structure specifies the channel number, mode, physical address and count as described for dma_param(K) above. An additional field specifies the address of a function to be called when the channel becomes free. The details of the transfer which have been stored in the dmareq structure can then be set using dma_param(K) and the DMA transfer initiated with a call to dma_enable(K).

When a DMA transfer has completed, an interrupt is raised and the dma_resid(K) function is called to determine how many bytes were not transferred, if any. The dma_relse(K) function should then be called to release the allocated DMA channel. This will wake any processes that are sleeping on the channel as a result of calling dma_start(K).

9.11 Raw I/O

Although the buffer cache provides some scope for reading and writing buffers of different sizes, this scope is limited and has an upward limit of 4 kbytes. It is not possible to perform transfers of only a few bytes or transfers up to many thousands of bytes.

Block device drivers can be extended to provide what is called a *raw interface* or simply *raw I/O*. This allows the kernel and driver to perform variable sized transfers outside of the buffer cache. Often, and more importantly, the I/O transfer is performed without data being copied from user mode to kernel mode before transfer to the device. This allows for a much greater throughput and is often the preferred method of I/O for many mainstream databases.

nterface is added to a block device driver by adding the XXread() and
erfaces and adding the driver to the cdevsw[] table. Access to the raw
......ace is achieved by adding a character special file in the filesystem namespace. The
dual access paths to the driver are shown in Figure 9.36.

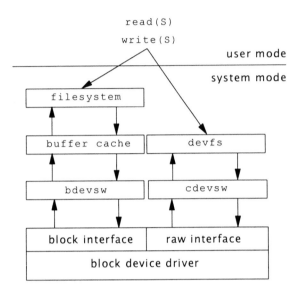

Figure 9.36 Block and character interfaces supported by the same device driver

As the figure suggests, from this logical view there appears to be little difference
between a driver supporting both block and character interfaces and two separate drivers.
The access paths to the driver are the same in both cases. However, since block-based
devices can be accessed only in fixed size quantities, the raw interface is heavily
dependent on the functionality of the block component of the driver.

As an example of issuing a read of only a few bytes through the raw interface of a
block driver, consider the following program, raw.c:

```
#include <fcntl.h>
#include <string.h>

main(int argc, char *argv[])
{
    int fd, n ;

    fd = open("/dev/fd0135ds18", O_WRONLY) ;
    if (fd < 0)
        pexit("floppy") ;

    n = write(fd, argv[0], strlen(argv[0])) ;

    printf("nbytes written = %d\n", n) ;
}
```

The program opens `/dev/fd0135ds18`, the block device entry for the floppy driver, and issues a `write(S)` system call to write the name of the program. As shown below, the number of bytes written is 4 (including the end of string character):

```
# ls -l /dev/fd0135ds18
brw-rw-rw-    2 bin        bin           2, 60 Jan 14 12:27 /dev/fd0135ds18
# raw
nbytes written = 4
```

Although the kernel wrote the 4 bytes requested, the floppy driver still needed to write 512 bytes, the sector size and minimal transfer size of the device. To write the 4 bytes the driver first has to read the sector or sectors which surround the 4 bytes, overwrite the 4 bytes to be written and then write the data back to the device.

Most utilities or applications which use raw devices always perform I/O transactions in multiples of the block size supported by the device to avoid this overhead.

9.11.1 Kernel support for raw I/O

There are a number of tasks to be performed by a driver supporting raw I/O. Tasks include checking that the user's pages holding the data to be transferred are present and locked in memory for the duration of the transfer and ensuring that the request can be handled by the underlying hardware.

The `physck(K)` and `physio(K)` kernel functions are available for handling raw I/O requests passed through the driver's `XXread()` and `XXwrite(K)` entry points.

Prototypes for both functions are as follows:

```
#include <sys/buf.h>
#include <sys/omti.h>

int physck(daddr_t nblocks, int rwflag) ;
void physio(int (*strategy)(struct buf *), struct buf *bp,
                                     dev_t dev, int rwflags) ;
```

The `nblocks` argument passed to `physck(K)` represents the number of 512 byte blocks that are present on the device. The number of blocks is converted to bytes and compared with the `u_offset` field which holds the byte offset within the device from which the transfer should start. If `physck(K)` completes successfully, 1 is returned, otherwise 0 is returned to indicate an error. There are three main checks performed by `physck(K)`:

- If `u_offset` is greater than the size of the device and the `rwflag` is set to `B_WRITE`, `u_error` is set to `ENXIO` and 0 is returned.

- If `u_offset` is greater than or equal to the limit and the `rwflag` is equal to `B_READ`, 0 is returned but no error is set.

- If `u_offset` + `u_count` is greater than the device limit, `u_count` is decremented so that `u_offset` + `u_count` falls within the boundaries of the device.

The processing performed by physio(K) is considerably more complex. It must further validate the request, lock the relevant pages of the process in memory and examine the driver attributes before it can issue the actual I/O request. It then invokes the strategy routine passed as an argument. The call to strategy may occur multiple times with different buffer headers, depending on the capabilities of the device.

The bp argument remains for historical reasons and should now be set to NULL. The dev argument specifies the major and minor numbers of the device. This is the dev argument passed to the XXread() or XXwrite() driver entry point.

The rwflags argument defines the I/O operation:

B_READ   A read operation should be performed.

B_WRITE   A write operation should be performed. This flag is not actually checked by physio(K) internally as it is assumed that a write should take place if B_READ is not set. The flag should still be set to anticipate any future changes.

B_BDEV   This flag indicates how physio(K) should find out the device properties. If it is set, the attributes will be determined by a call to getbattr(), otherwise the getcattr() function will be invoked.

B_NOSG   If this flag is set, physio(K) will not attempt to perform scatter/gather.

The following fields of the u_area should be initialised prior to calling physio(K):

u_base   The starting address of the user or kernel buffer from where the transfer should start.

u_count   The size of the transfer in bytes.

u_offset   The offset within the device from where the transfer should start.

u_segflg   If this field is set to 0, the transfer will take place to/from a user address. If it is set to 1, the transfer is internal to the kernel.

u_fmode   If the FBMODE flags is set, the u_offset field should be measured in 512 byte sectors, otherwise it is interpreted as a byte offset.

There are a number of checks to be performed by physio(K):

• If the device allows scatter/gather and the transfer would be most efficiently performed using scatter/gather, the driver will prepare scatter/gather lists before calling the specified strategy routine.

• If the device cannot support physical addresses above 16 Mbytes, physio(K) will use copy buffers to perform the transfer.

• A check will normally be made to see if, for partial writes, a full block read should be performed prior to writing. For example, this will occur when writing a number of bytes which is less than the physical block size of the device. This check can be disabled by setting appropriate flags in the mdevice file.

The following pseudo code shows how the `XXread()` driver function can be implemented using calls to `physck(K)` and `physio(K)`.

```
dcread(dev_t dev)
{
    if (physck(devSize(dev), B_READ) == 1)
        physio(dcstrategy, (buf_t *)0, dev, B_READ) ;
}
```

9.12 Summary and suggested reading

This chapter described the I/O subsystem, including the buffer cache which is the centre of most I/O activity. The different types of device drivers were explained, including the implementation of the TTY subsystem in SCO OpenServer.

Kettle and Statler (1993) provides excellent coverage of the I/O subsystem in SCO UNIX, describing in detail the STREAMS, TTY, block and character device driver environments. It also contains many practical, easy to follow examples.

The SCO OpenServer *Performance Guide* (1995) describes how to obtain the best performance from the buffer cache, including how to detect the amount of DMA'able memory and thus where the buffer cache should be placed in memory.

Bach (1986) provides a description of the operation of the buffer cache. Although the buffer cache he describes is based on UNIX System V Release 2, many of the principles are still the same today.

The SCO OpenServer *Advanced Hardware Developer's Kit* (1995) provides device driver writers with all of the information that they require for writing device drivers for SCO UNIX, including the complete set of functions available and information on linking and debugging drivers.

10

The STREAMS subsystem

This chapter describes the structures, functions and algorithms that comprise the STREAMS subsystem together with the mechanisms by which user processes and the rest of the kernel interface with STREAMS.

A STREAMS based driver and module are provided with details of how to add STREAMS drivers and modules to the kernel's link kit.

The chapter concludes by showing how to analyse live STREAMS stacks using the crash(ADM) command.

10.1 Introduction

The first documentation on STREAMS appeared in 1984 in Dennis Ritchie's paper 'A Stream Input–Output System'. The first commercial implementation of STREAMS appeared in UNIX System V Release 3.0 two years later.

The main aim behind the STREAMS architecture was to allow a clean separation between different network protocols. By providing a well-defined interface between protocols within the STREAMS environment, this allowed support for dynamic configuration of networking services. For example, UDP could be run over IP at the same time that TCP could be run over IP.

The use of STREAMS is still dominated by networking supported in SCO OpenServer Release 5. However, the STREAMS subsystem offers the flexibility to implement a number of other services including pipes and pseudo TTYs.

The STREAMS subsystem, while still retaining its architectural simplicity and elegance, is both large and complex. This chapter covers STREAMS in sufficient detail for users to write their own STREAMS drivers and modules, understand the procedures for linking drivers and modules into the kernel and analyse STREAMS structures with `crash(ADM)`.

10.1.1 The STREAMS toolkit

There are four toolkit examples in this chapter:

Toolkit 10.1 A STREAMS loopback driver, page 474
Toolkit 10.2 Accessing named STREAMS, page 482
Toolkit 10.3 Pushing and popping STREAMS modules, page 486
Toolkit 10.4 Walking through STREAMS stacks with `crash`, page 491

Toolkit 10.1 presents a simple loopback driver which demonstrates how the clone device can be used to open a STREAM. This example is used as a basis for the following two examples or can be used by readers to test their own modules, STREAMS based system calls, `crash(ADM)` functions, flow control and so on.

Toolkit 10.2 uses the loopback driver in conjunction with the `namefs` filesystem to show how named STREAMS can be constructed.

Toolkit 10.3 provides a simple module which is pushed onto the loopback driver. Again, it can be used as a basis for further experimentation.

Instructions are provided on how to link both STREAMS drivers and modules into the kernel link kit.

Toolkit 10.4 uses Toolkit 10.2 and `crash(ADM)` to show how `crash` commands can be used to walk through a STREAMS stack.

10.2 The STREAMS architecture

The STREAMS subsystem provides the mechanisms to construct a full duplex communication channel between a user process or the kernel and a STREAMS based device driver as shown in Figure 10.1. The STREAM head acts as an interface between the user/kernel and the STREAMS driver.

The user can access the STREAM using the traditional open(S), close(S), read(S), write(S) and ioctl(S) system calls or by using the getmsg(S), putmsg(S) and poll(S) system calls which were introduced specifically for accessing STREAMS. The details of how each function accesses the STREAM are described throughout the chapter.

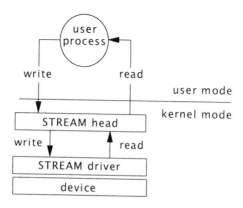

Figure 10.1   Accessing a STREAMS device

When the user issues a write(S) system call the data passes through the STREAM in a message which contains the data, a message type and control information.

One of the great strengths of the STREAMS architecture over character drivers is the ability to push *modules* onto the STREAM dynamically which can alter the content and flow of control of messages both *downstream* and *upstream*. The effect on the STREAM after pushing a module is shown in Figure 10.2.

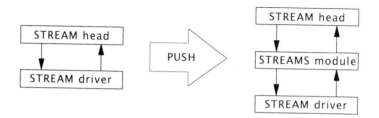

Figure 10.2   Pushing a module onto a STREAM

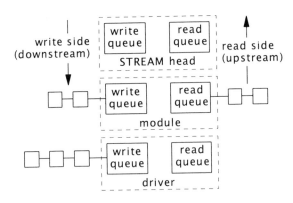

Figure 10.3   Flow of messages through a STREAM

Modules are always pushed onto the STREAM at the STREAM head. They cannot be inserted between an already existing module and driver. There is no theoretical limit to the number of modules that can be pushed onto the STREAM although performance and memory constraints will usually limit this number.

Each layer of the STREAM from head to module to driver is linked using a pair of queues to which messages may be attached as they flow through the STREAM. The queues provide module or driver specific procedures for processing messages and passing them through the STREAM. Figure 10.3 shows the flow of messages down the STREAM for writing data and up the STREAM when reading.

Data written to the STREAM passes *downstream* or down the *write side* of the STREAM. Data read from the STREAM passes *upstream* or up the *read side* of the STREAM.

STREAMS drivers are located in the `cdevsw[]` array although not all character device entry points are applicable to STREAMS drivers. The `cdevsw` structure, described in section 9.3.4, contains the field `d_str` which points to a `streamtab` structure. If this field is not `NULL` the driver is a STREAMS driver as shown in Figure 10.4. STREAMS modules are located in the `fmodsw[]` array. Section 10.4.3 describes how modules are accessed.

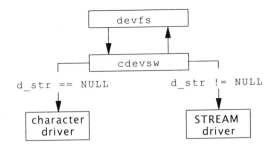

Figure 10.4   The difference between character and STREAMS drivers

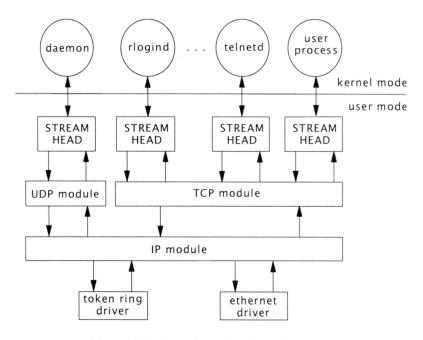

Figure 10.5   Network configuration using STREAMS

Unlike block or character drivers where the driver entry points are accessed through appropriate entries in the `bdevsw[]` and `cdevsw[]` tables, the interface between the kernel and STREAMS based drivers is through the STREAM *head*.

Figure 10.5 shows how STREAMS are used in SCO UNIX to implement TCP/IP and UDP/IP, the two most commonly used networking stacks.

The flow of messages both downstream and upstream is intercepted by each module in turn, allowing the module to perform its own specific data manipulation and control flow on the data it sees. For example, data flowing downstream will involve the construction of TCP packets which are then transformed into IP packets and so on.

10.3 The STREAM head

The STREAM head is the interface between the user/kernel and the STREAM and is responsible for a number of tasks including:

- Translating system call information into messages that are sent downstream to modules and drivers.

- Communicating errors and posting signals which have been sent upstream.

- Unpacking messages which have been sent upstream and copying data to a user or kernel supplied buffer.

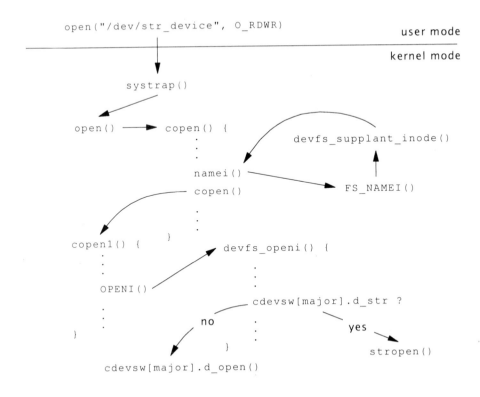

Figure 10.6   Opening a STREAMS device

The STREAM head is allocated on the first open of a STREAMS device and de-allocated on the last close. Figure 10.6 shows the flow of control through the kernel when performing an open(S) on a STREAMS device.

A STREAMS driver, like any other driver, is represented to the user as an entry in the filesystem namespace. The device special filename is passed by the user process as an argument to the open(S) system call.

When namei() is called by copen(), a device is detected so the inode which would be returned by namei() is replaced by a devfs inode through which all file operations will be subsequently directed.

The OPENI() call is then invoked to access the filesystem specific open routine, in this case, devfs_openi() which looks to see if the d_str field of the cdevsw[] entry for the device is set. If it is not NULL the device is a STREAMS device. In this case the stropen() function should be called to open the STREAMS device. Within stropen(), the driver's XXopen() will be called.

The stropen() function is responsible for creating the STREAM head on first open and connecting it with the driver. The STREAM head consists of a number of different structures which are linked together as shown in Figure 10.7.

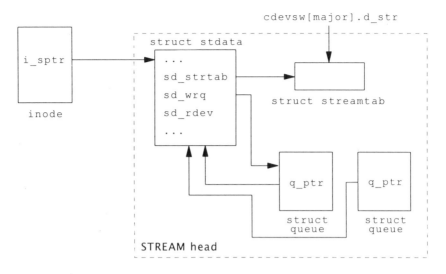

Figure 10.7   The STREAM head

Once a STREAM has been opened it is referenced by the `i_sptr` field of the inode returned by `namei()`. This field is used to locate the STREAM head when performing I/O operations on the STREAM.

The STREAM head is underpinned by the `stdata` structure which is used to interface the STREAM with the rest of the kernel when performing read, write or ioctl operations. The `i_sptr` field of the inode points to this structure. The major fields of the `stdata` structure are shown in Table 10.1.

Table 10.1   The `stdata` structure used to interface the STREAM with the rest of the kernel

`stdata` structure field		Description
`struct queue`	`*sd_wrq`	This field points to the write queue, the channel on which messages are sent downstream.
`struct msgb`	`*sd_iocblk`	The return block used for ioctl operations.
`dev_t`	`sd_rdev`	The device number of the STREAMS device taken from the inode for the device.
`ushort`	`sd_icnt`	Number of inodes which are pointing to the STREAM.
`struct streamtab`	`*sd_strtab`	A pointer to the `streamtab` structure which is associated with the STREAM.
`long`	`sd_iocid`	This field is used to record ioctl information when processing `ioctl(S)` system calls.
`ushort`	`sd_iocwait`	A count of the number of processes waiting to perform an ioctl command.
`short`	`sd_pgrp`	This field contains the process group ID which is used when signals need to be posted.
`unsigned char`	`sd_error`	This field contains any error codes which are used to set the `u.u_error` field.
`int`	`sd_pushcnt`	This field records the number of pushes that have been done on the STREAM.

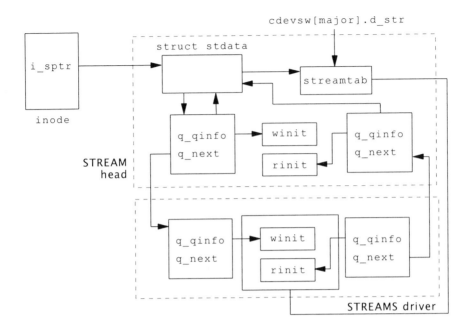

Figure 10.8   The STREAM after an open is complete

The `stdata_alloc()` function is called from `stropen()` to allocate the STREAM head if the STREAM has not already been opened. The `stdata` structures are held in the `streams[]` array, the size of which is governed by the `NSTREAM` kernel tuneable. Note, however, that if the number of STREAM heads reaches `NSTREAM`, the table will be dynamically grown.

The `stdata_alloc()` function calls `allocqs()` to allocate a pair of queue structures for the STREAM head and then calls `qattach()` to attach the STREAM head to the driver as shown in Figure 10.8. The `qattach()` function calls `allocqs()` to allocate a pair of queue structures which will be used by the driver.

The final task performed by `qattach()` is to call the driver's open routine which is located via the `q_qinfo` field of the read side queue. In Figure 10.8, this is located in the driver's structure marked `rinit`.

The procedures involved for pushing a module are very similar to the procedures followed above for attaching the STREAMS device to the STREAM head. Both call the `qattach()` function. For details of how modules are pushed onto a STREAM see section 10.4.3.

The `stdata` structures for either the whole `streams[]` array or an individual entry in the `streams[]` array can be displayed within `crash(ADM)` using the `stream` command as the following examples show.

```
> stream 1..10
STREAM TABLE SIZE = 1024
SLOT  WRQ IOCB INODE  PGRP      IOCID IOCWT WOFF  ERR FLAG
   1  105   -    50     0           0     0    0    0 plex 01000000
   2   97   -    47     0           0     0    0    0 plex 01000000
   3   93   -    46     0           0     0    0    0 plex 01000000
   4   89   -    45     0           0     0    0    0 plex 01000000
   5   85   -    44     0           0     0    0    0 plex 01000000
   6   81   -    43     0           0     0    0    0 plex 01000000
   7   77   -    39     0          11     0    0    0 plex 01000000
   8   73   -    41     0           0     0    0    0 plex 01000000
   9   69   -    40     0           0     0    0    0 plex 01000000
  10  109   -    -      0          15     0    0    0
> stream -f 3
STREAM TABLE SIZE = 1024
SLOT  WRQ IOCB INODE  PGRP      IOCID IOCWT WOFF  ERR FLAG
   3   93   -    46     0           0     0    0    0 plex 01000000
          STRTAB RCNT
       0xf01daeb8    0
       SIGFLAGS:
       SIGLIST:
       POLLFLAGS:
       POLLIST:
```

The first `stream` command displays a summary of the entries 1 to 10 in the `streams[]`
array. The second call displays the `stdata` structure in slot 3 in more detail. For further
details on using the `stream` command see Toolkit 10.4.

10.4 STREAMS modules

STREAMS modules are always pushed onto the STREAM between the STREAM head
and either the driver or the module which is currently below the STREAM head.

Shown earlier, both modules and drivers consists of two `queue` structures and a
number of functions which are attached to the `queue` structure for passing data
downstream and upstream. The `queue` structure is shown in Table 10.2.

The `queue` structure is used at all layers in the STREAM from the STREAM head to
the driver and by each module in between. The following sections describe the different
fields of the `queue` structure and how they are used to control the flow of data through
the STREAM.

Figure 10.9 shows how the STREAM head, STREAMS modules and STREAMS
drivers are linked together using the `q_next` field of the `queue` structure. The STREAM
head, each module and driver all have access to their own private data structures accessed
by the `q_ptr` field of the `queue` structure.

When a STREAM head is created, `stdata_alloc()` calls `allocqs()` to allocate a
pair of `queue` structures for use with the STREAM head. Queues are contained within the
`queue[]` array and `queue` structures which are in the free list are referenced by the
`qfreelist` kernel variable. Figure 10.10 shows the link between `queue[]` and
`qfreelist`.

Table 10.2   The queue structure used for passing messages within the STREAM

queue structure field		Description
struct qinit	*q_qinfo	Structure containing functions used for message handling.
struct msgb	*q_first	This field points to the first queued message.
struct msgb	*q_last	This field points to the last queued message.
struct queue	*q_next	This field points to the next queue structure to which messages should be passed.
struct queue	*q_link	This field points to the next queue for scheduling.
caddr_t	q_ptr	This field is used to point to private data.
ushort	q_count	This field is a count of the number of blocks on the queue.
ushort	q_flag	This field contains the queue state constructed from one or more of the following flags:
		QENAB The queue is already enabled to run.
		QWANTW A write to the queue is wanted.
		QWANTR A read from the queue is wanted.
		QFULL The queue is full.
short	q_minpsz	The minimum packet size accepted by this module.
short	q_maxpsz	The maximum packet size accepted by this module.
ushort	q_hiwat	The queue's high water mark.
ushort	q_lowat	The queue's low water mark.

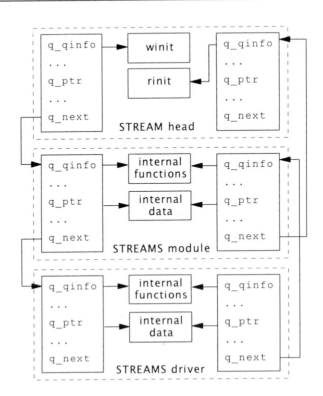

Figure 10.9   Modules and driver linked together using the queue structure

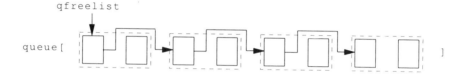

Figure 10.10   The free list used for queue structures

The chain of free queue structures is constructed using the q_next field linking every other queue structure in the queue[] array. If a pair of queue structures needs to be allocated, the first element is taken from the list and qfreelist is assigned to qfreelist->q_next. Since the queue structures are consecutive in memory, if the first structure referenced by qfreelist is used, its *pair* queue structure is always located next in memory.

The STREAMS queue structures can be displayed within crash(ADM) using the queue command as follows:

```
> queue ! head -8
QUEUE TABLE SIZE = 566
SLOT  INFO     NEXT LINK        PTR RCNT HD/TL MINP MAXP HIWT LOWT FLAGS
  0 0xf01deed0    2 - 0xf0852b00   0 -  -    0 16384 49152 8192 wr rr us
  1 0xf01deeec    - - 0xf0852b00   0 -  -    0 32739 32739 1024 wr us
  2 0xf01d900c    - - 0xf0863500   0 -  -    0    -1 16384 1024 rr us
  3 0xf01d9028    1 - 0xf0863500   0 -  -    0     0     0    0 us
  4 0xf01d74b8    6 - 0xf0223c30   0 -  -    0    -1  5120 1024 wr rr us
  5 0xf01d74d4   10 - 0xf0223c30   0 -  -    0    -1  5120 1024 wr us
```

Toolkit 10.4 uses the queue command in conjunction with other STREAMS based crash(ADM) commands to follow the links from the file descriptor, through the STREAM and back to the STREAM head.

10.4.1 The qinit structure

The flow of data both downstream and upstream is performed using the procedures held in the q_qinfo field of the queue structure which points to a qinit structure. Since the queue structures are linked together using the q_next field, it is easy for the kernel STREAM based routines to access the module to which the messages should be sent after processing.

The fields of the qinit structure are described briefly here. Each field will be described in more detail throughout the chapter.

int (*qi_putp)()   The put procedure is called by modules either upstream or downstream to request that the message is processed by the next module or driver in the STREAM. When a message needs to be forwarded to the next module the putnext(K_STR) function is called to call the put procedure of the next module or driver.

	There are certain circumstances under which the put procedure of the next module or driver cannot be invoked. For example, when messages are flowing downstream, modules located above the driver may have to wait while the driver outputs its current list of messages to the device. Messages that are flowing upstream may be blocked until a user issues a read request.
`int (*qi_srvp)()`	The `service` procedure is used in conjunction with the STREAMS scheduler to handle the case when a call to push the message onto the next queue on the STREAM is blocked by flow control. At some later stage when flow control has been relaxed, the STREAMS scheduler will call the service procedure to process waiting messages. STREAMS scheduling is described in section 10.9.
`int (*qi_qopen)()`	The `open` procedure is called each time a module is opened or pushed onto a STREAM.
`int (*qi_qclose)()`	The `close` procedure is called each time the module is closed or popped off the STREAM.

The tasks performed by these procedures will be described when discussing flow control through the STREAM in section 10.7.

10.4.2 The `streamtab` structure

STREAMS drivers and modules must each declare their own `streamtab` structure. Shown in Table 10.3, the `streamtab` structure is used by the kernel to locate the driver or module `qinit` structures from which the kernel can access the `put`, `service`, `open` and `close` procedures.

Table 10.3 The `streamtab` structure declared by STREAMS drivers and modules

streamtab structure field	Description
`struct qinit *st_rdinit`	The `qinit` structure referenced by `st_rdinit` points to the procedures used on the *read* side of the STREAM.
`struct qinit *st_wrinit`	The `qinit` structure referenced by `st_wrinit` points to the procedures used on the *write* side of the STREAM.
`struct qinit *st_muxrinit`	Used when performing an `I_LINK` ioctl to configure a multiplexed STREAM.
`struct qinit *st_muxwinit`	Used when performing an `I_LINK` ioctl to configure a multiplexed STREAM.

For STREAMS drivers, the `streamtab` structure is pointed to by the `d_str` field of the `cdevsw` structure at the entry in which the driver is stored in the `cdevsw[]` array. It is accessed when the STREAM is opened so that the `queue` structures allocated by `qattach()` reference `st_rdinit` and `st_wrinit`. The driver's open function is called by `qattach()` which locates it via `st_rdinit`.

STREAMS modules are located by the kernel in the `fmodsw[]` array which has only the following two fields:

```
char f_name[FMNAMESZ+1] ;
struct streamtab *f_str ;
```

The `f_name` field is used by STREAMS related ioctl commands such as pushing and popping the module, listing the modules on a STREAM and so on.

The following section shows how modules are located in the `fmodsw[]` array. Toolkit 10.3 describes how modules are configured into the kernel.

10.4.3 Pushing and popping modules

The structures declared by modules for interfacing with the kernel are identical to those used by a STREAMS driver. Pushing and popping STREAMS modules is not performed by the `open(S)` and `close(S)` system calls but by issuing `ioctl(S)` system calls to an already existing STREAM.

There are two ioctl commands recognised by STREAMS for pushing and popping modules, namely `I_PUSH` and `I_POP`. For example, consider the following:

```
fd = open("/dev/my_stream", O_RDWR) ;
ioctl(fd, I_PUSH, "my_module") ;
do_io() ;
ioctl(fd, I_POP, (char *)0) ;
close(fd) ;
```

The STREAM called `/dev/my_stream` is opened for reading and writing. An `ioctl(S)` system call is then made specifying that the module called `my_module` should be pushed onto the STREAM. After the `do_io()` function has returned, another `ioctl(S)` system call is invoked to pop the module off the STREAM before the STREAM is closed. Note that modules will be automatically popped on last close.

All `ioctl(S)` system calls are processed by `systrap()` which invokes the `ioctl()` kernel call which in turn locates the inode for the file descriptor and then calls the filesystem specific ioctl command through the `FS_IOCTL()` macro. For STREAMS devices this is the `devfs_ioctl()` function.

The entry for the STREAMS device is checked in the `cdevsw[]` table to see if the device passed is a STREAM (`d_str` is not `NULL`). In this case the STREAMS `strioctl()` command is called to process the ioctl command.

The tasks performed by `strioctl()` for an `I_PUSH` ioctl are:

- Call `copyin(K)` to copy the module name from user space.
- Invoke `findmod()` to search for the module name in `fmodsw[]`.
- Call `qattach()` to push the module onto the STREAM.

The name passed as an argument to `ioctl(S)` is checked against each entry in the `fmodsw[]` array by the `findmod()` function. This involves a string comparison with the `f_str` entry of each `fmodsw` structure.

If the module is found, `qattach()` is called to add the module to the top of the STREAM. The procedures followed by `qattach()` are identical for modules and drivers. For further details of `qattach()` see section 10.3.

The `I_POP` ioctl command is used to detach the module located at the top of the STREAM. The first check that `strioctl()` performs is to ensure that there is in fact a module at the top of the STREAM.

If a module is found, the `qdetach()` function is called to remove the module from the STREAM. The tasks performed by `qdetach()` are:

- For both the read and write side queues, call the `noenable(K_STR)`, `qdisable(K_STR)` and `flushq(K_STR)` functions.

- Detach the module by altering the `q_next` field of the STREAM head write queue to point to the next module or driver downstream and alter the `q_next` field of the next module or driver downstream to point to the read side queue in the STREAM head.

- Call `freeq()` to add the pair of queues to the free list headed by `qfreelist`.

10.5   STREAMS messages

All data passing through a STREAM is based on two categories of messages, *ordinary messages* and *priority messages*. The type of the message determines the order in which the message will be handled. When messages are queued for processing by the module or driver's service procedure, priority messages will be queued first with normal messages attached to the end of the queue. The details of how message queuing is handled are described in section 10.9.

Messages are accessed via a message control block and a number of message data blocks. Figure 10.11 shows the relationship between the various structures which are described throughout the next few sections.

10.5.1 Message structures

There are two basic structures used for constructing STREAMS messages. A pointer to a `msgb` (message block) structure, which is shown in Table 10.4, is passed to a module or driver's `put` procedure.

The message block points to a `datab` (data block) structure which in turn points to the buffer where the message data is actually stored.

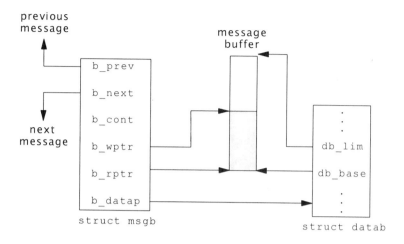

Figure 10.11   The structure of STREAMS messages

Table 10.4   The msgb structure used to describe STREAMS messages

msgb structure field		Description
struct msgb	*b_next	If messages are held on a queue for processing by the module or driver's service procedure, b_next and b_prev are used to link the message onto the queue using the q_first and q_last fields of the queue structure.
struct msgb	*b_prev	See above.
struct msgb	*b_cont	This field is used when messages are extended as they pass through the STREAM.
unsigned char	*b_rptr	When a message is allocated and data copied into the message buffer, this field points to the first location at which data should be read.
unsigned char	*b_wptr	As above but b_wptr points to the last location that data was written.
struct datab	*b_datap	This field points to the message data block.

If a module wishes to add new data to the message, a new message block can be allocated using the allocb(K_STR) function. Either the new message can be attached to the existing message using the b_cont field of the msgb structure with the additional data or a new message is allocated with the correct size, the data copied and the original message freed.

The data buffer is described by the datab structure as shown in Table 10.5.

Table 10.5   The `datab` structure used to describe the message data block

`datab` structure fields	Description
`unsigned char *db_base`	The address specified by `db_base` is the base address in memory of the data buffer.
`unsigned char *db_lim`	This address is the first location after the end of the data block. The size of the data block is `db_lim-db_base` bytes.
`unsigned char db_ref`	This field contains a reference count of the number of message blocks which are pointing to this data block.
`unsigned char db_type`	This field specifies the type of the message.

10.5.2 Message types

STREAMS messages are defined in the `<sys/stream.h>` header file. There are 18 messages in total, divided into normal messages and priority messages.

Table 10.6 shows the complete list of normal messages. Only a few messages will be described throughout the chapter. For further information see the SCO OpenServer *Advanced Hardware Developer's Kit* (1995).

Table 10.6   Ordinary STREAMS messages

Message type	Description
`M_DATA`	Used when a message contains ordinary data. For example, normal reads and writes result in `M_DATA` messages sent through the STREAM.
`M_PROTO`	An `M_PROTO` message contains protocol control and associated data. An `M_PROTO` message will be followed by zero or more `M_DATA` message blocks.
`M_BREAK`	This message is sent to a driver to request that a break is transmitted.
`M_PASSFP`	This message type is used to pass a file pointer from the STREAM head of one end of a STREAMS pipe to the other.
`M_SIG`	This message is generated by modules and drivers and sent upstream in order to post a signal to a process.
`M_DELAY`	This message is sent to a driver to introduce a time delay when transmitting characters to a device. This is usually performed to prevent transmitted data from exceeding the buffering capacity of slow devices.
`M_CTL`	Modules wishing to send messages to a particular module or type of module will use an `M_CTL` message. This is used only for inter-module communication since `M_CTL` messages will be discarded by the STREAM head.
`M_IOCTL`	This type of message is generated by the STREAM head in response to `I_STR`, `I_LINK`, `I_UNLINK`, `I_PLINK` and `I_PUNLINK` `ioctl(S)` based STREAM calls used for building multiplexed STREAMS.
`M_SETOPTS`	This message is used to set various characteristics of the STREAM head.
`M_RSE`	This message type is used for internal use. If modules or drivers see it, they should pass it on unchanged.

Ordinary messages are subject to *flow control*. The flow control within a STREAM is voluntary, that is, it is the responsibility of the STREAMS modules and drivers to enforce flow control. For example, when a message needs to be sent downstream or upstream, the module or driver must ensure that space is available in the next module before calling its put procedure. If the next module reaches its high water mark, the message will be placed on the current queue and the queue *enabled*. After a short interval, the STREAMS scheduler will call the module's service procedure which will then attempt once more to pass the message. In this scenario, messages can back up.

Priority messages are not subject to flow control. They will be forwarded to the next queue regardless of the number of messages that may be pending on that queue. The list of priority messages is shown in Table 10.7.

Table 10.7 Priority based STREAMS messages

Message type	Description
M_IOCACK	This message is used to acknowledge a previous M_IOCTL message. The STREAM head will pass any relevant data back to the user.
M_IOCNAK	When an ioctl(S) fails, this message is sent upstream. The STREAM head will return an error to the caller.
M_PCPROTO	This message is similar to the M_PROTO message with some additional attributes such as the ability to avoid flow control restrictions of normal messages.
M_PCSIG	This message is sent upstream in order to post a signal to a user process.
M_READ	This message is sent downstream when a read is requested but there is no data at the STREAM head.
M_FLUSH	When a module or driver receives this message, it should flush *all* messages from its queues based on the type of flush:

	FLUSHR Flush the read queue.
	    FLUSHW Flush the write queue.
	    FLUSHRW Flush both read and write queues.
	    FLUSHBAND Flush messages according to the message priority band.

	Each module must pass the message on to the next module.
M_STOP	This message is sent to stop transmission immediately.
M_START	This message is sent to restart transmission after a stop has occurred.
M_HANGUP	This message is sent upstream indicating that the driver can no longer send data upstream, usually owing to an error or the dropping of a remote line connection. Any subsequent write(S) or putmsg(S) system calls will fail with ENXIO.
M_ERROR	This message is sent upstream to report an error which occurred on the downstream side of the queue. All subsequent calls to the STREAM with the exception of close(S) and poll(S) will result in an error.
M_COPYIN	This message is sent upstream to request that the STREAM head should perform a copyin(K) in order to retrieve user data. It is valid only after receiving an M_IOCTL message and before an M_IOCACK or M_IOCNAK message.
M_COPYOUT	This message is sent upstream to request that the STREAM head performs a copyout(K) to pass data to a user process. It is valid only after receiving an M_IOCTL message and before an M_IOCACK or M_IOCNAK message.
M_IOCDATA	This message is generated by the STREAM head and sent downstream to respond to an M_COPYIN or M_COPYOUT message.
M_PCRSE	This message type is for internal use and if not recognised, it should be freed.

Section 10.9 describes the relationship between flow control and STREAMS scheduling.

10.5.3 Message allocation and de-allocation

Messages are allocated using the `allocb(K_STR)` function and de-allocated using `freeb(K_STR)` with additional functions available for message manipulation, all of which can be found in the `K_STR` section of the *Advanced Hardware Developer's Kit*:

```
#include <sys/stream.h>

mblk_t *allocb(int size, unsigned int pri) ;
mblk_t *dupb(mblk_t *bp) ;
mblk_t *dupmsg(mblk_t *mp) ;
mblk_t *copyb(mblk_t *bp) ;
mblk_t *copymsg(mblk_t *mp) ;
int     adjmsg(mblk_t *mp, int len) ;
void    linkb(mblk_t *mp1, mblk_t mp2) ;
void    freeb(mblk_t *bp) ;
void    freemsg(mblk_t *bp) ;
```

Most of the functions available take a message which has previously been allocated using the `allocb(K_STR)` function or these functions will call `allocb(K_STR)` themselves.

Calling `allocb(K_STR)` will result in an `M_DATA` message type of at least `size` bytes being allocated. The caller must then populate the data block which is attached to the message block via the `b_datap` field and adjust the `b_rptr` and `b_wptr` fields accordingly. The `pri` field specifies the priority of the allocation request as follows:

BPRI_LO   This is a *low* priority and may result in `allocb(K_STR)` failing even though a data buffer of the requested size may be available.

When write calls are issued to a STREAM, the STREAM head will use this priority, ensuring that messages that need to be allocated by modules and drivers to complete message processing will have higher priority and therefore ensuring that those messages will be able to flow through the STREAM with minimal hindrance.

BPRI_MED   The *medium* priority is usually used for normal data and control block allocation. It may also fail even though a data buffer of the correct size is available although requests with a priority of BPRI_LO are guaranteed to fail first.

BPRI_HI   This *high* priority request should be used only for allocation of critical control messages. All calls will succeed if a buffer of the correct size is available.

Since a buffer cannot be guaranteed to be allocated on a call to `allocb(K_STR)`, a module or driver can use `bufcall(K_STR)` to arrange to be notified when space becomes available. See section 10.5.4 for further details.

The `dupb(K_STR)` function duplicates the message block specified by `bp`, copying the fields into a newly allocated message block descriptor. Both new and old message blocks will point to the same data block using the `b_datap` field. A pointer to the newly allocated message block is returned.

The `dupmsg(K_STR)` function uses `dupb(K_STR)` to duplicate each message block descriptor in the message pointed to by `mp` and links each message block to form a new message. As with `dupb(K_STR)`, `dupmsg(K_STR)` does not duplicate the data blocks.

The `copyb(K_STR)` function copies the contents of the message block pointed to by `bp` using `allocb(K_STR)`. All the data between the `b_rptr` and `b_wptr` fields is copied to the new message block. A pointer to the new message block is returned.

The `copymsg(K_STR)` function uses `copyb(K_STR)` to copy each message block and data block which are then linked together to form a completely new message to which a pointer is returned.

The `adjmsg(K_STR)` can be used to trim `len` bytes from the message specified by `mp`. This function is used to remove unwanted space resulting from manipulation of message data where the amount of data is reduced.

The `linkb(K_STR)` function links the two messages pointed to by `mp1` and `mp2`. The message specified by `mp2` is appended to the message specified by `mp1`.

The `freeb(K_STR)` function is used to free the message block specified by `bp`. The reference count of the data block, specified in the `db_ref` field, will be decremented and if it reaches zero, the data block will be freed. The `freemsg(K_STR)` function can be called to free all message blocks linked together in the message specified by `bp`.

10.5.4 Recovering from failed buffer allocation

Since `allocb(K_STR)` is not guaranteed to succeed, the `bufcall(K_STR)` function is provided to allow invocation of a specified function when buffer space becomes available. The prototype for `bufcall(K_STR)` is:

```
#include <sys/stream.h>

int bufcall(unsigned int size, int pri, void (*func)(), long arg) ;
```

The `size` and `pri` arguments should be the same arguments that were passed to the failed `allocb(K_STR)`.

When a buffer of the correct size is available, the kernel will call the function specified by `func` with the `arg` argument. When `func` is called it should not make any assumptions about which context it is running in and should not therefore make reference to fields in the u_area.

`bufcall(K_STR)` cannot guarantee that the buffer will be available on a subsequent call to `allocb(K_STR)` since buffer space may be allocated in the meantime, for example during interrupt processing. Therefore, callers may need to make successive calls to `bufcall(K_STR)`.

10.5.5 Displaying message structures with `crash (ADM)`

The `mblock` and `mbfree` `crash(ADM)` commands can be used to display message block headers that are allocated and on the free list, respectively:

```
> mblock 10..20
MESSAGE BLOCK TABLE SIZE = 100
SLOT NEXT CONT PREV         RPTR        WPTR DATAB
  10   22   31    - 0xf0837000 0xf083700e     -
  11   43   38    - 0xf0837000 0xf083700e     -
  12   15    -    - 0xf0823036 0xf08235ea    67
  13   12    -    - 0xf08aa836 0xf08aadea    71
  14   29   25    - 0xfd197530 0xfd197534     -
  15   39    -    - 0xf0823836 0xf0823dea    66
  16   23   47    - 0xfd197530 0xfd197534     -
  17   47    -    - 0xf08371a0 0xf08371a0     -
  18   42    -    - 0xf083902a 0xf0839222     -
  19   52   18    - 0xf0837180 0xf083718e     -
  20   53    -    - 0xf08bc400 0xf08bc800     -
> mbfree ! head -10
SLOT NEXT CONT PREV         RPTR        WPTR DATAB
  31   37    -    - 0xf08371a0 0xf08371a0     -
  37   32    -    - 0xf083982a 0xf0839a22     -
  32   18    -    - 0xf083f694 0xf083f6a4     -
  18   42    -    - 0xf083902a 0xf0839222     -
  42   46    -    - 0xf0837094 0xf0837094     -
  46   17    -    - 0xf0837234 0xf0837234     -
  17   47    -    - 0xf08371a0 0xf08371a0     -
  47   16   17    - 0xf0837000 0xf083700e     -
  16   23   47    - 0xfd197530 0xfd197534     -
```

For further details on using the `mblock` command see Toolkit 10.4.

10.6 STREAMS drivers

STREAMS drivers and modules are similar in that they both must declare the same structures (`streamtab`, `qinit` and `module_info`) and provide the same interface. The three main differences between a driver and a module are:

- Only STREAMS drivers manage physical hardware and must therefore be responsible for handling interrupts if appropriate.

- A STREAMS driver may have multiple STREAMS connected to it. For example, refer to Figure 10.5.

- There is a difference in initialisation between drivers and modules. When an open of the STREAM occurs the driver `open` routine is called, while the module sees the open as an `I_PUSH` ioctl. The same is true for `close` when an `I_POP` ioctl is passed down the STREAM although the driver's `close` routine is called.

Each module and driver must declare `streamtab`, `qinit` and `module_info` structures. The interface to both modules and drivers is through the `qinit` structure. For both read and write sides, the `qinit` structures are referenced by the `streamtab` structure.

10.7 Accessing STREAMS

Each STREAM is opened and closed using the standard `open(S)` and `close(S)` system calls. The tasks performed by `open(S)` are described in section 10.3. Section 10.4.3 describes the tasks performed for popping modules. The procedures followed for `close(S)` are very similar so will not be described further here.

When reading from or writing to the STREAM there are two methods of access. The first method uses the standard file based system calls, `read(S)` and `write(S)`, with `ioctl(S)` available for device specific operations. Note that when closing a STREAM, modules will be automatically popped.

The second method involves using three system calls that were specifically added for STREAMS access, namely `getmsg(S)`, `putmsg(S)` and `poll(S)`.

10.7.1 Writing data to a STREAM

Writing data to a STREAM using the `write(S)` system call involves calling the `strwrite()` kernel function as shown in Figure 10.12.

When `strwrite()` is called it will break up the read request into messages which conform with the minimum and maximum message sizes that have been set by drivers and modules within the open STREAM. It will always attempt to use the largest buffer

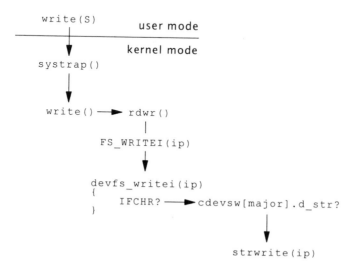

Figure 10.12   Kernel paths followed for writing to a STREAM

that will satisfy the request.

The main tasks performed by `strwrite()` are:

- The `stdata` structure in the STREAM head is located via the `i_sptr` field of the inode passed to `strwrite()`.

- The minimum and maximum packet sizes are determined by looking at the `q_minpsz` and `q_maxpsz` fields of the `queue` structure in the module or driver below the STREAM head. These values determine the size of the messages that will be created to send the data downstream and therefore the number of message transfers that will take place.

    Recall that the `sd_wrq` field of the `stdata` structure points to the write side queue from which the `q_next` field locates the next module downstream.

- The following tasks are performed repeatedly while data needs to be written to the STREAM. The amount of data is stored in `u.u_count` and the address in user space where the data is stored is held in `u.u_base`.

    ⇨ `canput(K_STR)` is called to see if space is available downstream in which to pass the message. If `canput(K_STR)` returns an error, `strwaitq()` is called to wait until space is available. This will result in a call to `sleep(K)`.

    ⇨ `strmakemsg()` is called to create a message of type `M_DATA` by calling `allocb(K_STR)` and copying data from user space.

    ⇨ The `u.u_base` and `u.u_count` fields are adjusted accordingly.

    ⇨ `putnext(K_STR)` is called to invoke the `put` procedure of the next module downstream.

The position at which the messages will be held in the STREAM when a call to `write(S)` returns is dependent on the modules and driver in the STREAM. If each `put` procedure in turn calls `putnext(K_STR)` and there are no blockages in the STREAM due to flow control, the messages will reach the driver and possibly the device before the `write(S)` returns.

However, most messages are subject to flow control restrictions and will impose flow control of their own by queuing messages for processing at a later time by the STREAM scheduler. The scheduler and flow control mechanisms are described in section 10.9.

10.7.2 Reading data from a STREAM

A `read(S)` system call will result in a call to the `strread()` kernel function after following the paths from `systrap()` shown in Figure 10.13.

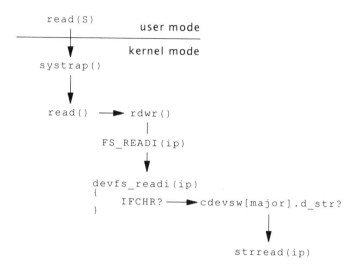

Figure 10.13   The kernel paths followed when reading data from a STREAM

When `strread()` is called it may encounter a number of different message types at the STREAM head including `M_DATA`, `M_PROTO`, `MPCPROTO` and `M_PASSFP`. The tasks performed by `strread()` for `M_DATA` messages are:

- The `stdata` structure in the STREAM head is located via the `i_sptr` field of the inode passed to `strread()`.

- The following tasks are called repeatedly until the number of bytes to be read (`u.u_count`) reaches zero or until an error occurs:

    ⇨ The `getq(K_STR)` function is called to retrieve a message from the read side queue at the STREAM head located through `RD(std->sd_wptr)`. If a message is not available, `strwaitq()` queue is called which will invoke `sleep(K)` until a message is available.

    ⇨ If the message is of type `M_DATA`, the data in the message will be copied to user space. Figure 10.14 shows how the copy is performed.

    ⇨ `freeb(K_STR)` is called to free the message block.

The amount of data transferred in Figure 10.14 is the entire message. If the amount of data requested by the user is less than the amount of data in the message body only the amount in `u.u_count` will be transferred.

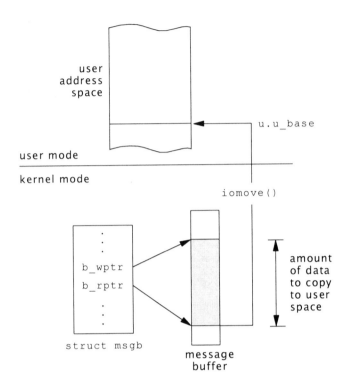

Figure 10.14   Transferring data to user space within `strread()`

10.7.3 Issuing `ioctl` commands to a STREAM

There are a number of `ioctl` commands which are applicable to STREAMS. The full list of commands is given in the `streamio`(M) manual page. Some of the more common commands are as follows:

I_PUSH   The module specified to `ioctl`(S) is pushed onto the STREAM. For details of pushing modules see section 10.4.3.

I_POP   The module at the top of the STREAM (just below the STREAM head) is removed from the STREAM. For details of popping modules see section 10.4.3.

I_LOOK   This command retrieves the name of the module below the STREAM head. The name returned is the module prefix as held in the `fmodsw[]` array.

I_FLUSH   This command is used to flush all input and output queues. An additional argument selects the read and/or write side queues.

I_SETSIG	This command is issued to inform the STREAM head that the user wishes to receive a SIGPOLL signal when a specified event occurs. Examples include when a non-priority message has arrived at the STREAM head or an M_ERROR or M_HANGUP message has reached the STREAM head.
I_FIND	This command is issued to check for presence of a specified module.
I_LIST	This command lists all modules on the specified STREAM.
I_STR	A user specified ioctl command which will be passed downstream.
I_LINK I_PLINK I_UNLINK I_PUNLINK	These commands are used in constructing multiplexed STREAMS. The details of these commands are discussed in section 10.10.2.

There are two types of STREAM ioctl commands: those that are handled directly by the strioctl() kernel function such as I_PUSH and I_POP, and ioctl commands which are packaged by strioctl() as M_IOCTL messages which are then passed downstream for processing by the modules and driver.

To generate an ioctl command that will be passed downstream, the caller specifies the I_STR command to ioctl(S). The additional argument passed to ioctl(S) must point to an strioctl structure, the fields of which are shown in Table 10.8.

Table 10.8   The strioctl structure used when issuing an I_STR ioctl(S) command

strioctl structure field		Description
int	ic_cmd	The ioctl command to be sent downstream.
int	ic_timout	This field specifies the number of seconds that an I_STR request will wait for acknowledgement before timing out.
int	ic_len	The length of the data argument.
char	ic_dp	A pointer to the data argument.

When an I_STR ioctl command is seen by strioctl() it copies the strioctl structure into kernel space and calls strdoioctl() to process the command. On return from strdoioctl() the contents of the strioctl structure are copied to user space. This allows the process to determine, through the ic_len field, how many bytes were returned.

strdoioctl() calls allocb(K_STR) to allocate a message block large enough to hold an iocblk structure. As well as holding the contents of the ic_cmd and ic_len fields of the strioctl structure specified by the user, it also contains the user and group IDs of the calling process. The message type is set to M_IOCTL.

The M_IOCTL message will be linked with zero or more messages of type M_DATA into which will be copied the user data accessible through the ic_dp field of the strioctl structure passed to ioctl(S).

If an `M_IOCTL` message is processed by a module or driver, an `M_IOCACK` or `M_IOCNAK` message will be returned upstream, usually by invoking the `qreply(K_STR)` function to send the message in the reverse direction (upstream).

If an acknowledgement needs to return data, the data will be stored in `M_DATA` messages linked to the `M_IOCACK` message which also contains an `iocblk` structure. The amount of data to be returned to the user is specified in the `ioc_count` field.

Drivers and modules may additionally send an `M_COPYIN` or `M_COPYOUT` message upstream to request the STREAM head to copy data to or from user space. These messages are valid only after an `M_IOCTL` message has been sent downstream and before an `M_IOCACK` or `M_IOCNAK` message has been returned.

When the `M_IOCTL` message is complete, `strdoioctl()` calls `putnext(K_STR)` to send the message downstream. Modules which do not recognise the `M_IOCTL` message should call `putnext(K_STR)` to pass the message further downstream. If the driver at the bottom of the STREAM does not recognise the `ioctl` command, it should invoke `qreply(K_STR)` to send the message upstream back to the STREAM head where `strdoioctl()` will generate an error to be returned to the user.

10.7.4 Writing data with `putmsg(S)`

The `putmsg(S)` and `putpmsg(S)` system calls are called to create messages to send data downstream. The prototypes of both system calls are:

```
#include <stropts.h>

int putmsg(int fd, const struct strbuf *ctlptr,
               const struct strbuf *dataptr, int flags) ;
int putpmsg(int fd, const struct strbuf *ctlptr,
               const struct strbuf *dataptr, int band, int flags) ;
```

The `putpmsg(S)` performs the same function as `putmsg(S)` with the exception of being able to specify different priority bands using the `band` argument.

The message to be created to be sent downstream can consist of a control part or a data part or both, as specified by the `ctlptr` and `dataptr` arguments.

The `strbuf` structure contains three fields of which only the `buf` and `len` fields are currently used. The `buf` field points to the buffer where the control or data buffer is located and the `len` field specifies the size of the data in bytes.

When `putmsg(S)` is invoked with a control part and the `flags` argument is set to `RS_HIPRI`, a high priority message is sent downstream.

For messages to be created for `putpmsg(S)`, the `flags` argument is a bit mask of `MSG_HIPRI` and `MSG_BAND`. If the `MSG_HIPRI` bit is set, a control part is specified and the `band` argument is set to zero, a high priority message is sent. When `MSG_BAND` is set, a message is sent in the priority band specified by `band`.

Both `putmsg(S)` and `putpmsg(S)` are handled within the kernel by the `msgio()` function. After validating the arguments, the control and/or data buffers are copied into the kernel address space and the `strputmsg()` function is called for `putmsg(S)` or the `strputpmsg()` function is called for `putpmsg(S)`. The `strputmsg()` function calls `strputpmsg()` with additional flags.

The tasks performed by `strputpmsg()` are similar to `strwrite()`, for example allocating a message block, checking for control flow and invoking `putnext(K_STR)` to pass the message downstream.

10.7.5 Reading data with `getmsg(S)`

The `getmsg(S)` and `getpmsg(S)` system calls are used to retrieve the contents of the next message at the STREAM head into a user supplied buffer. The prototypes for both functions are:

```
#include <stropts.h>

int getmsg(int fd, struct strbuf *ctlptr, struct strbuf *dataptr,
                                           int *flagsp) ;
int getpmsg(int fd, struct strbuf *ctlptr, struct strbuf *dataptr,
                                           int *band, int *flagsp) ;
```

The message must contain a data part or a control part or both. The control part of the message will be copied to the buffer pointed to by `ctlptr` and the data part will be copied to the buffer pointed to by the `dataptr`.

Each buffer to be copied to is specified by a `strbuf` structure as defined in section 10.7.4.

By default, `getmsg(S)` will receive the first available message attached to the STREAM head read queue. However, if the `flagsp` argument points to `RS_HIPRI`, it will retrieve only a high priority message.

As with `putpmsg(S)`, the `flagsp` argument of `getpmsg(P)` is a bit mask of the `MSG_HIPRI`, `MSG_BAND` and `MSG_ANY` flags.

If the STREAM is opened with neither the `O_NDELAY` nor the `O_NONBLOCK` flag, the process will sleep if no messages are available at the STREAM head.

Both `getmsg(S)` and `getpmsg(S)` are handled within the kernel by the `msgio()` function. After validating the system call arguments the `strgetmsg()` function is called for `getmsg(S)` or the `strgetpmsg()` function is called for `getpmsg(S)`. The `strgetmsg()` function calls `strgetpmsg()` with additional flags.

The tasks performed by `strgetpmsg()` are similar to `strread()`, described in section 10.7.2.

10.7.6 The `poll(S)` system call

The `poll(S)` system call allows a user process to multiplex I/O over a set of STREAMS simultaneously. The prototype for `poll(S)` is:

```
#include <stropts.h>
#include <poll.h>

int poll(struct pollfd fds[], unsigned long nfds, int timeout) ;
```

The STREAMS on which messages can be sent or received are specified in the `fds[]` array. The `pollfd` structure consists of three fields: `fd`, which is an open file descriptor, and the `events` and `revents` fields which are bit masks of the following event flags. The `events` field is used to specify requested events and the `revents` field contains events returned from `poll(S)`:

POLLIN	A non-priority message or a file descriptor passing message is present on the STREAM head's read queue. This flag is set in the `revents` field even if the message is of zero length. This flag is mutually exclusive with the `POLLPRI` flag.
POLLOUT	The first write queue downstream is not full. Priority control messages can therefore be sent using the `putmsg(S)` system call.
POLLPRI	This flag indicates that a priority message is present on the STREAM head read queue and is set even if the message is of zero length. In the `revents` field, this flag is mutually exclusive with `POLLIN`.
POLLERR	If an error message has arrived at the STREAM head, this flag is returned. This flag is valid only in the `revents` field.
POLLHUP	This flag indicates that a hang-up has occurred on the STREAM. This event and `POLLOUT` are mutually exclusive. A STREAM can never be written to if a hang-up has occurred. However, this event and `POLLIN` or `POLLPRI` are not mutually exclusive. This flag is valid only in the `revents` bit mask.
POLLNVAL	The specified file descriptor (`fd`) does not reference an open STREAM. This flag is valid only in the `revents` field.

For each of the `nfds` file descriptors, `poll(S)` will look to see if any of the events can be matched. Where a match is found, the appropriate bits are set in the `revents` field. If none of the defined events are true, `poll(S)` will wait for `timeout` milliseconds for an event to occur before returning. Figure 10.15 shows the paths followed when issuing a `poll(S)` system call.

For each entry in the array specified by `fds`, the `pollfd` structure is copied into kernel space and the `pollstr()` function invoked to perform poll processing. If the poll can be satisfied, the return events are copied back to user space.

If the poll cannot be satisfied by `pollstr()`, it sets a flag in the STREAM such that if any one of the events can be satisfied in future, the STREAM head will issue a `wakeup(K)` call.

If none of the events can be satisfied for any of the file descriptors, `poll()` sets a `timeout(K)` for the remaining time and calls `sleep(K)`. The process can then be awoken by two different mechanisms. Firstly, the timeout expires. In this case, the `poll(S)` system call has failed and an error will be returned to the caller. Each STREAM head is reset by calling `strpollreset()` so that they will not invoke any subsequent `wakeup(K)` calls.

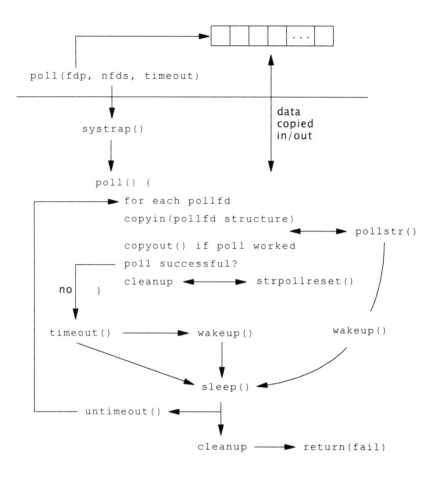

Figure 10.15   The kernel paths followed when performing poll(S)

The process may also wake up as a result of a wakeup(K) call being issued from the STREAM head to signal that the events specified can now be satisfied. If time remains, the timeout is cancelled with a call to untimeout(K) and the test for each file descriptor is repeated.

10.8 Device cloning

There are two basic methods for opening a STREAM. The first requires the caller to choose a unique, unused minor number which can be used by the STREAMS driver to establish the appropriate connection between the write side and the read side of the STREAM. The main problem with this method of access is highlighted with pseudo TTYs in section 9.8 where the user must loop through the range of minor numbers trying to open the device until an open succeeds.

The other method which is often used in the STREAMS environment is a technique called *device cloning*. With cloning, the user opens the device through a single device name and therefore without concerning the minor number. It is the responsibility of the STREAMS driver to manage the minor numbers internally to establish separate STREAMS for each open. The number of STREAMS provided by the driver is therefore limited not to the number of device entries in the filesystem namespace, but to internal configuration tables managed by the driver.

There are two methods by which a clone device can be created in the filesystem namespace. The first method involves using the *clone* driver which has a major device number of 40. The real driver's major number is used as the minor number for the clone driver as shown with some of the following drivers and modules:

```
crw-rw-rw-   1 root      sys        40, 30 Jan 15 11:18 arp
crw-rw-rw-   1 root      sys        40, 35 Jan 15 11:18 ip
crw-rw-rw-   1 root      sys        40, 39 Jan 15 11:18 llcloop
crw-rw-rw-   1 root      sys        40, 42 Jan 15 11:18 ptmx
crw-rw-rw-   1 root      sys        40, 36 Jan 15 11:18 rawip
crw-rw-rw-   1 root      sys        40, 60 Jan 15 11:18 spx
crw-rw-rw-   1 root      sys        40, 44 Jan 15 11:18 tcp
crw-rw-rw-   1 root      sys        40, 49 Jan 15 11:18 udp
```

The second method is for the driver to choose a particular minor number for use as the clone device. This may involve additional nodes in the namespace.

The clone driver is a fairly simple STREAMS driver offering only an open interface. When it is called it uses the minor number to locate the real driver in the cdevsw[] table, attaches the driver's qinit structures to the read and write queues (passed to open) and then calls the driver's open routine, setting the sflag argument to CLONEOPEN. This allows the driver to determine that the clone device was opened. The following toolkit example uses this mechanism.

Toolkit 10.1   A STREAMS loopback driver

The example presented in this toolkit provides a simple STREAMS driver which can be used in conjunction with the clone driver.

The driver performs little work other than to return messages upstream, although it will be used later in Toolkit 10.3 to demonstrate pushing of modules.

The main driver structures required by the kernel are shown in part of the following listing. This includes the module_info, streamtab and read/write side qinit structures. The functions referenced by the structures will be described later.

```
 1 #include <sys/sysmacros.h>
 2 #include <sys/types.h>
 3 #include <sys/param.h>
 4 #include <sys/stream.h>
 5 #include <sys/errno.h>
 6
 7 int loopopen(), loopclose(), loopput(), loopsrv() ;
 8
 9 struct module_info loop_info = { 77, "loop", 0, 512, 512, 128 } ;
10
```

```
11 struct qinit looprinit = {
12     NULL,
13     NULL,
14     loopopen,
15     loopclose,
16     NULL,
17     &loop_info,
18     NULL
19 } ;
20
21 struct qinit loopwinit = {
22     loopput,
23     loopsrv,
24     NULL,
25     NULL,
26     NULL,
27     &loop_info,
28     NULL
29 } ;
30
31 struct streamtab loopinfo = {
32     &looprinit,
33     &loopwinit,
34     NULL,
35     NULL
36 } ;
37
38 struct loop_clone {
39     queue_t *write_qp ;      /* write queue */
40     queue_t *read_qp ;       /* read queue   */
41 } ;
42
43 #define MAXLOOP 8
44
45 struct loop_clone lpclone[MAXLOOP] ;
46
```

The driver supports up to eight separate STREAMS through use of the `lpclone[]` array. Each entry in `lpclone[]` is a `loop_clone` structure.

For each open of the clone driver, one entry in `lpclone[]` will be allocated and both fields of the structure will be set to point to the read and write queues passed to open.

The details of how the `lpclone[]` array is used is shown in the following `loopopen()` function:

```
47 loopopen(queue_t *q, dev_t dev, int flag, int sflag)
48 {
49     dev_t lminor = minor(dev) ;
50     struct loop_clone *lc = NULL ;
51
52     if (sflag == CLONEOPEN) {
53         int x=0 ;
54         while (x < MAXLOOP) {
55             if (lpclone[x].write_qp == NULL) {
56                 lc = &lpclone[x] ;
57                 break ;
58             }
59             x++ ;
60         }
61         if (lc == NULL)
62             return(ENXIO) ;
```

```
63        }
64        else {
65            lc = &lpclone[lminor] ;
66            if (lc->write_qp != NULL)
67                return(ENXIO) ;
68        }
69
70        q->q_ptr = (caddr_t)lc ;
71        WR(q)->q_ptr = (caddr_t)lc ;
72
73        lc->read_qp = q ;
74        lc->write_qp = WR(q) ;
75
76        return(0) ;
77 }
78
```

Once the STREAM head has been created and the driver's read and write queues have been allocated, the kernel calls qattach() which in turn calls the driver open routine.

There are two routes through which loopopen() can be invoked. The first is through the clone driver for which the sflag argument will be set to CLONEOPEN. A check is made against this flag on line 52. For clone opens, loopopen() ignores the dev argument and searches through the lpclone[] array looking for an empty slot. This is shown in lines 54 to 60. If all slots are currently being used (line 61), ENXIO is returned.

If loopopen() has not been invoked through the clone driver, it should try to use the minor number of the dev_t passed (line 49) to allocate a specific slot in lpclone[]. This involves locating the entry on line 65 and checking to see if it is already in use. If the entry is used, ENXIO is returned.

Once an entry is found in lpclone[], the fields of this structure and the q_ptr field of the read and write queues are set to point to each other (lines 70 to 74).

Figure 10.16 shows the connection between the STREAM head and the loop driver after loopopen() has completed. Each call to open(S) using the clone driver involves allocating a new entry in lpclone[], allowing eight simultaneous STREAMS.

The following loopclose() function must break the connection between the queue structures passed to loopopen() and remove any messages that may be currently held on the write side queue.

```
79 loopclose(queue_t *q, int flag)
80 {
81        struct loop_clone *lc ;
82
83        lc = (struct loop_clone *)q->q_ptr ;
84        lc->write_qp == NULL ;
85        lc->read_qp == NULL ;
86        q->q_ptr = NULL ;
87        WR(q)->q_ptr = NULL ;
88
89        flushq(WR(q), FLUSHALL) ;
90 }
91
```

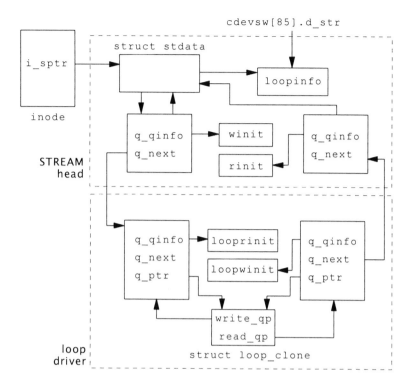

Figure 10.16   The loop STREAM after an open(S) has been performed

The queue structure passed to lpclose() points to the read side queue. The entry in lpclone[] is located in the q_ptr field and accessed on line 83.

The fields of the structure are then set to NULL on lines 84 and 85 indicating that a new STREAM may be allocated. The q_ptr fields of the read and write side queues are set to NULL and the flushq(K_STR) function is called on line 89 which will remove and free all messages that may be held on the write side queue (note that the read side queue will always be empty).

The loopput() and loopsrv() functions used by the write side of the driver are as follows:

```
 92 loopput(queue_t *q, mblk_t *mp)
 93 {
 94     putq(q, mp) ;
 95 }
 96
 97 loopsrv(queue_t *q)
 98 {
 99     mblk_t *mbp ;
100     queue_t *rsq = RD(q) ;
101
102     while ((mbp = getq(q)) != NULL) {
103         if (!canput(rsq->q_next)) {
```

```
104                    putbq(q, mbp) ;
105                    break ;
106                }
107                putnext(rsq, mbp) ;
108        }
109 }
```

The only task performed by loopput() is to call putq(K_STR) which will add the message specified by mp to the queue pointed to by q. The queue is then enabled so that the STREAMS scheduler, when run, will invoke the loopsrv() function to process any messages that are queued.

When loopsrv() is invoked it has no knowledge of how many messages it may have to process. It loops around lines 102 to 108 calling getq(K_STR) to retrieve the first message from the queue and invoking putnext(K_STR) to call the read side put procedure of the STREAM head (or module above) the driver.

Since there may not be space in the read side of the module above the driver, loopsrv() calls canput(K_STR) to determine whether space is available. If space is not available, putbq(K_STR) is called to put the message back on the queue and loopsrv() returns. loopsrv() will then invoked later by the STREAMS scheduler.

The method used for configuring the STREAMS driver into the kernel is almost identical to the method used for linking normal character drivers as the following example shows. Note that the -s option is passed to configure(ADM) to indicate that a STREAMS driver is being configured:

```
# mkdir /etc/conf/pack.d/loop
# cp Driver.o /etc/conf/pack.d/loop
# cd /etc/conf/cf.d
# ./configure -j NEXTMAJOR
85
# ./configure -a loopopen loopclose -c -s -m 85
# mknod /dev/loop c 85 0
# mknod /dev/cloop c 40 85
# ./link_unix
```

The following program is used to test the driver. If passed an additional argument starting with the letter c, the program will open the clone driver through the /dev/cloop device, otherwise the driver will be opened directly through /dev/loop.

The test program, ltest.c, then writes a message downstream and reads the same message back. The same file descriptor returned from open(S) is used for both reading from and writing to the STREAM.

```
#include <fcntl.h>
#include <string.h>

char write_buf[] = "A message to send down the STREAM" ;
char read_buf[256] ;

main(int argc, char **argv)
{
    int fd, n ;
```

```
    if (argc == 2 && argv[1][0] == 'c') {
        printf("Opening clone driver\n") ;
        fd = open("/dev/cloop", O_RDWR) ;
    }
    else {
        printf("Opening loop driver\n") ;
        fd = open("/dev/loop", O_RDWR) ;
    }

    if (fd < 0)
        pexit("/dev/loop") ;

    n = write(fd, write_buf, sizeof(write_buf)) ;
    printf("%d bytes written\n", n) ;

    n = read(fd, read_buf, 256) ;
    printf("%d bytes read [%s]\n", n, read_buf) ;
}
```

A run of the test program is:

```
$ ls -l /dev/loop
crw-rw-rw-  1 root      sys       85,  0 Feb  5 13:32 /dev/loop
$ ls -l /dev/cloop
crw-rw-rw-  1 root      sys       40, 85 Feb  5 13:27 /dev/cloop
$ ltest
Opening loop driver
34 bytes written
34 bytes read [A message to send down the STREAM]
$ ltest c
Opening clone driver
34 bytes written
34 bytes read [A message to send down the STREAM]
```

10.9 STREAMS flow control and scheduling

When a message enters a STREAM at the STREAM head it can potentially travel all the way downstream and back upstream without blocking by successive calls to the put procedure of the module or driver linked to the q_next field of the queue structure.

There are, however, a number of circumstances under which this flow of control will or can be interrupted:

- If a call to allocb(K_STR) to allocate a new message block fails the module or driver may call putq(K_STR) to add the current message to the queue for later scheduling. The service procedure may then retry to allocate a new message block or the bufcall(K_STR) function can be used in conjunction with the service procedure.

- Messages may start backing up as they reach the STREAM head. This may be a result of either a process repeatedly writing messages into the STREAM or the driver reading data from a device and sending data upstream but without any data being read from the STREAM.

A call to `canput(K_STR)` will determine whether the next `put` procedure in the STREAM can be called or whether `putq(K_STR)` should be called to add the message to the queue for later processing.

- The module or driver voluntarily calls `putq(K_STR)` to defer processing of messages to the `service` procedure. This can relinquish control of the kernel for processing of higher priority tasks. Such a decision must be left to the module or driver writer.

The `canput(K_STR)` function uses the high and low water marks specified in the `queue` structure to determine whether space is available in the queue or not.

When the `putq(K_STR)` function is invoked it adds the message to the specified queue and schedules the `service` procedure attached to the queue to be invoked by the STREAMS scheduler. The tasks performed by `putq(K_STR)` are:

- Determine the position at which the message will be placed on the queue. This depends on whether it is a priority, banded or normal message. For example, priority messages will be placed at the start of the queue while normal messages will be placed at the end of the queue.

- Add the message to the queue. Messages are linked using the `q_first` and `q_last` fields of the `queue` structure.

- Invoke the `qenable()` function to specify that the queue needs attention from the STREAMS scheduler.

The `qenable()` function sets the `q_flag` field of the `queue` structure to `QENABLE`, links the specified queue onto the STREAMS scheduling queue and sets `qrunflag` which will be checked by the scheduler to determine whether queue processing is required. The scheduling queue is a linked list of `queue` structures linked using the `q_link` field as shown in Figure 10.17.

The `qrunflag` flag is checked by the `runqueues()` function which is called from a number of places including:

- Whenever the `pswtch()` function is invoked as part of a context switch. See section 7.9 for further details of `pswtch()`.

- During processing of STREAMS related system calls such as `strread()`, `strwrite()` and `strioctl()`.

- Whenever a module is popped off a STREAM or the STREAM is closed.

The `runqueues()` function calls `queuerun()` to run the `service` procedure of each enabled queue. This walks through the list of queues headed by `qhead` and calls the `service` procedure of each queue to process the attached messages.

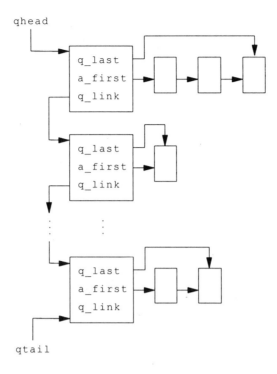

Figure 10.17   Queues linked together for processing by the STREAMS scheduler

10.10 Additional STREAMS features

This section covers some of the additional features and facilities that are available with
the STREAMS subsystem.

10.10.1 Named STREAMS with the `namefs` filesystem

The `fattach(S)` library function provides a mechanism whereby a STREAM based file
descriptor can be associated with an object in the filesystem namespace. The net effect of
calling `fattach(S)` is to build an association between a filename and an open
STREAM. This allows unrelated processes to communicate with each other in a similar
way to named pipes, although the flow of data is dependent on what the STREAM driver
and modules will do with the data sent through the STREAM.

   When `fattach(S)` is called, a `mount(S)` system call is made to mount the `namefs`
filesystem over the specified pathname. This creates a dummy inode so that further file
operations such as `read(S)` and `write(S)` will be redirected to the STREAM rather
than the file. For example, a `read(S)` system call will result in `rdwr()` calling
`FS_READI()`, which will call the `namefs_readi()` function. The real inode is retrieved
by `namefs_readi()` and control is passed to `strread()` to read data from the
STREAM.

The `fdettach(S)` library function breaks the connection between the STREAM and the file such that further file based operations will be applied to the real file.

The prototypes for both `fattach(S)` and `fdettach(S)` are:

```
int fattach(int fildes, char *path) ;
int fdettach(const char *path) ;
```

The filenames passed to `fattach(S)` and `fdettach(S)` must be identical.

Toolkit 10.2   Accessing named STREAMS

This toolkit provides an example which demonstrates how to use named STREAMS.

There are two programs, one which opens the STREAM and attaches it to a file in the filesystem namespace and another which will read data from the file.

The first program starts by opening the loop driver presented in Toolkit 10.1, calls `fattach(S)` to associate the STREAM with the file `/tmp/LOOP` and then writes data into the STREAM.

In the program, the `/tmp/LOOP` file must exist prior to the program being invoked. After writing data to the STREAM, the program calls `pause(S)` to prevent the STREAM from being closed. The `pause(S)` system call is actually unnecessary in this example since the STREAM will remain active after a call to `fattach(S)` even though the process that originally opened the STREAM has terminated.

```
 1 #include <fcntl.h>
 2 #include <unistd.h>
 3
 4 char write_buf[] = "A message to send down the STREAM" ;
 5
 6 main()
 7 {
 8     int fd, n ;
 9
10     printf("Opening loop driver\n") ;
11     fd = open("/dev/loop", O_WRONLY) ;
12
13     if (fd < 0)
14         pexit("/dev/loop") ;
15
16     n = write(fd, write_buf, sizeof(write_buf)) ;
17     printf("%d bytes written\n", n) ;
18
19     fattach(fd, "/tmp/LOOP") ;
20     pause() ;
21 }
```

The second program opens the `/tmp/LOOP` file and attempts to read 64 characters from it.

```
1 #include <fcntl.h>
2
3 char read_buf[256] ;
```

```
 4
 5 main()
 6 {
 7     int fd, n ;
 8
 9     printf("Opening named STREAM\n") ;
10     fd = open("/tmp/LOOP", O_RDONLY) ;
11
12     if (fd < 0)
13         pexit("/tmp/LOOP") ;
14
15     n = read(fd, read_buf, 256) ;
16     printf("%d bytes read [%s]\n", n, read_buf) ;
17 }
```

The program is run by starting `namewrite` in the background to establish an open connection to the STREAM and then by invoking `nameread` to read the characters from the file:

```
$ namewrite &
[1] 1294
$ Opening loop driver
34 bytes written

$ nameread
Opening named STREAM
34 bytes read [A message to send down the STREAM]
```

Of course, with such a scheme the STREAMS subsystem provides all the kernel based memory allocation, flow control and scheduling of data flowing through the named STREAM, while also allowing modules to be pushed and popped dynamically, altering the flow of data through the STREAM.

10.10.2 Multiplexing

A STREAMS multiplexor is a driver that has multiple STREAMS connected to it and allows messages to flow from one STREAM to another. Examples of where multiplexed STREAMS are useful are STREAMS based pipes, pseudo TTYs and the TCP/IP stack which will be described below.

Multiple open STREAMS are established above an existing driver with successive calls to `open(S)`, passing the name of the STREAMS device or the clone driver. There are two `ioctl(S)` system calls which are used to configure a multiplexed STREAM. For multiplexing drivers, the driver is responsible for establishing the connection between different STREAMS and routing data from one STREAM to another. Once a connection has been established, the flow of messages across the different STREAMS is performed using the same mechanisms as for a single STREAM.

There are two types of multiplexed STREAM configurations as shown in Figure 10.18.

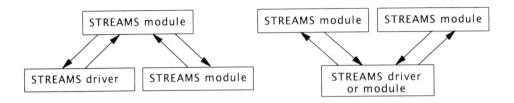

Figure 10.18   1-M and N-1 STREAMS multiplexor configurations

The STREAM on the left-hand side of Figure 10.18 is a 1:M multiplexor, also called a *lower* multiplexor configuration. The STREAM on the right-hand side of the figure is an N:1 multiplexor, also called an *upper* multiplexor configuration.

The most commonly used multiplexed STREAMS configuration is the TCP/IP stack shown in Figure 10.19 which is a 1:M and N:1 configuration.

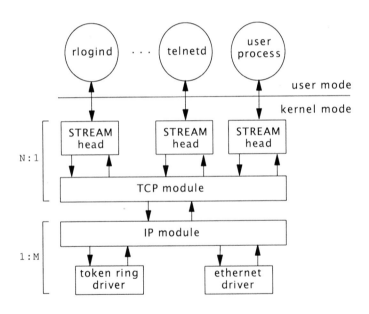

Figure 10.19   TCP/IP using multiplexed STREAMS

The IP STREAMS module routes a single STREAM from the TCP module to two STREAMS drivers below for the token ring and ethernet driver. The TCP module multiplexes multiple STREAMS from daemons and different user processes to a single STREAM to the IP module below.

There are four ioctl commands supported by the STREAMS subsystem which are used for establishing multiplexed STREAMS:

I_LINK   The file descriptor argument passed to `ioctl(S)` references the STREAM connected to the multiplexed driver. The second file descriptor which is passed as the `ioctl(S)` argument must reference the STREAM to be connected below the multiplexed driver.

I_PLINK   The `P_LINK` ioctl command performs the same function as I_LINK but allows the link to be persistent if the file descriptor is closed.

I_UNLINK   These two commands are used to disconnect the two STREAMS
I_PUNLINK   which were established by a previous call to I_LINK or I_PLINK.

                The file descriptor argument specifies the STREAM on which the previous I_LINK or I_PLINK was issued and the additional `ioctl(S)` argument specifies a multiplexor ID that was returned by I_LINK or I_PLINK.

To understand how these commands can be used consider the procedures that are followed during initialisation of the TCP/IP stack, as shown in Figure 10.20.

An initialisation daemon opens both the ethernet driver and the IP driver. By issuing an `ioctl(S)` system call specifying the I_LINK command, the IP module can be linked to the ethernet driver.

The daemon can now open the token ring driver and, by issuing another `ioctl(S)` system call, link the IP driver to the token ring driver.

In the same way that the IP driver is linked to the ethernet and token ring drivers, the TCP module can be linked to the IP module.

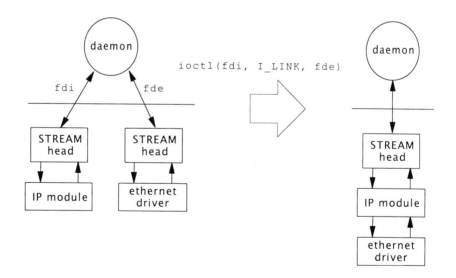

Figure 10.20   Linking the ethernet driver and IP driver

10.10.3 STREAMS error and trace logging

The `strlog(K_STR)` function is provided for STREAMS drivers and modules to submit messages to the `log(M)` device driver.

The log driver is a STREAMS software driver which is used in conjunction with the `sterr(ADM)` and `strace(ADM)` logging and event tracing programs. The log driver is opened through the `/dev/log` special file and for each open, a separate STREAM will be created. Messages generated through the use of `strlog(K_STR)` can be read from the log device and can therefore be used for tracing and error analysis:

```
#include <sys/types.h>
#include <sys/stream.h>
#include <sys/strlog.h>
#include <sys/log.h>

void
strlog(short mid, short sid, char level, ushort_t flags, char *fmt) ;
```

The `mid` argument is the identification number of the module which can be obtained using the `getmid(K_STR)` function. The `sid` argument specifies the minor number of the device which can be used to identify the caller of the message. The `level` argument specifies the tracing level which allows filtering of low priority messages. The `flags` argument is a bit mask which indicates the message type. It is constructed using the following flags:

SL_ERROR   The message is intended for use by the error logger `sterr(ADM)`.

SL_TRACE   The message is intended for use by the trace logger `strace(ADM)`.

SL_NOTIFY   The message should be mailed by the error logger to the system administrator.

SL_FATAL   This message indicates a fatal error.

The `fmt` argument is a formatted string which is similar to `printf(S)`, albeit with a limited number of formatting directives.

For further details of logging, see `log(M)`, `sterr(ADM)` and `strace(ADM)`.

Toolkit 10.3   Pushing and popping STREAMS modules

This toolkit provides a STREAMS module to be pushed onto the loopback STREAMS driver introduced in Toolkit 10.1.

The module performs no function on its write side other than to pass the message down to the driver. On the read side it will reverse the characters passed in the message so that any strings written to the STREAM will be reversed when read back. While this module does not provide any useful purpose it offers a useful test harness on which to try additional features.

The main module structures follow. Although the `service` procedure is common to both read and write sides, each queue requires its own `put` procedure:

```
 1 #include <sys/sysmacros.h>
 2 #include <sys/types.h>
 3 #include <sys/param.h>
 4 #include <sys/stream.h>
 5 #include <sys/errno.h>
 6
 7 int modopen(), modclose(), modrput(), modwput(), modsrv() ;
 8
 9 struct module_info mod_info = { 78, "mod", 0, 512, 512, 128 } ;
10
11 struct qinit modrinit = {
12     modrput,
13     modsrv,
14     modopen,
15     modclose,
16     NULL,
17     &mod_info,
18     NULL
19 } ;
20
21 struct qinit modwinit = {
22     modwput,
23     modsrv,
24     NULL,
25     NULL,
26     NULL,
27     &mod_info,
28     NULL
29 } ;
30
31 struct streamtab modinfo = {
32     &modrinit,
33     &modwinit,
34     NULL,
35     NULL
36 } ;
37
```

The `modopen()` and `modclose()` procedures are shown below. There is nothing specific that needs to be performed by the module on open so `modopen()` returns immediately. The `modclose()` function calls `flushq(K_STR)` for both read and write queues, specifying that all messages should be removed from the queue and freed:

```
38 modopen(queue_t *q, dev_t dev, int flag, int sflag)
39 {
40     return(0) ;
41 }
42
43 modclose(queue_t *q, int flag)
44 {
45     flushq(q, FLUSHALL) ;
46     flushq(WR(q), FLUSHALL) ;
47 }
48
```

The `modwput()` procedure calls `putq(K_STR)` which adds the message to the write side queue which is then enabled for scheduling.

When `modrput()` is called, it calls the `reverse()` function to reverse all characters in the message body, passing the address of the first character of the buffer and the number of characters. Note that the message buffer, which is allocated by the STREAM head, may well be bigger than the amount of data contained in the message.

```
49 reverse(char *str, int sz)
50 {
51      int i, c ;
52
53      for (i=0 ; i<=(sz / 2) ; i++) {
54          c = str[sz-i-1] ;
55          str[sz-i-1] = str[i] ;
56          str[i] = c ;
57      }
58 }
59
60 modrput(queue_t *q, mblk_t *mp)
61 {
62      reverse((char *)mp->b_rptr, (int)(mp->b_wptr - mp->b_rptr)) ;
63      putq(q, mp) ;
64 }
65
66 modwput(queue_t *q, mblk_t *mp)
67 {
68      putq(q, mp) ;
69 }
70
71 modsrv(queue_t *q)
72 {
73      mblk_t *mbp ;
74
75      while ((mbp = getq(q)) != NULL) {
76          if (!canput(q->q_next)) {
77              putbq(q, mbp) ;
78              break ;
79          }
80          putnext(q, mbp) ;
81      }
82 }
```

Figure 10.21 shows the effect on the message body after `modrput()` has called `reverse()`. All fields of the message block and data block structures remain unchanged. After `reverse()` has been called, `putq()` is called to add the message to the read side queue for later processing by `modsrv()`.

The `modsrv()` procedure loops repeatedly, calling `getq(K_STR)` to retrieve the first message from the queue (read or write side), calls `canput(K_STR)` to see if the next queue has space in which to receive the message and, if so, calls `putnext(K_STR)` to call the `put` procedure of the loopback driver for the write side of the STREAM or the `put` procedure of the STREAM head for the read side.

The steps taken for linking the module into the kernel are slightly different for a STREAMS module. Since the module is not contained in the `cdevsw[]` table, a free major number does not have to be located. The steps followed are:

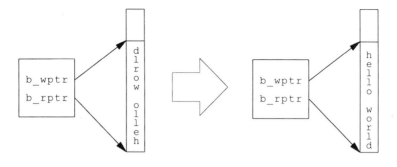

Figure 10.21   Reversing the characters in the message body

```
# mkdir /etc/conf/pack.d/mod
# cp Driver.o /etc/conf/pack.d/mod
# cd /etc/conf/cf.d
# ./configure -a modopen modclose -s -h mod
# ./link_unix
```

The -h option to `configure(ADM)` qualifies the -s (STREAM) option to indicate that
the driver is a STREAMS module and not a driver. The module prefix (`mod`) is required
by the -h option.

The following program is used to test the module. It is based on the test program
shown in Toolkit 10.1 which opened the loopback driver, wrote a string of characters to
the STREAM and read the same string back. The changes in this program are highlighted
in bold.

When the loopback STREAM is opened the module is pushed onto the STREAM and
the same string is written to and read from the STREAM.

```
#include <sys/types.h>
#include <sys/stropts.h>
#include <unistd.h>
#include <fcntl.h>
#include <string.h>

char write_buf[] = "A message to send down the STREAM" ;
char read_buf[256] ;

main(int argc, char **argv)
{
    int fd, n ;

    if (argc == 2 && argv[1][0] == 'c') {
        printf("Opening clone driver\n") ;
        fd = open("/dev/cloop", O_RDWR) ;
    }
    else {
        printf("Opening loop driver\n") ;
        fd = open("/dev/loop", O_RDWR) ;
    }
```

```
    if (fd < 0)
        pexit("/dev/loop") ;

    if (ioctl(fd, I_PUSH, "mod") < 0)
        pexit("I_PUSH(mod)") ;

    n = write(fd, write_buf, strlen(write_buf)) ;
    printf("%d bytes written\n", n) ;

    n = read(fd, read_buf, 256) ;
    printf("%d bytes read [%s]\n", n, read_buf) ;

    if (ioctl(fd, I_POP, (char *)0) < 0)
        pexit("I_POP") ;
}
```

When the program is run, the string read is reversed as expected:

```
$ mtest
Opening loop driver
33 bytes written
33 bytes read [MAERTS eht nwod dnes ot egassem A]
```

10.11 STREAMS statistics

There are some STREAMS related `crash(ADM)` features which, so far, have not been covered. The `strstat` command displays STREAMS statistics, including the number of allocated free numbers of STREAMS structures such as queues, message blocks and data blocks. For example:

```
> strstat
ITEM                    CONFIG  ALLOC  FREE    TOTAL  MAX  FAIL  BUFCALL
streams                   1024    106   918      203  111     0        –
queues                     566    496    70      456  516     0        –
message headers            100     57    43    71315   92     0        –
buffer headers             314    199   115    10527  203     0        0
data block size      64     64      2    62    27620    9     0        0
data block size     128     32      0    32    16534   15     0        0
data block size     256     16      5    11     1817    8     0        0
data block size     512     16      8     8     6202   10     0        0
data block size     1Kb     24      0    24      472   22     0        0
data block size     2Kb     20     18     2      173   20     0        0
data block size     4Kb      2      2     0       19    2     0        0
data block size     8Kb      1      0     1       19    1     0        0
data block size    16Kb      2      0     2       13    2     0        0
data block size    32Kb      0      0     0        0    0     0        0
data block size    64Kb      0      0     0        0    0     0        0
data block size   128Kb      0      0     0        0    0     0        0
data block size   256Kb      0      0     0        0    0     0        0
data block size   512Kb      0      0     0        0    0     0        0

Count of scheduled queues:       0
Number of unallocated pages:     462
Buffer splitting threshold:      100
Size of the interrupt pool:       20
Streams daemon (strd) flags:
```

For details on the fields displayed see chapter 14.

Toolkit 10.4   Walking through STREAMS stacks with `crash`

The example presented here is based on Toolkit 10.2 which was used to establish a name STREAM.

The `namewrite` program is run which sends a message downstream by invoking the `write(S)` system call. When `crash(ADM)` is run the message should have travelled downstream and back upstream and be attached to the STREAM head.

The intention of the example is to use `crash(ADM)` to display the link from the user process's file descriptor all the way through the STREAM to the STREAM head where the message will be held.

First, the process is located by using the `proc` command and invoking `grep(C)` to search for the appropriate program:

```
> proc ! grep namewrite
  64 s   670   445   670 13583  66   0 u          namewrite      load
```

The required process is located in slot `64` of the `proc[]` table as highlighted above.

The `user` command can then be used to display the open file descriptors associated with the process as follows. Note that not all fields of the u_area are displayed here.

```
> user #670
PER PROCESS USER AREA FOR PROCESS 64
USER ID's:  uid: 13583, gid: 50, real uid: 13583, real gid: 50
     supplementary gids: 50
OPEN FILES AND POFILE FLAGS:
     [ 0]: F#275   r    [ 1]: F#275    w  [ 2]: F#275     w
     [ 3]: F#284    w
```

File descriptor number 3 was returned from the `open(S)` system call which opened the loop driver; the other three file descriptors represent `stdin`, `stdout` and `stderr`.

This file descriptor references slot number `284` of the `file[]` table. The `file` command is used to display the contents of this entry:

```
> file 284
FILE TABLE SIZE = 341
SLOT  RCNT   I/FL      OFFSET  FLAGS
 284     1 I# 422        34 write
```

The entry shown indicates that the file table entry references slot number `422` of the in-core inode table. The `inode` command can be used to display this entry as follows:

```
> inode 422
INODE TABLE SIZE = 614
SLOT MAJ/MIN FS INUMB RCNT LINK   UID   GID  SIZE    MODE MNT M/ST FLAGS
 422  1,42   1  1231   3    1      0     3     0 c---000   0 S105
```

There are two fields of interest here. The file corresponds to a character device and the M/ST field indicates that it is a STREAMS device whose stdata structure is located in slot number 105 of the streams[] array.

The stream command can be used to display the structure as follows:

```
> stream 105
STREAM TABLE SIZE = 1024
SLOT  WRQ IOCB INODE  PGRP      IOCID IOCWT WOFF  ERR FLAG
105   521   -   422    0          0     0    0     0 01000000
```

Note that in the output displayed here, the inode which references this structure (422) is also displayed.

Recall that the stdata structure, described in section 10.3, only contains a pointer to the write side queue. In this output, the write side queue structure is held in slot 521.

Using the queue command, the contents of the queue structure can be displayed:

```
> queue 521
QUEUE TABLE SIZE = 566
SLOT  INFO     NEXT LINK    PTR RCNT HD TL MINP MAXP HIWT LOWT FLAGS
521 0xf01d799c 525   - 0xf02278b8  0  -  -   0    0    0    0  us
```

The NEXT field (q_next) points to the queue structure of the next module or driver. In this case, it should point to the write side queue of the loopback driver.

The queue command is run again to display the contents of the driver's write side queue as follows:

```
> queue 525
QUEUE TABLE SIZE = 566
SLOT      INFO NEXT LINK      PTR RCNT HD TL MINP MAXP HIWT LOWT FLAGS
 525 0xf01e0edc   -   - 0xf028d254  0  -  -   0  512  512  128 wr us
```

Since this is the bottom of the STREAM, the q_next field does not point to another queue. Recall from Toolkit 10.1 that for each open(S) made to the loopback driver, a loop_clone structure is allocated which contains a pointer to both the write side and read side queues.

The address of the loop_clone structure was stored in the q_ptr field of both the read and write side queues. The PTR field shows the address of this field.

The od command is used to display both pointers:

```
> od 0xf028d254 2
f028d254:  fcee89d4   fcee89b0
```

The address of the read side queue is highlighted. This time the queue command is called and passed the address of the queue rather than the slot number:

```
> queue @fcee89b0
QUEUE TABLE SIZE = 566
SLOT      INFO NEXT LINK      PTR RCNT HD TL MINP MAXP HIWT LOWT FLAGS
 524 0xf01e0ec0 520   - 0xf028d254  0  -  -   0  512  512  128 wr rr us
```

The NEXT field specifies the slot number of the next queue upstream, in this case the read side of the STREAM head.

The queue command is used once again to display the STREAM head read side queue:

```
> queue 520
QUEUE TABLE SIZE = 566
SLOT        INFO NEXT LINK   PTR  RCNT HD TL MINP MAXP HIWT LOWT FLAGS
 520 0xf01d7980    -   - 0xf02278b8 40  31 31  0  -1 5120 1024 wr rr us
```

The HD and TL (HEAD and TAIL) fields display the contents of the q_head and q_tail fields of the queue structure which are used to reference all attached messages. There is one message attached to the STREAM head whose message block can be displayed using the mblock command:

```
> mblock 31
MESSAGE BLOCK TABLE SIZE = 100
SLOT NEXT CONT PREV      RPTR      WPTR DATAB
  31    -    -    - 0xf0837080 0xf08370a2   181
```

The read and write pointers which point to the start and end addresses of data in the data buffer are highlighted.

Finally, the od command is used to display the contents of the data buffer:

```
> od -c 0xf0837080 40
f0837080:   A    m  e  s  s  a  g  e     t  o     s  e  n
f0837090:   d    d  o  w  n     t  h  e     S  T  R  E  A
f08370a0:   M \? \? \?     j  o  n
```

10.12 Summary and suggested reading

This chapter described the STREAMS architecture in SCO UNIX, including the kernel structures and functions available for supporting STREAMS. The chapter also showed an example STREAMS loopback driver and STREAMS module together with details of how to configure STREAMS modules and drivers into the kernel.

There are a large number of kernel tuneables for the STREAMS subsystem. The SCO OpenServer *Performance Guide* (1995) provides details of the tuneables available.

The SCO OpenServer *Advanced Hardware Developer's Kit* (1995) provides details of all the kernel functions available to driver writers, including a more complete description of STREAMS messages.

Kettle and Statler (1992) provides further information on STREAMS, including a more detailed loopback driver demonstrating the use of ioctl(S) on STREAMS and a simple STREAMS based mouse driver.

11

Inter-process communication

This chapter describes the main methods of inter-process communication (IPC) supported by SCO UNIX. The chapter concentrates on System V IPC which provides message queues, shared memory and semaphores. A toolkit example at the end of the chapter provides a program with similar functionality to `ipcs(ADM)` which can be used to display System V IPC object statistics.

In addition to shared memory, SCO UNIX provides another method of sharing memory between related processes using a combination of the `mmap(S)` system call and `/dev/zero`. Examples show how `/dev/zero` can be used and the different types of mappings that can be established.

The chapter concludes with a description of the different types of pipe implementations in the kernel including `HPPS`, the High Performance Pipe System, which provides significant advantages over traditional anonymous and named pipes.

11.1 Introduction

The term System V IPC (*Inter-process Communication*) is used to encompass shared memory, semaphores and message queues. While these traditional communication methods are still available, they are not the only means by which processes can communicate with each other. STREAMS, signals, `ptrace(S)` for debugging and file locking are four other methods by which processes can communicate and synchronise.

This chapter describes not only the traditional System V IPC mechanisms but also some old and new methods which are used for IPC, including anonymous and named pipes and the `mmap(S)` system call in conjunction with `/dev/zero`.

11.1.1 The IPC toolkit

Most sections throughout this chapter provide examples of use of the type of IPC being described. In addition there are three toolkit examples:

Toolkit 11.1 Sharing memory with `/dev/zero`, page 518
Toolkit 11.2 `mipcs` – an implementation of `ipcs(ADM)`, page 529
Toolkit 11.3 Analysing data flow through a pipe, page 539

Toolkit 11.1 describes the use of `mmap(S)` with `/dev/zero` for providing shared memory between related processes. Toolkit 11.2 provides an implementation of the `ipcs(ADM)` utility which can be used for displaying System V IPC statistics. Toolkit 11.3 shows how to use the `crash(ADM)` command to analyse data flow through anonymous pipes.

11.2 System V IPC

System V IPC combines shared memory, semaphores and message queues which will be described in subsequent chapters. There are, however, properties that are common to all three forms of System V IPC which will be described in this section.

11.2.1 IPC keys

An IPC *key* identifies an IPC object and is used to allow sharing of the object between multiple processes. In order to obtain access to a System V IPC object, whether it is a semaphore, message queue or shared memory segment, a process must have knowledge of the object's key.

A key is defined by the `key_t` data type which is an integral part of the data structures used to implement System V IPC. Each key is contained within an `ipc_perm` structure inside the kernel. Every active IPC object has its own `ipc_perm` structure. Table 11.1 shows the fields of the `ipc_perm` structure which includes the key.

Table 11.1   The `ipc_perm` structure used by all System V IPC objects

`ipc_perm` structure fields		Description
`uid_t`	`uid`	The IPC object owner's user ID.
`gid_t`	`gid`	The IPC object owner's group ID.
`uid_t`	`cuid`	The creator's user ID.
`gid_t`	`cgid`	The creator's group ID.
`mode_t`	`mode`	The access modes of the IPC object.
`unsigned short`	`seq`	The slot usage sequence number.
`key_t`	`key`	The key associated with the object.

The shared memory, semaphore and message queue subsystems all contain a pool of `ipc_perm` structures which are embedded within the object type they manage. For example, message queues are defined by the `msqid_ds` structure for which the `msg_perm` field is itself an `ipc_perm` structure.

The `mode` field is checked by the kernel each time a new IPC object is to be created or when an existing object is referenced. It consists of a bit mask of the following fields:

`IPC_ALLOC`	The object is currently allocated.
`IPC_CREAT`	The object can be created if the `key` does not exist.
`IPC_EXCL`	Object creation should fail if the `key` exists.
`IPC_NOWAIT`	Object creation will return an error if it must wait.

When an object is created the access permissions of the object are stored in the `mode` field. The details of how objects are accessed are described throughout the remainder of the chapter.

To allocate a key or return a pointer to an existing IPC object based on a specified key, the `ipcget()` kernel function is called. The actions taken by `ipcget()` depend on the key argument passed to `shmget(S)`, `semget(S)` or `msgget(S)`, the functions used to locate shared memory, semaphore or message queue objects. If the key is set to `IPC_PRIVATE`, the object should be created, otherwise an attempt is made to locate an existing object which matches the specified `key`.

The details of the `ipcget()` function are described in the context of allocating a message queue in section 11.3.5 and in subsequent sections on semaphores and message queues.

11.2.2 IPC get operations

All IPC mechanisms support the ability to create an IPC object or retrieve an existing IPC object based on a unique key and an additional flag argument.

If the key argument specifies an existing IPC object, the identifier associated with the object will be returned. For example, a call to `msgget(S)` may return an existing message queue identifier which can be used in subsequent calls to access or control the message queue.

If the key argument is set to `IPC_PRIVATE` or the specified key does not already have an associated IPC object and `(flag & IPC_CREAT)` is true, a new IPC object will be created and the identifier associated with the object will be returned. For example, a call of `shmget(IPC_PRIVATE, 0)` will result in a new shared memory segment being allocated and the shared memory identifier returned to the caller.

11.2.3 IPC control operations

Changing the attributes of an IPC object or deleting the object is performed through the object's control function. At a minimum, the control function allows a process to retrieve the status of the object, change its ownership or delete the object.

11.2.4 IPC operations

Each IPC object exports a number of *operation* functions. The operations that apply to semaphores are documented in the `semop(S)` manual page; operations that apply to message queues are documented in the `msgop(S)` manual page; and operations that apply to shared memory segments are documented in the `shmop(S)` manual page.

Each set of operations is specific to the IPC object in question. For example, `msgsnd(S)` and `msgrcv(S)` allow messages to be sent to and received from a message queue, while `shmat(S)` and `shmdt(S)` allow a shared memory segment to be attached and detached from a process's address space.

11.3 Message queues

Message queues were introduced prior to the advent of STREAMS and provided a reliable method of message passing between different processes.

11.3.1 The user view of message queues

This section describes the structures and functions available for creating, controlling and using message queues from the user perspective.

There are four message queue related library functions (Section 11.3.5 shows how each is handled by the kernel):

```
#include <sys/types.h>
#include <sys/ipc.h>
#include <sys/msg.h>

int msgget(key_t key, int msgflg) ;
int msgsnd(int msqid, struct msgbuf *msgp, int msgsz, int msgflg) ;
int msgrcv(int msqid, struct msgbuf *msgp, int msgsz, long msgtyp,
                                                      int msgflg) ;
int msgctl(int msqid, int cmd, struct msqid_ds *buf) ;
```

A message queue is created using the `msgget(S)` function which returns a message queue identifier to be used in subsequent calls to access the message queue. If a value is specified for `key`, `msgget(S)` will return the message queue identifier already associated

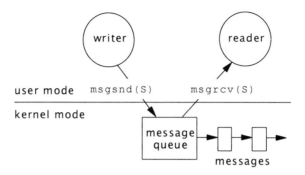

Figure 11.1   Using msgsnd(S) and msgrcv(S) to send and receive messages

with the key. If the key argument is set to IPC_PRIVATE or (msgflg & IPC_CREAT) is true, a message queue identifier and associated message queue are created.

The msgsnd(S) and msgrcv(S) functions are used to send a message to or read a message from the message queue specified by the msqid argument. The message to be sent or received, specified by the msgp, points to a msgbuf structure containing two fields, a long integer specifying the message type and an array of characters which is not required to be null terminated. The msgsz argument specifies the size of the message.

Figure 11.1 shows the flow of messages using msgsnd(S) and msgrcv(S).

When messages are sent to a queue using msgsnd(S) they are held in the kernel until a msgrcv(S) is issued on the same queue.

11.3.2 Using message queues

The following example shows how a message queue is established and how a message can be sent by one process and received by another.

The first fragment of the program shows the declarations needed and the main() function which establishes the message queue before calling fork(S) for the parent to send a message and for the child to receive the message.

The msgget(S) function is called to create a message queue and set the permissions for the queue. The message queue identifier is returned. This identifier is used both to send and receive messages. A call to msgctl(S) to remove the message queue identifier must be made before the process exits. It will not be removed automatically when the process terminates.

```
1 #include <sys/types.h>
2 #include <sys/ipc.h>
3 #include <sys/msg.h>
4
5 key_t mqid ;
6
7 main()
8 {
9     pid_t pid ;
```

```
10
11       mqid = msgget(IPC_PRIVATE, IPC_CREAT|0644) ;
12       if (mqid == -1) {
13           printf("couldn't allocate queue ID\n") ;
14           exit(-1) ;
15       }
16       printf("mqid = %d\n", mqid) ;
17
18       pid = fork() ;
19       if (pid == 0)
20           do_child() ;
21       else if (pid != -1)
22           do_parent() ;
23       else
24           pexit("fork") ;
25 }
```

The following do_parent() function builds a message in the message structure and calls msgsnd() to send the message to the queue specified by mqid. Since kernel message queue resources are not relinquished once the process terminates, the parent does not need to wait until the message has been read by the child before terminating.

```
27 do_parent()
28 {
29       int resp ;
30       char str[] = "Message to send through queue" ;
31       struct my_msg {
32           long mtype ;
33           char mdata[64] ;
34       } message ;
35
36       message.mtype = 7 ;                    /* an arbitrary value */
37       strcpy(message.mdata, str) ;
38
39       resp = msgsnd(mqid, &message, sizeof(message), IPC_NOWAIT) ;
40       if (resp == -1)
41           perror("msgsnd") ;
42 }
```

The child process calls msgrcv() to read the message. By setting the fourth argument to zero, any message on the queue will be returned.

Before it exits, do_child() calls msgctl(S) with the IPC_RMID to remove the message queue identifier and to destroy both the message queue and data structures associated with it.

```
44 do_child()
45 {
46       int resp ;
47       char buf[512] ;
48       struct msgbuf *msgr = (struct msgbuf *)buf ;
49
50       resp = msgrcv(mqid, msgr, 512, 0, !IPC_NOWAIT) ;
51       if (resp == -1)
52           perror("msgrcv") ;
53       else
54           printf("message received = %s\n", msgr->mtext) ;
55       msgctl(mqid, IPC_RMID, (struct msqid_ds *)0) ;
56 }
```

The output of the program for one particular run is:

```
$ msg
mqid = 300
message received = Message to send through queue
```

If the program is run repeatedly, despite the fact the message queue is deleted on each invocation, the message queue ID returned from `msgget(S)` increments in multiples of 50 on each call! This strange behaviour is explained in section 11.3.5.

11.3.3 The kernel interface for message queue handling

Before describing how each of the message queue functions is handled by the kernel, this section considers the main structures used by the kernel to implement message queues.

Figure 11.2 shows the message queue structures used by the kernel. Each message queue is represented by an `msqid_ds` structure which is one of a number of `msqid_ds` structures held in the `msgque[]` array. The `msg_perm` field is an `ipc_perm` structure which includes, among other things, the permissions of the queue and the associated key. The separation of the `ipc_perm` structure from the `msqid_ds` structure in Figure 11.2 is purely for presentation purposes, since it is not located in a separate part of memory but embedded within the `msqid_ds` structure.

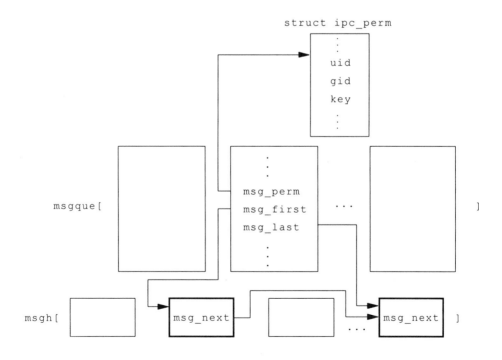

Figure 11.2   Kernel structures used to implement message queues

Each message queue also references a linked list of messages of type `struct msg` which are linked together using the `msg_next` field.

The fields of the `msqid_ds` structure are shown in Table 11.2. The `msg` and `ipc_perm` structures are described in more detail in later sections.

Table 11.2   The `msqid_ds` structure used for each message queue

msqid_ds structure field		Description
`struct ipc_perm`	`msg_perm`	The structure used to hold the key and various credentials used when issuing `msgsnd(S)` and `msgrcv(S)` system calls.
`struct msg`	`*msg_first`	Points to the first message on the queue.
`struct msg`	`*msg_last`	Points to the last message on the queue.
`unsigned short`	`msg_cbytes`	The current number of bytes on the queue.
`msgqnum_t`	`msg_qnum`	The current number of messages on the queue.
`msglen_t`	`msg_qbytes`	The maximum number of bytes that can be stored on the queue checked during processing of the `msgsnd(S)` system call.
`pid_t`	`msg_lspid`	The process ID of the last process to issue a `msgsnd(S)` system call.
`pid_t`	`msg_lrpid`	The process ID of the last process to issue a `msgrcv(S)` system call.
`time_t`	`msg_stime`	The time of the last `msgsnd(S)` system call.
`time_t`	`msg_rtime`	The time of the last `msgrcv(S)` system call.
`time_t`	`msg_ctime`	Set during creation time of the message queue or when the `msgctl(S)` system call is invoked with an `IPC_SET` command.

An `msqid_ds` structure, and thus a message queue, is allocated by invoking `msgget(S)` and will remain in existence until explicitly deleted with a call to `msgctl(S)`.

11.3.4 Message queue kernel initialisation

The `msginit()` kernel function is called from the kernel `main()` function during system initialisation. `msginit()` allocates memory and initialises its internal structures prior to providing message queue services. The tasks performed by `msginit()` are:

- Allocate memory for the message buffers by calling `sptalloc()` and assigning the base address of this buffer space to the `msg` variable.

- The message queue map specified by the `msgmap[]` array is initialised by a call to `mapinit[]`. The `msgmap[]` array is used to allocate subsequent memory for messages in response to `msgsnd(S)` calls.

- Link the message structures together to form a free list.

The last task links together each of the `msg` structures held in the `msgh[]` array and assigns the `msgfp` variable to point to the start of the list as shown in Figure 11.3.

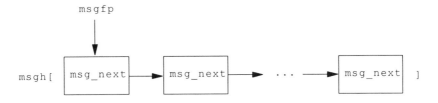

Figure 11.3   The free list of msg structures following msginit()

Each msg structure, referred to as the message header and accessed via the msg[] array, is allocated on a call to msgsnd(S) to describe the message which will be attached to the message queue ready for processing by subsequent calls to msgrcv(S).

The fields of the msg structure are shown in Table 11.3.

Table 11.3   The msg structure used to describe each message attached to a message queue

struct msg fields		Description
struct msg	*msg_next	The next (if any) message attached to the queue.
long	msg_type	The type of the message as specified to msgsnd(S).
short	msg_ts	The size of the message.
short	msg_spot	The location in msgmap[] where the data is stored.

Each message header allocated to a message queue is linked via the msg_next field. For details of how message headers are allocated see the next section.

11.3.5 Kernel handling of message queue calls

The four message queue functions each enter the kernel through the _msgsys library function which jumps through the kernel's system call gate. Once inside the kernel, the msgsys() function calls one of the msgget(), msgctl(), msgsnd() or msgrcv() functions to process the appropriate function as shown in Figure 11.4.

The following sections describe the tasks performed for each message queue function.

The msgget(S) system call

The msgget(S) system call can either retrieve an existing message queue identifier based on a specified key or create a new message queue. There are two circumstances under which a new message queue will be created:

1. The key argument passed to msgget(S) is set to IPC_PRIVATE.

2. There is currently no message queue associated with the specified key and (msgflg & IPC_CREAT) is true.

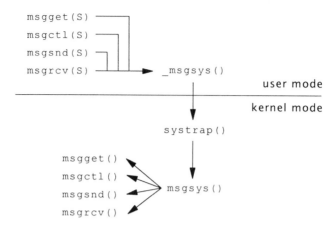

Figure 11.4   System call processing for message queues

Each message queue is represented by an `msqid_ds` structure held in the `msgque[]` array and each `msqid_ds` structure contains an embedded `ipc_perm` structure which is used to locate an existing or new message queue.

Figure 11.5 shows the arrangement of `msqid_ds` structures, each with an embedded `ipc_perm` structure. Using the size of the `msqid_ds` structure and the number of elements, it is easy for `ipcget()` to walk through the list.

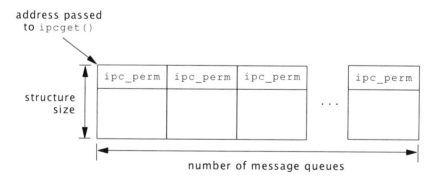

Figure 11.5   The physical arrangement of message queues and interpretation by `ipcget()`

The main bulk of processing performed for `msgget()` is done by the `ipcget()` function which takes the following parameters:

- The `key` and `msgflg` arguments passed to `msgget(S)`.
- A pointer to the first `ipc_perm` structure. This is the address of `msque[0]`.

- The number of `ipc_perm` structures which is the same as the size of the `msque[]` array.
- The size of each surrounding structure. For message queues, this is the size of the `msqid_ds` structure.

The `msqid_ds` structures are expected to be in consecutive memory locations so that `ipcget()` can use the size argument to add to the address of the first `ipc_perm` structure to locate the next one and so on.

If the `key` argument is set to `IPC_PRIVATE`, `ipcget()` will walk through the list of `ipc_perm` structures (and thus `msqid_ds` structures) looking for an empty slot. If the `mode` field of the `ipc_perm` structure is not set to `IPC_ALLOC`, the message queue is not currently being used. In this case the `mode` field is set to `IPC_ALLOC`, the `key` field is set to `IPC_PRIVATE` and the creator's user ID and group ID fields are set. The address of the `ipc_perm` structure, and thus the address of the newly allocated message queue, is then returned from `ipcget()`.

If the `key` field is not set to `IPC_PRIVATE`, the list is still searched. If a free slot is found, the `ipc_perm` structure is initialised as above and a pointer to it is returned to `msgget()`.

If a slot is occupied, the `key` field of the `ipc_perm` structure is equal to the `key` argument passed to `msgget(S)` and the `msgflg` argument is not set to `IPC_CREAT` or `IPC_EXCL`, a pointer is returned to the `ipc_perm` structure and thus, the required message queue.

The message queue identifier is returned to the user. This value is calculated as a product of the `ipc_perm seq` field and the total number of message queues.

The `msgsnd(S)` system call

The procedures to be followed by the `msgsnd()` kernel function are relatively straightforward in principle but complicated by numerous checks for the availability of kernel resources such as message headers, message buffer space, limits for the message queue and so on. This section shows the main paths through `msgsnd()`, assuming that the call will be successful, while highlighting where the main resource checks are made.

Figure 11.6 shows the main allocation of structures and flow of data when allocating kernel memory to store the second message sent to a specific queue. Refer to the figure when following the description of the tasks performed by `msgsnd()`.

The `msgsnd()` function is passed a pointer to the `msgsnd(S)` function arguments on the user's stack. The tasks performed by `msgsnd()` are:

- The `msgconv()` function is called to locate the message queue, given the message queue identifier passed to `msgsnd(S)`.
- The `ipcaccess()` function is called to check that the caller has the appropriate permissions to send the message. If the user does not have the appropriate permissions, an error is returned.
- The message size is checked to ensure that it does not exceed the maximum message size.

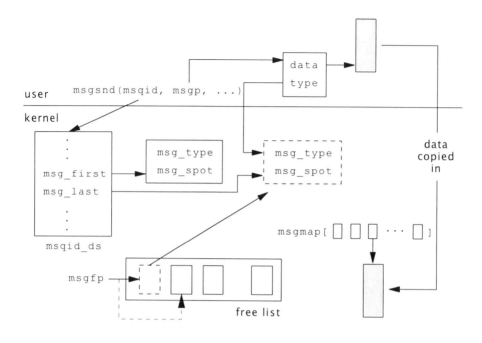

Figure 11.6   Allocation of kernel structures when processing `msgsnd(S)`

- If no space is available on the message queue and `IPC_NOWAIT` has been set in the `msgflg` argument passed to `msgsnd(S)`, `msgsnd()` will return, otherwise it will call `sleep(K)` to wait until space is available.

  A similar check is made against the message header free list which is pointed to by the `msgfp` kernel variable.

- At this stage space is available in the message queue and a message header is available. It is taken from the front of the free list headed by `msgfp` and added to the message queue (`msqid_ds`) using the `msg_first` and `msg_last` fields.

- The kernel `malloc()` function is called, passing the address of the `msgmap[]` array and the size of the data required. This function is used by all kernel subsystems which make use of the `map` structure. An appropriate entry is found in the `msgmap[]` array that can hold the data specified in the call to `msgsnd(S)`.

- The `msg` structure which will be used to describe the message is removed from the head of the free list and added to the message queue. The `msg_first` and `msg_last` fields are used to implement a FIFO of messages that have been sent to the queue.

- The message body data is copied from user space into the buffer space referenced from the `msgmap[]` array and the message header structure is initialised to increment the number of messages attached to the queue.

Toolkit 11.2 provides an implementation of ipcs(ADM) which displays the status of active message queues.

The msgrcv(S) system call

The tasks performed by the msgrcv() kernel function are more straightforward than for msgsnd(), assuming that the message queue already exists and messages are available.
The tasks performed by msgrcv() are:

- Call msgconv() to locate the message queue, given the message queue identifier passed to msgrcv(S).

- Call the ipcaccess() function to check that the caller has the appropriate permissions to receive a message from the requested message queue. If the user does not have the appropriate permissions an error is returned.

- Walk through the linked list of messages headed by the msg_first field of the msqid_ds structure looking for the first message that matches the msgtyp argument passed to msgrcv(S).

- If a message is found, the data component of the message, which is accessed via the msgmap[] array, is copied to user space and the msgfree() function is called to free the structures and space allocated to the message.

- If there are no messages associated with the specified message queue or there are no messages of the specified type, sleep(K) will be called with the address of the msg_qnum field of the msqid_ds structure if the IPC_NOWAIT flag has not been passed via the msgflg argument of msgrcv(S).

When a message has been removed from the queue, the msg_qnum field is decremented and the msg_cbytes field is decremented by the number of bytes that the message occupied.

The msgctl(S) system call

After calling msgconv() to locate the appropriate message queue, there are three paths that msgctl() can follow, depending on the value of the cmd argument passed:

IPC_RMID   This command specifies that the message queue identifier should be removed and that the message queue resources should be relinquished. This includes freeing any messages currently attached to the queue.

   To free messages involves walking through the list of messages headed by the msg_first field of the msqid_ds structure and calling msgfree() for each message. The fields of the msqid_ds structure should then be reset and the seq field of the ipc_perm structure should be incremented to ensure that the same message queue identifier will not be generated again.

IPC_SET   This command can be used to change the contents of the uid, gid and mode fields of the ipc_perm structure associated with the specified message queue and to increase msg_qbytes, the number of bytes that messages can occupy on a message queue.

IPC_STAT   This command is used to retrieve the contents of the msqid_ds structure corresponding to the specified message queue identifier.

11.3.6 Message queue tuneables

There are seven kernel tuneables which can be altered to tune the performance of message queues:

MSGMAP   This tuneable specifies the number of entries in the message queue map. Each entry in the map table indicates that there are MSGSEG / MSGMAP segments free, located via the address field in the map structure.

MSGMAX   The maximum size of a message for which the default is 128 bytes.

MSGMNB   The maximum number of bytes that messages can occupy for a single message queue.

MSGSEG   The number of MSGSSZ segments of memory allocated at kernel startup for holding messages.

MSGMNI   The total number of message queues that can be allocated. This tuneable specifies the size of the msque[] array.

MSGTQL   The maximum number of message headers that can exist simultaneously. This tuneable defines the size of the msgh[] array.

MSGSSZ   The number of bytes in a memory segment used for storing a message.

For further details on how to modify these kernel tuneables and re-link a new kernel, see the SCO OpenServer *Performance Guide* (1995).

11.4 Shared memory

The shared memory component of System V IPC provides a number of functions which allow two or more processes to share the same physical memory. The interfaces and their usage appears very similar to the interfaces used for handling message queues.

Shared memory segments are created and then attached to a process's address space. By specifying the shared memory identifier associated with the shared memory segment, any number of other processes can also attach the same segment to their address space.

The sharing actually occurs at the physical page level since shared memory segments can be attached at different virtual addresses in different processes.

11.4.1 The user view of shared memory

This section describes the structures and functions available for creating, controlling and using shared memory from the user perspective.

The following four library functions are available for using shared memory. Section 11.4.3 shows how each function is processed by the kernel.

```
#include <sys/shm.h>

int   shmget(key_y key, size_t size, int shmflg) ;
void *shmat(int shmid, const void *shmaddr, int shmflg) ;
int   shmdt(const void *shmaddr) ;
int   shmctl(int shmid, int cmd, struct shmid_ds *buf) ;
```

A shared memory identifier is created using the shmget(S) function or an existing shared memory identifier is returned by shmget(S) for the specified key. When a shared memory segment is created the size of the segment is passed as an argument to the shmget(S) system call.

The shmat(S) system call is used to attach the shared memory segment to the caller's address space, while the shmdt(S) system call is used to detach the segment from the caller's address space.

The shmctl(S) system call can be used to modify ownership of a shared memory segment, retrieve statistics about a segment or remove an existing segment.

11.4.2 Using shared memory

The example shown in this section demonstrates how shared memory segments are created, attached to multiple processes and then destroyed.

There are two separate programs. The first, called creat, creates a shared memory segment by invoking shmget(S) and then calls shmat(S) to attach the segment to its address space. It copies some data into the segment and then waits until it receives a SIGINT signal before calling shmctl(S) to remove the segment.

The second process, attach, also attaches the shared memory segment, prints out the string written by creat and then calls shmdt(S) to detach itself from the shared memory segment before terminating.

The sharing of the segment between both processes is shown in Figure 11.7.

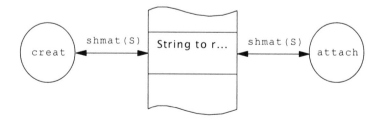

Figure 11.7   Sharing a shared memory segment

In the following `creat` program, the `sigset(S)` system call is invoked first on line 16 to connect the `sighdlr()` function to `SIGINT`.

The program then establishes the shared memory segment on line 18, specifying that it should be a single page in size.

```
 1 #include <sys/signal.h>
 2 #include <sys/shm.h>
 3
 4 int shmid ;
 5
 6 void
 7 sighdlr(int signo)
 8 {
 9      shmctl(shmid, IPC_RMID, (struct shmid_ds *)0) ;
10 }
11
12 main()
13 {
14      void *shmaddr ;
15
16      sigset(SIGINT, sighdlr) ;
17
18      shmid = shmget(IPC_PRIVATE, 4096, IPC_CREAT|0644) ;
19      if (shmid == -1)
20          pexit("shmget") ;
21      else
22          printf("Shared memory ID = %d\n", shmid) ;
23
24      shmaddr = shmat(shmid, (void *)0, 0) ;
25      if (shmaddr == -1)
26          pexit("shmat") ;
27      else {
28          printf("Shared memory attached at address %x\n", shmaddr) ;
29          strcpy((char *)shmaddr, "String to reside in shared memory");
30      }
31
32      sigpause(SIGINT) ;
33 }
```

The `shmat(S)` call is invoked on line 24 to attach the shared memory segment and a string is written to the address at which the segment is attached on line 29.

The program then calls `sigpause(S)` to wait for the arrival of a `SIGINT` signal for which the `sighdlr()` function will destroy the segment.

The following `attach` program expects the shared memory identifier associated with the shared memory segment created by `creat` to be passed as the first argument. It uses the identifier to call `shmat(S)` on line 14.

```
 1 #include <sys/shm.h>
 2 #include <sys/errno.h>
 3
 4 main(int argc, char *argv[])
 5 {
 6      int shmid ;
 7      void *shmaddr ;
 8
 9      if (argc != 2)
10          exit(EINVAL) ;
```

```
11
12      shmid = atoi(argv[1]) ;
13
14      shmaddr = shmat(shmid, (void *)0, 0) ;
15      if (shmaddr == -1)
16          pexit("shmat") ;
17      else {
18          printf("data = %s\n", (char *)shmaddr) ;
19          shmdt(shmaddr) ;
20      }
21 }
```

Using the address returned by `shmat(S)` it then calls `printf(S)` to display the string written to this address by `creat`.

When the `creat` program is run, it displays the shared memory identifier and the address at which the segment is attached in its address space:

```
$ creat &
[1]  357
Shared memory ID = 400
Shared memory attached at address 80000000

$ attach 400
data = String to reside in shared memory
$ ipcs -m
IPC status from /dev/kmem as of Wed Jun 21 06:10:54 1995
T     ID    KEY         MODE         OWNER     GROUP
Shared Memory:
m    400 0x00000000 --rw-r--r--     spate     group
$ kill -INT %1
[1] +  Done(255)             creat &
$ ipcs -m
IPC status from /dev/kmem as of Wed Jun 21 06:11:11 1995
T     ID    KEY         MODE         OWNER     GROUP
Shared Memory:
```

Using the identifier displayed by `creat`, the `attach` program displays the string and then terminates. The `ipcs(ADM)` is then run which shows the appropriate contents of the `shmid_ds` structure.

The `kill(C)` command is then run to send `SIGINT` to the `creat` process in order to destroy the shared memory segment. The `ipcs(ADM)` command is run once more to show that the segment has actually been removed.

Synchronisation between processes using shared memory can be achieved using semaphores. See section 11.5 for further details.

11.4.3 The kernel interface for shared memory

Each shared memory segment comprises two kernel structures, the `shmid_ds` structure, which describes the properties of the segment such as the permissions, size and the key, and a `region` structure, which describes the physical properties of the segment. A `region` structure is only associated with the `shmid_ds` structure following a call to `shmget(S)`.

Each `shmid_ds` structure is held in the `shmem[]` array which contains `SHMMNI` elements where `SHMMNI` is a kernel tuneable.

The fields of the `shmid_ds` structure are shown in Table 11.4.

Table 11.4   The `shmid_ds` structure used for each shared memory segment

`shmid_ds` structure field		Description
`struct ipc_perm`	`shm_perm`	Holds the key and credentials.
`int`	`shm_segsz`	Specifies the size of segment in bytes.
`struct region`	`*shm_reg`	A pointer to a `region` structure used to hold the data associated with the shared memory segment.
`pid_t`	`shm_lpid`	The process ID of the last process that issued a `shmat(S)` or `shmdt(S)` call.
`pid_t`	`shm_cpid`	The process ID of the creator.
`time_t`	`shm_atime`	The time of the last `shmat(S)` call.
`time_t`	`shm_dtime`	The time of the last `shmdt(S)` call.
`time_t`	`shm_ctime`	Specifies the time at which any contents of the `shmid_ds` structure were modified.

Since the structures used for implementing shared memory are relatively simple, there is no need for a shared memory initialisation routine. All memory required for implementing shared memory segments is performed by the memory management subsystem.

11.4.4 Kernel handling of shared memory calls

Each of the four functions available for creation and control of shared memory segments enter the kernel through a single system call as shown in Figure 11.8.

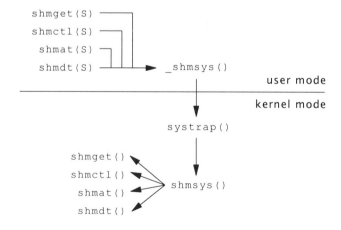

Figure 11.8   System call processing for shared memory

Each of the kernel functions which corresponds to its equivalent user space function is described in the sections that follow.

The `shmget(S)` system call

The `shmget(S)` system call is used to retrieve a shared memory identifier for an existing shared memory segment using a specified key or it can create a new shared memory segment. There are two cases where a new shared memory segment will be created:

1. The `key` argument passed to `shmget(S)` is set to `IPC_PRIVATE`.
2. There is currently no shared memory segment associated with the specified key and `(shmflg & IPC_CREAT)` is true.

Each shared memory segment is represented by a `shmid_ds` structure held in the `shmem[]` array and contains an embedded `ipc_perm` structure which is used to locate an existing shared memory segment or new shared memory segment.

To locate an existing shared memory segment or to create a new one, the `ipcget()` kernel function, which is common to shared memory, message queues and semaphores, is called. The tasks followed by `ipcget()` are described in section 11.3.5.

Prior to calling `ipcget()`, the `allocreg()` function is called to create a region which can be attached to a process's address space on a subsequent call to `shmat(S)`. Note that although the term 'segment' is used when describing shared memory, a process's address space is actually composed of multiple regions. For further details on memory allocation, see section 6.4.

On return from `ipcget()`, either an existing `shmid_ds` structure is found or a new structure has been allocated by marking the `mode` field of the `ipc_perm` structure to `IPC_ALLOC`. If a new segment is allocated, the fields of the `shmid_ds` structure must be initialised to set up the appropriate credentials, time-stamps and a pointer to the allocated `region` structure as shown in Figure 11.9.

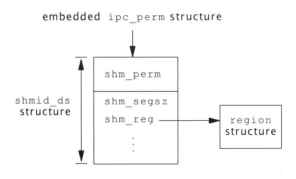

Figure 11.9   Allocation of a shared memory segment

The final task performed by `shmget()` is to return the shared memory identifier which is calculated as a product of the `ipc_perm seq` field and the total number of shared memory segments.

The `shmat(S)` system call

Since much of the hard work was performed in creating the shared memory segment and associated `region` structure during a call to `shmget(S)`, the tasks performed by `shmat(S)` consist mainly of checking to ensure that the region can actually be attached to the process's address space:

- The `shmconv()` function is called to convert the specified shared memory identifier into the corresponding `shmid_ds` structure.
- `ipcaccess()` is called to ensure that the caller has appropriate privileges to attach the region. This involves checking fields in the `ipc_perm` structure against the credentials of the caller.
- If the caller has not specified an address at which the region should be attached, `mmfindhole()` is called to locate an appropriate gap in the user's address space.
- The `chkpgrowth()` function is called to ensure that, by attaching the region, the maximum size of the process's address space will not be exceeded. See `getrlimit(S)` for further details of process limits.
- The `attachreg()` function is called to attach the region to the process's address space and various access time fields of the `shmid_ds` structure are updated.

The `crash(ADM)` command can be used to display the address space of the `creat` process before and after the call to `shmat(S)`.

Using `adb(CP)`, a breakpoint is set when the process reaches `main()` and the `crash(ADM)` `proc` and `pregion` commands can be used to display which regions are attached to the process.

First, `adb(CP)` is run and a breakpoint set at `main()` as follows:

```
$ adb creat
* main:br
* :r
creat: running
breakpoint  main:          jmp     near main+0xb6
```

The `:r` adb command runs the program which promptly hits the breakpoint and returns control to the debugger.

The `crash(ADM)` command is then run and the `proc` command is used to locate the process which is found in slot 66 of the process table:

```
> proc ! grep creat
  66 t    511    510    510 13583  45   0            creat        load trc
> pregion 66
SLOT PREG REG#       REGVA  TYPE FLAGS
```

```
66   0   603          0  text  rd ex cm
     1   602   0x400000  data  rd wr cm
     2   601 0x7fffe000 stack  rd wr cm
```

Running the `pregion` command at this point shows the three expected regions, text, data and stack, and their starting locations in memory.

Within `adb(CP)` the address at which the call to `shmat(S)` is made is displayed and a breakpoint is set at the address of the first instruction to be executed after the call to `shmat(S)`. Both addresses are highlighted:

```
* main,20?ia
main:                   jmp     near main+0xb6
main+0x5:   nop
main+0x6:   push    0x130
...
main+0x57:  push    0x0
main+0x59:  push    0x0
main+0x5b:  push    shmid
main+0x61:  call    near shmat
main+0x66:  add     esp,0xc
main+0x69:  mov     [ebp-0x4],eax
* main+0x66:br
* :co
creat: running
breakpoint  main+0x66:      add     esp,0xc
*
```

The program is then continued, resulting in the call to `shmat(S)` taking place before the breakpoint in the program is hit.

Running the `pregion` command within `crash` once more shows the newly attached shared memory region and the address at which it attached in memory:

```
> pregion 66
SLOT PREG REG#       REGVA  TYPE FLAGS
  66   0   603          0  text  rd ex cm
       1   602   0x400000  data  rd wr cm
       2   601 0x7fffe000 stack  rd wr cm
       3   662 0x80000000 shmem  rd wr cm
> region 662
REGION TABLE SIZE = 682
Region-list:

SLOT  PGSZ VALID  SMEM NONE SOFF   REF SWP NSW FORW BACK INOX TYPE FLAGS
 662    1    0      0    0    0     1   0   0  648 ract   -   shm  nofree
```

The `region` command is then run to display more details about the region, including the size which is displayed as one page (4096 bytes).

The `shmdt(S)` system call

To follow the tasks performed by `shmdt(S)`, consider the example process address space shown in Figure 11.10. The `shmdt(S)` system call is invoked with the address of the shared memory segment, in this case, the address `0x80000000`.

shmdt(0x80000000)

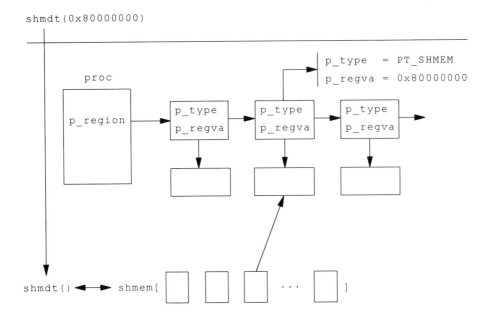

Figure 11.10   Removing a shared memory segment

When the shmdt() kernel function is entered, it performs the following tasks:

- Walk through the linked list of pregion structures looking for a pregion with a p_type field of PT_SHMEM (indicating shared memory) and the p_regva address which corresponds to the address passed to shmdt(S).

- The detachreg() function is called to detach the region from the process's address space.

- Using the address of the region which is held in the p_reg field of the pregion structure, shmdt() walks through the list of shared memory segments held in the shmem[] array until it finds the appropriate entry, at which point various fields are updated. Recall that the shm_reg field of the shmid_ds structure points to the region.

- The shm_dtime field is updated with the current time.

For more information on memory management see chapter 6.

The shmctl(S) system call

After calling shmconv() to locate the appropriate shared memory segment based on the identifier passed to shmctl(S), there are five paths that shmctl() can follow depending on the value of the cmd argument passed:

IPC_RMID   This command is used to remove the shared memory segment. After the fields of the `shmid_ds` structure have been reset, a check is made against the reference count of the `region` structure.

If the reference count is equal to zero, `freereg()` is called to free the region. If the reference count is not zero the region is still attached to at least one process's address space and therefore `rgnrele()` is called to decrement the reference count so that it will be freed when the last process that is using the region terminates.

IPC_SET   The `IPC_SET` command is used to set the `shm_perm.uid`, `shm_perm.gid` and `shm_perm.mode` fields of the `shmid_ds` structure. The only processing required by `IPC_SET` before the fields are set is to check that the caller has the appropriate privileges.

IPC_STAT   This command is used to retrieve a copy of the `shmid_ds` structure corresponding to the specified shared memory identifier.

The `ipcaccess()` function is called to check the caller's credentials and `copyout(K)` is then called to copy the contents of the structure to user space.

SHM_LOCK   The `SHM_LOCK` command is used to lock the shared memory segment in physical memory, that is, the physical pages which underpin the segment cannot be paged out.

The `pinregdown()` function is called to lock the region.

SM_UNLOCK   The `SHM_UNLOCK` command is used to unlock a previously locked shared memory segment through use of the `unpinreg()` function.

11.4.5 Shared memory tuneables

There are three tuneables available for configuring shared memory:

SHMMAX   This tuneable specifies the maximum size of a shared memory segment for which the default is 512 kbytes or 128 pages.

SHMMIN   The minimum size of a shared memory segment is specified by this kernel tuneable for which the default is 1 byte. Note, however, that in practice, the minimum amount of memory that can actually be allocated on the i386 is a single page which is equal to 4096 bytes.

SHMMNI   This tuneable specifies the maximum number of shared memory segments and thus defines the size of the `shmem[]` array.

For further details refer to the SCO OpenServer *Performance Guide* (1995).

11.4.6 Shared memory with /dev/zero

The /dev/zero pseudo driver provides a convenient method of supplying an endless stream of zeros. For example, consider the following program which attempts to read 256 bytes from /dev/zero:

```
#include <fcntl.h>

main()
{
    int n, fd ;
    char buf[256] ;

    fd = open("/dev/zero", O_RDONLY) ;
    n = read(fd, buf, 256) ;
    printf("number of bytes read = %d\n", n) ;
}
```

When the program is run it reads 256 bytes as expected:

```
$ zero
number of bytes read = 256
```

While this does not initially appear to be particularly interesting or anything more than an expensive implementation of bzero(), the more useful properties of /dev/zero come into play when using the mmap(S) system call.

If a user process maps /dev/zero into its address space, zero-filled pages will be allocated on demand as the process accesses them. This is similar in many respects to issuing a call to malloc(S), whereby the virtual address space is reserved by the kernel and physical pages are allocated on demand. One use of /dev/zero is in the creation of a process's BSS segment in memory. By using /dev/zero, pages will be allocated only if actually used.

Any virtual address space and corresponding physical pages allocated as a result of mapping /dev/zero are inherited across the fork(S) system call.

An interesting property of mapping /dev/zero comes into play when issuing a fork(S) system call after the mapping has been established by the parent. The behaviour of this mapping depends on the flags field passed to mmap(S).

If MAP_PRIVATE is specified, the parent and child will share the same physical pages while reading memory, but when one of them writes to a page of the mapping, a new physical page will be created thus exhibiting copy on write semantics.

If MAP_SHARED is specified, both parent and child will share the same physical pages regardless of whether read or write operations are performed.

Toolkit 11.1   Sharing memory with /dev/zero

The example provided here uses MAP_SHARED to show how a mapping can be shared by parent and child for read and write access.

The parent process opens /dev/zero for reading and writing on line 12 and then issues a call to mmap(S) on line 16 to create a one page mapping at a system chosen address. The mapping should be read/write and MAP_SHARED is specified so that the pages will be shared between parent and child.

```
 1 #include <sys/types.h>
 2 #include <sys/mman.h>
 3 #include <fcntl.h>
 4
 5 main()
 6 {
 7     pid_t pid ;
 8     int n, fd ;
 9     char buf[256] ;
10     caddr_t addr ;
11
12     fd = open("/dev/zero", O_RDWR) ;
13     if (fd < 0)
14         pexit("/dev/zero") ;
15
16     addr = mmap(0, 4096, PROT_READ|PROT_WRITE, MAP_SHARED, fd, 0);
17     if (addr == -1)
18         pexit("mmap") ;
19     *addr = 0x77 ;
20
21     pid = fork() ;
22
23     if (pid == 0)
24         printf("CHILD - contents of %x = %x\n", addr, *addr) ;
25     else
26         printf("PARENT - contents of %x = %x\n", addr, *addr) ;
27 }
```

The parent writes the value 0x77 to the address returned by mmap(S) and calls fork(S) to create a child process. The child then writes the value 0x78 to the same address and both parent and child display the contents of the address.

When the program is run the following output is displayed:

```
$ mapzero
CHILD - contents of 80001000 = 78
PARENT - contents of 80001000 = 78
```

Note that this example makes the assumption that the child will run first so that the parent will see the change from 0x77 to 0x78.

Chapter 8 shows how to analyse a process to see how pages are allocated and attached to a process region when mmap(S) is issued. Similar techniques are also shown in section 11.4.4 in which an allocated shared memory segment is attached to a process's address space.

11.5 Semaphores

Semaphores were first introduced by Dijkstra (1965) as a method of synchronisation between processes, by providing a means of mutual exclusion whereby one process can prevent another process from accessing a particular section of code or a particular data structure while a critical operation is performed.

Dijkstra used the terms *p* (wait) and *v* (signal) which come from the Dutch words *prolagen* (a compound of *proberen*, to try and *verlagen*, to decrease) and *verhogen* (to increase). They describe the two operations that can be applied to a semaphore, *sem*, as follows:

```
wait(sem) {
    if (sem != 0)
        sem--
    else
        wait until (sem != 0)
}

signal(sem) {
    if (waiting processes)
        wakeup first process
    sem++
}
```

Both the wait and signal operations must be atomic to avoid two processes acquiring the semaphore at the same time. Section 11.5.5 describes how this atomicity is achieved.

There are two types of semaphores, *binary semaphores*, which have only the values 0 and 1, and *multi-valued semaphores*, which can have a much wider range of values. The most common use of semaphores is in protecting critical regions of code, for which binary semaphores are usually used. The term *mutex* is also used to describe binary semaphores.

After establishing a semaphore with an initial value, which is usually 1 for binary semaphores, critical sections of code can be protected as follows:

```
wait(sem)
    perform critical section
signal(sem)
```

If two processes are trying to access the same critical section, one process will acquire the semaphore through a call to `wait` and the second process will be blocked until the `signal` operation is invoked.

Looking in greater detail, the first process issues a `wait` call which tests the value of `sem`, finds it is not zero and decrements it. When the second process issues a call to `wait`, it finds that the value of `sem` is equal to zero so it goes to sleep.

When the first process completes the critical section it calls `signal`, which wakes up the second process and increments the value of `sem`. The value of `sem` will be checked again by the second process. This time it is not equal to zero so the second process will decrement and acquire the semaphore and therefore enter the critical section.

11.5.1 The user view of semaphores

This section describes the functions available for creating, controlling and using semaphores from the user perspective. There are three functions available for using semaphores in SCO UNIX and other variants of System V UNIX:

```
#include <sys/types.h>
#include <sys/ipc.h>
#include <sys/sem.h>

int semget(key_t key, int nsems, int semflg) ;
int semop(int semid, struct sembuf *sops, unsigned nsops) ;
int semctl(int semid, int cmd, int semnum, union semun arg) ;
```

A semaphore identifier is created, or an existing semaphore identifier is returned, by the `semget(S)` system call. If an existing semaphore identifier is associated with the specified `key` argument, it is returned.

If the value of the `key` argument is set to `IPC_PRIVATE` or `(semflg & IPC_CREAT)` is true, a new semaphore identifier and associated data structure containing `nsems` semaphores is created by the kernel.

The `semop(S)` system call is used to perform an array of semaphore operations on a set of semaphores which are associated with the semaphore ID passed in the `semid` argument. Each `sembuf` structure has the following fields:

short	sem_num	The number of the semaphore.
short	sem_op	The operation to be performed on the semaphore.
short	sem_flg	The operation flags.

The `sem_num` field specifies the number of the semaphore in the semaphore set. For example, if the `nsems` argument to `semget(S)` is 2, a `sem_num` field set to 0 refers to the first semaphore in the set while a `sem_num` field set to 1 indicates the second semaphore.

There are three operations that can be performed on a semaphore based on the value set in the `sem_op` field. These operations are described in the context of binary semaphores to aid understanding and where semaphores are used in a more generalised manner this is explained as required:

1. If the value of `sem_op` is positive, the textbooks, and manual pages, usually indicate that this corresponds to the '*returning of resources*' by the process. In terms of binary semaphores, this corresponds to a *v* (signal) call. The returning of resources basically means that the process is about to exit a critical region or free up a resource which is managed by the semaphore, such as a shared memory segment.

   The action taken by `semop(S)` when the value of `sem_op` is greater than zero is to add the value of `sem_op` to the existing value of the semaphore. If there are processes waiting on the semaphore, they will be awoken. For a process to wait on a semaphore, it must have called `semop(S)` with `sem_op` either zero or less than zero.

2. If the `sem_op` field is less than zero, there are a number of actions that can be taken based on the following algorithm:

   ```
   if (sem_val >= abs(sem_op))
       sem_val = sem_val - abs(sem_op)
   ```

```
          else
             if (semop_flag & IPC_NOWAIT)
                 return -1
             else {
                 wait until sem_val >= abs(sem_op)
                 sem_val = sem_val - abs(sem_op)
             }
```

The example in the following section uses `semop(S)` with a value of `sem_op` equal to -1 to implement the `p()` operation.

3. If the value of `sem_op` is equal to zero then the value of the semaphore will not be altered and the process will sleep until the value of the semaphore reaches zero.

Trying to picture what happens between the different calls is difficult. In the implementation of `p()` and `v()` shown in section 11.5.2, the example attempts to simplify the usage and explanation of these calls. The best approach is to work through the example with a pen and paper!

The `semctl(S)` function provides a number of different operations. Most of the operations will be discussed when describing the kernel handling of this call. Like other System V IPC control operations, the semaphore set can be deleted and various statistics about the semaphore set can be read or modified.

11.5.2 Using semaphores

The example provided in this section uses System V semaphores to implement the `p()` and `v()` functions in order to provide an easier-to-use interface for binary semaphores.

The argument passed to both `p()` and `v()` is a semaphore identifier which was created and initialised in the `main()` function which is described later. In the description of `p()` and `v()` that follows, refer to the rules that apply to `semop()` described in section 11.5.1.

The `p()` function initialises a `sembuf` structure which it passes to `semop(S)`. The `sem_op` field of this structure is set to -1 to indicate that the process requests the resources held by the semaphore. If the value of the semaphore is set to 1, the value will be set to zero and the process will gain access to the critical region. If another process then calls `p()`, it will sleep until the value of the semaphore is incremented following a call to `v()`.

The `v()` function initialises a `sembuf` structure which it also passes to `semop(S)`. The `sem_op` field of this structure is set to 1. The kernel adds this value to the current value of the semaphore, which involves waking up any processes that will have slept on a call to `p()`.

```
1 #include <sys/types.h>
2 #include <sys/ipc.h>
3 #include <sys/sem.h>
4
5 void
6 p(int sem)
7 {
```

```
 8      struct sembuf pbuf ;
 9
10      pbuf.sem_num = 0 ;
11      pbuf.sem_op  = -1 ;
12      pbuf.sem_flg = SEM_UNDO ;
13
14      if (semop(sem, &pbuf, 1) == -1)
15          pexit("semop") ;
16 }
17
18 void
19 v(int sem)
20 {
21      struct sembuf vbuf ;
22
23      vbuf.sem_num = 0 ;
24      vbuf.sem_op  = 1 ;
25      vbuf.sem_flg = SEM_UNDO ;
26
27      if (semop(sem, &vbuf, 1) == -1)
28          pexit("semop") ;
29 }
```

The following `main()` function initialises a new semaphore by calling `semget(S)` on line 52. The `IPC_PRIVATE` argument ensures that a new semaphore will be created. The argument of 1 indicates that a single semaphore should be created.

The `semctl(S)` system call is invoked on line 57 to set the value of the single semaphore to the value passed in the `carg` argument (1).

```
31 repeat(int sem)
32 {
33      while (1) {
34          p(sem) ;
35
36          printf("%d entering critical section\n", getpid()) ;
37          sleep(2) ;
38
39          v(sem) ;
40      }
41 }
42
43 main()
44 {
45      int i, semid ;
46      union {
47          int            val ;
48          struct semid_ds *buf ;
49          ushort         *array ;
50      } carg;
51
52      semid = semget(IPC_PRIVATE, 1, 0666|IPC_CREAT) ;
53      if (semid == -1)
54          pexit("semget") ;
55
56      carg.val = 1;
57      if (semctl(semid, 0, SETVAL, carg) == -1)
58          pexit("semctl") ;
59
60      for (i=0 ; i<4 ; i++) {
61          if (fork() == 0)
```

```
62                  repeat(semid) ;
63      }
64      repeat(semid) ;
65  }
```

Lines 60 to 63 create four child processes which all call the `repeat()` function along with the parent. The `repeat()` function, shown on lines 31 to 41, loops forever, calling `p()` to protect entry to the lines of code on lines 36 and 37 and calling `v()` on line 39 to allow another process to obtain access.

When the program is run it shows successive print statements from the different processes as they acquire the semaphore. Since control is always given to the first process waiting on the semaphore, and issuing a `p()` call always puts the process on the end of the queue, the sequence displayed is always deterministic:

```
$ p_v
838 entering critical section
839 entering critical section
840 entering critical section
841 entering critical section
837 entering critical section    # original parent process
838 entering critical section
839 entering critical section
840 entering critical section
841 entering critical section
837 entering critical section
^D                               # ^D entered
```

11.5.3 The kernel interface for semaphore handling

There are a number of kernel structures used for managing semaphores which centre around the `semid_ds` structure which is allocated when a new semaphore identifier is allocated following a call to `semget(S)`.

The fields of the `semid_ds` structure are shown in Table 11.5. As with message queues and shared memory, the `semid_ds` structure contains an embedded `ipc_perm` structure used in generic operations for allocation and credentials checking.

Table 11.5 The `semid_ds` structure used to manage semaphore sets

semid_ds structure field		Description
struct ipc_perm	sem_perm	Holds the key and various credentials used when issuing semop(S) and semctl(S) functions.
struct sem	*sem_base	Contains a pointer to the first semaphore in the set.
unsigned short	sem_nsems	A count of the number of semaphores in the set.
time_t	sem_otime	The time of the last semop(S) system call.
time_t	sem_ctime	The time the semid_ds structure was last changed.

When a `semget(S)` system call is made, the number of semaphores in the set associated with the semaphore ID is specified as an argument. Each semaphore is described by the `sem` structure, the fields of which are shown in Table 11.6.

Table 11.6   The sem structure used to describe each semaphore

sem structure field		Description
unsigned short	semval	The current value of the semaphore which is always greater than or equal to zero.
pid_t	sempid	The process ID of the last process to issue a semop(S) operation on the semaphore.
unsigned short	semncnt	The number of processes which are awaiting an increase in the value of semval.
unsigned short	semzcnt	The number of processes which are waiting for the value of semval to reach zero.

11.5.4 Semaphore initialisation

The seminit() function is called from the kernel's main() function during kernel initialisation. Its main task is to set up the semmap[] array which is used to hold the semaphore sets which comprise a number of sem structures.

The tasks performed by seminit() are:

- The mapinit() function is called to initialise semmap[]. The size of the map is determined by the SEMMAP tuneable and therefore contains space for the total number of SEMMAP semaphores.

- The mfree() function is invoked to initialise semmap[] further by marking each entry in the map as free.

- Initialise the semfup[] array, which is used to manage the semaphore state in the event of process termination. These *undo* structures are described in the next section.

11.5.5 Kernel handling of semaphore calls

The three functions available for creating, controlling and using semaphores all enter the kernel through the _smsys library function as shown in Figure 11.11.

The following three sections describe each of the kernel semaphore calls.

The semget(S) system call

The semget(S) system call is used to retrieve a semaphore identifier associated with the specified key or to create a new semaphore identifier, associated kernel data structures and a set of semaphores, the number of which is specified by the nsems argument passed to semget(S). There are two cases where a new semaphore object will be created:

1. The key argument passed to semget(S) is set to IPC_PRIVATE.
2. There is currently no semaphore identifier associated with the specified key and (semflg & IPC_CREAT) is true.

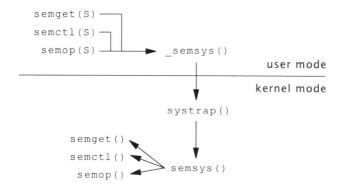

Figure 11.11   System call processing for semaphore functions

The term 'semaphore object', which is accessible through a semaphore identifier, is used here to refer to the set of semaphores created through a single `semget(S)` system call and represented by a single semaphore identifier.

Each semaphore object is represented by a `semid_ds` structure held in the `sema[]` array and each `semid_ds` structure contains an embedded `ipc_perm` structure which is used to locate an existing or new semaphore object.

To locate an existing semaphore object or to create a new semaphore object, the `ipcget()` kernel function, which is common to shared memory, message queues and semaphores, is called. The tasks followed by `ipcget()` are described in section 11.3.5.

On return from `ipcget()` either an existing `semid_ds` structure is found or a new structure has been allocated by marking the `mode` field of the `ipc_perm` structure to `IPC_ALLOC`. If a new semaphore object is allocated, the following tasks are performed:

- The size of the semaphore set specified by the `nsems` argument passed to `semget(S)` is checked against `SEMMSL`, a kernel tuneable which specifies the maximum size of a semaphore set.

- The kernel `malloc()` function is called with the address of the `semmap[]` array and the number of semaphores required, `nsems`. The `malloc()` function will check to see if an appropriate number of entries, and therefore space, is available in the map for storing the semaphore set.

- Appropriate fields of the `semid_ds` structure are updated to reflect the allocation.

At this point the appropriate kernel data structures associated with the semaphore object and the space required to store the semaphore set have been allocated but none of the semaphores in the set have been initialised.

If the semaphore object already exists, a check is made to ensure that the `nsems` argument passed to `semget(S)` does not exceed the size of the semaphore set associated with the semaphore object. If it does, `EINVAL` is returned to the user.

The final task performed by `semget()`, for either an existing semaphore object or a newly created semaphore object, is to return the semaphore identifier which is calculated as a product of the `ipc_perm seq` field and the maximum number of semaphore objects that can exist in the system, which is governed by the `SEMNMI` kernel tuneable.

The `semop(S)` system call

Much of the processing performed by the `semop()` function involves the handling of the `SEM_UNDO` flag which can be passed in the `sem_flag` field of each `sembuf` structure.

Calling `semop(S)` may establish an action to take place at some later date; for example, when passing `-1` as the value of `sem_op`, the process may sleep and when it is awoken it will decrement the value of the semaphore.

The `SEM_UNDO` flags informs the kernel that in the event of the process terminating, any scheduled operations should be undone.

The tasks performed by `semop()` are:

- Check that the number of `sembuf` structures does not exceed the system limit.

- Copy all the `sembuf` structures into kernel space.

- Call the `semconv()` function to convert the semaphore ID passed to `semop(S)` into a pointer to the appropriate `semid_ds` structure.

- Loop through each `sembuf` structure checking that the semaphore number is valid and call `ipcaccess()` to ensure that the caller has the appropriate privileges to access the semaphore.

- Loop through the `sembuf` structures once again and perform the following actions, depending on the value of the `sem_op` argument of each `sembuf` structure. The actions taken here correspond to the algorithm given in section 11.5.1.

    1. If the `sem_op` value is greater than zero, the `sem_op` field of the `sembuf` structure will be added to the `semval` field of the `sem` structure.

    2. If the value of `sem_op` is less than zero, there are two paths to be taken. If the value of `semval` is greater than or equal to the absolute value of `sem_op`, the absolute value of `sem_op` is decremented from `semval`.
       If the above condition is not true, the process will sleep until the condition is met. When it awakes, this step will be repeated.

    3. If the value of `sem_op` is equal to zero, and if the current value of `semval` is not equal to zero, `sleep(K)` will be called to put the process to sleep until this condition changes.

- At this stage, all operations have been completed. The only remaining task is to update the various statistical type fields of the `semid_ds` structure and loop through each `sembuf` once more to wake up any processes sleeping on changes in the value of the semaphore which has been satisfied by this call to `sem_op(S)`.

If the SEM_UNDO flag is specified for any of the operations, a check will be made to see if the process slept and was subsequently terminated. In this case the semundo() function is called to undo the operations specified to semop(S).

The semctl(S) system call

There are ten different commands that can be passed to semctl(S). Since, like the control operations for message queues and shared memory, the semctl() kernel function basically consists of a switch statement, this section describes only the functionality of the commands:

GETVAL This command retrieves the current value of semval.

SETVAL The only way to set the value of the semaphore is through calling semctl(S) with the SETVAL command.

GETPID This command returns the current value of sempid.

GETNCNT This command returns the current value of semcnt.

GETZCNT This command returns the current value of semzcnt.

GETALL The GETALL command copies all semaphore values into a user supplied buffer.

SETALL All semaphore values for a semaphore set can be set in one operation by calling semctl(S) with the SETALL command.

IPC_STAT This command copies the contents of the semid_ds structure into a user supplied buffer.

IPC_SET This command allows the caller to set the uid, gid and mode fields of the ipc_perm structure embedded within the semid_ds structure.

IPC_RMID This command removes all kernel state associated with the semaphore, including the semaphore ID, the semid_ds structure and each sem structure.

11.5.6 Semaphore tuneables

There are eight different tuneables associated with semaphores:

SEMMAP This tuneable determines the number of entries in the semaphore map, where each entry can store a single sem structure.

SEMMNI The number of semaphore sets in the kernel underpinned by semid_ds structures is specified by this tuneable.

SEMMNU The number of semaphore undo structures used when passing the SEM_UNDO flag to semop(S).

SEMMSL The maximum number of semaphores in a semaphore set. This governs the nsems argument passed to semget(S).

SEMOPM   The maximum number of semaphore operations that can be executed for each `semop(S)` system call.

SEMUME   The number of semaphore undo structures that a single process can use.

SEMVMX   The maximum value of `semval`.

11.6 System V IPC support functions

There are two commands which can be used for displaying statistics about System V IPC objects and removing objects which may have been left by a process which failed to remove them.

The `ipcs(ADM)` command prints a large amount of information about active IPC objects in the system. Without any arguments, most of the fields of each of the main kernel object structures are printed. For message queues, this is the `msqid_ds` structure, for shared memory it is the `shmid_ds` structure and for semaphores it is the `semid_ds` structure.

There are a wide variety of other arguments available for passing to `ipcs(ADM)`. The following toolkit provides a simple implementation of `ipcs(ADM)` which displays the default level of information.

The `ipcrm(ADM)` command is used to remove System V IPC resources. Unfortunately, unlike other resources that a process owns which are removed once a process terminates, System V IPC objects remain in existence after the process has terminated, producing a need for `ipcrm(ADM)`.

Toolkit 11.2   `mipcs` – an implementation of `ipcs(ADM)`

This toolkit example provides the basic structure of the `ipcs(ADM)` command. It prints the same amount of statistics about System V IPC objects as `ipcs(ADM)` when run without any additional arguments.

The header files included and the global variables and structures used by the program are shown on lines 1 to 35. The `nl[]` array on lines 13 to 20 declares the kernel symbols to be read by `mipcs`. The `#defines` on lines 22 to 27 provide access to the symbol values returned from `nlist(S)`, making the program easier to read.

The structures defined on lines 29 to 35 are used following calls to `nlist(S)` to read the required kernel structures. For example, the `msginfo.msgmni` field specifies the size of the `msqid_ds[]` array. Memory will be allocated, referenced by the `msqid_ds` variable declared on line 33, and the array will be read from the kernel.

```
1 #include <sys/types.h>
2 #include <sys/ipc.h>
3 #include <sys/msg.h>
4 #include <sys/shm.h>
5 #include <sys/sem.h>
6 #include <nlist.h>
7 #include <fcntl.h>
8 #include <stdlib.h>
9 #include <time.h>
```

```
10 #include <pwd.h>
11 #include <grp.h>
12
13 struct nlist nl[] = { { "msginfo", 0, 0, 0, 0, 0 },
14                       { "shminfo", 0, 0, 0, 0, 0 },
15                       { "seminfo", 0, 0, 0, 0, 0 },
16                       { "msgque", 0, 0, 0, 0, 0 },
17                       { "shmem", 0, 0, 0, 0, 0 },
18                       { "sema", 0, 0, 0, 0, 0 },
19                       { 0 }
20                     } ;
21
22 #define MSGINFO nl[0].n_value
23 #define SHMINFO nl[1].n_value
24 #define SEMINFO nl[2].n_value
25 #define MSG_DS  nl[3].n_value
26 #define SHM_DS  nl[4].n_value
27 #define SEM_DS  nl[5].n_value
28
29 struct msginfo msginfo ;
30 struct shminfo shminfo ;
31 struct seminfo seminfo ;
32
33 struct msqid_ds *msqid_ds ;
34 struct shmid_ds *shmid_ds ;
35 struct semid_ds *semid_ds ;
36
```

The `read_ipc_ds()` function is shown on lines 39 to 55. This function reads the IPC structures `msginfo`, `shminfo` and `seminfo`, all of which hold the size of their respective object arrays as described above.

The function starts by calling `nlist(S)` to retrieve the symbol addresses and then opens `/dev/kmem` to allow the structures to be read. For each structure, a call is made to `lseek(S)` and the contents of the structure are read.

```
37 int kfd ;
38
39 int
40 read_ipc_ds()
41 {
42     if (nlist("/unix", nl) == -1)
43         pexit("nlist") ;
44
45     kfd = open("/dev/kmem", O_RDONLY) ;
46     if (kfd == -1)
47         pexit("/dev/kmem") ;
48
49     lseek(kfd, MSGINFO, SEEK_SET) ;
50     read(kfd, (char *)&msginfo, sizeof(struct msginfo)) ;
51     lseek(kfd, SHMINFO, SEEK_SET) ;
52     read(kfd, (char *)&shminfo, sizeof(struct shminfo)) ;
53     lseek(kfd, SEMINFO, SEEK_SET) ;
54     read(kfd, (char *)&seminfo, sizeof(struct seminfo)) ;
55 }
56
```

The `read_ds()` function shown on lines 143 to 154 below reads the `msqid_ds[]`, `shmid_ds[]` and `semid_ds[]` arrays. For each array read, the functions `message_queues()`, `shared_memory()` and `semaphores()` print the contents of each element, formatting them as per the output expected of `ipcs(ADM)`.

```
57  char *
58  perms(char *pstr, int perms)
59  {
60      int x, p ;
61      perms &= (perms & ~(0107000)) ;
62
63      for (x=256, p=0 ; x>0 ; x= (x>>1), p++) {
64          if (!(x & perms))
65              pstr[p] = '-' ;
66          perms &= ~x ;
67      }
68
69      return(pstr) ;
70  }
71
72  message_queues()
73  {
74      int i, id ;
75      struct msqid_ds *ptr = msqid_ds ;
76      struct passwd *pass ;
77      struct group  *group ;
78      char   perm[] = "rw-rw-rw-" ;
79
80      printf("Message queues\n") ;
81
82      for (i=0 ; i<msginfo.msgmni ; i++) {
83          if (ptr->msg_perm.mode & IPC_ALLOC) {
84              strcpy(perm, "rw-rw-rw-") ;
85              id = ptr->msg_perm.seq*msginfo.msgmni + (ptr-msqid_ds) ;
86              pass = getpwuid(ptr->msg_perm.uid) ;
87              group = getgrgid(ptr->msg_perm.gid) ;
88              printf("q%7x 0x%08x --%s %8s %8s\n",id,ptr->msg_perm.key,
89                                      perms(perm, ptr->msg_perm.mode),
90                                      pass->pw_name, group->gr_name) ;
91          }
92          ptr++ ;
93      }
94  }
95
96  shared_memory()
97  {
98      int i, id ;
99      struct shmid_ds *ptr = shmid_ds ;
100     struct passwd *pass ;
101     struct group  *group ;
102     char   perm[] = "rw-rw-rw-" ;
103
104     printf("Shared memory\n") ;
105
106     for (i=0 ; i<shminfo.shmmni ; i++) {
107         if (ptr->shm_perm.mode & IPC_ALLOC) {
108             strcpy(perm, "rw-rw-rw-") ;
109             id = ptr->shm_perm.seq*shminfo.shmmni + (ptr-shmid_ds) ;
110             pass = getpwuid(ptr->shm_perm.uid) ;
111             group = getgrgid(ptr->shm_perm.gid) ;
112             printf("q%7x 0x%08x --%s %8s %8s\n",id,ptr->shm_perm.key,
113                                     perms(perm, ptr->shm_perm.mode),
114                                     pass->pw_name, group->gr_name) ; }
```

```
115          ptr++ ;
116      }
117 }
118
119 semaphores()
120 {
121     int i, id ;
122     struct semid_ds *ptr = semid_ds ;
123     struct passwd *pass ;
124     struct group  *group ;
125     char   perm[] = "ra-ra-ra-" ;
126
127     printf("Semaphores:\n") ;
128
129     for (i=0 ; i<seminfo.semmni ; i++) {
130         if (ptr->sem_perm.mode & IPC_ALLOC) {
131             strcpy(perm, "ra-ra-ra-") ;
132             pass = getpwuid(ptr->sem_perm.uid) ;
133             group = getgrgid(ptr->sem_perm.gid) ;
134             id = ptr->sem_perm.seq*seminfo.semmni + (ptr-semid_ds) ;
135             printf("q%7x 0x%08x --%s %8s %8s\n",id,ptr->sem_perm.key,
136                                     perms(perm, ptr->sem_perm.mode),
137                                     pass->pw_name, group->gr_name) ;
138         }
139         ptr++ ;
140     }
141 }
142
143 read_ds_arrays()
144 {
145     msqid_ds = malloc(msginfo.msgmni * sizeof(struct msqid_ds)) ;
146     shmid_ds = malloc(shminfo.shmmni * sizeof(struct shmid_ds)) ;
147     semid_ds = malloc(seminfo.semmni * sizeof(struct semid_ds)) ;
148     lseek(kfd, MSG_DS, SEEK_SET) ;
149     read(kfd, msqid_ds, msginfo.msgmni * sizeof(struct msqid_ds)) ;
150     lseek(kfd, SHM_DS, SEEK_SET) ;
151     read(kfd, shmid_ds, shminfo.shmmni*sizeof(struct shmid_ds));
152     lseek(kfd, SEM_DS, SEEK_SET) ;
153     read(kfd, semid_ds, seminfo.semmni*sizeof(struct semid_ds));
154 }
```

The `main()` function calls `read_ipc_ds()` and `read_ds_arrays()` to read the IPC object arrays, prints the initial header and then prints statistics for each of the IPC tables read:

```
157 main()
158 {
159     time_t tm ;
160
161     read_ipc_ds() ;
162     read_ds_arrays() ;
163
164     time(&tm) ;
165     printf("IPC status from /dev/kmem as of %s", ctime(&tm)) ;
166     printf("T    ID     KEY      MODE    OWNER    GROUP\n") ;
167
168     message_queues() ;
169     shared_memory() ;
170     semaphores() ;
171 }
```

The output of the program for one particular run is:

```
# mipcs
IPC status from /dev/kmem as of Sun Feb 18 13:53:47 1996
T     ID        KEY         MODE       OWNER     GROUP
Message queues
q     0 0x00000000 --rw-r--r--    spate     group
Shared memory
q     0 0x000018e5 --rw-rw-rw-    root      sys
Semaphores:
q     0 0x002a76d4 --ra-------    root      sys
q     1 0x000018e5 --ra-ra-ra-    root      sys
q     c 0x00000000 --ra-ra-ra-    spate     group
q     3 0x00000000 --ra-ra-ra-    spate     group
q     4 0x00000000 --ra-ra-ra-    spate     group
```

The output displayed is identical to the default output of ipcs(ADM). Since most of the information about IPC objects is retrieved by mipcs, the additional arguments passed to ipcs(ADM) are relatively straightforward to implement.

11.7 Pipes

Pipes are as old as UNIX itself, are provided by every version of UNIX and are still the most common method of communicating between two processes.

There are two types of pipes in UNIX, *traditional pipes*, also called *anonymous pipes* or just pipes, and *named pipes*, which are also called FIFOs (First In First Out).

11.7.1 Anonymous pipes

Pipes provide a half-duplex communication channel between two processes. One end of the pipe is used for writing and the other end for reading. The following pipe(S) system call is used create the pipe:

```
#include <unistd.h>

int pipe(int fildes[2]) ;
```

When a call to pipe(S) is successful, it returns two file descriptors; fildes[0] is opened for reading and fildes[1] is opened for writing. Of course, using a pipe internally within a single process is not particularly useful. The useful properties of the pipe come into play after the process which issued the pipe(S) system call issues a fork(S) system call to create a child process.

Since file descriptors are inherited by the child process, the child also has access to fildes[0] and fildes[1]. It is then usual for the parent to close fildes[0] and the child to close fildes[1], establishing the parent as the producer of data to the pipe and the child as the consumer. Of course the roles could be reversed so that the parent reads from the pipe while the child writes.

The flow of control through the pipe between processes is shown in Figure 11.12.

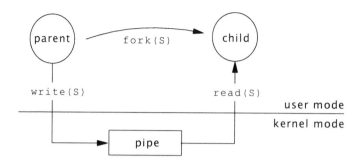

Figure 11.12   Establishing a pipe between parent and child

Each pipe can buffer up to a maximum of 5120 bytes of data. The pipe acts as a FIFO in that data is read from the pipe in the order that it is written.

In the following example, the `pipe(S)` system call is invoked followed by `fork(S)`. The parent then loops around lines 22 to 25 reading lines of characters from standard input and writing them to the pipe.

The child process loops around lines 13 to 17 reading data from the pipe until `read(S)` returns 0, indicating that the parent has terminated and the pipe has been closed.

```
 1 #include <unistd.h>
 2
 3 main()
 4 {
 5     char buffer[5120] ;
 6     int nread=1, fildes[2] ;
 7
 8     pipe(fildes) ;
 9
10     if (fork() == 0) { /* child */
11
12         close(fildes[1]) ;
13         do {
14             nread = read(fildes[0], buffer, 5120) ;
15             if (nread > 0)
16                 printf("data >> %s", buffer) ;
17         } while (nread != 0) ;
18
19     } else { /* parent */
20
21         close(fildes[0]) ;
22         do {
23             nread = read(0, buffer, 5120) ;
24             write(fildes[1], buffer, nread) ;
25         } while (nread != 0) ;
26     }
27 }
```

When the program is run, it will repeatedly read data from the keyboard (parent) and write the data to standard output (child) until an end-of-file character is detected by the parent:

```
$ mpipe
hello
data >> hello
world
data >> world
goodbye
data >> goodbye
^D$                        # ^D entered
```

Since pipes require buffering of data, they present a problem in terms of the amount of space that is required. The traditional solution to this problem was for the filesystem to provide support for pipes such that data written to the pipe involved a write of the data to disk. The details of this approach are shown here since this is the most common approach implemented in most UNIX variants. The other method involves storing the data in core, leading to a higher memory usage but a faster communication mechanism. The HPPS (High Performance Pipe System) filesystem in SCO UNIX uses such a mechanism and is described in section 11.7.5.

11.7.2 The `pipe(S)` system call

When the `pipe(S)` system call returns, both file descriptors reference different entries in the system file table. Both file table entries reference an inode for a file in the filesystem which is managing the pipe, whether it is HPPS or another filesystem.

The kernel function which is called by `systrap()` to handle the `pipe(S)` system call is the `pipe()` function. The tasks performed by `pipe()` are:

- Call `getpipeinode()` to allocate a new inode from the default pipe filesystem.

- The `falloc()` function is called twice to allocate two file table entries, one for reading from the pipe and one for writing. The `fildes[]` file descriptors are mapped to these file table entries. The `falloc()` function attaches each file structure to the inode returned by `getpipeinode()`.

- The `i_count` field of the `inode` structure is set to 2 to indicate that there are two references to the inode. When both ends of the pipe have been closed, the inode and any space allocated on disk can be freed.

The filesystem from which pipes are allocated is determined during kernel initialisation by examining the `pipedev` kernel variable. At any stage there can be multiple filesystems which will allow the kernel to call them to request allocation of an inode for use as a pipe. The number of filesystems available is held in the `npipedev` kernel variable and each filesystem identifier is held in the `pipetab[]` array. The functions `push_pipe_fs()` and `pop_pipe_fs()` are used by the kernel for adding and removing filesystems which support pipe access.

The `getpipeinode()` function which is called by `pipe()` has little work actually to perform. It loops through the `pipetab[]` array and calls each filesystem's `fs_getinode()` function in turn until an inode is returned. The `i_type` field of the inode allocated is set by the filesystem to `IFIFO`. If an inode cannot be returned, the `pipe(S)` system call will fail.

11.7.3 Reading and writing data using a pipe

As with access to regular files described in chapter 8, most of the work performed by the kernel for reading and writing data from and to a pipe is handled by the filesystem.

Figure 11.13 shows the flow of control through the kernel to reach the filesystem.

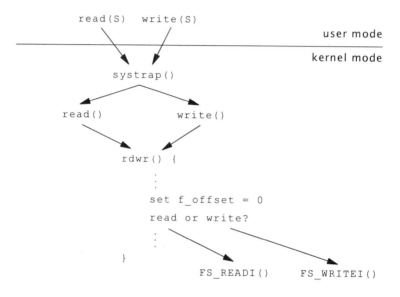

Figure 11.13   Reading from and writing to a pipe

How the read or write will be performed by the filesystem is filesystem specific. However, the following general tasks will be performed when writing data to a pipe:

- If space is not available in the pipe, `sleep(K)` will be called to wait until data has been read and free space becomes available again.

- Since there may already be data in the pipe, the filesystem must determine from where the write should start and allocate disk blocks if required.

- The data is copied into kernel space from the address passed to `write(S)` and written to disk through the buffer cache.

- The `i_size` field of the inode is updated to indicate how many bytes of data are in the pipe and can be read.

- If a process is sleeping and awaiting data, a `wakeup(K)` call is issued.

The following general tasks will be performed when reading from a pipe:

- If there is no data in the pipe, in which case `i_size` will be equal to zero, the kernel will issue a call to `sleep(K)` to put the process to sleep until a `write(S)` is invoked by another process to write data to the pipe.

- If data is available, the filesystem will issue a call to `getblk()` followed by `bread()` to read the data from disk through the buffer cache.
- The data is copied to the address specified to `read(S)`.
- The `i_size` field is adjusted to take into account the number of bytes read.
- If a different process cannot write data into the pipe because it is full, a `wakeup(S)` call is issued. Note that the amount of data to be written may still exceed the amount of space just freed.

Figure 11.14 summarises the flow of data through the kernel when reading from a pipe.

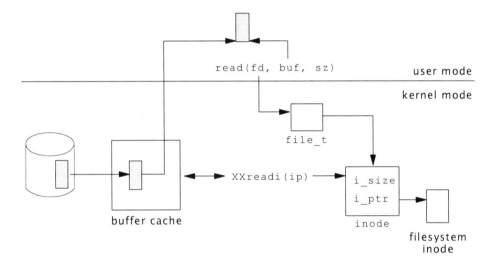

Figure 11.14   The flow of data when reading from a pipe

Note that since reading and writing of data through the pipe is likely to be performed in a short amount of time, there is a high chance of reading from the buffer cache and avoiding the hit of writing the data to disk. This increases the performance of the pipe.

11.7.4 Named pipes/FIFOs

One of the problems with anonymous pipes is that the sharing must be performed by related processes. Named pipes, often called FIFOs, avoid this problem by allowing any two processes to communicate through a pipe which is accessible in the filesystem namespace.

Named pipes are created by the `mknod(ADM)` command or with the `mkfifo(S)` function. The following example uses `mknod(ADM)` to create a named pipe called `FIFO`:

```
$ mknod FIFO p
$ ls -l FIFO
prw-------   1 spate     group        0 Feb 17 13:28 FIFO
```

The permissions of the named pipe can be altered to allow access as per normal files.

The other main difference between named pipes and anonymous pipes is that a named pipe is bi-directional so that read and write calls can be issued at both ends of the pipe.

The following two shell scripts can be used to test the duplex capabilities of named pipes. The script on the left reads a line of characters from the keyboard and writes it to the pipe. At the same time, the script on the right-hand side issues a `cat(C)` command to read from the pipe. Once data has been read, the roles of both scripts are reversed so that the script on the right-hand side writes to the pipe while the script on the left-hand side issues a `cat(S)` command to read from the pipe.

```
while [ true ]                        while [ true ]
do                                    do
    /bin/echo -n "left : "                cat < FIFO
    read left                             /bin/echo -n "right : "
    echo $left > FIFO                     read left
    sleep 1                               echo $left > FIFO
    cat < FIFO                            sleep 1
done                                  done
```

When a named pipe is opened, a single file table entry is allocated and marked as read/write, unlike the separate file table entries allocated with a call to `pipe(S)`.

The process for reading and writing from and to a FIFO is the same as for anonymous pipes. A process which writes data into the named pipe can also read the data back since the kernel does not make a distinction between who is reading and who is writing.

11.7.5 The High Performance Pipe System (HPPS)

As the preceding sections highlighted, pipe performance can be slow if data needs to be written to disk when writing to the pipe and read from disk when reading from the pipe. Of course the advantage with this approach is that it does not consume a large amount of physical memory.

For applications that require higher throughput when using pipes, the HPPS (High Performance Pipe System) filesystem can be used which implements pipes without any interaction with disk based filesystems.

Each pipe created by HPPS results in an HPPS inode being allocated which contains information such as the size of the pipe and the location in memory where data resides if the pipe is not empty. The structures used to implement HPPS pipes are shown in Figure 11.15. This figure should be compared and contrasted with the structures used for standard anonymous pipes shown in Figure 11.14.

There are a number of internal features of HPPS which not only improve the performance of pipes but also help in memory management. If the number of free pages starts to reach a predefined threshold, HPPS will not allow any further allocation of HPPS pipes but pass on further requests to disk based filesystems to allow the `pipe(S)` system call to succeed.

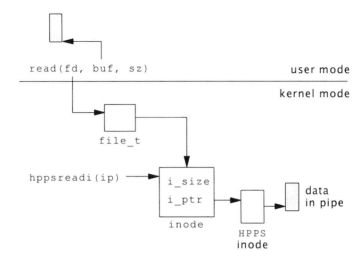

Figure 11.15   Structures used for hpps managed pipes

Toolkit 11.3   Analysing data flow through a pipe

There are a number of standard crash(ADM) commands which can be used to analyse the kernel structures used for implementing pipes. Where disk based pipes are used, the techniques shown in section 9.2 can be used to locate the pipe data in the buffer cache. In this example, a pipe implemented by HPPS will be analysed.

In order to establish an HPPS-managed pipe and write some data to the pipe, the following program is used. It calls pipe(S) to create an anonymous pipe, writes the string "hello world" into the pipe and calls pause(S):

```
#include <unistd.h>

main()
{
    char string[] = "hello world" ;
    int fildes[2] ;

    pipe(fildes) ;
    write(fildes[1], string, sizeof(string)) ;
    pause() ;
}
```

The program (expipe) can be searched for in crash(ADM) using the proc command as follows:

```
> proc ! grep expipe
   61 s  1700  1315  1700 13583  66   0 u           expipe      load
```

The process is located in slot 61 of the proc[] table. The u_area of the process needs to be displayed in order to obtain the list of open file descriptors. This is performed using the user command and passing the proc[] table entry of the process:

```
> user 61
PER PROCESS USER AREA FOR PROCESS 61
USER ID's:      uid: 13583, gid: 50, real uid: 13583, real gid: 50
        supplementary gids: 50
...
OPEN FILES AND POFILE FLAGS:
        [ 0]: F#247    r    [ 1]: F#247    w  [ 2]: F#247    w
        [ 3]: F#285         [ 4]: F#256    w
...
```

The first three file descriptors displayed represent the program's stdin, stdout and stderr streams. The next two file descriptors located in slots 3 and 4 of u_ofile[] reference separate entries in the system file table and are used to reference the read and write sides of the pipe.

The file command can be used to display the contents of both file_t structures:

```
> file 285
FILE TABLE SIZE = 341
SLOT   RCNT    I/FL        OFFSET  FLAGS
 285      1 I# 298              0 read
> file 256
FILE TABLE SIZE = 341
SLOT   RCNT    I/FL        OFFSET  FLAGS
 256      1 I# 298             12 write
```

Both file table entries reference slot 298 of the inode[] table. The inode command can be used to display the contents of this entry:

```
> inode -f 298
INODE TABLE SIZE = 665
SLOT MAJ/MIN FS INUMB RCNT LINK   UID   GID  SIZE    MODE MNT M/ST FLAGS
 298 255,255  3   16    2     0 13583    50     0 p---000  -    -
         FORW   BACK  AFOR  ABCK      MAPPAGES                   RDLOCKS
WANT
         298    298    -     -            0              0
         RMAJ/MIN    FSTYPP    FSPTR    FILOCKS    VCODE WCNT FS
         0,0      0xf01694e4 0xfc1f32d8       0        0    1 HPPS
```

The fields of interest which are highlighted indicate that the inode references an HPPS inode which is located at the address specified in the FSPTR field.

Unfortunately the HPPS inode structure cannot be displayed symbolically so the od command should be used in conjunction with the pipeinode structure definition located in the <sys/fs/hpps.h> header file:

```
> od 0xfc1f32d8 20
fc1f32d8:  f091b000   f091b00c   f091b000   00000000
fc1f32e8:  00000001   00000001   0000000c   3125e869
fc1f32f8:  3125e869   3125e869   00000000   00000000
fc1f3308:  fc1f33f0   00000001   f08cf000   f08cf000
fc1f3318:  f08cf000   00000000   00000000   00000000
```

The first field highlighted is the `read` field of the structure which points to the address in memory where the next read from the pipe will start. The contents of this address and thus the string written to the pipe are displayed below. The second highlighted field represents the `count` field of the structure which specifies the number of characters that are stored in the pipe:

```
> od -c f091b000 20
f091b000:   h   e   l   l   o       w   o   r   l   d \? \? \? \? \?
f091b010:  \? \? \? \?
```

11.8 Summary and suggested reading

This chapter described the main forms of inter-process communication, concentrating on System V IPC which is common to many versions of UNIX. The chapter also described the use of `mmap(S)` and `/dev/zero` to allow shared memory between related processes.

The chapter concluded by describing the different implementations of pipes in SCO UNIX including the High Performance Pipe System `HPPS`.

SCO OpenServer Release 5 also supports POSIX.1b semaphores as an additional upgrade. For details on these semaphores refer to the `sem_init(S)` manual page. Gallmeister (1985) provides a description of POSIX.1b semaphores.

12

Memory management policies

This chapter builds on chapter 6 which describes how the memory image of a UNIX process is constructed using facilities provided by the i386 processor and chapter 7 which describes how the kernel creates a process as a result of calling the `fork(S)` and `exec(S)` system calls.

This chapter describes in more detail the relationship between the virtual address space, physical memory and swap space and the actions taken by the kernel when moving pages between physical memory, swap space and the file from which the executable image is constructed or has been mapped.

The actions or *policies* implemented by the kernel are determined by the *paging* and *swapping* subsystems. The differences and functionality of both subsystems are described throughout the chapter.

12.1 Introduction

This chapter concentrates on *paging* and *swapping*, the two techniques used by the kernel to provide best overall performance in a system limited by the amount of physical memory. A description of how the kernel handles the various memory management related faults that the i386 family of processors generate is also given.

There are no toolkit examples in this chapter. Many of the examples in chapters 6 and 7 describe how to analyse the process memory image, displaying the process's regions, per region pages, copy on write techniques and so on.

Section 12.6 provides a simple program which is used in conjunction with the sar(ADM) command to analyse the effects of paging and swapping.

12.2 The differences between paging and swapping

For a process to be able to run, sufficient physical memory needs to be available. If the required amount of memory is not available, either the kernel must free already used memory before the process can run, or the fork(S) system call will fail.

The memory management policies of many older versions of UNIX were limited by constraints imposed by the underlying hardware. The usual method of making such space available was to move the contents of the current running process to backing store, copy the contents of the new process to run into memory and then pass control to it. Switching between different processes in this way is referred to as *swapping* and relies on disk space or some other medium on which to swap the process images to and from. This device is commonly referred to as the *swap device*.

Such a technique is still used to some degree in most UNIX kernels today. Fortunately, the memory management capabilities of hardware have improved considerably so that additional memory management policies can also be employed.

One key feature offered by most modern processors is support for *paging*. In a page based system memory is allocated in units of a *page* which, on the i386 family of processors, is 4 kbytes. Unlike swapping, where the whole process is either in memory or on the swap device, paging allows for a smaller subset of the process to be in memory at any one time.

The pages of a process that are in memory are those pages that have been accessed recently and are commonly referred to as the *working set*. If space needs to be made available to run a new process, the kernel can selectively choose pages to write to the swap device, typically those pages that have not been accessed recently. This operation is called paging out.

Consider Figure 12.1 which shows the separation of virtual and physical memory together with swap space.

The i386 family of processors support a 4 Gbyte virtual address space and therefore, in theory, it is possible to provide 4 Gbytes of physical memory, creating a one-to-one mapping between virtual and physical addresses.

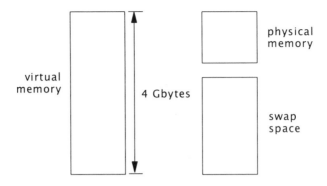

Figure 12.1   Separation of virtual memory, physical memory and swap space

Physical hardware constraints, limitations imposed by the kernel and the high cost of memory make such a system impractical for all but a few large installations. The amount of virtual memory that can actually be used is therefore governed by the amount of physical memory swap space available.

Recall from section 7.9.5 that each valid range of addresses for the kernel or a user processes is underpinned by page tables where each page table entry contains a bit indicating whether the page is present in physical memory or not.

If the kernel or user process accesses a page which does not have the present bit set, the processor generates a page fault for which the kernel will:

- Determine whether the address accessed is valid. For example, access by a user process to a kernel address is invalid and will result in a SIGSEGV signal being posted to the process.

- If the address is valid, the kernel must find a free physical page which is then mapped to the virtual address space covering the failed address.

- The contents of the page must be copied either from the swap device or from a file in the filesystem, or be zero-filled in the case of the process's BSS.

- The instruction which generated the page fault can then be retried.

Such paging policies are described in section 12.7.

The decision when to start paging is based on a set of kernel tuneables and *water marks* used to measure the amount of physical memory available. Swapping is a last resort attempt to free memory and will be invoked only when no memory is available.

When the system starts to page it does not mean that there is insufficient memory on which to run an effective workload. Pages which have been in memory for some time will be paged out to make space for new processes that need to run or for processes currently running but requiring more memory. However, if paging is persistent, there may be a noticeable degradation in performance.

If a system is permanently swapping, however, the performance of the system will start to become unacceptable. At this stage, tuning kernel resources to match the system load and adding more memory are usually the only solutions available. Miscovich and Simons (1994) describe how to detect paging and swapping activity and describe in more detail what actions can be taken. Section 12.6 shows how to use the `sar(ADM)` command to determine when the system starts paging and swapping.

12.2.1 The system memory map

The 4 Gbytes of virtual address space are divided between each user process and the kernel as shown in Figure 12.2.

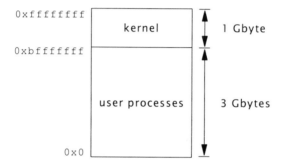

Figure 12.2   Division of the virtual address space between the kernel and user processes

The page table pointers in the page directory are altered on each context switch to point to the page tables for the new process that will run. The switching of page tables is described in section 7.9.5.

When a context switch occurs, the kernel virtual address range and underlying physical pages do not change. Kernel pages are always locked in memory and therefore are never paged out.

12.3 Management of physical memory

The amount of physical memory available to the system is passed to the kernel from `/boot` via the `bootinfo` structure described in chapter 4. Memory is set up during kernel initialisation so that each physical page of memory is described by a `pfdat` structure which is held in the `pfdat[]` array. The fields of the `pfdat` structure are shown in Table 12.1. The relevance of these fields with respect to paging and swapping will be described throughout the chapter.

Table 12.1   The `pfdat` structure used to describe each physical page of memory

pfdat structure field		Description
`dbd_t`	`pf_dbd`	A disk block descriptor used to describe the location of the page when not in memory.
`ushort`	`pf_ndref`	A reference count used for shared pages.
`ushort`	`pf_flags`	Flags describing the state of the page as described below.
`ulong`	`pf_inodex`	An index into the `inode[]` table for the file in which this page is located if the data is associated with a regular file.
`ushort`	`pf_lckcnt`	The number of processes which have locked this page .
`struct pfdat`	`*pf_next`	A pointer to the next free `pfdat` structure on the free list if the page of memory is not in use.
`struct pfdat`	`*pf_prev`	A pointer to the previous free `pfdat` structure if the page is on the free list.
`struct pfdat`	`*pf_hchain`	A hash chain link used for providing faster access to `pfdat` structures.
`ulong`	`pf_use`	The page shared-use count used to implement copy on write semantics for sharing of physical pages.

The `pf_flags` field consists of a bit mask of a number of the following flags:

`P_QUEUE`	The page is on the free list.
`P_BAD`	This page of memory has been detected bad and should not be used.
`P_HASH`	The page is in use and on the hash queue.
`P_DONE`	An I/O operation on the page has completed.
`P_WAIT`	A process is waiting for an I/O operation on this page.
`P_DMA`	The page of memory is DMA'able.
`P_MOD`	This page of memory has been modified and will need writing back to disk before being freed.

When `/boot` loads the kernel it places a `bootinfo` structure at a well-known place in physical memory as described in chapter 4. Within this structure is an array of `bootmem` structures which specify the start address and size of each contiguous set of physical pages, called an *extent*. Memory is discontiguous mainly due to decisions taken historically, such as the placement of video RAM and various BIOS routines between 640 kbytes and 1 Mbyte.

Within the kernel, the extents are represented by `mfmap` structures held in the `mfmap[]` array. There are three fields in the `mfmap` structure:

`paddr_t`	`base`	The base physical address of the extent.
`ulong`	`extent`	The size of the extent.
`struct pfdat *pf`		A pointer to the first `pfdat` structure describing the first physical page in this extent.

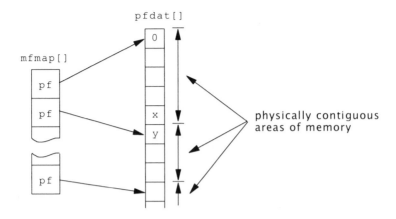

pfdat[]

Figure 12.3   The relationship between the mfmap[] array and pfdat[] array

The relationship between the mfmap[] array and the pfdat[] array is established during kernel initialisation by calling the meminit() function from mlstartup(). The pfdat[] array contains an entry for each usable physical page such that pfdat[0] represents the first usable physical page, pfdat[1] represents the next usable physical page and so on.

The pf field of each mfmap structure is used to point to the first pfdat structure which describes the physical page in the extent which the mfmap structure covers. For example, consider Figure 12.3 which shows the mapping between the mfmap[] and pfdat[] arrays.

The pfdat structure in pfdat[0] represents the first usable page of physical memory. Note, however, that the pages referenced by pfdat[x] and pfdat[y] are not physically contiguous.

The tasks performed by the kernel meminit() routine are:

- Call imemget() to allocate space for the pfdat[] array and the phash[] array.
- Establish the relationship between the mfmap[] and pfdat[] arrays.
- Construct a hash queue of pfdat structures referenced by the phash[] array from which the kernel can quickly locate a pfdat structure using a hash function which takes an index into the inode[] table and the block number of the page in the file or on the swap device.
- Set up the kernel variables that are used to measure the amount of physical memory, the amount of swap space and so on.
- Set up the paging parameters that are used to determine when to page and swap.

A number of kernel variables are used in the management of memory. The totmem variable counts the total amount of usable physical memory on the machine. Since some memory is always allocated by the kernel, the `maxmem` variable measures the maximum amount of physical memory that can be made available. The `freemem` variable measures the actual amount of free memory available at any one time. The `freeswap` variable measures the amount of free space available on the swap device.

12.3.1 Disk block descriptors

The `pfdat` structure is used to describe the properties of a physical page. Embedded within the `pfdat` structure is a *disk block descriptor* underpinned by the `dbd` (`dbd_t`) structure which is used to describe the location of the page when it is not in physical memory. The fields of the `dbd` structure are shown in Table 12.2.

Table 12.2   The disk block descriptor used to locate pages not in memory

dbd struct field	Description
dbd_pv	Copy of the page present bit. If this bit is zero, the dbd is valid.
dbd_rw	Copy of the page table entry read/write bit.
dbd_type	The type of dbd as described below.
dbd_swpi	An index into the swaptab[] array for the device this page is on if the dbd_type field is set to DBD_SWAP.
dbd_blkno	This field represents the disk or file block number.

The disk block descriptor is used when the kernel has detected, usually through a page fault or a need to swap a process into memory, that the page is not present and needs to be created or copied from disk to satisfy a read or write request. The `dbd_type` field is used to determine whether the page already exists on disk and where it is located:

DBD_NONE   This flag indicates that there is no copy of this page on disk. A page fault on this type of page may involve terminating the process.

DBD_PAGE   This flag indicates that the page table entry is correct even if the page present bit is not set.

DBD_FILE   The page can be located in the file specified by the `r_iptr` field of the `region` structure starting at block `dbd_blkno`.

DBD_SWAP   The page can be found on the swap device starting at the block specified by `dbd_blkno` of `swaptab[dbd_swpi]`.

DBD_DZERO   This is a demand-zero page which will be filled with zeros when a page fault occurs.

DBD_DFILL   This is a demand-fill page which will be filled after a page fault.

The following sections will describe how the `dbd_type` field is used to locate pages when a page fault occurs.

12.3.2 Page lists and hash lists

The *page cache* is similar in principle to the buffer cache, whereby pages that are not currently referenced are held in memory with valid contents until either re-used for another purpose or the same page of data is required once again.

Active pages, that is, pages that are in use, reside on a hash queue established within meminit() during kernel initialisation. Each hash queue is located in the phash[] array. The size of the hash queue is calculated dynamically during meminit(), based on the amount of usable physical memory available in the machine.

A pfdat structure is added to the hash list using the pinsert() function which takes an inode pointer and disk block descriptor in addition to a pfdat structure. Using the PHASH() hash function, it locates the appropriate position on the hash queue and adds the pfdat structure to the front of the queue as shown in Figure 12.4.

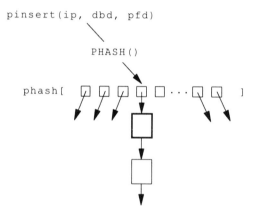

Figure 12.4   Linking a pfdat structure to the hash queue

The pfdat structures on each hash queue are linked using the pf_chain field. After a pfdat structure has been linked onto a hash queue, the P_HASH flag is set in the pf_flags field.

The main use of the hash queue is when the pfind() function is called to check whether a page is present in the cache or not. The use of the pfind() function is described throughout the chapter.

The premove() function takes a pointer to a pfdat structure and removes it from the hash queue. This is called whenever the association between the page and its disk representation changes.

12.4 Process paging

Memory allocated by the kernel when loading a process, or allocated dynamically during process execution, for example by calling malloc(), mmap(S) and so on, may not have physical pages underpinning the allocated virtual address space. Either the pages may be allocated on demand to reduce unnecessary wastage of memory if the process never uses them or the pages may have been allocated and then subsequently *stolen* to satisfy the needs of another process or the kernel.

The first scenario involves the use of *demand paging*, whereby pages are allocated and filled with their contents only when required. For example, the instructions executed by a process tend to be localised and much of the process's text and data segments will not be accessed.

When free memory is low, the physical pages used by one process may be re-used to satisfy the memory needs of another process. Before the pages are stolen from the process, the page contents must sometimes be saved to disk (paged out) so that subsequent access to a virtual address that previously accessed the physical page can be satisfied by allocating another page and reloading the contents from disk. Accessing pages that were previously stolen involves the same page fault recovery techniques as demand paging.

12.4.1 Demand paging

Since the i386 memory management architecture provides support for page level manipulation, the kernel can support demand paging. As described in section 12.2, the physical pages which underpin a process address space may be completely in memory, on a swap device, in the original binary image or a combination of all three.

One of the simplest examples of where demand paging can yield benefits is when a process exits prematurely without having used much of its address space. For example, consider the following program:

```
char buf[1024 * 1024] ;

main(int argc, char *argv[])
{
    if (argc != 2) {
        perror("usage: filename <arg>\n") ;
        exit(-1) ;
    }
    .
    .
    .
```

If the number of arguments passed to the program is not equal to 2, the program will exit immediately. Allocating 1 Mbyte of physical memory for the buf array in this case is therefore wasteful.

One theme that is common to the process regardless of the location of the underlying pages is the layout of the virtual address space, created by the kernel when the process is loaded, which remains unchanged throughout the execution of the process. The only changes that occur are as the result of allocating new memory or growing the process stack. For example, consider Figure 12.5 which shows a simplified portion of a process's address space.

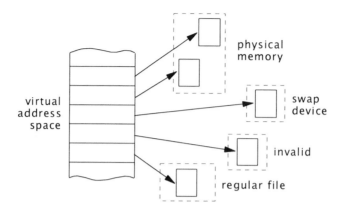

Figure 12.5   The possible locations of physical pages

The user process sees only virtual addresses. There are four possible locations where the physical pages/data corresponding to the virtual address space can reside:

1. A physical page is associated with the virtual address. Accessing a virtual address within this range accesses the corresponding physical address.

2. The page has been moved to a swap device to free space required by another process. Accessing an address here will result in a page fault, allocation of a new physical page, reading of the data from swap and setting the appropriate page table entry so that the virtual address range accesses the new physical page.

3. There is no association between the page and physical memory or a disk based copy. Such an example may include a BSS page which will result in a zero-filled page being allocated when the process accesses the corresponding virtual page causing a page fault.

4. The data is located in the file from which the process has been loaded or in a file that has been mapped into the process address space using the mmap(S) system call. A page fault caused by accessing this virtual page results in allocation of a new physical page, reading the data from the file and setting the appropriate page table entry so that the virtual page accesses the new physical page.

Demand paging covers all cases where the physical page of data underpinning the virtual page is not in physical memory. The mechanics of demand paging involve most kernel subsystems. The details of memory management, including memory management capabilities of the i386 family of processor, are described in chapter 6.

For details on how the process address space is established across the fork(S) and exec(S) system calls see chapter 7.

Chapter 8 describes how block list maps are created to aid demand paging. Handling of page faults by the kernel is described in section 12.7.

12.4.2 Page stealing

During the processing of each clock tick, the `clock()` interrupt handler checks to see if the number of free pages falls below the value specified by the `GPGSLO` kernel tuneable. By calling the kernel `needmem()` function, the number of pages required to be freed is returned. If this number of pages is greater than zero, `clock()` wakes the kernel process `vhand`, called the *page stealer*, whose task is to free memory. If zero is returned from `needmem()`, there is no shortage of memory and clock processing continues without waking `vhand`.

The `vhand` kernel process is created during processing of the kernel's `main()` function and loops repeatedly within the `vhand()` kernel function.

The purpose of `vhand` is to select pages that can either be discarded, in the case of pages read directly from an executable file, or written to the swap device, thus increasing the amount of available physical memory. There are two kernel tuneables which dictate when `vhand` runs:

GPGSLO   If the number of free pages available falls below the value held in `GPGSLO`, `vhand` will be awoken to push pages to the swap device in order to increase the amount of available physical memory. `GPGSLO` is usually set to approximately 1/16 of the total pageable memory.

GPGSHI   When the number of available free pages exceeds the value held in the `GPGSHI` kernel tuneable, `vhand` will stop stealing pages to write to swap. The value of `GPGSHI` is usually set to approximately 1/10 of the total pageable memory.

Figure 12.6 shows the relationship between `vhand`, `GPGSLO` and `GPGSHI`.

The `vhand` kernel process relies on a number of support functions to determine which pages can be paged out, to allocate swap space and to write the actual pages.

The main body of `vhand` loops repeatedly, performing the following tasks:

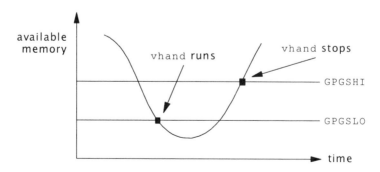

Figure 12.6   The relationship between `vhand`, `GPGSLO` and `GPGSHI`

- Obtain a pointer to the first active `region` structure which is pointed to by the `ractive` kernel variable and lock the region. Active regions are those which are currently being accessed, that is, have a reference count greater than zero.

- If the pages underpinning the region are not eligible for paging, move to the next active region.

- Call `ageregion()` to modify the age properties of each page which will be used to determine those pages in the region which can be paged out.

- Call `getpages()` to build a list of pages for paging out, during which `needmem()` is repeatedly called to avoid paging out too many pages.

- Release the region lock and re-arrange the list of active regions so that the region just processed does not get processed before other active regions. This provides a level of fairness between processes.

- Call `pglstflush()` to allocate swap space and perform the actual write of the page list to the swap device.

- If at this stage `needmem()` still returns pages to be written out, the `strd` daemon is woken up to attempt reclaiming of STREAMS buffers.

- Call `sleep(K)` which will cause `vhand` to sleep until awoken by the `clock()` interrupt handler when memory becomes low again.

The following sections describe some of the more detailed tasks performed during processing of `vhand`. Figure 12.7 summarises the tasks performed by `vhand()`.

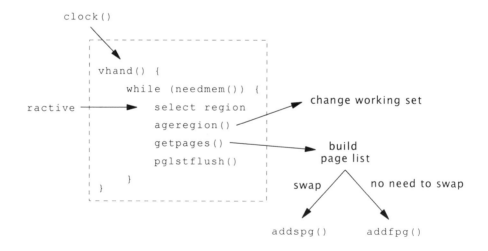

Figure 12.7   The steps taken by `vhand()` to free physical pages

12.4.3 Region ageing

The ageregion() function is called by vhand to determine which pages of a region are eligible for paging out. This is the method by which the kernel dynamically modifies the working set of a process, that is, the set of pages which have been used recently and therefore the core set of pages needed for the process to run without causing too many page faults.

Ageing the region involves analysing the page table entry and its corresponding pfdat structure as shown in Figure 12.8, for each page in the region.

Each page table entry is defined by the pde_t structure declared in the <sys/immu.h> header file. The ageing procedure involves use of the *referenced* bit (pg_ref) in the page table entry that is set by hardware when the page is referenced and bit 9 of each page table entry (pg_ndref) which is not used by the processor and therefore is available for use by the kernel.

If a page has been referenced, the accessed bit of the page table entry will have been set by hardware. This bit alone provides a limited level of ageing. However, to provide finer level of control, the following checks are made by ageregion() for each valid page within the region:

- If the pg_ref bit of the pte is set, the pg_ndref field of the pte is cleared, the pg_ref is cleared and the pf_ndref field of the pfdat structure is incremented.

- If the pg_ref bit of the pte is clear and if the pg_ndref field of the pte is set, the pf_ndref field of the pfdat is incremented and the pg_ndref field of the pte is cleared.

- If both the pg_ref bit and pg_ndref bits of the pte are clear, the pf_ndref field of the pfdat structure is incremented.

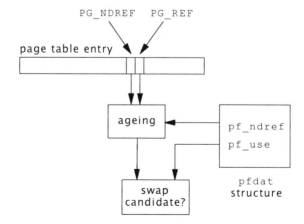

Figure 12.8   The page table entry and pfdat structure used in region ageing

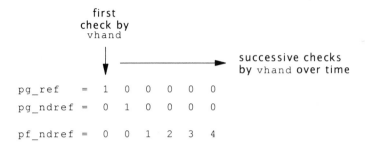

Figure 12.9   Successive checks on a page by vhand

Note that only one of these conditions will be true. As vhand makes repeated calls over time to analyse the pages in the region, only pages that have not been modified recently will be aged. Figure 12.9 shows a page that has been accessed since vhand last ran but will not be accessed again.

Table 12.3 shows how the fields of the pte and pfdat structures are set using the rules above. Each row in the table shows the modification of each field after processing by ageregion(). In the table an X means any value. The column on the right-hand side indicates whether the page is then eligible for paging or not.

Table 12.3   Modifying the age properties of a valid page

pg_ref	pg_ndref	pf_ndref	Pageable?
1 ↪ 0	X ↪ 1	X ↪ 0	✗
0 ↪ 0	1 ↪ 0	X ↪ $X+1$	✓
0 ↪ 0	0 ↪ 0	X ↪ $X+1$	✓

Another field in the pfdat structure, the pf_use field, is used to determine finally whether the page will be paged out. This field specifies the number of references to the page. If the above conditions hold true and pf_ndref is less than or equal to pf_use, the page will be paged out.

12.4.4 Building page lists for swapping

Once a region has been aged, vhand calls getpages() to build a list of eligible pages that can be either written to swap or simply discarded.

getpages() walks through the pages of the region and checks the pfdat and pte for each page to determine whether the page can be paged out based on the ageing process performed by ageregion(). For eligible pages, the dbd_type field of the disk block descriptor embedded within the `pfdat` structure is checked to determine the actions to be taken with the page. The following actions are performed:

DBD_NONE The page is currently not associated with any backing store on disk, therefore `addspg()` is called to add the page to the swap list.

DBD_SWAP This page already has space allocated on the swap device. If the page has not been modified, the `addfpg()` function is called to add the page to the free list since there is no need to write the data back to swap. If the page has been modified, `addspg()` is called to add the page to the swap list.

DBD_FILE The page is associated with a disk based file, for example a program's text segment. Since the page can be retrieved from the file, the `addfpg()` function is called to add the page to the free list.

The swap list is an array of `pglst_t` structures accessed by `spglst[]`. Included in the `pglst_t` structure is a pointer to the region to which the page belongs and a pointer to the page table entry.

12.4.5 Flushing pages to swap

After the list of pages to be paged out has been constructed by `getpages()`, `pglstflush()` is called to write the pages to the swap device.

The operations performed by `pglstflush()` are almost identical to the operations performed when swapping out a process which are described in section 12.5. Figure 12.10 summarises the main steps taken by `vhand` to write the pages to the swap device.

The `swapchunk()`, `swalloc()`, `swap()` and `swapseg()` functions are described in detail in the next section. Collectively, these functions take a list of `pglst_t` structures, allocate swap space for them, determine the fastest path to disk and write the pages out.

When `swapchunk()` returns, the data has been successfully written to swap so the `memfree()` function is called to add the pages to the free list. The `spgIndx` variable which is used to measure the number of `pglst_t` structures in the `spglst[]` array is then reset to zero before `pglstflush()` returns.

12.5 Process swapping

Swapping is performing by the `sched` kernel process which occupies slot zero of the `proc[]` table. Chapter 4 shows how the kernel `main()` function becomes the swapper by invoking `sched()` as the last function it calls.

The swapper is called whenever the amount of free memory hits zero or is sufficiently low that even trivial requests for memory cannot be satisfied, or when a process chosen to run has been previously swapped out. In the latter case the `p_flag` field of the `proc` structure will not have the SLOAD flag set.

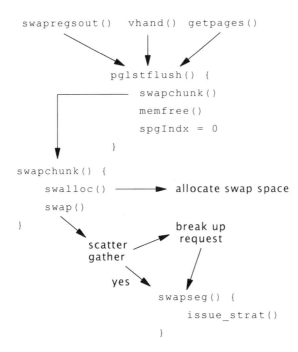

Figure 12.10   Writing a page list to the swap device

When the swapper will run and whether it will swap in or swap out is determined by the variables `runin` and `runout`. The swapper will sleep on the `runin` variable when there is not enough space to swap in a process or after a process has been swapped in. It will sleep on `runout` when there are no processes to swap in.

The use of `runin` and `runout` is described in more detail later in this section.

12.5.1 Allocation of swap space

Swap space is initially allocated during processing of the kernel's `main()` function early during kernel initialisation. Additional swap space may be allocated at any stage during the lifetime of the system.

Each active swap device is represented in the kernel by a `swaptab` structure shown in Table 12.4. Each `swaptab` structure is held in the `swaptab[]` array.

When the kernel is entered from /boot the `swaptab[]` array is empty. The `swapdev` variable which indicates the swap device to use is passed by /boot to the kernel. During the kernel's `main()` function a call is made to `swapadd()` to add the device specified by `swapdev` to the `swaptab[]` array. The device referenced by `swapdev` is assigned to the `st_dev` field. Other arguments passed to `swapadd()` include the starting block which is assigned to the `st_swplo` field and the number of swap blocks which is converted into pages before being assigned to the `st_npgs` field.

Table 12.4   The swaptab structure used to describe each active swap device

swaptab structure field		Description
dev_t	st_dev	The device number of the swap device.
short	st_flags	Various flags used to define the state of the device.
use_t	*st_ucnt	A pointer to the *used count* array for pages on swap.
use_t	*st_next	A pointer to the next page to start searching.
int	st_swplo	The first block number on the device to be used for swapping.
int	st_npgs	The number of pages of swap space on the device.
int	st_nfpgs	The number of free pages left on the device.
struct inode	*st_ip	The inode pointer used to access the device.

The swap(ADM) command allows the caller to add and remove swap devices to and from the swaptab[] array or to display the list of currently accessible swap devices.

Each time a swap device is added, the freeswap variable is incremented by the number of pages available on the swap device.

The tasks performed by swapadd() are:

- A check is made to ensure that the specified device is not mounted.

- A scan is made through the swaptab[] array looking for an unused entry.

- The fields of the swaptab structure found are initialised with the arguments passed to swapadd(). This includes the st_dev, st_npgs and st_swplo fields.

- The device open routine is called to specify that the device will be accessed for reading and writing.

- The sptalloc() function is called to allocate an array of use_t elements which will be used to record which pages of the swap device are in use. The bzero() function is called to clear the array.

- The freeswap variable used to record the number of free swap pages is incremented by the number of pages available on the device.

The array allocated by sptalloc() is referenced by the st_ucnt field of the swaptab structure. When the swap device is in use, the st_next field is used as the location in the array to start the next search for free pages. For example, consider the swap device allocated in Figure 12.11.

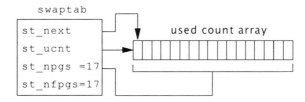

Figure 12.11   A swaptab structure after calling swapadd()

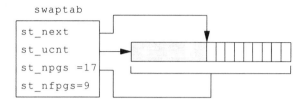

Figure 12.12   The same `swaptab` structure following allocation of eight pages

If eight pages are allocated, the `swaptab` structure will be modified as shown in Figure 12.12.

The `st_next` field is set to point to the next free location in the `st_ucnt` array and the `st_nfpgs` field is decremented to show how many free pages are left on the swap device.

Allocation of pages on swap is requested both by `sched` and `vhand` using the `swalloc()` function. The arguments passed to `swalloc()` include a list of `pglst_t` structures representing the pages that will be written to swap and the number of pages. The tasks performed by `swalloc()` are:

- The `swapfind()` function is called to see if a contiguous area of swap can be allocated. If such a contiguous area cannot be found, the caller of `swalloc()` will call `swapfind()` multiple times, once for each page to be swapped out.

- The fields in the appropriate `swaptab` structure are updated to reflect the number of pages allocated.

- The amount of free space held in the `freeswap` variable is decremented.

- The disk block descriptor associated with each `pglst_t` structure is updated to reference the position on the swap device where the page will reside.

At this stage swap space is allocated so the pages that need to be swapped can be written to the device.

12.5.2 Finding processes to swap in and out

The actual swapping in or out of processes is a relatively straightforward task built on the functions already covered in this chapter and additional functions described in the next two sections. The `sched()` routine loops repeatedly between the following tasks:

1.   When `sched()` is first called it walks through the `proc[]` table and locates all processes which are currently swapped out. The processes are ordered by the time they have been swapped out and placed in the `outprocs[]` array. If there are no processes to swap in, `sched` will increment the `runout` variable and call `sleep(K)`, passing its address.

2. When `sched` reaches this point there is at least one process to swap in. A loop is made through `outprocs[]` and, for each process, the `swapin()` function is called to move the required parts of the process from the swap device back into main memory.

   At some stage there may not be enough memory to swap a process in. `sched` must then locate processes eligible for swapping out to make room for those processes which need to be swapped in. The tasks performed in step 3 are then called.

3. When `sched` reaches this point there is at least one process to swap out. A scan is made through `proc[]`, this time looking for the process that has been in memory for the longest period of time. An attempt is always made to locate processes that are sleeping before choosing those processes that are on the run queue. When a process is located, the `swapout()` function is called to swap the process out. If `swapout()` fails due to lack of swap space, `sched` will increment the `runin` variable and call `sleep(K)`, passing its address.

   The `clock()` interrupt handler checks every second to see if the `runin` variable is set and, if so, issues a `wakeup(.)` call to start `sched` running again. It is hoped at this stage that a memory resident process may have terminated, thus freeing physical memory. This allows a process currently on the swap device to be swapped in, allowing a subsequent call to `swapout()` to succeed.

   When `sched` awakes it will start running the tasks in point 1 to locate candidates for swapping in.

When `sched` is active, memory resources, both physical memory and swap space, can become so scarce that `sched` will be consuming large amounts of processor time, resulting in significant delays between scheduling of one process and another. This situation is called *thrashing*. The net effect is a noticeable degradation in performance. Section 12.6 provides an example which demonstrates how slow the system can become as a result of paging and swapping.

If swapping occurs regularly, the amount of swap space should be increased. In practice, if swapping is persistent, the most practical solution is to increase the amount of physical memory. See Miscovich and Simons (1994) for further details.

12.5.3 Swapping processes out

`sched` is called to swap processes out when requests for memory cannot be satisfied. If the `ptmemall()` function cannot allocate the requested number pages for a process owing to lack of memory, it will call the `sxbrknswtch()` function.

The `p_stat` field of the `proc[]` structure is set to SXBRK by `sxbrknswtch()` and a check is made on `runout` to ensure that `sched` is able to create space by swapping out the oldest resident process, thus freeing the required space.

The `swapout()` function is called by `sched` to swap out the chosen process. The tasks performed by `swapout()` are as follows:

- The SLOAD bit is turned off in the p_stat field of the proc structure. This indicates that the process is no longer resident in memory.
- The calcregsout() function is called to calculate how many pages on swap are needed to swap out the process's regions.
- The swalloc() function is called to allocate the required number of swap pages.
- The swapregsout() function is called which will write out all of the pages attached to the process's regions to the allocated swap space.
- The swap() function is called, specifying an argument of B_WRITE. This function is passed a list of pglst_t structures which specify all remaining pages to be written to swap. The swap() function determines the capabilities of the underlying device to find the most efficient method of writing the data and then calls swapseg() which will issue a call to the driver's strategy routine.

12.5.4 Swapping processes in

There are a number of places where sched is awoken to swap a process in:

- The clock() interrupt handler checks to see if sched is sleeping on runin. Recall from section 12.5.1 that this occurs only when there is no space in memory to swap in a process or a process has just been swapped in.
- The wakeup() function wakes a process which has been swapped out, in which case the p_flag will not be set to SLOAD. A check is made to ensure that sched is sleeping on runout.
- The setrun() function is called to schedule a process which is swapped out. The same procedures are followed as for wakeup().
- The killprocs() function is about to terminate a process that is swapped out. Again, the same procedures are followed as for wakeup().

The swapin() function is called by sched to swap a process from the swap device into main memory, following the procedures outlined in section 12.5.2. The tasks performed by swapin() are, not surprisingly, almost the reverse of the tasks performed by swapout(). For completeness, the tasks are:

- The ptmemalloc() function is called to allocate pages for the u_area.
- The swap() function is called to swap in the specified process. This time, the B_READ argument is passed to swap().
- The swapregsin() function is called to read in the process's regions.
- The p_stat field of the proc structure is set to SLOAD to indicate that the process is now resident in memory and therefore eligible for execution.
- The ubptswap() function is finally called to free the swap space previously allocated to the process.

12.6 Analysing paging and swapping activity

Detecting when paging and swapping occurs is easy; solving the problem of persistent paging and swapping is more difficult. If a system spends much of its time swapping, although the kernel and application profiles may be tuned for better matching of system resources, adding more memory is usually the best way to reduce swapping and therefore improve performance.

The example program shows how paging and swapping can be invoked and detected using the sar(ADM) command.

The program forks 24 children (line 10) each of which allocates a megabyte of memory and walks through page by page writing a value to each page to ensure that physical memory is allocated.

```
 1 #include <sys/types.h>
 2 #include <sys/immu.h>
 3 #include <stdlib.h>
 4
 5 main()
 6 {
 7     int pid, x, np, i, npgs = (1024 * 1024) / NBPP ;
 8     char *addr, *touch ;
 9
10     for (np=0 ; np<24 ; np++) {
11         pid = fork() ;
12         if (pid == 0) { /* child */
13             addr = malloc(1024*1024) ;
14             if (addr == -1)
15                 pexit("malloc") ;
16
17             for (x=0 ; x<8 ; x++) {
18                 touch = addr ;
19                 for (i=0 ; i<npgs; i++) {
20                     *touch = 0x77 ;
21                     touch += NBPP ;
22                 }
23                 sleep(1) ;
24             }
25             exit(0) ;
26         } else if (pid == -1)
27             printf("couldn't fork child %d\n", np) ;
28     }
29 }
```

The sar(ADM) command is run with the -w option which instructs sar to display swapping and paging activity. The fields displayed by sar are:

swpin/s   The number of transfers from the swap device into memory per second.

bswin/s   The number of 4 kbyte transfers from swap into memory per second.

swpot/s   The number of transfers from memory to swap per second.

bswot/s   The number of 4 kbyte transfers from memory to swap per second.

pswch/s   The number of context switches per second.

The additional arguments passed to sar below are the time between samples (1) and the number of samples that should be taken (20).

```
# sar -w 1 20

SCO_SV xian 3.2v5.0.0 Pentium     02/22/96

09:04:12 swpin/s bswin/s swpot/s bswot/s pswch/s
09:04:13    0.00     0.0    0.00     0.0      43
09:04:14    0.00     0.0    0.00     0.0      30
09:04:15    0.00     0.0    0.00     0.0      46
09:04:16    0.00     0.0   10.78   502.0     112
09:04:17   14.29   114.3   20.41  1102.0     119
09:04:20   19.03   155.2   17.16   976.1      91
09:04:23   22.90   186.3   12.60   769.5      65
09:04:24    8.82    70.6   21.57  1380.4      52
09:04:25   46.08   384.3    9.80   525.5      91
09:04:26   54.90   462.7    0.00     0.0      86
09:04:27   56.86   454.9    0.00     0.0      75
09:04:28   74.51   596.1    0.00     0.0      97
09:04:29  119.80   958.4    0.00     0.0     143
09:04:30   62.75   502.0    0.00     0.0      77
09:04:31    0.00     0.0    0.00     0.0      15
09:04:32    0.00     0.0    0.00     0.0      15
09:04:33    0.00     0.0    0.00     0.0      16
09:04:34    3.92    31.4    0.00     0.0      23
09:04:35    1.92    15.4    0.00     0.0      15
09:04:36    0.00     0.0    0.00     0.0       8

Average    23.80   192.7    6.00   345.2      63
```

Before the program is run there is no paging or swapping activity. Since all processes are memory intensive, it takes little time before vhand starts running. This is shortly followed by sched.

The results obtained depend greatly on the number of processes that are run and the amount of memory allocated. For example, try running the program with a few less processes or a few more processes and observe the effects.

12.7 Page fault handling

The previous sections have described the management of a process address space as consisting of pages of data which can be either in memory, on a swap device or within the file or files from which they have been loaded or mapped.

Accessing a page which is not present in memory will result in a page fault in which normal execution of the CPU is interrupted, the reason for failure is saved and a kernel provided exception handler is invoked.

There are two circumstances under which a page fault will be generated:

- The page is marked not present. This is determined by bit 0 of the page table entry being set to 0. This type of fault is called a validity fault and is handled by the `vfault()` function.

- The process which is currently running on the CPU has attempted to access an address in memory for which it does not have the appropriate privileges. This type of fault is called a protection fault and is handled by the `pfault()` function.

When a page fault occurs, the processor pushes an error code onto the stack to allow the kernel's exception handler to determine why the page fault occurred. The exception handler must determine:

- Whether the exception was due to an attempt to read from or write to an invalid memory address.

- What invoked the exception, the kernel or a user process.

- Whether the exception was due to a valid page not being present or whether the caller did not have sufficient access privileges.

The address being accessed at the time of the exception is stored in the `cr2` register. Using this address and the information provided above, the kernel can determine the appropriate course of action to take.

The processor locates which kernel function to invoke using the *Interrupt Descriptor Table* (IDT). The entry in this table which corresponds to page faults is the `pftrap()` function. There are a number of functions invoked prior to `vfault()` or `pfault()` as shown in Figure 12.13.

Most types of exceptions are handled by the `cmntrap()` routine. Depending on whether the page fault occurred while in kernel mode or user mode, the `kern_trap()` or `user_trap()` function will be invoked. Each transfers control to `k_trap()` and `u_trap()`, respectively.

The actions taken by the kernel differ when a page fault occurs, depending on whether the page fault occurs when running in user mode or kernel mode. For example, a page fault which cannot be resolved when running in user mode will result in the process being terminated. Such unresolved page faults are invalid when running in kernel mode and may result in a kernel panic.

When the `usrxmemflt()` function is invoked it is passed the exception code, which is 14 for page faults, and the address which caused the fault. If the page to which the virtual address belongs is valid, `vfault()` is called.

If the page is not valid, `usrxmemflt()` must assume that a write fault occurred to an otherwise valid page. In this case it calls the `pfault()` function.

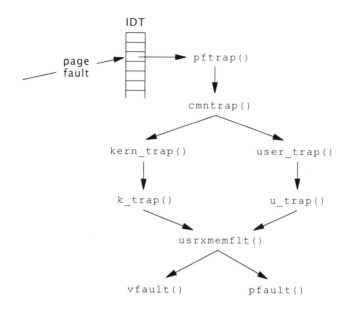

Figure 12.13   The route taken from a page fault through to `vfault()` or `pfault()`

12.7.1 Validity faults

When the page is valid but not present the `vfault()` kernel function is used to locate and read in the page of data from either swap or the file with which it may be associated. When `vfault()` is called by `usrxmemflt()`, it is passed the virtual address which resulted in the exception and a pointer to the `pregion` structure which references the appropriate region, and therefore the range of virtual addresses, which span the failed virtual address.

Figure 12.14 shows how the arguments passed to `vfault()` are used to locate the missing page within a process region.

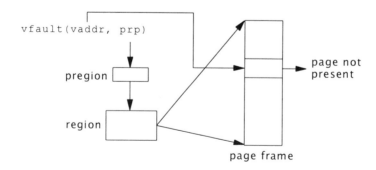

Figure 12.14   The validity fault handler called to resolve pages marked not present

Although the actual manipulation of page directory and page table entries, together with management of the page cache, involves complex processing by `vfault()` the principles are relatively straightforward:

- A pointer to the `region` structure associated with the `pregion` is obtained via the `p_reg` field of the `pregion` structure passed to `vfault()`. If the page needs to be read from a regular file, the `r_iptr` field of the `region` structure points to the in-core inode and thus allows `vfault()` to invoke the filesystem to read the data. This path is described later.

- The `uptaddr()` function is called to retrieve the page directory entry which points to the page table and thus the page table entry of the page which caused the fault.

- The disk block descriptor field of the `pfdat` structure is examined to determine the type of the page in order to decide where to read the data from or whether the page is invalid. There are three possibilities:

  ⇨ The page is of type `DBD_FILE`. In this case, the `pfind()` function is called, passing the `pfdat` structure. The page cache is searched to determine whether the required page is in memory.

  ⇨ The page is of type `DBD_SWAP`. As with pages of type `DBD_FILE`, the `pfind()` function is called, passing the appropriate `pfdat` structure to search the page cache for the required page.

  ⇨ The page is of type `DBD_NONE`. In this case there is no backing store associated with the page and therefore the read or write which caused the page fault cannot be satisfied. This type of access may be a result of invoking `mmap(S)` and specifying an address which is beyond the end of the file. In this case, return to `usrxmemflt()` will result in a `SIGBUS` signal being posted to the process which caused the exception.

- If the page is not found in the page cache, the `ptmemall()` function is called to allocate a new page. Since this page will not have the required contents, the `pagerw()` function is called to read the data from the file for `DBD_FILE` pages or from swap for `DBD_SWAP` pages. If the page is of type `DBD_DZERO`, the page will be zero filled.

If the page is found in the page cache and is on the free list, it is unlinked and inserted into the `pfdat` hash queue.

Before calling `pagerw()`, `vfault()` calls `pfntopfdat()` to modify the page attributes such as the swap block number or file block number.

If the page is located on a swap device, the `swap()` function is called to read the page of data from swap, otherwise `FS_READMAP()` is called to read the page from the regular file specified by the region's inode.

12.7.2 Protection faults

When a protection violation occurs, the `pfault()` function is called either to allocate a physical page to allow the instruction to be restarted or to post a signal to the process if the address is invalid. There are two circumstances under which a protection fault occurs:

1. The address accessed is not part of the process's address space. In this case an appropriate signal will be sent to the process for which the default behaviour is to terminate the process.

2. The page has been marked as a *copy on write* page. This is the usual mechanism used across the `fork(S)` system call so that pages are shared between parent and child for as long as possible. Separate physical pages are created only if one of the processes attempts to write to the page. The principles of copy on write are described in section 7.5 and the actions taken when a protection fault occurs are described below.

Protection faults are handled by `pfault()` which is passed the faulting virtual address and a pointer to a `pregion` structure in which the address is located.

The main tasks performed by `pfault()` are:

- If the `p_flags` field of the `pregion` structure is not set to `PF_READ` or `PF_WRITE`, return to `usrxmemflt()`. This will result in `SIGSEGV` being sent to the process.

- The `uptaddr()` function is called to obtain the appropriate page table followed by a call to `pfntopfdat()` to locate the `pfdat` for the failed page.

- If the `pf_use` field of the `pfdat` structure is greater than 1, `pfault()` is dealing with a copy on write page. This involves performing the following steps:

  ⇨ `ptmemall()` is called to allocate a new physical page.

  ⇨ `bcopy()` is called to copy the data from the valid page to the new page, creating a per process copy on which the write can be performed.

  ⇨ The page table entry is modified to reference the new physical page.

  ⇨ The `pf_use` field of the `pfdat` structure corresponding to the original physical page is decremented.

12.8 Summary and suggested reading

This chapter described how the kernel manages physical memory and swap space and the actions taken when the amount of free memory becomes scarce.

The chapter then described the actions taken by the kernel in response to page faults in order to implement demand paging policies.

The SCO *Performance Guide* (1995) provides information on how to tune the SCO UNIX kernel. Since much of the book centres around the use of `sar(ADM)`, the approach followed in this book should also be applicable to other UNIX kernels.

13

Application debugging with adb(CP)

Since adb(CP) is used throughout the book in conjunction with crash(ADM) to analyse active processes, this chapter briefly describes adb(CP), a powerful command line debugger used for setting breakpoints, single stepping user programs and displaying memory and registers.

13.1 Introduction

The absolute debugger, `adb`, is a powerful program used for both analysing and debugging C and assembly language programs. It provides features such as:

- Displaying program instructions and data.
- Displaying memory segment properties and machine registers.
- Setting and clearing breakpoints.
- Running and single stepping programs.
- Analysing core files.
- Patching both program instructions and data.
- Displaying program stack traces.
- Establishing arbitrary memory maps.

Most people would agree that the features provided by newer debuggers available today, such as multiple graphical windows, far surpass the old command line style interface of debuggers such as `adb` and `sdb`, for example the window based debugger `Argus`. However, `adb`, with its simple user interface and small but powerful set of commands, is an ideal tool for examining program execution at a level close to the underlying machine, thus the choice of `adb` to demonstrate programs and kernel analysis techniques throughout this book.

While this is not an exhaustive tutorial on the capabilities of `adb`, it demonstrates a sufficient level of detail in order to follow the examples used throughout the book.

13.2 Getting started

Invoking `adb` is straightforward since there are only a few command line options to remember. The complete syntax for starting an `adb` session is:

```
adb [-w] [-p prompt] [object_file [corefile]]
```

To invoke `adb` for the `object_file` called `myprog`, the command line to be entered is:

```
$ adb myprog
*
```

If `object_file` is not given, `adb` looks by default in the current directory for the standard compiler output file, `a.out`.

The prompt `*` indicates that `adb` is ready to start receiving commands. The `object_file` is usually an executable file in ELF or COFF format. However, there is no restriction on the file type for `object_file`. It may even be a plain text file.

To ease debugging, the file should contain a symbol table although this is not essential. An executable file will contain a symbol table by default unless the `-s` option is passed to the compiler/link editor or the strip(CP) program is run on the file, which explicitly removes all data from the executable file which is not required for execution.

The corefile is the core image produced during an unsuccessful run of the program. If the corefile is not specified, adb will use the file core by default. If a core file is produced by executing a program other than object_file, it will be used by adb although a warning will be printed as follows:

```
$ prog1
Floating exception(coredump)          # Error message from prog1
$ adb prog2
adb: core file ("prog1") doesn't match object "prog2"
*
```

When prog1 was run it generated an exception resulting from, in this example, division by zero. Invoking adb with prog2 results in the warning message but allows the session to continue.

If the -w option is specified to adb, the object_file is opened for writing. The main use for this option is to allow *patching* of executables without invoking a recompilation. If object_file and corefile do not exist, they are created if necessary. The -w option is described in section 13.6.

The adb prompt can be set to an alternative character or string of characters by using the -p option. For example, to invoke adb for an executable file a.out with the prompt ok>, the following command is typed at the shell prompt:

```
$ adb -p "ok>" a.out
ok>
```

To exit adb either ^D (control-D) or the $q command should be typed at the prompt as follows:

```
ok> $q
$
```

13.3 Analysing text and data segments

Much of the time within an adb session is spent issuing requests to read program text and data. Each request takes the following format:

```
[address] [,count] [command] [;]
```

The address, which is an expression of the form [segment:]offset, is the location at which the command should be applied. adb supports the notion of a *current* address '.' which is referred to as dot. If the address used in the last command typed is valid, dot is set to address.

The segment component of the address is a *segment selector* through which an area of memory can be specified in terms of a base address, limit (end address) and various protection properties. Segment selectors are described in section 6.3.2. The `offset` component of the `address` specifies an offset within the segment.

There are three commands available for displaying text and data:

?f   The contents of the *text* address are displayed in format `f`.
/f   The contents of the *data* address are displayed in the format `f`.
=f   The `address` itself is displayed in the format `f`.

There are many different formats available, each specified by a single character, which can be combined to produce various different outputs.

The format is used to specify how to display the `address` for the = command, or the contents of the address for the / and ? commands. Some of the more commonly used formats are shown in Table 13.1.

Table 13.1   Subset of data formats for displaying addresses of text or data

Format	Description
i	Machine instruction mnemonics.
d	2 bytes in decimal.
D	4 bytes in decimal.
c	1 byte as a character.
s	A null terminated string.
x	2 bytes in hexadecimal.
X	4 bytes in hexadecimal.
b	1 byte in octal.
a	The address is displayed in symbolic form.

13.3.1 An adb session

To demonstrate the `adb` features described so far, this section shows the use of the ?, / and = commands and various formats using the following program:

```
char hw[] = "hello world" ;

main()
{
    printf("%s\n", hw) ;
}
```

Note that for this example to be effective, the object file must contain a symbol table. If the symbol table is not present, even a simple example like this would give the more experienced `adb` user problems to decompose and understand.

The example session is shown with a description:

```
1    $ adb a.out                    # enter adb
2    * main=X                       # display address of main()
3                     0x128
4    * .=X                          # display current address (dot)
5                     0x128
```

```
6     * main,4?i                   # display instructions from main
7       main:     push    ebp
8                 mov     ebp,esp
9                 sub     esp,0x0
10                push    ebx
11    * hw/s                        # display string at address hw
12      hw:       hello world
13    * hw/c                        # display single character at hw
14      hw:       h
15    * hw,b/c                      # display 11 characters
16      hw:       hello world
17    * $q                          # exit from adb
18    $
```

The commands entered and their output are as follows:

Line 1   The adb session is entered using the object_file called a.out.

Line 2   The address of the symbol main is displayed in hexadecimal format.

Line 4   Since the address of main() is valid, dot is set to this address and also displayed in hexadecimal format.

Line 6   The memory contents starting at the address of main() are displayed using the *instruction* format. The first four instructions are displayed as specified by the count argument.

Line 11   The contents starting at the address specified by the symbol hw are displayed in string format. Note that the string must be null terminated.

Line 13   The difference between various formats is demonstrated here. The same starting address is used as in line 11 but only a single character is displayed by using the c format.

Line 15   The use of count is demonstrated, producing the same effect as the s format as shown in line 11.

Later examples will further demonstrate the use of these commands and formats.

13.4 Constructing expressions

When invoking commands within adb, the address (segment and offset) and count arguments are formed by constructing expressions. The examples shown so far use the most simplistic form of expression, an integer or symbol.

However, expressions in adb can consist of more than just symbols or integers as the following sections show.

13.4.1 Address variables

adb maintains four internal variables which can be used for forming addresses. These are shown in Table 13.2.

Table 13.2   adb internal variables used to form addresses

Expression	Description
.	The value currently assigned to dot.
+	The value of dot plus the current increment.
^	The value of dot decremented by the current increment.
–	Decrements dot by one.
=	The last address typed.

dot is often referred to as the *current address* and is the last address used in a command, for example:

```
* main?i                        # this is the same as main,1?i
main:     push    ebp
```

sets dot to the address of main().

Typing a newline at the adb prompt increments dot. The most appropriate way to demonstrate this is using the ? or / commands. Using the program described earlier:

```
1      * main?i
2      main:         push    ebp
3      *                                    # return pressed
4      main+0x1:     mov     ebp,esp
5      *                                    # return pressed
6      main+0x3:     sub     esp,0x0
7      * hw/c
8      hw:           h
9      *                                    # return pressed
10     hw+0x1:       e
11     *                                    # return pressed
12     hw+0x2:       l
```

After the request is made to disassemble one instruction from main() on line 1, a newline is typed on lines 3 and 5. This has the effect of incrementing dot and displaying the instruction at the new value of dot. The same effect is shown for displaying characters starting at the address specified by the symbol hw on lines 7 to 12.

Note that when using the + and ^ address variables the value of the increment is dependent on the previous format. If an instruction is displayed then + will point to the address of the next instruction. If a character is displayed, + will point to dot plus one.

13.4.2 Symbol names

A symbol is the name of either a function or a global variable and is found in the program's symbol table if present. The addresses of symbols within an executable program can be found using the nm(CP) command.

Local (automatic) variables in C are held on the user's stack and have no entry in the program's symbol table.

13.4.3 Registers

The current values of the machine registers can be used in expressions by prefixing the register name with the < character. The register names can be displayed with the $r command as follows:

```
$ $r
eax        0x400544        efl    0x206
ebx        0x0             eip    0x128
ecx        0x0             cs     0x17
edx        0x406d54        ds     0x1f
esi        0x406d38        es     0x1f
edi        0x406d54        fs     0x0
ebp        0x7ffffec4      gs     0x0
esp        0x7ffffeb4      ss     0x1f
main:          push     ebp
```

This example shows the register values part way through program execution. Displaying registers prior to program execution will display all registers with values of 0.

13.4.4 adb variables

adb maintains its own internal set of variables which hold various addresses and data regarding the program's location, state, execution and so on.

The variables can be displayed with the $v command as shown. The output shows the named variables which are initialised during startup of adb.

```
* $v
variables
0 = 0x13e             # last value printed
1 = 0x4022a8          # last offset part of an instruction source
b = 0x1f:0x0          # base address of the data segment
d = 0x20e8            # size of the data segment
e = 0x17:0xd4         # entry address of the program
m = 0x14c             # execution type (magic number)
t = 0x43c8            # size of the program text
```

Only those variables that are initialised to a value other than 0 will be printed.

The adb variables can be used within expressions by prefixing them with the < character. For example, the first few instructions executed at the start of the program can be displayed as follows:

```
* <e,3?ia
_start:        push     0x0
_start+0x2:    push     0x0
_start+0x4:    mov      ebp,esp
_start+0x6:
```

13.5 Program execution

Programs are initiated within adb using the :r or :R commands as follows:

```
[address][,count]:r[arguments]
[address][,count]:R[arguments]
```

The arguments are passed directly to the program by using the :r command. If the :R command is used, the arguments are passed through the shell for wildcard expansion prior to execution.

The following program demonstrates passing arguments:

```
main(int argc, char *argv[])
{
    int x ;

    for (x=0 ; x<argc ; x++)
        printf("%s\n", argv[x]) ;
}
```

The following session within adb shows how command line arguments can be passed to the program when issuing the :r command:

```
*  :r
a.out: running
a.out
adb: process terminated
*  :r one two three
a.out: running
a.out
one
two
three
adb: process terminated
```

13.5.1 Controlling execution

Breakpoints are used during program execution to stop the normal flow of control at a specific address. This allows variables, registers, stack traces and so on to be displayed. Breakpoints are set by the :br command as follows:

```
address [,count]:br command
```

The address is constructed in the same manner as other addresses in adb, by composition of a segment and offset.

To demonstrate the use of breakpoints, consider the following program which loops repeatedly, calling the inc() function which increments and returns the argument passed. The value of the global variable i will be increased with each call:

```
int
inc(int x)
{
    return(x+1) ;
}

int i=0 ;

main()
{
    while(1)
        i=inc(i) ;
}
```

In the `adb` session that follows, the `main()` function is disassembled and a breakpoint placed on the first instruction executed after return from the `inc()` function:

```
$ adb brk
* main,8?ia
main:                   push    ebp
main+0x1:    push    edi
main+0x2:    push    esi
main+0x3:    mov     esi,0x4007d8
main+0x8:    push    ebx
main+0x9:    mov     edx,[esi]
main+0xb:    push    edx
main+0xc:    call    near inc
main+0x11:
* main+0x11:br
* :r
brk: running
breakpoint  main+0x11:       mov     [esi],eax
```

When the program is run with the `:r` command, the program stops when it hits the breakpoint. The value of `i` can be printed as follows:

```
* i/d
i:          0
```

The value returned from `inc()` is held in the `eax` register and therefore will be assigned to `i` when the next instruction is executed.

The program is continued using the `:co` command which will result in the `inc()` function being called again. The loop is repeated twice as shown below:

```
* :co
brk: running
breakpoint  main+0x11:       mov     [esi],eax
* i/d
i:          1
* :co
brk: running
breakpoint  main+0x11:       mov     [esi],eax
* i/d
i:          2
```

Breakpoints can be displayed with the `$b` command and cleared with the `$d1` command. See the SCO OpenServer Release 5 *Programming Tools Guide* (1995) for further details.

13.5.2 Single stepping execution

A program can be single stepped, one instruction at a time, by use of the `:s` and `:S` commands. Using the example program, a breakpoint is placed on the `main()` function and the program is single stepped up to the point where the `inc()` function is entered:

```
* main:br
* :r
brk: running
breakpoint  main:            push    ebp
* :s
brk: running
```

```
stopped        at        main+0x2:      push    esi
*  :s
brk: running
stopped        at        main+0x3:      mov     esi,0x4007d8
*  :s
brk: running
stopped        at        main+0x8:      push    ebx
*  :s
brk: running
stopped        at        main+0x9:      mov     edx,[esi]
*  :s
brk: running
stopped        at        main+0xb:      push    edx
*  :s
brk: running
stopped        at        main+0xc:      call    near inc
*  :s
brk: running
stopped        at        inc:           push    ebp
*
```

Each time the :s is entered adb shows the instruction to be executed next.

13.6 Program patching

adb can be used to make changes to the file on which it is currently operating by use of the -w option passed as a command line option. If the file is not currently executing, for example just after initial entry to adb, any changes made are reflected in the disk copy of the file. If the program is part way through execution, the changes are made only to memory and are not reflected on disk.

The w and W commands are used to modify either program text or data according to the following syntax:

```
address?[w|W]
address/[w|W]
```

The address must fall on an even byte boundary. The ? specifier is used when modifying data in segments containing text, while / is used for segments containing data.

The w command is used to write 2 bytes of data to the specified address while the W command writes 4 bytes of data. The following C program can be used to demonstrate the effects of patching:

```
int gvar ;

main()
{
    printf("%d\n", gvar) ;
}
```

The following adb session demonstrates the effect of patching:

```
 1    $ a.out
 2    0
 3    $ adb a.out
 4    * gvar/W1
 5    gvar:         0x0adb: Not in write mode
 6    * $q
 7
 8    $ adb -w a.out
 9    * gvar/W1
10    gvar:         0x0=    0x1
11    * $q
12
13    $ a.out
14    1
```

Lines 1–2   The program is executed showing the expected result.

Lines 3–5   Without use of the -w command line option, adb denies write access.

Lines 8–10   adb is entered with write access and the patch is applied. The old, overwritten value is displayed, followed by the new value.

Lines 13–14   Running the program outside of adb confirms that the patch was successfully applied.

13.6.1 Patching program text

Although adb provides mechanisms to patch the program's text segments, this is a facility which is seldom used. There are a number of operating system vendors who provide software upgrades in *patch* format for which there are two main reasons:

- To fix a critical bug without performing a complete or even partial upgrade.

- To *repair* dynamically the text or data of a currently executing operating system or application without the need for down time. This is critical in many real-time and mission critical environments.

There are other techniques in operation, namely:

- Distribute a small object module which can be linked with the already existing object modules. This suffers from a requirement for application or system down time which is often unacceptable.

- Extend the replaceable module mechanism; for example, if the kernel is pageable, text can be replaced by paging out the faulty text and paging in the new modified text page.

These few points barely touch the surface of what is a complex issue, but they highlight the possibilities.

13.7 Summary and suggested reading

For many application writers, debugging programs purely at source level is often sufficient to produce good, bug free applications. However, the more knowledge of the underlying hardware that an application writer has, the greater the potential to write applications with greater performance.

This chapter has described the mapping of applications onto the i386 architecture in sufficient detail to follow the examples used throughout the book where `adb(CP)` is usually used in conjunction with `crash(ADM)` for analysing processes part way through execution.

For further details of `adb` refer to both the `adb(CP)` manual page and the SCO OpenServer Release 5 *Programming Tools Guide* (1995).

14

Diagnostic analysis using `crash` (ADM)

This chapter describes how to analyse both an *active* kernel and a *crash dump* using the `crash` (ADM) diagnostic utility.

The `crash` utility is the most effective tool for analysing kernel data structures and flow of control through the kernel, next to some of the kernel debuggers which are not usually available to most users. Once you have uncovered the power of `crash` and overcome its screenfulls of terse output, you are half way there!

14.1 Introduction

This chapter describes how to use `crash(ADM)`, one of the most talked about but little used diagnostic tools. It is often surprising to see how few people can or do use `crash(ADM)`, including many of the kernel engineers who have been involved in its creation or have added extensions over the years.

Perhaps one of the drawbacks of `crash` on nearly every UNIX system is the lack of good documentation. Most manual pages provide an adequate description of the commands and their arguments but do not give any examples of the output one might expect to see or how the commands can be used together to analyse the flow of control through the kernel. This chapter shows the type of output produced by each command in abbreviated and full formats.

The chapter should be used conjunction with the many practical examples shown throughout the book. When describing the different `crash` commands, cross-references are given to show where they are used throughout the book.

14.1.1 Command cross-references

Table 14.1 below lists all of the `crash` commands available and provides the page number where the command is described in this chapter.

Table 14.1   `crash` commands and references

Command	Page	Command	Page	Command	Page	Command	Page
b (buffer)	600	findslot	590	pbpool	618	stack	611
base	587	fs	602	pcb	613	stat	594
boot	597	help	590	pdt	605	stream	619
buf(bufhdr)	599	i (inode)	601	pfdat	605	strstat	620
buffer	600	inode	601	plock	592	t (trace)	612
bufhdr	599	kfp	611	pregion	610	trace	612
c (callout)	598	ksp	611	proc	607	ts	595
callout	598	l (lck)	602	q (quit)	592	tss	613
cblock	614	lck	602	qrun	619	tty	614
curproc	588	linkblk	617	queue	619	u (user)	609
dbfree	616	m (mount)	602	quit	592	user	609
dblock	616	map	599	rd (od)	591	v (var)	595
defproc	588	mbfree	617	redirect	593	var	595
dis	589	mblock	617	region	606	vtop	597
ds	589	mode	590	rp (rtop)	606	ldt	604
ep (eproc)	609	mount	602	rtop	606	idt	604
eproc	609	nm	591	runq	611	gdt	603
eval (base)	587	od	591	s (stack)	611	panic	592
f (file)	600	p (proc)	607	sdt	607	?	587
file	600	pbfree	618	search	593	!cmd	587
findaddr	589	pblock	618	size	593		

14.2 Getting started

Since the crash command displays many kernel structures and provides the ability to modify the kernel address space, crash is accessible only by the superuser. It can be invoked with the following options:

```
# /etc/crash [ -d dump ] [ -n namelist ] [ -w file ]
```

-d dump   This option defines dump as the file containing the system memory image, which is also referred to as a *panic dump*. If the -d option is not used, the default dump file is /dev/mem, which provides access to the physical memory of the system.

                       If the system panics, the *system* or *crash dump* is saved to a dump file which can then be specified to crash with this option when the system is reloaded.

-n namelist   This option defines the namelist argument as the program file that contains the symbol table information needed for access to the system memory image to be examined. The default file used to extract the namelist is /unix.

-w filename   Directs the output from crash to the file specified by filename. If the -w option is omitted, standard output is used.

The following example shows the typical way in which crash is invoked. All arguments are defaulted, which instructs crash to obtain the required namelist from /unix and use the mem driver (/dev/mem) to read and write data from and to physical memory:

```
# crash
dumpfile = /dev/mem, namelist = /unix, outfile = stdout
> ?
b (buffer)          findslot          pbpool            stack
base                fs                pcb               stat
boot                help              pdt               stream
buf (bufhdr)        i (inode)         pfdat             strstat
buffer              inode             plock             t (trace)
bufhdr              kfp               pregion           trace
c (callout)         ksp               proc              ts
callout             l (lck)           q (quit)          tss
cblock              lck               qrun              tty
curproc (defproc)   linkblk           queue             u (user)
dbfree              m (mount)         quit              user
dblock              map               rd (od)           v (var)
defproc             mbfree            redirect          var
dis                 mblock            region            vtop
ds                  mode              rp (rtop)         ldt
ep (eproc)          mount             rtop              idt
eproc               nm                runq              gdt
eval (base)         od                s (stack)         panic
f (file)            p (proc)          sdt               test
file                pbfree            search            ?
findaddr            pblock            size              !cmd
```

The ? command displays a basic help menu showing the crash commands available.

14.3 Interactive usage with `crash`

The `crash` utility provides a large set of commands for examining the system image. Input lines are entered to `crash` which take the following form:

```
command [ argument ... ]
```

where the `command` is one of the `crash` commands shown in section 14.2 and the arguments are used to qualify the command by indicating which items of the system image are to be displayed.

When `crash` is entered it displays the file it is using to read the kernel image from, the file from which it retrieves symbol table information and to where the output is redirected. Entering `crash` with no arguments displays the defaults as previously described:

```
# /etc/crash
dumpfile = /dev/mem, namelist = /unix, outfile = stdout
>
```

Note that the > character is the `crash` prompt.

14.3.1 Sending `crash` output to a file or another UNIX command

The output of `crash` commands can be sent to a file using the redirection operators > and >> in the same way that they are used in the Korn, C or Bourne shells. For example, consider the following command:

```
> ? >> /tmp/file
```

This invokes the help command and the >> operator appends the output to the file specified by /tmp/file if it already exists, or creates the file if it did not exist previously. The > operator overwrites a file with its output and removes any existing contents.

The pipe operator specified by the | character is also available, allowing external commands to filter the output from `crash`:

```
command [ argument ... ] | command ...
```

For example, the following command is frequently used throughout the book to display the `proc` table and search for the specified program:

```
> proc | grep prog_name
```

The same effect can also be achieved by using ! in place of |.

14.3.2 Default `crash` objects

The default process for a `crash` session is the process that is currently running. Some commands will run without any arguments, in which case they assume that the command should be applied to the current process.

If `crash` is being used on a system dump, the default process is the one that was executing at the time the system invoked a panic call.

14.3.3 Evaluation of expressions

Many of the `crash` commands accept expressions as arguments. Most of the operators that exist in the C programming language are allowed by `crash` with the exception of the logical operators `!`, `<`, `<=`, `==`, `!=`, `>` or `>=`, and the unary operators `&`, `++` and `--`.

The operators provided have precedence and associativity similar to C. An additional binary operator `#` is provided such that `a#b` rounds `a` up to the next nearest multiple of `b`.

Table 14.2 shows the operators available in `crash`, together with their associativity in decreasing order of precedence:

Table 14.2   Operators used for evaluating expressions

Operator	Associativity	Description
`–  ~  *  ()`	right to left	unary operators
`*  /  %  #`	left to right	binary operators
`+  –`	left to right	
`<<  >>`	left to right	
`&`	left to right	
`^`	left to right	
`|`	left to right	
`=  +=  -=  *=  /=`	right to left	assignment operators
`#=  %=  &=.  |=  ^=`		
`>>=  <<=`		

Identifiers (symbols) are always treated as pointers with the exception of the `od` command. To de-reference the pointer and obtain the value stored at that address apply the `*` unary operator which always returns a long word value. For example, `*addr` is evaluated as the long word stored at the address referenced by `addr`. If the `od` command is used to print the value stored at an address, the de-reference is implicit.

No address scaling is performed. For example, `address-1` is not the address of the object preceding `address` but the address of the byte preceding `address`.

Commands that return table information accept a table entry number (a slot) or a range of table entries. Commands make a heuristic choice if it is ambiguous whether an expression refers to a slot or an address. To force `crash` to interpret an expression as an address, prefix the expression with `@`. The prefix `=` forces interpretation as a slot number.

A range of table slots, `A` through `B`, is specified as `A..B`.

14.3.4 Specifying a radix

Depending on the context in which a command is used, numeric arguments that do not specify a radix are assumed to be hexadecimal for addresses, and decimal for counts and table slots. A table slot number larger than the size of the table will not be interpreted correctly. The `findslot` command can be used to translate from an address to a table slot number. The following C prefixes for designating the bases of numbers are recognised:

`0`	octal
`0b`	binary
`0d or 0t`	decimal
`0x`	hexadecimal

14.3.5 Abbreviated commands

Most commands can be entered in full but also have an abbreviated form. The abbreviated form of the command name can be obtained by omitting the characters within the square brackets. For example, `h` is the short form of `h[elp]`.

14.3.6 Abbreviated arguments

There are three abbreviated arguments to many of the `crash` commands:

process	Processes may be identified by their slot numbers in the process table or by their process ID if prefixed by the `#` character. For example, `#2729` refers to process ID `2729`. If the `#` is used on its own, it specifies the currently defined process.
table_entry	Table entries are identified by their slot number, a range of slot numbers, or a mixture of both, for example, `2 4 6..8`.
start_addr	A start address is expressed as a numeric value, a symbol, or an expression, for example, `symbol+offset`.

14.3.7 Common command options

The following command options are available to `crash` commands wherever valid:

`e`	Display every entry in a table.
`f`	Display the full structure.
`p`	Interpret all address arguments as physical addresses.
`s process`	Specify a process other than the default. The process may be specified by its process table slot or its process ID prefixed by `#`.

-w file   Redirect the output of a command to `file`. This is an alternative to using the redirection operator >>. All `crash` commands accept the -w option except the `plock` and `quit` commands.

The `crash` commands `mode`, `defproc` and `redirect` correspond to the command options -p, -s and -w. They affect all subsequent output until reset. The -w file option has been omitted from the command syntax through the chapter for clarity.

14.4 General purpose commands

This section describes the general purpose `crash` commands that do not fit into a specific category such a process management, memory management and so on.

?

List all available commands. The output of this command was shown earlier.

!command

Escape to the shell to execute `command`. This involves forking a shell which in turn forks a new process to run the command. For example, when reading inode numbers, it is often useful to run the `ncheck` (ADM) utility to check to which file an inode number refers. The inode command which is described later displays the inode structures or the full inode[] table. One of the fields displayed is the file's inode number which can be passed to `ncheck` (ADM) to locate the filename as follows:

```
> inode 508
INODE TABLE SIZE = 768
SLOT MAJ/MIN FS INUMB RCNT LINK   UID   GID SIZE    MODE MNT M/ST FLAGS
 508   1,42   5   75    1    1 13583    50    0 c---600   0   -
> !ncheck -i 75
/dev/root:
75      /dev/ttyp0
```

---

bas[e] expression ...

ev[al] expression ...

Both commands evaluate an expression in each of the following formats:

- hexadecimal
- decimal
- unsigned decimal
- octal
- ASCII

- binary
- date/time stamp

The hexadecimal, decimal, unsigned decimal and octal formats display each expression as one long word, two short words (least significant first) and four bytes (least significant first). Both commands display the same output.

The following example shows the output when `eval` is passed the `u` kernel variable:

```
> eval u
RADIX:          LONGWORD      WORDS (LSW MSW)       BYTES (LSB .. MSB)
hex:            0xe0000000        0  0xe000      0    0    0 0xe0
decimal:        -536870912        0   -8192      0    0    0  -32
(unsigned)      3758096384        0   57344      0    0    0  224
octal:          034000000000      0 0160000      0    0    0 0340
ascii:                                           ^@   ^@   ^@  M-`
binary:         11100000000000000000000000000000
date/time: Sat Dec 26 00:11:28 1952
```

An address must be de-referenced in order to display the value at the address. For example, `eval  runrun` displays the address associated with `runrun` while `eval *runrun` displays the value of `runrun`.

If the `od` command is used, the de-reference is implicit such that `od  runrun` displays the value of `runrun`.

```
cu[rproc] [ -c | process ]

de[fproc] [ -c | process ]
```

Set the value of the *current* process on which many commands operate by default to a slot in the process table. If no argument is entered, the value of the previously set slot number is printed. The current process at the start of a `crash` session is the value of the kernel variable `curproc` found in the dump file; the `-c` option re-selects this process. Both commands are identical in behaviour.

In the following example the current process is displayed. Since this process is currently running, it is not possible to display the process's TSS which results in the warning message displayed.

```
> curproc
Procslot = 23
> tss
PER PROCESS TSS FOR PROCESS 23:
This is the current process on active system
> curproc 20
Procslot = 20
> tss
PER PROCESS TSS FOR PROCESS 20:
cs:eip=0158:f00d8216 Flags=006
ds = 0160    es = 0160    fs = 0000    gs = 0000    ss = 0160
esi= 00000000    edi= fb118ae0    ebp= e0000d58    esp= e0000d3c
eax= fb118020    ebx= 00000007    ecx= 00000000    edx= 00000148
```

The current process is then assigned to the process in slot 20 of the process table. Running the tss command again displays the TSS for this process.

For further information on the notion of the current process see section 7.2.2.

`ds virtual_addr ...`

The ds command prints the data symbol whose address is closest to, but not greater than, the virtual address entered. When the eval command was issued earlier it displayed the address of the u variable (u_area) as 0xe0000000.

The ds command takes the address of the u_area and displays the symbol associated with the address:

```
> ds e0000000
u          + 0
```

This command is particularly useful when analysing panic dumps where data structures contain pointers whose symbolic value is required.

`di[s] [ -a ] start_addr [ count ]`

Disassemble from the address specified by start_addr for count instructions. The default count is 1. The -a option displays a symbolic disassembly in addition to the bytes that comprise the instructions.

The example shows disassembly of the first four instructions of the kernel systrap() function with and without the -a option:

```
> dis systrap 4
systrap              pushl   %ebp
systrap+0x1          movl    %esp,%ebp
systrap+0x3          subl    $0x14,%esp
systrap+0x6          pushl   %edi
> dis -a systrap 4
0xf00d1fc8:   55              pushl   %ebp
0xf00d1fc9:   8b ec           movl    %esp,%ebp
0xf00d1fcb:   83 ec 14        subl    $0x14,%esp
0xf00d1fce:   57              pushl   %edi
```

A symbol or expression may be specified for start_addr. Suitable symbols, such as the name of the function systrap(), are the names of routines and assembler routine labels; these are listed by the nm -e command as being of type .text.

`finda[ddr] table slot`

Print the address of slot in table. Only tables recognised by the size command (described later) are available to findaddr.

In this example, the addresses of proc[0], file[0] and inode[0] are displayed:

```
> findaddr proc 0
0xfb117000
> findaddr file 0
0xfb83c000
> findaddr inode 0
0xfb8f8000
```

finds[lot] virtual_addr ...

Print the table, entry slot number and offset for the address entered. Only tables recognised by the size command are available to findslot.

Use of the findslot command is shown in the following example with the address returned by findaddr proc 0 demonstrated above:

```
> findslot 0xfb117000
proc, slot 0, offset 0
```

h[elp] command ...

The help command prints the syntax of command, a short description, and any aliases (equivalent commands).

The example shows the use of the help command to display the syntax for both the proc and inode commands:

```
> help proc
proc [-e] [-f] [-q | -l] [-wfilename] [([-p] tbl_entry | #[procid])[s]
                    | -r)] tbl_entry = [=]slot | [@]address | slot..slot
process table
alias: p
      acceptable aliases are uniquely identifiable initial substrings
> help inode
inode [-e] [-f] [-l] [-r] [-wfilename] [[-p] tbl_entry[s]]
        tbl_entry = [=]slot | [@]address | slot..slot
inode table
alias: i
      acceptable aliases are uniquely identifiable initial substrings
```

mod[e] [p | v]

With the v argument, all address arguments are assumed to be virtual addresses, and all addresses are shown as virtual addresses.

With the p argument, all address arguments are assumed to be physical addresses, and all addresses are shown as physical addresses.

When no arguments are specified, crash prints the current address mode which is virtual at the start of a crash session.

```
n[m] symbol ... | -e
```

The `nm` command prints the address and type of `symbol`. The `-e` option prints the value and type of all symbols. The output from `nm` can be piped through a command such as `awk`(C), `grep`(C), `sed`(C) or `sort`(C) in order to filter it. The following example produces a sorted list of all symbols that start with the letters a or z:

```
> nm -e | grep '^[az]' | sort
a_flg           0xf014d0a2  .data (static)
able8042        0xf002e764  .text
accept          0xf00659fc  .text
accepted        0xf00faffc  .text (static)
accessmech      0xf0175744  .bss (static)
acct            0xf014a170  .text
acctbuf         0xf0226568  .bss
acctp           0xf0226588  .bss
ackflushtlb     0xf00106a8  .text
acktlbspins     0xf0227c64  .bss
...
```

```
o[d] [ -p ] [ format ] [ mode ] [ -s process ][ -p ] start_addr [ count ]

rd [ -p ] [ format ] [ mode ] [ -s process ][ -p ] start_addr [ count ]
```

The `od` and `rd` commands print `count` symbol values beginning at the address specified by `start_addr`. The following formats may be selected:

`-a`	ASCII
`-c`	character
`-d`	decimal
`-h`	hexadecimal and character (mode not needed)
`-o`	octal
`-x`	hexadecimal

and one of the following modes:

`-b`	byte; default mode for character and ASCII formats
`-l`	long; default mode for decimal, hexadecimal, and octal formats
`-t`	short

If `format` or `mode` is omitted, the previous setting is used. At the start of a `crash` session, the `format` is hexadecimal and the `mode` is long. The default `count` is 1.

The following example dumps the first four long words starting at virtual address 0x0:

```
> od 0 4
00000000:  0008014c   256471ed   00000000   00000000
```

The next example uses `findaddr` to display the address of the first entry in the `inode` table, dumps 20 words starting at the address returned and then calls the `inode` command to display also the contents of `inode[0]`:

```
> findaddr inode 0
0xfb8f8000
> od 0xfb8f8000 20
fb8f8000:   f0225f88    f0225f88    fb901ce0    fb8fb0c0
fb8f8010:   fc3aacc0    000013fe    00054000    00000200
fb8f8020:   00030000    00000000    00090000    012a0000
fb8f8030:   fbf2e000    00000000    f0151590    00000000
fb8f8040:   00000000    00000000    00000000    00000000
> inode 0
INODE TABLE SIZE = 768
SLOT MAJ/MIN FS INUMB RCNT LINK    UID   GID  SIZE    MODE MNT M/ST FLAGS
   0   1,42   5 5118    0    9      0     3   512 d---755   0    -
```

It is necessary to use the appropriate structure definitions located in their respective header files when using the od command. Also, inode and other commands do not display structure data in the order in which they are declared in the structure.

Part of the inode structure associated with the addresses and contents shown above is shown below. For example, the i_number field is located at address 0xfb8f8014. The data stored at this address is 0x000013fe which in decimal is 5118, the inode number displayed by the inode command.

```
typedef struct inode
{
    struct  inode   *i_forw;        fb8f8000
    struct  inode   *i_back;        fb8f8004
    struct  inode   *av_forw;       fb8f8008
    struct  inode   *av_back;       fb8f800c
    int             *i_fsptr;       fb8f8010
    ino32_t         i_number;       fb8f8014
    ushort          i_ftype;        fb8f8018
    short           i_fstyp;        fb8f801a
    off_t           i_size;         fb8f801c
```

pa[nic]

The panic command prints the most recent system notices, warnings and panic messages from the limited circular buffer kept in memory. Section 14.16 shows use of the panic command.

pl[ock] [-d | -t | -u]

Without options, plock locks the entire crash process (text, data and stack segments) in memory. The -d option locks its data and stack segments, and -t locks its text in memory. The -u option removes any locks.

q[uit]

Exit the crash session.

red[irect] [-c | file]

The `redirect` command redirects output of a `crash` session to `file`. If no argument is given, `crash` prints the filename to which it is currently redirecting output. The `-c` option closes the output file and redirects output to the standard output.

The following example uses the `redirect` command to redirect `crash` output to the file called `filex`:

```
> redirect
outfile = stdout
> redirect filex
outfile = filex
> redirect
outfile = filex
> inode 0
> !cat filex
outfile = filex

> redirect
outfile = filex

> inode 0
INODE TABLE SIZE = 563
SLOT MAJ/MIN FS INUMB RCNT LINK   UID   GID  SIZE     MODE MNT M/ST FLAGS
   0   1,42  5   296    0    1     2     2 26756 f---711   0    -
>
```

---

se[arch] [-m mask] [-s process] pattern [-p] start_addr count

The `search` command prints `count` long words in memory that match `pattern`, beginning at `start_addr`. `crash`, performs a bit-wise AND (&) of each memory word with `mask` and compares the result with `pattern`. The default `mask` is `0xffffffff`.

The example searches for long words from the address `0x0` that have the pattern `0xed` in their next to lowest order byte:

```
> od 0 4
00000000:  0008ed4c   0004014c   2c7aabae   2564ed71
> se -m 0xff00 0xed00 0 4
MASK = 0xff00, PATTERN = 0xed00, START = 0, LENGTH = 0x4 (4)

MATCH AT      0x0: 0x0008ed4c
MATCH AT      0xc: 0x2564ed71
```

---

si[ze] [-x] [structure ...]

The `size` command prints the size of the `structure` given as a name or symbol. The `-x` option prints the size in hexadecimal. If no argument is given, a list of the structure names for which sizes are available is printed.

The `size` command understands the following structures:

size argument	Structure name	Header file	crash command
buf	buf	/usr/include/sys/buf.h	buffer
callo	callo	/usr/include/sys/callo.h	callout
callout	callo	/usr/include/sys/callo.h	callout
datab	extdatab	/usr/include/sys/stream.h	dblock
dblk	extdatab	/usr/include/sys/stream.h	dblock
dblock	extdatab	/usr/include/sys/stream.h	dblock
edblock	extdatab	/usr/include/sys/stream.h	dblock
eproc	eproc	/usr/include/sys/eproc.h	eproc
file	file	/usr/include/sys/file.h	file
flckinfo	flckinfo	/usr/include/sys/flock.h	lck
filock	filock	/usr/include/sys/flock.h	lck
flox	filock	/usr/include/sys/flock.h	lck
fsinfo	fsinfo	/usr/include/sys/conf.h	fs
fstypsw	fstypsw	/usr/include/sys/conf.h	inode
hinode	hinode	/usr/include/sys/inode.h	inode
inode	inode	/usr/include/sys/inode.h	inode
linkblk	linkblk	/usr/include/sys/stream.h	linkblk
mblk	msgb	/usr/include/sys/stream.h	mblock
mblock	msgb	/usr/include/sys/stream.h	mblock
mount	mount	/usr/include/sys/mount.h	mount
msgb	msgb	/usr/include/sys/stream.h	mblock
pageb	pageb	/usr/include/sys/stream.h	pblock
pblock	pageb	/usr/include/sys/stream.h	pblock
pblk	pageb	/usr/include/sys/stream.h	pblock
pfdat	pfdat	/usr/include/sys/pfdat.h	pfdat
proc	proc	/usr/include/sys/proc.h	proc
queue	queue	/usr/include/sys/stream.h	queue
region	region	/usr/include/sys/region.h	region
s5inode	s5inode	/usr/include/sys/fs/s5inode.h	inode
stdata	stdata	/usr/include/sys/stream.h	stream
stream	stdata	/usr/include/sys/stream.h	stream
tty	tty	/usr/include/sys/tty.h	tty

The following example shows use of the `size` command:

```
> size
buf             callo           callout         eproc
file            flckinfo        filock          flox
fsinfo          fstypsw         hinode          inode
mount           pfdat           proc            region
s5inode         htinode         dtnode          tty
datab           dblk            dblock          edblock
linkblk         mblk            mblock          msgb
pageb           pblock          pblk            queue
stdata          streams
> size inode
80
> size -x inode
0x50
```

stat

The `stat` command prints information about the operating system including:

- System, node, and machine names.
- Operating system release and version numbers.
- Serial number, machine bus type, and kernel ID.
- Maximum number of licensed users.
- Number of CPUs.
- The time of the latest crash and how long the system was up prior to the crash.

The output of `stat` on one particular machine is:

```
> stat
                   UNIX UTS     XENIX UTS       SCO UTS
system name:      SCO_SV       SCO_SV         SCO_SV
release:          3.2          3.2            3.2v5.0.0
node name:        xian         xian           xian
version:          2            2              --
machine name:     i386         Pentium        Pentium
system origin:     --                    1              1
system oem:        --                    0              0
serial number:     --               0x4c0   LTD001216
bustype:           --                --     EISA
kernel id:         --                --     95/04/19
number users:      --                --     5-user
number cpus:       --                --              1
time of crash:   Wed Dec 27 11:54:24 1995
age of system:   2 hr., 1 min.
panicstr:
```

---

ts virtual_addr ...

This command prints the text symbol closest to, but not greater than, the virtual address specified by `virtual_addr`.

In the following example, the `nm` command is used to print the address and the type of the `systrap` symbol. The `ts` command is then used to locate the text symbol associated with the address displayed by `nm`.

```
> nm systrap
systrap           0xf014370c   .text
> ts 0xf014370c
systrap   + 0
```

---

v[ar]

The `var` command prints the values of the members of the kernel structure `v` that holds the tuneable system parameters and the current size of the dynamic kernel tables. The structure `v` and the equivalent tuneable parameters for each of its members are defined in the file <sys/var.h>.

In Table 14.3 the contents of the `var` structure are shown together with typical values, the tuneable corresponding to the field and a description of each field.

Table 14.3   `var` structure fields

var field	Value	Tuneable	Description
v_buf	736	NBUF	Number of I/O buffers
v_clist	170	NCLIST	Number of clists allocated
v_maxup	100	MAXUP	Maximum processes per user
v_hbuf	512	NHBUF	Number of hash buffers
v_hmask	511	–	Hash mask for buffers
v_nofiles	110	NOFILES	Maximum number of files per process
v_inode	153	MAX_INODE	Size of the in-core inode table
v_file	341	MAX_FILE	Size of the file table
v_mount	8	MAX_MOUNT	Size of the mount table
v_proc	47	MAX_PROC	Size of the proc table
v_region	170	MAX_REGION	Number of regions allocated
v_sptmap	200	SPTMAP	Size of kernel virtual space allocation map
v_nstream	896	NSTREAM	STREAMS head structures
v_nqueue	110	–	STREAMS queues
v_autoup	10	NAUTOUP	Time between bdflush running
v_ulimit	2097151	ULIMIT	Largest file size a user can write
v_scrn	12	NSCRN	Number of multiscreens
v_emap	10	NEMAP	Number of I/O mappings
v_sxt	6	NUMSXT	Shell layers channels
v_xsdsegs	25	XSDSEGS	Number of shared data segments
v_xsdslots	3	XSDSLOTS	Slots in `xsdtab[]` per segment
v_scrnmem	17	SCRNMEM	Pages for multiscreens
v_kbtype	0	KBTYPE	Keyboard type
v_disk	3	MAX_DISK	Maximum number of disks supported
v_evqueues	72	EVQUEUES	Number of event queues
v_evdevs	80	EVDEVS	Number of event devices
v_evdevsperq	3	EVDEVSPERQ	Maximum events devs per event queue
v_ngroups	8	NGROUPS	Maximum supplementary groups
v_bfreemin	0	BFREEMEM	Minium number of free buffer cache blocks left on the free list when allocating via `getblk(K)`
v_mpbuf	40	NMPBUF	Multi-physical buffers
v_mpheadbuf	84	–	Standalone multi-physical buffer headers
v_hinode	128	NHINODE	Hash inodes
v_nstrpages	500	NSTRPAGES	Maximum memory pages for STREAMS
v_tablemap	100	TBLMAP	Size of dynamic kernel table map
v_table_pages	0	TBLPAGES	Maximum number of pages for tables
v_table_limit	70	TBLLIMIT	Maximum % of TBLPAGES per table
v_table_dma_pages	100	TBLDMAPAGES	Maximum number of DMA pages used by dynamic tables
v_table_sys_limit	25	TBLSYSLIMIT	Maximum % of user memory for dynamic tables

The `var` command is used to print a number of tuneables:

```
> v ! head -8
v_buf: 684
v_clist: 170
v_maxup: 100
v_hbuf: 512
v_hmask: 511
v_nofiles: 110
v_inode: 204        ve_inode: 204
v_file: 341         ve_file: 341
```

```
vt[op] [ -s process ] start_addr ...
```

The `vtop` command prints the physical address corresponding to the specified virtual address `start_addr`. This example finds the physical address corresponding to the virtual address `0x0` for the current process. The `od` command is then used to demonstrate that these addresses reference the same memory location:

```
> vtop 0
VIRTUAL  PHYSICAL
0x0   0x1eb000
> od -p 0x1eb000 4
001eb000:  0008014c   256471ed   00000000   00000000
> od 0x0 4
001eb000:  0008014c   256471ed   00000000   00000000
```

Note that if the memory locations being dumped cross a page boundary, there is no guarantee that the corresponding physical memory locations are contiguous. Kernel memory is usually physically contiguous. Memory used by user processes may or may not be physically contiguous.

14.5 Boot structures

The `boot` command is used to print information that is passed to the kernel when the system is booted.

```
bo[ot] [ -ef ] [ -p boot_info [ boot_misc [ boot_apm ] ] ]
```

The following boot configuration information is displayed:

- The inode number of the booted kernel.
- The amount of base and extended memory.
- A map of all memory segments after booting.
- BIOS-APM information (if any).
- PCI bus configuration information (if any).

`boot_info`, `boot_misc` and `boot_apm` can be used to specify the addresses of the `bootinfo`, `bootmisc` and `bootapm` structures:

```
> boot -f bootinfo
BOOT INFORMATION
    checksum: 2880991120, bootstrlen: 68, size: misc 18 apm 0
    magic: 0xfeedbac (valid)
    flags: at i486
    vendor: 0x5, model: 0xfc, submodel: 0x1
    kernel inode: 11
    pci: numbuses: 0, accessmech: 0
    apm: \000\000 v0.0, check:
    ac: off, battery: high, 0%
    connect: 0, pm32: 0:0, pm16: 0, data: 0
    basemem: 654336 (639k), extmem: 7340032 (7m)
memavail memory map (6 segments used; 8 free):
NUM  SYNOPSIS                  BASE -> LAST ADDR      BYTES FLAGS
  0. 0k-32k/r                     0 ->    0x7fff    0x8000 reserved
  1. 32k-636k                0x8000 ->    0x9efff   0x97000
  2. 1m-7000k              0x100000 ->    0x6d5fff  0x5d6000
  3. 7000k-7280k           0x6d6000 ->    0x71bfff  0x46000 bss
  4. 7280k-7376k           0x71c000 ->    0x733fff  0x18000 data
  5. 7376k-8m              0x734000 ->    0x7fffff  0xcc000 text
memused memory map (4 segments used; 10 free):
NUM  SYNOPSIS                  BASE -> LAST ADDR      BYTES FLAGS
  0. 0k-32k/r                     0 ->    0x7fff    0x8000 reserved
  1. 7000k-7280k           0x6d6000 ->    0x71bfff  0x46000 bss
  2. 7280k-7376k           0x71c000 ->    0x733fff  0x18000 data
  3. 7376k-8m              0x734000 ->    0x7fffff  0xcc000 text
```

The `boot` command uses the structures `bootinfo`, `bootmem` and `bootmisc` defined in the header file `<sys/boot.h>`, and the `bootapm` structure defined in the header file `<sys/apm.h>`.

The procedures followed during system bootstrap are described in chapter 4.

14.6 The callout table

The callout table contains entries for functions that will be called after a specified number of clock ticks has elapsed. The `timeout(K)` kernel function is used to establish timeouts.

`c[allout]`

The `callout` command prints each entry of the callout table. The `callout` command uses the `callo` structure defined in the `<sys/callo.h>` header file.

The output of one particular run of `callout` is:

```
> callout
FUNCTION           ARGUMENT          TIME           ID         PROC
wdtimeout                 0            89         5578            0
epi_poker        0xc0139000          210         5579            0
unselect         0xfb117c18         1030         5538            0
unselect         0xfb118178          783         5539            0
kmwakeup                  0        26262         4919            0
```

For further details on the use of timeouts and the `callout` command see section 7.8.4.

14.7 System memory maps

Memory maps maintain a resource such as free memory and dynamic kernel space. They are used by the kernel when allocating memory by calls such as `sptalloc(K)` and `kmem_alloc(K)`.

`ma[p] mapname ...`

The `map` structure specified by `mapname` will be displayed. The following examples display the `sptmap` and `tablemap` which are used for kernel memory allocation:

```
> map sptmap

sptmap:
MAPSIZE: 197        SLEEP VALUE: 0

   SIZE        ADDRESS
   1974        0xf084a
1 SEGMENTS, 1974 UNITS
> map tablemap

tablemap:
MAPSIZE: 97 SLEEP VALUE: 0

   SIZE        ADDRESS
   10296       0xfd3c8
1 SEGMENTS, 10296 UNITS
```

For `sptmap` there is one unallocated segment of `1974` pages. For `tablemap` there is one unallocated segment of `10296` pages.

The `map` command uses the `map` structure defined in the `<sys/map.h>` header file.

14.8 Filesystem buffers

The following two commands are used to display the contents of buffers and their associated buffer headers in the system buffer cache.

`buf[hdr] [ -f ] [ [ -p ] table_entry ... ]`

The `bufhdr` command displays buffer cache buffer headers using the `buf` structure defined in the `<sys/buf.h>` header file.

The first example displays the first four buffer headers in abbreviated form. The second example displays the specified buffer in full format.

```
> bufhdr ! head -6
BUFFER HEADER TABLE SIZE = 684
  SLOT MAJ/MIN       BLOCK      ADDRESS      FOR   BCK   AVF   AVB FLAGS
     0   1,42        86198 0xc009e000      681     -    241   369 read   done
     1   1,42        58058 0xc009e400        -     -    197   327 read   done
     2   1,40        12310 0xc009e800        -   384      3   283 read   done
     3   1,40        12312 0xc009ec00      230     -    608     2 read   done
```

```
> bufhdr -f 2
BUFFER HEADER TABLE SIZE = 684
 SLOT MAJ/MIN       BLOCK    ADDRESS    FOR    BCK    AVF    AVB FLAGS
    2   1,40        12310 0xc009e800     -     384      3    283 read  done
   BCNT ERR RESI    START PROC  RELTIME        INUM WANT
   1024   0   0    0x133c   -    0x2f4a6         -
   BSIZ   IODONE    BWRITE DWFOR DWBCK FFORW FBACK  FSDATA
   1024     -          -     -     -     -     -       -
```

b[uffer] [format] table_entry | [-p] start_addr

This command prints the contents of a buffer in one of the following formats:

-b	byte
-c	character
-d	decimal
-x	hexadecimal
-o	octal
-r	directory
-i	inode list

If no format is specified, the previously used format is used. The default format at the beginning of a crash session is hexadecimal.

The example displays the contents of the buffer associated with the buffer header located in buf[3] in character format:

```
> buffer -c 3 | head -8
BUFFER 3:

00000:     r   a   p \?   i   n   v   t   s   s   t   r   a   p \?   s
00010:     e   g   n   p   t   r   a   p \?   i   n   v   a   l   t   r
00020:     a   p \?   v   8   6   g   p   t   r   a   p \?   s   y   s
00030:     e   r   r   t   r   a   p \?   s   i   g   _   c   l   e   a
00040:     n \?   s   u   d   s   _   c   a   l   l \?   c   l   k   i
00050:     n   t   _   m   c \?   i   o   _   k   e   n   t   e   r \?
```

Toolkit 9.1 shows how to use the buffer command to display the contents of a buffer containing data recently read from disk for a specified file and also describes each of the buf structure fields.

14.9 Filesystem tables

The commands described in this section return information about the files that each process has open and the filesystems that the kernel has mounted.

f[ile] [-e] [[-p] table_entry ...]

The file command is used to print the file table. References to entries in the in-core inode table are prefixed by I#. The flags displayed for each slot control file access and correspond to the flags defined in the <sys/fcntl.h> header file; for example, the read flag is equivalent to FREAD.

The file command uses the file structure defined in <sys/file.h>. An example output is:

```
> file 10-15
FILE TABLE SIZE = 341
SLOT   RCNT    I/FL        OFFSET  FLAGS
  10      1 I#     8            0  read
  11      1 I#    77            4  read
  12      1 I#    77           16  write
  13      1 I#    29            0  read
  14      1 I#    76            0  read
  15      1 I#    76            0  write
```

For further details of the file table, see section 8.3.

---

i[node] [-eflr] [[-p] table_entry ...]

The inode command prints elements in the in-core inode table. The abbreviated form of the inode command is:

```
> inode 20-25
INODE TABLE SIZE = 204
SLOT MAJ/MIN FS INUMB RCNT LINK   UID  GID   SIZE      MODE MNT M/ST FLAGS
  20   1,42   1    29   1    1     2    15      0 c---000   0  -
  21   1,42   3  3123   6    2     2     2 152320 f---111   0  R 63 tx
  22   1,42   3  2974   2    1     0     0 517712 f---500   0  R 26 tx
  23   1,42   3    29   1    1     2    15      0 c---600   0  -
  24   1,42   3 21938   1    7 13583    50    512 d---755   0  -
  25   1,42   3    63   1    1     0     3      0 c---666   0  -
```

The -f option displays a full listing of an inode structure plus additional per filesystem specific information as the example shows:

```
> inode -f 22
INODE TABLE SIZE = 204
SLOT MAJ/MIN FS INUMB RCNT LINK  UID  GID    SIZE      MODE MNT M/ST FLAGS
  22   1,42   3  2974   2    1    0    0  517712 f---500   0  R 26 tx
      FORW    BACK AFOR ABCK    MAPPAGES          RDLOCKS          WANT
      { 30}    139   -    -          49               0
     RMAJ/MIN      FSTYPP      FSPTR       FILOCKS      VCODE WCNT FS
       0,0    0xf00f507c 0xfc1f4368           0             0  -1 HTFS
HTFS INODE:
     FLAGS: used
        LASTREAD    MAP/DOFF            DADDRS
          0xe8   0xf0830000        [ 0] 36992    [ 1] 36993
        [ 2] 36994     [ 3] 36995  [ 4] 36996    [ 5] 36997
        [ 6] 36998     [ 7] 37671  [ 8] 37672    [ 9] 37673
        [10] 37674     [11] 37931
```

The -r option displays inodes that are on the free list. The -l option lists the number of in-core inodes that are in use, on the free list, on the free list with a non-zero reference count, or in an unknown state.

The inode command uses structures inode and hinode defined in the <sys/inode.h> header file; the dtnode structure defined in the <sys/fs/dtnode.h> header file; the htinode structure defined in the <sys/fs/htinode.h> header file; and the s5inode structure defined in the <sys/fs/s5inode.h> header file.

```
fs [ [ -p ] table_entry ... ]
```

The fs command prints the filesystem information table, as the example shows:

```
> fs
FILE SYSTEM INFORMATION TABLE SIZE = 3
SLOT          NAME        PIPE       NOTIFY  FLAGS
    1 DEVFS                 -                noic
    2 DOS                   -         sk     noic
    3 HTFS                  0         sk
```

On the system where the command is run there are three filesystems linked into the kernel. The fs command uses the fsinfo structure which is defined in the <sys/conf.h> header file.

```
m[ount] [ -e ] [ [ -p ] table_entry ... ]
```

The mount command can be used to print the active mount table entries, as the example shows:

```
> mount
MOUNT TABLE SIZE = 8
SLOT FS  BSZ MAJ/MIN  BUFPTR BCOUNT IPTR MPTR RFLAG RD FLAGS NAME
   0  3 1024 1,42 0xc0135000      0  -     50 ---- rw inuse notrunc HTFS
   1  3 1024 1,40 0xc0139000      0  28    14 ---- ro inuse notrunc EAFS
```

The mount command uses the mount structure which is defined in the <sys/mount.h> header file. For further details of the mount structure see section 8.6.2.

14.10 Record locks

Record locks provide a mechanism by which a process can gain exclusive access to part or all of a file. The lck command is used to display active record locks.

```
l[ck] [ -e ] [ [ -p ] table_entry ... ]
```

If the -e option or a table range is specified, crash prints the required list of record locks. If no arguments are given, crash prints information on all active locks.

The example displays output for one particular run of `lck`:

```
> lck
ACTIVE LOCKS:
  INO TYP W       START       LEN PROC  EPID  SYSID       WAIT PREV NEXT
   33  W  0           0         1   18   214      0          0   -    -

SLEEP LOCKS:
TYP W       START     LEN LPRC  EPID  SYSID BPRC  EPID  SYSID PREV NEXT

CONFIGURED RECORD LOCKS:
RECS   RECCNT  RECOVF  RECTOT
 128      1       0      36

ACTUAL RECORD LOCKS:
TOTAL   ACTIVE  FREE  SLEEP
 128       1    127     0
```

The `lck` command uses the structures `filock` and `flckinfo` defined in the `<sys/flock.h>` header file. For further information on file and record locking and use of the `lck` command, see section 8.5.

14.11 Processor specific structures

The `crash` commands in this section examine structures that are specific to the way that i386, i486 and Pentium processors handle memory management and interrupts.

The system maintains two tables of virtual memory segments per CPU:

- The *Global Descriptor Table* (GDT) defines the objects used by the kernel, including its data and text segments.

- The *Interrupt Descriptor Table* (IDT) defines where trap and interrupt handler routines may be found in the kernel's text segment.

Each user process also has a *Local Descriptor Table* (LDT) that defines the objects it uses, including its text and data segments.

`g[dt] [ -e ] [ -c cpu ] [ slot [ count ] ]`

This command prints the contents of the GDT using the `dscr` structure defined in the `<sys/seg.h>` header file. The output for one particular run of `gdt` is:

```
> gdt
iAPX386 GDT
CPU SLOT      SELECTOR OFFSET    TYPE       DPL  ACCESSBITS
  0    1      f00dd114 000002d0  DSEG         0  ACCS'D R&W
  0    2      f00dc114 00000800  DSEG         0  R&W
  0    3      00000500 0000005f  LDT          0
  0    4      00000640 00000067  TSS386       0
  0   40      e0001600 00000807  LDT          0
```

```
0   41      e0001514 000000e7 TSS386     0
0   42      f00dd450 00000068 TSS386     0
0   43      00000000 fffff000 XSEG       0   ACCS'D R&X DFLT G4096
0   44      00000000 fffff000 DSEG       0   ACCS'D R&W BIG  G4096
0   45      f00dd4b8 00000068 TSS386     0
0   46      dffeb514 000000e7 TSS386     0
0   49      00110000 00000000 TSS386     0
0   50      f0820000 00005177 XSEG       0   ACCS'D R&X CONF DFLT
0   55      00000000 0000ffff XSEG       0   R&X DFLT
0   56      00000000 0000ffff XSEG       0   R&X
0   57      00000000 0000ffff DSEG       0   R&W BIG
```

For further information on the GDT see section 6.3.2.

---

id[t] [-e] [-c cpu] [slot [count]]

This command prints the contents of the IDT. See trap(M) for a description of the various traps, interrupts and exceptions. Output for one particular run of idt is:

```
> idt ! head -8
iAPX386 IDT
CPU SLOT      SELECTOR OFFSET    TYPE       DPL   ACCESSBITS
  0   0       0158 f0011004 TGATE386    0    CNT=0
  0   1       0158 f0011010 TGATE386    0    CNT=0
  0   2       0158 f001101c IGATE386    0    CNT=0
  0   3       0158 f0011028 TGATE386    3    CNT=0
  0   4       0158 f0011038 TGATE386    3    CNT=0
  0   5       0158 f0011044 TGATE386    0    CNT=0
```

The idt command uses the dscr structure defined in the <sys/seg.h> header file. For further information on the IDT see section 9.4.

---

ld[t] [-e] [process [slot [count]]]

The ldt command prints the LDT for a specified process using the dscr structure defined in the <sys/seg.h> header file. The output when running the ldt command to display the LDT for the current process is:

```
> ldt
iAPX386 LDT for process 20
SLOT      BASE/SEL LIM/OFF   TYPE       DPL   ACCESSBITS
  0       0158 f00d84f4 CGATE386    3    CNT=1
  1       0158 f00102e8 CGATE386    3    CNT=1
  2       00000000 bffff000 XSEG       3    ACCS'D R&X DFLT G4096
  3       00000000 ffc0f000 DSEG       3    ACCS'D R&W BIG  G4096
  4       00000000 ffc0f000 DSEG       3    R&W BIG  G4096
  5       e0000e80 00000180 DSEG       3    ACCS'D R&W BIG
  7       0158 f0010394 CGATE386    3    CNT=1
```

For further information on the LDT see section 6.3.2 and section 7.3.

14.12 Memory management related tables

The following commands display information about memory usage by processes on the system.

---

pd[t] [-e] [-s process] [-p] slot | start_addr [count]

The pdt command displays count page table entries of the page table specified by the slot or start_addr. This command prints the virtual and physical addresses of the page frames, and their corresponding entries in the page table.

The sdt command may be used to examine the page directory entries of a specific process although a process's page tables cannot be printed if it has been swapped out.

The example displays the page table entries for curproc:

```
> pdt curproc
Page Table for Process 69
SLOT    OFFSET PFDAT PHYSADDR ----------- FLAGS ----------- TYPE   BLKNO
     2 00002000    - 00000000 pres                          none      -
     3 00003000    - 00000000 pres                          none      -
     8 00008000    - fffbf000 pres rw    ref mod ndref lock none      -
    13 0000d000    - 00030000 pres rw                       none      -
    26 0001a000    - 00000000 nval     us ref mod           none      -
    37 00025000    - f0166000 nval     us          ndref    none      -
    40 00028000    - f0169000 nval     us     ref  ndref lock none     -
    53 00035000    - 00000000 pres     us ref           lock none     -
    54 00036000    - 00000000 pres rw  us ref      ndref    none      -
   147 00093000 5829 01baf000 pres            mod           none      -
   149 00095000    - 0002c000 pres        ref      ndref    none      -
   165 000a5000    - 00004000 pres rw  us ref mod      lock none      -
```

The pdt command uses the pde structure defined in the <sys/immu.h> header file. For further details on page directory and page table entries see section 6.3.4.

---

pfd[at] [-e] [[-p] table_entry ...]

Associated with each usable page of physical memory is a pfdat structure. The pfdat command can be used to print the entries of the pfdat[] array:

```
> pfdat ! head -6
PFDATA TABLE SIZE: 1239
SLOT TYPE     BLKNO INOX   USE NRF LCK   NEXT  PREV  HASH FLAGS
    25 file     288   80     1   0   0                853 hsh don dma
    27 file     288   21     0   0   0    369   117   168 que hsh don dma
    28 file     304   80     1   0   0                329 hsh don dma
    29 file      88   17     1   1   0                834 hsh don dma
```

The pfdat command uses the pfdat structure defined in the <sys/pfdat.h> header file. For further information about the pfdat structure see section 12.3.

---

reg[ion] [-ef] [[-p] table_entry ...]

The region command prints the elements of region[] table. Using the -f option, the region command also prints information about the associated page table and disk block descriptor entries.

The example shows both the abbreviated and full format listings of region[] table structures:

```
> region ! head -10
REGION TABLE SIZE = 170
Region-list:

SLOT PGSZ VALID SMEM SOFF REF SWP NSW FORW BACK INOX TYPE FLAGS
   0    6     6    6   82   1   0   0    1    3   37 priv nosh
   1   10     8    0   72   1   0   0    2    0   37 stxt nosh nosmem
   2    2     1    1   70   1   0   0  117    1    - priv nosh stack
   3   80    37    0    1   1   0   0    0    4   31 map  nosh nosmem
   4   10     9    9   81   1   0   0    3   32   31 map  nosh
   5    1     1    0   92   1   0   0  157    6   27 map  nosh nosmem
> region -f 4
REGION TABLE SIZE = 170
Region-list:

SLOT  PGSZ VALID  SMEM NONE SOFF  REF SWP NSW FORW BACK INOX TYPE FLAGS
   4    10     9     9    0   81    1   0   0    3   32   31 map  nosh

Page-tables:

LIST fa0001a0  1146 0059e000 pres rw us                    none     -
SLOT   OFFSET PFDAT PHYSADDR ----------- FLAGS ----------- TYPE  BLKNO
  81 00000000  1137 00595000 pres    us                    none     -
  82 00001000  1134 00592000 pres    us                    none     -
  83 00002000  1092 00568000 pres    us                    none     -
  84 00003000  1132 00590000 pres    us                    none     -
  85 00004000  1130 0058e000 pres    us                    none     -
  86 00005000  1128 0058c000 pres    us                    none     -
  87 00006000     -        -  nval                          file   688
  88 00007000  1142 0059a000 pres    us                    none     -
  89 00008000  1079 0055b000 pres rw us       mod          none     -
  90 00009000  1126 0058a000 pres    us                    none     -
```

The region command uses the region structure defined in the <sys/region.h> header file, the pde structure defined in the <sys/immu.h> header file and the dbd structure defined in the <sys/region.h> header file.

For further information on the region structure refer to section 6.4.2.

---

rt[op] [-l | -q] [-p] [table_entry ...]

The rtop command prints the process table entries of all processes that are using the specified region[] table entries. The -l and -q options have the same effect as for the proc command.

The following example displays the processes that are accessing region[] table entries 28 to 34:

```
> rtop 28..34
SLOT ST PID  PPID  PGRP  UID PRI CPU EVENT             NAME      FLAGS
Region 28:
  12 s    68    1    57    0  75   0 0xfcee43f0        strerr    load
Region 29:
  14 s    50   42    50    0  76   0 selwait           sco_cpd   load
Region 30:
  20 s   212    1     0    0  76   0 selwait           dlpid     load nxec
Region 31:
   8 s    37    1    36    0  76   0 selwait           syslogd   load nxec
Region 32:
   9 s    41    1    41    0  73   0 region_end+0xc8   ifor_pmd  load nxec
  10 s    42   41    41    0  76   0 selwait           ifor_pmd  load nxec
Region 33:
  16 s   402    1   402    0  75   0 cn_tty+0xd0       getty     load
Region 34:
  28 s   403    1   403    0  75   0 cn_tty+0x138      getty     load
```

The `rtop` command uses the `pregion` structure defined in the `<sys/region.h>` header file, and the `proc` structure defined in the `<sys/proc.h>` header file.

For further details of the `pregion` and `region` structures see section 6.4.2.

---

sd[t] [-ef] [-s process] [-p] [slot | start_addr [count]]

The `sdt` command prints the page directory entries for a process. By default, `sdt` prints information from the page directory pointed to by control register `cr3`, also known as the page directory base register (`pdbr`). Note that there is only one page directory per system which is shared by the kernel and all processes.

The example displays a subset of the page directory for the current process:

```
> sdt ! head -6
Page Table Directory for Process 69
SLOT   VIRTUAL PFDAT PHYSADDR ---------- FLAGS ----------  TYPE   BLKNO
  32 08000000  5844 01bbe000 pres rw us ref               none     -
 512 80000000  3417 01243000 pres rw us ref               none     -
 768 c0000000     - 01ea9000 pres rw    ref mod           none     -
 769 c0400000     - 01ea8000 pres rw    ref mod           none     -
```

The `sdt` command uses the `pde` structure defined in the `<sys/immu.h>` header file. For further details on page directory and page table entries see section 6.3.4.

14.13 Per process related structures

The kernel maintains a process table, `proc[]`, that contains information for every process in the system. This table is always present in memory, unlike a process's u_area which can be swapped out. The entries in the `proc[]` table, the process's u_area and other process management related structures are described in this section.

`p[roc] [-ef ] [ -q | -l ] [ [ -p ] process ... | -r ]`

The `proc` command prints entries in the process table `proc[]`. Process table information can be specified using a mixture of process table slot numbers and process IDs. A process ID, as reported by `ps (C)`, must be prefixed by a #.

The `-r` option reports information only for processes that are executing or are on the run queue. With the `-f` option, `proc` displays most of the information in the process table, and also the `pregion` table for the specified process.

The `-l` option selects the wakeup channel value in the EVENT column to be displayed as a symbolic name plus an offset address. The `-q` option selects it to be displayed as an address. The setting is remembered for the next `proc` command. The initial setting is `-l`.

In the example, entries 20 to 25 of the `proc[]` table are displayed:

```
> proc 20-25
PROC TABLE SIZE = 47
SLOT ST PID PPID PGRP   UID PRI CPU EVENT            NAME    FLAGS
  20  s 250  214  250     0  73   0 region_end+0x1ae0 sh     load
  21  s 317  250  317     0  73   0 region_end+0x1c38 ksh    load
  22  s 235  202  235 13583  75   0 cn_tty+0x1a0      ksh    load ntrc
  23  s 340  317  340     0  75   0 cn_tty           script  load
  24  s 341  340  340     0  75   4 spt_tty+0x1c     script  load nxec
  25  s 342  341  342     0  73   0 region_end+0x2198 ksh    load
```

A full listing of a single `proc` structure produced with the `-f` option is:

```
> proc -l 23
PROC TABLE SIZE = 47
SLOT ST PID   PPID  PGRP   UID PRI CPU EVENT      NAME       FLAGS
  23 r   340   317   340     0  50   2             script     load
     time: 10, nice: 20, exit: 0, sid: 198
     clktim: 0, suid: 0, sgid: 3, size: 200
     flink:   - , blink:   - , mlink:   -
     parent: P#21, child: P#24, sibling:   -
     utime: 333, stime: 191
     sig#  sig  mask  hold chold flags, cursig: 0
       1:   -    -     -     -    sigaction
       2:   -    -     -     -    sigaction
       ...
      30:   -    -     -     -    sigaction
      31:   -    -     -     -    sigaction
     ptracep:   - , controlp:   - , controllink:   -
     trace:   - , whystop:      -    , whatstop: 0
     mempts: 0, swppts: 0, epid: 340, sysid: 0
     ldt: 0xe0001600, eproc: 0xfb657b80, v86: 0, sdp: 0
     usize: 2, ubptbl:  0: 0x402007   1: 0x1e2003
     PREG REG#     REGVA   TYPE FLAGS
        0  128  0x8046000 stack rd wr cm
        1  135  0x8048000  text rd ex cm
        2  147  0x804e000  data rd wr cm
        3  129 0x80001000 lbtxt rd ex pr
        4  149 0x80051000 lbdat rd wr ex pr
        5  126 0x8005c000 shfil rd
        6   49 0x8005e000 lbtxt rd ex pr
        7  114 0x80080000 lbdat rd wr ex pr
        8  131 0x8008f000 shfil rd
        9  112 0x80091000 lbtxt rd ex pr
       10  125 0x800b7000 lbdat rd wr ex pr
```

The `proc` command uses the `proc` structure defined in the `<sys/proc.h>` header file and the `pregion` structure defined in the `<sys/region.h>` header file.

For further details of the `proc` structure see section 7.2.2.

`ep[roc] [ -ef ] [ [ -p ] process ... | [ -r ] ]`

This command prints the entries in the extended process table, which contains per process information that is not held in the `proc` structure.

The example displays the `eproc` structure for the current process:

```
> curproc
Procslot = 69
> eproc 69
EPROC TABLE SIZE = 83
SLOT HAS   RQ NOR   PR LPR PRO SLP PCTCPU CLK FLAGS
  69   0   82    0    0   0   0   0  0x26c    1 selpoll elf
```

The `eproc` command uses the `eproc` structure defined in the `<sys/eproc.h>` header file and the `proc` structure defined in the `<sys/proc.h>` header file.

`u[ser] [ -f ] [ process ... ]`

The `user` command prints information about the u_area of a process. The abbreviated form of the `user` command is below for the current process:

```
> user
PER PROCESS USER AREA FOR PROCESS 27
USER ID's:  uid: 0, gid: 3, real uid: 0, real gid: 3
     supplementary gids: 3 0 1
PROCESS TIMES:     user: 210, sys: 21, child user: 0, child sys: 0
PROCESS MISC:
     command: crash, psargs: /etc/crash
     proc: P#27, cntrl tty:   58,0
     start: Sun Jun 18 06:55:07 1995
     mem: 0x9f92, type: exec
     proc/text lock: none
     current directory: I#74
OPEN FILES AND POFILE FLAGS:
     [ 0]: F#59    r    [ 1]: F#59     w  [ 2]: F#59     w
     [ 3]: F#64    r
FILE I/O:
     u_base: 0x80ab578, file offset: 6251936, bytes: 4096
     segment: data, cmask: 0022, ulimit: 2097151
     file mode(s): read
SIGNAL DISPOSITION:
     sig#       signal oldmask sigmask
       2:   0x805eb50     -     2 13
      16: ignore          -
      17: ignore          -
```

The `-f` option can be used to display a full listing of the u_area plus additional useful information about the process. The example displays the u_area for the current running process (`crash`):

```
> user -f
PER PROCESS USER AREA FOR PROCESS 27
USER ID's:   uid: 0, gid: 3, real uid: 0, real gid: 3
       supplementary gids: 3 0 1
PROCESS TIMES:       user: 210, sys: 30, child user: 0, child sys: 0
PROCESS MISC:
       command: crash, psargs: /etc/crash
       proc: P#27, cntrl tty:  58,0
       start: Sun Jun 18 06:55:07 1995
       mem: 0xa6eb, type: exec
       proc/text lock: none
       current directory: I#74
OPEN FILES AND POFILE FLAGS:
       [ 0]: F#59   r   [ 1]: F#59    w  [ 2]: F#59    w
       [ 3]: F#64   r
FILE I/O:
       u_base: 0x80ab578, file offset: 6251936, bytes: 4096
       segment: data, cmask: 0022, ulimit: 2097151
       file mode(s): read
SIGNAL DISPOSITION:
       sig#       signal oldmask sigmask
         1:     default    -
         2:     0x805eb50   -       2 13
       ...
        31:     default    -
       ux_uid: 0, ux_gid: 0, ux_mode:
       comp: 0xe0000d0b, nextcp: 0xe0000d0f
       bsize: 1024, pgproc: 0, qsav: 0xe0000e34, error: -266966692
       ap: 0xe0001148, u_r: 0, pbsize: 878
       pboff: 0, pbdev:   1,40 , rablock: 0, errcnt: 12
       dirp: 0x4c, dent.d_ino: 0 dent.d_name: unix, pdir: I#152
       ttyip:   - , tsize: 0x6a, dsize: 0x65, ssize: 0x2
       arg[0]:        0x4c, arg[1]:        0x179, arg[2]:   0x80aa578
       arg[3]:       0x12000, arg[4]:        0x4, arg[5]:          0
       syscall: 0x32, ar0: 0xe0000e34, ttyp: 0xf017355a, ticks: 0xd68b0
       pr_base: 0, pr_size: 0, pr_off: 0, pr_scale: 0
       ior: 0x1, iow: 0, iosw: 0xb, ioch: 0x2ce1d
       sysabort: 0, systrap: 0
       callgatep: 0, callgate[0]: 0, callgate[1]: 0
       debugpend: 0, debugon: 0
       dr[0]:          0,  dr[1]:          0,  dr[2]:          0
       dr[3]:          0,  dr[4]:          0,  dr[5]:          0
       dr[6]:          0,  dr[7]:          0
       entrymask: 00000000 00000000 00000000 00000000
       exitmask:  00000000 00000000 00000000 00000000
EXDATA:
       ip:I#80, tsize: 0x19be4, dsize: 0xed78, bsize: 0x2094, lsize: 0
       magic#:011065, toffset: 0x34, doffset: 0x19c18, loffset: 0
       txtorg:0x8048034, datorg: 0x8062c18, entloc: 0x80014480, nshlibs: 0
       execsz:0x30, ldtmodified: 0, ldtlimit: 256
```

A swapped out u_area can be examined only on a live system. The `user` command uses the `user` structure defined in the `<sys/user.h>` header file.

For further information on the u_area see section 7.2.2.

---

pre[gion] [-e] [-p] process ...

The `pregion` command prints the `pregion` entries for a process which describe the regions attached to the process.

The example displays the pregion structures for the process whose process ID is 446:

```
> pregion #446
SLOT PREG REG#      REGVA  TYPE FLAGS
  60    0  616  0x8046000 stack rd wr cm
       1  618  0x8048000  text rd ex cm
       2  617  0x8069000  data rd wr cm
       3  615 0x80001000 lbtxt rd ex pr
       4  614 0x80051000 lbdat rd wr ex pr
       5  613 0x8005c000 shfil rd
       6  612 0x8005e000 lbtxt rd ex pr
       7  611 0x80084000 lbdat rd wr ex pr
```

The pregion command uses the pregion structure defined in the <sys/region.h> header file and the proc structure defined in the <sys/proc.h> header file. For further details of the pregion structure and pregion command see section 6.4.2.

---

ru[nq]

The runq command prints details of processes that are on the run queue using the short format of the proc command.

---

kf[p] [-s process] [-r | kfp]

The kfp command prints the frame pointer for the start of a kernel (system) stack trace. The kernel frame pointer is set to the value of kfp if specified. The -r option sets the kernel frame pointer to the base of the kernel stack for the current process.
    The kfp command uses the t_ebp member of the tss386 structure defined in the <sys/tss.h> header file.

---

ks[p] [-s process] [-r | ks]

The ksp command prints the kernel stack pointer which is set to the value of ks if specified. The -r option resets the kernel stack pointer to the top of the kernel stack for the current process.

```
> ksp
ksp: 0000000000
> ksp 68
ksp: 0x0000000068
```

The ksp command uses the t_esp member of the tss386 structure defined in the <sys/tss.h> header file.

```
s[tack] [ -u | -k | -l ] [ process ... ]
```

The `stack` command dumps the user or kernel stack for the specified process. The `-k` option prints a hexadecimal dump of the system stack while the `-l` option prints a more detailed dump including translation of function calls into symbols and offsets. If no arguments are passed, `stack` prints the kernel stack for the current process as though the `-l` option were specified. The `-u` option prints a hexadecimal dump of the user stack.

The user and kernel stacks associated with the current process are not accessible on a running system. The following example displays the kernel stack for a specified process:

```
> proc ! grep sleep
  26 s    358    235    358 13583   66   0 u    sleep      load omsk ntrc
> stack #358
KERNEL STACK FOR PROCESS 26:
FP: e0000dc0
LOWER BOUND: e0000da4

e0000da4:  sleep+0x205         00000000      region_end+0x22f0 0000002a
e0000db4:  region_end+0x158 u+0xdc4          00000200          u+0xdd0
e0000dc4:  pause+0x12          u             00000127          u+0xdf0
e0000dd4:  sigsuspend+0x72     region_end+0x24  ffbfffff       region_end
e0000de4:  ffffeff             cxentry+0x150    00000000       u+0xe00
e0000df4:  cxenix+0x6f         sysent+0x140     u+0xe34        u+0xe28
e0000e04:  systrap+0x1ce       8005828c         00000000       00000000
e0000e14:  u+0xe28             u+0xe74          s_trap+0x90    00000011
e0000e24:  01660000            u+0xe34          scall_noke+0xe u+0xe34
e0000e34:  00000000            00000000         0000001f       0000001f
e0000e44:  00000000            00000000         08047e1c       u+0xe64
e0000e54:  8005828c            00000000         80058dec       00002a28
e0000e64:  00000212            00002a28         80030d04       00000017
e0000e74:  00000206            08047dac         0000001f

STACK FRAME:
    ARGN ... ARG1  EIP'  EBP'  (REGS)  LOCAL1 ...
    FP (=EBP) -----------^
```

The `stack` command uses the `proc` structure defined in the `<sys/proc.h>` header file, the `tss386` structure defined in the `<sys/tss.h>` header file and the `user` structure defined in the `<sys/user.h>` header file.

```
t[race] [ -e ] [ -q | -l ] [ -r ] [ process ... ]
```

This command prints a kernel stack trace. The `-r` option causes `trace` to examine the stack frame set by the `kfp` command. The `-l` option translates function arguments into symbols and offsets and the `-q` option suppresses this translation.

Following an interrupt or exception, the kernel creates an additional stack frame on the system stack for the interrupt handler to use. If there is an interrupt outstanding on the crashed system being examined, `crash` also displays this interrupt stack.

If no arguments are entered, `trace` prints the kernel stack trace for the current process as though the `-l` option were specified.

A stack backtrace for the process whose process ID is 358 is:

```
> trace #358
KERNEL STACK TRACE FOR PROCESS 26:
STKADDR    FRAMEPTR   FUNCTION   POSSIBLE ARGUMENTS
e0000da4   e0000dc0   jmptotss   (u,0x127)
e0000dc8   e0000dd0   pause      (region_end+0x2364,0xffbfffff,
                                  region_end+0x2364,0xffffffeff)
e0000dd8   e0000df0   sigsuspend (sysent+0x140,u+0xe34)
e0000df8   e0000e00   cxenix     (0x8005828c,0,0,u+0xe28)
e0000e08   e0000e28   systrap    (u+0xe34)
           e0000e34   scall_noke from 0x80030d04
    ax:    2a28 cx:80058dec dx:      0 bx:8005828c fl:    206 ds:  1f fs:   0
    sp:e0000e64 bp: 8047e1c si:       0 di:       0 err:  2a28 es:  1f gs:   0
```

The trace command uses the proc structure defined in the <sys/proc.h> header file, the tss386 structure defined in the <sys/tss.h> header file and the user structure defined in the <sys/user.h> header file.

---

tss [-u | -k] [process] | -i [-p] start_addr

pc[b] [-u | -k] [process] | -i [-p] start_addr

The tss and pcb commands print the *Task State Segment* (TSS) of a process, also known as the *Process Control Block* (PCB). With no arguments tss prints the kernel's TSS pointed to by the u_tss member in the u_area of the current process. The -k option also prints the kernel's TSS.

The -u option prints a process's TSS. This is always saved on the kernel stack in the process's u_area following every fault.

The -i option prints a process's TSS that is saved to the user stack when an interrupt or trap is encountered in user mode. This option requires the start address of the TSS to be provided.

In the following example, running the tss command without any arguments attempts to print the TSS for the current running process. Since the process is running, the contents of the TSS as pointed to by the u_tss field of the u_area is out of date and the contents displayed consist of the machine registers which would be altered as a process of displaying them. The TSS for the processes in slots 10 and 20 of the proc[] table are then displayed:

```
> tss
PER PROCESS TSS FOR PROCESS 70:
This is the current process on active system
> tss 10
PER PROCESS TSS FOR PROCESS 10:
cs:eip=0158:f015e6f2 Flags=087
ds = 0160    es = 0160    fs = 0000    gs = 0000    ss = 0160
esi= 00000000   edi= fb117d70   ebp= e0000d58   esp= e0000d3c
eax= fb11ce10   ebx= 00000007   ecx= 00000000   edx= 00000148
> tss 20
```

```
PER PROCESS TSS FOR PROCESS 20:
cs:eip=0158:f015e6f2 Flags=012
ds = 0160    es = 0160    fs = 0000    gs = 0000    ss = 0160
esi= 00000000   edi= fb118ae0   ebp= e0000d1c   esp= e0000d00
eax= fb1186d8   ebx= 00000007   ecx= 00000000   edx= 00000148
```

The `tss` command uses the `proc` structure defined in the `<sys/proc.h>` header file, the `tss386` structure defined in the `<sys/tss.h>` header file, and the `user` structure defined in the `<sys/user.h>` header file.

14.14 `cblock` and `tty` structures

The `cblock` structures are used to implement the raw input, canonical input and output character list (`clist`) data queues, and the transmit and receive control blocks for the clist based console and terminal drivers. The system maintains a `tty` structure for each console and terminal device known to it.

---

cb[lock] [-eft] [-p] table_entry ...]

The `cblock` command prints `cblock` structures. The `-f` option additionally prints the contents of the `cblock` in hexadecimal and character format. The `-t` option prints the chain of `cblock` entries that form a `clist`, starting with `table_entry`.

The following example displays the contents of a `cblock` which was used to display messages when the system bootstrapped:

```
> cblock -f 168
SLOT      ADDRESS         NEXT   FIRST  LAST
 168   0xfc0d0f40           0       0    64
 54 68 65 20 73 79 73 74 65 6d 20 69 73 20 63 6f  The.system.is.co
 6d 69 6e 67 20 75 70 2e 20 20 50 6c 65 61 73 65  ming.up...Please
 20 77 61 69 74 2e 0a 65 64 20 73 75 62 73 79 73  .wait..ed.subsys
 74 65 6d 20 64 61 74 61 62 61 73 65 73 20 2e 2e  tem.databases...
```

The `cblock` command uses the `cblock` structure defined in the `<sys/tty.h>` header file. Toolkit 9.5 shows the flow of control through the console driver using the `cblock` command.

---

tt[y] [-ef] [-t type [[-p] table_entry ...] | [-p] start_addr]]

The `tty` command prints entries in the `tty` table. The `-f` flag can be used to display a full listing of the `tty` structure. The `-t` option prints the table for the `tty` type specified which includes:

cn   console multiscreens

pa   parallel ports

sio   serial ports

spt   pseudo TTYs

Without any arguments, as the following example shows, the `tty` command displays an abbreviated `tty` structure associated with each console multiscreen:

```
> tty
cn TABLE SIZE = 12
SLOT OUT RAW CAN DEL  PGRP STATE
   0   0   0   0   0   421 isop carr islp
   1   0   0   0   0   328 isop carr
   2   0   0   0   0   422 isop carr islp
   3   0   0   0   0   423 isop carr islp
   4   0   0   0   0   424 isop carr islp
   5   0   0   0   0   425 isop carr islp
   6   0   0   0   0   426 isop carr islp
   7   0   0   0   0   427 isop carr islp
   8   0   0   0   0   428 isop carr islp
   9   0   0   0   0   429 isop carr islp
  10   0   0   0   0   430 isop carr islp
  11   0   0   0   0   431 isop carr islp

sio TABLE SIZE = 24
SLOT OUT RAW CAN DEL  PGRP STATE
   0   0   0   0   0     0 isop carr xdly

spt TABLE SIZE = 32
SLOT OUT RAW CAN DEL  PGRP STATE
   0   0   0   0   0   466 isop carr islp
   1   0   0   0   0   465 isop carr
   2   0   0   0   0  3833 isop carr islp
   3   0   0   0   0  1138 isop carr
   4 207   0   0   0  3885 isop carr
```

The following example displays in full a single `tty` structure:

```
> tty -f -tspt -p 0
spt TABLE SIZE = 32
SLOT OUT RAW CAN DEL  PGRP STATE
   0   0   0   0   0   466 isop carr islp
     rawq.cf:         0, rawq.cl:        0
     canq.cf:         0, canq.cl:        0
     outq.cf:         0, outq.cl:        0
                  c_ptr  count  size
     tbuf:            0      0      0
     rbuf:   0xfc0d0b56     64     64
          proc line term   termflag col row vrow lrow hqcnt dstat
        sptproc    0    0          0   7   0    0    0     0     0
     intr:    ^C    quit:    ^\    erase:   ^H    kill:    ^U
     eof:     ^[    eol:     ^M    eol2:    ^D    swtch:   ^@
     susp:    ^Z    start:   ^Q    stop:    ^S    ceof:    ^@
     ceol:    ^@
     iflag: brkint ignpar inlcr ixon
     oflag: opost onlcr nl0 cr0 tab0 bs0 vt0 ff0
     cflag: b9600 cs8 cread parenb hupcl
     lflag: isig icanon echo echoe echok iexten
```

The `tty` command uses the `tty` structure defined in the `<sys/tty.h>` header file. For further information about `tty` structures see section 9.7.6.

14.15 STREAMS structures

The STREAMS environment is commonly used by networking software to implement layered protocol stacks as modules within device drivers. This section describes the commands available for displaying STREAMS related data structures.

---

dbf[ree] [class ...]

The `dbfree` command prints STREAMS data block headers in the `edblock` free list. Data block headers are printed only for the specified buffer class; if none are specified, `dbfree` prints data block headers for all buffer classes as follows:

```
> dbfree ! head -8
CLASS = 0   SIZE = 16
SLOT CLASS RCNT TYPE      BASE       LIMIT FREEP PREV ADJ DMA FUNC  ARG
 436    0    0 data 0xfd198690 0xfd1986a0   439    -   -   N    -    -
 439    0    0 data 0xfd1986f0 0xfd198700   437    -   -   N    -    -
 437    0    0 data 0xfd1986b0 0xfd1986c0   438    -   -   N    -    -
 438    0    0 data 0xfd1986d0 0xfd1986e0   434    -   -   N    -    -
 434    0    0 data 0xfd198650 0xfd198660   435    -   -   N    -    -
```

The `dbfree` command uses the `extdatab` structure defined in the `<sys/stream.h>` header file. For further information on STREAMS see chapter 10.

---

dbl[ock] [-e] [-c class ... | [-p] table_entry ...]

The `dblock` command prints allocated STREAMS data block headers. The `-c` option prints only data block headers for the specified buffer class.

The default output displayed by `dblock` is:

```
> dblock ! head -8
DATA BLOCK TABLE SIZE = 442
SLOT CLASS RCNT TYPE      BASE       LIMIT FREEP PREV ADJ DMA FUNC ARG
  58    6    1 data 0xf08b0800 0xf08b1000    -    -    -   Y    -    -
  59    6    1 data 0xf08b0000 0xf08b0800   58    -   58   Y    -    -
  60    6    1 data 0xf08af800 0xf08b0000    -    -    -   Y    -    -
  61    6    1 data 0xf08af000 0xf08af800   60    -   60   Y    -    -
  62    6    1 data 0xf08b3000 0xf08b3800  309    -  309   N    -    -
  63    6    1 data 0xf08ae000 0xf08ae800   73    -   73   Y    -    -
```

The `dblock` command uses the `extdatab` structure defined in the `<sys/stream.h>` header file. For further information on STREAMS see chapter 10.

```
li[nkblk] [ -e ] [ [ -p ] table_entry ... ]
```

The `linkblk` command prints the contents of the `linkblk` table. A `linkblk` structure stores triples of multiplexed STREAMS).

The output of `linkblk` for one particular run is:

```
> linkblk
LINKBLK TABLE SIZE = 192
SLOT          QTOP          QBOT INDEX
   0             0           105     1
   1             0            97     2
   2             0            93     3
   3             0            89     4
   4             0            85     5
   5             0            81     6
   6             0            73     8
   7             0            69     9
   8             0            77     7
```

The `linkblk` command uses the `linkblk` structure defined in the `<sys/stream.h>` header file. For further information on STREAMS see chapter 10.

```
mbf[ree]
```

The `mbfree` command prints STREAMS message block headers in the `mblock` free list as the following example shows:

```
> mbfree ! head -8
SLOT NEXT CONT PREV       RPTR        WPTR DATAB
 214  242   -    - 0xf08371e8 0xf08371e8    -
 242  234  214   - 0xf083f200 0xf083f224    -
 234  213  242   - 0xf08d5000 0xf08d5000    -
 213  248   -    - 0xf083902a 0xf0839222    -
 248  260  234   - 0xfd1986d0 0xfd1986d4    -
 260  212   -    - 0xf08e27f8 0xf08e27f8    -
 212  222   -    - 0xf08371d4 0xf08371d4    -
```

The `mbfree` command uses the `msgb` structure defined in the `<sys/stream.h>` header file. For further information on STREAMS see chapter 10.

```
mbl[ock] [ -e ] [ [ -p ] table_entry ... ]
```

The `mblock` command prints allocated STREAMS message block headers as the example shows:

```
> mblock 1..8
MESSAGE BLOCK TABLE SIZE = 271
SLOT NEXT CONT PREV       RPTR        WPTR DATAB
   1   57   -    - 0xf08bfa18 0xf08bfc22   69
   2  237   -    - 0xf08d3420 0xf08d3421  252
```

```
3    16     –     – 0xf08b9218 0xf08b9422    298
4    207   223    – 0xfd1986b0 0xfd1986b4     –
5    10     –     – 0xf08b8218 0xf08b8422    301
6    230    –     – 0xf08fd000 0xf08fe000    192
7    17     –     – 0xf08b7a18 0xf08b7c22    300
8    53     –     – 0xf08de000 0xf08df000    237
```

The mblock command uses the msgb structure defined in the <sys/stream.h> header file. For further information on STREAMS see chapter 10.

---

pbf[ree]

The pbfree command prints STREAMS page descriptor entries which are held on the pageb free list:

```
> pbfree ! head -4
STREAMS PAGE TABLE SIZE = 1000
SLOT NEXT CLASS DBLOCK      PTR
901  900    –      –       null
900  899    –      –       null
```

The pbfree command uses the pageb structure defined in the <sys/stream.h> header file. For further information on STREAMS see chapter 10.

---

pbl[ock] [-e] [-c class ... | [-p] table_entry ...]

The pblock command prints elements of the STREAMS page table. Entries in this table are descriptors for pages of memory allocated to STREAMS buffers. The -c option displays entries for memory allocated to the specified buffer class.
    The following default output is displayed when pblock is run:

```
> pblock ! head -6
STREAMS PAGE TABLE SIZE = 1000
SLOT NEXT CLASS DBLOCK      PTR
902  903    7     440       –
903  904    7     441       –
904  905    7     198       –
905  906    7     186       –
```

The pblock command uses the pageb structure defined in the <sys/stream.h> header file. For further information on STREAMS see chapter 10.

---

pbp[ool]

The pbpool command prints STREAMS page descriptor entries allocated to the pool of memory reserved for interrupt time allocations:

```
> pbpool ! head -6
STREAMS PAGE TABLE SIZE = 1000
SLOT NEXT CLASS DBLOCK        PTR SIZE
 999   -     -       - 0xf0823000   20
```

The `pbpool` command uses the `pageb` structure defined in the `<sys/stream.h>` header file. For further information on STREAMS see chapter 10.

---

qr[un]

The `qrun` command prints the list of STREAMS `queue` slots that are scheduled for service using the `queue` structure defined in the `<sys/stream.h>` header file.

For further information on STREAMS see chapter 10.

---

que[ue] [-e] [[-p] table_entry ...]

The `queue` command prints the table of allocated STREAMS queues. The example displays a subset of the allocated `queue` structures:

```
> queue 1..8
QUEUE TABLE SIZE = 566
SLOT        INFO NEXT LINK     PTR RCNT HD TL MINP MAXP HIWT LOWT FLAGS
   1 0xf01deeec   -  - 0xf0853b00   0  -  -  0 32739 32739 1024 wr us
   2 0xf01d900c   -  - 0xf0867500   0  -  -  0    -1 16384 1024 rr us
   3 0xf01d9028   1  - 0xf0867500   0  -  -  0     0     0    0 us
   4 0xf01d74b8   6  - 0xf0223c30   0  -  -  0    -1  5120 1024 wr rr us
   5 0xf01d74d4  10  - 0xf0223c30   0  -  -  0    -1  5120 1024 wr us
   6 0xf01d7980   -  - 0xf0226878   0  -  -  0    -1  5012 1024 wr rr us
   7 0xf01d799c   5  - 0xf0226878   0  -  -  0     0     0    0 us
   8 0xf01d74b8  10  - 0xf0223c20   0  -  -  0    -1  5120 1024 wr rr us
```

The `queue` command uses the `queue` structure defined in the `<sys/stream.h>` header file. For further information on STREAMS see chapter 10.

---

stre[am] [-ef] [[-p] table_entry ...]

The `stream` command prints allocated slots in the STREAMS table. In the example, the first six entries of the STREAMS table are displayed in summary format:

```
> stream ! head -8
STREAM TABLE SIZE = 1024
SLOT   WRQ IOCB INODE  PGRP     IOCID IOCWT WOFF  ERR FLAG
   0   101   -    -      0        18    0     0    0
   1   105   -   50      0         0    0     0    0 plex 01000000
   2    97   -   47      0         0    0     0    0 plex 01000000
   3    93   -   46      0         0    0     0    0 plex 01000000
   4    89   -   45      0         0    0     0    0 plex 01000000
   5    85   -   44      0         0    0     0    0 plex 01000000
```

In the following example, entry number 1 is displayed in full format:

```
> stream -f 1
STREAM TABLE SIZE = 1024
SLOT  WRQ IOCB INODE  PGRP       IOCID IOCWT WOFF  ERR FLAG
   1  105   -    50     0            0     0    0    0 plex 01000000
          STRTAB RCNT
       0xf01e17d0     0
       SIGFLAGS:
       SIGLIST:
       POLLFLAGS:
       POLLIST:
```

The `stream` command uses the `stdata` and `strevent` structures defined in the `<sys/stream.h>` header file. For further information on STREAMS see chapter 10.

---

strs[tat]

The `strstat` command prints STREAMS statistics, including the allocated and free numbers of STREAMS, STREAMS queues, message and buffer headers, and data blocks of different sizes.

The `strstat` command uses the `stdata`, `queue` and `pagestat` structures defined in the `<sys/stream.h>` header file, and the `strstat` structure defined in the `<sys/strstat.h>` header file. The output displayed by `strstat` is shown in section 10.11. For further information on STREAMS see chapter 10.

14.16 Panic dump analysis

This section provides a basic insight into how to determine the reason for a kernel panic. The dummy driver presented in section 9.3 will be used to invoke a panic. The `dmread()` driver entry point has been modified as shown:

```
dmread(dev_t dev)
{
    printf("dmread() called\n") ;
    cmn_err(CE_PANIC, "dmread: for analysing core dump") ;
}
```

When `dmread()` is called, it displays a message on the console using `printf()` and then calls `cmn_err(K)`, resulting in a kernel panic.

The device special file used to access the dummy driver is:

```
# ls -l /dev/dummy
crw-rw-rw-   1 root     sys       81,  0 Jan 11 12:20 /dev/dummy
```

To invoke a panic, the device `read` routine can be invoked as follows. This results in the dummy driver entry point message being displayed, followed by the panic message and then an attempt to dump the contents of memory to the dump device. In most cases the dump is written over the contents of the swap division.

```
# cat < /dev/dummy
dmopen() called
dmread() called

PANIC: dmread: for analysing core dump
Trying to dump 8096 pages to dumpdev hd (1/41) at block 0, 102 pages per
`.'
............................................................
8096 pages dumped


**   Safe to Power Off    **
          - or -
** Press Any Key to Reboot **
```

When the system is next bootstrapped it looks in the swap division to see if a dump was written when the system was last operational. If a dump is found, the following messages are displayed:

```
There may be a system dump memory image in the swap device.
Do you want to save a copy of it? (y/n) n
Do you want to remove the dump from the swap device now? (y/n) n
```

The answers given in this case are no to both questions. This allows the dump to be saved at a later date using the dd(C) command as follows:

```
# dd if=/dev/swap of=/tmp/DUMP
```

To run crash, the name of the dump file is specified as follows:

```
# crash -d /tmp/DUMP
dumpfile = /tmp/DUMP, namelist = /unix, outfile = stdout
> curproc
Procslot = 16
> p 16
PROC TABLE SIZE = 47
SLOT ST PID   PPID  PGRP   UID PRI CPU EVENT        NAME          FLAGS
  16 p   101    83    83     0  50   3              cat           load
```

When crash is entered, the curproc kernel variable should point to the process that was running when the panic occurred. The curproc command run above returns the process which is located in slot 16. When the proc command was run the process that was running was the cat(C) command, the command which was run to read from the dummy device.

The panic command can be used to give clues as to which part of the kernel resulted in a panic.

```
> panic
System Messages:

mem: total = 32384k, kernel = 6932k, user = 25452k
swapdev = 1/41, swplo = 0, nswap = 98000, swapmem = 49000k
```

```
M rootdev = 1/42, pipedev = 1/42, dumpdev = 1/41
kernel: Hz = 100, i/o bufs = 3084k

dmopen() called
dmread() called

PANIC: dmread: for analysing core dump
Trying to dump 8096 pages to dumpdev hd (1/41) at block 0, 102 pages per
'.'
. . . . . . . . . . . . . . . . . . . . . . . . . . . . . . . .

Panic String: dmread: for analysing core dump
```

The string passed to `cmn_err(K)` is displayed as the *panic string*. This has now isolated the error to a specific part of the kernel. Of course there may be multiple code paths which could result in `cmn_err(K)` being invoked. The `trace` command can therefore be used to display a stack backtrace of the kernel stack. This shows the functions invoked with the arguments passed to them as follows:

```
> trace
KERNEL STACK TRACE FOR PROCESS 16:
STKADDR     FRAMEPTR   FUNCTION    POSSIBLE ARGUMENTS
e0000cb4    e0000d28   prf_task_s  (0x4,0,inode+0x2260,0x1)
e0000d30    e0000d48   cmn_err     (0x3,ramd_valid+0xa0)
e0000d50    e0000d58   dmread      (0x5100,0x51,0x4,inode+0x2260)
e0000d60    e0000d8c   devfs_read  (inode+0x2260,inode+0x2260,0x8,0)
e0000d94    e0000df4   rdwr        (0x1)
e0000dfc    e0000e00   read        (0x8047f38,0x2,0,u+0xe28)
e0000e08    e0000e28   systrap     (u+0xe34)
            e0000e34   scall_noke from 0x8002f56c
   ax:        3 cx:80058c24 dx:80058dec bx: 8047f38 fl: 246 ds: 1f  fs: 0
   sp:e0000e64 bp: 8047e04 si:        2 di:   0     err: 3 es: 1f  gs: 0
```

From here, the task gets more difficult. The path to the failure is known, and the user process is known, but the exact reason for failure may not be visible at this stage.

It is at this point that the large number of `crash` commands become useful to analyse specific structures to pinpoint the error further.

14.17 Summary and suggested reading

This chapter described the `crash(ADM)` utility which can be used to analyse both a live kernel and a panic dump. Each command is briefly described with example output and a cross-reference to examples in the book where the commands are used.

For further information regarding kernel tuneables see the SCO OpenServer *Performance Guide* (1995).

Bibliography

ANSI (1989). *American National Standard for Information Systems – Programming Language C*, X3.159-1989, ANSI (Dec).

The ANSI standard C programming language specification.

Bach M. (1986). *The Design of the UNIX Operating System*. Englewood Cliffs, NJ: Prentice-Hall.

For a number of years this book was the only published reference of the UNIX kernel architecture. Although based on System V Release 2, many of the concepts and algorithms described are still valid today.

Comer D. (1984). *Operating System Design: The XINU Approach*. Englewood Cliffs, NJ: Prentice-Hall.

This book describes a UNIX-like operating system written for the LSI-11 microcomputer. The book includes the operating system source code.

Dijkstra E.W. (1965). Solution of a problem in concurrent programming control. *Communications of the ACM*, vol. 8, Sep. 1965, pp. 569–578.

Description of Dijkstra's semaphores.

Dunphy E. (1991). *The UNIX Industry, Evolution, Concepts, Architecture, Applications and Standards*. Wellesley, MA: QED Technical Publishing.

This book provides a wealth of information on UNIX from magazines and books to UNIX operating system concepts to the UNIX marketplace.

Gallmeister B.O. (1995). *POSIX.4: Programming for the Real World*. Sebastopol, CA: O'Reilly & Associates.

A description of the POSIX.1b real-time standard including worked examples.

Gircys G.R. (1988). *Understanding and Using COFF*. Newton, MA: O'Reilly & Associates.

A comprehensive description of the features of COFF including many examples of how to interpret COFF files.

Goodheart B. and Cox J. (1994). *The Magic Garden Explained: The Internals of UNIX System V Release 4, An Open Systems Design*. Sydney: Prentice-Hall.

Provides comprehensive coverage of the internals of SVR4.

Intel (1991). *Intel386 Family Binary Compatibility Specification 2*. Mt. Prospect, IL: Intel Corporation.

This book defines the standard for executable files for System V, based on COFF. It provides coverage of COFF and also describes system call sequences, stack frames and library formats.

Intel (1992). *Intel486 Microprocessor Family: Programmer's Reference Manual*. Mt. Prospect, IL: Intel Corporation.

Despite the many other books published on the Intel i386 family of processors, this book, together with the other processor manuals, provides the definitive description of the i386 family covering details of memory management, I/O, multitasking and so on.

Intel (1993). *Pentium Processor User's Manual. Volume 3: Architecture and Programming Manual*. Mt. Prospect, IL: Intel Corporation.

The definitive reference for the Intel Pentium processor.

Kernighan B.W. and Ritchie D.M. (1978). *The C Programming Language*. Englewood Cliffs, NJ: Prentice-Hall.

The first available book on the C language.

Kettle P. and Statler S. (1992). *Writing Device Drivers for SCO UNIX: A Practical Approach*. Wokingham, England: Addison-Wesley.

Provides many examples of device drivers written for SCO UNIX.

Leffler S.J., McKusick M.K., Karels M.J. and Quarterman J.S. (1989). *The Design and Implementation of the 4.3BSD UNIX Operating System*. Reading, MA: Addison-Wesley.

Written by four of the authors of BSD UNIX, this book describes the internals of the 4.3BSD version of UNIX.

Messmer H.P. (1995). *The Indispensable PC Hardware Book,* 2nd edition. Harlow, England: Addison-Wesley.

An excellent source of information on all aspects of PC hardware.

Miscovich G. and Simons D. (1994). *The SCO Performance Tuning Handbook*. Englewood Cliffs, NJ: Prentice-Hall.

Covers numerous case studies and describes how to detect performance problems and to tune the SCO UNIX kernel.

Nohr M.L. (1994). *Understanding ELF Object Files and Debugging Tools*. Englewood Cliffs, NJ: Prentice-Hall.

Comprehensive description of ELF and the tools available for analysing ELF files.

POSIX (1990). *Portable Operating System Interface (POSIX) – Part 1: System Application Programming Interface (API) [C Language]*. ISO/IEC 9945-1, IEE Std 1003.1, First edition 1990-12-07.

The POSIX.1 standard.

POSIX.1b (1993). *Portable Operating System Interface (POSIX) – Part 1: System Application Programming Interface (API) [C Language]. Amendment 1: Realtime Extension [C Language]*.

An extension to POSIX.1 including real-time support, formerly POSIX.4.

Presotto D.L. and Ritchie D.M. (1985). *Interprocess Communication in the Eighth Edition Unix System*. Proceedings of the 1985 Summer USENIX Conference. Portland, OR, pp. 309–316.

A description of STREAM based IPC facilities.

Rago S.A. (1993). *UNIX System V Network Programming*. Reading, MA: Addison-Wesley.

A must for STREAMS programmers. This book contains many examples.

Ritchie D.M. and Thompson K. (1974). The UNIX Timesharing System. *Communications of the ACM*: vol. 17, no. 7. July 1974, pp. 365–375.

A description of Fourth Edition UNIX.

Salus P.H. (1994). *A Quarter Century of UNIX*. Reading, MA: Addison-Wesley.

An historical view of the first 25 years of UNIX.

SCO OpenServer. (1995). *Performance Guide*. The Santa Cruz Operation.

How to tune SCO OpenServer. This book describes all the kernel tuneables available.

SCO OpenServer. (1995). *Programmer's Reference Manual – Volumes 1 and 2*. The Santa Cruz Operation.

Specifies and describes all system calls and library functions.

SCO OpenServer. (1995). *Operating System Administrator's Reference - Volumes 1 and 2*. The Santa Cruz Operation.

Contains many useful descriptions of system files.

SCO OpenServer Development System. (1995). *Developer's Topics*. The Santa Cruz Operation.

A good description of COFF and ELF.

SCO OpenServer Development System. (1995). *Programming Tools Guide*. The Santa Cruz Operation.

A detailed description of C language support, COFF, ELF and tools such as lex, yacc and make.

SCO OpenServer. (1995). *Advanced Hardware Developer's Kit*, The Santa Cruz Operation.

Contains all the device driver APIs that can be used.

Stevens W.R. (1990). *UNIX Network Programming*. Englewood Cliffs, NJ: Prentice-Hall.

A good introduction to network programming with many example programs.

Stevens W.R. (1992). *Advanced Programming in the UNIX Environment*. Reading, MA: Addison-Wesley.

An excellent description of the UNIX programming environment.

Tanenbaum A.S. (1987). *Operating Systems: Design and Implementation*. Englewood Cliffs, NJ: Prentice-Hall.

A good introduction to operating systems which also describes Minix, a UNIX-like operating system. The book contains complete source code.

Vann K. (1995). *Essential SCO System Administration*. Englewood Cliffs, NJ: Prentice-Hall.

A good source of information on SCO system administration.

X/Open (1994). *System Interfaces and Headers Issue 4, Version 2*. Berkshire, England. The X/Open Company Limited.

The X/Open XPG4.2 specification.

Index